#13   791 REYT $ 35⁰⁰

CIVIL WAR GENERALS

CIVIL WAR GENERALS

Categorical Listings and a Biographical Directory

Compiled by
James Spencer

GREENWOOD PRESS
New York • Westport, Connecticut • London

LIBRARY OF CONGRESS CATALOGING-IN-PUBLICATION DATA

Spencer, James, 1937-
   Civil War generals.

   Includes index.
   1. Generals—United States—Registers. 2. Generals—
United States—Biography. 3. United States—History—
Civil War, 1861-1865—Registers. 4. United States—
History—Civil War, 1861-1865—Biography. 5. United
States. Army—Registers. 6. United States. Army—
Biography. I. Title.
E467.S78   1986   973.7′4   86-19391
ISBN 0-313-25423-0 (lib. bdg. : alk. paper)

Library of Congress Catalog Card Number: 86-19391
ISBN: 0-313-25423-0

First published in 1986

Greenwood Press, Inc.
88 Post Road West, Westport, Connecticut 06881

Printed in the United States of America

The paper used in this book complies with the
Permanent Paper Standard issued by the National
Information Standards Organization (Z39.48-1984).

10 9 8 7 6 5 4 3 2 1

Contents

Dedicated to my wife Russetta, and children James David,
Nina Eleanor and Joseph Christopher. Thanks for the en-
couragement and faith.

Introduction

Since the end of the American Civil War, countless volumes have minutely examined, discussed and diagnosed the conflict. Each battle, skirmish and action, however minor, has been thoroughly critiqued. One of the areas which has not received as much attention as the military aspects of the war, however, is the personal lives of the leaders of the two great armies. To be sure, the great and famous generals on both sides, such as Robert E. Lee, Ulysses Grant, Stonewall Jackson, George Custer and Jeb Stuart, have been well covered, but little has been said about the majority of the other, lesser known generals.

Where did the generals come from? How many generals did each state furnish? How many foreign-born generals were there? Who was the youngest general? Who was the oldest? How many generals were West Point graduates? How many were killed in battles? Which generals were they? Which battles? Did many generals attend college? Which colleges? What were the most common professions of generals before the war? After the war? What were the most commonly used first names of the generals? Middle names? Last names?

The foremost objective in arranging the material in this book is to answer these questions and many more. The following chapters list the generals of the Civil War in sixteen different categories. The last chapter is a concise biography of each general in alphabetical order.

Some of the generals, too old or not in physical condition for field command, were involved only in support duties such as supply, communications and other important functions. Other officers were appointed as Brigadier Generals by their superiors, exercised the rank in field command, but were never confirmed by the Senate. Generals in these categories are included in the following lists.

In some cases, officers were promoted to general officer rank following their death in battle. An example of this was Colonel Joshua Blackwood Howell, who died September 14, 1864 after his horse fell on him. Seven months later he was appointed Brigadier General, to rank from the date of his accident, and his name duly appears on the list of Civil War generals. His name, and others of similar circumstances, was not included in this book.

Several other men appearing on the official roster of
Civil War generals were promoted following the end of hostilities, some as late as November 20, 1865. Only those who held
the rank of general officer during wartime are listed here, and
the highest rank attained by each general during actual wartime
is the only rank used in these lists.

There is little problem determining which of the Confederate generals actually served during wartime; there were no post-
war promotions to sort out, as their army was disbanded immme-
diately following the war. Some of the promotions were never
confirmed by the Confederate Senate, but if they exercised general officer rank, they are included here.

The Union side presents quite a different situation. According to the official roster, there were 1,989 Union generals.
The difficulty of ascertaining exactly which of these actually
served in general officer capacity during the war is further
compounded by the liberal use of brevet rank by the Union.

An officer could be appointed to brevet rank for any number
of reasons, but usually it was as a reward for services rendered
or gallantry in battle. This brevet rank was more or less an
honorary title, and carried with it none of the authority or pay
of the full rank. Under certain specified circumstances (such
as court-martial duty), an officer could claim his brevet rank.
At the end of the war, approximately 1,700 Union soldiers were
awarded brevet rank of Brigadier or Major General. Most of these
"promotions" were backdated to be effective March 13, 1865.
Brevet appointments are not considered in these lists.

Further complicating the Union rank structure was the des-
ignations U.S. Army and U.S. Volunteers. Because promotion
there was much more rapid, many regular army officers resigned
from the U.S. Army to accept higher rank in the U.S. Volunteers.
Following the end of hostilities, if they desired to continue
an army career, they reentered the U.S. Army, usually at their
former rank.

The highest rank in the Union army during the Civil War
was Lieutenant General, which was not instituted until late in
the war when it was conferred on Ulysses S. Grant.

The Confederate rank structure was entirely different from
that of the Union.   Of the 420 general officers, there were
eight full rank Generals and seventeen Lieutenant Generals in
addition to the ranks of Major Generals and Brigadiers.

The insignia of rank also differed greatly between the
two armies. The Union retained the indications of rank on
shoulder straps, while the Confederacy placed their insignia
on the officer's collars. In the northern army, one star on
the shoulder strap indicated a Brigadier General, two stars
a Major General, and three stars for Lieutenant General. In
the Confederate army, however, all generals, Brigadier through
full General, were marked by the same insignia: three stars on
the collar surrounded by a wreath. In most cases, the star in
the middle was larger than the other two.

The generals came from a wide variety of pre-war work
backgrounds. One might be curious as to how a person who was
a store clerk or farmer would be qualified to be a general.
In some cases, perhaps, they weren't qualified, but many times
future Civil War generals had gained valuable war experience

and influence by serving in the Mexican War.

Promotions in the army before the Civil War were extremely slow, and many officers resigned from the army shortly after graduation from West Point to follow other, more lucrative pursuits. In many cases, these fields were either engineering or law. When war broke out, governments on both sides eagerly sought out West Point graduates and men with previous army experience. The majority of these recruits were appointed to general officer rank.

Because the Civil War was so political in nature, many Congressmen, Senators and other influential politicians were appointed as generals, merely to aid in gaining the support of their state or political party. Likewise, the Lincoln administration endeavored to make sure each nationality was represented by at least one general.

Often, this was not in the best interests of the North. A case in point is that of Brigadier General Alexander Schimmelfennig, a representative of the German immigrants. Appointed a Brigadier of U.S. Volunteers on November 29, 1862, he served without distinction during the spring campaign of 1863. On the first day of battle at Gettysburg, it is alleged he took refuge and hid out in a pigsty for two days until the fighting was over.

Other political appointments, however, worked more favorably for the Union. Major General Franz Sigel, another German immigrant, was responsible for thousands of recruits from among his people.

To fully examine the performance and qualifications of each general is not the intention of this book. The primary purpose is to group the "working" generals of the Civil War and set them down in convenient classifications for research and informational purposes.

Abbreviations

Agt.	Agent		Mgr.	Manager
A/	Assistant		Manuf.	Manufacturer
AR	Arkansas		MD	Maryland
B	Brigadier		Mass.	Massachusetts
Brig.	Brigadier		M.A.	Military Academy
Bus.	Business		M.I.	Military Institute
Ch.	Church		Min.	Minister
Coll.	College		MS	Mississippi
Collect.	Collector		N/	North
Co.	Company		NC	North Carolina
Cty	County		NM	New Mexico
Dist.	District		NY	New York
Dr.	Doctor		Off.	Officer
Exam.	Examiner		Oper.	Operator
G	General		PA	Pennsylvania
Gen.	General		Pres.	President
GA	Georgia		Prof.	Professor
Govt.	Government		RR	Railroad
Gov.	Governor		Rep.	Representative
IN	Indiana		Sec'y	Secretary
Insp.	Inspector		Serv.	Service
Inst.	Institute		Sher.	Sheriff
I.R.	Internal Revenue		S/	South
Invest.	Investment		SC	South Carolina
Just.	Justice		St.	State
KY	Kentucky		Supt.	Superintendent
/L	Lawyer		TN	Tennessee
L	Lieutenant		Treas.	Treasurer
Lt.	Lieutenant		U.S.	United States
LA	Louisiana		Univ.	University
M	Major		VA	Virginia
Maj.	Major			

CIVIL WAR GENERALS

Civil War Generals
by Rank

The generals from both sides are listed in this chapter first
in order of rank, then alphabetically within each rank structure. Dates of birth and death are included for comparative
purposes. In some cases, the complete dates are not available.

CONFEDERATE FULL GENERALS

GENERAL	DATE BORN	DATE OF DEATH
Pierre G.T. Beauregard	May 28, 1818	February 20, 1893
Braxton Bragg	March 22, 1817	September 27, 1876
Samuel Cooper	June 12, 1798	December 3, 1876
John Bell Hood	June 1, 1831	August 30, 1879
Albert Sidney Johnston	February 2, 1803	April 6, 1862
Joseph E. Johnston	February 3, 1807	March 21, 1891
Robert Edward Lee	January 19, 1807	October 12, 1870
Edmund Kirby Smith	May 16, 1824	March 28, 1893

CONFEDERATE LIEUTENANT GENERALS

Richard Heron Anderson	October 7, 1821	June 26, 1879
Simon Bolivar Buckner	April 1, 1823	January 8, 1914
Jubal Anderson Early	November 3, 1816	March 2, 1894
Richard Stoddert Ewell	February 8, 1817	January 25, 1872
Nathan Bedford Forrest	July 13, 1821	October 29, 1877
Wade Hampton	March 28, 1818	April 11, 1902
William Joseph Hardee	October 12, 1815	November 6, 1873
Ambrose Powell Hill	November 9, 1825	April 2, 1865
Daniel Harvey Hill	July 12, 1821	September 24, 1889
Theophilus H. Holmes	November 13, 1804	June 21, 1880
Thomas Jonathon Jackson	January 21, 1824	May 10, 1863
Stephen Dill Lee	September 22, 1833	May 28, 1908
James Longstreet	January 8, 1821	January 2, 1904
John Clifford Pemberton	August 10, 1814	July 13, 1881
Leonidas Polk	April 10, 1806	June 14, 1864
Alexander Peter Stewart	October 2, 1821	August 30, 1908
Richard Taylor	January 27, 1826	April 12, 1879

UNION LIEUTENANT GENERAL

Ulysses Simpson Grant	April 27, 1822	July 23, 1885

CONFEDERATE MAJOR GENERALS

James Patton Anderson	February 16, 1822	September 20, 1872
William Brimage Bate	October 7, 1826	March 9, 1905
John Stevens Bowen	October 30, 1830	July 13, 1863
John C. Breckinridge	January 15, 1821	May 17, 1875
John Calvin Brown	January 6, 1827	August 17, 1889
Matthew C. Butler	March 8, 1836	April 14, 1909
Benjamin F. Cheatham	October 20, 1820	September 4, 1886
Thomas James Churchill	March 10, 1824	May 14, 1905
Henry DeLamar Clayton	March 7, 1827	October 13, 1889
Patrick R. Cleburne	March 17, 1828	November 30, 1864
Howell Cobb	September 7, 1815	October 9, 1868
George Bibb Crittenden	March 20, 1812	November 27, 1880
Daniel Smith Donelson	June 23, 1801	April 17, 1863
Arnold Elzey	December 18, 1816	February 21, 1871
James Fleming Fagan	March 1, 1828	September 1, 1893
Charles William Field	April 6, 1828	April 9, 1892
John Horace Forney	August 12, 1829	September 13, 1902
Samuel Gibbs French	November 22, 1818	April 20, 1910
Franklin Gardner	January 29, 1823	April 29, 1873
Jeremy Francis Gilmer	February 23, 1818	December 1, 1883
John Brown Gordon	February 6, 1832	January 9, 1904
Bryan Grimes	November 2, 1828	August 14, 1880
Harry Thompson Hays	April 14, 1820	August 21, 1876
Henry Heth	December 16, 1825	September 27, 1899
Thomas C. Hindman	January 28, 1828	September 28, 1868
Robert Frederick Hoke	May 27, 1837	July 3, 1912
Benjamin Huger	November 22, 1805	December 7, 1877
Bushrod Rust Johnson	October 7, 1817	September 12, 1880
Edward Johnson	April 16, 1816	March 2, 1873
David Rumph Jones	April 5, 1825	January 15, 1863
Samuel Jones	December 17, 1819	July 31, 1887
James Lawson Kemper	June 11, 1823	April 7, 1895
Joseph Brevard Kershaw	January 5, 1822	April 13, 1894
Fitzhugh Lee	November 19, 1835	April 28, 1905
George Washington Lee	September 16, 1832	February 18, 1913
William Henry F. Lee	May 31, 1837	October 15, 1891
Lunsford Lindsay Lomax	November 4, 1835	May 28, 1913
William Wing Loring	December 4, 1818	December 30, 1886
Mansfield Lovell	October 20, 1822	June 1, 1884
John Bankhead Magruder	May 1, 1807	February 18, 1871
William Mahone	December 1, 1826	October 8, 1895
John S. Marmaduke	March 14, 1833	December 28, 1887
William Thompson Martin	March 25, 1823	March 16, 1910
Dabney Herndon Maury	May 21, 1822	January 11, 1900
Samuel Bell Maxey	March 30, 1825	August 16, 1895
John Porter McCown	August 19, 1815	January 22, 1879
Lafayette McLaws	January 15, 1821	July 24, 1897
Mosby Monroe Parsons	May 21, 1822	August 15, 1865
William Dorsey Pender	February 6, 1834	July 18, 1863
George Edward Pickett	January 28, 1825	July 30, 1875

Camille A.J.M.Polignac	February 16, 1832	November 15, 1913
Sterling Price	September 20, 1809	September 29, 1867
Stephen Dodson Ramseur	May 31, 1837	October 20, 1864
Robert Ransom,Jr.	February 12, 1828	January 14, 1892
Robert Emmett Rodes	March 29, 1829	September 19, 1864
Thomas Lafayette Rosser	October 15, 1836	March 29, 1910
Gustavus Woodson Smith	November 30, 1821	June 24, 1896
Martin Luther Smith	September 9, 1819	July 29, 1866
William Smith	September 6, 1797	May 18, 1887
Carter L. Stevenson	September 21, 1817	August 15, 1888
James Ewell Stuart	February 6, 1833	May 12, 1864
William B. Taliaferro	December 28, 1822	December 27, 1898
Isaac Ridgeway Trimble	May 15, 1802	January 2, 1888
David Emanuel Twiggs	1790	July 15, 1862
Earl Van Dorn	September 17, 1820	May 7, 1863
John George Walker	July 22, 1822	July 20, 1893
William Henry Walker	November 26, 1816	July 22, 1864
Edward Cary Walthall	April 4, 1831	April 21, 1898
John Austin Wharton	July 3, 1828	April 6, 1865
Joseph Wheeler	September 10, 1836	January 25, 1906
William Henry Whiting	March 22, 1824	March 10, 1865
Cadmus M. Wilcox	May 29, 1824	December 2, 1890
Jones Mitchell Withers	January 12, 1814	March 13, 1890
Ambrose Ransom Wright	April 26, 1826	December 21, 1872
Pierce Manning Young	November 15, 1836	July 6, 1896

UNION MAJOR GENERALS

Christopher C. Augur	July 10, 1821	January 16, 1898
Edward Dickinson Baker	February 24, 1811	October 21, 1861
Nathaniel P. Banks	January 30, 1816	September 1, 1894
Hiram Gregory Berry	August 27, 1824	May 3, 1863
David Bell Birney	May 29, 1825	October 18, 1864
Francis P. Blair,Jr.	February 19, 1821	July 8, 1875
James Gillpatrick Blunt	July 21, 1826	July 27, 1881
William Thomas Brooks	January 28, 1821	July 19, 1870
Don Carlos Buell	March 23, 1818	November 19, 1898
Ambrose Everett Burnside	May 23, 1824	September 13, 1881
Benjamin F. Butler	November 5, 1818	January 11, 1893
Daniel Butterfield	October 31, 1831	July 17, 1901
George Cadwalader	May 16, 1806	February 3, 1879
Edward Richard S. Canby	November 9, 1817	April 11, 1873
Silas Casey	July 12, 1807	January 22, 1882
Cassius Marcellus Clay	October 19, 1810	July 22, 1903
Darius Nash Couch	July 23, 1822	February 12, 1897
Jacob Dolson Cox	October 27, 1828	August 4, 1900
Thomas L. Crittenden	May 15, 1819	October 23, 1893
George Crook	September 8, 1828	March 21, 1890
Samuel Ryan Curtis	February 3, 1805	December 26, 1866
Napoleon Jackson Dana	April 15, 1822	July 15, 1905
John Adams Dix	July 24, 1798	April 21, 1879
Grenville Mellen Dodge	April 12, 1831	January 3, 1916
John Gray Foster	May 27, 1823	September 2, 1874
John Charles Fremont	January 21, 1813	July 13, 1890
William Henry French	January 13, 1815	May 20, 1881
James Abram Garfield	November 19, 1831	September 19, 1881

John Gibbon	April 20, 1827	February 6, 1896
Quincy Adams Gillmore	February 28, 1825	April 7, 1888
Gordon Granger	November 6, 1822	January 10, 1876
Charles Griffin	December 18, 1825	September 15, 1867
Henry Wager Halleck	January 16, 1815	January 9, 1872
Charles Smith Hamilton	November 16, 1822	April 17, 1891
Schuyler Hamilton	July 25, 1822	March 8, 1903
Winfield Scott Hancock	February 14, 1824	February 9, 1886
George Lucas Hartsuff	May 28, 1830	1874
William Babcock Hazen	September 27, 1830	January 16, 1887
Samuel P. Heintzelman	September 30, 1805	May 1, 1880
Francis Jay Herron	February 17, 1837	January 8, 1902
Ethan Allen Hitchcock	May 18, 1798	August 5, 1870
Joseph Hooker	November 13, 1814	October 31, 1879
Oliver Otis Howard	November 8, 1830	October 26, 1909
Andrew A. Humphreys	November 2, 1810	December 27, 1883
David Hunter	July 21, 1802	February 2, 1886
Stephen A. Hurlbut	November 29, 1815	March 27, 1882
Philip Kearny	June 2, 1815	September 1, 1862
Erasmus Darwin Keyes	May 29, 1810	October 14, 1895
John Alexander Logan	February 9, 1826	December 26, 1886
George B. McClellan	December 3, 1826	October 29, 1885
John Alexander McClernand	May 30, 1812	September 20, 1890
Alexander McDowell McCook	April 22, 1831	June 12, 1903
Irvin McDowell	October 15, 1818	May 4, 1885
James B. McPherson	November 14, 1828	July 22, 1864
George Gordon Meade	December 31, 1815	November 6, 1872
Wesley Merritt	June 16, 1834	December 3, 1910
Robert Huston Milroy	June 11, 1816	March 29, 1890
Ormsby MacKnight Mitchel	July 28, 1809	October 30, 1862
George Webb Morell	January 8, 1815	February 11, 1883
Edwin Denison Morgan	February 8, 1811	February 14, 1883
Joseph Anthony Mower	August 22, 1827	January 6, 1870
James Scott Negley	December 22, 1826	August 7, 1901
William Nelson	September 27, 1824	September 29, 1862
John Newton	August 25, 1822	May 1, 1895
Richard James Oglesby	July 25, 1824	April 24, 1899
Edward Otho C. Ord	October 18, 1818	July 22, 1883
Peter Joseph Osterhaus	January 4, 1823	January 2, 1917
John McCauley Palmer	September 13, 1817	September 25, 1900
John Grubb Parke	September 22, 1827	December 16, 1900
John James Peck	January 4, 1821	April 21, 1878
Alfred Pleasonton	July 7, 1824	February 17, 1897
John Pope	March 16, 1822	September 23, 1892
Fitz John Porter	August 31, 1822	May 21, 1901
Benjamin M. Prentiss	November 23, 1819	February 8, 1901
Jesse Lee Reno	June 20, 1823	September 14, 1862
John Fulton Reynolds	September 20, 1820	July 1, 1863
Joseph Jones Reynolds	January 4, 1822	February 25, 1899
Israel Bush Richardson	December 26, 1815	November 3, 1862
William S. Rosecrans	September 6, 1819	March 11, 1898
Lovell Harrison Rousseau	August 4, 1818	January 7, 1869
Robert Cumming Schenck	October 4, 1809	March 23, 1890
John M. Schofield	September 29, 1831	March 4, 1906
Carl Schurz	March 2, 1829	May 14, 1906
Winfield Scott	June 13, 1786	May 29, 1866

John Sedgwick	September 13, 1813	May 9, 1864
Philip Henry Sheridan	March 6, 1831	August 5, 1888
William T. Sherman	February 8, 1820	February 14, 1891
Daniel Edgar Sickles	October 20, 1819	May 3, 1914
Franz Sigel	November 18, 1824	August 21, 1902
Henry Warner Slocum	September 24, 1827	April 14, 1894
Andrew Jackson Smith	April 28, 1815	January 30, 1897
Charles Ferguson Smith	April 24, 1807	April 25, 1862
William Farrar Smith	February 17, 1824	February 28, 1903
Julius Stahel	November 5, 1825	December 4, 1912
David Sloane Stanley	June 1, 1828	March 13, 1902
James Blair Steedman	July 29, 1817	October 18, 1883
Frederick Steele	January 14, 1819	January 12, 1868
George Stoneman	August 22, 1822	September 5, 1894
Edwin Vose Sumner	January 30, 1797	March 21, 1863
George Sykes	October 9, 1822	February 8, 1880
Alfred Howe Terry	November 10, 1827	December 16, 1890
George Henry Thomas	July 31, 1816	March 28, 1870
Lewis Wallace	April 10, 1827	February 15, 1905
Gouverneur Kemble Warren	January 8, 1830	August 8, 1882
Cadwallader C. Washburn	April 22, 1818	May 14, 1882
Godfrey Weitzel	November 1, 1835	March 19, 1884
Thomas John Wood	September 25, 1823	February 25, 1906
John Ellis Wool	February 29, 1784	November 10, 1869
Horatio G. Wright	March 6, 1820	July 2, 1899

CONFEDERATE BRIGADIER GENERALS

Daniel Weisiger Adams	June 1821	June 13, 1872
John Adams	July 1, 1825	November 30, 1864
William Wirt Adams	March 22, 1819	May 1, 1888
Edward Porter Alexander	May 26, 1835	April 28, 1910
Henry Watkins Allen	April 29, 1820	April 22, 1866
William Wirt Allen	September 11, 1835	November 24, 1894
George Burgwyn Anderson	April 12, 1831	October 16, 1862
George Thomas Anderson	February 3, 1824	April 4, 1901
Joseph Reid Anderson	February 16, 1813	September 7, 1892
Robert Houstoun Anderson	October 1, 1835	February 8, 1888
Samuel Read Anderson	February 17, 1804	January 2, 1883
James Jay Archer	December 19, 1817	October 24, 1864
Lewis Addison Armistead	October 18, 1817	July 5, 1863
Frank C. Armstrong	November 22, 1835	September 8, 1909
Turner Ashby	October 23, 1828	June 6, 1862
Alpheus Baker	May 28, 1828	October 2, 1891
Laurence Simmons Baker	May 15, 1830	April 10, 1907
William Edwin Baldwin	July 28, 1827	February 19, 1864
William Barksdale	August 21, 1821	July 3, 1863
Rufus Barringer	December 2, 1821	February 3, 1895
John Decatur Barry	June 21, 1839	March 24, 1867
Seth Maxwell Barton	September 8, 1829	April 11, 1900
Cullen Andrews Battle	June 1, 1829	April 8, 1905
Richard Lee T. Beale	May 22, 1819	April 21, 1893
William Nelson R. Beall	March 20, 1825	July 25, 1883
Barnard Elliott Bee	February 8, 1824	July 22, 1861
Hamilton Prioleau Bee	July 22, 1822	October 3, 1897
Tyree Harris Bell	September 5, 1815	September 1, 1902

Henry Lewis Benning	April 2, 1814	July 10, 1875
Albert G. Blanchard	September 10, 1810	June 21, 1891
William Robertson Boggs	March 18, 1829	September 11, 1911
Milledge Luke Bonham	December 25, 1813	August 27, 1890
Lawrence O. Branch	November 28, 1820	September 17, 1862
William Lindsay Brandon	1802	October 8, 1890
William Felix Brantley	March 12, 1830	November 2, 1870
John Bratton	March 7, 1831	January 12, 1898
Theodore W. Brevard	August 26, 1835	June 20, 1882
William Montague Browne	1823	April 28, 1883
Goode Bryan	August 31, 1811	August 16, 1885
Abraham Buford	January 18, 1820	June 9, 1884
Robert Bullock	December 8, 1828	July 27, 1905
William Lewis Cabell	January 1, 1827	February 22, 1911
Alexander W. Campbell	June 4, 1828	June 13, 1893
James Cantey	December 30, 1818	June 30, 1874
Ellison Capers	October 14, 1837	April 22, 1908
William Henry Carroll	1810	May 3, 1868
John Carpenter Carter	December 19, 1837	November 30, 1864
James Ronald Chalmers	January 11, 1831	April 9, 1898
John R. Chambliss,Jr.	January 23, 1833	August 16, 1864
James Chesnut, Jr.	January 18, 1815	February 1, 1885
Robert Hall Chilton	February 25, 1815	February 18, 1879
James Holt Clanton	January 8, 1827	September 27, 1871
Charles Clark	May 24, 1811	December 18, 1877
John Bullock Clark,Jr.	January 14, 1831	September 7, 1903
Thomas Lanier Clingman	July 27, 1812	November 3, 1897
Thomas Reade Rootes Cobb	April 10, 1823	December 13, 1862
Philip St.George Cocke	April 17, 1809	December 26, 1861
Francis Marion Cockrell	October 1, 1834	December 13, 1915
Alfred Holt Colquitt	April 20, 1824	March 26, 1894
Raleigh Edward Colston	October 31, 1825	July 29, 1896
James Conner	September 1, 1829	June 26, 1883
Philip Cook	July 31, 1817	May 21, 1894
John Rogers Cooke	June 9, 1833	April 10, 1891
Douglas Hancock Cooper	November 1, 1815	April 29, 1879
Montgomery Dent Corse	March 14, 1816	February 11, 1895
George Blake Cosby	January 19, 1830	June 29, 1909
William Ruffin Cox	March 11, 1832	December 26, 1919
Alfred Cumming	January 30, 1829	December 5, 1910
Junius Daniel	June 27, 1828	May 13, 1864
Henry Brevard Davidson	January 28, 1831	March 4, 1899
Joseph Robert Davis	January 12, 1825	September 15, 1896
William George M. Davis	May 9, 1812	March 11, 1898
James Dearing	April 25, 1840	April 23, 1865
Zachariah Cantey Deas	October 25, 1819	March 6, 1882
Julius Adolph deLagnel	July 24, 1827	June 3, 1912
James Deshler	February 18, 1833	September 20, 1863
George Gibbs Dibrell	April 12, 1822	May 9, 1888
Thomas P. Dockery	December 18, 1833	February 27, 1898
George Pierce Doles	May 14, 1830	June 2, 1864
Thomas Fenwick Drayton	August 24, 1808	February 18, 1891
Dudley McIver DuBose	October 28, 1834	March 2, 1883
Basil Wilson Duke	May 28, 1838	September 16, 1916
Johnson Kelly Duncan	March 19, 1827	December 18, 1862
John Dunovant	March 5, 1825	October 1, 1864

John Echols	March 20, 1823	May 24, 1896
Matthew Duncan Ector	February 28, 1822	October 29, 1879
Stephen Elliott,Jr.	October 26, 1830	February 21, 1866
Clement Anselm Evans	February 25, 1833	July 2, 1911
Nathan George Evans	February 3, 1824	November 23, 1868
Winfield S. Featherston	August 8, 1820	May 28, 1891
Samuel Wragg Ferguson	November 3, 1834	February 3, 1917
Joseph Finegan	November 17, 1814	October 29, 1885
Jesse Johnson Finley	November 18, 1812	November 6, 1904
John Buchanan Floyd	June 1, 1806	August 26, 1863
William Henry Forney	November 9, 1823	January 16, 1894
John Wesley Frazer	January 6, 1827	March 31, 1906
Daniel Marsh Frost	August 9, 1823	October 29, 1900
Birkett Davenport Fry	June 24, 1822	January 21, 1891
Richard Montgomery Gano	June 17, 1830	March 27, 1913
William Montgomery Gardner	June 8, 1824	June 16, 1901
Samuel Garland,Jr.	December 16, 1830	September 14, 1862
Richard Brooke Garnett	November 21, 1817	July 3, 1863
Robert Selden Garnett	December 16, 1819	July 3, 1861
Lucius Jeremiah Gartrell	January 7, 1821	April 7, 1891
Martin Witherspoon Gary	March 25, 1831	April 9, 1881
Richard Caswell Gatlin	January 18, 1809	September 8, 1896
Samuel Jameson Gholson	May 19, 1808	October 16, 1883
Randall Lee Gibson	September 10, 1832	December 15, 1892
Victor Jean B. Girardey	June 26, 1837	August 16, 1864
States Rights Gist	September 3, 1831	November 30, 1864
Adley Hogan Gladden	October 28, 1810	April 12, 1862
Archibald Campbell Godwin	1832	September 19, 1864
James Monroe Goggin	October 23, 1820	October 10, 1889
George Washington Gordon	October 5, 1836	August 9, 1911
James Byron Gordon	November 2, 1822	May 18, 1864
Josiah Gorgas	July 1, 1818	May 15, 1883
Daniel Chevilette Govan	July 4, 1829	March 12, 1911
Archibald Gracie,Jr.	December 1, 1832	December 2, 1864
Hiram Bronson Granbury	March 1, 1831	November 30, 1864
Henry Gray	January 19, 1816	December 11, 1892
John B. Grayson	October 18, 1806	October 21, 1861
Martin Edwin Green	June 3, 1815	June 25, 1863
Thomas Green	January 8, 1814	April 12, 1864
Elkanah Brackin Greer	October 11, 1825	March 25, 1877
John Gregg	September 28, 1828	October 7, 1864
Maxcy Gregg	August 1, 1814	December 15, 1862
Richard Griffith	January 11, 1814	June 29, 1862
Johnson Hagood	February 21, 1829	January 4, 1898
Roger Weightman Hanson	August 27, 1827	January 4, 1863
William Polk Hardeman	November 4, 1816	April 8, 1898
Nathaniel H. Harris	August 22, 1834	August 23, 1900
James Edward Harrison	April 24, 1815	February 23, 1875
Thomas Harrison	May 1, 1823	July 14, 1891
Robert Hopkins Hatton	November 2, 1826	May 31, 1862
James Morrison Hawes	January 7, 1824	November 22, 1889
Alexander T. Hawthorne	January 10, 1825	May 31, 1899
Louis Hebert	March 13, 1820	January 7, 1901
Paul Octave Hebert	December 12, 1818	August 29, 1880
Benjamin Hardin Helm	June 2, 1831	September 20, 1863
Edward Higgins	1821	January 31, 1875

Benjamin Jefferson Hill	June 13, 1825	January 5, 1880
George Baird Hodge	April 8, 1828	August 1, 1892
Joseph Lewis Hogg	September 13, 1806	May 16, 1862
James T. Holtzclaw	December 17, 1833	July 19, 1893
William Young Conn Humes	May 1, 1830	September 11, 1882
Benjamin Grubb Humphreys	August 24, 1808	December 20, 1882
Eppa Hunton	September 22, 1822	October 11, 1908
John Daniel Imboden	February 16, 1823	August 15, 1895
Alfred Iverson,Jr.	February 14, 1829	March 31, 1911
Alfred Eugene Jackson	January 11, 1807	October 30, 1889
Henry Rootes Jackson	June 24, 1820	May 23, 1898
John King Jackson	February 8, 1828	February 27, 1866
William Hicks Jackson	October 1, 1835	March 30, 1903
William Lowther Jackson	February 3, 1825	March 24, 1890
Albert G. Jenkins	November 10, 1830	May 21, 1864
Micah Jenkins	December 1, 1835	May 6, 1864
Adam Rankin Johnson	February 8, 1834	October 20, 1922
Bradley Tyler Johnson	September 29, 1829	October 5, 1903
George Doherty Johnston	May 30, 1832	December 8, 1910
Robert Daniel Johnston	March 19, 1837	February 1, 1919
John Marshall Jones	July 26, 1820	May 5, 1864
John Robert Jones	March 12, 1827	April 1, 1901
William Edmonson Jones	May 9, 1824	June 5, 1864
Thomas Jordan	September 30, 1819	November 27, 1895
John Herbert Kelly	March 31, 1840	September 4, 1864
John Doby Kennedy	January 5, 1840	April 14, 1896
William W. Kirkland	February 13, 1833	May 12, 1915
James Henry Lane	July 28, 1833	September 21, 1907
Walter Paye Lane	February 18, 1817	January 28, 1892
Evander McIvor Law	August 7, 1836	October 31, 1920
Alexander Robert Lawton	November 4, 1818	July 2, 1896
Danville Leadbetter	August 26, 1811	September 26, 1866
Edwin Gray Lee	May 27, 1836	August 24, 1870
Collett Leventhorpe	May 15, 1815	December 1, 1889
Joseph Horace Lewis	October 29, 1824	July 6, 1904
William Gaston Lewis	September 3, 1835	January 7, 1901
St.John R. Liddell	September 6, 1815	February 14, 1870
Robert Doak Lilley	January 28, 1836	November 12, 1886
Lewis Henry Little	March 19, 1817	September 19, 1862
Thomas Muldrup Logan	November 3, 1840	August 11, 1914
Armistead Lindsay Long	September 3, 1825	April 29, 1891
Mark Perrin Lowrey	December 30, 1828	February 27, 1885
Robert Lowry	March 10, 1830	January 19, 1910
Hylan Benton Lyon	February 22, 1836	April 25, 1907
William Whann Mackall	January 18, 1817	August 12, 1891
William MacRae	September 9, 1834	February 11, 1882
James Patrick Major	May 14, 1836	May 7, 1877
George Ear Maney	August 24, 1826	February 9, 1901
Arthur M. Manigault	October 26, 1824	August 17, 1886
Humphrey Marshall	January 13, 1812	March 28, 1872
James Green Martin	February 14, 1819	October 4, 1878
John McCausland	September 13, 1836	January 22, 1927
William McComb	November 21, 1828	July 21, 1918
Ben McCulloch	November 11, 1811	March 7, 1862
Henry E. McCulloch	December 6, 1816	March 12, 1895
Samuel McGowan	October 9, 1819	August 9, 1897

James McQueen McIntosh	1828	March 7, 1862
Evander McNair	April 15, 1820	November 13, 1902
Dandridge McRae	October 10, 1829	April 23, 1899
Hugh Weedon Mercer	November 27, 1808	June 9, 1877
William Miller	August 3, 1820	August 8, 1909
Young Marshall Moody	June 23, 1822	September 18, 1866
John Creed Moore	February 28, 1824	December 31, 1910
Patrick T. Moore	September 22, 1821	February 19, 1883
John Hunt Morgan	June 1, 1825	September 4, 1864
John Tyler Morgan	June 20, 1824	June 11, 1907
Jean Jacques Mouton	February 18, 1829	April 8, 1864
Allison Nelson	March 11, 1822	October 7, 1862
Francis Redding Nicholls	August 20, 1834	January 4, 1912
Lucius B. Northrop	September 8, 1811	February 9, 1894
Richard Lucian Page	December 20, 1807	August 9, 1901
Joseph Benjamin Palmer	November 1, 1825	November 4, 1890
Elisha Franklin Paxton	March 4, 1828	May 3, 1863
William Henry F. Payne	January 27, 1830	March 29, 1904
William Raine Peck	January 31, 1818	January 22, 1871
John Pegram	January 24, 1832	February 6, 1865
William N. Pendleton	December 26, 1809	January 15, 1883
Abner Monroe Perrin	February 2, 1827	May 12, 1864
Edward Aylesworth Perry	March 15, 1831	October 15, 1889
William Flank Perry	March 12, 1823	December 18, 1901
James Johnston Pettigrew	July 4, 1828	July 17, 1863
Edmund Winston Pettus	July 6, 1821	July 27, 1907
Albert Pike	December 29, 1809	April 2, 1891
Gideon Johnson Pillow	June 8, 1806	October 8, 1878
Lucius Eugene Polk	July 10, 1833	December 1, 1892
Carnot Posey	August 5, 1818	November 13, 1863
John Smith Preston	April 20, 1809	May 1, 1881
William Preston	October 16, 1816	September 21, 1887
Roger Atkinson Pryor	July 19, 1828	March 14, 1919
William Andrew Quarles	July 4, 1825	December 28, 1893
Gabriel James Rains	June 4, 1803	August 6, 1881
James Edwards Rains	April 10, 1833	December 31, 1862
George Wythe Randolph	March 10, 1818	April 3, 1867
Matt Whitaker Ransom	October 8, 1826	October 8, 1904
Alexander Welch Reynolds	April 1816	May 26, 1876
Daniel Harris Reynolds	December 14, 1832	March 14, 1902
Robert Richardson	November 4, 1820	January 5, 1870
Roswell Sabine Ripley	March 14, 1823	March 29, 1887
John Selden Roane	January 8, 1817	April 8, 1867
William Paul Roberts	July 11, 1841	March 28, 1910
Beverly Holcombe Robertson	June 5, 1827	November 12, 1910
Felix Huston Robertson	March 9, 1839	April 20, 1928
Jerome Bonaparte Robertson	March 14, 1815	January 7, 1891
Philip Dale Roddey	April 2, 1826	July 20, 1897
Lawrence Sullivan Ross	September 27, 1838	January 3, 1898
Daniel Ruggles	January 31, 1810	June 1, 1897
Albert Rust	1818	April 4, 1870
John Caldwell C. Sanders	April 4, 1840	August 21, 1864
Alfred Moore Scales	November 26, 1827	February 8, 1892
Thomas Moore Scott	1829	April 21, 1876
William Read Scurry	February 10, 1821	April 30, 1864
Claudius Wistar Sears	November 8, 1817	February 15, 1891

Name	Birth	Death
Paul Jones Semmes	June 4, 1815	July 10, 1863
Jacob Hunter Sharp	February 6, 1833	September 15, 1907
Joseph Orville Shelby	December 12, 1830	February 13, 1897
Charles Miller Shelley	December 28, 1833	January 20, 1907
Francis Asbury Shoup	March 22, 1834	September 4, 1896
Henry Hopkins Sibley	May 25, 1816	August 23, 1886
James Phillip Simms	January 16, 1837	May 30, 1887
William Yarnel Slack	August 1, 1816	March 21, 1862
James Edwin Slaughter	June 0, 1827	January 1, 1901
James Argyle Smith	July 1, 1831	December 6, 1901
Preston Smith	December 25, 1823	September 19, 1863
Thomas Benton Smith	February 24, 1838	May 21, 1923
William Duncan Smith	July 28, 1825	October 4, 1862
Gilbert Moxley Sorrel	February 23, 1838	August 10, 1901
Isaac Munroe St.John	November 19, 1827	April 7, 1880
Leroy Augustus Stafford	April 13, 1822	May 8, 1864
Peter Burwell Starke	1815	July 13, 1888
William Edwin Starke	1814	September 16, 1862
William Steele	May 1, 1819	January 12, 1885
George Hume Steuart	August 24, 1828	November 22, 1903
Clement Hoffman Stevens	August 14, 1821	July 25, 1864
Walter Husted Stevens	August 24, 1827	November 12, 1867
Marcellus Stovall	September 18, 1818	August 4, 1895
Otho French Strahl	June 3, 1831	November 30, 1864
James Camp Tappan	September 9, 1825	March 19, 1906
Thomas Hart Taylor	July 31, 1825	April 12, 1901
William Terry	August 14, 1824	September 5, 1888
William Richard Terry	March 12, 1827	March 28, 1897
Allen Thomas	December 14, 1830	December 3, 1897
Bryan Morel Thomas	May 8, 1836	July 16, 1905
Edward Lloyd Thomas	March 23, 1825	March 8, 1898
Lloyd Tilghman	January 26, 1816	May 16, 1863
Robert Augustus Toombs	July 2, 1810	December 15, 1885
Thomas Fentress Toon	June 10, 1840	February 19, 1902
Edward Dorr Tracy	November 5, 1833	May 1, 1863
James Heyward Trapier	November 24, 1815	December 21, 1865
William Feimster Tucker	May 9, 1827	September 14, 1881
Robert Charles Tyler	1833	April 16, 1865
Robert Brank Vance	April 24, 1828	November 28, 1899
Alfred Jefferson Vaughan,Jr	May 10, 1830	October 1, 1899
John Crawford Vaughn	February 24, 1824	September 10, 1875
John Bordenave Villepigue	July 2, 1830	November 9, 1862
Henry Harrison Walker	October 15, 1832	March 22, 1912
James Alexander Walker	August 27, 1832	October 20, 1901
Leroy Pope Walker	February 7, 1817	August 22, 1884
Lucius Marshall Walker	October 18, 1829	September 7, 1863
Reuben Lindsay Walker	May 29, 1827	June 7, 1890
William Stephen Walker	April 13, 1822	June 7, 1899
William Henry Wallace	March 24, 1827	March 21, 1901
Richard Waterhouse	January 12, 1832	March 20, 1876
Stand Watie	December 12, 1806	September 9, 1871
Thomas Neville Waul	January 5, 1813	July 28, 1903
Henry Constantine Wayne	September 18, 1815	March 15, 1883
David Addison Weisiger	December 23, 1818	February 23, 1899
Gabriel Colvin Wharton	July 23, 1824	May 12, 1906
John Wilkins Whitfield	March 11, 1818	October 27, 1879

Williams Carter Wickham	September 21, 1820	July 23, 1888
Louis Trezevant Wigfall	April 21, 1816	February 18, 1874
John Stuart Williams	July 10, 1818	July 17, 1898
Charles Sidney Winder	October 18, 1829	August 9, 1862
John Henry Winder	February 21, 1800	February 7, 1865
Henry Alexander Wise	December 3, 1806	September 12, 1876
William Tatum Wofford	June 28, 1824	May 22, 1884
Sterling Alexander M. Wood	March 17, 1823	January 26, 1891
Marcus Joseph Wright	June 5, 1831	December 27, 1922
Zebulon York	October 10, 1819	August 5, 1900
William Hugh Young	January 1, 1838	November 28, 1901
Felix Kirk Zollicoffer	May 19, 1812	January 19, 1862

UNION BRIGADIER GENERALS

John Joseph Abercrombie	March 4, 1798	January 3, 1877
Robert Allen	March 15, 1811	August 5, 1886
Benjamin Alvord	August 18, 1813	October 16, 1884
Adelbert Ames	October 31, 1835	April 13, 1833
Jacob Ammen	January 7, 1806	February 6, 1894
Robert Anderson	June 14, 1805	October 26, 1871
Christopher C. Andrews	October 27, 1829	September 21, 1922
George Leonard Andrews	August 31, 1828	April 4, 1899
Lewis Golding Arnold	January 15, 1817	September 21, 1871
Richard Arnold	April 12, 1828	November 8, 1882
Alexander Sandor Asboth	December 18, 1811	January 21, 1868
William Woods Averell	November 5, 1832	February 3, 1900
Romeyn Beck Ayres	December 20, 1825	December 4, 1888
Joseph Bailey	May 6, 1825	March 21, 1867
Absalom Baird	August 20, 1824	June 14, 1905
Francis Channing Barlow	October 19, 1834	January 11, 1896
John Gross Barnard	May 19, 1815	May 14, 1882
James Barnes	December 28, 1801	February 12, 1869
Joseph K. Barnes	July 21, 1817	June 30, 1882
William Farquhar Barry	August 18, 1818	July 18, 1879
Joseph Jackson Bartlett	November 21, 1834	January 14, 1893
William Francis Bartlett	June 6, 1840	December 17, 1876
Henry Baxter	September 8, 1821	December 30, 1873
George Dashiell Bayard	December 18, 1835	December 14, 1862
George Lafayette Beal	May 21, 1825	December 11, 1896
John Beatty	December 16, 1828	December 21, 1914
Samuel Beatty	December 16, 1820	May 26, 1885
William Worth Belknap	September 22, 1829	October 13, 1890
Henry Washington Benham	April 17, 1813	June 1, 1884
William Plummer Benton	December 25, 1828	March 14, 1867
Daniel Davidson Bidwell	August 12, 1819	October 19, 1864
Henry Warner Birge	August 25, 1825	June 1, 1888
William Birney	May 28, 1819	August 14, 1907
Louis Ludwig Blenker	May 12, 1812	October 31, 1863
Henry Bohlen	October 22, 1810	August 22, 1862
James Bowen	February 25, 1808	September 29, 1886
Jerimiah Tilford Boyle	May 22, 1818	July 28, 1871
Luther Prentice Bradley	December 8, 1822	March 13, 1910
Edward Stuyvesant Bragg	February 20, 1827	June 20, 1912
John Milton Brannan	July 1, 1819	December 16, 1892
Mason Brayman	May 23, 1813	February 27, 1895

Henry Shaw Briggs	August 1, 1824	September 23, 1887
John Rutter Brooke	July 21, 1838	September 5, 1926
Egbert Benson Brown	October 4, 1816	February 11, 1902
Robert Christie Buchanan	March 1, 1811	November 29, 1878
Catharinus Buckingham	March 14, 1808	August 30, 1888
Ralph Pomeroy Buckland	January 20, 1812	May 27, 1892
John Buford	March 4, 1826	December 16, 1863
Napoleon Bonaparte Buford	January 13, 1807	March 28, 1883
Stephen Gano Burbridge	August 19, 1831	December 2, 1894
Hiram Burnham	1814	September 29, 1864
William Wallace Burns	September 3, 1825	April 19, 1892
Cyrus Bussey	October 5, 1833	March 2, 1915
Richard Busteed	February 16, 1822	September 14, 1898
John Curtis Caldwell	April 17, 1833	August 31, 1912
Robert Alexander Cameron	February 22, 1828	March 15, 1894
Charles Thomas Campbell	August 10, 1823	April 15, 1895
William Bowen Campbell	February 1, 1807	August 19, 1867
James Henry Carleton	December 27, 1814	January 7, 1873
William Passmore Carlin	November 24, 1829	October 4, 1903
Eugene Asa Carr	March 20, 1830	December 2, 1910
Joseph Bradford Carr	August 16, 1828	February 24, 1895
Henry Beebee Carrington	March 2, 1824	October 26, 1912
Samuel Sprigg Carroll	September 21, 1832	January 28, 1893
Samuel Powhatan Carter	August 6, 1819	May 26, 1891
Joshua Chamberlain	September 8, 1828	February 24, 1914
Alexander Chambers	August 23, 1832	January 2, 1888
Stephen Gardner Champlin	July 1, 1827	January 24, 1864
George Henry Chapman	November 22, 1832	June 16, 1882
Augustus Louis Chetlain	December 26, 1824	March 15, 1914
Powell Clayton	August 7, 1833	August 25, 1914
Gustave Paul Cluseret	June 13, 1823	August 22, 1900
John Cochrane	August 27, 1813	February 7, 1898
Patrick Edward Connor	March 17, 1820	December 17, 1891
Selden Connor	January 25, 1839	July 9, 1917
John Cook	June 12, 1825	October 13, 1910
Philip St.George Cooke	June 13, 1809	March 20, 1895
James Cooper	May 8, 1810	March 28, 1863
Joseph Alexander Cooper	November 25, 1823	May 20, 1910
Joseph Tarr Copeland	May 6, 1813	May 6, 1893
Michael Corcoran	September 21, 1827	December 22, 1863
John Murray Corse	April 27, 1835	April 27, 1893
Robert Cowdin	September 18, 1805	July 9, 1874
James Craig	February 28, 1817	October 21, 1888
Samuel Wylie Crawford	November 8, 1829	November 3, 1892
Thomas Turpin Crittenden	October 16, 1825	September 5, 1905
Marcellus Monroe Crocker	February 6, 1830	August 26, 1865
John Thomas Croxton	November 20, 1836	April 16, 1874
Charles Cruft	January 12, 1826	March 23, 1883
George Cullum	February 25, 1809	February 29, 1892
Newton Martin Curtis	May 21, 1835	January 8, 1910
George Armstrong Custer	December 5, 1839	June 25, 1876
Lysander Cutler	February 16, 1807	July 30, 1866
John Wynn Davidson	August 18, 1824	June 26, 1881
Henry Eugene Davies	July 2, 1836	September 7, 1894
Thomas Alfred Davies	December 3, 1809	August 19, 1899
Edmund Jackson Davis	October 2, 1827	February 7, 1883

Jefferson Columbus Davis	March 2, 1828	November 30, 1879
George Deitzler	November 30, 1826	April 11, 1884
Richard Delafield	September 1, 1798	November 5, 1873
Elias Smith Dennis	December 4, 1812	December 17, 1894
James William Denver	October 23, 1817	August 9, 1892
Gustavus DeRussy	November 3, 1818	May 29, 1891
Philippe Regis deTrobriand	June 4, 1816	July 15, 1897
Charles Devens,Jr.	April 4, 1820	January 7, 1891
Thomas Casimer Devin	December 10, 1822	April 4, 1878
Charles Cleveland Dodge	September 16, 1841	November 4, 1910
Charles Camp Doolittle	March 16, 1832	February 20, 1903
Abner Doubleday	June 26, 1819	January 26, 1893
Neal Dow	March 20, 1804	October 2, 1897
Alfred Napoleon Duffie	May 1, 1835	November 8, 1880
Ebenezer Dumont	November 23, 1814	April 16, 1871
Abram Duryee	April 29, 1815	September 27, 1890
Isaac Hardin Duval	September 1, 1824	July 10, 1902
William Dwight	July 14, 1831	April 21, 1888
Alexander Brydie Dyer	January 10, 1815	May 20, 1874
Amos Beebe Eaton	May 12, 1806	February 21, 1877
John Edwards	October 24, 1815	April 8, 1894
Thomas Wilberforce Egan	June 14, 1834	February 24, 1887
Alfred Washington Ellet	November 11, 1820	January 9, 1895
Washington Elliott	March 31, 1825	June 29, 1888
William Hemsley Emory	September 7, 1811	December 1, 1887
Henry Lawrence Eustis	February 1, 1819	January 11, 1885
Hugh Boyle Ewing	October 31, 1826	June 30, 1905
Thomas Ewing,Jr.	August 7, 1829	January 21, 1896
Lucius Fairchild	December 27, 1831	May 23, 1896
Elon John Farnsworth	July 30, 1837	July 3, 1863
John Franklin Farnsworth	March 27, 1820	July 14, 1897
Edward Ferrero	January 18, 1831	December 11, 1899
Orris Sanford Ferry	August 15, 1823	November 21, 1875
Francis Fessenden	March 18, 1839	January 2, 1906
James Deering Fessenden	September 28, 1833	November 18, 1882
Clinton Bowen Fisk	December 8, 1828	July 9, 1890
Manning Ferguson Force	December 17, 1824	May 8, 1899
Robert Sanford Foster	January 27, 1834	March 3, 1903
William Buel Franklin	February 27, 1823	March 8, 1903
James Barnet Fry	February 22, 1827	July 11, 1894
Speed Smith Fry	September 9, 1817	August 1, 1892
John Wallace Fuller	July 28, 1827	March 12, 1891
Kenner Garrard	September 30, 1827	May 15, 1879
Theophilus Toulmin Garrard	June 7, 1812	March 15, 1902
John White Geary	December 30, 1819	January 18, 1873
George Washington Getty	October 2, 1819	October 1, 1901
Alfred Gibbs	April 22, 1823	December 26, 1868
Charles Champion Gilbert	March 1, 1822	January 17, 1903
James Isham Gilbert	July 16, 1823	February 9, 1884
Alvan Cullem Gillem	July 29, 1830	December 2, 1875
George Henry Gordon	July 19, 1823	August 30, 1886
Willis Arnold Gorman	January 12, 1816	May 20, 1876
Charles Kinnaird Graham	June 3, 1824	April 15, 1889
Lawrence Pike Graham	January 8, 1815	September 12, 1905
Robert Seaman Granger	May 24, 1816	April 25, 1894
Lewis Addison Grant	January 17, 1828	March 20, 1918

Name	Born	Died
George Sears Greene	May 6, 1801	January 28, 1899
David McMurtrie Gregg	April 10, 1833	August 7, 1916
Walter Quintin Gresham	March 17, 1832	May 28, 1895
Benjamin Henry Grierson	July 8, 1826	September 1, 1911
Simon Goodell Griffin	August 9, 1824	January 14, 1902
William Grose	December 16, 1812	July 30, 1900
Cuvier Grover	July 29, 1828	June 6, 1885
Pleasant Adam Hackleman	November 15, 1814	October 3, 1862
Andrew Jackson Hamilton	January 28, 1815	April 11, 1875
Cyrus Hamlin	April 26, 1839	August 28, 1867
William Alexander Hammond	August 28, 1828	January 5, 1900
James Allen Hardie	May 5, 1823	December 14, 1876
Martin Davis Hardin	June 26, 1837	December 12, 1923
Abner Clark Harding	February 10, 1807	July 19, 1874
Charles Garrison Harker	December 2, 1835	June 26, 1864
Edward Harland	June 24, 1832	March 9, 1915
William Selby Harney	August 27, 1800	May 9, 1889
Thomas Maley Harris	June 17, 1817	September 30, 1906
William Harrow	November 14, 1822	September 27, 1872
John Frederick Hartranft	December 16, 1830	October 17, 1889
Milo Smith Hascall	August 5, 1829	August 30, 1904
Joseph Abel Haskin	June 21, 1818	August 3, 1874
Edward Hatch	December 22, 1832	April 11, 1889
John Porter Hatch	January 9, 1822	April 12, 1901
Herman Haupt	March 26, 1817	December 14, 1905
John Parker Hawkins	September 29, 1830	February 7, 1914
Joseph Roswell Hawley	October 31, 1826	March 18, 1905
Joseph Hayes	September 14, 1835	August 19, 1912
Rutherford Birchard Hayes	October 4, 1822	January 13, 1893
Isham Nicholas Haynie	November 18, 1824	May 22, 1868
Alexander Hays	July 8, 1819	May 5, 1864
William Hays	May 9, 1819	February 7, 1875
Charles Adam Heckman	December 3, 1822	January 14, 1896
Edward Winslow Hincks	May 30, 1830	February 14, 1894
Edward Henry Hobson	July 11, 1825	September 14, 1901
Joseph Holt	January 6, 1807	August 1, 1894
Alvin Peterson Hovey	September 26, 1821	November 23, 1891
Charles Edward Hovey	April 26, 1827	November 17, 1897
Albion Parris Howe	March 13, 1818	January 25, 1897
Henry Jackson Hunt	September 14, 1819	February 11, 1889
Lewis Cass Hunt	February 23, 1824	September 6, 1886
Rufus Ingalls	August 23, 1818	January 15, 1893
Conrad Feger Jackson	September 11, 1813	December 13, 1862
James Streshly Jackson	September 27, 1823	October 8, 1862
Nathaniel James Jackson	July 28, 1818	April 21, 1892
Charles Davis Jameson	February 24, 1827	November 6, 1862
Andrew Johnson	December 29, 1808	July 31, 1875
Richard W. Johnson	February 27, 1827	April 21, 1897
Henry Moses Judah	June 12, 1821	January 14, 1866
Thomas Leiper Kane	January 27, 1822	December 26, 1883
August Valentine Kautz	January 5, 1828	September 4, 1895
William High Keim	June 25, 1813	May 18, 1862
Benjamin Franklin Kelley	April 10, 1807	July 16, 1891
John Reese Kenly	January 11, 1818	December 20, 1891
William Scott Ketchum	July 7, 1813	June 28, 1871
James Lawlor Kiernan	October 26, 1837	November 29, 1869

Hugh Judson Kilpatrick	January 14, 1836	December 4, 1881
Nathan Kimball	November 22, 1822	January 21, 1898
John Haskell King	February 19, 1820	April 7, 1888
Rufus King	January 26, 1814	October 13, 1876
Edward Needles Kirk	February 29, 1828	July 21, 1863
Joseph Farmer Knipe	March 30, 1823	August 18, 1901
Wladimir Krzyzanowski	July 8, 1824	January 31, 1887
Frederick West Lander	December 17, 1821	March 2, 1862
Jacob Gartner Lauman	January 20, 1813	February 9, 1867
Michael Kelly Lawler	November 16, 1814	July 26, 1882
James Hewett Ledlie	April 14, 1832	August 15, 1882
Albert Lindley Lee	January 16, 1834	December 31, 1907
Mortimer Dormer Leggett	April 19, 1821	January 6, 1896
Joseph Andrew Lightburn	September 21, 1824	May 17, 1901
Henry Hayes Lockwood	August 17, 1814	December 7, 1899
Eli Long	June 16, 1837	January 5, 1903
Thomas John Lucas	September 9, 1826	November 16, 1908
Nathaniel Lyon	July 14, 1818	August 10, 1861
William Haines Lytle	November 2, 1826	September 20, 1863
Ranald Slidell Mackenzie	July 27, 1840	January 19, 1889
Jasper Adalmorn Maltby	November 3, 1826	December 12, 1867
Joseph King F. Mansfield	December 22, 1803	September 18, 1862
Mahlon Dickerson Manson	February 20, 1820	February 4, 1895
Randolph Barnes Marcy	April 9, 1812	November 2, 1887
Gilman Marston	August 20, 1811	July 3, 1890
John Henry Martindale	March 20, 1815	December 13, 1881
John Sanford Mason	August 21, 1824	November 29, 1897
Charles Leopold Matthies	May 31, 1824	October 16, 1868
John McArthur	November 17, 1826	May 15, 1906
George Archibald McCall	March 16, 1802	February 26, 1868
Edward Moody McCook	June 15, 1833	September 9, 1909
Robert Latimer McCook	December 28, 1827	August 6, 1862
George Francis McGinnis	March 19, 1826	May 29, 1910
John Baillie McIntosh	June 6, 1829	June 29, 1888
Thomas Jefferson McKean	August 21, 1810	April 19, 1870
Justus McKinstry	July 6, 1814	December 11, 1897
Nathaniel Collins McLean	February 2, 1815	January 4, 1905
James Winning McMillan	April 28, 1825	March 9, 1903
John McNeil	February 14, 1813	June 8, 1891
Thomas Francis Meagher	August 3, 1823	July 1, 1867
Montgomery Cunningham Meigs	May 3, 1816	January 2, 1892
Solomon Meredith	May 29, 1810	October 2, 1875
Sullivan Amory Meredith	July 4, 1816	December 26, 1874
Nelson Appleton Miles	August 8, 1839	May 15, 1925
John Franklin Miller	November 21, 1831	March 8, 1886
Stephen Miller	January 7, 1816	August 18, 1881
John Grant Mitchell	November 6, 1838	November 7, 1894
Robert Byington Mitchell	April 4, 1823	January 26, 1882
William Reading Montgomery	July 10, 1801	June 1, 1871
George W. Morgan	September 20, 1820	July 26, 1893
James Dada Morgan	August 1, 1810	September 12, 1896
William Hopkins Morris	April 22, 1827	August 26, 1900
James St.Clair Morton	September 24, 1829	June 17, 1864
Gershom Mott	April 7, 1822	November 29, 1884
James Nagle	April 5, 1822	August 22, 1866
Henry Morris Naglee	January 15, 1815	March 5, 1886

Thomas Hewson Neill	April 9, 1826	March 12, 1885
Franklin S. Nickerson	August 27, 1826	January 23, 1917
John Morrison Oliver	September 6, 1828	March 30, 1872
William Ward Orme	February 17, 1832	September 13, 1866
Joshua Thomas Owen	March 29, 1821	November 7, 1887
Charles Jackson Paine	August 26, 1833	August 12, 1916
Eleazer Arthur Paine	September 10, 1815	December 16, 1882
Halbert Eleazer Paine	February 4, 1826	April 14, 1905
Innis Newton Palmer	March 30, 1824	September 9, 1900
Marsena Rudolph Patrick	March 11, 1811	July 27, 1888
Francis Engle Patterson	May 7, 1821	November 22, 1862
Gabriel Rene Paul	March 22, 1813	May 5, 1886
John Smith Phelps	December 22, 1814	November 20, 1886
John Wolcott Phelps	November 13, 1813	February 2, 1885
Abram Sanders Piatt	May 2, 1821	March 16, 1808
Byron Root Pierce	September 20, 1829	July 10, 1824
William Anderson Pile	February 11, 1829	July 7, 1889
Thomas Gamble Pitcher	October 23, 1824	October 21, 1895
Joseph Bennett Plummer	November 15, 1816	August 9, 1862
Orlando Metcalfe Poe	March 7, 1832	October 2, 1895
Andrew Porter	July 10, 1820	January 3, 1872
Edward Elmer Potter	June 21, 1823	June 1, 1889
Robert Brown Potter	July 16, 1829	February 19, 1887
Benjamin Franklin Potts	January 29, 1836	June 17, 1887
William Henry Powell	May 10, 1825	December 26, 1904
Calvin Edward Pratt	January 23, 1828	August 3, 1896
Henry Prince	June 19, 1811	August 19, 1892
Issac Ferdinand Quinby	January 29, 1821	September 18, 1891
George Douglas Ramsay	February 21, 1802	May 23, 1882
Thomas Edward G. Ransom	November 29, 1834	October 29, 1864
Green Berry Raum	December 3, 1829	December 18, 1909
John Aaron Rawlins	February 13, 1831	September 6, 1869
Hugh Thompson Reid	October 18, 1811	August 21, 1874
James William Reilly	May 20, 1828	November 6, 1905
Joseph Warren Revere	May 17, 1812	April 20, 1880
Elliott Warren Rice	November 16, 1835	June 22, 1887
James Clay Rice	December 27, 1829	May 10, 1864
Samuel Allen Rice	January 27, 1828	July 6, 1864
James Brewerton Ricketts	June 21, 1817	September 22, 1887
James Wolfe Ripley	December 10, 1794	March 15, 1870
Benjamin Stone Roberts	November 18, 1810	January 29, 1875
James Sidney Robinson	October 14, 1827	January 14, 1892
John Cleveland Robinson	April 10, 1817	February 18, 1897
Isaac Peace Rodman	August 18, 1822	September 30, 1862
Leonard Fulton Ross	July 18, 1823	January 17, 1901
Thomas Algeo Rowley	October 5, 1808	May 14, 1892
Daniel Henry Rucker	April 28, 1812	January 6, 1910
Thomas Howard Ruger	April 2, 1833	June 3, 1907
David Allen Russell	December 10, 1820	September 19, 1864
Friedrich Salomon	April 7, 1826	March 8, 1897
John Benjamin Sanborn	December 5, 1826	May 16, 1904
William Price Sanders	August 12, 1833	November 19, 1863
Rufus Saxton	October 19, 1824	February 23, 1908
Eliakim Parker Scammon	December 27, 1816	December 7, 1894
Alexander Schimmelfennig	July 20, 1824	September 5, 1865
Albin Francisco Schoepf	March 1, 1822	May 10, 1886

William Henry Seward,Jr.	June 18, 1839	April 26, 1920
Truman Seymour	September 24, 1824	October 30, 1891
James Murrell Shackelford	July 7, 1827	September 7, 1909
Alexander Shaler	March 19, 1827	December 28, 1911
Isaac Fitzgerald Shepard	July 7, 1816	August 25, 1889
George Foster Shepley	January 1, 1819	July 20, 1878
Thomas West Sherman	March 26, 1813	March 16, 1879
James Shields	May 10, 1810	June 1, 1879
Henry Hastings Sibley	February 29, 1811	February 18, 1891
Joshua Woodrow Sill	December 6, 1831	December 31, 1862
James Richard Slack	September 28, 1818	July 28, 1881
Adam Jacoby Slemmer	January 24, 1829	October 7, 1868
John Potts Slough	February 1, 1829	December 17, 1867
Giles Alexander Smith	September 29, 1829	November 5, 1876
Green Clay Smith	July 4, 1826	June 29, 1895
Gustavus Adolphus Smith	December 26, 1820	December 11, 1885
John Eugene Smith	August 3, 1816	January 29, 1897
Morgan Lewis Smith	March 8, 1821	December 28, 1874
Thomas Church Smith	March 24, 1819	April 8, 1897
Thomas Kilby Smith	September 23, 1820	December 14, 1887
William Sooy Smith	July 22, 1830	March 4, 1916
Thomas Alfred Smyth	December 25, 1832	April 7, 1865
James Gallant Spears	March 29, 1816	July 22, 1869
Francis Barretto Spinola	March 19, 1821	1890
John Wilson Sprague	April 4, 1817	December 24, 1893
George Jerrison Stannard	October 20, 1820	June 1, 1886
John Converse Starkweather	May 11, 1830	November 14, 1890
Isaac Ingalls Stevens	March 25, 1818	September 1, 1862
John Dunlap Stevenson	June 8, 1821	January 22, 1897
Thomas Greely Stevenson	February 3, 1836	May 10, 1864
Charles John Stolbrand	May 11, 1821	February 3, 1894
Charles Pomeroy Stone	September 30, 1824	January 24, 1887
Edwin Henry Stoughton	June 23, 1838	December 25, 1868
George Crockett Strong	October 16, 1832	July 30, 1863
William Kerley Strong	April 30, 1805	March 16, 1867
David Stuart	March 12, 1816	September 11, 1868
Frederick Stumbaugh	April 14, 1817	February 25, 1897
Samuel Davis Sturgis	June 11, 1822	September 28, 1889
Jeremiah Cutler Sullivan	October 1, 1830	October 21, 1890
Alfred Sully	May 22, 1820	April 27, 1879
Wager Swayne	November 10, 1834	December 18, 1902
Thomas William Sweeny	December 25, 1820	April 10, 1892
George William Taylor	November 22, 1808	September 1, 1862
Joseph Pannell Taylor	May 4, 1796	June 29, 1864
Nelson Taylor	June 8, 1821	January 16, 1894
William Rufus Terrill	April 21, 1834	October 8, 1862
Henry Dwight Terry	March 16, 1812	June 22, 1869
John Milton Thayer	January 24, 1820	March 19, 1906
Henry Goddard Thomas	April 4, 1837	January 23, 1897
Lorenzo Thomas	October 26, 1804	March 2, 1875
Charles Mynn Thruston	February 22, 1798	February 18, 1873
Davis Tillson	April 14, 1830	April 30, 1895
John Blair Smith Todd	April 4, 1814	January 5, 1872
Alfred Thomas A. Torbert	July 1, 1833	August 29, 1880
Joseph Gilbert Totten	April 17, 1788	April 22, 1864
Zealous Bates Tower	January 12, 1819	March 20, 1900

John Basil Turchin	January 30, 1822	June 19, 1901
John Wesley Turner	July 19, 1833	April 8, 1899
James Madison Tuttle	September 24, 1823	October 24, 1892
Daniel Tyler	January 7, 1799	November 30, 1882
Erastus Barnard Tyler	April 24, 1822	January 9, 1891
Robert Ogden Tyler	December 22, 1831	December 1, 1874
George Hector Tyndale	March 24, 1821	March 19, 1880
Daniel Ullmann	April 28, 1810	September 20, 1892
Adin Ballou Underwood	May 19, 1828	January 24, 1888
Emory Upton	August 27, 1839	March 15, 1881
James Henry Van Alen	August 17, 1819	July 22, 1886
Horatio Van Cleve	November 23, 1809	April 24, 1891
Ferdinand Van Derveer	February 27, 1823	November 5, 1892
Stewart Van Vliet	July 21, 1815	March 28, 1901
William Vandever	March 31, 1817	July 23, 1893
James Clifford Veatch	December 19, 1819	December 22, 1895
Egbert Ludovicus Viele	June 17, 1825	April 22, 1902
Francis Laurens Vinton	June 1, 1835	October 6, 1879
Israel Vogdes	August 4, 1816	December 7, 1889
Adolph Von Steinwehr	September 25, 1822	February 25, 1877
Melancthon Smith Wade	December 2, 1802	August 11, 1868
James Samuel Wadsworth	October 30, 1807	May 8, 1864
George Day Wagner	September 22, 1829	February 13, 1869
Charles Carroll Walcutt	February 12, 1838	May 2, 1898
William Harvey Wallace	July 8, 1821	April 10, 1862
John Henry Hobart Ward	June 17, 1823	July 24, 1903
William Thomas Ward	August 9, 1808	October 12, 1878
Fitz-Henry Warren	January 11, 1816	June 21, 1878
Alexander Stewart Webb	February 15, 1835	February 12, 1911
Max Weber	August 27, 1824	June 15, 1901
Joseph Dana Webster	August 25, 1811	March 12, 1876
Stephen Hinsdale Weed	November 17, 1831	July 2, 1863
Thomas Welsh	May 5, 1824	August 14, 1863
Henry Walton Wessells	February 20, 1809	January 12, 1889
Joseph Rodman West	September 19, 1822	October 31, 1898
Frank Wheaton	May 8, 1833	June 18, 1903
Amiel Weeks Whipple	October 15, 1816	May 7, 1863
William Denison Whipple	August 2, 1826	April 1, 1902
Walter Chiles Whitaker	August 8, 1823	July 9, 1887
Julius White	September 23, 1816	May 12, 1890
Edward Augustus Wild	November 25, 1825	August 28, 1891
Orlando Bolivar Willcox	April 16, 1823	May 10, 1907
Alpheus Williams	September 20, 1810	December 21, 1878
David Henry Williams	March 19, 1819	June 1, 1891
Seth Williams	March 22, 1822	March 23, 1866
Thomas Williams	January 10, 1815	August 5, 1862
James Williamson	February 8, 1829	September 7, 1902
August Willich	November 19, 1810	January 22, 1878
James Harrison Wilson	September 2, 1837	February 23, 1925
Isaac Jones Wistar	November 14, 1827	September 18, 1905
Daniel Phineas Woodbury	December 16, 1812	August 15, 1864
Charles Robert Woods	February 19, 1827	February 26, 1885
George Wright	October 21, 1801	July 30, 1865
Samuel Kosciuszko Zook	March 27, 1821	July 3, 1863

2

Civil War Generals
by First Names

The first names of the generals are listed here in alphabetical order, first by their first names, then by last. Generals with no middle names are listed first.

GENERAL	FOUGHT FOR	RANK
Abner Doubleday	Union	Brigadier General
Abner Clark Harding	Union	Brigadier General
Abner Monroe Perrin	Confederacy	Brigadier General
Abraham Buford	Confederacy	Brigadier General
Abram Duryee	Union	Brigadier General
Abram Sanders Piatt	Union	Brigadier General
Absalom Baird	Union	Brigadier General
Adam Rankin Johnson	Confederacy	Brigadier General
Adam Jacoby Slemmer	Union	Brigadier General
Adelbert Ames	Union	Brigadier General
Adley Hogan Gladden	Confederacy	Brigadier General
Adin Ballou Underwood	Union	Brigadier General
Adolph Wilhelm von Steinwehr	Union	Brigadier General
Albert Pike	Confederacy	Brigadier General
Albert Rust	Confederacy	Brigadier General
Albert Gallatin Blanchard	Confederacy	Brigadier General
Albert Gallatin Jenkins	Confederacy	Brigadier General
Albert Sidney Johnston	Confederacy	General
Albert Lindley Lee	Union	Brigadier General
Albin Francisco Schoepf	Union	Brigadier General
Albion Parris Howe	Union	Brigadier General
Alexander Chambers	Union	Brigadier General
Alexander Hays	Union	Brigadier General
Alexander Shaler	Union	Brigadier General
Alexander Sandor Asboth	Union	Brigadier General
Alexander William Campbell	Confederacy	Brigadier General
Alexander Brydie Dyer	Union	Brigadier General
Alexander Travis Hawthorne	Confederacy	Brigadier General
Alexander Robert Lawton	Confederacy	Brigadier General
Alexander McDowell McCook	Union	Major General
Alexander Welch Reynolds	Confederacy	Brigadier General
Alexander Schimmelfennig	Union	Brigadier General
Alexander Peter Stewart	Confederacy	Lieutenant General

Alexander Stewart Webb	Union	Brigadier General
Alfred Cumming	Confederacy	Brigadier General
Alfred Gibbs	Union	Brigadier General
Alfred Iverson,Jr.	Confederacy	Brigadier General
Alfred Pleasonton	Union	Major General
Alfred Sully	Union	Brigadier General
Alfred Holt Colquitt	Confederacy	Brigadier General
Alfred Napoleon A. Duffie	Union	Brigadier General
Alfred Washington Ellet	Union	Brigadier General
Alfred Eugene Jackson	Confederacy	Brigadier General
Alfred Moore Scales	Confederacy	Brigadier General
Alfred Howe Terry	Union	Major General
Alfred Thomas A. Torbert	Union	Brigadier General
Alfred Jefferson Vaughan,Jr	Confederacy	Brigadier General
Allen Thomas	Confederacy	Brigadier General
Allison Nelson	Confederacy	Brigadier General
Alpheus Baker	Confederacy	Brigadier General
Alpheus Starkey Williams	Union	Brigadier General
Alvan Cullem Gillem	Union	Brigadier General
Alvin Peterson Hovey	Union	Brigadier General
Ambrose Everett Burnside	Union	Major General
Ambrose Powell Hill	Confederacy	Lieutenant General
Ambrose Ransom Wright	Confederacy	Major General
Amiel Weeks Whipple	Union	Brigadier General
Amos Beebe Eaton	Union	Brigadier General
Andrew Johnson	Union	Brigadier General
Andrew Porter	Union	Brigadier General
Andrew Jackson Hamilton	Union	Brigadier General
Andrew Atkinson Humphreys	Union	Major General
Andrew Jackson Smith	Union	Major General
Archibald Gracie,Jr.	Confederacy	Brigadier General
Archibald Campbell Godwin	Confederacy	Brigadier General
Armistead Lindsay Long	Confederacy	Brigadier General
Arnold Elzey	Confederacy	Major General
Arthur Middleton Manigault	Confederacy	Brigadier General
August Willich	Union	Brigadier General
August Valentine Kautz	Union	Brigadier General
Augustus Louis Chetlain	Union	Brigadier General
Barnard Elliott Bee	Confederacy	Brigadier General
Basil Wilson Duke	Confederacy	Brigadier General
Ben McCulloch	Confederacy	Brigadier General
Benjamin Alvord	Union	Brigadier General
Benjamin Huger	Confederacy	Major General
Benjamin Franklin Butler	Union	Major General
Benjamin Franklin Cheatham	Confederacy	Major General
Benjamin Henry Grierson	Union	Brigadier General
Benjamin Hardin Helm	Confederacy	Brigadier General
Benjamin Jefferson Hill	Confederacy	Brigadier General
Benjamin Grubb Humphreys	Confederacy	Brigadier General
Benjamin Franklin Kelley	Union	Brigadier General
Benjamin Franklin Potts	Union	Brigadier General
Benjamin Mayberry Prentiss	Union	Major General
Benjamin Stone Roberts	Union	Brigadier General
Beverly Holcombe Robertson	Confederacy	Brigadier General
Birkett Davenport Fry	Confederacy	Brigadier General
Bradley Tyler Johnson	Confederacy	Brigadier General

Braxton Bragg	Confederacy	General
Bryan Grimes	Confederacy	Major General
Bryan Morel Thomas	Confederacy	Brigadier General
Bushrod Rust Johnson	Confederacy	Major General
Byron Root Pierce	Union	Brigadier General
Cadmus Marcellus Wilcox	Confederacy	Major General
Cadwallader Colden Washburn	Union	Major General
Calvin Edward Pratt	Union	Brigadier General
Camille A.J.M.P. Polignac	Confederacy	Major General
Carl Schurz	Union	Major General
Carnot Posey	Confederacy	Brigadier General
Carter Littlepage Stevenson	Confederacy	Major General
Cassius Marcellus Clay	Union	Major General
Catharinus Putnam Buckingham	Union	Brigadier General
Charles Clark	Confederacy	Brigadier General
Charles Cruft	Union	Brigadier General
Charles Devens,Jr.	Union	Brigadier General
Charles Griffin	Union	Major General
Charles Thomas Campbell	Union	Brigadier General
Charles Cleveland Dodge	Union	Brigadier General
Charles Camp Doolittle	Union	Brigadier General
Charles William Field	Confederacy	Major General
Charles Champion Gilbert	Union	Brigadier General
Charles Kinnaird Graham	Union	Brigadier General
Charles Smith Hamilton	Union	Major General
Charles Garrison Harker	Union	Brigadier General
Charles Adam Heckman	Union	Brigadier General
Charles Edward Hovey	Union	Brigadier General
Charles Davis Jameson	Union	Brigadier General
Charles Leopold Matthies	Union	Brigadier General
Charles Jackson Paine	Union	Brigadier General
Charles Miller Shelley	Confederacy	Brigadier General
Charles Ferguson Smith	Union	Major General
Charles John Stolbrand	Union	Brigadier General
Charles Pomeroy Stone	Union	Brigadier General
Charles Mynn Thruston	Union	Brigadier General
Charles Carroll Walcutt	Union	Brigadier General
Charles Sidney Winder	Confederacy	Brigadier General
Charles Robert Woods	Union	Brigadier General
Christopher Columbus Andrews	Union	Brigadier General
Christopher Columbus Augur	Union	Major General
Claudius Wistar Sears	Confederacy	Brigadier General
Clement Anselm Evans	Confederacy	Brigadier General
Clement Hoffman Stevens	Confederacy	Brigadier General
Clinton Bowen Fisk	Union	Brigadier General
Collett Leventhorpe	Confederacy	Brigadier General
Conrad Feger Jackson	Union	Brigadier General
Cullen Andrews Battle	Confederacy	Brigadier General
Cuvier Grover	Union	Brigadier General
Cyrus Bussey	Union	Brigadier General
Cyrus Hamlin	Union	Brigadier General
Dabney Herndon Maury	Confederacy	Major General
Dandridge McRae	Confederacy	Brigadier General
Daniel Butterfield	Union	Major General
Daniel Ruggles	Confederacy	Brigadier General
Daniel Tyler	Union	Brigadier General

Daniel Ullmann	Union	Brigadier General
Daniel Weisiger Adams	Confederacy	Brigadier General
Daniel Davidson Bidwell	Union	Brigadier General
Daniel Smith Donelson	Confederacy	Major General
Daniel Marsh Frost	Confederacy	Brigadier General
Daniel Chevilette Govan	Confederacy	Brigadier General
Daniel Harvey Hill	Confederacy	Lieutenant General
Daniel Harris Reynolds	Confederacy	Brigadier General
Daniel Henry Rucker	Union	Brigadier General
Daniel Edgar Sickles	Union	Major General
Daniel Phineas Woodbury	Union	Brigadier General
Danville Leadbetter	Confederacy	Brigadier General
Darius Nash Couch	Union	Major General
David Hunter	Union	Major General
David Stuart	Union	Brigadier General
David Bell Birney	Union	Major General
David McMurtrie Gregg	Union	Brigadier General
David Rumph Jones	Confederacy	Major General
David Allen Russell	Union	Brigadier General
David Sloane Stanley	Union	Major General
David Emanuel Twiggs	Confederacy	Major General
David Addison Weisiger	Confederacy	Brigadier General
David Henry Williams	Union	Brigadier General
Davis Tillson	Union	Brigadier General
Don Carlos Buell	Union	Major General
Douglas Hancock Cooper	Confederacy	Brigadier General
Dudley McIver DuBose	Confederacy	Brigadier General
Earl Van Dorn	Confederacy	Major General
Ebenezer Dumont	Union	Brigadier General
Edmund Jackson Davis	Union	Brigadier General
Edmund Winston Pettus	Confederacy	Brigadier General
Edmund Kirby Smith	Confederacy	General
Edward Ferrero	Union	Brigadier General
Edward Harland	Union	Brigadier General
Edward Hatch	Union	Brigadier General
Edward Higgins	Confederacy	Brigadier General
Edward Johnson	Confederacy	Major General
Edward Porter Alexander	Confederacy	Brigadier General
Edward Dickinson Baker	Union	Major General
Edward Stuyvesant Bragg	Union	Brigadier General
Edward Richard S. Canby	Union	Major General
Edward Winslow Hincks	Union	Brigadier General
Edward Henry Hobson	Union	Brigadier General
Edward Needles Kirk	Union	Brigadier General
Edward Moody McCook	Union	Brigadier General
Edward Otho C. Ord	Union	Major General
Edward Aylesworth Perry	Confederacy	Brigadier General
Edward Elmer Potter	Union	Brigadier General
Edward Lloyd Thomas	Confederacy	Brigadier General
Edward Dorr Tracy	Confederacy	Brigadier General
Edward Cary Walthall	Confederacy	Major General
Edward Augustus Wild	Union	Brigadier General
Edwin Gray Lee	Confederacy	Brigadier General
Edwin Denison Morgan	Union	Major General
Edwin Henry Stoughton	Union	Brigadier General
Edwin Vose Sumner	Union	Major General

Egbert Benson Brown	Union	Brigadier General
Egbert Ludovicus Viele	Union	Brigadier General
Eleazer Arthur Paine	Union	Brigadier General
Eli Long	Union	Brigadier General
Eliakim Parker Scammon	Union	Brigadier General
Elias Smith Dennis	Union	Brigadier General
Elisha Franklin Paxton	Confederacy	Brigadier General
Elkanah Brackin Greer	Confederacy	Brigadier General
Elliott Warren Rice	Union	Brigadier General
Ellison Capers	Confederacy	Brigadier General
Elon John Farnsworth	Union	Brigadier General
Emory Upton	Union	Brigadier General
Eppa Hunton	Confederacy	Brigadier General
Erasmus Darwin Keyes	Union	Major General
Erastus Barnard Tyler	Union	Brigadier General
Ethan Allen Hitchcock	Union	Major General
Eugene Asa Carr	Union	Brigadier General
Evander McNair	Confederacy	Brigadier General
Evander McIvor Law	Confederacy	Brigadier General
Felix Huston Robertson	Confederacy	Brigadier General
Felix Kirk Zollicoffer	Confederacy	Brigadier General
Ferdinand Van Derveer	Union	Brigadier General
Fitz John Porter	Union	Major General
Fitz Henry Warren	Union	Brigadier General
Fitzhugh Lee	Confederacy	Major General
Francis Fessenden	Union	Brigadier General
Francis Channing Barlow	Union	Brigadier General
Francis Preston Blair,Jr.	Union	Major General
Francis Marion Cockrell	Confederacy	Brigadier General
Francis Jay Herron	Union	Major General
Francis Redding T. Nicholls	Confederacy	Brigadier General
Francis Engle Patterson	Union	Brigadier General
Francis Asbury Shoup	Confederacy	Brigadier General
Francis Barretto Spinola	Union	Brigadier General
Francis Laurens Vinton	Union	Brigadier General
Frank Wheaton	Union	Brigadier General
Frank Crawford Armstrong	Confederacy	Brigadier General
Franklin Gardner	Confederacy	Major General
Franklin Stillman Nickerson	Union	Brigadier General
Franz Sigel	Union	Major General
Frederick Steele	Union	Major General
Frederick West Lander	Union	Brigadier General
Frederick Shearer Stumbaugh	Union	Brigadier General
Friedrich Salomon	Union	Brigadier General
Gabriel Rene Paul	Union	Brigadier General
Gabriel James Rains	Confederacy	Brigadier General
Gabriel Colvin Wharton	Confederacy	Brigadier General
George Cadwalader	Union	Major General
George Crook	Union	Major General
George Stoneman	Union	Major General
George Sykes	Union	Major General
George Wright	Union	Brigadier General
George Burgwyn Anderson	Confederacy	Brigadier General
George Thomas Anderson	Confederacy	Brigadier General
George Leonard Andrews	Union	Brigadier General
George Dashiell Bayard	Union	Brigadier General

George Lafayette Beal	Union	Brigadier General
George Henry Chapman	Union	Brigadier General
George Blake Cosby	Confederacy	Brigadier General
George Bibb Crittenden	Confederacy	Major General
George Washington Cullum	Union	Brigadier General
George Armstrong Custer	Union	Brigadier General
George Washington Deitzler	Union	Brigadier General
George Gibbs Dibrell	Confederacy	Brigadier General
George Pierce Doles	Confederacy	Brigadier General
George Washington Getty	Union	Brigadier General
George Henry Gordon	Union	Brigadier General
George Washington Gordon	Confederacy	Brigadier General
George Sears Greene	Union	Brigadier General
George Lucas Hartsuff	Union	Major General
George Baird Hodge	Confederacy	Brigadier General
George Doherty Johnston	Confederacy	Brigadier General
George Washington C. Lee	Confederacy	Major General
George Ear Maney	Confederacy	Brigadier General
George Archibald McCall	Union	Brigadier General
George Brinton McClellan	Union	Major General
George Francis McGinnis	Union	Brigadier General
George Gordon Meade	Union	Major General
George Webb Morell	Union	Major General
George Washington Morgan	Union	Brigadier General
George Edward Pickett	Confederacy	Major General
George Douglas Ramsay	Union	Brigadier General
George Wythe Randolph	Confederacy	Brigadier General
George Foster Shepley	Union	Brigadier General
George Jerrison Stannard	Union	Brigadier General
George Hume Steuart	Confederacy	Brigadier General
George Crockett Strong	Union	Brigadier General
George William Taylor	Union	Brigadier General
George Henry Thomas	Union	Major General
George Hector Tyndale	Union	Brigadier General
George Day Wagner	Union	Brigadier General
Gershom Mott	Union	Brigadier General
Gideon Johnson Pillow	Confederacy	Brigadier General
Gilbert Moxley Sorrel	Confederacy	Brigadier General
Giles Alexander Smith	Union	Brigadier General
Gilman Marston	Union	Brigadier General
Godfrey Weitzel	Union	Major General
Goode Bryan	Confederacy	Brigadier General
Gordon Granger	Union	Major General
Gouverneur Kemble Warren	Union	Major General
Green Berry Raum	Union	Brigadier General
Green Clay Smith	Union	Brigadier General
Grenville Mellen Dodge	Union	Major General
Gustave Paul Cluseret	Union	Brigadier General
Gustavus Adolphus DeRussy	Union	Brigadier General
Gustavus Adolphus Smith	Union	Brigadier General
Gustavus Woodson Smith	Confederacy	Major General
Halbert Eleazer Paine	Union	Brigadier General
Hamilton Prioleau Bee	Confederacy	Brigadier General
Harry Thompson Hays	Confederacy	Major General
Henry Baxter	Union	Brigadier General
Henry Bohlen	Union	Brigadier General

Henry Gray	Confederacy	Brigadier General
Henry Heth	Confederacy	Major General
Henry Prince	Union	Brigadier General
Henry Watkins Allen	Confederacy	Brigadier General
Henry Washington Benham	Union	Brigadier General
Henry Lewis Benning	Confederacy	Brigadier General
Henry Warner Birge	Union	Brigadier General
Henry Shaw Briggs	Union	Brigadier General
Henry Beebee Carrington	Union	Brigadier General
Henry DeLamar Clayton	Confederacy	Major General
Henry Brevard Davidson	Confederacy	Brigadier General
Henry Eugene Davies	Union	Brigadier General
Henry Lawrence Eustis	Union	Brigadier General
Henry Wager Halleck	Union	Major General
Henry Jackson Hunt	Union	Brigadier General
Henry Rootes Jackson	Confederacy	Brigadier General
Henry Moses Judah	Union	Brigadier General
Henry Hayes Lockwood	Union	Brigadier General
Henry Eustace McCulloch	Confederacy	Brigadier General
Henry Morris Naglee	Union	Brigadier General
Henry Hastings Sibley	Union	Brigadier General
Henry Hopkins Sibley	Confederacy	Brigadier General
Henry Warner Slocum	Union	Major General
Henry Dwight Terry	Union	Brigadier General
Henry Goddard Thomas	Union	Brigadier General
Henry Harrison Walker	Confederacy	Brigadier General
Henry Constantine Wayne	Confederacy	Brigadier General
Henry Walton Wessells	Union	Brigadier General
Henry Alexander Wise	Confederacy	Brigadier General
Herman Haupt	Union	Brigadier General
Hiram Burnham	Union	Brigadier General
Hiram Gregory Berry	Union	Major General
Hiram Bronson Granbury	Confederacy	Brigadier General
Horatio Phillips Van Cleve	Union	Brigadier General
Horatio Gouverneur Wright	Union	Major General
Howell Cobb	Confederacy	Major General
Hugh Boyle Ewing	Union	Brigadier General
Hugh Judson Kilpatrick	Union	Brigadier General
Hugh Weedon Mercer	Confederacy	Brigadier General
Hugh Thompson Reid	Union	Brigadier General
Humphrey Marshall	Confederacy	Brigadier General
Hylan Benton Lyon	Confederacy	Brigadier General
Innis Newton Palmer	Union	Brigadier General
Irvin McDowell	Union	Major General
Isaac Hardin Duval	Union	Brigadier General
Isaac Peace Rodman	Union	Brigadier General
Isaac Fitzgerald Shepard	Union	Brigadier General
Isaac Ingalls Stevens	Union	Brigadier General
Isaac Munroe St.John	Confederacy	Brigadier General
Isaac Ridgeway Trimble	Confederacy	Major General
Isaac Jones Wistar	Union	Brigadier General
Isham Nicholas Haynie	Union	Brigadier General
Israel Vogdes	Union	Brigadier General
Israel Bush Richardson	Union	Major General
Issac Ferdinand Quinby	Union	Brigadier General
Jacob Ammen	Union	Brigadier General

Jacob Dolson Cox	Union	Major General
Jacob Gartner Lauman	Union	Brigadier General
Jacob Hunter Sharp	Confederacy	Brigadier General
James Barnes	Union	Brigadier General
James Bowen	Union	Brigadier General
James Cantey	Confederacy	Brigadier General
James Chesnut, Jr.	Confederacy	Brigadier General
James Conner	Confederacy	Brigadier General
James Cooper	Union	Brigadier General
James Craig	Union	Brigadier General
James Dearing	Confederacy	Brigadier General
James Deshler	Confederacy	Brigadier General
James Longstreet	Confederacy	Lieutenant General
James Nagle	Union	Brigadier General
James Shields	Union	Brigadier General
James Patton Anderson	Confederacy	Major General
James Jay Archer	Confederacy	Brigadier General
James Gillpatrick Blunt	Union	Major General
James Henry Carleton	Union	Brigadier General
James Ronald Chalmers	Confederacy	Brigadier General
James Holt Clanton	Confederacy	Brigadier General
James William Denver	Union	Brigadier General
James Fleming Fagan	Confederacy	Major General
James Deering Fessenden	Union	Brigadier General
James Barnet Fry	Union	Brigadier General
James Abram Garfield	Union	Major General
James Isham Gilbert	Union	Brigadier General
James Monroe Goggin	Confederacy	Brigadier General
James Byron Gordon	Confederacy	Brigadier General
James Allen Hardie	Union	Brigadier General
James Edward Harrison	Confederacy	Brigadier General
James Morrison Hawes	Confederacy	Brigadier General
James Thadeus Holtzclaw	Confederacy	Brigadier General
James Streshly Jackson	Union	Brigadier General
James Lawson Kemper	Confederacy	Major General
James Lawlor Kiernan	Union	Brigadier General
James Henry Lane	Confederacy	Brigadier General
James Hewett Ledlie	Union	Brigadier General
James Patrick Major	Confederacy	Brigadier General
James Green Martin	Confederacy	Brigadier General
James McQueen McIntosh	Confederacy	Brigadier General
James Winning McMillan	Union	Brigadier General
James Birdseye McPherson	Union	Major General
James Dada Morgan	Union	Brigadier General
James St.Clair Morton	Union	Brigadier General
James Scott Negley	Union	Major General
James Johnston Pettigrew	Confederacy	Brigadier General
James Edwards Rains	Confederacy	Brigadier General
James William Reilly	Union	Brigadier General
James Clay Rice	Union	Brigadier General
James Brewerton Ricketts	Union	Brigadier General
James Wolfe Ripley	Union	Brigadier General
James Sidney Robinson	Union	Brigadier General
James Murrell Shackelford	Union	Brigadier General
James Phillip Simms	Confederacy	Brigadier General
James Richard Slack	Union	Brigadier General

James Edwin Slaughter	Confederacy	Brigadier General
James Argyle Smith	Confederacy	Brigadier General
James Gallant Spears	Union	Brigadier General
James Blair Steedman	Union	Major General
James Ewell Brown Stuart	Confederacy	Major General
James Camp Tappan	Confederacy	Brigadier General
James Heyward Trapier	Confederacy	Brigadier General
James Madison Tuttle	Union	Brigadier General
James Henry VanAlen	Union	Brigadier General
James Clifford Veatch	Union	Brigadier General
James Samuel Wadsworth	Union	Brigadier General
James Alexander Walker	Confederacy	Brigadier General
James Alexander Williamson	Union	Brigadier General
James Harrison Wilson	Union	Brigadier General
Jasper Adalmorn Maltby	Union	Brigadier General
Jean Jacques A.A. Mouton	Confederacy	Brigadier General
Jefferson Columbus Davis	Union	Brigadier General
Jeremy Francis Gilmer	Confederacy	Major General
Jerimiah Tilford Boyle	Union	Brigadier General
Jeremiah Cutler Sullivan	Union	Brigadier General
Jerome Bonaparte Robertson	Confederacy	Brigadier General
Jesse Johnson Finley	Confederacy	Brigadier General
Jesse Lee Reno	Union	Major General
John Adams	Confederacy	Brigadier General
John Beatty	Union	Brigadier General
John Bratton	Confederacy	Brigadier General
John Buford	Union	Brigadier General
John Cochrane	Union	Brigadier General
John Cook	Union	Brigadier General
John Dunovant	Confederacy	Brigadier General
John Echols	Confederacy	Brigadier General
John Edwards	Union	Brigadier General
John Gibbon	Union	Major General
John Gregg	Confederacy	Brigadier General
John McArthur	Union	Brigadier General
John McCausland	Confederacy	Brigadier General
John McNeil	Union	Brigadier General
John Newton	Union	Major General
John Pegram	Confederacy	Brigadier General
John Pope	Union	Major General
John Sedgwick	Union	Major General
John Joseph Abercrombie	Union	Brigadier General
John Gross Barnard	Union	Brigadier General
John Decatur Barry	Confederacy	Brigadier General
John Stevens Bowen	Confederacy	Major General
John Milton Brannan	Union	Brigadier General
John Cabell Breckinridge	Confederacy	Major General
John Rutter Brooke	Union	Brigadier General
John Calvin Brown	Confederacy	Major General
John Curtis Caldwell	Union	Brigadier General
John Carpenter Carter	Confederacy	Brigadier General
John Randolph Chambliss,Jr.	Confederacy	Brigadier General
John Bullock Clark,Jr.	Confederacy	Brigadier General
John Rogers Cooke	Confederacy	Brigadier General
John Murray Corse	Union	Brigadier General
John Thomas Croxton	Union	Brigadier General

John Wynn Davidson	Union	Brigadier General
John Adams Dix	Union	Major General
John Franklin Farnsworth	Union	Brigadier General
John Buchanan Floyd	Confederacy	Brigadier General
John Horace Forney	Confederacy	Major General
John Gray Foster	Union	Major General
John Wesley Frazer	Confederacy	Brigadier General
John Charles Fremont	Union	Major General
John Wallace Fuller	Union	Brigadier General
John White Geary	Union	Brigadier General
John Brown Gordon	Confederacy	Major General
John Breckinridge Grayson	Confederacy	Brigadier General
John Frederick Hartranft	Union	Brigadier General
John Porter Hatch	Union	Brigadier General
John Parker Hawkins	Union	Brigadier General
John Bell Hood	Confederacy	General
John Daniel Imboden	Confederacy	Brigadier General
John King Jackson	Confederacy	Brigadier General
John Marshall Jones	Confederacy	Brigadier General
John Robert Jones	Confederacy	Brigadier General
John Herbert Kelly	Confederacy	Brigadier General
John Reese Kenly	Union	Brigadier General
John Doby Kennedy	Confederacy	Brigadier General
John Haskell King	Union	Brigadier General
John Alexander Logan	Union	Major General
John Bankhead Magruder	Confederacy	Major General
John Sappington Marmaduke	Confederacy	Major General
John Henry Martindale	Union	Brigadier General
John Sanford Mason	Union	Brigadier General
John Alexander McClernand	Union	Major General
John Porter McCown	Confederacy	Major General
John Baillie McIntosh	Union	Brigadier General
John Franklin Miller	Union	Brigadier General
John Grant Mitchell	Union	Brigadier General
John Creed Moore	Confederacy	Brigadier General
John Hunt Morgan	Confederacy	Brigadier General
John Tyler Morgan	Confederacy	Brigadier General
John Morrison Oliver	Union	Brigadier General
John McCauley Palmer	Union	Major General
John Grubb Parke	Union	Major General
John James Peck	Union	Major General
John Clifford Pemberton	Confederacy	Lieutenant General
John Smith Phelps	Union	Brigadier General
John Wolcott Phelps	Union	Brigadier General
John Smith Preston	Confederacy	Brigadier General
John Aaron Rawlins	Union	Brigadier General
John Fulton Reynolds	Union	Major General
John Selden Roane	Confederacy	Brigadier General
John Cleveland Robinson	Union	Brigadier General
John Benjamin Sanborn	Union	Brigadier General
John Caldwell C. Sanders	Confederacy	Brigadier General
John McAllister Schofield	Union	Major General
John Potts Slough	Union	Brigadier General
John Eugene Smith	Union	Brigadier General
John Wilson Sprague	Union	Brigadier General
John Converse Starkweather	Union	Brigadier General

John Dunlap Stevenson	Union	Brigadier General
John Milton Thayer	Union	Brigadier General
John Blair Smith Todd	Union	Brigadier General
John Basil Turchin	Union	Brigadier General
John Wesley Turner	Union	Brigadier General
John Crawford Vaughn	Confederacy	Brigadier General
John Bordenave Villepigue	Confederacy	Brigadier General
John George Walker	Confederacy	Major General
John Henry Hobart Ward	Confederacy	Brigadier General
John Austin Wharton	Confederacy	Major General
John Wilkins Whitfield	Confederacy	Brigadier General
John Stuart Williams	Confederacy	Brigadier General
John Henry Winder	Confederacy	Brigadier General
John Ellis Wool	Union	Major General
Johnson Hagood	Confederacy	Brigadier General
Johnson Kelly Duncan	Confederacy	Brigadier General
Jones Mitchell Withers	Confederacy	Major General
Joseph Bailey	Union	Brigadier General
Joseph Finegan	Confederacy	Brigadier General
Joseph Hayes	Union	Brigadier General
Joseph Holt	Union	Brigadier General
Joseph Hooker	Union	Major General
Joseph Wheeler	Confederacy	Major General
Joseph Reid Anderson	Confederacy	Brigadier General
Joseph K. Barnes	Union	Brigadier General
Joseph Jackson Bartlett	Union	Brigadier General
Joseph Bradford Carr	Union	Brigadier General
Joseph Alexander Cooper	Union	Brigadier General
Joseph Tarr Copeland	Union	Brigadier General
Joseph Robert Davis	Confederacy	Brigadier General
Joseph Abel Haskin	Union	Brigadier General
Joseph Roswell Hawley	Union	Brigadier General
Joseph Lewis Hogg	Confederacy	Brigadier General
Joseph Eggleston Johnston	Confederacy	General
Joseph Brevard Kershaw	Confederacy	Major General
Joseph Farmer Knipe	Union	Brigadier General
Joseph Horace Lewis	Confederacy	Brigadier General
Joseph Andrew J. Lightburn	Union	Brigadier General
Joseph King F. Mansfield	Union	Brigadier General
Joseph Anthony Mower	Union	Major General
Joseph Benjamin Palmer	Confederacy	Brigadier General
Joseph Bennett Plummer	Union	Brigadier General
Joseph Warren Revere	Union	Brigadier General
Joseph Jones Reynolds	Union	Major General
Joseph Orville Shelby	Confederacy	Brigadier General
Joseph Pannell Taylor	Union	Brigadier General
Joseph Gilbert Totten	Union	Brigadier General
Joseph Dana Webster	Union	Brigadier General
Joseph Rodman West	Union	Brigadier General
Joshua Lawrence Chamberlain	Union	Brigadier General
Joshua Thomas Owen	Union	Brigadier General
Joshua Woodrow Sill	Union	Brigadier General
Josiah Gorgas	Confederacy	Brigadier General
Jubal Anderson Early	Confederacy	Lieutenant General
Julius Stahel	Union	Major General
Julius White	Union	Brigadier General

Julius Adolph deLagnel	Confederacy	Brigadier General
Junius Daniel	Confederacy	Brigadier General
Justus McKinstry	Union	Brigadier General
Kenner Garrard	Union	Brigadier General
Lafayette McLaws	Confederacy	Major General
Laurence Simmons Baker	Confederacy	Brigadier General
Lawrence O'Bryan Branch	Confederacy	Brigadier General
Lawrence Pike Graham	Union	Brigadier General
Lawrence Sullivan Ross	Confederacy	Brigadier General
Leonard Fulton Ross	Union	Brigadier General
Leonidas Polk	Confederacy	Lieutenant General
Leroy Augustus Stafford	Confederacy	Brigadier General
Leroy Pope Walker	Confederacy	Brigadier General
Lewis Wallace	Union	Major General
Lewis Addison Armistead	Confederacy	Brigadier General
Lewis Golding Arnold	Union	Brigadier General
Lewis Addison Grant	Union	Brigadier General
Lewis Cass Hunt	Union	Brigadier General
Lewis Henry Little	Confederacy	Brigadier General
Lloyd Tilghman	Confederacy	Brigadier General
Lorenzo Thomas	Union	Brigadier General
Louis Hebert	Confederacy	Brigadier General
Louis Ludwig Blenker	Union	Brigadier General
Louis Trezevant Wigfall	Confederacy	Brigadier General
Lovell Harrison Rousseau	Union	Major General
Lucius Fairchild	Union	Brigadier General
Lucius Jeremiah Gartrell	Confederacy	Brigadier General
Lucius Bellinger Northrop	Confederacy	Brigadier General
Lucius Eugene Polk	Confederacy	Brigadier General
Lucius Marshall Walker	Confederacy	Brigadier General
Lunsford Lindsay Lomax	Confederacy	Major General
Luther Prentice Bradley	Union	Brigadier General
Lysander Cutler	Union	Brigadier General
Mahlon Dickerson Manson	Union	Brigadier General
Manning Ferguson Force	Unionn	Brigadier General
Mansfield Lovell	Confederacy	Major General
Marcellus Monroe Crocker	Union	Brigadier General
Marcellus Augustus Stovall	Confederacy	Brigadier General
Marcus Joseph Wright	Confederacy	Brigadier General
Mark Perrin Lowrey	Confederacy	Brigadier General
Marsena Rudolph Patrick	Union	Brigadier General
Martin Witherspoon Gary	Confederacy	Brigadier General
Martin Edwin Green	Confederacy	Brigadier General
Martin Davis Hardin	Union	Brigadier General
Martin Luther Smith	Confederacy	Major General
Mason Brayman	Union	Brigadier General
Matt Whitaker Ransom	Confederacy	Brigadier General
Matthew Calbraith Butler	Confederacy	Major General
Matthew Duncan Ector	Confederacy	Brigadier General
Max Weber	Union	Brigadier General
Maxcy Gregg	Confederacy	Brigadier General
Melancthon Smith Wade	Union	Brigadier General
Micah Jenkins	Confederacy	Brigadier General
Michael Corcoran	Union	Brigadier General
Michael Kelly Lawler	Union	Brigadier General
Milledge Luke Bonham	Confederacy	Brigadier General

Milo Smith Hascall	Union	Brigadier General
Montgomery Dent Corse	Confederacy	Brigadier General
Montgomery Cunningham Meigs	Union	Brigadier General
Morgan Lewis Smith	Union	Brigadier General
Mortimer Dormer Leggett	Union	Brigadier General
Mosby Monroe Parsons	Confederacy	Major General
Napoleon Bonaparte Buford	Union	Brigadier General
Napoleon Jackson T. Dana	Union	Major General
Nathan Kimball	Union	Brigadier General
Nathan Bedford Forrest	Confederacy	Lieutenant General
Nathan George Evans	Confederacy	Brigadier General
Nathaniel Lyon	Union	Brigadier General
Nathaniel Prentiss Banks	Union	Major General
Nathaniel Harrison Harris	Confederacy	Brigadier General
Nathaniel James Jackson	Union	Brigadier General
Nathaniel Collins McLean	Union	Brigadier General
Neal Dow	Union	Brigadier General
Nelson Taylor	Union	Brigadier General
Nelson Appleton Miles	Union	Brigadier General
Newton Martin Curtis	Union	Brigadier General
Oliver Otis Howard	Union	Major General
Orlando Metcalfe Poe	Union	Brigadier General
Orlando Bolivar Willcox	Union	Brigadier General
Ormsby MacKnight Mitchel	Union	Major General
Orris Sanford Ferry	Union	Brigadier General
Otho French Strahl	Confederacy	Brigadier General
Patrick Ronayne Cleburne	Confederacy	Major General
Patrick Edward Connor	Union	Brigadier General
Patrick Theodore Moore	Confederacy	Brigadier General
Paul Jones Semmes	Confederacy	Brigadier General
Paul Octave Hebert	Confederacy	Brigadier General
Peter Joseph Osterhaus	Union	Major General
Peter Burwell Starke	Confederacy	Brigadier General
Philip Cook	Confederacy	Brigadier General
Philip Kearny	Union	Major General
Philip St.George Cocke	Confederacy	Brigadier General
Philip St.George Cooke	Union	Brigadier General
Philip Dale Roddey	Confederacy	Brigadier General
Philip Henry Sheridan	Union	Major General
Philippe Regis deTrobriand	Union	Brigadier General
Pierce Manning B. Young	Confederacy	Major General
Pierre Gustave Beauregard	Confederacy	General
Pleasant Adam Hackleman	Union	Brigadier General
Powell Clayton	Union	Brigadier General
Preston Smith	Confederacy	Brigadier General
Quincy Adams Gillmore	Union	Major General
Raleigh Edward Colston	Confederacy	Brigadier General
Ralph Pomeroy Buckland	Union	Brigadier General
Ranald Slidell Mackenzie	Union	Brigadier General
Randall Lee Gibson	Confederacy	Brigadier General
Randolph Barnes Marcy	Union	Brigadier General
Reuben Lindsay Walker	Confederacy	Brigadier General
Richard Arnold	Union	Brigadier General
Richard Busteed	Union	Brigadier General
Richard Delafield	Union	Brigadier General
Richard Griffith	Confederacy	Brigadier General

Richard Taylor	Confederacy	Lieutenant General
Richard Waterhouse	Confederacy	Brigadier General
Richard Heron Anderson	Confederacy	Lieutenant General
Richard Lee T. Beale	Confederacy	Brigadier General
Richard Stoddert Ewell	Confederacy	Lieutenant General
Richard Montgomery Gano	Confederacy	Brigadier General
Richard Brooke Garnett	Confederacy	Brigadier General
Richard Caswell Gatlin	Confederacy	Brigadier General
Richard W. Johnson	Union	Brigadier General
Richard James Oglesby	Union	Major General
Richard Lucian Page	Confederacy	Brigadier General
Robert Allen	Union	Brigadier General
Robert Anderson	Union	Brigadier General
Robert Bullock	Confederacy	Brigadier General
Robert Cowdin	Union	Brigadier General
Robert Lowry	Confederacy	Brigadier General
Robert Ransom,Jr.	Confederacy	Major General
Robert Houstoun Anderson	Confederacy	Brigadier General
Robert Christie Buchanan	Union	Brigadier General
Robert Alexander Cameron	Union	Brigadier General
Robert Hall Chilton	Confederacy	Brigadier General
Robert Sanford Foster	Union	Brigadier General
Robert Selden Garnett	Confederacy	Brigadier General
Robert Seaman Granger	Confederacy	Brigadier General
Robert Hopkins Hatton	Confederacy	Brigadier General
Robert Frederick Hoke	Confederacy	Major General
Robert Daniel Johnston	Confederacy	Brigadier General
Robert Edward Lee	Confederacy	General
Robert Doak Lilley	Confederacy	Brigadier General
Robert Latimer McCook	Union	Brigadier General
Robert Huston Milroy	Union	Major General
Robert Byington Mitchell	Union	Brigadier General
Robert Brown Potter	Union	Brigadier General
Robert Vinkler Richardson	Confederacy	Brigadier General
Robert Emmett Rodes	Confederacy	Major General
Robert Cumming Schenck	Union	Major General
Robert Augustus Toombs	Confederacy	Brigadier General
Robert Charles Tyler	Confederacy	Brigadier General
Robert Ogden Tyler	Union	Brigadier General
Robert Brank Vance	Confederacy	Brigadier General
Roger Weightman Hanson	Confederacy	Brigadier General
Roger Atkinson Pryor	Confederacy	Brigadier General
Romeyn Beck Ayres	Union	Brigadier General
Roswell Sabine Ripley	Confederacy	Brigadier General
Rufus Barringer	Confederacy	Brigadier General
Rufus Ingalls	Union	Brigadier General
Rufus King	Union	Brigadier General
Rufus Saxton	Union	Brigadier General
Rutherford Birchard Hayes	Union	Brigadier General
Samuel Beatty	Union	Brigadier General
Samuel Cooper	Confederacy	General
Samuel Garland,Jr.	Confederacy	Brigadier General
Samuel Jones	Confederacy	Major General
Samuel McGowan	Confederacy	Brigadier General
Samuel Read Anderson	Confederacy	Brigadier General
Samuel Sprigg Carroll	Union	Brigadier General

Samuel Powhatan Carter	Union	Brigadier General
Samuel Wylie Crawford	Union	Brigadier General
Samuel Ryan Curtis	Union	Major General
Samuel Wragg Ferguson	Confederacy	Brigadier General
Samuel Gibbs French	Confederacy	Major General
Samuel Jameson Gholson	Confederacy	Brigadier General
Samuel Peter Heintzelman	Union	Major General
Samuel Bell Maxey	Confederacy	Major General
Samuel Allen Rice	Union	Brigadier General
Samuel Davis Sturgis	Union	Brigadier General
Samuel Kosciuszko Zook	Union	Brigadier General
Schuyler Hamilton	Union	Major General
Selden Connor	Union	Brigadier General
Seth Williams	Union	Brigadier General
Seth Maxwell Barton	Confederacy	Brigadier General
Silas Casey	Union	Major General
Simon Bolivar Buckner	Confederacy	Lieutenant General
Simon Goodell Griffin	Union	Brigadier General
Solomon Meredith	Union	Brigadier General
Speed Smith Fry	Union	Brigadier General
St.John Richardson Liddell	Confederacy	Brigadier General
Stand Watie	Confederacy	Brigadier General
States Rights Gist	Confederacy	Brigadier General
Stephen Elliott,Jr.	Confederacy	Brigadier General
Stephen Miller	Union	Brigadier General
Stephen Gano Burbridge	Union	Brigadier General
Stephen Gardner Champlin	Union	Brigadier General
Stephen Augustus Hurlbut	Union	Major General
Stephen Dill Lee	Confederacy	Lieutenant General
Stephen Dodson Ramseur	Confederacy	Major General
Stephen Hinsdale Weed	Union	Brigadier General
Sterling Price	Confederacy	Major General
Sterling Alexander M. Wood	Confederacy	Brigadier General
Stewart Van Vliet	Union	Brigadier General
Sullivan Amory Meredith	Union	Brigadier General
Theodore Washington Brevard	Confederacy	Brigadier General
Theophilus Toulmin Garrard	Union	Brigadier General
Theophilus Hunter Holmes	Confederacy	Lieutenant General
Thomas Ewing,Jr.	Union	Brigadier General
Thomas Green	Confederacy	Brigadier General
Thomas Harrison	Confederacy	Brigadier General
Thomas Jordan	Confederacy	Brigadier General
Thomas Welsh	Union	Brigadier General
Thomas Williams	Union	Brigadier General
Thomas James Churchill	Confederacy	Major General
Thomas Lanier Clingman	Confederacy	Brigadier General
Thomas Reade Rootes Cobb	Confederacy	Brigadier General
Thomas Leonidas Crittenden	Union	Major General
Thomas Turpin Crittenden	Union	Brigadier General
Thomas Alfred Davies	Union	Brigadier General
Thomas Casimer Devin	Union	Brigadier General
Thomas Pleasant Dockery	Confederacy	Brigadier General
Thomas Fenwick Drayton	Confederacy	Brigadier General
Thomas Wilberforce Egan	Union	Brigadier General
Thomas Maley Harris	Union	Brigadier General
Thomas Carmichael Hindman	Confederacy	Major General

Thomas Jonathon Jackson	Confederacy	Lieutenant General
Thomas Leiper Kane	Union	Brigadier General
Thomas Muldrup Logan	Confederacy	Brigadier General
Thomas John Lucas	Union	Brigadier General
Thomas Jefferson McKean	Union	Brigadier General
Thomas Francis Meagher	Union	Brigadier General
Thomas Hewson Neill	Union	Brigadier General
Thomas Gamble Pitcher	Union	Brigadier General
Thomas Edward G. Ransom	Union	Brigadier General
Thomas Lafayette Rosser	Confederacy	Major General
Thomas Algeo Rowley	Union	Brigadier General
Thomas Howard Ruger	Union	Brigadier General
Thomas Moore Scott	Confederacy	Brigadier General
Thomas West Sherman	Union	Brigadier General
Thomas Benton Smith	Confederacy	Brigadier General
Thomas Church H. Smith	Union	Brigadier General
Thomas Kilby Smith	Union	Brigadier General
Thomas Alfred Smyth	Union	Brigadier General
Thomas Greely Stevenson	Union	Brigadier General
Thomas William Sweeny	Union	Brigadier General
Thomas Hart Taylor	Confederacy	Brigadier General
Thomas Fentress Toon	Confederacy	Brigadier General
Thomas Neville Waul	Confederacy	Brigadier General
Thomas John Wood	Union	Major General
Truman Seymour	Union	Brigadier General
Turner Ashby	Confederacy	Brigadier General
Tyree Harris Bell	Confederacy	Brigadier General
Ulysses Simpson Grant	Union	Lieutenant General
Victor Jean B. Girardey	Confederacy	Brigadier General
Wade Hampton	Confederacy	Lieutenant General
Wager Swayne	Union	Brigadier General
Walter Quintin Gresham	Union	Brigadier General
Walter Paye Lane	Confederacy	Brigadier General
Walter Husted Stevens	Confederacy	Brigadier General
Walter Chiles Whitaker	Union	Brigadier General
Washington Lafayette Elliott	Union	Brigadier General
Wesley Merritt	Union	Major General
William Barksdale	Confederate	Brigadier General
William Birney	Union	Brigadier General
William Dwight	Union	Brigadier General
William Grose	Union	Brigadier General
William Harrow	Union	Brigadier General
William Hays	Union	Brigadier General
William MacRae	Confederate	Brigadier General
William Mahone	Confederate	Major General
William McComb	Confederate	Brigadier General
William Miller	Confederate	Brigadier General
William Nelson	Union	Major General
William Preston	Confederate	Brigadier General
William Smith	Confederate	Major General
William Steele	Confederate	Brigadier General
William Terry	Confederate	Brigadier General
William Vandever	Union	Brigadier General
William Wirt Adams	Confederate	Brigadier General
William Wirt Allen	Confederate	Brigadier General
William Woods Averell	Union	Brigadier General

William Edwin Baldwin	Confederate	Brigadier General
William Farquhar Barry	Union	Brigadier General
William Francis Bartlett	Union	Brigadier General
William Brimage Bate	Confederacy	Major General
William Nelson R. Beall	Confederacy	Brigadier General
William Worth Belknap	Union	Brigadier General
William Plummer Benton	Union	Brigadier General
William Robertson Boggs	Confederacy	Brigadier General
William Lindsay Brandon	Confederacy	Brigadier General
William Felix Brantley	Confederacy	Brigadier General
William Thomas H. Brooks	Union	Major General
William Montague Browne	Confederacy	Brigadier General
William Wallace Burns	Union	Brigadier General
William Lewis Cabell	Confederacy	Brigadier General
William Bowen Campbell	Union	Brigadier General
William Passmore Carlin	Union	Brigadier General
William Henry Carroll	Confederacy	Brigadier General
William Ruffin Cox	Confederacy	Brigadier General
William George M. Davis	Confederacy	Brigadier General
William Hemsley Emory	Union	Brigadier General
William Henry Forney	Confederacy	Brigadier General
William Buel Franklin	Union	Brigadier General
William Henry French	Union	Major General
William Montgomery Gardner	Confederacy	Brigadier General
William Alexander Hammond	Union	Brigadier General
William Joseph Hardee	Confederacy	Lieutenant General
William Polk Hardeman	Confederacy	Brigadier General
William Selby Harney	Union	Brigadier General
William Babcock Hazen	Union	Major General
William Young Conn Humes	Confederacy	Brigadier General
William Hicks Jackson	Confederacy	Brigadier General
William Lowther Jackson	Confederacy	Brigadier General
William Edmonson Jones	Confederacy	Brigadier General
William High Keim	Union	Brigadier General
William Scott Ketchum	Union	Brigadier General
William Whedbee Kirkland	Confederacy	Brigadier General
William Henry F. Lee	Confederacy	Major General
William Gaston Lewis	Confederacy	Brigadier General
William Wing Loring	Confederacy	Major General
William Haines Lytle	Union	Brigadier General
William Whann Mackall	Confederacy	Brigadier General
William Thompson Martin	Confederacy	Major General
William Reading Montgomery	Union	Brigadier General
William Hopkins Morris	Union	Brigadier General
William Ward Orme	Union	Brigadier General
William Henry F. Payne	Confederacy	Brigadier General
William Raine Peck	Confederacy	Brigadier General
William Dorsey Pender	Confederacy	Major General
William Nelson Pendleton	Confederacy	Brigadier General
William Flank Perry	Confederacy	Brigadier General
William Anderson Pile	Union	Brigadier General
William Henry Powell	Union	Brigadier General
William Andrew Quarles	Confederacy	Brigadier General
William Paul Roberts	Confederacy	Brigadier General
William Starke Rosecrans	Union	Major General
William Price Sanders	Union	Brigadier General

William Read Scurry	Confederacy	Brigadier General
William Henry Seward,Jr.	Union	Brigadier General
William Tecumseh Sherman	Union	Major General
William Duncan Smith	Confederacy	Brigadier General
William Farrar Smith	Union	Major General
William Sooy Smith	Union	Brigadier General
William Yarnel Slack	Confederacy	Brigadier General
William Edwin Starke	Confederacy	Brigadier General
William Kerley Strong	Union	Brigadier General
William Booth Taliaferro	Confederacy	Major General
William Rufus Terrill	Union	Brigadier General
William Richard Terry	Confederacy	Brigadier General
William Feimster Tucker	Confederacy	Brigadier General
William Henry T. Walker	Confederacy	Major General
William Stephen Walker	Confederacy	Brigadier General
William Harvey L. Wallace	Union	Brigadier General
William Henry Wallace	Confederacy	Brigadier General
William Thomas Ward	Union	Brigadier General
William Denison Whipple	Union	Brigadier General
William Henry C. Whiting	Confederacy	Major General
Williams Carter Wickham	Confederacy	Brigadier General
William Tatum Wofford	Confederacy	Brigadier General
William Hugh Young	Confederacy	Brigadier General
Willis Arnold Gorman	Union	Brigadier General
Winfield Scott	Union	Major General
Winfield Scott Featherston	Confederacy	Brigadier General
Winfield Scott Hancock	Union	Major General
Wladimir Krzyzanowski	Union	Brigadier General
Young Marshall Moody	Confederacy	Brigadier General
Zachariah Cantey Deas	Confederacy	Brigadier General
Zealous Bates Tower	Union	Brigadier General
Zebulon York	Confederacy	Brigadier General

3

Civil War Generals
by Middle Names

In this chapter the middle names are arranged alphabetically, then within each group of the same middle name, by the last names. Only those generals which had middle names are included here.

GENERAL	FOUGHT FOR	RANK
John Aaron Rawlins	North	Brigadier General
Joseph Abel Haskin	North	Brigadier General
James Abram Garfield	North	Major General
Jasper Adalmorn Maltby	North	Brigadier General
Pleasant Adam Hackleman	North	Brigadier General
Charles Adam Heckman	North	Brigadier General
John Adams Dix	North	Major General
Quincy Adams Gillmore	North	Major General
Lewis Addison Armistead	South	Brigadier General
Lewis Addison Grant	North	Brigadier General
David Addison Weisiger	South	Brigadier General
Julius Adolph deLagnel	South	Brigadier General
Gustavus Adolphus DeRussy	North	Brigadier General
Gustavus Adolphus Smith	North	Brigadier General
Robert Alexander Cameron	North	Brigadier General
Joseph Alexander Cooper	North	Brigadier General
William Alexander Hammond	North	Brigadier General
John Alexander Logan	North	Major General
John Alexander McClernand	North	Major General
Giles Alexander Smith	North	Brigadier General
James Alexander Walker	South	Brigadier General
James Alexander Williamson	North	Brigadier General
Henry Alexander Wise	South	Brigadier General
Sterling Alexander M. Wood	South	Brigadier General
Thomas Alfred Davies	North	Brigadier General
Thomas Alfred Smyth	North	Brigadier General
Thomas Algeo Rowley	North	Brigadier General
James Allen Hardie	North	Brigadier General
Ethan Allen Hitchcock	North	Brigadier General
Samuel Allen Rice	North	Brigadier General
David Allen Russell	North	Brigadier General
Sullivan Amory Meredith	North	Brigadier General

Jubal Anderson Early	South	Lieutenant General
William Anderson Pile	North	Brigadier General
Joseph Andrew J. Lightburn	North	Brigadier General
William Andrew Quarles	South	Brigadier General
Cullen Andrews Battle	South	Brigadier General
Clement Anselm Evans	South	Brigadier General
Joseph Anthony Mower	North	Major General
Nelson Appleton Miles	North	Brigadier General
George Archibald McCall	North	Brigadier General
James Argyle Smith	South	Brigadier General
George Armstrong Custer	North	Brigadier General
Willis Arnold Gorman	North	Brigadier General
Eleazer Arthur Paine	North	Brigadier General
Eugene Asa Carr	North	Brigadier General
Francis Asbury Shoup	South	Brigadier General
Andrew Atkinson Humphreys	North	Major General
Roger Atkinson Pryor	South	Brigadier General
Stephen Augustus Hurlbut	North	Major General
Leroy Augustus Stafford	South	Brigadier General
Marcellus Augustus Stovall	South	Brigadier General
Robert Augustus Toombs	South	Brigadier General
Edward Augustus Wild	North	Brigadier General
John Austin Wharton	South	Major General
Edward Aylesworth Perry	South	Brigadier General
William Babcock Hazen	North	Major General
John Baillie McIntosh	North	Brigadier General
George Baird Hodge	South	Brigadier General
Adin Ballou Underwood	North	Brigadier General
John Bankhead Magruder	South	Major General
Erastus Barnard Tyler	North	Brigadier General
Randolph Barnes Marcy	North	Brigadier General
James Barnet Fry	North	Brigadier General
Francis Barretto Spinola	North	Brigadier General
John Basil Turchin	North	Brigadier General
Zealous Bates Tower	North	Brigadier General
Romeyn Beck Ayres	North	Brigadier General
Nathan Bedford Forrest	South	Lieutenant General
Amos Beebe Eaton	North	Brigadier General
Henry Beebee Carrington	North	Brigadier General
David Bell Birney	North	Major General
John Bell Hood	South	General
Samuel Bell Maxey	South	Major General
Lucius Bellinger Northrop	South	Brigadier General
Joseph Benjamin Palmer	South	Brigadier General
John Benjamin Sanborn	North	Brigadier General
Joseph Bennett Plummer	North	Brigadier General
Egbert Benson Brown	North	Brigadier General
Hylan Benton Lyon	South	Brigadier General
Thomas Benton Smith	South	Brigadier General
Green Berry Raum	North	Brigadier General
George Bibb Crittenden	South	Major General
Rutherford Birchard Hayes	North	Brigadier General
James Birdseye McPherson	North	Major General
George Blake Cosby	South	Brigadier General
James Blair Steedman	North	Major General
John Blair Smith Todd	North	Brigadier General

Simon Bolivar Buckner	South	Lieutenant General
Orlando Bolivar Willcox	North	Brigadier General
Napoleon Bonaparte Buford	North	Brigadier General
Jerome Bonaparte Robertson	South	Brigadier General
William Booth Taliaferro	South	Major General
John Bordenave Villepigue	South	Brigadier General
William Bowen Campbell	North	Brigadier General
Clinton Bowen Fisk	North	Brigadier General
Hugh Boyle Ewing	North	Brigadier General
Elkanah Brackin Greer	South	Brigadier General
Joseph Bradford Carr	North	Brigadier General
Robert Brank Vance	South	Brigadier General
John Breckinridge Grayson	South	Brigadier General
Henry Brevard Davidson	South	Brigadier General
Joseph Brevard Kershaw	South	Major General
James Brewerton Ricketts	North	Brigadier General
William Brimage Bate	South	Major General
George Brinton McClellan	North	Major General
Hiram Bronson Granbury	South	Brigadier General
Richard Brooke Garnett	South	Brigadier General
John Brown Gordon	South	Major General
Robert Brown Potter	North	Brigadier General
Alexander Brydie Dyer	North	Brigadier General
John Buchanan Floyd	South	Brigadier General
William Buel Franklin	North	Brigadier General
John Bullock Clark,Jr.	South	Brigadier General
George Burgwyn Anderson	South	Brigadier General
Peter Burwell Starke	South	Brigadier General
Israel Bush Richardson	North	Major General
Robert Byington Mitchell	North	Brigadier General
James Byron Gordon	South	Brigadier General
John Cabell Breckinridge	South	Major General
Matthew Calbraith Butler	South	Major General
John Caldwell C. Sanders	South	Brigadier General
John Calvin Brown	South	Major General
Charles Camp Doolittle	North	Brigadier General
James Camp Tappan	South	Brigadier General
Archibald Campbell Godwin	South	Brigadier General
Zachariah Cantey Deas	South	Brigadier General
Don Carlos Buell	North	Major General
Thomas Carmichael Hindman	South	Major General
John Carpenter Carter	South	Brigadier General
Charles Carroll Walcutt	North	Brigadier General
Williams Carter Wickham	South	Brigadier General
Edward Cary Walthall	South	Major General
Thomas Casimer Devin	North	Brigadier General
Lewis Cass Hunt	North	Brigadier General
Richard Caswell Gatlin	South	Brigadier General
Charles Champion Gilbert	North	Brigadier General
Francis Channing Barlow	North	Brigadier General
John Charles Fremont	North	Major General
Robert Charles Tyler	South	Brigadier General
Daniel Chevilette Govan	South	Brigadier General
Walter Chiles Whitaker	North	Brigadier General
Robert Christie Buchanan	North	Brigadier General
Thomas Church H. Smith	North	Brigadier General

Abner Clark Harding	North	Brigadier General
James Clay Rice	North	Brigadier General
Green Clay Smith	North	Brigadier General
Charles Cleveland Dodge	North	Brigadier General
John Cleveland Robinson	North	Brigadier General
John Clifford Pemberton	South	Lieutenant General
James Clifford Veatch	North	Brigadier General
Cadwallader Colden Washburn	North	Major General
Nathaniel Collins McLean	North	Brigadier General
Christopher Columbus Andrews	North	Brigadier General
Christopher Columbus Augur	North	Major General
Jefferson Columbus Davis	North	Brigadier General
Gabriel Colvin Wharton	South	Brigadier General
Henry Constantine Wayne	South	Brigadier General
John Converse Starkweather	North	Brigadier General
Frank Crawford Armstrong	South	Brigadier General
John Crawford Vaughn	South	Brigadier General
John Creed Moore	South	Brigadier General
George Crockett Strong	North	Brigadier General
Alvan Cullem Gillem	North	Brigadier General
Robert Cumming Schenck	North	Major General
Montgomery Cunningham Meigs	North	Brigadier General
John Curtis Caldwell	North	Brigadier General
Jeremiah Cutler Sullivan	North	Brigadier General
James Dada Morgan	North	Brigadier General
Philip Dale Roddey	South	Brigadier General
Joseph Dana Webster	North	Brigadier General
John Daniel Imboden	South	Brigadier General
Robert Daniel Johnston	South	Brigadier General
Erasmus Darwin Keyes	North	Major General
George Dashiell Bayard	North	Brigadier General
Birkett Davenport Fry	South	Brigadier General
Daniel Davidson Bidwell	North	Brigadier General
Martin Davis Hardin	North	Brigadier General
Charles Davis Jameson	North	Brigadier General
Samuel Davis Sturgis	North	Brigadier General
George Day Wagner	North	Brigadier General
John Decatur Barry	South	Brigadier General
James Deering Fessenden	North	Brigadier General
Henry DeLamar Clayton	South	Major General
Edwin Denison Morgan	North	Major General
William Denison Whipple	North	Brigadier General
Montgomery Dent Corse	South	Brigadier General
Mahlon Dickerson Manson	North	Brigadier General
Edward Dickinson Baker	North	Major General
Stephen Dill Lee	South	Lieutenant General
Robert Doak Lilley	South	Brigadier General
John Doby Kennedy	South	Brigadier General
Stephen Dodson Ramseur	South	Major General
George Doherty Johnston	South	Brigadier General
Jacob Dolson Cox	North	Major General
Mortimer Dormer Leggett	North	Brigadier General
Edward Dorr Tracy	South	Brigadier General
William Dorsey Pender	South	Major General
George Douglas Ramsay	North	Brigadier General
Matthew Duncan Ector	South	Brigadier General

William Duncan Smith	South	Brigadier General
John Dunlap Stevenson	North	Brigadier General
Henry Dwight Terry	North	Brigadier General
George Ear Maney	South	Brigadier General
Daniel Edgar Sickles	North	Major General
William Edmonson Jones	South	Brigadier General
Raleigh Edward Colston	South	Brigadier General
Patrick Edward Connor	North	Brigadier General
James Edward Harrison	South	Brigadier General
Charles Edward Hovey	North	Brigadier General
Robert Edward Lee	South	General
George Edward Pickett	South	Major General
Calvin Edward Pratt	North	Brigadier General
James Edwards Rains	South	Brigadier General
Thomas Edward G. Ransom	North	Brigadier General
William Edwin Baldwin	South	Brigadier General
Martin Edwin Green	South	Brigadier General
James Edwin Slaughter	South	Brigadier General
William Edwin Starke	South	Brigadier General
Joseph Eggleston Johnston	South	General
Halbert Eleazer Paine	North	Brigadier General
Barnard Elliott Bee	South	Brigadier General
John Ellis Wool	North	Major General
Edward Elmer Potter	North	Brigadier General
David Emanuel Twiggs	South	Major General
Robert Emmett Rodes	South	Major General
Francis Engle Patterson	North	Brigadier General
Henry Eugene Davies	North	Brigadier General
Alfred Eugene Jackson	South	Brigadier General
Lucius Eugene Polk	South	Brigadier General
John Eugene Smith	North	Brigadier General
Henry Eustace McCulloch	South	Brigadier General
Ambrose Everett Burnside	North	Major General
James Ewell Brown Stuart	South	Major General
Joseph Farmer Knipe	North	Brigadier General
William Farquhar Barry	North	Brigadier General
William Farrar Smith	North	Major General
Conrad Feger Jackson	North	Brigadier General
William Feimster Tucker	South	Brigadier General
William Felix Brantley	South	Brigadier General
Thomas Fentress Toon	South	Brigadier General
Thomas Fenwick Drayton	South	Brigadier General
Issac Ferdinand Quinby	North	Brigadier General
Manning Ferguson Force	North	Brigadier General
Charles Ferguson Smith	North	Major General
Isaac Fitzgerald Shepard	North	Brigadier General
William Flank Perry	South	Brigadier General
James Fleming Fagan	South	Major General
George Foster Shepley	North	Brigadier General
William Francis Bartlett	North	Brigadier General
Jeremy Francis Gilmer	South	Major General
George Francis McGinnis	North	Brigadier General
Thomas Francis Meagher	North	Brigadier General
Albin Francisco Schoepf	North	Brigadier General
Benjamin Franklin Butler	North	Major General
Benjamin Franklin Cheatham	South	Major General

John Franklin Farnsworth	North	Brigadier General
Benjamin Franklin Kelley	North	Brigadier General
John Franklin Miller	North	Brigadier General
Elisha Franklin Paxton	South	Brigadier General
Benjamin Franklin Potts	North	Brigadier General
John Frederick Hartranft	North	Brigadier General
Robert Frederick Hoke	South	Major General
Otho French Strahl	South	Brigadier General
John Fulton Reynolds	North	Major General
Leonard Fulton Ross	North	Brigadier General
James Gallant Spears	North	Brigadier General
Albert Gallatin Blanchard	South	Brigadier General
Albert Gallatin Jenkins	South	Brigadier General
Thomas Gamble Pitcher	North	Brigadier General
Stephen Gano Burbridge	North	Brigadier General
Stephen Gardner Champlin	North	Brigadier General
Charles Garrison Harker	North	Brigadier General
Jacob Gartner Lauman	North	Brigadier General
William Gaston Lewis	South	Brigadier General
William George M. Davis	South	Brigadier General
Nathan George Evans	South	Brigadier General
John George Walker	South	Major General
George Gibbs Dibrell	South	Brigadier General
Samuel Gibbs French	South	Major General
Joseph Gilbert Totten	North	Brigadier General
James Gillpatrick Blunt	North	Major General
Henry Goddard Thomas	North	Brigadier General
Lewis Golding Arnold	North	Brigadier General
Simon Goodell Griffin	North	Brigadier General
George Gordon Meade	North	Major General
Horatio Gouverneur Wright	North	Major General
John Grant Mitchell	North	Brigadier General
John Gray Foster	North	Major General
Edwin Gray Lee	South	Brigadier General
Thomas Greely Stevenson	North	Brigadier General
James Green Martin	South	Brigadier General
Hiram Gregory Berry	North	Major General
John Gross Barnard	North	Brigadier General
Benjamin Grubb Humphreys	South	Brigadier General
John Grubb Parke	North	Major General
Pierre Gustave T. Beauregard	South	General
William Haines Lytle	North	Brigadier General
Robert Hall Chilton	South	Brigadier General
Douglas Hancock Cooper	South	Brigadier General
Isaac Hardin Duval	North	Brigadier General
Benjamin Hardin Helm	South	Brigadier General
Tyree Harris Bell	South	Brigadier General
Daniel Harris Reynolds	South	Brigadier General
Nathaniel Harrison Harris	South	Brigadier General
Lovell Harrison Rousseau	North	Major General
Henry Harrison Walker	South	Brigadier General
James Harrison Wilson	North	Brigadier General
Thomas Hart Taylor	South	Brigadier General
Daniel Harvey Hill	South	Lieutenant General
William Harvey L. Wallace	North	Brigadier General
John Haskell King	North	Brigadier General

Henry Hastings Sibley	North	Brigadier General
Henry Hayes Lockwood	North	Brigadier General
George Hector Tyndale	North	Brigadier General
William Hemsley Emory	North	Brigadier General
James Henry Carleton	North	Brigadier General
William Henry Carroll	South	Brigadier General
George Henry Chapman	North	Brigadier General
William Henry Forney	South	Brigadier General
William Henry French	North	Major General
George Henry Gordon	North	Brigadier General
Benjamin Henry Grierson	North	Brigadier General
Edward Henry Hobson	North	Brigadier General
James Henry Lane	South	Brigadier General
William Henry F. Lee	South	Major General
Lewis Henry Little	South	Brigadier General
John Henry Martindale	North	Brigadier General
William Henry F. Payne	South	Brigadier General
William Henry Powell	North	Brigadier General
Daniel Henry Rucker	North	Brigadier General
William Henry Seward,Jr.	North	Brigadier General
Philip Henry Sheridan	North	Major General
Edwin Henry Stoughton	North	Brigadier General
George Henry Thomas	North	Major General
James Henry Van Alen	North	Brigadier General
William Henry T. Walker	South	Major General
William Henry Wallace	South	Brigadier General
John Henry Hobart Ward	North	Brigadier General
William Henry C. Whiting	South	Major General
David Henry Williams	North	Brigadier General
John Henry Winder	South	Brigadier General
John Herbert Kelly	South	Brigadier General
Dabney Herndon Maury	South	Major General
Richard Heron Anderson	South	Lieutenant General
James Hewett Ledlie	North	Brigadier General
Thomas Hewson Neill	North	Brigadier General
James Heyward Trapier	South	Brigadier General
William Hicks Jackson	South	Brigadier General
William High Keim	North	Brigadier General
Stephen Hinsdale Weed	North	Brigadier General
Clement Hoffman Stevens	South	Brigadier General
Adley Hogan Gladden	South	Brigadier General
Beverly Holcombe Robertson	South	Brigadier General
James Holt Clanton	South	Brigadier General
Alfred Holt Colquitt	South	Brigadier General
Robert Hopkins Hatton	South	Brigadier General
William Hopkins Morris	North	Brigadier General
Henry Hopkins Sibley	South	Brigadier General
John Horace Forney	South	Major General
Joseph Horace Lewis	South	Brigadier General
Robert Houstoun Anderson	South	Brigadier General
Thomas Howard Ruger	North	Brigadier General
Alfred Howe Terry	North	Major General
William Hugh Young	South	Brigadier General
George Hume Steuart	South	Brigadier General
John Hunt Morgan	South	Brigadier General
Theophilus Hunter Holmes	South	Lieutenant General

Jacob Hunter Sharp	South	Brigadier General
Walter Husted Stevens	South	Brigadier General
Robert Huston Milroy	North	Major General
Felix Huston Robertson	South	Brigadier General
Isaac Ingalls Stevens	North	Brigadier General
James Isham Gilbert	North	Brigadier General
Joseph Jackson Bartlett	North	Brigadier General
Napoleon Jackson T. Dana	North	Major General
Edmund Jackson Davis	North	Brigadier General
Andrew Jackson Hamilton	North	Brigadier General
Henry Jackson Hunt	North	Brigadier General
Charles Jackson Paine	North	Brigadier General
Andrew Jackson Smith	North	Major General
Adam Jacoby Slemmer	North	Brigadier General
Jean Jacques A.A. Mouton	South	Brigadier General
Thomas James Churchill	South	Major General
Nathaniel James Jackson	North	Brigadier General
Richard James Oglesby	North	Major General
John James Peck	North	Major General
Gabriel James Rains	South	Brigadier General
Samuel Jameson Gholson	South	Brigadier General
James Jay Archer	South	Brigadier General
Francis Jay Herron	North	Major General
Victor Jean B. Girardey	South	Brigadier General
Benjamin Jefferson Hill	South	Brigadier General
Thomas Jefferson McKean	North	Brigadier General
Alfred Jefferson Vaughan,Jr	South	Brigadier General
Lucius Jeremiah Gartrell	South	Brigadier General
George Jerrison Stannard	North	Brigadier General
Elon John Farnsworth	North	Brigadier General
Thomas John Lucas	North	Brigadier General
Fitz John Porter	North	Major General
Charles John Stolbrand	North	Brigadier General
Thomas John Wood	North	Major General
Jesse Johnson Finley	South	Brigadier General
Gideon Johnson Pillow	South	Brigadier General
James Johnston Pettigrew	South	Brigadier General
Thomas Jonathon Jackson	South	Lieutenant General
Joseph Jones Reynolds	North	Major General
Paul Jones Semmes	South	Brigadier General
Isaac Jones Wistar	North	Brigadier General
John Joseph Abercrombie	North	Brigadier General
William Joseph Hardee	South	Lieutenant General
Peter Joseph Osterhaus	North	Major General
Marcus Joseph Wright	South	Brigadier General
Hugh Judson Kilpatrick	North	Brigadier General
Johnson Kelly Duncan	South	Brigadier General
Michael Kelly Lawler	North	Brigadier General
Gouverneur Kemble Warren	North	Major General
William Kerley Strong	North	Brigadier General
Thomas Kilby Smith	North	Brigadier General
John King Jackson	South	Brigadier General
Joseph King F. Mansfield	North	Brigadier General
Charles Kinnaird Graham	North	Brigadier General
Edmund Kirby Smith	South	General
Felix Kirk Zollicoffer	South	Brigadier General

Samuel Kosciuszko Zook	North	Brigadier General
George Lafayette Beal	North	Brigadier General
Washington Lafayette Elliott	North	Brigadier General
Thomas Lafayette Rosser	South	Major General
Thomas Lanier Clingman	South	Brigadier General
Robert Latimer McCook	North	Brigadier General
Francis Laurens Vinton	North	Brigadier General
James Lawlor Kiernan	North	Brigadier General
Joshua Lawrence Chamberlain	North	Brigadier General
Henry Lawrence Eustis	North	Brigadier General
James Lawson Kemper	South	Major General
Richard Lee T. Beale	South	Brigadier General
Randall Lee Gibson	South	Brigadier General
Jesse Lee Reno	North	Major General
Thomas Leiper Kane	North	Brigadier General
George Leonard Andrews	North	Brigadier General
Thomas Leonidas Crittenden	North	Major General
Charles Leopold Matthies	North	Brigadier General
Henry Lewis Benning	South	Brigadier General
William Lewis Cabell	South	Brigadier General
Joseph Lewis Hogg	South	Brigadier General
Morgan Lewis Smith	North	Brigadier General
Albert Lindley Lee	North	Brigadier General
William Lindsay Brandon	South	Brigadier General
Lunsford Lindsay Lomax	South	Major General
Armistead Lindsay Long	South	Brigadier General
Reuben Lindsay Walker	South	Brigadier General
Carter Littlepage Stevenson	South	Major General
Edward Lloyd Thomas	South	Brigadier General
Augustus Louis Chetlain	North	Brigadier General
William Lowther Jackson	South	Brigadier General
George Lucas Hartsuff	North	Major General
Richard Lucian Page	South	Brigadier General
Egbert Ludovicus Viele	North	Brigadier General
Louis Ludwig Blenker	North	Brigadier General
Milledge Luke Bonham	South	Brigadier General
Martin Luther Smith	South	Major General
Ormsby MacKnight Mitchel	North	Major General
James Madison Tuttle	North	Brigadier General
Thomas Maley Harris	North	Brigadier General
Pierce Manning B. Young	South	Major General
Cassius Marcellus Clay	North	Major General
Cadmus Marcellus Wilcox	South	Major General
Francis Marion Cockrell	South	Brigadier General
Daniel Marsh Frost	South	Brigadier General
John Marshall Jones	South	Brigadier General
Young Marshall Moody	South	Brigadier General
Lucius Marshall Walker	South	Brigadier General
Newton Martin Curtis	North	Brigadier General
Benjamin Mayberry Prentiss	North	Major General
Seth Maxwell Barton	South	Brigadier General
John McAllister Schofield	North	Major General
John McCauley Palmer	North	Major General
Alexander McDowell McCook	North	Major General
Dudley McIver DuBose	South	Brigadier General
Evander McIvor Law	South	Brigadier General

David McMurtrie Gregg	North	Brigadier General
James McQueen McIntosh	South	Brigadier General
Grenville Mellen Dodge	North	Major General
Orlando Metcalfe Poe	North	Brigadier General
Arthur Middleton Manigault	South	Brigadier General
Charles Miller Shelley	South	Brigadier General
John Milton Brannan	North	Brigadier General
John Milton Thayer	North	Brigadier General
Jones Mitchell Withers	South	Major General
Marcellus Monroe Crocker	North	Brigadier General
James Monroe Goggin	South	Brigadier General
Mosby Monroe Parsons	South	Major General
Abner Monroe Perrin	South	Brigadier General
William Montague Browne	South	Brigadier General
Richard Montgomery Gano	South	Brigadier General
William Montgomery Gardner	South	Brigadier General
Edward Moody McCook	North	Brigadier General
Alfred Moore Scales	South	Brigadier General
Thomas Moore Scott	South	Brigadier General
Bryan Morel Thomas	South	Brigadier General
Henry Morris Naglee	North	Brigadier General
James Morrison Hawes	South	Brigadier General
John Morrison Oliver	North	Brigadier General
Henry Moses Judah	North	Brigadier General
Gilbert Moxley Sorrel	South	Brigadier General
Thomas Muldrup Logan	South	Brigadier General
Isaac Munroe St.John	South	Brigadier General
John Murray Corse	North	Brigadier General
James Murrell Shackelford	North	Brigadier General
Charles Mynn Thruston	North	Brigadier General
Alfred Napoleon A. Duffie	North	Brigadier General
Darius Nash Couch	North	Major General
Edward Needles Kirk	North	Brigadier General
William Nelson R. Beall	South	Brigadier General
William Nelson Pendleton	South	Brigadier General
Thomas Neville Waul	South	Brigadier General
Innis Newton Palmer	North	Brigadier General
Isham Nicholas Haynie	North	Brigadier General
Lawrence O'Bryan Branch	South	Brigadier General
Paul Octave Hebert	South	Brigadier General
Robert Ogden Tyler	North	Brigadier General
Joseph Orville Shelby	South	Brigadier General
Edward Otho C. Ord	North	Major General
Oliver Otis Howard	North	Major General
Joseph Pannell Taylor	North	Brigadier General
John Parker Hawkins	North	Brigadier General
Eliakim Parker Scammon	North	Brigadier General
Albion Parris Howe	North	Brigadier General
William Passmore Carlin	North	Brigadier General
James Patrick Major	South	Brigadier General
James Patton Anderson	South	Major General
Gustave Paul Cluseret	North	Brigadier General
William Paul Roberts	South	Brigadier General
Walter Paye Lane	South	Brigadier General
Isaac Peace Rodman	North	Brigadier General
Mark Perrin Lowrey	South	Brigadier General

Samuel Peter Heintzelman	North	Major General
Alexander Peter Stewart	South	Lieutenant General
Alvin Peterson Hovey	North	Brigadier General
James Phillip Simms	South	Brigadier General
Horatio Phillips Van Cleve	North	Brigadier General
Daniel Phineas Woodbury	North	Brigadier General
George Pierce Doles	South	Brigadier General
Lawrence Pike Graham	North	Brigadier General
Thomas Pleasant Dockery	South	Brigadier General
William Plummer Benton	North	Brigadier General
William Polk Hardeman	South	Brigadier General
Ralph Pomeroy Buckland	North	Brigadier General
Charles Pomeroy Stone	North	Brigadier General
Leroy Pope Walker	South	Brigadier General
Edward Porter Alexander	South	Brigadier General
John Porter Hatch	North	Brigadier General
John Porter McCown	South	Major General
John Potts Slough	North	Brigadier General
Ambrose Powell Hill	South	Lieutenant General
Samuel Powhatan Carter	North	Brigadier General
Luther Prentice Bradley	North	Brigadier General
Nathaniel Prentiss Banks	North	Major General
Francis Preston Blair,Jr.	North	Major General
William Price Sanders	North	Brigadier General
Hamilton Prioleau Bee	South	Brigadier General
Catharinus Putnam Buckingham	North	Brigadier General
Walter Quintin Gresham	North	Brigadier General
William Raine Peck	South	Brigadier General
John Randolph Chambliss,Jr.	South	Brigadier General
Adam Rankin Johnson	South	Brigadier General
Ambrose Ransom Wright	South	Major General
Samuel Read Anderson	South	Brigadier General
William Read Scurry	South	Brigadier General
Thomas Reade Rootes Cobb	South	Brigadier General
William Reading Montgomery	North	Brigadier General
Francis Redding T. Nicholls	South	Brigadier General
John Reese Kenly	North	Brigadier General
Philippe Regis deTrobriand	North	Brigadier General
Joseph Reid Anderson	South	Brigadier General
Gabriel Rene Paul	North	Brigadier General
Edward Richard S. Canby	North	Major General
James Richard Slack	North	Brigadier General
William Richard Terry	South	Brigadier General
St.John Richardson Liddell	South	Brigadier General
Isaac Ridgeway Trimble	South	Major General
States Rights Gist	South	Brigadier General
Joseph Robert Davis	South	Brigadier General
John Robert Jones	South	Brigadier General
Alexander Robert Lawton	South	Brigadier General
Charles Robert Woods	North	Brigadier General
William Robertson Boggs	South	Brigadier General
Joseph Rodman West	North	Brigadier General
John Rogers Cooke	South	Brigadier General
James Ronald Chalmers	South	Brigadier General
Patrick Ronayne Cleburne	South	Major General
Byron Root Pierce	North	Brigadier General

Henry Rootes Jackson	South	Brigadier General
Joseph Roswell Hawley	North	Brigadier General
Marsena Rudolph Patrick	North	Brigadier General
William Ruffin Cox	South	Brigadier General
William Rufus Terrill	North	Brigadier General
David Rumph Jones	South	Major General
Bushrod Rust Johnson	South	Major General
John Rutter Brooke	North	Brigadier General
Samuel Ryan Curtis	North	Major General
Roswell Sabine Ripley	South	Brigadier General
James Samuel Wadsworth	North	Brigadier General
Abram Sanders Piatt	North	Brigadier General
Alexander Sandor Asboth	North	Brigadier General
Orris Sanford Ferry	North	Brigadier General
Robert Sanford Foster	North	Brigadier General
John Sanford Mason	North	Brigadier General
John Sappington Marmaduke	South	Major General
Winfield Scott Featherston	South	Brigadier General
Winfield Scott Hancock	North	Major General
William Scott Ketchum	North	Brigadier General
James Scott Negley	North	Major General
Robert Seaman Granger	North	Brigadier General
George Sears Greene	North	Brigadier General
William Selby Harney	North	Brigadier General
Robert Selden Garnett	South	Brigadier General
John Selden Roane	South	Brigadier General
Henry Shaw Briggs	North	Brigadier General
Frederick Shearer Stumbaugh	North	Brigadier General
Albert Sidney Johnston	South	General
James Sidney Robinson	North	Brigadier General
Charles Sidney Winder	South	Brigadier General
Laurence Simmons Baker	South	Brigadier General
Ulysses Simpson Grant	North	Lieutenant General
Ranald Slidell Mackenzie	North	Brigadier General
David Sloane Stanley	North	Major General
Elias Smith Dennis	North	Brigadier General
Daniel Smith Donelson	South	Major General
Speed Smith Fry	North	Brigadier General
Charles Smith Hamilton	North	Major General
Milo Smith Hascall	North	Brigadier General
John Smith Phelps	North	Brigadier General
John Smith Preston	South	Brigadier General
Melancthon Smith Wade	North	Brigadier General
William Sooy Smith	North	Brigadier General
Samuel Sprigg Carroll	North	Brigadier General
James St.Clair Morton	North	Brigadier General
Philip St.George Cocke	South	Brigadier General
Philip St.George Cooke	North	Brigadier General
William Starke Rosecrans	North	Major General
Alpheus Starkey Williams	North	Brigadier General
William Stephen Walker	South	Brigadier General
John Stevens Bowen	South	Major General
Alexander Stewart Webb	North	Brigadier General
James Streshly Jackson	North	Brigadier General
Franklin Stillman Nickerson	North	Brigadier General
Richard Stoddert Ewell	South	Lieutenant General

Benjamin Stone Roberts	North	Brigadier General
John Stuart Williams	South	Brigadier General
Edward Stuyvesant Bragg	North	Brigadier General
Lawrence Sullivan Ross	South	Brigadier General
Joseph Tarr Copeland	North	Brigadier General
William Tatum Wofford	South	Brigadier General
William Tecumseh Sherman	North	Major General
James Thadeus Holtzclaw	South	Brigadier General
Patrick Theodore Moore	South	Brigadier General
George Thomas Anderson	South	Brigadier General
William Thomas H. Brooks	North	Major General
Charles Thomas Campbell	North	Brigadier General
John Thomas Croxton	North	Brigadier General
Joshua Thomas Owen	North	Brigadier General
Alfred Thomas A. Torbert	North	Brigadier General
William Thomas Ward	North	Brigadier General
Harry Thompson Hays	South	Major General
William Thompson Martin	South	Major General
Hugh Thompson Reid	North	Brigadier General
Jerimiah Tilford Boyle	North	Brigadier General
Theophilus Toulmin Garrard	North	Brigadier General
Alexander Travis Hawthorne	South	Brigadier General
Louis Trezevant Wigfall	South	Brigadier General
Thomas Turpin Crittenden	North	Brigadier General
Bradley Tyler Johnson	South	Brigadier General
John Tyler Morgan	South	Brigadier General
August Valentine Kautz	North	Brigadier General
Robert Vinkler Richardson	South	Brigadier General
Edwin Vose Sumner	North	Major General
Henry Wager Halleck	North	Major General
William Wallace Burns	North	Brigadier General
John Wallace Fuller	North	Brigadier General
Henry Walton Wessells	North	Brigadier General
William Ward Orme	North	Brigadier General
Henry Warner Birge	North	Brigadier General
Henry Warner Slocum	North	Major General
Joseph Warren Revere	North	Brigadier General
Elliott Warren Rice	North	Brigadier General
Henry Washington Benham	North	Brigadier General
Theodore Washington Brevard	South	Brigadier General
George Washington Cullum	North	Brigadier General
George Washington Deitzler	North	Brigadier General
Alfred Washington Ellet	North	Brigadier General
George Washington Getty	North	Brigadier General
George Washington Gordon	South	Brigadier General
George Washington C. Lee	South	Major General
George Washington Morgan	North	Brigadier General
Henry Watkins Allen	South	Brigadier General
George Webb Morell	North	Major General
Hugh Weedon Mercer	South	Brigadier General
Amiel Weeks Whipple	North	Brigadier General
Roger Weightman Hanson	South	Brigadier General
Daniel Weisiger Adams	South	Brigadier General
Alexander Welch Reynolds	South	Brigadier General
John Wesley Frazer	South	Brigadier General
John Wesley Turner	North	Brigadier General

Frederick West Lander	North	Brigadier General
Thomas West Sherman	North	Brigadier General
William Whann Mackall	South	Brigadier General
William Whedbee Kirkland	South	Brigadier General
Matt Whitaker Ransom	South	Brigadier General
John White Geary	North	Brigadier General
Thomas Wilberforce Egan	North	Brigadier General
Adolph Wilhelm von Steinwehr	North	Brigadier General
John Wilkins Whitfield	South	Brigadier General
Alexander William Campbell	South	Brigadier General
James William Denver	North	Brigadier General
Charles William Field	South	Major General
James William Reilly	North	Brigadier General
Thomas William Sweeny	North	Brigadier General
George William Taylor	North	Brigadier General
Basil Wilson Duke	South	Brigadier General
John Wilson Sprague	North	Brigadier General
William Wing Loring	South	Major General
James Winning McMillan	North	Brigadier General
Edward Winslow Hincks	North	Brigadier General
Edmund Winston Pettus	South	Brigadier General
William Wirt Adams	South	Brigadier General
William Wirt Allen	South	Brigadier General
Claudius Wistar Sears	South	Brigadier General
Martin Witherspoon Gary	South	Brigadier General
John Wolcott Phelps	North	Brigadier General
James Wolfe Ripley	North	Brigadier General
Joshua Woodrow Sill	North	Brigadier General
William Woods Averell	North	Brigadier General
Gustavus Woodson Smith	South	Major General
William Worth Belknap	North	Brigadier General
Samuel Wragg Ferguson	South	Brigadier General
Samuel Wylie Crawford	North	Brigadier General
John Wynn Davidson	North	Brigadier General
George Wythe Randolph	South	Brigadier General
William Yarnel Slack	South	Brigadier General
William Young Conn Humes	South	Brigadier General

4

Civil War Generals
by Hometowns and Homestates

The town and state where each general was born is listed below
in alphabetical order, first by state or country, then by town
or city. In many cases only the county or district where the
general originated is known. There are also isolated cases
where only the state or country is available. The best available information is stated here. Where possible the current
name of a town or state is used, as in some cases the town either does not exist today or has changed names. Some of the
states, such as West Virginia, were not yet states when the
generals were born.

GENERALS	SIDE/RANK	HOMETOWN	HOMESTATE
Dandridge McRae	S/B	Baldwin County	Alabama
John Herbert Kelly	S/B	Carrollton	Alabama
Alexander Hawthorne	S/B	Evergreen	Alabama
Sterling Alexander Wood	S/B	Florence	Alabama
William Felix Brantley	S/B	Greene County	Alabama
David Bell Birney	N/M	Huntsville	Alabama
Thomas Crittenden	N/B	Huntsville	Alabama
Andrew Jackson Hamilton	N/B	Huntsville	Alabama
John Hunt Morgan	S/B	Huntsville	Alabama
Leroy Pope Walker	S/B	Huntsville	Alabama
Thomas Harrison	S/B	Jefferson County	Alabama
John Gregg	S/B	Lawrence County	Alabama
Edmund Winston Pettus	S/B	Limestone County	Alabama
William Birney	N/B	Madison County	Alabama
Jones Mitchell Withers	S/M	Madison County	Alabama
Philip Dale Roddey	S/B	Moulton	Alabama
Jacob Hunter Sharp	S/B	Pickensville	Alabama
John Caldwell Sanders	S/B	Tuscaloosa	Alabama
James Deshler	S/B	Tuscumbia	Alabama
Theodore Brevard	S/B	Tuskegee	Alabama
John Franklin Farnsworth	N/B	Eaton	Canada
Jacob Dolson Cox	N/M	Montreal	Canada
Nathaniel Lyon	N/B	Ashford	Connecticut
Orris Sanford Ferry	N/B	Bethel	Connecticut
Daniel Tyler	N/B	Brooklyn	Connecticut
Horatio Wright	N/M	Clinton	Connecticut

John Sedgwick	N/M	Cornwall Hollow	Connecticut
Abner Clark Harding	N/B	East Hampton	Connecticut
Alexander Shaler	N/B	Haddam	Connecticut
Henry Warner Birge	N/B	Hartford	Connecticut
Alfred Howe Terry	N/M	Hartford	Connecticut
Henry Dwight Terry	N/B	Hartford	Connecticut
Henry Walton Wessells	N/B	Litchfield	Connecticut
Henry Washington Benham	N/B	Meriden	Connecticut
Luther Prentice Bradley	N/B	New Haven	Connecticut
Joseph King Mansfield	N/B	New Haven	Connecticut
Joseph Gilbert Totten	N/B	New Haven	Connecticut
William Scott Ketchum	N/B	Norwalk	Connecticut
Nelson Taylor	N/B	Norwalk	Connecticut
Edward Harland	N/B	Norwich	Connecticut
Clement Hoffman Stevens	S/B	Norwich	Connecticut
Alpheus Starkey Williams	N/B	Saybrook	Connecticut
John Smith Phelps	N/B	Simsbury	Connecticut
Henry Beebee Carrington	N/B	Wallingford	Connecticut
James Wolfe Ripley	N/B	Windham County	Connecticut
Richard Stoddert Ewell	S/L	Georgetown	D.C.
George Washington Getty	N/B	Georgetown	D.C.
John Milton Brannan	N/B	Washington	D.C.
Samuel Sprigg Carroll	N/B	Washington	D.C.
Manning Ferguson Force	N/B	Washington	D.C.
David Hunter	N/M	Washington	D.C.
Mansfield Lovell	S/M	Washington	D.C.
William Ward Orme	N/B	Washington	D.C.
Alfred Pleasonton	N/M	Washington	D.C.
George Sykes	N/M	Dover	Delaware
Alfred Thomas Torbert	N/B	Georgetown	Delaware
Henry Hayes Lockwood	N/B	Kent County	Delaware
Lorenzo Thomas	N/B	New Castle	Delaware
Daniel Ullmann	N/B	Wilmington	Delaware
Collett Leventhorpe	S/B	Devonshire	England
John Wallace Fuller	N/B	Harston	England
Edward Dickinson Baker	N/M	London	England
John Baillie McIntosh	N/B	Fort Brooke	Florida
Edmund Jackson Davis	N/B	St.Augustine	Florida
Edmund Kirby Smith	S/G	St.Augustine	Florida
James McQueen McIntosh	S/B	Tampa	Florida
Victor Jean Girardey	S/B	Lauw	France
Camille A.J.M. Polignac	S/M	Millemont	France
Raleigh Edward Colston	S/B	Paris	France
Alfred Napoleon Duffie	N/B	Paris	France
Gustave Paul Cluseret	N/B	Suresnes	France
Philippe deTrobriand	N/B	Tours	France
Henry Rootes Jackson	S/B	Athens	Georgia
Thomas Moore Scott	S/B	Athens	Georgia
William Robertson Boggs	S/B	Augusta	Georgia
Alfred Cumming	S/B	Augusta	Georgia
William Gardner	S/B	Augusta	Georgia
John King Jackson	S/B	Augusta	Georgia
Lafayette McLaws	S/M	Augusta	Georgia
Montgomery Meigs	N/B	Augusta	Georgia
William Duncan Smith	S/B	Augusta	Georgia
Isaac Munroe St.John	S/B	Augusta	Georgia

William Henry Walker	S/M	Augusta	Georgia
Joseph Wheeler	S/M	Augusta	Georgia
William Joseph Hardee	S/L	Camden County	Georgia
Edward Lloyd Thomas	S/B	Clarke County	Georgia
Alfred Iverson,Jr.	S/B	Clinton	Georgia
Henry Lewis Benning	S/B	Columbia County	Georgia
James Holt Clanton	S/B	Columbia County	Georgia
George Thomas Anderson	S/B	Covington	Georgia
James Phillip Simms	S/B	Covington	Georgia
Allison Nelson	S/B	Fulton County	Georgia
William Tatum Wofford	S/B	Habersham County	Georgia
Goode Bryan	S/B	Hancock County	Georgia
William Flank Perry	S/B	Jackson County	Georgia
Howell Cobb	S/M	Jefferson County	Georgia
Thomas Reade Rootes Cobb	S/B	Jefferson County	Georgia
Ambrose Ransom Wright	S/M	Louisville	Georgia
Edward Dorr Tracy	S/B	Macon	Georgia
James Thadeus Holtzclaw	S/B	McDonough	Georgia
George Pierce Doles	S/B	Milledgeville	Georgia
Bryan Morel Thomas	S/B	Milledgeville	Georgia
Alfred Holt Colquitt	S/B	Monroe	Georgia
Joseph Lewis Hogg	S/B	Morgan County	Georgia
Cullen Andrews Battle	S/B	Powelton	Georgia
Henry DeLamar Clayton	S/M	Pulaski County	Georgia
Matthew Duncan Ector	S/B	Putnam County	Georgia
David Emanuel Twiggs	S/M	Richmond County	Georgia
Stand Watie	S/B	Rome	Georgia
Robert Houstoun Anderson	S/B	Savannah	Georgia
John Stevens Bowen	S/M	Savannah	Georgia
John Charles Fremont	N/M	Savannah	Georgia
Gilbert Moxley Sorrel	S/B	Savannah	Georgia
Henry Constantine Wayne	S/B	Savannah	Georgia
Marcellus Stovall	S/B	Sparta	Georgia
Clement Anselm Evans	S/B	Stewart County	Georgia
Philip Cook	S/B	Twiggs County	Georgia
John Brown Gordon	S/M	Upson County	Georgia
Edward Porter Alexander	S/B	Washington	Georgia
John Carpenter Carter	S/B	Waynesboro	Georgia
Lucius Jeremiah Gartrell	S/B	Wilkes County	Georgia
Paul Jones Semmes	S/B	Wilkes County	Georgia
Robert Augustus Toombs	S/B	Wilkes County	Georgia
Max Weber	N/B	Achern	Germany
August Valentine Kautz	N/B	Baden	Germany
Adolph von Steinwehr	N/B	Blankenburg	Germany
August Willich	N/B	Braunsberg	Germany
Henry Bohlen	N/B	Bremen	Germany
Charles Leopold Matthies	N/B	Bromberg	Germany
Peter Joseph Osterhaus	N/M	Coblenz	Germany
Carl Schurz	N/M	Liblar	Germany
Alexander Schimmelfennig	N/B	Lithauen	Germany
Wladimir Krzyzanowski	N/B	Raznova	Germany
Franz Sigel	N/M	Sinsheim	Germany
Friedrich Salomon	N/B	Strobeck	Germany
Louis Ludwig Blenker	N/B	Worms	Germany
Alexander Sandor Asboth	N/B	Keszthely	Hungary
Julius Stahel	N/M	Szeged	Hungary

John Cook	N/B	Belleville	Illinois
William Passmore Carlin	N/B	Carrollton	Illinois
James Barnet Fry	N/B	Carrollton	Illinois
John Aaron Rawlins	N/B	Galena	Illinois
Green Berry Raum	N/B	Golconda	Illinois
John Alexander Logan	N/M	Jackson County	Illinois
Martin Davis Hardin	N/B	Jacksonville	Illinois
Leonard Fulton Ross	N/B	Lewistown	Illinois
James Harrison Wilson	N/B	Shawneetown	Illinois
Lewis Wallace	N/M	Brookville	Indiana
Jefferson Columbus Davis	N/B	Clark County	Indiana
James Clifford Veatch	N/B	Elizabethtown	Indiana
Marcellus Monroe Crocker	N/B	Franklin	Indiana
Pleasant Adam Hackleman	N/B	Franklin County	Indiana
Nathan Kimball	N/B	Fredericksburg	Indiana
John Parker Hawkins	N/B	Indianapolis	Indiana
William Anderson Pile	N/B	Indianapolis	Indiana
Walter Quintin Gresham	N/B	Lanesville	Indiana
Francis Asbury Shoup	S/B	Laurel	Indiana
Thomas John Lucas	N/B	Lawrenceburg	Indiana
Ambrose Everett Burnside	N/M	Liberty	Indiana
Jeremiah Cutler Sullivan	N/B	Madison	Indiana
Alvin Peterson Hovey	N/B	Mt.Vernon	Indiana
Thomas Gamble Pitcher	N/B	Rockport	Indiana
Robert Huston Milroy	N/M	Salem	Indiana
John Franklin Miller	N/B	South Bend	Indiana
Charles Cruft	N/B	Terre Haute	Indiana
Hugh Thompson Reid	N/B	Union County	Indiana
Robert Sanford Foster	N/B	Vernon	Indiana
Ebenezer Dumont	N/B	Vevay	Indiana
Lawrence Sullivan Ross	S/B	Bentonsport	Iowa
Patrick Ronayne Cleburne	S/M	Bridgepark Cottage	Ireland
Michael Corcoran	N/B	Carrowkeel	Ireland
Richard Busteed	N/B	Cavan	Ireland
Joseph Finegan	S/B	Clones	Ireland
Walter Paye Lane	S/B	County Cork	Ireland
Thomas Alfred Smyth	N/B	County Cork	Ireland
Thomas William Sweeny	N/B	County Cork	Ireland
Patrick Edward Connor	N/B	County Kerry	Ireland
Michael Kelly Lawler	N/B	County Kildare	Ireland
James Shields	N/B	County Tyrone	Ireland
William Montague Browne	S/B	Dublin	Ireland
James Lawlor Kiernan	N/B	Galway	Ireland
Patrick Theodore Moore	S/B	Galway	Ireland
Thomas Francis Meagher	N/B	Waterford	Ireland
James Williamson	N/B	Adair County	Kentucky
William Nelson Beall	S/B	Bardstown	Kentucky
Benjamin Hardin Helm	S/B	Bardstown	Kentucky
John Thomas Croxton	N/B	Bourbon County	Kentucky
Richard Montgomery Gano	S/B	Bourbon County	Kentucky
Speed Smith Fry	N/B	Boyle County	Kentucky
Joseph Holt	N/B	Breckinridge County	Kentucky
Hylan Benton Lyon	S/B	Caldwell Cty	Kentucky
James Fleming Fagan	S/M	Clark County	Kentucky
Roger Weightman Hanson	S/B	Clark County	Kentucky
James Winning McMillan	N/B	Clark County	Kentucky

Joseph Alexander Cooper	N/B	Cumberland Falls	Kentucky
Kenner Garrard	N/B	Fairfield	Kentucky
John B. Grayson	S/B	Fayette County	Kentucky
James Streshly Jackson	N/B	Fayette County	Kentucky
George Baird Hodge	S/B	Fleming County	Kentucky
Willis Arnold Gorman	N/B	Flemingsburg	Kentucky
Joseph Jones Reynolds	N/M	Flemingsburg	Kentucky
Daniel Weisiger Adams	S/B	Frankfort	Kentucky
William Wirt Adams	S/B	Frankfort	Kentucky
Humphrey Marshall	S/B	Frankfort	Kentucky
William Price Sanders	N/B	Frankfort	Kentucky
Thomas Hart Taylor	S/B	Frankfort	Kentucky
Gustavus Woodson Smith	S/M	Georgetown	Kentucky
Joseph Horace Lewis	S/B	Glasgow	Kentucky
William Thompson Martin	S/M	Glasgow	Kentucky
Edward Henry Hobson	N/B	Greensburg	Kentucky
John McClernand	N/M	Hardinsburg	Kentucky
Simon Bolivar Buckner	S/L	Hart County	Kentucky
Adam Rankin Johnson	S/B	Henderson	Kentucky
Thomas James Churchill	S/M	Jefferson County	Kentucky
Charles Clark	S/B	Lebanon	Kentucky
Francis Preston Blair	N/M	Lexington	Kentucky
John Cabell Breckinridge	S/M	Lexington	Kentucky
James Morrison Hawes	S/B	Lexington	Kentucky
Joseph Orville Shelby	S/B	Lexington	Kentucky
Charles Mynn Thruston	N/B	Lexington	Kentucky
John Blair Smith Todd	N/B	Lexington	Kentucky
James Shackelford	N/B	Lincoln County	Kentucky
Robert Anderson	N/B	Louisville	Kentucky
George Blake Cosby	S/B	Louisville	Kentucky
John Edwards	N/B	Louisville	Kentucky
James Isham Gilbert	N/B	Louisville	Kentucky
John Pope	N/M	Louisville	Kentucky
William Preston	S/B	Louisville	Kentucky
Joseph Pannell Taylor	N/B	Louisville	Kentucky
Richard Taylor	S/L	Louisville	Kentucky
Cassius Marcellus Clay	N/M	Madison County	Kentucky
Samuel Jameson Gholson	S/B	Madison County	Kentucky
Theophilus Garrard	N/B	Manchester	Kentucky
William Yarnel Slack	S/B	Mason County	Kentucky
William Nelson	N/M	Maysville	Kentucky
Jerimiah Tilford Boyle	N/B	Mercer County	Kentucky
Ormsby Mitchel	N/M	Morganfield	Kentucky
John Stuart Williams	S/B	Mount Sterling	Kentucky
Thomas John Wood	N/M	Munfordville	Kentucky
Richard James Oglesby	N/M	Oldham County	Kentucky
John Bell Hood	S/G	Owingsville	Kentucky
Edward Richard Canby	N/M	Piatt's Landing	Kentucky
Green Clay Smith	N/B	Richmond	Kentucky
George Bibb Crittenden	S/M	Russellville	Kentucky
Thomas Crittenden	N/M	Russellville	Kentucky
Stephen Gano Burbridge	N/B	Scott County	Kentucky
Basil Wilson Duke	S/B	Scott County	Kentucky
John McCauley Palmer	N/M	Scott County	Kentucky
Walter Chiles Whitaker	N/B	Shelbyville	Kentucky
Richard W. Johnson	N/B	Smithland	Kentucky

Lovell Harrison Rousseau	N/M	Stanford	Kentucky
Samuel Bell Maxey	S/M	Tompkinsville	Kentucky
Randall Lee Gibson	S/B	Versailles	Kentucky
Albert Sidney Johnston	S/G	Washington	Kentucky
William Harrow	N/B	Winchester	Kentucky
Abraham Buford	S/B	Woodford County	Kentucky
John Buford	N/B	Woodford County	Kentucky
Napoleon Buford	N/B	Woodford County	Kentucky
Charles William Field	S/M	Woodford County	Kentucky
Eli Long	N/B	Woodford County	Kentucky
Jerome Robertson	S/B	Woodford County	Kentucky
Leroy Augustus Stafford	S/B	Cheneyville	Louisiana
Francis Redding Nicholls	S/B	Donaldsonville	Louisiana
Louis Hebert	S/B	Iberville Parish	Louisiana
Paul Octave Hebert	S/B	Iberville Parish	Louisiana
Henry Hopkins Sibley	S/B	Natchitoches	Louisiana
Joseph Rodman West	N/B	New Orleans	Louisiana
Jean Jacques Mouton	S/B	Opelousas	Louisiana
Pierre Beauregard	S/G	St.Bernard Parish	Louisiana
Seth Williams	N/B	Augusta	Maine
Zebulon York	S/B	Avon	Maine
Edward Hatch	N/B	Bangor	Maine
Cuvier Grover	N/B	Bethel	Maine
Joshua Chamberlain	N/B	Brewer	Maine
Edward Winslow Hincks	N/B	Bucksport	Maine
Rufus Ingalls	N/B	Denmark	Maine
Napoleon Jackson Dana	N/M	Eastport	Maine
Henry Prince	N/B	Eastport	Maine
Selden Connor	N/B	Fairfield	Maine
Francis Laurens Vinton	N/B	Fort Preble	Maine
Cyrus Hamlin	N/B	Hampden	Maine
Oliver Otis Howard	N/M	Leeds	Maine
Danville Leadbetter	S/B	Leeds	Maine
Cadwallader Washburn	N/M	Livermore	Maine
James Henry Carleton	N/B	Lubec	Maine
Hiram Burnham	N/B	Narraguagus	Maine
Joseph Tarr Copeland	N/B	Newcastle	Maine
George Lafayette Beal	N/B	Norway	Maine
Charles Davis Jameson	N/B	Orono	Maine
Neal Dow	N/B	Portland	Maine
Francis Fessenden	N/B	Portland	Maine
Henry Goddard Thomas	N/B	Portland	Maine
Adelbert Ames	N/B	Rockland	Maine
Hiram Gregory Berry	N/M	Rockland	Maine
Davis Tillson	N/B	Rockland	Maine
George Foster Shepley	N/B	Saco	Maine
Joseph Hayes	N/B	South Berwick	Maine
Albion Parris Howe	N/B	Standish	Maine
Franklin Nickerson	N/B	Swanville	Maine
James Gillpatrick Blunt	N/M	Trenton	Maine
James Deering Fessenden	N/B	Westbrook	Maine
Eliakim Parker Scammon	N/B	Whitefield	Maine
William Hammond	N/B	Annapolis	Maryland
John Joseph Abercrombie	N/B	Baltimore	Maryland
Robert Christie Buchanan	N/B	Baltimore	Maryland
William Henry French	N/M	Baltimore	Maryland

John Reese Kenly	N/B	Baltimore	Maryland
Lewis Henry Little	S/B	Baltimore	Maryland
George Hume Steuart	S/B	Baltimore	Maryland
Lloyd Tilghman	S/B	Baltimore	Maryland
Robert Charles Tyler	S/B	Baltimore	Maryland
William Vandever	N/B	Baltimore	Maryland
James Jay Archer	S/B	Bel Air	Maryland
William Whann Mackall	S/B	Cecil County	Maryland
Edward Otho C. Ord	N/M	Cumberland	Maryland
Bradley Tyler Johnson	S/B	Frederick	Maryland
James Cooper	N/B	Frederick County	Maryland
Allen Thomas	S/B	Howard County	Maryland
William Plummer Benton	N/B	New Market	Maryland
William Hemsley Emory	N/B	Queen Annes Cty.	Maryland
Henry Moses Judah	N/B	Snow Hill	Maryland
Arnold Elzey	S/M	Somerset County	Maryland
John Henry Winder	S/B	Somerset County	Maryland
Charles Sidney Winder	S/B	Talbot County	Maryland
Jacob Gartner Lauman	N/B	Taneytown	Maryland
Thomas Church H. Smith	N/B	Acushnet	Massachusetts
Isaac Ingalls Stevens	N/B	Andover	Massachusetts
Joseph Bennett Plummer	N/B	Barre	Massachusetts
Daniel Ruggles	S/B	Barre	Massachusetts
John Milton Thayer	N/B	Bellingham	Massachusetts
Henry Lawrence Eustis	N/B	Boston	Massachusetts
George Francis McGinnis	N/B	Boston	Massachusetts
James Dada Morgan	N/B	Boston	Massachusetts
Charles Jackson Paine	N/B	Boston	Massachusetts
Albert Pike	S/B	Boston	Massachusetts
Joseph Warren Revere	N/B	Boston	Massachusetts
Thomas Greely Stevenson	N/B	Boston	Massachusetts
Edwin Vose Sumner	N/M	Boston	Massachusetts
George Leonard Andrews	N/B	Bridgewater	Massachusetts
Erasmus Darwin Keyes	N/M	Brimfield	Massachusetts
Fitz-Henry Warren	N/B	Brimfield	Massachusetts
Edward Augustus Wild	N/B	Brookline	Massachusetts
Albert Blanchard	S/B	Charlestown	Massachusetts
Charles Devens, Jr.	N/B	Charlestown	Massachusetts
George Henry Gordon	N/B	Charlestown	Massachusetts
Zealous Bates Tower	N/B	Cohasset	Massachuseets
Grenville Mellen Dodge	N/M	Danvers	Massachusetts
Thomas Kilby Smith	N/B	Dorchester	Massachusetts
Rufus Saxton	N/B	Greenfield	Massachusetts
Charles Pomeroy Stone	N/B	Greenfield	Massachusetts
Randolph Barnes Marcy	N/B	Greenwich	Massachusetts
Amiel Weeks Whipple	N/B	Greenwich	Massachusetts
Joseph Hooker	N/M	Hadley	Massachusetts
William Francis Bartlett	N/B	Haverhill	Massachusetts
George Henry Chapman	N/B	Holland	Massachusetts
Henry Shaw Briggs	N/B	Lanesboro	Massachusetts
Ralph Pomeroy Buckland	N/B	Leyden	Massachusetts
Adin Ballou Underwood	N/B	Milford	Massachusetts
Isaac Fitzgerald Shepard	N/B	Natick	Massachusetts
Nathaniel James Jackson	N/B	Newburyport	Massachusetts
James Camp Tappan	S/B	Newburyport	Massachusetts
Claudius Wistar Sears	S/B	Peru	Massachusetts

Edward Aylesworth Perry	S/B	Richmond	Massachusetts
Frederick West Lander	N/B	Salem	Massachusetts
John Gross Barnard	N/B	Sheffield	Massachusetts
Calvin Edward Pratt	N/B	Shrewsbury	Massachusetts
William Dwight	N/B	Springfield	Massachusetts
Nathaniel Prentiss Banks	N/M	Waltham	Massachusetts
Edwin Denison Morgan	N/M	Washington	Massachusetts
Nelson Appleton Miles	N/B	Westminster	Massachusetts
Lysander Cutler	N/B	Worcester County	Massachusetts
James Clay Rice	N/B	Worthington	Massachusetts
Henry Jackson Hunt	N/B	Detroit	Michigan
Henry Hastings Sibley	N/B	Detroit	Michigan
Orlando Bolivar Willcox	N/B	Detroit	Michigan
Elon John Farnsworth	N/B	Green Oak	Michigan
Douglas Hancock Cooper	S/B	Amite County	Mississippi
William Henry C. Whiting	S/M	Biloxi	Mississippi
Benjamin Grubb Humphreys	S/B	Claiborne County	Mississippi
Hiram Bronson Granbury	S/B	Copiah County	Mississippi
Nathaniel Harris	S/B	Natchez	Mississippi
Earl Van Dorn	S/M	Port Gibson	Mississippi
William Lindsay Brandon	S/B	Washington	Mississippi
Carnot Posey	S/B	Wilkinson County	Mississippi
Joseph Robert Davis	S/B	Woodville	Mississippi
St.John Liddell	S/B	Woodville	Mississippi
John Marmaduke	S/M	Arrow Rock	Missouri
William Hugh Young	S/B	Booneville	Missouri
John George Walker	S/M	Cole County	Missouri
John Bullock Clark,Jr.	S/B	Fayette	Missouri
James Patrick Major	S/B	Fayette	Missouri
John Rogers Cooke	S/B	Jefferson Barracks	Missouri
Augustus Louis Chetlain	N/B	St.Louis	Missouri
John McCausland	S/B	St.Louis	Missouri
Gabriel Rene Paul	N/B	St.Louis	Missouri
Francis Marion Cockrell	S/B	Warrensburg	Missouri
John Adams Dix	N/M	Boscawen	New Hampshire
Benjamin Franklin Butler	N/M	Deerfield	New Hampshire
John Benjamin Sanborn	N/B	Epsom	New Hampshire
Joseph Dana Webster	N/B	Hampton	New Hampshire
Christopher Andrews	N/B	Hillsboro	New Hampshire
Simon Goodell Griffin	N/B	Nelson	New Hampshire
Benjamin Franklin Kelley	N/B	New Hampton	New Hampshire
Daniel Phineas Woodbury	N/B	New London	New Hampshire
Gilman Marston	N/B	Orford	New Hampshire
Fitz John Porter	N/M	Portsmouth	New Hampshire
John Gray Foster	N/M	Whitefield	New Hampshire
Daniel Henry Rucker	N/B	Belleville	New Jersey
Hugh Judson Kilpatrick	N/B	Deckertown	New Jersey
Samuel Gibbs French	S/M	Gloucester County	New Jersey
Samuel Cooper	S/G	Hackensack	New Jersey
George William Taylor	N/B	Hunterdon County	New Jersey
Gershom Mott	N/B	Lamberton	New Jersey
William Montgomery	N/B	Monmouth County	New Jersey
Issac Ferdinand Quinby	N/B	Morristown	New Jersey
Julius Adolph deLagnel	S/B	Newark	New Jersey
Lewis Golding Arnold	N/B	Perth Amboy	New Jersey
Charles Cleveland Dodge	N/B	Plainfield	New Jersey

Name	Code	Town	State
Horatio Van Cleve	N/B	Princeton	New Jersey
Charles Garrison Harker	N/B	Swedesboro	New Jersey
Joseph Bradford Carr	N/B	Albany	New York
Philip Henry Sheridan	N/M	Albany	New York
William Steele	S/B	Albany	New York
Thomas Williams	N/B	Albany	New York
Alfred Gibbs	N/B	Astoria	New York
William Henry Seward,Jr.	N/B	Auburn	New York
Abner Doubleday	N/B	Ballston Spa	New York
Emory Upton	N/B	Batavia	New York
Joseph Jackson Bartlett	N/B	Binghamton	New York
John Cleveland Robinson	N/B	Binghamton	New York
Daniel Davidson Bidwell	N/B	Black Rock	New York
Francis Channing Barlow	N/B	Brooklyn	New York
Robert Cameron	N/B	Brooklyn	New York
Gustavus DeRussy	N/B	Brooklyn	New York
David Stuart	N/B	Brooklyn	New York
Egbert Benson Brown	N/B	Brownsville	New York
Mason Brayman	N/B	Buffalo	New York
Innis Newton Palmer	N/B	Buffalo	New York
George Stoneman	N/M	Busti	New York
William Woods Averell	N/B	Cameron	New York
Amos Beebe Eaton	N/B	Catskill	New York
Samuel Allen Rice	N/B	Cattaraugus County	New York
Julius White	N/B	Cazenovia	New York
Samuel Ryan Curtis	N/M	Clinton County	New York
Gouverneur Warren	N/M	Cold Spring	New York
Justus McKinstry	N/B	Columbia County	New York
George Webb Morell	N/M	Cooperstown	New York
John Starkweather	N/B	Cooperstown	New York
Martin Luther Smith	S/M	Danby	New York
Frederick Steele	N/M	Delhi	New York
Henry Warner Slocum	N/M	Delphi	New York
Newton Martin Curtis	N/B	DePeyster	New York
William Kerley Strong	N/B	Duanesburg	New York
Byron Root Pierce	N/B	East Bloomfield	New York
Romeyn Beck Ayres	N/B	East Creek	New York
Eugene Asa Carr	N/B	Erie County	New York
Albert Lindley Lee	N/B	Fulton	New York
James Samuel Wadsworth	N/B	Geneseo	New York
John Schofield	N/M	Gerry	New York
Alexander Chambers	N/B	Great Valley	New York
John Henry Martindale	N/B	Hudson Falls	New York
Robert Ogden Tyler	N/B	Hunter	New York
Mortimer Dormer Leggett	N/B	Ithaca	New York
William Miller	S/B	Ithaca	New York
Giles Alexander Smith	N/B	Jefferson County	New York
Gordon Granger	N/M	Joy	New York
Christopher Augur	N/M	Kendall	New York
James Henry Van Alen	N/B	Kinderhook	New York
Stephen Gardner Champlin	N/B	Kingston	New York
Milo Smith Hascall	N/B	LeRoy	New York
Thomas Howard Ruger	N/B	Lima	New York
John James Peck	N/M	Manlius	New York
Morgan Lewis Smith	N/B	Mexico	New York
William Denison Whipple	N/B	Nelson	New York

William Wirt Allen	S/B	New York City	New York
William Farquhar Barry	N/B	New York City	New York
James Bowen	N/B	New York City	New York
George Washington Cullum	N/B	New York City	New York
Henry Eugene Davies	N/B	New York City	New York
Richard Delafield	N/B	New York City	New York
Thomas Casimer Devin	N/B	New York City	New York
Abram Duryee	N/B	New York City	New York
Franklin Gardner	S/M	New York City	New York
Archibald Gracie,Jr.	S/B	New York City	New York
Charles Kinnaird Graham	N/B	New York City	New York
Schuyler Hamilton	N/M	New York City	New York
James Allen Hardie	N/B	New York City	New York
Philip Kearny	N/M	New York City	New York
Rufus King	N/B	New York City	New York
Wesley Merritt	N/M	New York City	New York
William Hopkins Morris	N/B	New York City	New York
Edward Elmer Potter	N/B	New York City	New York
James Brewerton Ricketts	N/B	New York City	New York
Daniel Edgar Sickles	N/M	New York City	New York
John Henry Hobart Ward	N/B	New York City	New York
Alexander Stewart Webb	N/B	New York City	New York
William Worth Belknap	N/B	Newburgh	New York
Elias Smith Dennis	N/B	Newburgh	New York
John Ellis Wool	N/M	Newburgh	New York
Walter Husted Stevens	S/B	Penn Yan	New York
John Porter Hatch	N/B	Oswego	New York
David Henry Williams	N/B	Otsego County	New York
John Cochrane	N/B	Palatine	New York
John Morrison Oliver	N/B	Penn Yan	New York
Stephen Hinsdale Weed	N/B	Potsdam	New York
Darius Nash Couch	N/M	Putnam County	New York
John Haskell King	N/B	Sackets Harbor	New York
David Allen Russell	N/B	Salem	New York
John Wesley Turner	N/B	Saratoga	New York
Robert Brown Potter	N/B	Schenectady	New York
Daniel Marsh Frost	S/B	Schenectady County	New York
George Dashiell Bayard	N/B	Seneca Falls	New York
Henry Baxter	N/B	Sidney Plains	New York
Thomas Alfred Davies	N/B	St.Lawrence County	New York
Francis Barretto Spinola	N/B	Stony Brook	New York
Joseph Abel Haskin	N/B	Troy	New York
George Lucas Hartsuff	N/M	Tyre	New York
Edward Stuyvesant Bragg	N/B	Unadilla	New York
Daniel Butterfield	N/M	Utica	New York
James Hewett Ledlie	N/B	Utica	New York
Egbert Ludovicus Viele	N/B	Waterford	New York
Marsena Rudolph Patrick	N/B	Watertown	New York
Thomas Wilberforce Egan	N/B	Watervliet	New York
Erastus Barnard Tyler	N/B	West Bloomfield	New York
Ranald Mackenzie	N/B	Westchester County	New York
Henry Wager Halleck	N/M	Westernville	New York
Charles Smith Hamilton	N/M	Westernville	New York
John Wilson Sprague	N/B	White Creek	New York
Clinton Bowen Fisk	N/B	York	New York
John McNeil	N/B	Halifax	Nova Scotia

Robert Brank Vance	S/B	Buncombe County	North Carolina
Rufus Parringer	S/B	Cabarrus County	North Carolina
Thomas Fentress Toon	S/B	Columbus County	North Carolina
Gabriel James Rains	S/B	Craven County	North Carolina
William Dorsey Pender	S/M	Edgecomb County	North Carolina
James Green Martin	S/B	Elizabeth County	North Carolina
Lawrence O'Bryan Branch	S/B	Enfield	North Carolina
Laurence Simmons Baker	S/B	Gates County	North Carolina
William Paul Roberts	S/B	Gates County	North Carolina
Robert Richardson	S/B	Granville County	North Carolina
Robert Bullock	S/B	Greenville	North Carolina
Jeremy Francis Gilmer	S/M	Guilford County	North Carolina
Solomon Meredith	N/B	Guilford County	North Carolina
Junius Daniel	S/B	Halifax	North Carolina
George Burgwyn Anderson	S/B	Hillsboro	North Carolina
George Doherty Johnston	S/B	Hillsboro	North Carolina
William Whedbee Kirkland	S/B	Hillsboro	North Carolina
Thomas Lanier Clingman	S/B	Huntsville	North Carolina
William Feimster Tucker	S/B	Iredell County	North Carolina
Richard Caswell Gatlin	S/B	Lenoir County	North Carolina
Robert Daniel Johnston	S/B	Lincoln County	North Carolina
John Horace Forney	S/M	Lincolnton	North Carolina
William Henry Forney	S/B	Lincolnton	North Carolina
Robert Frederick Hoke	S/M	Lincolnton	North Carolina
Stephen Dodson Ramseur	S/M	Lincolnton	North Carolina
Thomas Pleasant Dockery	S/B	Montgomery County	North Carolina
Lewis Addison Armistead	S/B	New Bern	North Carolina
Daniel Chevilette Govan	S/B	Northampton Cty.	North Carolina
Bryan Grimes	S/M	Pitt County	North Carolina
Andrew Johnson	N/B	Raleigh	North Carolina
Leonidas Polk	S/L	Raleigh	North Carolina
Alfred Moore Scales	S/B	Reidsville	North Carolina
Evander McNair	S/B	Richmond County	North Carolina
William Gaston Lewis	S/B	Rocky Mountain	North Carolina
Lucius Eugene Polk	S/B	Salisbury	North Carolina
Theophilus Hunter Holmes	S/L	Sampson County	North Carolina
William Ruffin Cox	S/B	Scotland Neck	North Carolina
Joseph Roswell Hawley	N/B	Stewartsville	North Carolina
James Johnston Pettigrew	S/B	Tyrrell County	North Carolina
Matt Whitaker Ransom	S/B	Warren County	North Carolina
Robert Ransom,Jr.	S/M	Warren County	North Carolina
Braxton Bragg	S/G	Warrenton	North Carolina
Cadmus Marcellus Wilcox	S/M	Wayne County	North Carolina
James Byron Gordon	S/B	Wilkesboro	North Carolina
John Decatur Barry	S/B	Wilmington	North Carolina
William Wing Loring	S/M	Wilmington	North Carolina
William MacRae	S/B	Wilmington	North Carolina
James William Reilly	N/B	Akron	Ohio
Bushrod Rust Johnson	S/M	Belmont County	Ohio
Ferdinand Van Derveer	N/B	Butler County	Ohio
Benjamin Franklin Potts	N/B	Carroll County	Ohio
David Sloane Stanley	N/M	Cedar Valley	Ohio
Daniel Harris Reynolds	S/B	Centerburg	Ohio
Halbert Eleazer Paine	N/B	Chardon	Ohio
Joshua Woodrow Sill	N/B	Chillicothe	Ohio
William Haines Lytle	N/B	Cincinnati	Ohio

Abram Sanders Piatt	N/B	Cincinnati	Ohio
John Potts Slough	N/B	Cincinnati	Ohio
Melancthon Smith Wade	N/B	Cincinnati	Ohio
Godfrey Weitzel	N/M	Cincinnati	Ohio
James Birdseye McPherson	N/M	Clyde	Ohio
Alexander McCook	N/M	Columbiana County	Ohio
Irvin McDowell	N/M	Columbus	Ohio
Wager Swayne	N/B	Columbus	Ohio
Charles Carroll Walcutt	N/B	Columbus	Ohio
William Wallace Burns	N/B	Coshocton	Ohio
James Abram Garfield	N/M	Cuyahoga County	Ohio
George Crook	N/M	Dayton	Ohio
William Grose	N/B	Dayton	Ohio
Rutherford Hayes	N/B	Delaware	Ohio
William Starke Rosecrans	N/M	Delaware County	Ohio
Robert Cumming Schenck	N/M	Franklin	Ohio
Charles Griffin	N/M	Granville	Ohio
Cyrus Bussey	N/B	Hubbard	Ohio
Edward Needles Kirk	N/B	Jefferson County	Ohio
Jasper Adalmorn Maltby	N/B	Kingsville	Ohio
Hugh Boyle Ewing	N/B	Lancaster	Ohio
Thomas Ewing,Jr.	N/B	Lancaster	Ohio
William Sherman	N/M	Lancaster	Ohio
William Thomas Brooks	N/M	Lisbon	Ohio
Quincy Adams Gillmore	N/M	Lorain	Ohio
Don Carlos Buell	N/M	Lowell	Ohio
Robert Mitchell	N/B	Mansfield	Ohio
James Sidney Robinson	N/B	Mansfield	Ohio
Otho French Strahl	S/B	McConnelsville	Ohio
Orlando Metcalfe Poe	N/B	Navarre	Ohio
Charles Robert Woods	N/B	Newark	Ohio
Robert Latimer McCook	N/B	New Lisbon	Ohio
George Armstrong Custer	N/B	New Rumley	Ohio
Eleazer Arthur Paine	N/B	Parkman	Ohio
Joseph Bailey	N/B	Pennsville	Ohio
Mahlon Dickerson Manson	N/B	Piqua	Ohio
John Grant Mitchell	N/B	Piqua	Ohio
Ulysses Simpson Grant	N/L	Point Pleasant	Ohio
Lucius Fairchild	N/B	Portage County	Ohio
Nathaniel Collins McLean	N/B	Ridgeville	Ohio
George Day Wagner	N/B	Ross County	Ohio
John Beatty	N/B	Sandusky	Ohio
John Sanford Mason	N/B	Steubenville	Ohio
Edward Moody McCook	N/B	Steubenville	Ohio
James Madison Tuttle	N/B	Summerfield	Ohio
William Sooy Smith	N/B	Tarlton	Ohio
William Harvey Wallace	N/B	Urbana	Ohio
Robert Allen	N/B	West Point	Ohio
Roswell Sabine Ripley	S/B	Worthington	Ohio
Robert Hopkins Hatton	S/B	Youngstown	Ohio
Catharinus Buckingham	N/B	Zanesville	Ohio
Charles Champion Gilbert	N/B	Zanesville	Ohio
Robert Seaman Granger	N/B	Zanesville	Ohio
Frank Armstrong	S/B	Scullyville	Oklahoma
Conrad Feger Jackson	N/B	Alsace	Pennsylvania
James Richard Slack	N/B	Bucks County	Pennsylvania

Andrew Jackson Smith	N/M	Bucks County	Pennsylvania
Thomas Jefferson McKean	N/B	Burlington	Pennsylvania
Washington Elliott	N/B	Carlisle	Pennsylvania
Stephen Miller	N/B	Carroll	Pennsylvania
Samuel Kosciuszko Zook	N/B	Chester County	Pennsylvania
John Grubb Parke	N/M	Coatesville	Pennsylvania
Thomas Welsh	N/B	Columbia	Pennsylvania
Powell Clayton	N/B	Delaware County	Pennsylvania
Charles Adam Heckman	N/B	Easton	Pennsylvania
Alexander Hays	N/B	Franklin	Pennsylvania
Charles Thomas Campbell	N/B	Franklin County	Pennsylvania
Samuel Wylie Crawford	N/B	Franklin County	Pennsylvania
David McMurtrie Gregg	N/B	Huntingdon	Pennsylvania
Andrew Porter	N/B	Lancaster	Pennsylvania
John Fulton Reynolds	N/M	Lancaster	Pennsylvania
Samuel Heintzelman	N/M	Manheim	Pennsylvania
William McComb	S/B	Mercer County	Pennsylvania
Samuel Beatty	N/B	Mifflin County	Pennsylvania
John Rutter Brooke	N/B	Montgomery County	Pennsylvania
Adam Jacoby Slemmer	N/B	Montgomery County	Pennsylvania
Winfield Scott Hancock	N/M	Montgomery Square	Pennsylvania
Joseph Farmer Knipe	N/B	Mount Joy	Pennsylvania
John White Geary	N/B	Mount Pleasant	Pennsylvania
James Blair Steedman	N/M	Northumberland Cty	Pennsylvania
Alfred Washington Ellet	N/B	Penn's Manor	Pennsylvania
Joseph K. Barnes	N/B	Philadelphia	Pennsylvania
George Cadwalader	N/M	Philadelphia	Pennsylvania
John Gibbon	N/M	Philadelphia	Pennsylvania
Richard Griffith	S/B	Philadelphia	Pennsylvania
Herman Haupt	N/B	Philadelphia	Pennsylvania
Andrew Humphreys	N/M	Philadelphia	Pennsylvania
Thomas Leiper Kane	N/B	Philadelphia	Pennsylvania
George Archibald McCall	N/B	Philadelphia	Pennsylvania
George McClellan	N/M	Philadelphia	Pennsylvania
Sullivan Amory Meredith	N/B	Philadelphia	Pennsylvania
James St.Clair Morton	N/B	Philadelphia	Pennsylvania
Henry Morris Naglee	N/B	Philadelphia	Pennsylvania
Thomas Hewson Neill	N/B	Philadelphia	Pennsylvania
Francis Engle Patterson	N/B	Philadelphia	Pennsylvania
John Clifford Pemberton	S/L	Philadelphia	Pennsylvania
Charles Ferguson Smith	N/M	Philadelphia	Pennsylvania
Gustavus Adolphus Smith	N/B	Philadelphia	Pennsylvania
Alfred Sully	N/B	Philadelphia	Pennsylvania
George Hector Tyndale	N/B	Philadelphia	Pennsylvania
Isaac Jones Wistar	N/B	Philadelphia	Pennsylvania
George Deitzler	N/B	Pine Grove	Pennsylvania
John Murray Corse	N/B	Pittsburgh	Pennsylvania
Benjamin Henry Grierson	N/B	Pittsburgh	Pennsylvania
Francis Jay Herron	N/M	Pittsburgh	Pennsylvania
James Scott Negley	N/M	Pittsburgh	Pennsylvania
Elliott Warren Rice	N/B	Pittsburgh	Pennsylvania
Thomas Algeo Rowley	N/B	Pittsburgh	Pennsylvania
William Stephen Walker	S/B	Pittsburgh	Pennsylvania
John Hartranft	N/B	Pottstown	Pennsylvania
William High Keim	N/B	Reading	Pennsylvania
James Nagle	N/B	Reading	Pennsylvania

Josiah Gorgas	S/B Running Pumps	Pennsylvania
Frederick Stumbaugh	N/B Shippensburg	Pennsylvania
Samuel Davis Sturgis	N/B Shippensburg	Pennsylvania
Absalom Baird	N/B Washington	Pennsylvania
James Craig	N/B Washington County	Pennsylvania
George Morgan	N/B Washington County	Pennsylvania
Joseph Andrew Lightburn	N/B Webster	Pennsylvania
Israel Vogdes	N/B Willistown	Pennsylvania
Johnson Kelly Duncan	S/B York	Pennsylvania
William Buel Franklin	N/B York	Pennsylvania
Albin Francisco Schoepf	N/B Podgorz	Poland
George Sears Greene	N/B Apponaug	Rhode Island
Silas Casey	N/M East Greenwich	Rhode Island
Lunsford Lindsay Lomax	S/M Newport	Rhode Island
Thomas West Sherman	N/B Newport	Rhode Island
Richard Arnold	N/B Providence	Rhode Island
Frank Wheaton	N/B Providence	Rhode Island
Isaac Peace Rodman	N/B South Kingstown	Rhode Island
John Basil Turchin	N/B Don	Russia
John McArthur	N/B Erskine	Scotland
Alpheus Baker	S/B Abbeville Dist.	South Carolina
Johnson Hagood	S/B Barnwell	South Carolina
Stephen Elliott,Jr.	S/B Beaufort	South Carolina
Alexander Robert Lawton	S/B Beaufort Dist.	South Carolina
James Cantey	S/B Camden	South Carolina
James Chestnut, Jr.	S/B Camden	South Carolina
Zachariah Cantey Deas	S/B Camden	South Carolina
John Doby Kennedy	S/B Camden	South Carolina
Joseph Brevard Kershaw	S/M Camden	South Carolina
John Villepigue	S/B Camden	South Carolina
Barnard Elliott Bee	S/B Charleston	South Carolina
Hamilton Prioleau Bee	S/B Charleston	South Carolina
Ellison Capers	S/B Charleston	South Carolina
James Conner	S/B Charleston	South Carolina
Thomas Fenwick Drayton	S/B Charleston	South Carolina
Samuel Wragg Ferguson	S/B Charleston	South Carolina
Maxcy Gregg	S/B Charleston	South Carolina
Wade Hampton	S/L Charleston	South Carolina
Benjamin Huger	S/M Charleston	South Carolina
Stephen Augustus Hurlbut	N/M Charleston	South Carolina
Stephen Dill Lee	S/L Charleston	South Carolina
Thomas Muldrup Logan	S/B Charleston	South Carolina
Arthur Manigault	S/B Charleston	South Carolina
Lucius Northrop	S/B Charleston	South Carolina
John Dunovant	S/B Chester	South Carolina
Robert Lowry	S/B Chesterfield Dist.	South Carolina
Martin Witherspoon Gary	S/B Cokesbury	South Carolina
Evander McIvor Law	S/B Darlington	South Carolina
Louis Trezevant Wigfall	S/B Edgefield	South Carolina
Milledge Luke Bonham	S/B Edgefield Dist.	South Carolina
James Longstreet	S/L Edgefield Dist.	South Carolina
Abner Monroe Perrin	S/B Edgefield Dist.	South Carolina
Micah Jenkins	S/B Edisto Island	South Carolina
Adley Hogan Gladden	S/B Fairfield Dist.	South Carolina
James Heyward Trapier	S/B Georgetown	South Carolina
Matthew Calbraith Butler	S/M Greenville	South Carolina

James Edward Harrison	S/B	Greenville Dist.	South Carolina
Henry Gray	S/B	Laurens Dist.	South Carolina
Samuel McGowan	S/B	Laurens Dist.	South Carolina
William Henry Wallace	S/B	Laurens Dist.	South Carolina
Nathan George Evans	S/B	Marion	South Carolina
David Rumph Jones	S/M	Orangeburg Dist.	South Carolina
Pierce Manning B. Young	S/M	Spartanburg	South Carolina
William Edwin Baldwin	S/B	Statesburg	South Carolina
Richard Heron Anderson	S/L	Sumter County	South Carolina
Thomas Neville Waul	S/B	Sumter District	South Carolina
States Rights Gist	S/B	Union District	South Carolina
John Bratton	S/B	Winnsboro	South Carolina
Daniel Harvey Hill	S/L	York District	South Carolina
William Henry Powell	N/B	Pontypool	South Wales
Edward Ferrero	N/B	Granada	Spain
George Gordon Meade	N/M	Cadiz	Spain
Charles John Stolbrand	N/B	Kristianstad	Sweden
John Eugene Smith	N/B	Berne	Switzerland
John Tyler Morgan	S/B	Athens	Tennessee
Nathan Bedford Forrest	S/L	Bedford County	Tennessee
James Gallant Spears	N/B	Bledsoe County	Tennessee
William Brimage Bate	S/M	Bledsoe's Lick	Tennessee
Lucius Marshall Walker	S/B	Columbia	Tennessee
Tyree Harris Bell	S/B	Covington	Tennessee
Alfred Eugene Jackson	S/B	Davidson County	Tennessee
Isham Nicholas Haynie	N/B	Dover	Tennessee
Samuel Powhatan Carter	N/B	Elizabethton	Tennessee
George Ear Maney	S/B	Franklin	Tennessee
John Wilkins Whitfield	S/B	Franklin	Tennessee
James Patton Anderson	S/M	Franklin County	Tennessee
Alvan Cullem Gillem	N/B	Gainesboro	Tennessee
William Read Scurry	S/B	Gallatin	Tennessee
John Calvin Brown	S/M	Giles County	Tennessee
George Washington Gordon	S/B	Giles County	Tennessee
Preston Smith	S/B	Giles County	Tennessee
John Wesley Frazer	S/B	Hardin County	Tennessee
William Selby Harney	N/B	Haysboro	Tennessee
John Creed Moore	S/B	Hawkins County	Tennessee
William Raine Peck	S/B	Jefferson County	Tennessee
Thomas Hindman	S/M	Knoxville	Tennessee
James Argyle Smith	S/B	Maury County	Tennessee
Felix Kirk Zollicoffer	S/B	Maury County	Tennessee
Benjamin Jefferson Hill	S/B	McMinnville	Tennessee
Thomas Benton Smith	S/B	Mechanicsville	Tennessee
Winfield Featherston	S/B	Murfreesboro	Tennessee
John Adams	S/B	Nashville	Tennessee
Alexander Campbell	S/B	Nashville	Tennessee
William Henry Carroll	S/B	Nashville	Tennessee
Benjamin Cheatham	S/M	Nashville	Tennessee
James Edwards Rains	S/B	Nashville	Tennessee
John Austin Wharton	S/M	Nashville	Tennessee
Mark Perrin Lowrey	S/B	NcNairy County	Tennessee
Elkanah Brackin Greer	S/B	Paris	Tennessee
William Hicks Jackson	S/B	Paris	Tennessee
Marcus Joseph Wright	S/B	Purdy	Tennessee
Richard Waterhouse	S/B	Rhea County	Tennessee

John Crawford Vaughn	S/B	Roane County	Tennessee
Alexander Peter Stewart	S/L	Rogersville	Tennessee
Ben McCulloch	S/B	Rutherford County	Tennessee
Henry Eustace McCulloch	S/B	Rutherford County	Tennessee
Joseph Benjamin Palmer	S/B	Rutherford County	Tennessee
John Porter McCown	S/M	Sevierville	Tennessee
Dudley McIver DuBose	S/B	Shelby County	Tennessee
Henry Brevard Davidson	S/B	Shelbyville	Tennessee
William Barksdale	S/B	Smyrna	Tennessee
George Gibbs Dibrell	S/B	Sparta	Tennessee
Charles Miller Shelley	S/B	Sullivan County	Tennessee
William Bowen Campbell	N/B	Sumner County	Tennessee
Daniel Smith Donelson	S/M	Sumner County	Tennessee
William Polk Hardeman	S/B	Williamson County	Tennessee
Gideon Johnson Pillow	S/B	Williamson County	Tennessee
Jesse Johnson Finley	S/B	Wilson County	Tennessee
Harry Thompson Hays	S/M	Wilson County	Tennessee
John Selden Roane	S/B	Wilson County	Tennessee
Felix Huston Robertson	S/B	Washington	Texas
Charles Camp Doolittle	N/B	Burlington	Vermont
Truman Seymour	N/B	Burlington	Vermont
Edwin Henry Stoughton	N/B	Chester	Vermont
Israel Bush Richardson	N/M	Fairfax	Vermont
Stewart Van Vliet	N/B	Ferrisburg	Vermont
George Stannard	N/B	Georgia	Vermont
John Wolcott Phelps	N/B	Guilford	Vermont
Robert Cowdin	N/B	Jamaica	Vermont
John Curtis Caldwell	N/B	Lowell	Vermont
Benjamin Stone Roberts	N/B	Manchester	Vermont
Thomas Edward G. Ransom	N/B	Norwich	Vermont
George Wright	N/B	Norwich	Vermont
Benjamin Alvord	N/B	Rutland	Vermont
William Farrar Smith	N/M	St.Albans	Vermont
George Crockett Strong	N/B	Stockbridge	Vermont
Charles Edward Hovey	N/B	Thetford	Vermont
Ethan Allen Hitchcock	N/M	Vergennes	Vermont
William Babcock Hazen	N/M	West Hartford	Vermont
Lewis Addison Grant	N/B	Winhall	Vermont
Joseph Anthony Mower	N/M	Woodstock	Vermont
William Young Conn Humes	S/B	Abingdon	Virginia
John Smith Preston	S/B	Abingdon	Virginia
Montgomery Dent Corse	S/B	Alexandria	Virginia
Lawrence Pike Graham	N/B	Amelia County	Virginia
Thomas Green	S/B	Amelia County	Virginia
Beverly Robertson	S/B	Amelia County	Virginia
William Thomas Ward	N/B	Amelia County	Virginia
William Terry	S/B	Amherst County	Virginia
William Henry F. Lee	S/M	Arlington	Virginia
Samuel Read Anderson	S/B	Bedford County	Virginia
James Monroe Goggin	S/B	Bedford County	Virginia
Jacob Ammen	N/B	Botetourt County	Virginia
Joseph Reid Anderson	S/B	Botetourt County	Virginia
Peter Burwell Starke	S/B	Brunswick County	Virginia
William Edwin Starke	S/B	Brunswick County	Virginia
James Dearing	S/B	Campbell County	Virginia
Armistead Lindsay Long	S/B	Campbell County	Virginia

Thomas Lafayette Rosser	S/M	Campbell County	Virginia
James Edwin Slaughter	S/B	Cedar Mountain	Virginia
John Marshall Jones	S/B	Charlottesville	Virginia
Mosby Monroe Parsons	S/M	Charlottesville	Virginia
George Wythe Randolph	S/B	Charlottesville	Virginia
Henry Heth	S/M	Chesterfield County	Virginia
Young Marshall Moody	S/B	Chesterfield County	Virginia
David Addison Weisiger	S/B	Chesterfield County	Virginia
Richard Lucian Page	S/B	Clarke County	Virginia
Alexander Welch Reynolds	S/B	Clarke County	Virginia
William Rufus Terrill	N/B	Covington	Virginia
Ambrose Powell Hill	S/L	Culpeper	Virginia
Isaac Ridgeway Trimble	S/M	Culpeper County	Virginia
Gabriel Colvin Wharton	S/B	Culpeper County	Virginia
William Lewis Cabell	S/B	Danville	Virginia
Alfred Vaughan, Jr	S/B	Dinwiddie County	Virginia
Henry Alexander Wise	S/B	Drummondtown	Virginia
George Douglas Ramsay	N/B	Dumfries	Virginia
Richard Brooke Garnett	S/B	Essex County	Virginia
Robert Selden Garnett	S/B	Essex County	Virginia
John Wynn Davidson	N/B	Fairfax County	Virginia
Fitzhugh Lee	S/M	Fairfax County	Virginia
Joseph Johnston	S/G	Farmville	Virginia
Turner Ashby	S/B	Fauquier County	Virginia
Martin Edwin Green	S/B	Fauquier County	Virginia
Eppa Hunton	S/B	Fauquier County	Virginia
William Henry F. Payne	S/B	Fauquier County	Virginia
Albert Rust	S/B	Fauquier County	Virginia
Philip St.George Cocke	S/B	Fluvanna County	Virginia
George Washington Lee	S/M	Fortress Monroe	Virginia
Jubal Anderson Early	S/L	Franklin County	Virginia
Seth Maxwell Barton	S/B	Fredericksburg	Virginia
Dabney Herndon Maury	S/M	Fredericksburg	Virginia
Hugh Weedon Mercer	S/B	Fredericksburg	Virginia
Carter Stevenson	S/M	Fredericksburg	Virginia
William Booth Taliaferro	S/M	Gloucester County	Virginia
Robert Doak Lilley	S/B	Greenville	Virginia
James Ronald Chalmers	S/B	Halifax County	Virginia
John Robert Jones	S/B	Harrisonburg	Virginia
Richard Lee T. Beale	S/B	Hickory Hill	Virginia
John Chambliss, Jr.	S/B	Hicksford	Virginia
William Andrew Quarles	S/B	Jamestown	Virginia
William Smith	S/M	King George Cty.	Virginia
Edwin Gray Lee	S/B	Leeland	Virginia
Philip St.George Cooke	N/B	Leesburg	Virginia
William Richard Terry	S/B	Liberty	Virginia
Reuben Lindsay Walker	S/B	Logan	Virginia
Robert Hall Chilton	S/B	Loudoun County	Virginia
Thomas Jordan	S/B	Luray	Virginia
John Echols	S/B	Lynchburg	Virginia
Samuel Garland, Jr.	S/B	Lynchburg	Virginia
Robert Emmett Rodes	S/M	Lynchburg	Virginia
James Lawson Kemper	S/M	Madison County	Virginia
James Henry Lane	S/B	Mathews Court Hse.	Virginia
John Buchanan Floyd	S/B	Montgomery County	Virginia
James Alexander Walker	S/B	Mt.Sidney	Virginia

Archibald Godwin	S/B	Nansemond County	Virginia
Edward Higgins	S/B	Norfolk	Virginia
John Newton	N/M	Norfolk	Virginia
James Ewel Stuart	S/M	Patrick County	Virginia
John Pegram	S/B	Petersburg	Virginia
Roger Atkinson Pryor	S/B	Petersburg	Virginia
Winfield Scott	N/M	Petersburg	Virginia
John Bankhead Magruder	S/M	Port Royal	Virginia
William George Davis	S/B	Portsmouth	Virginia
Samuel Jones	S/M	Powhatan County	Virginia
Henry Watkins Allen	S/B	Prince Edward Cty.	Virginia
Sterling Price	S/M	Prince Edward Cty.	Virginia
Alexander Brydie Dyer	N/B	Richmond	Virginia
William Hays	N/B	Richmond	Virginia
William Nelson Pendleton	S/B	Richmond	Virginia
George Edward Pickett	S/M	Richmond	Virginia
Edward Cary Walthall	S/M	Richmond	Virginia
Williams Carter Wickham	S/B	Richmond	Virginia
Elisha Franklin Paxton	S/B	Rockbridge County	Virginia
Edward Johnson	S/M	Salisbury	Virginia
William Mahone	S/M	Southampton Cty.	Virginia
George Henry Thomas	N/M	Southampton Cty.	Virginia
John Daniel Imboden	S/B	Staunton	Virginia
John Dunlap Stevenson	N/B	Staunton	Virginia
Henry Harrison Walker	S/B	Sussex County	Virginia
William Edmonson Jones	S/B	Washington County	Virginia
Robert Edward Lee	S/G	Westmoreland Cty.	Virginia
James William Denver	N/B	Winchester	Virginia
Joshua Thomas Owen	N/B	Caermarthen	Wales
Benjamin Prentiss	N/M	Belleville	West Virginia
Albert Gallatin Jenkins	S/B	Cabell County	West Virginia
Thomas Jonathon Jackson	S/L	Clarksburg	West Virginia
William Lowther Jackson	S/B	Clarksburg	West Virginia
Birkett Davenport Fry	S/B	Kanawha County	West Virginia
Isaac Hardin Duval	N/B	Wellsburg	West Virginia
Jesse Lee Reno	N/M	Wheeling	West Virginia
Thomas Maley Harris	N/B	Wood County	West Virginia
Lewis Cass Hunt	N/B	Green Bay	Wisconsin

5

Civil War Generals
by Date of Birth

The generals are arranged here in the order that they were born.
In some cases the exact date of birth is unknown. All available
information is listed. In some cases this is only the year.

DATE BORN	GENERAL	SIDE/RANK
February 29, 1784	John Ellis Wool	N/Maj.Gen.
June 13, 1786	Winfield Scott	N/Maj.Gen.
April 17, 1788	Joseph Gilbert Totten	N/Brig.Gen.
1790	David Emanuel Twiggs	S/Maj.Gen.
December 10, 1794	James Wolfe Ripley	N/Brig.Gen.
May 4, 1796	Joseph Pannell Taylor	N/Brig.Gen.
January 30, 1797	Edwin Vose Sumner	N/Maj.Gen.
September 6, 1797	William Smith	S/Maj.Gen.
February 22, 1798	Charles Mynn Thruston	N/Brig.Gen.
March 4, 1798	John Joseph Abercrombie	N/Brig.Gen.
May 18, 1798	Ethan Allen Hitchcock	N/Maj.Gen.
June 12, 1798	Samuel Cooper	S/General
July 24, 1798	John Adams Dix	N/Maj.Gen.
September 1, 1798	Richard Delafield	N/Brig.Gen.
January 7, 1799	Daniel Tyler	N/Brig.Gen.
February 21, 1800	John Henry Winder	S/Brig.Gen.
August 27, 1800	William Selby Harney	N/Brig.Gen.
May 6, 1801	George Sears Greene	N/Brig.Gen.
June 23, 1801	Daniel Smith Donelson	S/Maj.Gen.
July 10, 1801	William Montgomery	N/Brig.Gen.
October 21, 1801	George Wright	N/Brig.Gen.
December 28, 1801	James Barnes	N/Brig.Gen.
1802	William Lindsay Brandon	S/Brig.Gen.
February 21, 1802	George Douglas Ramsay	N/Brig.Gen.
March 16, 1802	George Archibald McCall	N/Brig.Gen.
May 15, 1802	Isaac Ridgeway Trimble	S/Maj.Gen.
July 21, 1802	David Hunter	N/Maj.Gen.
December 2, 1802	Melancthon Smith Wade	N/Brig.Gen.
February 2, 1803	Albert Sidney Johnston	S/General
June 4, 1803	Gabriel James Rains	S/Brig.Gen.
December 22, 1803	Joseph King F. Mansfield	N/Brig.Gen.
February 17, 1804	Samuel Read Anderson	S/Brig.Gen.
March 20, 1804	Neal Dow	N/Brig.Gen.

October 26, 1804	Lorenzo Thomas	N/Brig.Gen.
November 13, 1804	Theophilus Hunter Holmes	S/Lt.Gen.
February 3, 1805	Samuel Ryan Curtis	N/Maj.Gen.
April 30, 1805	William Kerley Strong	N/Brig.Gen.
June 14, 1805	Robert Anderson	N/Brig.Gen.
September 18, 1805	Robert Cowdin	N/Brig.Gen.
September 30, 1805	Samuel Peter Heintzelman	N/Maj.Gen.
November 22, 1805	Benjamin Huger	S/Maj.Gen.
January 7, 1806	Jacob Ammen	N/Brig.Gen.
April 10, 1806	Leonidas Polk	S/Lt.Gen.
May 12, 1806	Amos Beebe Eaton	N/Brig.Gen.
May 16, 1806	George Cadwalader	N/Maj.Gen.
June 1, 1806	John Buchanan Floyd	S/Brig.Gen.
June 8, 1806	Gideon Johnson Pillow	S/Brig.Gen.
September 13, 1806	Joseph Lewis Hogg	S/Brig.Gen.
October 18, 1806	John Breckinridge Grayson	S/Brig.Gen.
December 3, 1806	Henry Alexander Wise	S/Brig.Gen.
December 12, 1806	Stand Watie	S/Brig.Gen.
January 6, 1807	Joseph Holt	N/Brig.Gen.
January 11, 1807	Alfred Eugene Jackson	S/Brig.Gen.
January 13, 1807	Napoleon Bonaparte Buford	N/Brig.Gen.
January 19, 1807	Robert Edward Lee	S/General
February 1, 1807	William Bowen Campbell	N/Brig.Gen.
February 3, 1807	Joseph Eggleston Johnston	S/General
February 10, 1807	Abner Clark Harding	N/Brig.Gen.
February 16, 1807	Lysander Cutler	N/Brig.Gen.
April 10, 1807	Benjamin Franklin Kelley	N/Brig.Gen.
April 24, 1807	Charles Ferguson Smith	N/Maj.Gen.
May 1, 1807	John Bankhead Magruder	S/Maj.Gen.
July 12, 1807	Silas Casey	N/Maj.Gen.
October 30, 1807	James Samuel Wadsworth	N/Brig.Gen.
December 20, 1807	Richard Lucian Page	S/Brig.Gen.
February 25, 1808	James Bowen	N/Brig.Gen.
March 14, 1808	Catharinus Buckingham	N/Brig.Gen.
May 19, 1808	Samuel Jameson Gholson	S/Brig.Gen.
August 9, 1808	William Thomas Ward	N/Brig.Gen.
August 24, 1808	Thomas Fenwick Drayton	S/Brig.Gen.
August 24, 1808	Benjamin Grubb Humphreys	S/Brig.Gen.
October 5, 1808	Thomas Algeo Rowley	N/Brig.Gen.
November 22, 1808	George William Taylor	N/Brig.Gen.
November 27, 1808	Hugh Weedon Mercer	S/Brig.Gen.
December 29, 1808	Andrew Johnson	N/Brig.Gen.
January 18, 1809	Richard Caswell Gatlin	S/Brig.Gen.
February 20, 1809	Henry Walton Wessells	N/Brig.Gen.
February 25, 1809	George Washington Cullum	N/Brig.Gen.
April 17, 1809	Philip St.George Cocke	S/Brig.Gen.
April 20, 1809	John Smith Preston	S/Brig.Gen.
June 13, 1809	Philip St.George Cooke	N/Brig.Gen.
July 28, 1809	Ormsby MacKnight Mitchel	N/Maj.Gen.
September 20, 1809	Sterling Price	S/Maj.Gen.
October 4, 1809	Robert Cumming Schenck	N/Maj.Gen.
November 23, 1809	Horatio Phillips Van Cleve	N/Brig.Gen.
December 3, 1809	Thomas Alfred Davies	N/Brig.Gen.
December 26, 1809	William Nelson Pendleton	S/Brig.Gen.
December 29, 1809	Albert Pike	S/Brig.Gen.
1810	William Henry Carroll	S/Brig.Gen.

January 31, 1810	Daniel Ruggles	S/Brig.Gen.
April 28, 1810	Daniel Ullmann	N/Brig.Gen.
May 8, 1810	James Cooper	N/Brig.Gen.
May 10, 1810	James Shields	N/Brig.Gen.
May 29, 1810	Erasmus Darwin Keyes	N/Maj.Gen.
May 29, 1810	Solomon Meredith	N/Brig.Gen.
July 2, 1810	Robert Augustus Toombs	S/Brig.Gen.
August 1, 1810	James Dada Morgan	N/Brig.Gen.
August 21, 1810	Thomas Jefferson McKean	N/Brig.Gen.
September 10, 1810	Albert Gallatin Blanchard	S/Brig.Gen.
September 20, 1810	Alpheus Starkey Williams	N/Brig.Gen.
October 19, 1810	Cassius Marcellus Clay	N/Maj.Gen.
October 22, 1810	Henry Bohlen	N/Brig.Gen.
October 28, 1810	Adley Hogan Gladden	S/Brig.Gen.
November 2, 1810	Andrew Atkinson Humphreys	N/Maj.Gen.
November 18, 1810	Benjamin Stone Roberts	N/Brig.Gen.
November 19, 1810	August Willich	N/Brig.Gen.
February 8, 1811	Edwin Denison Morgan	N/Maj.Gen.
February 24, 1811	Edward Dickinson Baker	N/Maj.Gen.
February 29, 1811	Henry Hastings Sibley	N/Brig.Gen.
March 1, 1811	Robert Christie Buchanan	N/Brig.Gen.
March 11, 1811	Marsena Rudolph Patrick	N/Brig.Gen.
March 15, 1811	Robert Allen	N/Brig.Gen.
May 24, 1811	Charles Clark	S/Brig.Gen.
June 19, 1811	Henry Prince	N/Brig.Gen.
August 20, 1811	Gilman Marston	N/Brig.Gen.
August 25, 1811	Joseph Dana Webster	N/Brig.Gen.
August 26, 1811	Danville Leadbetter	S/Brig.Gen.
August 31, 1811	Goode Bryan	S/Brig.Gen.
September 7, 1811	William Hemsley Emory	N/Brig.Gen.
September 8, 1811	Lucius Bellinger Northrop	S/Brig.Gen.
October 18, 1811	Hugh Thompson Reid	N/Brig.Gen.
November 11, 1811	Ben McCulloch	S/Brig.Gen.
December 18, 1811	Alexander Sandor Asboth	N/Brig.Gen.
January 13, 1812	Humphrey Marshall	S/Brig.Gen.
January 20, 1812	Ralph Pomeroy Buckland	N/Brig.Gen.
March 16, 1812	Henry Dwight Terry	N/Brig.Gen.
March 20, 1812	George Bibb Crittenden	S/Maj.Gen.
April 9, 1812	Randolph Barnes Marcy	N/Brig.Gen.
April 28, 1812	Daniel Henry Rucker	N/Brig.Gen.
May 9, 1812	William George M. Davis	S/Brig.Gen.
May 12, 1812	Louis Ludwig Blenker	N/Brig.Gen.
May 17, 1812	Joseph Warren Revere	N/Brig.Gen.
May 19, 1812	Felix Kirk Zollicoffer	S/Brig.Gen.
May 30, 1812	John Alexander McClernand	N/Maj.Gen.
June 7, 1812	Theophilus Garrard	N/Brig.Gen.
July 27, 1812	Thomas Lanier Clingman	S/Brig.Gen.
November 18, 1812	Jesse Johnson Finley	S/Brig.Gen.
December 4, 1812	Elias Smith Dennis	N/Brig.Gen.
December 16, 1812	William Grose	N/Brig.Gen.
December 16, 1812	Daniel Phineas Woodbury	N/Brig.Gen.
January 5, 1813	Thomas Neville Waul	S/Brig.Gen.
January 20, 1813	Jacob Gartner Lauman	N/Brig.Gen.
January 21, 1813	John Charles Fremont	N/Maj.Gen.
February 14, 1813	John McNeil	N/Brig.Gen.
February 16, 1813	Joseph Reid Anderson	S/Brig.Gen.

March 22, 1813	Gabriel Rene Paul	N/Brig.Gen.
March 26, 1813	Thomas West Sherman	N/Brig.Gen.
April 17, 1813	Henry Washington Benham	N/Brig.Gen.
May 6, 1813	Joseph Tarr Copeland	N/Brig.Gen.
May 23, 1813	Mason Brayman	N/Brig.Gen.
June 25, 1813	William High Keim	N/Brig.Gen.
July 7, 1813	William Scott Ketchum	N/Brig.Gen.
August 18, 1813	Benjamin Alvord	N/Brig.Gen.
August 27, 1813	John Cochrane	N/Brig.Gen.
September 11, 1813	Conrad Feger Jackson	N/Brig.Gen.
September 13, 1813	John Sedgwick	N/Maj.Gen.
November 13, 1813	John Wolcott Phelps	N/Brig.Gen.
December 25, 1813	Milledge Luke Bonham	S/Brig.Gen
1814	Hiram Burnham	N/Brig.Gen.
1814	William Edwin Starke	S/Brig.Gen.
January 8, 1814	Thomas Green	S/Brig.Gen.
January 11, 1814	Richard Griffith	S/Brig.Gen.
January 12, 1814	Jones Mitchell Withers	S/Maj.Gen.
January 26, 1814	Rufus King	N/Brig.Gen.
April 2, 1814	Henry Lewis Benning	S/Brig.Gen.
April 4, 1814	John Blair Smith Todd	N/Brig.Gen.
July 6, 1814	Justus McKinstry	N/Brig.Gen.
August 1, 1814	Maxcy Gregg	S/Brig.Gen.
August 10, 1814	John Clifford Pemberton	S/Lt.Gen.
August 17, 1814	Henry Hayes Lockwood	N/Brig.Gen.
November 13, 1814	Joseph Hooker	N/Maj.Gen.
November 15, 1814	Pleasant Adam Hackleman	N/Brig.Gen.
November 16, 1814	Michael Kelly Lawler	N/Brig.Gen.
November 17, 1814	Joseph Finegan	S/Brig.Gen.
November 23, 1814	Ebenezer Dumont	N/Brig.Gen.
December 22, 1814	John Smith Phelps	N/Brig.Gen.
December 27, 1814	James Henry Carleton	N/Brig.Gen.
1815	Peter Burwell Starke	S/Brig.Gen.
January 8, 1815	Lawrence Pike Graham	N/Brig.Gen.
January 8, 1815	George Webb Morell	N/Maj.Gen.
January 10, 1815	Alexander Brydie Dyer	N/Brig.Gen.
January 10, 1815	Thomas Williams	N/Brig.Gen.
January 13, 1815	William Henry French	N/Maj.Gen.
January 15, 1815	Henry Morris Naglee	N/Brig.Gen.
January 16, 1815	Henry Wager Halleck	N/Maj.Gen.
January 18, 1815	James Chesnut, Jr.	S/Brig.Gen.
January 28, 1815	Andrew Jackson Hamilton	N/Brig.Gen.
February 2, 1815	Nathaniel Collins McLean	N/Brig.Gen.
February 25, 1815	Robert Hall Chilton	S/Brig.Gen.
March 14, 1815	Jerome Robertson	S/Brig.Gen.
March 20, 1815	John Henry Martindale	N/Brig.Gen.
April 24, 1815	James Edward Harrison	S/Brig.Gen.
April 28, 1815	Andrew Jackson Smith	N/Maj.Gen.
April 29, 1815	Abram Duryee	N/Brig.Gen.
May 15, 1815	Collett Leventhorpe	S/Brig.Gen.
May 19, 1815	John Gross Barnard	N/Brig.Gen.
June 2, 1815	Philip Kearny	N/Maj.Gen.
June 3, 1815	Martin Edwin Green	S/Brig.Gen.
June 4, 1815	Paul Jones Semmes	S/Brig.Gen.
July 21, 1815	Stewart Van Vliet	N/Brig.Gen.
August 19, 1815	John Porter McCown	S/Maj.Gen.

September 5, 1815	Tyree Harris Bell	S/Brig.Gen.
September 6, 1815	St.John Liddell	S/Brig.Gen.
September 7, 1815	Howell Cobb	S/Maj.Gen.
September 10, 1815	Eleazer Arthur Paine	N/Brig.Gen.
September 18, 1815	Henry Constantine Wayne	S/Brig.Gen.
October 12, 1815	William Joseph Hardee	S/Lt.Gen.
October 24, 1815	John Edwards	N/Brig.Gen.
November 1, 1815	Douglas Hancock Cooper	S/Brig.Gen.
November 24, 1815	James Heyward Trapier	S/Brig.Gen.
November 29, 1815	Stephen Augustus Hurlbut	N/Maj.Gen.
December 26, 1815	Israel Bush Richardson	N/Maj.Gen.
December 31, 1815	George Gordon Meade	N/Maj.Gen.
January 7, 1816	Stephen Miller	N/Brig.Gen.
January 11, 1816	Fitz-Henry Warren	N/Brig.Gen.
January 12, 1816	Willis Arnold Gorman	N/Brig.Gen.
January 19, 1816	Henry Gray	S/Brig.Gen.
January 26, 1816	Lloyd Tilghman	S/Brig.Gen.
January 30, 1816	Nathaniel Prentiss Banks	N/Maj.Gen.
March 12, 1816	David Stuart	N/Brig.Gen.
March 14, 1816	Montgomery Dent Corse	S/Brig.Gen.
March 29, 1816	James Gallant Spears	N/Brig.Gen.
April 1816	Alexander Welch Reynolds	S/Brig.Gen.
April 16, 1816	Edward Johnson	S/Maj.Gen.
April 21, 1816	Louis Trezevant Wigfall	S/Brig.Gen.
May 3, 1816	Montgomery Meigs	N/Brig.Gen.
May 24, 1816	Robert Seaman Granger	N/Brig.Gen.
May 25, 1816	Henry Hopkins Sibley	S/Brig.Gen.
June 4, 1816	Philippe deTrobriand	N/Brig.Gen.
June 11, 1816	Robert Huston Milroy	N/Maj.Gen.
July 4, 1816	Sullivan Amory Meredith	N/Brig.Gen.
July 7, 1816	Isaac Fitzgerald Shepard	N/Brig.Gen.
July 31, 1816	George Henry Thomas	N/Maj.Gen.
August 1, 1816	William Yarnel Slack	S/Brig.Gen.
August 3, 1816	John Eugene Smith	N/Brig.Gen.
August 4, 1816	Israel Vogdes	N/Brig.Gen.
September 23, 1816	Julius White	N/Brig.Gen.
October 4, 1816	Egbert Benson Brown	N/Brig.Gen.
October 15, 1816	Amiel Weeks Whipple	N/Brig.Gen.
October 16, 1816	William Preston	S/Brig.Gen.
November 3, 1816	Jubal Anderson Early	S/Lt.Gen.
November 4, 1816	William Polk Hardeman	S/Brig.Gen.
November 15, 1816	Joseph Bennett Plummer	N/Brig.Gen.
November 26, 1816	William Henry T. Walker	S/Maj.Gen.
December 6, 1816	Henry Eustace McCulloch	S/Brig.Gen.
December 18, 1816	Arnold Elzey	S/Maj.Gen.
December 27, 1816	Eliakim Parker Scammon	N/Brig.Gen.
January 8, 1817	John Selden Roane	S/Brig.Gen.
January 15, 1817	Lewis Golding Arnold	N/Brig.Gen.
January 18, 1817	William Whann Mackall	S/Brig.Gen.
February 7, 1817	Leroy Pope Walker	S/Brig.Gen.
February 8, 1817	Richard Stoddert Ewell	S/Lt.Gen.
February 18, 1817	Walter Paye Lane	S/Brig.Gen.
February 28, 1817	James Craig	N/Brig.Gen.
March 19, 1817	Lewis Henry Little	S/Brig.Gen.
March 22, 1817	Braxton Bragg	S/General
March 26, 1817	Herman Haupt	N/Brig.Gen.

March 31, 1817	William Vandever	N/Brig.Gen.
April 4, 1817	John Wilson Sprague	N/Brig.Gen.
April 10, 1817	John Cleveland Robinson	N/Brig.Gen.
April 14, 1817	Frederick Stumbaugh	N/Brig.Gen.
June 17, 1817	Thomas Maley Harris	N/Brig.Gen.
July 21, 1817	Joseph K. Barnes	N/Brig.Gen.
June 21, 1817	James Brewerton Ricketts	N/Brig.Gen.
July 29, 1817	James Blair Steedman	N/Maj.Gen.
July 31, 1817	Philip Cook	S/Brig.Gen.
September 9, 1817	Speed Smith Fry	N/Brig.Gen.
September 13, 1817	John McCauley Palmer	N/Maj.Gen.
September 21, 1817	Carter Stevenson	S/Maj.Gen.
October 7, 1817	Bushrod Rust Johnson	S/Maj.Gen.
October 18, 1817	Lewis Addison Armistead	S/Brig.Gen.
October 23, 1817	James William Denver	N/Brig.Gen.
November 8, 1817	Claudius Wistar Sears	S/Brig.Gen.
November 9, 1817	Edward Richard S. Canby	N/Maj.Gen.
November 21, 1817	Richard Brooke Garnett	S/Brig.Gen.
December 19, 1817	James Jay Archer	S/Brig.Gen.
1818	Albert Rust	S/Brig.Gen.
January 11, 1818	John Reese Kenly	N/Brig.Gen.
January 31, 1818	William Raine Peck	S/Brig.Gen.
February 23, 1818	Jeremy Francis Gilmer	S/Maj.Gen.
March 10, 1818	George Wythe Randolph	S/Brig.Gen.
March 11, 1818	John Wilkins Whitfield	S/Brig.Gen.
March 13, 1818	Albion Parris Howe	N/Brig.Gen.
March 23, 1818	Don Carlos Buell	N/Maj.Gen.
March 25, 1818	Isaac Ingalls Stevens	N/Brig.Gen.
March 28, 1818	Wade Hampton	S/Lt.Gen.
April 22, 1818	Cadwallader Washburn	N/Maj.Gen.
May 22, 1818	Jerimiah Tilford Boyle	N/Brig.Gen.
May 28, 1818	Pierre Gustave Beauregard	S/General
June 21, 1818	Joseph Abel Haskin	N/Brig.Gen.
July 1, 1818	Josiah Gorgas	S/Brig.Gen.
July 10, 1818	John Stuart Williams	S/Brig.Gen.
July 14, 1818	Nathaniel Lyon	N/Brig.Gen.
July 28, 1818	Nathaniel James Jackson	N/Brig.Gen.
August 4, 1818	Lovell Harrison Rousseau	N/Maj.Gen.
August 5, 1818	Carnot Posey	S/Brig.Gen.
August 18, 1818	William Farquhar Barry	N/Brig.Gen.
August 23, 1818	Rufus Ingalls	N/Brig.Gen.
September 18, 1818	Marcellus Augustus Stovall	S/Brig.Gen.
September 28, 1818	James Richard Slack	N/Brig.Gen.
October 15, 1818	Irvin McDowell	N/Maj.Gen.
October 18, 1818	Edward Otho C. Ord	N/Maj.Gen.
November 3, 1818	Gustavus Adolphus DeRussy	N/Brig.Gen.
November 4, 1818	Alexander Robert Lawton	S/Brig.Gen.
November 5, 1818	Benjamin Franklin Butler	N/Maj.Gen.
November 22, 1818	Samuel Gibbs French	S/Maj.Gen.
December 4, 1818	William Wing Loring	S/Maj.Gen.
December 12, 1818	Paul Octave Hebert	S/Brig.Gen.
December 23, 1818	David Addison Weisiger	S/Brig.Gen.
December 30, 1818	James Cantey	S/Brig.Gen.
January 1, 1819	George Foster Shepley	N/Brig.Gen.
January 12, 1819	Zealous Bates Tower	N/Brig.Gen.
January 14, 1819	Frederick Steele	N/Maj.Gen.

February 1, 1819	Henry Lawrence Eustis	N/Brig.Gen.
February 14, 1819	James Green Martin	S/Brig.Gen.
March 19, 1819	David Henry Williams	N/Brig.Gen.
March 22, 1819	William Wirt Adams	S/Brig.Gen.
March 24, 1819	Thomas Church H. Smith	N/Brig.Gen.
May 1, 1819	William Steele	S/Brig.Gen.
May 9, 1819	William Hays	N/Brig.Gen.
May 15, 1819	Thomas Leonidas Crittenden	N/Maj.Gen.
May 22, 1819	Richard Lee T. Beale	S/Brig.Gen.
May 28, 1819	William Birney	N/Brig.Gen.
June 26, 1819	Abner Doubleday	N/Brig.Gen.
July 1, 1819	John Milton Brannan	N/Brig.Gen.
July 8, 1819	Alexander Hays	N/Brig.Gen.
August 6, 1819	Samuel Powhatan Carter	N/Brig.Gen.
August 12, 1819	Daniel Davidson Bidwell	N/Brig.Gen.
August 17, 1819	James Henry Van Alen	N/Brig.Gen.
September 6, 1819	William Starke Rosecrans	N/Maj.Gen.
September 9, 1819	Martin Luther Smith	S/Maj.Gen.
September 14, 1819	Henry Jackson Hunt	N/Brig.Gen.
September 30, 1819	Thomas Jordan	S/Brig.Gen.
October 2, 1819	George Washington Getty	N/Brig.Gen.
October 9, 1819	Samuel McGowan	S/Brig.Gen.
October 10, 1819	Zebulon York	S/Brig.Gen.
October 20, 1819	Daniel Edgar Sickles	N/Maj.Gen.
October 25, 1819	Zachariah Cantey Deas	S/Brig.Gen.
November 23, 1819	Benjamin Mayberry Prentiss	N/Maj.Gen.
December 16, 1819	Robert Selden Garnett	S/Brig.Gen.
December 17, 1819	Samuel Jones	S/Maj.Gen.
December 19, 1819	James Clifford Veatch	N/Brig.Gen.
December 30, 1819	John White Geary	N/Brig.Gen.
January 18, 1820	Abraham Buford	S/Brig.Gen.
January 24, 1820	John Milton Thayer	N/Brig.Gen.
February 8, 1820	William Tecumseh Sherman	N/Maj.Gen.
February 19, 1820	John Haskell King	N/Brig.Gen.
February 20, 1820	Mahlon Dickerson Manson	N/Brig.Gen.
March 6, 1820	Horatio Gouverneur Wright	N/Maj.Gen.
March 13, 1820	Louis Hebert	S/Brig.Gen.
March 17, 1820	Patrick Edward Connor	N/Brig.Gen.
March 27, 1820	John Franklin Farnsworth	N/Brig.Gen.
April 4, 1820	Charles Devens,Jr.	N/Brig.Gen.
April 14, 1820	Harry Thompson Hays	S/Maj.Gen.
April 15, 1820	Evander McNair	S/Brig.Gen.
April 29, 1820	Henry Watkins Allen	S/Brig.Gen.
May 22, 1820	Alfred Sully	N/Brig.Gen.
June 24, 1820	Henry Rootes Jackson	S/Brig.Gen.
July 10, 1820	Andrew Porter	N/Brig.Gen.
July 26, 1820	John Marshall Jones	S/Brig.Gen.
August 3, 1820	William Miller	S/Brig.Gen.
August 8, 1820	Winfield Scott Featherston	S/Brig.Gen.
September 17, 1820	Earl Van Dorn	S/Maj.Gen.
September 20, 1820	George Washington Morgan	N/Brig.Gen.
September 20, 1820	John Fulton Reynolds	N/Maj.Gen.
September 21, 1820	Williams Carter Wickham	S/Brig.Gen.
September 23, 1820	Thomas Kilby Smith	N/Brig.Gen.
October 20, 1820	Benjamin Franklin Cheatham	S/Maj.Gen.
October 20, 1820	George Jerrison Stannard	N/Brig.Gen.

October 23, 1820	James Monroe Goggin	S/Brig.Gen.
November 4, 1820	Robert Vinkler Richardson	S/Brig.Gen.
November 11, 1820	Alfred Washington Ellet	N/Brig.Gen.
November 28, 1820	Lawrence O'Bryan Branch	S/Brig.Gen.
December 10, 1820	David Allen Russell	N/Brig.Gen.
December 16, 1820	Samuel Beatty	N/Brig.Gen.
December 25, 1820	Thomas William Sweeny	N/Brig.Gen.
December 26, 1820	Gustavus Adolphus Smith	N/Brig.Gen.
1821	Edward Higgins	S/Brig.Gen.
January 4, 1821	John James Peck	N/Maj.Gen.
January 7, 1821	Lucius Jeremiah Gartrell	S/Brig.Gen.
January 8, 1821	James Longstreet	S/Lt.Gen.
January 15, 1821	John Cabell Breckinridge	S/Maj.Gen.
January 15, 1821	Lafayette McLaws	S/Maj.Gen.
January 28, 1821	William Thomas H. Brooks	N/Maj.Gen.
January 29, 1821	Issac Ferdinand Quinby	N/Brig.Gen.
February 10, 1821	William Read Scurry	S/Brig.Gen.
February 19, 1821	Francis Preston Blair,Jr.	N/Maj.Gen.
March 8, 1821	Morgan Lewis Smith	N/Brig.Gen.
March 19, 1821	Francis Barretto Spinola	N/Brig.Gen.
March 24, 1821	George Hector Tyndale	N/Brig.Gen.
March 27, 1821	Samuel Kosciuszko Zook	N/Brig.Gen.
March 29, 1821	Joshua Thomas Owen	N/Brig.Gen.
April 19, 1821	Mortimer Dormer Leggett	N/Brig.Gen.
May 2, 1821	Abram Sanders Piatt	N/Brig.Gen.
May 7, 1821	Francis Engle Patterson	N/Brig.Gen.
May 11, 1821	Charles John Stolbrand	N/Brig.Gen.
June 1821	Daniel Weisiger Adams	S/Brig.Gen.
June 8, 1821	John Dunlap Stevenson	N/Brig.Gen.
June 8, 1821	Nelson Taylor	N/Brig.Gen.
June 12, 1821	Henry Moses Judah	N/Brig.Gen.
July 6, 1821	Edmund Winston Pettus	S/Brig.Gen.
July 8, 1821	William Harvey L. Wallace	N/Brig.Gen.
July 10, 1821	Christopher Columbus Augur	N/Maj.Gen.
July 12, 1821	Daniel Harvey Hill	S/Lt.Gen.
July 13, 1821	Nathan Bedford Forrest	S/Lt.Gen.
August 14, 1821	Clement Hoffman Stevens	S/Brig.Gen.
August 21, 1821	William Barksdale	S/Brig.Gen.
September 8, 1821	Henry Baxter	N/Brig.Gen.
September 22, 1821	Patrick Theodore Moore	S/Brig.Gen.
September 26, 1821	Alvin Peterson Hovey	N/Brig.Gen.
October 2, 1821	Alexander Peter Stewart	S/Lt.Gen.
October 7, 1821	Richard Heron Anderson	S/Lt.Gen.
November 30, 1821	Gustavus Woodson Smith	S/Maj.Gen.
December 2, 1821	Rufus Barringer	S/Brig.Gen.
December 17, 1821	Frederick West Lander	N/Brig.Gen.
January 4, 1822	Joseph Jones Reynolds	N/Maj.Gen.
January 5, 1822	Joseph Brevard Kershaw	S/Maj.Gen.
January 9, 1822	John Porter Hatch	N/Brig.Gen.
January 27, 1822	Thomas Leiper Kane	N/Brig.Gen.
January 30, 1822	John Basil Turchin	N/Brig.Gen.
February 16, 1822	James Patton Anderson	S/Maj.Gen.
February 16, 1822	Richard Busteed	N/Brig.Gen.
February 28, 1822	Matthew Duncan Ector	S/Brig.Gen.
March 1, 1822	Charles Champion Gilbert	N/Brig.Gen.
March 1, 1822	Albin Francisco Schoepf	N/Brig.Gen.

March 11, 1822	Allison Nelson	S/Brig.Gen.
March 16, 1822	John Pope	N/Maj.Gen.
March 22, 1822	Seth Williams	N/Brig.Gen.
April 5, 1822	James Nagle	N/Brig.Gen.
April 7, 1822	Gershom Mott	N/Brig.Gen.
April 12, 1822	George Gibbs Dibrell	S/Brig.Gen.
April 13, 1822	Leroy Augustus Stafford	S/Brig.Gen.
April 13, 1822	William Stephen Walker	S/Brig.Gen.
April 15, 1822	Napoleon Jackson T. Dana	N/Maj.Gen.
April 24, 1822	Erastus Barnard Tyler	N/Brig.Gen.
April 27, 1822	Ulysses Simpson Grant	N/Lt.Gen.
May 21, 1822	Dabney Herndon Maury	S/Maj.Gen.
May 21, 1822	Mosby Monroe Parsons	S/Maj.Gen.
June 11, 1822	Samuel Davis Sturgis	N/Brig.Gen.
June 23, 1822	Young Marshall Moody	S/Brig.Gen.
June 24, 1822	Birkett Davenport Fry	S/Brig.Gen.
July 22, 1822	Hamilton Prioleau Bee	S/Brig.Gen.
July 22, 1822	John George Walker	S/Maj.Gen.
July 23, 1822	Darius Nash Couch	N/Maj.Gen.
July 25, 1822	Schuyler Hamilton	N/Maj.Gen.
August 18, 1822	Isaac Peace Rodman	N/Brig.Gen.
August 22, 1822	George Stoneman	N/Maj.Gen.
August 25, 1822	John Newton	N/Maj.Gen.
August 31, 1822	Fitz John Porter	N/Maj.Gen.
September 19, 1822	Joseph Rodman West	N/Brig.Gen.
September 22, 1822	Eppa Hunton	S/Brig.Gen.
September 25, 1822	Adolph von Steinwehr	N/Brig.Gen.
October 4, 1822	Rutherford Birchard Hayes	N/Brig.Gen.
October 9, 1822	George Sykes	N/Maj.Gen.
October 20, 1822	Mansfield Lovell	S/Maj.Gen.
November 2, 1822	James Byron Gordon	S/Brig.Gen.
November 6, 1822	Gordon Granger	N/Maj.Gen.
November 14, 1822	William Harrow	N/Brig.Gen.
November 16, 1822	Charles Smith Hamilton	N/Maj.Gen.
November 22, 1822	Nathan Kimball	N/Brig.Gen.
December 3, 1822	Charles Adam Heckman	N/Brig.Gen.
December 8, 1822	Luther Prentice Bradley	N/Brig.Gen.
December 10, 1822	Thomas Casimer Devin	N/Brig.Gen.
December 28, 1822	William Booth Taliaferro	S/Maj.Gen.
1823	William Montague Browne	S/Brig.Gen.
January 4, 1823	Peter Joseph Osterhaus	N/Maj.Gen.
January 29, 1823	Franklin Gardner	S/Maj.Gen.
February 16, 1823	John Daniel Imboden	S/Brig.Gen.
February 27, 1823	Ferdinand Van Derveer	N/Brig.Gen.
February 27, 1823	William Buel Franklin	N/Brig.Gen.
March 12, 1823	William Flank Perry	S/Brig.Gen.
March 14, 1823	Roswell Sabine Ripley	S/Brig.Gen.
March 17, 1823	Sterling Alexander M. Wood	S/Brig.Gen.
March 20, 1823	John Echols	S/Brig.Gen.
March 25, 1823	William Thompson Martin	S/Maj.Gen.
March 30, 1823	Joseph Farmer Knipe	N/Brig.Gen.
April 1, 1823	Simon Bolivar Buckner	S/Lt.Gen.
April 4, 1823	Robert Byington Mitchell	N/Brig.Gen.
April 10, 1823	Thomas Reade Rootes Cobb	S/Brig.Gen.
April 16, 1823	Orlando Bolivar Willcox	N/Brig.Gen.
April 22, 1823	Alfred Gibbs	N/Brig.Gen.

Date	Name	Rank
May 1, 1823	Thomas Harrison	S/Brig.Gen.
May 5, 1823	James Allen Hardie	N/Brig.Gen.
May 27, 1823	John Gray Foster	N/Maj.Gen.
June 11, 1823	James Lawson Kemper	S/Maj.Gen.
June 13, 1823	Gustave Paul Cluseret	N/Brig.Gen.
July 16, 1823	James Isham Gilbert	N/Brig.Gen.
June 17, 1823	John Henry Hobart Ward	N/Brig.Gen.
June 20, 1823	Jesse Lee Reno	N/Maj.Gen.
June 21, 1823	Edward Elmer Potter	N/Brig.Gen.
July 18, 1823	Leonard Fulton Ross	N/Brig.Gen.
July 19, 1823	George Henry Gordon	N/Brig.Gen.
August 3, 1823	Thomas Francis Meagher	N/Brig.Gen.
August 8, 1823	Walter Chiles Whitaker	N/Brig.Gen.
August 9, 1823	Daniel Marsh Frost	S/Brig.Gen.
August 10, 1823	Charles Thomas Campbell	N/Brig.Gen.
August 15, 1823	Orris Sanford Ferry	N/Brig.Gen.
September 24, 1823	James Madison Tuttle	N/Brig.Gen.
September 25, 1823	Thomas John Wood	N/Maj.Gen.
September 27, 1823	James Streshly Jackson	N/Brig.Gen.
November 9, 1823	William Henry Forney	S/Brig.Gen.
November 25, 1823	Joseph Alexander Cooper	N/Brig.Gen.
December 25, 1823	Preston Smith	S/Brig.Gen.
January 7, 1824	James Morrison Hawes	S/Brig.Gen.
January 21, 1824	Thomas Jonathon Jackson	S/Lt.Gen.
February 3, 1824	George Thomas Anderson	S/Brig.Gen.
February 3, 1824	Nathan George Evans	S/Brig.Gen.
February 8, 1824	Barnard Elliott Bee	S/Brig.Gen.
February 14, 1824	Winfield Scott Hancock	N/Maj.Gen.
February 17, 1824	William Farrar Smith	N/Maj.Gen.
February 23, 1824	Lewis Cass Hunt	N/Brig.Gen.
February 24, 1824	John Crawford Vaughn	S/Brig.Gen.
February 28, 1824	John Creed Moore	S/Brig.Gen.
March 2, 1824	Henry Beebee Carrington	N/Brig.Gen.
March 10, 1824	Thomas James Churchill	S/Maj.Gen.
March 22, 1824	William Henry C. Whiting	S/Maj.Gen.
March 30, 1824	Innis Newton Palmer	N/Brig.Gen.
April 20, 1824	Alfred Holt Colquitt	S/Brig.Gen.
May 5, 1824	Thomas Welsh	N/Brig.Gen.
May 9, 1824	William Edmonson Jones	S/Brig.Gen.
May 16, 1824	Edmund Kirby Smith	S/General
May 23, 1824	Ambrose Everett Burnside	N/Maj.Gen.
May 29, 1824	Cadmus Marcellus Wilcox	S/Maj.Gen.
May 31, 1824	Charles Leopold Matthies	N/Brig.Gen.
June 3, 1824	Charles Kinnaird Graham	N/Brig.Gen.
June 8, 1824	William Gardner	S/Brig.Gen.
June 20, 1824	John Tyler Morgan	S/Brig.Gen.
June 28, 1824	William Tatum Wofford	S/Brig.Gen.
July 7, 1824	Alfred Pleasonton	N/Maj.Gen.
July 8, 1824	Wladimir Krzyzanowski	N/Brig.Gen.
July 20, 1824	Alexander Schimmelfennig	N/Brig.Gen.
July 23, 1824	Gabriel Colvin Wharton	S/Brig.Gen.
July 25, 1824	Richard James Oglesby	N/Maj.Gen.
August 1, 1824	Henry Shaw Briggs	N/Brig.Gen.
August 9, 1824	Simon Goodell Griffin	N/Brig.Gen.
August 14, 1824	William Terry	S/Brig.Gen.
August 18, 1824	John Wynn Davidson	N/Brig.Gen.

August 20, 1824	Absalom Baird	N/Brig.Gen.
August 21, 1824	John Sanford Mason	N/Brig.Gen.
August 27, 1824	Hiram Gregory Berry	N/Maj.Gen.
August 27, 1824	Max Weber	N/Brig.Gen.
September 1, 1824	Isaac Hardin Duval	N/Brig.Gen.
September 21, 1824	Joseph Andrew Lightburn	N/Brig.Gen.
September 24, 1824	Truman Seymour	N/Brig.Gen.
September 27, 1824	William Nelson	N/Maj.Gen.
September 30, 1824	Charles Pomeroy Stone	N/Brig.Gen.
October 19, 1824	Rufus Saxton	N/Brig.Gen.
October 23, 1824	Thomas Gamble Pitcher	N/Brig.Gen.
October 26, 1824	Arthur Manigault	S/Brig.Gen.
October 29, 1824	Joseph Horace Lewis	S/Brig.Gen.
November 18, 1824	Isham Nicholas Haynie	N/Brig.Gen.
November 18, 1824	Franz Sigel	N/Maj.Gen.
December 17, 1824	Manning Ferguson Force	N/Brig.Gen.
December 26, 1824	Augustus Louis Chetlain	N/Brig.Gen.
January 10, 1825	Alexander Hawthorne	S/Brig.Gen.
January 12, 1825	Joseph Robert Davis	S/Brig.Gen.
January 28, 1825	George Edward Pickett	S/Maj.Gen.
February 3, 1825	William Lowther Jackson	S/Brig.Gen.
February 28, 1825	Quincy Adams Gillmore	N/Maj.Gen.
March 5, 1825	John Dunovant	S/Brig.Gen.
March 20, 1825	William Nelson R. Beall	S/Brig.Gen.
March 23, 1825	Edward Lloyd Thomas	S/Brig.Gen.
March 30, 1825	Samuel Bell Maxey	S/Maj.Gen.
March 31, 1825	Washington Elliott	N/Brig.Gen.
April 5, 1825	David Rumph Jones	S/Maj.Gen.
April 28, 1825	James Winning McMillan	N/Brig.Gen.
May 6, 1825	Joseph Bailey	N/Brig.Gen.
May 10, 1825	William Henry Powell	N/Brig.Gen.
May 21, 1825	George Lafayette Beal	N/Brig.Gen.
May 29, 1825	David Bell Birney	N/Maj.Gen.
June 1, 1825	John Hunt Morgan	S/Brig.Gen.
June 12, 1825	John Cook	N/Brig.Gen.
June 13, 1825	Benjamin Jefferson Hill	S/Brig.Gen.
June 17, 1825	Egbert Ludovicus Viele	N/Brig.Gen.
July 1, 1825	John Adams	S/Brig.Gen.
July 4, 1825	William Andrew Quarles	S/Brig.Gen.
July 11, 1825	Edward Henry Hobson	N/Brig.Gen.
July 28, 1825	William Duncan Smith	S/Brig.Gen.
July 31, 1825	Thomas Hart Taylor	S/Brig.Gen.
August 25, 1825	Henry Warner Birge	N/Brig.Gen.
September 3, 1825	William Wallace Burns	N/Brig.Gen.
September 3, 1825	Armistead Lindsay Long	S/Brig.Gen.
September 9, 1825	James Camp Tappan	S/Brig.Gen.
October 11, 1825	Elkanah Brackin Greer	S/Brig.Gen.
October 16, 1825	Thomas Turpin Crittenden	N/Brig.Gen.
October 31, 1825	Raleigh Edward Colston	S/Brig.Gen.
November 1, 1825	Joseph Benjamin Palmer	S/Brig.Gen.
November 5, 1825	Julius Stahel	N/Maj.Gen.
November 9, 1825	Ambrose Powell Hill	S/Lt.Gen.
November 25, 1825	Edward Augustus Wild	N/Brig.Gen.
December 16, 1825	Henry Heth	S/Maj.Gen.
December 18, 1825	Charles Griffin	N/Maj.Gen.
December 20, 1825	Romeyn Beck Ayres	N/Brig.Gen.

January 12, 1826	Charles Cruft	N/Brig.Gen.
January 27, 1826	Richard Taylor	S/Lt.Gen.
February 4, 1826	Halbert Eleazer Paine	N/Brig.Gen.
February 9, 1826	John Alexander Logan	N/Maj.Gen.
March 4, 1826	John Buford	N/Brig.Gen.
March 19, 1826	George Francis McGinnis	N/Brig.Gen.
April 2, 1826	Philip Dale Roddey	S/Brig.Gen.
April 7, 1826	Friedrich Salomon	N/Brig.Gen.
April 9, 1826	Thomas Hewson Neill	N/Brig.Gen.
April 26, 1826	Ambrose Ransom Wright	S/Maj.Gen.
July 4, 1826	Green Clay Smith	N/Brig.Gen.
July 8, 1826	Benjamin Henry Grierson	N/Brig.Gen.
July 21, 1826	James Gillpatrick Blunt	N/Maj.Gen.
August 2, 1826	William Denison Whipple	N/Brig.Gen.
August 24, 1826	George Ear Maney	S/Brig.Gen.
August 27, 1826	Franklin Nickerson	N/Brig.Gen.
September 9, 1826	Thomas John Lucas	N/Brig.Gen.
October 7, 1826	William Brimage Bate	S/Maj.Gen.
October 8, 1826	Matt Whitaker Ransom	S/Brig.Gen.
October 31, 1826	Hugh Boyle Ewing	N/Brig.Gen.
October 31, 1826	Joseph Roswell Hawley	N/Brig.Gen.
November 2, 1826	Robert Hopkins Hatton	S/Brig.Gen.
November 2, 1826	William Haines Lytle	N/Brig.Gen.
November 3, 1826	Jasper Adalmorn Maltby	N/Brig.Gen.
November 17, 1826	John McArthur	N/Brig.Gen.
November 30, 1826	George Deitzler	N/Brig.Gen.
December 1, 1826	William Mahone	S/Maj.Gen.
December 3, 1826	George Brinton McClellan	N/Maj.Gen.
December 5, 1826	John Benjamin Sanborn	N/Brig.Gen.
December 22, 1826	James Scott Negley	N/Maj.Gen.
January 1, 1827	William Lewis Cabell	S/Brig.Gen.
January 6, 1827	John Calvin Brown	S/Maj.Gen.
January 6, 1827	John Wesley Frazer	S/Brig.Gen.
January 8, 1827	James Holt Clanton	S/Brig.Gen.
February 2, 1827	Abner Monroe Perrin	S/Brig.Gen.
February 19, 1827	Charles Robert Woods	N/Brig.Gen.
February 20, 1827	Edward Stuyvesant Bragg	N/Brig.Gen.
February 22, 1827	James Barnet Fry	N/Brig.Gen.
February 24, 1827	Charles Davis Jameson	N/Brig.Gen.
February 27, 1827	Richard W. Johnson	N/Brig.Gen.
March 7, 1827	Henry DeLamar Clayton	S/Maj.Gen.
March 12, 1827	John Robert Jones	S/Brig.Gen.
March 12, 1827	William Richard Terry	S/Brig.Gen.
March 19, 1827	Johnson Kelly Duncan	S/Brig.Gen.
March 19, 1827	Alexander Shaler	N/Brig.Gen.
March 24, 1827	William Henry Wallace	S/Brig.Gen.
April 10, 1827	Lewis Wallace	N/Maj.Gen.
April 20, 1827	John Gibbon	N/Maj.Gen.
April 22, 1827	William Hopkins Morris	N/Brig.Gen.
April 26, 1827	Charles Edward Hovey	N/Brig.Gen.
May 9, 1827	William Feimster Tucker	S/Brig.Gen.
May 29, 1827	Reuben Lindsay Walker	S/Brig.Gen.
June 1827	James Edwin Slaughter	S/Brig.Gen.
June 5, 1827	Beverly Robertson	S/Brig.Gen.
July 1, 1827	Stephen Gardner Champlin	N/Brig.Gen.
July 7, 1827	James Shackelford	N/Brig.Gen.

July 24, 1827	Julius Adolph deLagnel	S/Brig.Gen.
July 28, 1827	William Edwin Baldwin	S/Brig.Gen.
July 28, 1827	John Wallace Fuller	N/Brig.Gen.
August 22, 1827	Joseph Anthony Mower	N/Maj.Gen.
August 24, 1827	Walter Husted Stevens	S/Brig.Gen.
August 27, 1827	Roger Weightman Hanson	S/Brig.Gen.
September 21, 1827	Michael Corcoran	N/Brig.Gen.
September 22, 1827	John Grubb Parke	N/Maj.Gen.
September 24, 1827	Henry Warner Slocum	N/Maj.Gen.
September 30, 1827	Kenner Garrard	N/Brig.Gen.
October 2, 1827	Edmund Jackson Davis	N/Brig.Gen.
October 14, 1827	James Sidney Robinson	N/Brig.Gen.
November 10, 1827	Alfred Howe Terry	N/Maj.Gen.
November 14, 1827	Isaac Jones Wistar	N/Brig.Gen.
November 19, 1827	Isaac Munroe St.John	S/Brig.Gen.
November 26, 1827	Alfred Moore Scales	S/Brig.Gen.
December 28, 1827	Robert Latimer McCook	N/Brig.Gen.
1828	James McQueen McIntosh	S/Brig.Gen.
January 5, 1828	August Valentine Kautz	N/Brig.Gen.
January 17, 1828	Lewis Addison Grant	N/Brig.Gen.
January 23, 1828	Calvin Edward Pratt	N/Brig.Gen.
January 27, 1828	Samuel Allen Rice	N/Brig.Gen.
January 28, 1828	Thomas Carmichael Hindman	S/Maj.Gen.
February 8, 1828	John King Jackson	S/Brig.Gen.
February 12, 1828	Robert Ransom,Jr.	S/Maj.Gen.
February 22, 1828	Robert Alexander Cameron	N/Brig.Gen.
February 29, 1828	Edward Needles Kirk	N/Brig.Gen.
March 1, 1828	James Fleming Fagan	S/Maj.Gen.
March 2, 1828	Jefferson Columbus Davis	N/Brig.Gen.
March 4, 1828	Elisha Franklin Paxton	S/Brig.Gen.
March 17, 1828	Patrick Ronayne Cleburne	S/Maj.Gen.
April 6, 1828	Charles William Field	S/Maj.Gen.
April 8, 1828	George Baird Hodge	S/Brig.Gen.
April 12, 1828	Richard Arnold	N/Brig.Gen.
April 24, 1828	Robert Brank Vance	S/Brig.Gen.
May 19, 1828	Adin Ballou Underwood	N/Brig.Gen.
May 20, 1828	James William Reilly	N/Brig.Gen.
May 28, 1828	Alpheus Baker	S/Brig.Gen.
June 1, 1828	David Sloane Stanley	N/Maj.Gen.
June 4, 1828	Alexander William Campbell	S/Brig.Gen.
June 27, 1828	Junius Daniel	S/Brig.Gen.
July 3, 1828	John Austin Wharton	S/Maj.Gen.
July 4, 1828	James Johnston Pettigrew	S/Brig.Gen.
July 19, 1828	Roger Atkinson Pryor	S/Brig.Gen.
July 29, 1828	Cuvier Grover	N/Brig.Gen.
August 16, 1828	Joseph Bradford Carr	N/Brig.Gen.
August 24, 1828	George Hume Steuart	S/Brig.Gen.
August 28, 1828	William Alexander Hammond	N/Brig.Gen.
August 31, 1828	George Leonard Andrews	N/Brig.Gen.
September 6, 1828	John Morrison Oliver	N/Brig.Gen.
September 8, 1828	Joshua Chamberlain	N/Brig.Gen.
September 8, 1828	George Crook	N/Maj.Gen.
September 28, 1828	John Gregg	S/Brig.Gen.
October 23, 1828	Turner Ashby	S/Brig.Gen.
October 27, 1828	Jacob Dolson Cox	N/Maj.Gen.
November 2, 1828	Bryan Grimes	S/Maj.Gen.

November 14, 1828	James Birdseye McPherson	N/Maj.Gen.
November 21, 1828	William McComb	S/Brig.Gen.
December 8, 1828	Robert Bullock	S/Brig.Gen.
December 8, 1828	Clinton Bowen Fisk	N/Brig.Gen.
December 16, 1828	John Beatty	N/Brig.Gen.
December 25, 1828	William Plummer Benton	N/Brig.Gen.
December 30, 1828	Mark Perrin Lowrey	S/Brig.Gen.
1829	Thomas Moore Scott	S/Brig.Gen.
January 24, 1829	Adam Jacoby Slemmer	N/Brig.Gen.
January 30, 1829	Alfred Cumming	S/Brig.Gen.
February 1, 1829	John Potts Slough	N/Brig.Gen.
February 8, 1829	James Williamson	N/Brig.Gen.
February 11, 1829	William Anderson Pile	N/Brig.Gen.
February 14, 1829	Alfred Iverson,Jr.	S/Brig.Gen.
February 18, 1829	Jean Jacques Mouton	S/Brig.Gen.
February 21, 1829	Johnson Hagood	S/Brig.Gen.
March 2, 1829	Carl Schurz	N/Maj.Gen.
March 18, 1829	William Robertson Boggs	S/Brig.Gen.
March 29, 1829	Robert Emmett Rodes	S/Maj.Gen.
June 1, 1829	Cullen Andrews Battle	S/Brig.Gen.
June 6, 1829	John Baillie McIntosh	N/Brig.Gen.
July 4, 1829	Daniel Chevilette Govan	S/Brig.Gen.
July 16, 1829	Robert Brown Potter	N/Brig.Gen.
August 5, 1829	Milo Smith Hascall	N/Brig.Gen.
August 7, 1829	Thomas Ewing,Jr.	N/Brig.Gen.
August 12, 1829	John Horace Forney	S/Maj.Gen.
September 1, 1829	James Conner	S/Brig.Gen.
September 8, 1829	Seth Maxwell Barton	S/Brig.Gen.
September 20, 1829	Byron Root Pierce	N/Brig.Gen.
September 22, 1829	William Worth Belknap	N/Brig.Gen.
September 22, 1829	George Day Wagner	N/Brig.Gen.
September 24, 1829	James St.Clair Morton	N/Brig.Gen.
September 29, 1829	Bradley Tyler Johnson	S/Brig.Gen.
September 29, 1829	Giles Alexander Smith	N/Brig.Gen.
October 10, 1829	Dandridge McRae	S/Brig.Gen.
October 18, 1829	Lucius Marshall Walker	S/Brig.Gen.
October 18, 1829	Charles Sidney Winder	S/Brig.Gen.
October 27, 1829	Christopher Andrews	N/Brig.Gen.
November 8, 1829	Samuel Wylie Crawford	N/Brig.Gen.
November 24, 1829	William Passmore Carlin	N/Brig.Gen.
December 3, 1829	Green Berry Raum	N/Brig.Gen.
December 27, 1829	James Clay Rice	N/Brig.Gen.
January 8, 1830	Gouverneur Kemble Warren	N/Maj.Gen.
January 19, 1830	George Blake Cosby	S/Brig.Gen.
January 27, 1830	William Henry F. Payne	S/Brig.Gen.
February 6, 1830	Marcellus Monroe Crocker	N/Brig.Gen.
March 10, 1830	Robert Lowry	S/Brig.Gen.
March 12, 1830	William Felix Brantley	S/Brig.Gen.
March 20, 1830	Eugene Asa Carr	N/Brig.Gen.
April 14, 1830	Davis Tillson	N/Brig.Gen.
May 1, 1830	William Young Conn Humes	S/Brig.Gen.
May 10, 1830	Alfred Jefferson Vaughan	S/Brig.Gen.
May 11, 1830	John Converse Starkweather	N/Brig.Gen.
May 14, 1830	George Pierce Doles	S/Brig.Gen.
May 15, 1830	Laurence Simmons Baker	S/Brig.Gen.
May 28, 1830	George Lucas Hartsuff	N/Maj.Gen.

May 30, 1830	Edward Winslow Hincks	N/Brig.Gen.
June 17, 1830	Richard Montgomery Gano	S/Brig.Gen.
July 2, 1830	John Bordenave Villepigue	S/Brig.Gen.
July 22, 1830	William Sooy Smith	N/Brig.Gen.
July 29, 1830	Alvan Cullem Gillem	N/Brig.Gen.
September 27, 1830	William Babcock Hazen	N/Maj.Gen.
September 29, 1830	John Parker Hawkins	N/Brig.Gen.
October 1, 1830	Jeremiah Cutler Sullivan	N/Brig.Gen.
October 26, 1830	Stephen Elliott,Jr.	S/Brig.Gen.
October 30, 1830	John Stevens Bowen	S/Maj.Gen.
November 8, 1830	Oliver Otis Howard	N/Maj.Gen.
November 10, 1830	Albert Gallatin Jenkins	S/Brig.Gen.
December 12, 1830	Joseph Orville Shelby	S/Brig.Gen.
December 14, 1830	Allen Thomas	S/Brig.Gen.
December 16, 1830	Samuel Garland,Jr.	S/Brig.Gen.
December 16, 1830	John Frederick Hartranft	N/Brig.Gen.
1831	Archibald Campbell Godwin	S/Brig.Gen.
January 11, 1831	James Ronald Chalmers	S/Brig.Gen.
January 14, 1831	John Bullock Clark,Jr.	S/Brig.Gen.
January 18, 1831	Edward Ferrero	N/Brig.Gen.
January 28, 1831	Henry Brevard Davidson	S/Brig.Gen.
February 13, 1831	John Aaron Rawlins	N/Brig.Gen.
March 1, 1831	Hiram Bronson Granbury	S/Brig.Gen.
March 6, 1831	Philip Henry Sheridan	N/Maj.Gen.
March 7, 1831	John Bratton	S/Brig.Gen.
March 15, 1831	Edward Aylesworth Perry	S/Brig.Gen.
March 25, 1831	Martin Witherspoon Gary	S/Brig.Gen.
April 4, 1831	Edward Cary Walthall	S/Maj.Gen.
April 12, 1831	George Burgwyn Anderson	S/Brig.Gen.
April 12, 1831	Grenville Mellen Dodge	N/Maj.Gen.
April 22, 1831	Alexander McDowell McCook	N/Maj.Gen.
June 1, 1831	John Bell Hood	S/General
June 2, 1831	Benjamin Hardin Helm	S/Brig.Gen.
June 3, 1831	Otho French Strahl	S/Brig.Gen.
June 5, 1831	Marcus Joseph Wright	S/Brig.Gen.
July 1, 1831	James Argyle Smith	S/Brig.Gen.
July 14, 1831	William Dwight	N/Brig.Gen.
August 19, 1831	Stephen Gano Burbridge	N/Brig.Gen.
September 3, 1831	States Rights Gist	S/Brig.Gen.
September 29, 1831	John McAllister Schofield	N/Maj.Gen.
October 31, 1831	Daniel Butterfield	N/Maj.Gen.
November 17, 1831	Stephen Hinsdale Weed	N/Brig.Gen.
November 19, 1831	James Abram Garfield	N/Maj.Gen.
November 21, 1831	John Franklin Miller	N/Brig.Gen.
December 6, 1831	Joshua Woodrow Sill	N/Brig.Gen.
December 22, 1831	Robert Ogden Tyler	N/Brig.Gen.
December 27, 1831	Lucius Fairchild	N/Brig.Gen.
January 12, 1832	Richard Waterhouse	S/Brig.Gen.
January 24, 1832	John Pegram	S/Brig.Gen.
February 6, 1832	John Brown Gordon	S/Maj.Gen.
February 16, 1832	Camille A.J.M.P. Polignac	S/Maj.Gen.
February 17, 1832	William Ward Orme	N/Brig.Gen.
March 7, 1832	Orlando Metcalfe Poe	N/Brig.Gen.
March 11, 1832	William Ruffin Cox	S/Brig.Gen.
March 16, 1832	Charles Camp Doolittle	N/Brig.Gen.
March 17, 1832	Walter Quintin Gresham	N/Brig.Gen.

April 14, 1832	James Hewett Ledlie	N/Brig.Gen.
May 30, 1832	George Doherty Johnston	S/Brig.Gen.
June 24, 1832	Edward Harland	N/Brig.Gen.
August 23, 1832	Alexander Chambers	N/Brig.Gen.
August 27, 1832	James Alexander Walker	S/Brig.Gen.
September 10, 1832	Randall Lee Gibson	S/Brig.Gen.
September 16, 1832	George Washington C. Lee	S/Maj.Gen.
September 21, 1832	Samuel Sprigg Carroll	N/Brig.Gen.
October 15, 1832	Henry Harrison Walker	S/Brig.Gen.
October 16, 1832	George Crockett Strong	N/Brig.Gen.
November 5, 1832	William Woods Averell	N/Brig.Gen.
November 22, 1832	George Henry Chapman	N/Brig.Gen.
December 1, 1832	Archibald Gracie,Jr.	S/Brig.Gen.
December 14, 1832	Daniel Harris Reynolds	S/Brig.Gen.
December 22, 1832	Edward Hatch	N/Brig.Gen.
December 25, 1832	Thomas Alfred Smyth	N/Brig.Gen.
1833	Robert Charles Tyler	S/Brig.Gen.
January 23, 1833	John Randolph Chambliss	S/Brig.Gen.
February 6, 1833	James Ewell Brown Stuart	S/Maj.Gen.
February 6, 1833	Jacob Hunter Sharp	S/Brig.Gen.
February 13, 1833	William Whedbee Kirkland	S/Brig.Gen.
February 18, 1833	James Deshler	S/Brig.Gen.
February 25, 1833	Clement Anselm Evans	S/Brig.Gen.
March 14, 1833	John Sappington Marmaduke	S/Maj.Gen.
April 2, 1833	Thomas Howard Ruger	N/Brig.Gen.
April 10, 1833	David McMurtrie Gregg	N/Brig.Gen.
April 10, 1833	James Edwards Rains	S/Brig.Gen.
April 17, 1833	John Curtis Caldwell	N/Brig.Gen.
May 8, 1833	Frank Wheaton	N/Brig.Gen.
June 9, 1833	John Rogers Cooke	S/Brig.Gen.
June 15, 1833	Edward Moody McCook	N/Brig.Gen.
July 1, 1833	Alfred Thomas A. Torbert	N/Brig.Gen.
July 10, 1833	Lucius Eugene Polk	S/Brig.Gen.
July 19, 1833	John Wesley Turner	N/Brig.Gen.
July 28, 1833	James Henry Lane	S/Brig.Gen.
August 7, 1833	Powell Clayton	N/Brig.Gen.
August 12, 1833	William Price Sanders	N/Brig.Gen.
August 26, 1833	Charles Jackson Paine	N/Brig.Gen.
September 22, 1833	Stephen Dill Lee	S/Lt.Gen.
September 28, 1833	James Deering Fessenden	N/Brig.Gen.
October 5, 1833	Cyrus Bussey	N/Brig.Gen.
November 5, 1833	Edward Dorr Tracy	S/Brig.Gen.
December 17, 1833	James Thadeus Holtzclaw	S/Brig.Gen.
December 18, 1833	Thomas Pleasant Dockery	S/Brig.Gen.
December 28, 1833	Charles Miller Shelley	S/Brig.Gen.
January 16, 1834	Albert Lindley Lee	N/Brig.Gen.
January 27, 1834	Robert Sanford Foster	N/Brig.Gen.
February 6, 1834	William Dorsey Pender	S/Maj.Gen.
February 8, 1834	Adam Rankin Johnson	S/Brig.Gen.
March 22, 1834	Francis Asbury Shoup	S/Brig.Gen.
April 21, 1834	William Rufus Terrill	N/Brig.Gen.
June 14, 1834	Thomas Wilberforce Egan	N/Brig.Gen.
June 16, 1834	Wesley Merritt	N/Maj.Gen.
August 20, 1834	Francis Redding Nicholls	S/Brig.Gen.
August 22, 1834	Nathaniel Harrison Harris	S/Brig.Gen.
September 9, 1834	William MacRae	S/Brig.Gen.

October 1, 1834	Francis Marion Cockrell	S/Brig.Gen.
October 19, 1834	Francis Channing Barlow	N/Brig.Gen.
October 28, 1834	Dudley McIver DuBose	S/Brig.Gen.
November 3, 1834	Samuel Wragg Ferguson	S/Brig.Gen.
November 10, 1834	Wager Swayne	N/Brig.Gen.
November 21, 1834	Joseph Jackson Bartlett	N/Brig.Gen.
November 29, 1834	Thomas Edward G. Ransom	N/Brig.Gen.
February 15, 1835	Alexander Stewart Webb	N/Brig.Gen.
April 27, 1835	John Murray Corse	N/Brig.Gen.
May 1, 1835	Alfred Napoleon A. Duffie	N/Brig.Gen.
May 21, 1835	Newton Martin Curtis	N/Brig.Gen.
May 26, 1835	Edward Porter Alexander	S/Brig.Gen.
June 1, 1835	Francis Laurens Vinton	N/Brig.Gen.
August 26, 1835	Theodore Washington Brevard	S/Brig.Gen.
September 3, 1835	William Gaston Lewis	S/Brig.Gen.
September 11, 1835	William Wirt Allen	S/Brig.Gen.
September 14, 1835	Joseph Hayes	N/Brig.Gen.
October 1, 1835	Robert Houstoun Anderson	S/Brig.Gen.
October 1, 1835	William Hicks Jackson	S/Brig.Gen.
October 31, 1835	Adelbert Ames	N/Brig.Gen.
November 1, 1835	Godfrey Weitzel	N/Maj.Gen.
November 4, 1835	Lunsford Lindsay Lomax	S/Maj.Gen.
November 16, 1835	Elliott Warren Rice	N/Brig.Gen.
November 19, 1835	Fitzhugh Lee	S/Maj.Gen.
November 22, 1835	Frank Crawford Armstrong	S/Brig.Gen.
December 1, 1835	Micah Jenkins	S/Brig.Gen.
December 2, 1835	Charles Garrison Harker	N/Brig.Gen.
December 18, 1835	George Dashiell Bayard	N/Brig.Gen.
January 14, 1836	Hugh Judson Kilpatrick	N/Brig.Gen.
January 28, 1836	Robert Doak Lilley	S/Brig.Gen.
January 29, 1836	Benjamin Franklin Potts	N/Brig.Gen.
February 3, 1836	Thomas Greely Stevenson	N/Brig.Gen.
February 22, 1836	Hylan Benton Lyon	S/Brig.Gen.
March 8, 1836	Matthew Calbraith Butler	S/Maj.Gen.
May 8, 1836	Bryan Morel Thomas	S/Brig.Gen.
May 14, 1836	James Patrick Major	S/Brig.Gen.
May 27, 1836	Edwin Gray Lee	S/Brig.Gen.
July 2, 1836	Henry Eugene Davies	N/Brig.Gen.
August 7, 1836	Evander McIvor Law	S/Brig.Gen.
September 10, 1836	Joseph Wheeler	S/Maj.Gen.
September 13, 1836	John McCausland	S/Brig.Gen.
October 5, 1836	George Washington Gordon	S/Brig.Gen.
October 15, 1836	Thomas Lafayette Rosser	S/Maj.Gen.
November 15, 1836	Pierce Manning B. Young	S/Maj.Gen.
November 20, 1836	John Thomas Croxton	N/Brig.Gen.
January 16, 1837	James Phillip Simms	S/Brig.Gen.
February 17, 1837	Francis Jay Herron	N/Maj.Gen.
March 19, 1837	Robert Daniel Johnston	S/Brig.Gen.
April 4, 1837	Henry Goddard Thomas	N/Brig.Gen.
May 27, 1837	Robert Frederick Hoke	S/Maj.Gen.
May 31, 1837	Stephen Dodson Ramseur	S/Maj.Gen.
May 31, 1837	William Henry F. Lee	S/Maj.Gen.
June 16, 1837	Eli Long	N/Brig.Gen.
June 26, 1837	Victor Jean B. Girardey	S/Brig.Gen.
June 26, 1837	Martin Davis Hardin	N/Brig.Gen.
July 30, 1837	Elon John Farnsworth	N/Brig.Gen.

September 2, 1837	James Harrison Wilson	N/Brig.Gen.
October 14, 1837	Ellison Capers	S/Brig.Gen.
October 26, 1837	James Lawlor Kiernan	N/Brig.Gen.
December 19, 1837	John Carpenter Carter	S/Brig.Gen.
January 1, 1838	William Hugh Young	S/Brig.Gen.
February 12, 1838	Charles Carroll Walcutt	N/Brig.Gen.
February 23, 1838	Gilbert Moxley Sorrel	S/Brig.Gen.
February 24, 1838	Thomas Benton Smith	S/Brig.Gen.
May 28, 1838	Basil Wilson Duke	S/Brig.Gen.
June 23, 1838	Edwin Henry Stoughton	N/Brig.Gen.
July 21, 1838	John Rutter Brooke	N/Brig.Gen.
September 27, 1838	Lawrence Sullivan Ross	S/Brig.Gen.
November 6, 1838	John Grant Mitchell	N/Brig.Gen.
January 25, 1839	Selden Connor	N/Brig.Gen.
March 9, 1839	Felix Huston Robertson	S/Brig.Gen.
March 18, 1839	Francis Fessenden	N/Brig.Gen.
April 26, 1839	Cyrus Hamlin	N/Brig.Gen.
June 18, 1839	William Henry Seward,Jr.	N/Brig.Gen.
June 21, 1839	John Decatur Barry	S/Brig.Gen.
August 8, 1839	Nelson Appleton Miles	N/Brig.Gen.
August 27, 1839	Emory Upton	N/Brig.Gen.
December 5, 1839	George Armstrong Custer	N/Brig.Gen.
January 5, 1840	John Doby Kennedy	S/Brig.Gen.
March 31, 1840	John Herbert Kelly	S/Brig.Gen.
April 4, 1840	John Caldwell C. Sanders	S/Brig.Gen.
April 25, 1840	James Dearing	S/Brig.Gen.
June 6, 1840	William Francis Bartlett	N/Brig.Gen.
June 10, 1840	Thomas Fentress Toon	S/Brig.Gen.
July 27, 1840	Ranald Slidell Mackenzie	N/Brig.Gen.
November 3, 1840	Thomas Muldrup Logan	S/Brig.Gen.
July 11, 1841	William Paul Roberts	S/Brig.Gen.
September 16, 1841	Charles Cleveland Dodge	N/Brig.Gen.

6

Civil War Generals
by Month of Birth

The generals are listed below first according to the month they were born, then by the day of the month, and finally by the year. There are thirteen generals where the month of birth was not able to be determined; these are ommitted. Some of the men have only the month listed, with the day unknown.

DATE OF BIRTH	GENERAL	SIDE/RANK
January 1, 1819	George Foster Shepley	N/Brig.Gen.
January 1, 1827	William Lewis Cabell	S/Brig.Gen.
January 1, 1838	William Hugh Young	S/Brig.Gen.
January 4, 1821	John James Peck	N/Maj.Gen.
January 4, 1822	Joseph Jones Reynolds	N/Maj.Gen.
January 4, 1823	Peter Joseph Osterhaus	N/Maj.Gen.
January 5, 1813	Thomas Neville Waul	S/Brig.Gen.
January 5, 1822	Joseph Brevard Kershaw	S/Maj.Gen.
January 5, 1828	August Valentine Kautz	N/Brig.Gen.
January 5, 1840	John Doby Kennedy	S/Brig.Gen.
January 6, 1807	Joseph Holt	N/Brig.Gen.
January 6, 1827	John Calvin Brown	S/Maj.Gen.
January 6, 1827	John Wesley Frazer	S/Brig.Gen.
January 7, 1799	Daniel Tyler	N/Brig.Gen.
January 7, 1806	Jacob Ammen	N/Brig.Gen.
January 7, 1816	Stephen Miller	N/Brig.Gen.
January 7, 1821	Lucius Jeremiah Gartrell	S/Brig.Gen.
January 7, 1824	James Morrison Hawes	S/Brig.Gen.
January 8, 1814	Thomas Green	S/Brig.Gen.
January 8, 1815	Lawrence Pike Graham	N/Brig.Gen.
January 8, 1815	George Webb Morell	N/Maj.Gen.
January 8, 1817	John Selden Roane	S/Brig.Gen.
January 8, 1821	James Longstreet	S/Lt.Gen.
January 8, 1827	James Holt Clanton	S/Brig.Gen.
January 8, 1830	Gouverneur Kemble Warren	N/Maj.Gen.
January 9, 1822	John Porter Hatch	N/Brig.Gen.
January 10, 1815	Alexander Brydie Dyer	N/Brig.Gen.
January 10, 1815	Thomas Williams	N/Brig.Gen.
January 10, 1825	Alexander Travis Hawthorne	S/Brig.Gen.
January 11, 1807	Alfred Eugene Jackson	S/Brig.Gen.
January 11, 1814	Richard Griffith	S/Brig.Gen.

January 11, 1816	Fitz-Henry Warren	N/Brig.Gen.
January 11, 1818	John Reese Kenly	N/Brig.Gen.
January 11, 1831	James Ronald Chalmers	S/Brig.Gen.
January 12, 1814	Jones Mitchell Withers	S/Maj.Gen.
January 12, 1816	Willis Arnold Gorman	N/Brig.Gen.
January 12, 1819	Zealous Bates Tower	N/Brig.Gen.
January 12, 1825	Joseph Robert Davis	S/Brig.Gen.
January 12, 1826	Charles Cruft	N/Brig.Gen.
January 12, 1832	Richard Waterhouse	S/Brig.Gen.
January 13, 1807	Napoleon Bonaparte Buford	N/Brig.Gen.
January 13, 1812	Humphrey Marshall	S/Brig.Gen.
January 13, 1815	William Henry French	N/Maj.Gen.
January 14, 1819	Frederick Steele	N/Maj.Gen.
January 14, 1831	John Bullock Clark,Jr.	S/Brig.Gen.
January 14, 1836	Hugh Judson Kilpatrick	N/Brig.Gen.
January 15, 1815	Henry Morris Naglee	N/Brig.Gen.
January 15, 1817	Lewis Golding Arnold	N/Brig.Gen.
January 15, 1821	John Cabell Breckinridge	S/Maj.Gen.
January 15, 1821	Lafayette McLaws	S/Maj.Gen.
January 16, 1815	Henry Wager Halleck	N/Maj.Gen.
January 16, 1834	Albert Lindley Lee	N/Brig.Gen.
January 16, 1837	James Phillip Simms	S/Brig.Gen.
January 17, 1828	Lewis Addison Grant	N/Brig.Gen.
January 18, 1809	Richard Caswell Gatlin	S/Brig.Gen.
January 18, 1815	James Chesnut, Jr.	S/Brig.Gen.
January 18, 1817	William Whann Mackall	S/Brig.Gen.
January 18, 1820	Abraham Buford	S/Brig.Gen.
January 18, 1831	Edward Ferrero	N/Brig.Gen.
January 19, 1807	Robert Edward Lee	S/General
January 19, 1816	Henry Gray	S/Brig.Gen.
January 19, 1830	George Blake Cosby	S/Brig.Gen.
January 20, 1812	Ralph Pomeroy Buckland	N/Brig.Gen.
January 20, 1813	Jacob Gartner Lauman	N/Brig.Gen.
January 21, 1813	John Charles Fremont	N/Maj.Gen.
January 21, 1824	Thomas Jonathon Jackson	S/Lt.Gen.
January 23, 1828	Calvin Edward Pratt	N/Brig.Gen.
January 23, 1833	John Randolph Chambliss	S/Brig.Gen.
January 24, 1820	John Milton Thayer	N/Brig.Gen.
January 24, 1829	Adam Jacoby Slemmer	N/Brig.Gen.
January 24, 1832	John Pegram	S/Brig.Gen.
January 25, 1839	Selden Connor	N/Brig.Gen.
January 26, 1814	Rufus King	N/Brig.Gen.
January 26, 1816	Lloyd Tilghman	S/Brig.Gen.
January 27, 1822	Thomas Leiper Kane	N/Brig.Gen.
January 27, 1826	Richard Taylor	S/Lt.Gen.
January 27, 1828	Samuel Allen Rice	N/Brig.Gen.
January 27, 1830	William Henry F. Payne	S/Brig.Gen.
January 27, 1834	Robert Sanford Foster	N/Brig.Gen.
January 28, 1815	Andrew Jackson Hamilton	N/Brig.Gen.
January 28, 1821	William Thomas H. Brooks	N/Maj.Gen.
January 28, 1825	George Edward Pickett	S/Maj.Gen.
January 28, 1828	Thomas Carmichael Hindman	S/Maj.Gen.
January 28, 1831	Henry Brevard Davidson	S/Brig.Gen.
January 28, 1836	Robert Doak Lilley	S/Brig.Gen.
January 29, 1821	Issac Ferdinand Quinby	N/Brig.Gen.
January 29, 1823	Franklin Gardner	S/Maj.Gen.

January 29, 1836	Benjamin Franklin Potts	N/Brig.Gen.
January 30, 1797	Edwin Vose Sumner	N/Maj.Gen.
January 30, 1816	Nathaniel Prentiss Banks	N/Maj.Gen.
January 30, 1822	John Basil Turchin	N/Brig.Gen.
January 30, 1829	Alfred Cumming	S/Brig.Gen.
January 31, 1810	Daniel Ruggles	S/Brig.Gen.
January 31, 1818	William Raine Peck	S/Brig.Gen.
February 1, 1807	William Bowen Campbell	N/Brig.Gen.
February 1, 1819	Henry Lawrence Eustis	N/Brig.Gen.
February 1, 1829	John Potts Slough	N/Brig.Gen.
February 2, 1803	Albert Sidney Johnston	S/General
February 2, 1815	Nathaniel Collins McLean	N/Brig.Gen.
February 2, 1827	Abner Monroe Perrin	S/Brig.Gen.
February 3, 1805	Samuel Ryan Curtis	N/Maj.Gen.
February 3, 1807	Joseph Johnston	S/General
February 3, 1824	George Thomas Anderson	S/Brig.Gen.
February 3, 1824	Nathan George Evans	S/Brig.Gen.
February 3, 1825	William Lowther Jackson	S/Brig.Gen.
February 3, 1836	Thomas Greely Stevenson	N/Brig.Gen.
February 4, 1826	Halbert Eleazer Paine	N/Brig.Gen.
February 6, 1830	Marcellus Monroe Crocker	N/Brig.Gen.
February 6, 1832	John Brown Gordon	S/Maj.Gen.
February 6, 1833	Jacob Hunter Sharp	S/Brig.Gen.
February 6, 1833	James Ewell Brown Stuart	S/Maj.Gen.
February 6, 1834	William Dorsey Pender	S/Maj.Gen.
February 7, 1817	Leroy Pope Walker	S/Brig.Gen.
February 8, 1811	Edwin Denison Morgan	N/Maj.Gen.
February 8, 1817	Richard Stoddert Ewell	S/Lt.Gen.
February 8, 1820	William Tecumseh Sherman	N/Maj.Gen.
February 8, 1824	Barnard Elliott Bee	S/Brig.Gen.
February 8, 1828	John King Jackson	S/Brig.Gen.
February 8, 1829	James Alexander Williamson	N/Brig.Gen.
February 8, 1834	Adam Rankin Johnson	S/Brig.Gen.
February 9, 1826	John Alexander Logan	N/Maj.Gen.
February 10, 1807	Abner Clark Harding	N/Brig.Gen.
February 10, 1821	William Read Scurry	S/Brig.Gen.
February 11, 1829	William Anderson Pile	N/Brig.Gen.
February 12, 1828	Robert Ransom,Jr.	S/Maj.Gen.
February 12, 1838	Charles Carroll Walcutt	N/Brig.Gen.
February 13, 1831	John Aaron Rawlins	N/Brig.Gen.
February 13, 1833	William Whedbee Kirkland	S/Brig.Gen.
February 14, 1813	John McNeil	N/Brig.Gen.
February 14, 1819	James Green Martin	S/Brig.Gen.
February 14, 1824	Winfield Scott Hancock	N/Maj.Gen.
February 14, 1829	Alfred Iverson,Jr.	S/Brig.Gen.
February 15, 1835	Alexander Stewart Webb	N/Brig.Gen.
February 16, 1807	Lysander Cutler	N/Brig.Gen.
February 16, 1813	Joseph Reid Anderson	S/Brig.Gen.
February 16, 1822	James Patton Anderson	S/Maj.Gen.
February 16, 1822	Richard Busteed	N/Brig.Gen.
February 16, 1823	John Daniel Imboden	S/Brig.Gen.
February 16, 1832	Camille A.J.M.P. Polignac	S/Maj.Gen.
February 17, 1804	Samuel Read Anderson	S/Brig.Gen.
February 17, 1824	William Farrar Smith	N/Maj.Gen.
February 17, 1832	William Ward Orme	N/Brig.Gen.
February 17, 1837	Francis Jay Herron	N/Maj.Gen.

February 18, 1817	Walter Paye Lane	S/Brig.Gen.
February 18, 1829	Jean Jacques A.A. Mouton	S/Brig.Gen.
February 18, 1833	James Deshler	S/Brig.Gen.
February 19, 1820	John Haskell King	N/Brig.Gen.
February 19, 1821	Francis Preston Blair,Jr.	N/Maj.Gen.
February 19, 1827	Charles Robert Woods	N/Brig.Gen.
February 20, 1809	Henry Walton Wessells	N/Brig.Gen.
February 20, 1820	Mahlon Dickerson Manson	N/Brig.Gen.
February 20, 1827	Edward Stuyvesant Bragg	N/Brig.Gen.
February 21, 1800	John Henry Winder	S/Brig.Gen.
February 21, 1802	George Douglas Ramsay	N/Brig.Gen.
February 21, 1829	Johnson Hagood	S/Brig.Gen.
February 22, 1798	Charles Mynn Thruston	N/Brig.Gen.
February 22, 1827	James Barnet Fry	N/Brig.Gen.
February 22, 1828	Robert Alexander Cameron	N/Brig.Gen.
February 22, 1836	Hylan Benton Lyon	S/Brig.Gen.
February 23, 1818	Jeremy Francis Gilmer	S/Maj.Gen.
February 23, 1824	Lewis Cass Hunt	N/Brig.Gen.
February 23, 1838	Gilbert Moxley Sorrel	S/Brig.Gen.
February 24, 1811	Edward Dickinson Baker	N/Maj.Gen.
February 24, 1824	John Crawford Vaughn	S/Brig.Gen.
February 24, 1827	Charles Davis Jameson	N/Brig.Gen.
February 24, 1838	Thomas Benton Smith	S/Brig.Gen.
February 25, 1808	James Bowen	N/Brig.Gen.
February 25, 1809	George Washington Cullum	N/Brig.Gen.
February 25, 1815	Robert Hall Chilton	S/Brig.Gen.
February 25, 1833	Clement Anselm Evans	S/Brig.Gen.
February 27, 1823	William Buel Franklin	N/Brig.Gen.
February 27, 1823	Ferdinand Van Derveer	N/Brig.Gen.
February 27, 1827	Richard W. Johnson	N/Brig.Gen.
February 28, 1817	James Craig	N/Brig.Gen.
February 28, 1822	Matthew Duncan Ector	S/Brig.Gen.
February 28, 1824	John Creed Moore	S/Brig.Gen.
February 28, 1825	Quincy Adams Gillmore	N/Maj.Gen.
February 29, 1784	John Ellis Wool	N/Maj.Gen.
February 29, 1811	Henry Hastings Sibley	N/Brig.Gen.
February 29, 1828	Edward Needles Kirk	N/Brig.Gen.
March 1, 1811	Robert Christie Buchanan	N/Brig.Gen.
March 1, 1822	Charles Champion Gilbert	N/Brig.Gen.
March 1, 1822	Albin Francisco Schoepf	N/Brig.Gen.
March 1, 1828	James Fleming Fagan	S/Maj.Gen.
March 1, 1831	Hiram Bronson Granbury	S/Brig.Gen.
March 2, 1824	Henry Beebee Carrington	N/Brig.Gen.
March 2, 1828	Jefferson Columbus Davis	N/Brig.Gen.
March 2, 1829	Carl Schurz	N/Maj.Gen.
March 4, 1798	John Joseph Abercrombie	N/Brig.Gen.
March 4, 1826	John Buford	N/Brig.Gen.
March 4, 1828	Elisha Franklin Paxton	S/Brig.Gen.
March 5, 1825	John Dunovant	S/Brig.Gen.
March 6, 1820	Horatio Gouverneur Wright	N/Maj.Gen.
March 6, 1831	Philip Henry Sheridan	N/Maj.Gen.
March 7, 1827	Henry DeLamar Clayton	S/Maj.Gen.
March 7, 1831	John Bratton	S/Brig.Gen.
March 7, 1832	Orlando Metcalfe Poe	N/Brig.Gen.
March 8, 1821	Morgan Lewis Smith	N/Brig.Gen.
March 8, 1836	Matthew Calbraith Butler	S/Maj.Gen.

March 9, 1839	Felix Huston Robertson	S/Brig.Gen.
March 10, 1818	George Wythe Randolph	S/Brig.Gen.
March 10, 1824	Thomas James Churchill	S/Maj.Gen.
March 10, 1830	Robert Lowry	S/Brig.Gen.
March 11, 1811	Marsena Rudolph Patrick	N/Brig.Gen.
March 11, 1818	John Wilkins Whitfield	S/Brig.Gen.
March 11, 1822	Allison Nelson	S/Brig.Gen.
March 11, 1832	William Ruffin Cox	S/Brig.Gen.
March 12, 1816	David Stuart	N/Brig.Gen.
March 12, 1823	William Flank Perry	S/Brig.Gen.
March 12, 1827	John Robert Jones	S/Brig.Gen.
March 12, 1827	William Richard Terry	S/Brig.Gen.
March 12, 1830	William Felix Brantley	S/Brig.Gen.
March 13, 1818	Albion Parris Howe	N/Brig.Gen.
March 13, 1820	Louis Hebert	S/Brig.Gen.
March 14, 1808	Catharinus Buckingham	N/Brig.Gen.
March 14, 1815	Jerome Bonaparte Robertson	S/Brig.Gen.
March 14, 1816	Montgomery Dent Corse	S/Brig.Gen.
March 14, 1823	Roswell Sabine Ripley	S/Brig.Gen.
March 14, 1833	John Sappington Marmaduke	S/Maj.Gen.
March 15, 1811	Robert Allen	N/Brig.Gen.
March 15, 1831	Edward Aylesworth Perry	S/Brig.Gen.
March 16, 1802	George Archibald McCall	N/Brig.Gen.
March 16, 1812	Henry Dwight Terry	N/Brig.Gen.
March 16, 1822	John Pope	N/Maj.Gen.
March 16, 1832	Charles Camp Doolittle	N/Brig.Gen.
March 17, 1820	Patrick Edward Connor	N/Brig.Gen.
March 17, 1823	Sterling Alexander Wood	S/Brig.Gen.
March 17, 1828	Patrick Ronayne Cleburne	S/Maj.Gen.
March 17, 1832	Walter Quintin Gresham	N/Brig.Gen.
March 18, 1829	William Robertson Boggs	S/Brig.Gen.
March 18, 1839	Francis Fessenden	N/Brig.Gen.
March 19, 1817	Lewis Henry Little	S/Brig.Gen.
March 19, 1819	David Henry Williams	N/Brig.Gen.
March 19, 1821	Francis Barretto Spinola	N/Brig.Gen.
March 19, 1826	George Francis McGinnis	N/Brig.Gen.
March 19, 1827	Johnson Kelly Duncan	S/Brig.Gen.
March 19, 1827	Alexander Shaler	N/Brig.Gen.
March 19, 1837	Robert Daniel Johnston	S/Brig.Gen.
March 20, 1804	Neal Dow	N/Brig.Gen.
March 20, 1812	George Bibb Crittenden	S/Maj.Gen.
March 20, 1815	John Henry Martindale	N/Brig.Gen.
March 20, 1823	John Echols	S/Brig.Gen.
March 20, 1825	William Nelson R. Beall	S/Brig.Gen.
March 20, 1830	Eugene Asa Carr	N/Brig.Gen.
March 22, 1813	Gabriel Rene Paul	N/Brig.Gen.
March 22, 1817	Braxton Bragg	S/General
March 22, 1819	William Wirt Adams	S/Brig.Gen.
March 22, 1822	Seth Williams	N/Brig.Gen.
March 22, 1824	William Henry C. Whiting	S/Maj.Gen.
March 22, 1834	Francis Asbury Shoup	S/Brig.Gen.
March 23, 1818	Don Carlos Buell	N/Maj.Gen.
March 23, 1825	Edward Lloyd Thomas	S/Brig.Gen.
March 24, 1819	Thomas Church H. Smith	N/Brig.Gen.
March 24, 1821	George Hector Tyndale	N/Brig.Gen.
March 24, 1827	William Henry Wallace	S/Brig.Gen.

March 25, 1818	Isaac Ingalls Stevens	N/Brig.Gen.
March 25, 1823	William Thompson Martin	S/Maj.Gen.
March 25, 1831	Martin Witherspoon Gary	S/Brig.Gen.
March 26, 1813	Thomas West Sherman	N/Brig.Gen.
March 26, 1817	Herman Haupt	N/Brig.Gen.
March 27, 1820	John Franklin Farnsworth	N/Brig.Gen.
March 27, 1821	Samuel Kosciuszko Zook	N/Brig.Gen.
March 28, 1818	Wade Hampton	S/Lt.Gen.
March 29, 1816	James Gallant Spears	N/Brig.Gen.
March 29, 1821	Joshua Thomas Owen	N/Brig.Gen.
March 29, 1829	Robert Emmett Rodes	S/Maj.Gen.
March 30, 1823	Joseph Farmer Knipe	N/Brig.Gen.
March 30, 1824	Innis Newton Palmer	N/Brig.Gen.
March 30, 1825	Samuel Bell Maxey	S/Maj.Gen.
March 31, 1817	William Vandever	N/Brig.Gen.
March 31, 1825	Washington Elliott	N/Brig.Gen.
March 31, 1840	John Herbert Kelly	S/Brig.Gen.
April 1816	Alexander Welch Reynolds	S/Brig.Gen.
April 1, 1823	Simon Bolivar Buckner	S/Lt.Gen.
April 2, 1814	Henry Lewis Benning	S/Brig.Gen.
April 2, 1826	Philip Dale Roddey	S/Brig.Gen.
April 2, 1833	Thomas Howard Ruger	N/Brig.Gen.
April 4, 1814	John Blair Smith Todd	N/Brig.Gen.
April 4, 1817	John Wilson Sprague	N/Brig.Gen.
April 4, 1820	Charles Devens,Jr.	N/Brig.Gen.
April 4, 1823	Robert Byington Mitchell	N/Brig.Gen.
April 4, 1831	Edward Cary Walthall	S/Maj.Gen.
April 4, 1837	Henry Goddard Thomas	N/Brig.Gen.
April 4, 1840	John Caldwell C. Sanders	S/Brig.Gen.
April 5, 1822	James Nagle	N/Brig.Gen.
April 5, 1825	David Rumph Jones	S/Maj.Gen.
April 6, 1828	Charles William Field	S/Maj.Gen.
April 7, 1822	Gershom Mott	N/Brig.Gen.
April 7, 1826	Friedrich Salomon	N/Brig.Gen.
April 8, 1828	George Baird Hodge	S/Brig.Gen.
April 9, 1812	Randolph Barnes Marcy	N/Brig.Gen.
April 9, 1826	Thomas Hewson Neill	N/Brig.Gen.
April 10, 1806	Leonidas Polk	S/Lt.Gen.
April 10, 1807	Benjamin Franklin Kelley	N/Brig.Gen.
April 10, 1817	John Cleveland Robinson	N/Brig.Gen.
April 10, 1823	Thomas Reade Rootes Cobb	S/Brig.Gen.
April 10, 1827	Lewis Wallace	N/Maj.Gen.
April 10, 1833	David McMurtrie Gregg	N/Brig.Gen.
April 10, 1833	James Edwards Rains	S/Brig.Gen.
April 12, 1822	George Gibbs Dibrell	S/Brig.Gen.
April 12, 1828	Richard Arnold	N/Brig.Gen.
April 12, 1831	George Burgwyn Anderson	S/Brig.Gen.
April 12, 1831	Grenville Mellen Dodge	N/Maj.Gen.
April 13, 1822	Leroy Augustus Stafford	S/Brig.Gen.
April 13, 1822	William Stephen Walker	S/Brig.Gen.
April 14, 1817	Frederick Stumbaugh	N/Brig.Gen.
April 14, 1820	Harry Thompson Hays	S/Maj.Gen.
April 14, 1830	Davis Tillson	N/Brig.Gen.
April 14, 1832	James Hewett Ledlie	N/Brig.Gen.
April 15, 1820	Evander McNair	S/Brig.Gen.
April 15, 1822	Napoleon Jackson T. Dana	N/Maj.Gen.

April 16, 1816	Edward Johnson	S/Maj.Gen.
April 16, 1823	Orlando Bolivar Willcox	N/Brig.Gen.
April 17, 1788	Joseph Gilbert Totten	N/Brig.Gen.
April 17, 1809	Philip St.George Cocke	S/Brig.Gen.
April 17, 1813	Henry Washington Benham	N/Brig.Gen.
April 17, 1833	John Curtis Caldwell	N/Brig.Gen.
April 19, 1821	Mortimer Dormer Leggett	N/Brig.Gen.
April 20, 1809	John Smith Preston	S/Brig.Gen.
April 20, 1824	Alfred Holt Colquitt	S/Brig.Gen.
April 20, 1827	John Gibbon	N/Maj.Gen.
April 21, 1816	Louis Trezevant Wigfall	S/Brig.Gen.
April 21, 1834	William Rufus Terrill	N/Brig.Gen.
April 22, 1818	Cadwallader Washburn	N/Maj.Gen.
April 22, 1823	Alfred Gibbs	N/Brig.Gen.
April 22, 1827	William Hopkins Morris	N/Brig.Gen.
April 22, 1831	Alexander McDowell McCook	N/Maj.Gen.
April 24, 1807	Charles Ferguson Smith	N/Maj.Gen.
April 24, 1815	James Edward Harrison	S/Brig.Gen.
April 24, 1822	Erastus Barnard Tyler	N/Brig.Gen.
April 24, 1828	Robert Brank Vance	S/Brig.Gen.
April 25, 1840	James Dearing	S/Brig.Gen.
April 26, 1826	Ambrose Ransom Wright	S/Maj.Gen.
April 26, 1827	Charles Edward Hovey	N/Brig.Gen.
April 26, 1839	Cyrus Hamlin	N/Brig.Gen.
April 27, 1822	Ulysses Simpson Grant	N/Lt.Gen.
April 27, 1835	John Murray Corse	N/Brig.Gen.
April 28, 1810	Daniel Ullmann	N/Brig.Gen.
April 28, 1812	Daniel Henry Rucker	N/Brig.Gen.
April 28, 1815	Andrew Jackson Smith	N/Maj.Gen.
April 28, 1825	James Winning McMillan	N/Brig.Gen.
April 29, 1815	Abram Duryee	N/Brig.Gen.
April 29, 1820	Henry Watkins Allen	S/Brig.Gen.
April 30, 1805	William Kerley Strong	N/Brig.Gen.
May 1, 1807	John Bankhead Magruder	S/Maj.Gen.
May 1, 1819	William Steele	S/Brig.Gen.
May 1, 1823	Thomas Harrison	S/Brig.Gen.
May 1, 1830	William Young Conn Humes	S/Brig.Gen.
May 1, 1835	Alfred Napoleon A. Duffie	N/Brig.Gen.
May 2, 1821	Abram Sanders Piatt	N/Brig.Gen.
May 3, 1816	Montgomery Meigs	N/Brig.Gen.
May 4, 1896	Joseph Pannell Taylor	N/Brig.Gen.
May 5, 1823	James Allen Hardie	N/Brig.Gen.
May 5, 1824	Thomas Welsh	N/Brig.Gen.
May 6, 1801	George Sears Greene	N/Brig.Gen.
May 6, 1813	Joseph Tarr Copeland	N/Brig.Gen.
May 6, 1825	Joseph Bailey	N/Brig.Gen.
May 7, 1821	Francis Engle Patterson	N/Brig.Gen.
May 8, 1810	James Cooper	N/Brig.Gen.
May 8, 1833	Frank Wheaton	N/Brig.Gen.
May 8, 1836	Bryan Morel Thomas	S/Brig.Gen.
May 9, 1812	William George M. Davis	S/Brig.Gen.
May 9, 1819	William Hays	N/Brig.Gen.
May 9, 1824	William Edmonson Jones	S/Brig.Gen.
May 9, 1827	William Feimster Tucker	S/Brig.Gen.
May 10, 1810	James Shields	N/Brig.Gen.
May 10, 1825	William Henry Powell	N/Brig.Gen.

May 10, 1830	Alfred Jefferson Vaughan	S/Brig.Gen.
May 11, 1821	Charles John Stolbrand	N/Brig.Gen.
May 11, 1830	John Converse Starkweather	N/Brig.Gen.
May 12, 1806	Amos Beebe Eaton	N/Brig.Gen.
May 12, 1812	Louis Ludwig Blenker	N/Brig.Gen.
May 14, 1830	George Pierce Doles	S/Brig.Gen.
May 14, 1836	James Patrick Major	S/Brig.Gen.
May 15, 1802	Isaac Ridgeway Trimble	S/Maj.Gen.
May 15, 1815	Collett Leventhorpe	S/Brig.Gen.
May 15, 1819	Thomas Leonidas Crittenden	N/Maj.Gen.
May 15, 1830	Laurence Simmons Baker	S/Brig.Gen.
May 16, 1806	George Cadwalader	N/Maj.Gen.
May 16, 1824	Edmund Kirby Smith	S/General
May 17, 1812	Joseph Warren Revere	N/Brig.Gen.
May 18, 1898	Ethan Allen Hitchcock	N/Maj.Gen.
May 19, 1808	Samuel Jameson Gholson	S/Brig.Gen.
May 19, 1812	Felix Kirk Zollicoffer	S/Brig.Gen.
May 19, 1815	John Gross Barnard	N/Brig.Gen.
May 19, 1828	Adin Ballou Underwood	N/Brig.Gen.
May 20, 1828	James William Reilly	N/Brig.Gen.
May 21, 1822	Dabney Herndon Maury	S/Maj.Gen.
May 21, 1822	Mosby Monroe Parsons	S/Maj.Gen.
May 21, 1825	George Lafayette Beal	N/Brig.Gen.
May 21, 1835	Newton Martin Curtis	N/Brig.Gen.
May 22, 1818	Jerimiah Tilford Boyle	N/Brig.Gen.
May 22, 1819	Richard Lee T. Beale	S/Brig.Gen.
May 22, 1820	Alfred Sully	N/Brig.Gen.
May 23, 1813	Mason Brayman	N/Brig.Gen.
May 23, 1824	Ambrose Everett Burnside	N/Maj.Gen.
May 24, 1811	Charles Clark	S/Brig.Gen.
May 24, 1816	Robert Seaman Granger	N/Brig.Gen.
May 25, 1816	Henry Hopkins Sibley	S/Brig.Gen.
May 26, 1835	Edward Porter Alexander	S/Brig.Gen.
May 27, 1823	John Gray Foster	N/Maj.Gen.
May 27, 1836	Edwin Gray Lee	S/Brig.Gen.
May 27, 1837	Robert Frederick Hoke	S/Maj.Gen.
May 28, 1818	Pierre Gustave Beauregard	S/General
May 28, 1819	William Birney	N/Brig.Gen.
May 28, 1828	Alpheus Baker	S/Brig.Gen.
May 28, 1830	George Lucas Hartsuff	N/Maj.Gen.
May 28, 1838	Basil Wilson Duke	S/Brig.Gen.
May 29, 1810	Erasmus Darwin Keyes	N/Maj.Gen.
May 29, 1810	Solomon Meredith	N/Brig.Gen.
May 29, 1824	Cadmus Marcellus Wilcox	S/Maj.Gen.
May 29, 1825	David Bell Birney	N/Maj.Gen.
May 29, 1827	Reuben Lindsay Walker	S/Brig.Gen.
May 30, 1812	John Alexander McClernand	N/Maj.Gen.
May 30, 1830	Edward Winslow Hincks	N/Brig.Gen.
May 30, 1832	George Doherty Johnston	S/Brig.Gen.
May 31, 1824	Charles Leopold Matthies	N/Brig.Gen.
May 31, 1837	William Henry F. Lee	S/Maj.Gen.
May 31, 1837	Stephen Dodson Ramseur	S/Maj.Gen.
June 1821	Daniel Weisiger Adams	S/Brig.Gen.
June 1827	James Edwin Slaughter	S/Brig.Gen.
June 1, 1806	John Buchanan Floyd	S/Brig.Gen.
June 1, 1825	John Hunt Morgan	S/Brig.Gen.

June 1, 1828	David Sloane Stanley	N/Maj.Gen.
June 1, 1829	Cullen Andrews Battle	S/Brig.Gen.
June 1, 1831	John Bell Hood	S/General
June 1, 1835	Francis Laurens Vinton	N/Brig.Gen.
June 2, 1815	Philip Kearny	N/Maj.Gen.
June 2, 1831	Benjamin Hardin Helm	S/Brig.Gen.
June 3, 1815	Martin Edwin Green	S/Brig.Gen.
June 3, 1831	Otho French Strahl	S/Brig.Gen.
June 3, 1824	Charles Kinnaird Graham	N/Brig.Gen.
June 4, 1803	Gabriel James Rains	S/Brig.Gen.
June 4, 1815	Paul Jones Semmes	S/Brig.Gen.
June 4, 1816	Philippe Regis deTrobriand	N/Brig.Gen.
June 4, 1828	Alexander William Campbell	S/Brig.Gen.
June 5, 1827	Beverly Holcombe Robertson	S/Brig.Gen.
June 5, 1831	Marcus Joseph Wright	S/Brig.Gen.
June 6, 1829	John Baillie McIntosh	N/Brig.Gen.
June 6, 1840	William Francis Bartlett	N/Brig.Gen.
June 7, 1812	Theophilus Toulmin Garrard	N/Brig.Gen.
June 8, 1806	Gideon Johnson Pillow	S/Brig.Gen.
June 8, 1821	John Dunlap Stevenson	N/Brig.Gen.
June 8, 1821	Nelson Taylor	N/Brig.Gen.
June 8, 1824	William Montgomery Gardner	S/Brig.Gen.
June 9, 1833	John Rogers Cooke	S/Brig.Gen.
June 10, 1840	Thomas Fentress Toon	S/Brig.Gen.
June 11, 1816	Robert Huston Milroy	N/Maj.Gen.
June 11, 1822	Samuel Davis Sturgis	N/Brig.Gen.
June 11, 1823	James Lawson Kemper	S/Maj.Gen.
June 12, 1798	Samuel Cooper	S/General
June 12, 1821	Henry Moses Judah	N/Brig.Gen.
June 12, 1825	John Cook	N/Brig.Gen.
June 13, 1786	Winfield Scott	N/Maj.Gen.
June 13, 1809	Philip St.George Cooke	N/Brig.Gen.
June 13, 1823	Gustave Paul Cluseret	N/Brig.Gen.
June 13, 1825	Benjamin Jefferson Hill	S/Brig.Gen.
June 14, 1805	Robert Anderson	N/Brig.Gen.
June 14, 1834	Thomas Wilberforce Egan	N/Brig.Gen.
June 15, 1833	Edward Moody McCook	N/Brig.Gen.
June 16, 1834	Wesley Merritt	N/Maj.Gen.
June 16, 1837	Eli Long	N/Brig.Gen.
June 17, 1817	Thomas Maley Harris	N/Brig.Gen.
June 17, 1823	John Henry Hobart Ward	N/Brig.Gen.
June 17, 1825	Egbert Ludovicus Viele	N/Brig.Gen.
June 17, 1830	Richard Montgomery Gano	S/Brig.Gen.
June 18, 1839	William Henry Seward,Jr.	N/Brig.Gen.
June 19, 1811	Henry Prince	N/Brig.Gen.
June 20, 1823	Jesse Lee Reno	N/Maj.Gen.
June 20, 1824	John Tyler Morgan	S/Brig.Gen.
June 21, 1817	James Brewerton Ricketts	N/Brig.Gen.
June 21, 1818	Joseph Abel Haskin	N/Brig.Gen.
June 21, 1823	Edward Elmer Potter	N/Brig.Gen.
June 21, 1839	John Decatur Barry	S/Brig.Gen.
June 23, 1801	Daniel Smith Donelson	S/Maj.Gen.
June 23, 1822	Young Marshall Moody	S/Brig.Gen.
June 23, 1838	Edwin Henry Stoughton	N/Brig.Gen.
June 24, 1820	Henry Rootes Jackson	S/Brig.Gen.
June 24, 1822	Birkett Davenport Fry	S/Brig.Gen.

June 24, 1832	Edward Harland	N/Brig.Gen.
June 25, 1813	William High Keim	N/Brig.Gen.
June 26, 1819	Abner Doubleday	N/Brig.Gen.
June 26, 1837	Victor Jean B. Girardey	S/Brig.Gen.
June 26, 1837	Martin Davis Hardin	N/Brig.Gen.
June 27, 1828	Junius Daniel	S/Brig.Gen.
June 28, 1824	William Tatum Wofford	S/Brig.Gen.
July 1, 1818	Josiah Gorgas	S/Brig.Gen.
July 1, 1819	John Milton Brannan	N/Brig.Gen.
July 1, 1825	John Adams	S/Brig.Gen.
July 1, 1827	Stephen Gardner Champlin	N/Brig.Gen.
July 1, 1831	James Argyle Smith	S/Brig.Gen.
July 1, 1833	Alfred Thomas A. Torbert	N/Brig.Gen.
July 2, 1810	Robert Augustus Toombs	S/Brig.Gen.
July 2, 1830	John Bordenave Villepigue	S/Brig.Gen.
July 2, 1836	Henry Eugene Davies	N/Brig.Gen.
July 3, 1828	John Austin Wharton	S/Maj.Gen.
July 4, 1816	Sullivan Amory Meredith	N/Brig.Gen.
July 4, 1825	William Andrew Quarles	S/Brig.Gen.
July 4, 1826	Green Clay Smith	N/Brig.Gen.
July 4, 1828	James Johnston Pettigrew	S/Brig.Gen.
July 4, 1829	Daniel Chevilette Govan	S/Brig.Gen.
July 6, 1814	Justus McKinstry	N/Brig.Gen.
July 6, 1821	Edmund Winston Pettus	S/Brig.Gen.
July 7, 1813	William Scott Ketchum	N/Brig.Gen.
July 7, 1816	Isaac Fitzgerald Shepard	N/Brig.Gen.
July 7, 1824	Alfred Pleasonton	N/Maj.Gen.
July 7, 1827	James Murrell Shackelford	N/Brig.Gen.
July 8, 1819	Alexander Hays	N/Brig.Gen.
July 8, 1821	William Harvey L. Wallace	N/Brig.Gen.
July 8, 1824	Wladimir Krzyzanowski	N/Brig.Gen.
July 8, 1826	Benjamin Henry Grierson	N/Brig.Gen.
July 10, 1801	William Reading Montgomery	N/Brig.Gen.
July 10, 1818	John Stuart Williams	S/Brig.Gen.
July 10, 1820	Andrew Porter	N/Brig.Gen.
July 10, 1821	Christopher Columbus Augur	N/Maj.Gen.
July 10, 1833	Lucius Eugene Polk	S/Brig.Gen.
July 11, 1825	Edward Henry Hobson	N/Brig.Gen.
July 11, 1841	William Paul Roberts	S/Brig.Gen.
July 12, 1807	Silas Casey	N/Maj.Gen.
July 12, 1821	Daniel Harvey Hill	S/Lt.Gen.
July 13, 1821	Nathan Bedford Forrest	S/Lt.Gen.
July 14, 1818	Nathaniel Lyon	N/Brig.Gen.
July 14, 1831	William Dwight	N/Brig.Gen.
July 16, 1823	James Isham Gilbert	N/Brig.Gen.
July 16, 1829	Robert Brown Potter	N/Brig.Gen.
July 18, 1823	Leonard Fulton Ross	N/Brig.Gen.
July 19, 1823	George Henry Gordon	N/Brig.Gen.
July 19, 1828	Roger Atkinson Pryor	S/Brig.Gen.
July 19, 1833	John Wesley Turner	N/Brig.Gen.
July 20, 1824	Alexander Schimmelfennig	N/Brig.Gen.
July 21, 1802	David Hunter	N/Maj.Gen.
July 21, 1815	Stewart Van Vliet	N/Brig.Gen.
July 21, 1817	Joseph K. Barnes	N/Brig.Gen.
July 21, 1826	James Gillpatrick Blunt	N/Maj.Gen.
July 21, 1838	John Rutter Brooke	N/Brig.Gen.

July 22, 1822	Hamilton Prioleau Bee	S/Brig.Gen.
July 22, 1822	John George Walker	S/Maj.Gen.
July 22, 1830	William Sooy Smith	N/Brig.Gen.
July 23, 1822	Darius Nash Couch	N/Maj.Gen.
July 23, 1824	Gabriel Colvin Wharton	S/Brig.Gen.
July 24, 1798	John Adams Dix	N/Maj.Gen.
July 24, 1827	Julius Adolph deLagnel	S/Brig.Gen.
July 25, 1822	Schuyler Hamilton	N/Maj.Gen.
July 25, 1824	Richard James Oglesby	N/Maj.Gen.
July 26, 1820	John Marshall Jones	S/Brig.Gen.
July 27, 1812	Thomas Lanier Clingman	S/Brig.Gen.
July 27, 1840	Ranald Slidell Mackenzie	N/Brig.Gen.
July 28, 1809	Ormsby MacKnight Mitchel	N/Maj.Gen.
July 28, 1818	Nathaniel James Jackson	N/Brig.Gen.
July 28, 1825	William Duncan Smith	S/Brig.Gen.
July 28, 1827	William Edwin Baldwin	S/Brig.Gen.
July 28, 1827	John Wallace Fuller	N/Brig.Gen.
July 28, 1833	James Henry Lane	S/Brig.Gen.
July 29, 1817	James Blair Steedman	N/Maj.Gen.
July 29, 1828	Cuvier Grover	N/Brig.Gen.
July 29, 1830	Alvan Cullem Gillem	N/Brig.Gen.
July 30, 1837	Elon John Farnsworth	N/Brig.Gen.
July 31, 1816	George Henry Thomas	N/Maj.Gen.
July 31, 1817	Philip Cook	S/Brig.Gen.
July 31, 1825	Thomas Hart Taylor	S/Brig.Gen.
August 1, 1810	James Dada Morgan	N/Brig.Gen.
August 1, 1814	Maxcy Gregg	S/Brig.Gen.
August 1, 1816	William Yarnel Slack	S/Brig.Gen.
August 1, 1824	Henry Shaw Briggs	N/Brig.Gen.
August 2, 1826	William Denison Whipple	N/Brig.Gen.
August 3, 1816	John Eugene Smith	N/Brig.Gen.
August 3, 1820	William Miller	S/Brig.Gen.
August 3, 1823	Thomas Francis Meagher	N/Brig.Gen.
August 4, 1816	Israel Vogdes	N/Brig.Gen.
August 4, 1818	Lovell Harrison Rousseau	N/Maj.Gen.
August 5, 1818	Carnot Posey	S/Brig.Gen.
August 5, 1829	Milo Smith Hascall	N/Brig.Gen.
August 6, 1819	Samuel Powhatan Carter	N/Brig.Gen.
August 7, 1829	Thomas Ewing,Jr.	N/Brig.Gen.
August 7, 1833	Powell Clayton	N/Brig.Gen.
August 7, 1836	Evander McIvor Law	S/Brig.Gen.
August 8, 1820	Winfield Scott Featherston	S/Brig.Gen.
August 8, 1823	Walter Chiles Whitaker	N/Brig.Gen.
August 8, 1839	Nelson Appleton Miles	N/Brig.Gen.
August 9, 1808	William Thomas Ward	N/Brig.Gen.
August 9, 1823	Daniel Marsh Frost	S/Brig.Gen.
August 9, 1824	Simon Goodell Griffin	N/Brig.Gen.
August 10, 1814	John Clifford Pemberton	S/Lt.Gen.
August 10, 1823	Charles Thomas Campbell	N/Brig.Gen.
August 12, 1819	Daniel Davidson Bidwell	N/Brig.Gen.
August 12, 1829	John Horace Forney	S/Maj.Gen.
August 12, 1833	William Price Sanders	N/Brig.Gen.
August 14, 1821	Clement Hoffman Stevens	S/Brig.Gen.
August 14, 1824	William Terry	S/Brig.Gen.
August 15, 1823	Orris Sanford Ferry	N/Brig.Gen.
August 16, 1828	Joseph Bradford Carr	N/Brig.Gen.

August 17, 1814	Henry Hayes Lockwood	N/Brig.Gen.
August 17, 1819	James Henry Van Alen	N/Brig.Gen.
August 18, 1813	Benjamin Alvord	N/Brig.Gen.
August 18, 1818	William Farquhar Barry	N/Brig.Gen.
August 18, 1822	Isaac Peace Rodman	N/Brig.Gen.
August 18, 1824	John Wynn Davidson	N/Brig.Gen.
August 19, 1815	John Porter McCown	S/Maj.Gen.
August 19, 1831	Stephen Gano Burbridge	N/Brig.Gen.
August 20, 1811	Gilman Marston	N/Brig.Gen.
August 20, 1824	Absalom Baird	N/Brig.Gen.
August 20, 1834	Francis Redding T. Nicholls	S/Brig.Gen.
August 21, 1810	Thomas Jefferson McKean	N/Brig.Gen.
August 21, 1821	William Barksdale	S/Brig.Gen.
August 21, 1824	John Sanford Mason	N/Brig.Gen.
August 22, 1822	George Stoneman	N/Maj.Gen.
August 22, 1827	Joseph Anthony Mower	N/Maj.Gen.
August 22, 1834	Nathaniel Harrison Harris	S/Brig.Gen.
August 23, 1818	Rufus Ingalls	N/Brig.Gen.
August 23, 1832	Alexander Chambers	N/Brig.Gen.
August 24, 1808	Thomas Fenwick Drayton	S/Brig.Gen.
August 24, 1808	Benjamin Grubb Humphreys	S/Brig.Gen.
August 24, 1826	George Ear Maney	S/Brig.Gen.
August 24, 1827	Walter Husted Stevens	S/Brig.Gen.
August 24, 1828	George Hume Steuart	S/Brig.Gen.
August 25, 1811	Joseph Dana Webster	N/Brig.Gen.
August 25, 1822	John Newton	N/Maj.Gen.
August 25, 1825	Henry Warner Birge	N/Brig.Gen.
August 26, 1811	Danville Leadbetter	S/Brig.Gen.
August 26, 1833	Charles Jackson Paine	N/Brig.Gen.
August 26, 1835	Theodore Washington Brevard	S/Brig.Gen.
August 27, 1800	William Selby Harney	N/Brig.Gen.
August 27, 1813	John Cochrane	N/Brig.Gen.
August 27, 1824	Hiram Gregory Berry	N/Maj.Gen.
August 27, 1824	Max Weber	N/Brig.Gen.
August 27, 1826	Franklin Stillman Nickerson	N/Brig.Gen.
August 27, 1827	Roger Weightman Hanson	S/Brig.Gen.
August 27, 1832	James Alexander Walker	S/Brig.Gen.
August 27, 1839	Emory Upton	N/Brig.Gen.
August 28, 1828	William Alexander Hammond	N/Brig.Gen.
August 31, 1811	Goode Bryan	S/Brig.Gen.
August 31, 1822	Fitz John Porter	N/Maj.Gen.
August 31, 1828	George Leonard Andrews	N/Brig.Gen.
September 1, 1898	Richard Delafield	N/Brig.Gen.
September 1, 1824	Isaac Hardin Duval	N/Brig.Gen.
September 1, 1829	James Conner	S/Brig.Gen.
September 2, 1837	James Harrison Wilson	N/Brig.Gen.
September 3, 1825	William Wallace Burns	N/Brig.Gen.
September 3, 1825	Armistead Lindsay Long	S/Brig.Gen.
September 3, 1831	States Rights Gist	S/Brig.Gen.
September 3, 1835	William Gaston Lewis	S/Brig.Gen.
September 5, 1815	Tyree Harris Bell	S/Brig.Gen.
September 6, 1797	William Smith	S/Maj.Gen.
September 6, 1815	St.John Richardson Liddell	S/Brig.Gen.
September 6, 1819	William Starke Rosecrans	N/Maj.Gen.
September 6, 1828	John Morrison Oliver	N/Brig.Gen.
September 7, 1811	William Hemsley Emory	N/Brig.Gen.

September 7, 1815	Howell Cobb	S/Maj.Gen.
September 8, 1811	Lucius Bellinger Northrop	S/Brig.Gen.
September 8, 1821	Henry Baxter	N/Brig.Gen.
September 8, 1828	Joshua Lawrence Chamberlain	N/Brig.Gen.
September 8, 1828	George Crook	N/Maj.Gen.
September 8, 1829	Seth Maxwell Barton	S/Brig.Gen.
September 9, 1817	Speed Smith Fry	N/Brig.Gen.
September 9, 1819	Martin Luther Smith	S/Maj.Gen.
September 9, 1825	James Camp Tappan	S/Brig.Gen.
September 9, 1826	Thomas John Lucas	N/Brig.Gen.
September 9, 1834	William MacRae	S/Brig.Gen.
September 10, 1810	Albert Gallatin Blanchard	S/Brig.Gen.
September 10, 1815	Eleazer Arthur Paine	N/Brig.Gen.
September 10, 1832	Randall Lee Gibson	S/Brig.Gen.
September 10, 1836	Joseph Wheeler	S/Maj.Gen.
September 11, 1813	Conrad Feger Jackson	N/Brig.Gen.
September 11, 1835	William Wirt Allen	S/Brig.Gen.
September 13, 1806	Joseph Lewis Hogg	S/Brig.Gen.
September 13, 1813	John Sedgwick	N/Maj.Gen.
September 13, 1817	John McCauley Palmer	N/Maj.Gen.
September 13, 1836	John McCausland	S/Brig.Gen.
September 14, 1819	Henry Jackson Hunt	N/Brig.Gen.
September 14, 1835	Joseph Hayes	N/Brig.Gen.
September 16, 1832	George Washington C. Lee	S/Maj.Gen.
September 16, 1841	Charles Cleveland Dodge	N/Brig.Gen.
September 17, 1820	Earl Van Dorn	S/Maj.Gen.
September 18, 1805	Robert Cowdin	N/Brig.Gen.
September 18, 1815	Henry Constantine Wayne	S/Brig.Gen.
September 18, 1818	Marcellus Augustus Stovall	S/Brig.Gen.
September 19, 1822	Joseph Rodman West	N/Brig.Gen.
September 20, 1809	Sterling Price	S/Maj.Gen.
September 20, 1810	Alpheus Starkey Williams	N/Brig.Gen.
September 20, 1820	George Washington Morgan	N/Brig.Gen.
September 20, 1820	John Fulton Reynolds	N/Maj.Gen.
September 20, 1829	Byron Root Pierce	N/Brig.Gen.
September 21, 1817	Carter Littlepage Stevenson	S/Maj.Gen.
September 21, 1820	Williams Carter Wickham	S/Brig.Gen.
September 21, 1824	Joseph Andrew J. Lightburn	N/Brig.Gen.
September 21, 1827	Michael Corcoran	N/Brig.Gen.
September 21, 1832	Samuel Sprigg Carroll	N/Brig.Gen.
September 22, 1821	Patrick Theodore Moore	S/Brig.Gen.
September 22, 1822	Eppa Hunton	S/Brig.Gen.
September 22, 1827	John Grubb Parke	N/Maj.Gen.
September 22, 1829	William Worth Belknap	N/Brig.Gen.
September 22, 1829	George Day Wagner	N/Brig.Gen.
September 22, 1833	Stephen Dill Lee	S/Lt.Gen.
September 23, 1816	Julius White	N/Brig.Gen.
September 23, 1820	Thomas Kilby Smith	N/Brig.Gen.
September 24, 1823	James Madison Tuttle	N/Brig.Gen.
September 24, 1824	Truman Seymour	N/Brig.Gen.
September 24, 1827	Henry Warner Slocum	N/Maj.Gen.
September 24, 1829	James St.Clair Morton	N/Brig.Gen.
September 25, 1822	Adolph von Steinwehr	N/Brig.Gen.
September 25, 1823	Thomas John Wood	N/Maj.Gen.
September 26, 1821	Alvin Peterson Hovey	N/Brig.Gen.
September 27, 1823	James Streshly Jackson	N/Brig.Gen.

September 27, 1824	William Nelson	N/Maj.Gen.
September 27, 1830	William Babcock Hazen	N/Maj.Gen.
September 27, 1838	Lawrence Sullivan Ross	S/Brig.Gen.
September 28, 1818	James Richard Slack	N/Brig.Gen.
September 28, 1828	John Gregg	S/Brig.Gen.
September 28, 1833	James Deering Fessenden	N/Brig.Gen.
September 29, 1829	Bradley Tyler Johnson	S/Brig.Gen.
September 29, 1829	Giles Alexander Smith	N/Brig.Gen.
September 29, 1830	John Parker Hawkins	N/Brig.Gen.
September 29, 1831	John McAllister Schofield	N/Maj.Gen.
September 30, 1805	Samuel Peter Heintzelman	N/Maj.Gen.
September 30, 1819	Thomas Jordan	S/Brig.Gen.
September 30, 1824	Charles Pomeroy Stone	N/Brig.Gen.
September 30, 1827	Kenner Garrard	N/Brig.Gen.
October 1, 1830	Jeremiah Cutler Sullivan	N/Brig.Gen.
October 1, 1834	Francis Marion Cockrell	S/Brig.Gen.
October 1, 1835	Robert Houstoun Anderson	S/Brig.Gen.
October 1, 1835	William Hicks Jackson	S/Brig.Gen.
October 2, 1819	George Washington Getty	N/Brig.Gen.
October 2, 1821	Alexander Peter Stewart	S/Lt.Gen.
October 2, 1827	Edmund Jackson Davis	N/Brig.Gen.
October 4, 1809	Robert Cumming Schenck	N/Maj.Gen.
October 4, 1816	Egbert Benson Brown	N/Brig.Gen.
October 4, 1822	Rutherford Birchard Hayes	N/Brig.Gen.
October 5, 1808	Thomas Algeo Rowley	N/Brig.Gen.
October 5, 1833	Cyrus Bussey	N/Brig.Gen.
October 5, 1836	George Washington Gordon	S/Brig.Gen.
October 7, 1817	Bushrod Rust Johnson	S/Maj.Gen.
October 7, 1821	Richard Heron Anderson	S/Lt.Gen.
October 7, 1826	William Brimage Bate	S/Maj.Gen.
October 8, 1826	Matt Whitaker Ransom	S/Brig.Gen.
October 9, 1819	Samuel McGowan	S/Brig.Gen.
October 9, 1822	George Sykes	N/Maj.Gen.
October 10, 1819	Zebulon York	S/Brig.Gen.
October 10, 1829	Dandridge McRae	S/Brig.Gen.
October 11, 1825	Elkanah Brackin Greer	S/Brig.Gen.
October 12, 1815	William Joseph Hardee	S/Lt.Gen.
October 14, 1827	James Sidney Robinson	N/Brig.Gen.
October 14, 1837	Ellison Capers	S/Brig.Gen.
October 15, 1816	Amiel Weeks Whipple	N/Brig.Gen.
October 15, 1818	Irvin McDowell	N/Maj.Gen.
October 15, 1832	Henry Harrison Walker	S/Brig.Gen.
October 15, 1836	Thomas Lafayette Rosser	S/Maj.Gen.
October 16, 1816	William Preston	S/Brig.Gen.
October 16, 1825	Thomas Turpin Crittenden	N/Brig.Gen.
October 16, 1832	George Crockett Strong	N/Brig.Gen.
October 18, 1806	John Breckinridge Grayson	S/Brig.Gen.
October 18, 1811	Hugh Thompson Reid	N/Brig.Gen.
October 18, 1817	Lewis Addison Armistead	S/Brig.Gen.
October 18, 1818	Edward Otho C. Ord	N/Maj.Gen.
October 18, 1829	Charles Sidney Winder	S/Brig.Gen.
October 18, 1829	Lucius Marshall Walker	S/Brig.Gen.
October 19, 1810	Cassius Marcellus Clay	N/Maj.Gen.
October 19, 1824	Rufus Saxton	N/Brig.Gen.
October 19, 1834	Francis Channing Barlow	N/Brig.Gen.
October 20, 1819	Daniel Edgar Sickles	N/Maj.Gen.

October 20, 1820	Benjamin Franklin Cheatham	S/Maj.Gen.
October 20, 1820	George Jerrison Stannard	N/Brig.Gen.
October 20, 1822	Mansfield Lovell	S/Maj.Gen.
October 21, 1801	George Wright	N/Brig.Gen.
October 22, 1810	Henry Bohlen	N/Brig.Gen.
October 23, 1817	James William Denver	N/Brig.Gen.
October 23, 1820	James Monroe Goggin	S/Brig.Gen.
October 23, 1824	Thomas Gamble Pitcher	N/Brig.Gen.
October 23, 1828	Turner Ashby	S/Brig.Gen.
October 24, 1815	John Edwards	N/Brig.Gen.
October 25, 1819	Zachariah Cantey Deas	S/Brig.Gen.
October 26, 1804	Lorenzo Thomas	N/Brig.Gen.
October 26, 1824	Arthur Middleton Manigault	S/Brig.Gen.
October 26, 1830	Stephen Elliott,Jr.	S/Brig.Gen.
October 26, 1837	James Lawlor Kiernan	N/Brig.Gen.
October 27, 1828	Jacob Dolson Cox	N/Maj.Gen.
October 27, 1829	Christopher Andrews	N/Brig.Gen.
October 28, 1810	Adley Hogan Gladden	S/Brig.Gen.
October 28, 1834	Dudley McIver DuBose	S/Brig.Gen.
October 29, 1824	Joseph Horace Lewis	S/Brig.Gen.
October 30, 1807	James Samuel Wadsworth	N/Brig.Gen.
October 30, 1830	John Stevens Bowen	S/Maj.Gen.
October 31, 1825	Raleigh Edward Colston	S/Brig.Gen.
October 31, 1826	Hugh Boyle Ewing	N/Brig.Gen.
October 31, 1826	Joseph Roswell Hawley	N/Brig.Gen.
October 31, 1831	Daniel Butterfield	N/Maj.Gen.
October 31, 1835	Adelbert Ames	N/Brig.Gen.
November 1, 1815	Douglas Hancock Cooper	S/Brig.Gen.
November 1, 1825	Joseph Benjamin Palmer	S/Brig.Gen.
November 1, 1835	Godfrey Weitzel	N/Maj.Gen.
November 2, 1810	Andrew Atkinson Humphreys	N/Maj.Gen.
November 2, 1822	James Byron Gordon	S/Brig.Gen.
November 2, 1826	Robert Hopkins Hatton	S/Brig.Gen.
November 2, 1826	William Haines Lytle	N/Brig.Gen.
November 2, 1828	Bryan Grimes	S/Maj.Gen.
November 3, 1816	Jubal Anderson Early	S/Lt.Gen.
November 3, 1818	Gustavus Adolphus DeRussy	N/Brig.Gen.
November 3, 1826	Jasper Adalmorn Maltby	N/Brig.Gen.
November 3, 1834	Samuel Wragg Ferguson	S/Brig.Gen.
November 3, 1840	Thomas Muldrup Logan	S/Brig.Gen.
November 4, 1816	William Polk Hardeman	S/Brig.Gen.
November 4, 1818	Alexander Robert Lawton	S/Brig.Gen.
November 4, 1820	Robert Vinkler Richardson	S/Brig.Gen.
November 4, 1835	Lunsford Lindsay Lomax	S/Maj.Gen.
November 5, 1818	Benjamin Franklin Butler	N/Maj.Gen.
November 5, 1825	Julius Stahel	N/Maj.Gen.
November 5, 1832	William Woods Averell	N/Brig.Gen.
November 5, 1833	Edward Dorr Tracy	S/Brig.Gen.
November 6, 1822	Gordon Granger	N/Maj.Gen.
November 6, 1838	John Grant Mitchell	N/Brig.Gen.
November 8, 1817	Claudius Wistar Sears	S/Brig.Gen.
November 8, 1829	Samuel Wylie Crawford	N/Brig.Gen.
November 8, 1830	Oliver Otis Howard	N/Maj.Gen.
November 9, 1817	Edward Richard S. Canby	N/Maj.Gen.
November 9, 1823	William Henry Forney	S/Brig.Gen.
November 9, 1825	Ambrose Powell Hill	S/Lt.Gen.

November 10, 1827	Alfred Howe Terry	N/Maj.Gen.
November 10, 1830	Albert Gallatin Jenkins	S/Brig.Gen.
November 10, 1834	Wager Swayne	N/Brig.Gen.
November 11, 1811	Ben McCulloch	S/Brig.Gen.
November 11, 1820	Alfred Washington Ellet	N/Brig.Gen.
November 13, 1804	Theophilus Hunter Holmes	S/Lt.Gen.
November 13, 1813	John Wolcott Phelps	N/Brig.Gen.
November 13, 1814	Joseph Hooker	N/Maj.Gen.
November 14, 1822	William Harrow	N/Brig.Gen.
November 14, 1827	Isaac Jones Wistar	N/Brig.Gen.
November 14, 1828	James Birdseye McPherson	N/Maj.Gen.
November 15, 1814	Pleasant Adam Hackleman	N/Brig.Gen.
November 15, 1816	Joseph Bennett Plummer	N/Brig.Gen.
November 15, 1836	Pierce Manning B. Young	S/Maj.Gen.
November 16, 1814	Michael Kelly Lawler	N/Brig.Gen.
November 16, 1822	Charles Smith Hamilton	N/Maj.Gen.
November 16, 1835	Elliott Warren Rice	N/Brig.Gen.
November 17, 1814	Joseph Finegan	S/Brig.Gen.
November 17, 1826	John McArthur	N/Brig.Gen.
November 17, 1831	Stephen Hinsdale Weed	N/Brig.Gen.
November 18, 1810	Benjamin Stone Roberts	N/Brig.Gen.
November 18, 1812	Jesse Johnson Finley	S/Brig.Gen.
November 18, 1824	Isham Nicholas Haynie	N/Brig.Gen.
November 18, 1824	Franz Sigel	N/Maj.Gen.
November 19, 1810	August Willich	N/Brig.Gen.
November 19, 1827	Isaac Munroe St.John	S/Brig.Gen.
November 19, 1831	James Abram Garfield	N/Maj.Gen.
November 19, 1835	Fitzhugh Lee	S/Maj.Gen.
November 20, 1836	John Thomas Croxton	N/Brig.Gen.
November 21, 1817	Richard Brooke Garnett	S/Brig.Gen.
November 21, 1828	William McComb	S/Brig.Gen.
November 21, 1831	John Franklin Miller	N/Brig.Gen.
November 21, 1834	Joseph Jackson Bartlett	N/Brig.Gen.
November 22, 1805	Benjamin Huger	S/Maj.Gen.
November 22, 1808	George William Taylor	N/Brig.Gen.
November 22, 1818	Samuel Gibbs French	S/Maj.Gen.
November 22, 1822	Nathan Kimball	N/Brig.Gen.
November 22, 1832	George Henry Chapman	N/Brig.Gen.
November 22, 1835	Frank Crawford Armstrong	S/Brig.Gen.
November 23, 1809	Horatio Phillips Van Cleve	N/Brig.Gen.
November 23, 1814	Ebenezer Dumont	N/Brig.Gen.
November 23, 1819	Benjamin Mayberry Prentiss	N/Maj.Gen.
November 24, 1815	James Heyward Trapier	S/Brig.Gen.
November 24, 1829	William Passmore Carlin	N/Brig.Gen.
November 25, 1823	Joseph Alexander Cooper	N/Brig.Gen.
November 25, 1825	Edward Augustus Wild	N/Brig.Gen.
November 26, 1816	William Henry T. Walker	S/Maj.Gen.
November 26, 1827	Alfred Moore Scales	S/Brig.Gen.
November 27, 1808	Hugh Weedon Mercer	S/Brig.Gen.
November 28, 1820	Lawrence O'Bryan Branch	S/Brig.Gen.
November 29, 1815	Stephen Augustus Hurlbut	N/Maj.Gen.
November 29, 1834	Thomas Edward G. Ransom	N/Brig.Gen.
November 30, 1821	Gustavus Woodson Smith	S/Maj.Gen.
November 30, 1826	George Washington Deitzler	N/Brig.Gen.
December 1, 1826	William Mahone	S/Maj.Gen.
December 1, 1832	Archibald Gracie,Jr.	S/Brig.Gen.

Date	Name	Rank
December 1, 1835	Micah Jenkins	S/Brig.Gen.
December 2, 1802	Melancthon Smith Wade	N/Brig.Gen.
December 2, 1821	Rufus Barringer	S/Brig.Gen.
December 2, 1835	Charles Garrison Harker	N/Brig.Gen.
December 3, 1806	Henry Alexander Wise	S/Brig.Gen.
December 3, 1809	Thomas Alfred Davies	N/Brig.Gen.
December 3, 1822	Charles Adam Heckman	N/Brig.Gen.
December 3, 1826	George Brinton McClellan	N/Maj.Gen.
December 3, 1829	Green Berry Raum	N/Brig.Gen.
December 4, 1812	Elias Smith Dennis	N/Brig.Gen.
December 4, 1818	William Wing Loring	S/Maj.Gen.
December 5, 1826	John Benjamin Sanborn	N/Brig.Gen.
December 5, 1839	George Armstrong Custer	N/Brig.Gen.
December 6, 1816	Henry Eustace McCulloch	S/Brig.Gen.
December 6, 1831	Joshua Woodrow Sill	N/Brig.Gen.
December 8, 1822	Luther Prentice Bradley	N/Brig.Gen.
December 8, 1828	Robert Bullock	S/Brig.Gen.
December 8, 1828	Clinton Bowen Fisk	N/Brig.Gen.
December 10, 1794	James Wolfe Ripley	N/Brig.Gen.
December 10, 1820	David Allen Russell	N/Brig.Gen.
December 10, 1822	Thomas Casimer Devin	N/Brig.Gen.
December 12, 1806	Stand Watie	S/Brig.Gen.
December 12, 1818	Paul Octave Hebert	S/Brig.Gen.
December 12, 1830	Joseph Orville Shelby	S/Brig.Gen.
December 14, 1830	Allen Thomas	S/Brig.Gen.
December 14, 1832	Daniel Harris Reynolds	S/Brig.Gen.
December 16, 1812	William Grose	N/Brig.Gen.
December 16, 1812	Daniel Phineas Woodbury	N/Brig.Gen.
December 16, 1819	Robert Selden Garnett	S/Brig.Gen.
December 16, 1820	Samuel Beatty	N/Brig.Gen.
December 16, 1825	Henry Heth	S/Maj.Gen.
December 16, 1828	John Beatty	N/Brig.Gen.
December 16, 1830	Samuel Garland,Jr.	S/Brig.Gen.
December 16, 1830	John Frederick Hartranft	N/Brig.Gen.
December 17, 1819	Samuel Jones	S/Maj.Gen.
December 17, 1821	Frederick West Lander	N/Brig.Gen.
December 17, 1824	Manning Ferguson Force	N/Brig.Gen.
December 17, 1833	James Thadeus Holtzclaw	S/Brig.Gen.
December 18, 1811	Alexander Sandor Asboth	N/Brig.Gen.
December 18, 1816	Arnold Elzey	S/Maj.Gen.
December 18, 1825	Charles Griffin	N/Maj.Gen.
December 18, 1833	Thomas Pleasant Dockery	S/Brig.Gen.
December 18, 1835	George Dashiell Bayard	N/Brig.Gen.
December 19, 1817	James Jay Archer	S/Brig.Gen.
December 19, 1819	James Clifford Veatch	N/Brig.Gen.
December 19, 1837	John Carpenter Carter	S/Brig.Gen.
December 20, 1807	Richard Lucian Page	S/Brig.Gen.
December 20, 1825	Romeyn Beck Ayres	N/Brig.Gen.
December 22, 1803	Joseph King F. Mansfield	N/Brig.Gen.
December 22, 1814	John Smith Phelps	N/Brig.Gen.
December 22, 1826	James Scott Negley	N/Maj.Gen.
December 22, 1831	Robert Ogden Tyler	N/Brig.Gen.
December 22, 1832	Edward Hatch	N/Brig.Gen.
December 23, 1818	David Addison Weisiger	S/Brig.Gen.
December 25, 1813	Milledge Luke Bonham	S/Brig.Gen.
December 25, 1820	Thomas William Sweeny	N/Brig.Gen.

December 25, 1823	Preston Smith	S/Brig.Gen.
December 25, 1828	William Plummer Benton	N/Brig.Gen.
December 25, 1832	Thomas Alfred Smyth	N/Brig.Gen.
December 26, 1809	William Nelson Pendleton	S/Brig.Gen.
December 26, 1815	Israel Bush Richardson	N/Maj.Gen.
December 26, 1820	Gustavus Adolphus Smith	N/Brig.Gen.
December 26, 1824	Augustus Louis Chetlain	N/Brig.Gen.
December 27, 1814	James Henry Carleton	N/Brig.Gen.
December 27, 1816	Eliakim Parker Scammon	N/Brig.Gen.
December 27, 1829	James Clay Rice	N/Brig.Gen.
December 27, 1831	Lucius Fairchild	N/Brig.Gen.
December 28, 1801	James Barnes	N/Brig.Gen.
December 28, 1822	William Booth Taliaferro	S/Maj.Gen.
December 28, 1827	Robert Latimer McCook	N/Brig.Gen.
December 28, 1833	Charles Miller Shelley	S/Brig.Gen.
December 29, 1808	Andrew Johnson	N/Brig.Gen.
December 29, 1809	Albert Pike	S/Brig.Gen.
December 30, 1818	James Cantey	S/Brig.Gen.
December 30, 1819	John White Geary	N/Brig.Gen.
December 30, 1828	Mark Perrin Lowrey	S/Brig.Gen.
December 31, 1815	George Gordon Meade	N/Maj.Gen.

7

Civil War Generals
by Colleges

Those generals who attended college are listed below, first
by the colleges (which are arranged alphabetically), then alphabetically by general under each individual college. Many
of the generals did not complete a course of study or graduate
from the colleges. If it was determined from their biography
that a general attended a college for any period of time, he
is listed here.

COLLEGE	GENERAL	SIDE/RANK
University of Alabama	Cullen Andrews Battle	S/Brig.Gen.
University of Alabama	William Henry Forney	S/Brig.Gen.
University of Alabama	John Caldwell C. Sanders	S/Brig.Gen.
University of Alabama	Jacob Hunter Sharp	S/Brig.Gen.
University of Alabama	Leroy Pope Walker	S/Brig.Gen.
Albany Academy	Egbert Ludovicus Viele	N/Brig.Gen.
Allegheny College	Alexander Hays	N/Brig.Gen.
Amherst College	John Curtis Caldwell	N/Brig.Gen.
Amherst College	Henry Goddard Thomas	N/Brig.Gen.
Amherst College	Amiel Weeks Whipple	N/Brig.Gen.
Asbury College	Francis Asbury Shoup	S/Brig.Gen.
Bacon College	Richard Montgomery Gano	S/Brig.Gen.
Baylor University	Felix Huston Robertson	S/Brig.Gen.
Berlin M.A.	August Willich	N/Brig.Gen.
Bethany College	Walter Chiles Whitaker	N/Brig.Gen.
Bloomington College	Hugh Thompson Reid	N/Brig.Gen.
Bonn University	Carl Schurz	N/Maj.Gen.
Bowdoin College	Joshua Chamberlain	N/Brig.Gen.
Bowdoin College	Francis Fessenden	N/Brig.Gen.
Bowdoin College	James Deering Fessenden	N/Brig.Gen.
Bowdoin College	Oliver Otis Howard	N/Maj.Gen.
Bristol Academy	Alfred Washington Ellet	N/Brig.Gen.
Brown University	John Milton Thayer	N/Brig.Gen.
Brown University	Adin Ballou Underwood	N/Brig.Gen.
Brown University	Frank Wheaton	N/Brig.Gen.
Brunswick M.A.	Adolph von Steinwehr	N/Brig.Gen.
Capt.Partridge M.A.	George William Taylor	N/Brig.Gen.
Capt.Partridge M.A.	George Wright	N/Brig.Gen.
Capt.Partridge M.A.	Robert Huston Milroy	N/Maj.Gen.

Carroll College	Lucius Fairchild	N/Brig.Gen.
Cazenovia Seminary	Henry Warner Slocum	N/Maj.Gen.
Centre College	John Cabell Breckinridge	S/Maj.Gen.
Centre College	Abraham Buford	S/Brig.Gen.
Centre College	Basil Wilson Duke	S/Brig.Gen.
Centre College	Matthew Duncan Ector	S/Brig.Gen.
Centre College	Joseph Holt	N/Brig.Gen.
Centre College	James Streshly Jackson	N/Brig.Gen.
Centre College	Joseph Horace Lewis	S/Brig.Gen.
Centre College	William Thompson Martin	S/Maj.Gen.
Centre College	Thomas Hart Taylor	S/Brig.Gen.
Chapel Hill College	Francis Marion Cockrell	S/Brig.Gen.
Charleston College	John Charles Fremont	N/Maj.Gen.
Cincinnati College	Thomas Kilby Smith	N/Brig.Gen.
Clinton College	Edmund Winston Pettus	S/Brig.Gen.
Colby College	Benjamin Franklin Butler	N/Maj.Gen.
Colby College	Cyrus Hamlin	N/Brig.Gen.
Columbia University	Henry Eugene Davies	N/Brig.Gen.
Columbia University	Philip Kearny	N/Maj.Gen.
Columbia University	Edward Elmer Potter	N/Brig.Gen.
Cumberland University	Robert Hopkins Hatton	S/Brig.Gen.
Cumberland University	George Doherty Johnston	S/Brig.Gen.
Cumberland University	John Selden Roane	S/Brig.Gen.
Dartmouth College	Alfred Gibbs	N/Brig.Gen.
Dartmouth College	Charles Edward Hovey	N/Brig.Gen.
Dartmouth College	John Benjamin Sanborn	N/Brig.Gen.
Dartmouth College	George Foster Shepley	N/Brig.Gen.
Dartmouth College	Joseph Dana Webster	N/Brig.Gen.
Dartmouth College	Daniel Phineas Woodbury	N/Brig.Gen.
DePauw University	Nathan Kimball	N/Brig.Gen.
Dickinson College	Washington Elliott	N/Brig.Gen.
Emory & Henry College	Henry DeLamar Clayton	S/Maj.Gen.
Emory & Henry College	James Byron Gordon	S/Brig.Gen.
Emory & Henry College	William Edmonson Jones	S/Brig.Gen.
Emory & Henry College	John Creed Moore	S/Brig.Gen.
Emory & Henry College	William Feimster Tucker	S/Brig.Gen.
Emory College	George Thomas Anderson	S/Brig.Gen.
Emory College	Edward Lloyd Thomas	S/Brig.Gen.
Frankfort M.A.	Eli Long	N/Brig.Gen.
Franklin College	Lucius Jeremiah Gartrell	S/Brig.Gen.
Franklin College	Elliott Warren Rice	N/Brig.Gen.
Georgetown University	Stephen Gano Burbridge	N/Brig.Gen.
University of Georgia	Henry Lewis Benning	S/Brig.Gen.
University of Georgia	Howell Cobb	S/Maj.Gen.
University of Georgia	Thomas Reade Rootes Cobb	S/Brig.Gen.
University of Georgia	John Brown Gordon	S/Maj.Gen.
Granville College	Erastus Barnard Tyler	N/Brig.Gen.
Halle University	Charles Leopold Matthies	N/Brig.Gen.
Hamilton College	John Cochrane	N/Brig.Gen.
Hamilton College	Joseph Roswell Hawley	N/Brig.Gen.
Hampden-Sydney College	Sterling Price	S/Maj.Gen.
Hampden-Sydney College	Roger Atkinson Pryor	S/Brig.Gen.
Harvard Law School	Christopher Andrews	N/Brig.Gen.
Harvard Law School	Rutherford Birchard Hayes	N/Brig.Gen.
Harvard Law School	Alexander Robert Lawton	S/Brig.Gen.
Harvard Law School	Nelson Taylor	N/Brig.Gen.

Harvard University	Francis Channing Barlow	N/Brig.Gen.
Harvard University	William Francis Bartlett	N/Brig.Gen.
Harvard University	John Rogers Cooke	S/Brig.Gen.
Harvard University	Joseph Tarr Copeland	N/Brig.Gen.
Harvard University	Charles Devens,Jr.	N/Brig.Gen.
Harvard University	Henry Lawrence Eustis	N/Brig.Gen.
Harvard University	Manning Ferguson Force	N/Brig.Gen.
Harvard University	Kenner Garrard	N/Brig.Gen.
Harvard University	Martin Witherspoon Gary	S/Brig.Gen.
Harvard University	Joseph Hayes	N/Brig.Gen.
Harvard University	William Henry F. Lee	S/Maj.Gen.
Harvard University	Gilman Marston	N/Brig.Gen.
Harvard University	Nathaniel Collins McLean	N/Brig.Gen.
Harvard University	Charles Jackson Paine	N/Brig.Gen.
Harvard University	John Smith Preston	S/Brig.Gen.
Harvard University	William Preston	S/Brig.Gen.
Harvard University	Isaac Fitzgerald Shepard	N/Brig.Gen.
Harvard University	Thomas Church H. Smith	N/Brig.Gen.
Harvard University	James Samuel Wadsworth	N/Brig.Gen.
Harvard University	Edward Augustus Wild	N/Brig.Gen.
Haverford College	Isaac Jones Wistar	N/Brig.Gen.
Hobart College	Edward Stuyvesant Bragg	N/Brig.Gen.
Holy Cross Academy	Frank Crawford Armstrong	S/Brig.Gen.
Imperial M.A.	John Basil Turchin	N/Brig.Gen.
Indiana Medical College	Robert Alexander Cameron	N/Brig.Gen.
Indiana University	Ebenezer Dumont	N/Brig.Gen.
Jackson College	John Calvin Brown	S/Maj.Gen.
Jackson College	Preston Smith	S/Brig.Gen.
Jacksonville College	Leonard Fulton Ross	N/Brig.Gen.
Jefferson College	John White Geary	N/Brig.Gen.
Jefferson College	Louis Hebert	S/Brig.Gen.
Jefferson College	Paul Octave Hebert	S/Brig.Gen.
Jefferson College	Albert Gallatin Jenkins	S/Brig.Gen.
Jefferson College	Joshua Thomas Owen	N/Brig.Gen.
Jesuit College	John George Walker	S/Maj.Gen.
Jesuit College	Sterling Alexander Wood	S/Brig.Gen.
Karlsruhe M.A.	Max Weber	N/Brig.Gen.
Kentucky Law School	Isham Nicholas Haynie	N/Brig.Gen.
Kentucky M.I.	Robert Frederick Hoke	S/Maj.Gen.
Kentucky M.I.	Charles Carroll Walcutt	N/Brig.Gen.
Kenyon College	John Grant Mitchell	N/Brig.Gen.
Kenyon College	Robert Byington Mitchell	N/Brig.Gen.
Knox College	James Alexander Williamson	N/Brig.Gen.
LaGrange College	John Gregg	S/Brig.Gen.
Lancaster Academy	John Fulton Reynolds	N/Maj.Gen.
Univ.of Louisiana	Nathaniel Harrison Harris	S/Brig.Gen.
Univ.of Louisiana	William Miller	S/Brig.Gen.
Univ.of Louisiana	Francis Redding Nicholls	S/Brig.Gen.
Univ.of Louisiana	Zebulon York	S/Brig.Gen.
Marion College	Henry Watkins Allen	S/Brig.Gen.
Marion County Seminary	George Henry Chapman	N/Brig.Gen.
McKendree College	James Harrison Wilson	N/Brig.Gen.
Miami University	Joseph Robert Davis	S/Brig.Gen.
Miami University	Robert Cumming Schenck	N/Maj.Gen.
Miami University	John Stuart Williams	S/Brig.Gen.
Univ.of Michigan	Elon John Farnsworth	N/Brig.Gen.

Univ.of Mississippi	Dudley McIver DuBose	S/Brig.Gen.
Univ.of Missouri	John Bullock Clark,Jr.	S/Brig.Gen.
Mt.St.Mary's College	William Ward Orme	N/Brig.Gen.
Mt.St.Mary's College	James William Reilly	N/Brig.Gen.
Nashville M.I.	Thomas Benton Smith	S/Brig.Gen.
Nashville University	William Barksdale	S/Brig.Gen.
Nashville University	Thomas Green	S/Brig.Gen.
Nashville University	George Ear Maney	S/Brig.Gen.
Nashville University	Gideon Johnson Pillow	S/Brig.Gen.
Nashville University	Cadmus Marcellus Wilcox	S/Maj.Gen.
National University	William Montague Browne	S/Brig.Gen.
New Baltimore Academy	Eppa Hunton	S/Brig.Gen.
New York Medical Coll.	William Alexander Hammond	N/Brig.Gen.
New York Medical Coll.	James Lawlor Kiernan	N/Brig.Gen.
New York University	Daniel Edgar Sickles	N/Maj.Gen.
Univ.of North Carolina	George Burgwyn Anderson	S/Brig.Gen.
Univ.of North Carolina	Rufus Barringer	S/Brig.Gen.
Univ.of North Carolina	John Decatur Barry	S/Brig.Gen.
Univ.of North Carolina	Thomas Lanier Clingman	S/Brig.Gen.
Univ.of North Carolina	Richard Caswell Gatlin	S/Brig.Gen.
Univ.of North Carolina	Bryan Grimes	S/Maj.Gen.
Univ.of North Carolina	Robert Daniel Johnston	S/Brig.Gen.
Univ.of North Carolina	William Gaston Lewis	S/Brig.Gen.
Univ.of North Carolina	James Johnston Pettigrew	S/Brig.Gen.
Univ.of North Carolina	Matt Whitaker Ransom	S/Brig.Gen.
Univ.of North Carolina	Alfred Moore Scales	S/Brig.Gen.
Norwalk Academy	James Birdseye McPherson	N/Maj.Gen.
Norwich Academy	Joseph Anthony Mower	N/Maj.Gen.
Norwich University	Edward Hatch	N/Brig.Gen.
Norwich University	William Nelson	N/Maj.Gen.
Norwich University	Thomas Edward G. Ransom	N/Brig.Gen.
Norwich University	Truman Seymour	N/Brig.Gen.
Oakland College	Hiram Bronson Granbury	S/Brig.Gen.
Oberlin College	Jacob Dolson Cox	N/Maj.Gen.
Oberlin College	Emory Upton	N/Brig.Gen.
Oglethorpe University	Philip Cook	S/Brig.Gen.
University of Ohio	Richard Griffith	S/Brig.Gen.
University of Ohio	William Sooy Smith	N/Brig.Gen.
Ohio Wesleyan Univ.	Otho French Strahl	S/Brig.Gen.
Ohio Wesleyan Univ.	Daniel Harris Reynolds	S/Brig.Gen.
Univ.of Pennsylvania	Joseph K. Barnes	N/Brig.Gen.
Univ.of Pennsylvania	Samuel Wylie Crawford	N/Brig.Gen.
Univ.of Pennsylvania	George Brinton McClellan	N/Maj.Gen.
Univ.of Pennsylvania	Montgomery Meigs	N/Brig.Gen.
Univ.of Pennsylvania	James St.Clair Morton	N/Brig.Gen.
Univ.of Pennsylvania	Thomas Hewson Neill	N/Brig.Gen.
Univ.of Pennsylvania	John Grubb Parke	N/Maj.Gen.
Univ.of Pennsylvania	Joseph Rodman West	N/Brig.Gen.
Philips-Andover Academy	Isaac Ingalls Stevens	N/Brig.Gen.
Pitt University	Francis Jay Herron	N/Maj.Gen.
Pitt University	James Scott Negley	N/Maj.Gen.
Princeton University	William Wirt Allen	S/Brig.Gen.
Princeton University	James Jay Archer	S/Brig.Gen.
Princeton University	William Worth Belknap	N/Brig.Gen.
Princeton University	Francis Preston Blair	N/Maj.Gen.
Princeton University	Jerimiah Tilford Boyle	N/Brig.Gen.

Princeton University	Lawrence O'Bryan Branch	S/Brig.Gen.
Princeton University	William Lindsay Brandon	S/Brig.Gen.
Princeton University	Samuel Powhatan Carter	N/Brig.Gen.
Princeton University	James Chesnut, Jr.	S/Brig.Gen.
Princeton University	Alfred Holt Colquitt	S/Brig.Gen.
Princeton University	Bradley Tyler Johnson	S/Brig.Gen.
Princeton University	Allen Thomas	S/Brig.Gen.
Princeton University	Horatio Phillips Van Cleve	N/Brig.Gen.
Randolph-Macon College	Nathan George Evans	S/Brig.Gen.
Rhinebeck Academy	Stephen Gardner Champlin	N/Brig.Gen.
Sharon Academy	John Sedgwick	N/Maj.Gen.
Shurtleff College	John McCauley Palmer	N/Maj.Gen.
South Carolina M.A.	Ellison Capers	S/Brig.Gen.
South Carolina M.A.	Johnson Hagood	S/Brig.Gen.
South Carolina M.A.	Micah Jenkins	S/Brig.Gen.
South Carolina M.A.	Evander McIvor Law	S/Brig.Gen.
Univ.of South Carolina	Milledge Luke Bonham	S/Brig.Gen.
Univ.of South Carolina	John Bratton	S/Brig.Gen.
Univ.of South Carolina	James Cantey	S/Brig.Gen.
Univ.of South Carolina	James Ronald Chalmers	S/Brig.Gen.
Univ.of South Carolina	James Conner	S/Brig.Gen.
Univ.of South Carolina	Stephen Elliott,Jr.	S/Brig.Gen.
Univ.of South Carolina	John Buchanan Floyd	S/Brig.Gen.
Univ.of South Carolina	States Rights Gist	S/Brig.Gen.
Univ.of South Carolina	Daniel Chevilette Govan	S/Brig.Gen.
Univ.of South Carolina	Henry Gray	S/Brig.Gen.
Univ.of South Carolina	Maxcy Gregg	S/Brig.Gen.
Univ.of South Carolina	Wade Hampton	S/Lt.Gen.
Univ.of South Carolina	John King Jackson	S/Brig.Gen.
Univ.of South Carolina	John Doby Kennedy	S/Brig.Gen.
Univ.of South Carolina	Thomas Muldrup Logan	S/Brig.Gen.
Univ.of South Carolina	Samuel McGowan	S/Brig.Gen.
Univ.of South Carolina	Dandridge McRae	S/Brig.Gen.
Univ.of South Carolina	John Dunlap Stevenson	N/Brig.Gen.
Univ.of South Carolina	William Henry Wallace	S/Brig.Gen.
Univ.of South Carolina	Thomas Neville Waul	S/Brig.Gen.
Univ.of South Carolina	John Austin Wharton	S/Maj.Gen.
Univ.of South Carolina	Louis Trezevant Wigfall	S/Brig.Gen.
St.Cyr M.A.	Alfred Napoleon Duffie	N/Brig.Gen.
St.John's College	John Morrison Oliver	N/Brig.Gen.
St.Mary's College	Thomas James Churchill	S/Maj.Gen.
St.Mary's College	Harry Thompson Hays	S/Maj.Gen.
St.Mary's College	William Thomas Ward	N/Brig.Gen.
Stanislaus College	Camille A.J.M. Polignac	S/Maj.Gen.
Transylvania Univ.	Thomas Turpin Crittenden	N/Brig.Gen.
Transylvania Univ.	Albert Sidney Johnston	S/General
Transylvania Univ.	John Hunt Morgan	S/Brig.Gen.
Transylvania Univ.	Jerome Robertson	S/Brig.Gen.
Transylvania Univ.	Joseph Orville Shelby	S/Brig.Gen.
Transylvania Univ.	Green Clay Smith	N/Brig.Gen.
Trinity College	John Smith Phelps	N/Brig.Gen.
Tufts College	Selden Connor	N/Brig.Gen.
Union College	Daniel Butterfield	N/Maj.Gen.
Union College	Henry Wager Halleck	N/Maj.Gen.
Union College	John Frederick Hartranft	N/Brig.Gen.
Union College	James Hewett Ledlie	N/Brig.Gen.

Union College	Albert Lindley Lee	N/Brig.Gen.
Union College	Joseph Benjamin Palmer	S/Brig.Gen.
Union College	Robert Brown Potter	N/Brig.Gen.
Union College	Samuel Allen Rice	N/Brig.Gen.
Union College	John Starkweather	N/Brig.Gen.
Union College	Robert Augustus Toombs	S/Brig.Gen.
Virginia M.I.	Raleigh Edward Colston	S/Brig.Gen.
Virginia M.I.	Birkett Davenport Fry	S/Brig.Gen.
Virginia M.I.	William Young Conn Humes	S/Brig.Gen.
Virginia M.I.	John Robert Jones	S/Brig.Gen.
Virginia M.I.	William Mahone	S/Maj.Gen.
Virginia M.I.	John McCausland	S/Brig.Gen.
Virginia M.I.	Robert Emmett Rodes	S/Maj.Gen.
Virginia M.I.	James Edwin Slaughter	S/Brig.Gen.
Virginia M.I.	Alfred Jefferson Vaughan	S/Brig.Gen.
Virginia M.I.	Reuben Lindsay Walker	S/Brig.Gen.
Virginia M.I.	Gabriel Colvin Wharton	S/Brig.Gen.
Univ.of Virginia	Richard Lee T. Beale	S/Brig.Gen.
Univ.of Virginia	Theodore Brevard	S/Brig.Gen.
Univ.of Virginia	John Carpenter Carter	S/Brig.Gen.
Univ.of Virginia	Douglas Hancock Cooper	S/Brig.Gen.
Univ.of Virginia	Samuel Garland,Jr.	S/Brig.Gen.
Univ.of Virginia	James Henry Lane	S/Brig.Gen.
Univ.of Virginia	Dabney Herndon Maury	S/Maj.Gen.
Univ.of Virginia	William Henry Payne	S/Brig.Gen.
Univ.of Virginia	Lucius Eugene Polk	S/Brig.Gen.
Univ.of Virginia	Carnot Posey	S/Brig.Gen.
Univ.of Virginia	William Andrew Quarles	S/Brig.Gen.
Univ.of Virginia	George Wythe Randolph	S/Brig.Gen.
Univ.of Virginia	Paul Jones Semmes	S/Brig.Gen.
Univ.of Virginia	William Terry	S/Brig.Gen.
Univ.of Virginia	William Richard Terry	S/Brig.Gen.
Univ.of Virginia	James Alexander Walker	S/Brig.Gen.
Univ.of Virginia	Williams Carter Wickham	S/Brig.Gen.
Univ.of Virginia	William Hugh Young	S/Brig.Gen.
Wabash College	Joseph Jones Reynolds	N/Maj.Gen.
Wake Forrest College	Thomas Fentress Toon	S/Brig.Gen.
Wabash College	Edward Richard S. Canby	N/Maj.Gen.
Wabash College	Charles Cruft	N/Brig.Gen.
Wabash College	Speed Smith Fry	N/Brig.Gen.
Washington College	Absalom Baird	N/Brig.Gen.
Washington College	James Cooper	N/Brig.Gen.
Washington College	John Echols	S/Brig.Gen.
Washington College	John Daniel Imboden	S/Brig.Gen.
Washington College	Alfred Eugene Jackson	S/Brig.Gen.
Washington College	James Lawson Kemper	S/Maj.Gen.
Washington College	Robert Doak Lilley	S/Brig.Gen.
Washington College	Henry Alexander Wise	S/Brig.Gen.
Wesleyan University	Lawrence Sullivan Ross	S/Brig.Gen.
Westbrook Seminary	George Lafayette Beal	N/Brig.Gen.
West Tennessee College	William Hicks Jackson	S/Brig.Gen.
West Tennessee College	Alexander William Campbell	S/Brig.Gen.
Western M.I.	George Washington Gordon	S/Brig.Gen.
Western Reserve Univ.	Halbert Eleazer Paine	N/Brig.Gen.
William & Mary College	Edwin Gray Lee	S/Brig.Gen.
William & Mary College	Winfield Scott	N/Maj.Gen.

William & Mary College	William Booth Taliaferro	S/Maj.Gen.
Williams College	Henry Shaw Briggs	N/Brig.Gen.
Williams College	James Abram Garfield	N/Maj.Gen.
Williams College	Ranald Slidell Mackenzie	N/Brig.Gen.
Yale Law School	Alfred Howe Terry	N/Maj.Gen.
Yale University	Henry Washington Benham	N/Brig.Gen.
Yale University	Henry Beebee Carrington	N/Brig.Gen.
Yale University	Cassius Marcellus Clay	N/Maj.Gen.
Yale University	John Thomas Croxton	N/Brig.Gen.
Yale University	Orris Sanford Ferry	N/Brig.Gen.
Yale University	Randall Lee Gibson	S/Brig.Gen.
Yale University	Edward Harland	N/Brig.Gen.
Yale University	Alexander Hawthorne	S/Brig.Gen.
Yale University	Henry Rootes Jackson	S/Brig.Gen.
Yale University	Elisha Franklin Paxton	S/Brig.Gen.
Yale University	James Edwards Rains	S/Brig.Gen.
Yale University	James Clay Rice	N/Brig.Gen.
Yale University	Isaac Munroe St.John	S/Brig.Gen.
Yale University	Wager Swayne	N/Brig.Gen.
Yale University	James Camp Tappan	S/Brig.Gen.
Yale University	Richard Taylor	S/Lt.Gen.
Yale University	Daniel Ullmann	N/Brig.Gen.
Yale University	Alpheus Starkey Williams	N/Brig.Gen.

8

Civil War Generals by Graduation from U.S. Military Academy

Generals in this chapter are listed first by the year they graduated from West Point, then alphabetically within each year. Dates of birth are listed for comparative purposes.

YEAR	GENERAL	SIDE/RANK	DATE OF BIRTH
1805	Joseph Gilbert Totten	N/Brig.Gen.	April 17, 1788
1814	James Wolfe Ripley	N/Brig.Gen.	December 10, 1794
1814	Charles Mynn Thruston	N/Brig.Gen.	February 22, 1798
1815	Samuel Cooper	S/General	June 12, 1798
1817	Ethan Allen Hitchcock	N/Maj.Gen.	May 18, 1798
1818	Richard Delafield	N/Brig.Gen.	September 1, 1798
1819	Daniel Tyler	N/Brig.Gen.	January 7, 1799
1820	George Douglas Ramsay	N/Brig.Gen.	February 21, 1802
1820	John Henry Winder	S/Brig.Gen.	February 21, 1800
1822	John J. Abercrombie	N/Brig.Gen.	March 4, 1798
1822	David Hunter	N/Maj.Gen.	July 21, 1802
1822	Joseph King Mansfield	N/Brig.Gen.	December 22, 1803
1822	Isaac Ridgeway Trimble	S/Maj.Gen.	May 15, 1802
1822	George Wright	N/Brig.Gen.	October 21, 1801
1823	George Sears Greene	N/Brig.Gen.	May 6, 1801
1823	Lorenzo Thomas	N/Brig.Gen.	October 26, 1804
1825	Robert Anderson	N/Brig.Gen.	June 14, 1805
1825	Daniel Smith Donelson	S/Maj.Gen.	June 23, 1801
1825	Benjamin Huger	S/Maj.Gen.	November 22, 1805
1825	George A. McCall	N/Brig.Gen.	March 16, 1802
1825	William Montgomery	N/Brig.Gen.	July 10, 1801
1825	Charles Smith	N/Maj.Gen.	April 24, 1807
1826	Silas Casey	N/Maj.Gen.	July 12, 1807
1826	Amos Beebe Eaton	N/Brig.Gen.	May 12, 1806
1826	John Grayson	S/Brig.Gen.	October 18, 1806
1826	Samuel Heintzelman	N/Maj.Gen.	September 30, 1805
1826	Albert Johnston	S/General	February 2, 1803
1827	Napoleon Buford	N/Brig.Gen.	January 13, 1807
1827	Philip Cooke	N/Brig.Gen.	June 13, 1809
1827	Leonidas Polk	S/Lt.Gen.	April 10, 1806
1827	Gabriel James Rains	S/Brig.Gen.	June 4, 1803
1828	Thomas Drayton	S/Brig.Gen.	August 24, 1808
1828	Hugh Weedon Mercer	S/Brig.Gen.	November 27, 1808

1829	James Barnes	N/Brig.Gen.	December 28, 1801
1829	Albert Blanchard	S/Brig.Gen.	September 10, 1810
1829	Catharinus Buckingham	N/Brig.Gen.	March 14, 1808
1829	Thomas Alfred Davies	N/Brig.Gen.	December 3, 1809
1829	Theophilus Holmes	S/Lt.Gen.	November 13, 1804
1829	Joseph Johnston	S/General	February 3, 1807
1829	Robert Edward Lee	S/General	January 19, 1807
1829	Ormsby Mitchel	N/Maj.Gen.	July 28, 1809
1830	Robert Buchanan	N/Brig.Gen.	March 1, 1811
1830	John Magruder	S/Maj.Gen.	May 1, 1807
1830	William Pendleton	S/Brig.Gen.	December 26, 1809
1831	Jacob Ammen	N/Brig.Gen.	January 7, 1806
1831	Samuel Ryan Curtis	N/Maj.Gen.	February 3, 1805
1831	William Emory	N/Brig.Gen.	September 7, 1811
1831	Andrew Humphreys	N/Maj.Gen.	November 2, 1810
1831	Thomas McKean	N/Brig.Gen.	August 21, 1810
1831	Lucius Northrop	S/Brig.Gen.	September 8, 1811
1831	Horatio Van Cleve	N/Brig.Gen.	November 23, 1809
1832	Philip Cocke	S/Brig.Gen.	April 17, 1809
1832	George Crittenden	S/Maj.Gen.	March 20, 1812
1832	Richard Gatlin	S/Brig.Gen.	January 18, 1809
1832	Erasmus Darwin Keyes	N/Maj.Gen.	May 29, 1810
1832	Randolph Barnes Marcy	N/Brig.Gen.	April 9, 1812
1832	Humphrey Marshall	S/Brig.Gen.	January 13, 1812
1833	Benjamin Alvord	N/Brig.Gen.	August 18, 1813
1833	John Gross Barnard	N/Brig.Gen.	May 19, 1815
1833	George Cullum	N/Brig.Gen.	February 25, 1809
1833	Rufus King	N/Brig.Gen.	January 26, 1814
1833	Daniel Ruggles	S/Brig.Gen.	January 31, 1810
1833	Henry Walton Wessells	N/Brig.Gen.	February 20, 1809
1834	Goode Bryan	S/Brig.Gen.	August 31, 1811
1834	William Scott Ketchum	N/Brig.Gen.	July 7, 1813
1834	Gabriel Rene Paul	N/Brig.Gen.	March 22, 1813
1835	Herman Haupt	N/Brig.Gen.	March 26, 1817
1835	John Henry Martindale	N/Brig.Gen.	March 20, 1815
1835	George Gordon Meade	N/Maj.Gen.	December 31, 1815
1835	George Webb Morell	N/Maj.Gen.	January 8, 1815
1835	Henry Morris Naglee	N/Brig.Gen.	January 15, 1815
1835	Marsena Patrick	N/Brig.Gen.	March 11, 1811
1835	Henry Prince	N/Brig.Gen.	June 19, 1811
1835	Benjamin Roberts	N/Brig.Gen.	November 18, 1810
1835	Jones Withers	S/Maj.Gen.	January 12, 1814
1836	Robert Allen	N/Brig.Gen.	March 15, 1811
1836	Joseph Reid Anderson	S/Brig.Gen.	February 16, 1813
1836	Danville Leadbetter	S/Brig.Gen.	August 26, 1811
1836	Henry Hayes Lockwood	N/Brig.Gen.	August 17, 1814
1836	Montgomery Meigs	N/Brig.Gen.	May 3, 1816
1836	John Wolcott Phelps	N/Brig.Gen.	November 13, 1813
1836	Thomas West Sherman	N/Brig.Gen.	March 26, 1813
1836	Lloyd Tilghman	S/Brig.Gen.	January 26, 1816
1836	Daniel Woodbury	N/Brig.Gen.	December 16, 1812
1837	Lewis Golding Arnold	N/Brig.Gen.	January 15, 1817
1837	Henry Benham	N/Brig.Gen.	April 17, 1813
1837	Braxton Bragg	S/General	March 22, 1817
1837	Robert Hall Chilton	S/Brig.Gen.	February 25, 1815
1837	Alexander Dyer	N/Brig.Gen.	January 10, 1815

1837	Jubal Anderson Early	S/Lt.Gen.	November 3, 1816
1837	Arnold Elzey	S/Maj.Gen.	December 18, 1816
1837	William Henry French	N/Maj.Gen.	January 13, 1815
1837	Joseph Hooker	N/Maj.Gen.	November 13, 1814
1837	William Whann Mackall	S/Brig.Gen.	January 18, 1817
1837	John Pemberton	S/Lt.Gen.	August 10, 1814
1837	Eliakim Scammon	N/Brig.Gen.	December 27, 1816
1837	John Sedgwick	N/Maj.Gen.	September 13, 1813
1837	John Blair Todd	N/Brig.Gen.	April 4, 1814
1837	Israel Vogdes	N/Brig.Gen.	August 4, 1816
1837	William Henry Walker	S/Maj.Gen.	November 26, 1816
1837	Thomas Williams	N/Brig.Gen.	January 10, 1815
1838	William Farquhar Barry	N/Brig.Gen.	August 18, 1818
1838	Pierre Beauregard	S/General	May 28, 1818
1838	Robert Seaman Granger	N/Brig.Gen.	May 24, 1816
1838	William Joseph Hardee	S/Lt.Gen.	October 12, 1815
1838	Edward Johnson	S/Maj.Gen.	April 16, 1816
1838	Irvin McDowell	N/Maj.Gen.	October 15, 1818
1838	Justus McKinstry	N/Brig.Gen.	July 6, 1814
1838	Alexander Reynolds	S/Brig.Gen.	April 0, 1816
1838	Henry Sibley	S/Brig.Gen.	May 25, 1816
1838	Andrew Jackson Smith	N/Maj.Gen.	April 28, 1815
1838	Carter Stevenson	S/Maj.Gen.	September 21, 1817
1838	James Trapier	S/Brig.Gen.	November 24, 1815
1838	Henry Wayne	S/Brig.Gen.	September 18, 1815
1839	Edward Richard Canby	N/Maj.Gen.	November 9, 1817
1839	Jeremy Francis Gilmer	S/Maj.Gen.	February 23, 1818
1839	Henry Wager Halleck	N/Maj.Gen.	January 16, 1815
1839	Joseph Abel Haskin	N/Brig.Gen.	June 21, 1818
1839	Henry Jackson Hunt	N/Brig.Gen.	September 14, 1819
1839	Alexander Lawton	S/Brig.Gen.	November 4, 1818
1839	Edward Otho C. Ord	N/Maj.Gen.	October 18, 1818
1839	Eleazer Arthur Paine	N/Brig.Gen.	September 10, 1815
1839	James Ricketts	N/Brig.Gen.	June 21, 1817
1839	Isaac Ingalls Stevens	N/Brig.Gen.	March 25, 1818
1840	Richard Ewell	S/Lt.Gen.	February 8, 1817
1840	George Getty	N/Brig.Gen.	October 2, 1819
1840	William Hays	N/Brig.Gen.	May 9, 1819
1840	Paul Octave Hebert	S/Brig.Gen.	December 12, 1818
1840	Bushrod Rust Johnson	S/Maj.Gen.	October 7, 1817
1840	Thomas Jordan	S/Brig.Gen.	September 30, 1819
1840	James Green Martin	S/Brig.Gen.	February 14, 1819
1840	John Porter McCown	S/Maj.Gen.	August 19, 1815
1840	William Sherman	N/Maj.Gen.	February 8, 1820
1840	William Steele	S/Brig.Gen.	May 1, 1819
1840	George Henry Thomas	N/Maj.Gen.	July 31, 1816
1840	Stewart Van Vliet	N/Brig.Gen.	July 21, 1815
1841	John Milton Brannan	N/Brig.Gen.	July 1, 1819
1841	William Brooks	N/Maj.Gen.	January 28, 1821
1841	Don Carlos Buell	N/Maj.Gen.	March 23, 1818
1841	Abraham Buford	S/Brig.Gen.	January 18, 1820
1841	Richard Brooke Garnett	S/Brig.Gen.	November 21, 1817
1841	Robert Selden Garnett	S/Brig.Gen.	December 16, 1819
1841	Josiah Gorgas	S/Brig.Gen.	July 1, 1818
1841	Schuyler Hamilton	N/Maj.Gen.	July 25, 1822
1841	Albion Parris Howe	N/Brig.Gen.	March 13, 1818

1841	John Marshall Jones	S/Brig.Gen.	July 26, 1820
1841	Samuel Jones	S/Maj.Gen.	December 17, 1819
1841	Nathaniel Lyon	N/Brig.Gen.	July 14, 1818
1841	Joseph Bennett Plummer	N/Brig.Gen.	November 15, 1816
1841	John Fulton Reynolds	N/Maj.Gen.	September 20, 1820
1841	Israel Bush Richardson	N/Maj.Gen.	December 26, 1815
1841	Claudius Wistar Sears	S/Brig.Gen.	November 8, 1817
1841	Alfred Sully	N/Brig.Gen.	May 22, 1820
1841	Zealous Bates Tower	N/Brig.Gen.	January 12, 1819
1841	Amiel Weeks Whipple	N/Brig.Gen.	October 15, 1816
1841	Horatio Wright	N/Maj.Gen.	March 6, 1820
1842	Richard Heron Anderson	S/Lt.Gen.	October 7, 1821
1842	Napoleon Jackson Dana	N/Maj.Gen.	April 15, 1822
1842	Abner Doubleday	N/Brig.Gen.	June 26, 1819
1842	Henry Lawrence Eustis	N/Brig.Gen.	February 1, 1819
1842	Daniel Harvey Hill	S/Lt.Gen.	July 12, 1821
1842	James Longstreet	S/Lt.Gen.	January 8, 1821
1842	Mansfield Lovell	S/Maj.Gen.	October 20, 1822
1842	Lafayette McLaws	S/Maj.Gen.	January 15, 1821
1842	John Newton	N/Maj.Gen.	August 25, 1822
1842	John Pope	N/Maj.Gen.	March 16, 1822
1842	William Rosecrans	N/Maj.Gen.	September 6, 1819
1842	Gustavus Smith	S/Maj.Gen.	November 30, 1821
1842	Martin Luther Smith	S/Maj.Gen.	September 9, 1819
1842	Alexander Stewart	S/Lt.Gen.	October 2, 1821
1842	George Sykes	N/Maj.Gen.	October 9, 1822
1842	Earl Van Dorn	S/Maj.Gen.	September 17, 1820
1842	Seth Williams	N/Brig.Gen.	March 22, 1822
1843	Christopher Augur	N/Maj.Gen.	July 10, 1821
1843	William Buel Franklin	N/Brig.Gen.	February 27, 1823
1843	Samuel Gibbs French	S/Maj.Gen.	November 22, 1818
1843	Franklin Gardner	S/Maj.Gen.	January 29, 1823
1843	Ulysses Simpson Grant	N/Lt.Gen.	April 27, 1822
1843	Charles Smith Hamilton	N/Maj.Gen.	November 16, 1822
1843	James Allen Hardie	N/Brig.Gen.	May 5, 1823
1843	Rufus Ingalls	N/Brig.Gen.	August 23, 1818
1843	Henry Moses Judah	N/Brig.Gen.	June 12, 1821
1843	John James Peck	N/Maj.Gen.	January 4, 1821
1843	Issac Quinby	N/Brig.Gen.	January 29, 1821
1843	Joseph Jones Reynolds	N/Maj.Gen.	January 4, 1822
1843	Roswell Sabine Ripley	S/Brig.Gen.	March 14, 1823
1843	Frederick Steele	N/Maj.Gen.	January 14, 1819
1844	Simon Bolivar Buckner	S/Lt.Gen.	April 1, 1823
1844	Daniel Marsh Frost	S/Brig.Gen.	August 9, 1823
1844	Winfield Hancock	N/Maj.Gen.	February 14, 1824
1844	Alexander Hays	N/Brig.Gen.	July 8, 1819
1844	Alfred Pleasonton	N/Maj.Gen.	July 7, 1824
1845	Barnard Elliott Bee	S/Brig.Gen.	February 8, 1824
1845	John Wynn Davidson	N/Brig.Gen.	August 18, 1824
1845	Gordon Granger	N/Maj.Gen.	November 6, 1822
1845	John Porter Hatch	N/Brig.Gen.	January 9, 1822
1845	James Morrison Hawes	S/Brig.Gen.	January 7, 1824
1845	Louis Hebert	S/Brig.Gen.	March 13, 1820
1845	George Baird Hodge	S/Brig.Gen.	April 8, 1828
1845	Thomas Gamble Pitcher	N/Brig.Gen.	October 23, 1824
1845	Fitz John Porter	N/Maj.Gen.	August 31, 1822

1845	David Allen Russell	N/Brig.Gen.	December 10, 1820
1845	Edmund Kirby Smith	S/General	May 16, 1824
1845	William Farrar Smith	N/Maj.Gen.	February 17, 1824
1845	Charles Pomeroy Stone	N/Brig.Gen.	September 30, 1824
1845	Thomas John Wood	N/Maj.Gen.	September 25, 1823
1845	William Henry Whiting	S/Maj.Gen.	March 22, 1824
1846	John Adams	S/Brig.Gen.	July 1, 1825
1846	Samuel Powhatan Carter	N/Brig.Gen.	August 6, 1819
1846	Darius Nash Couch	N/Maj.Gen.	July 23, 1822
1846	John Gray Foster	N/Maj.Gen.	May 27, 1823
1846	William Gardner	S/Brig.Gen.	June 8, 1824
1846	Alfred Gibbs	N/Brig.Gen.	April 22, 1823
1846	Charles Gilbert	N/Brig.Gen.	March 1, 1822
1846	George Henry Gordon	N/Brig.Gen.	July 19, 1823
1846	Thomas Jackson	S/Lt.Gen.	January 21, 1824
1846	David Rumph Jones	S/Maj.Gen.	April 5, 1825
1846	Dabney Herndon Maury	S/Maj.Gen.	May 21, 1822
1846	Samuel Bell Maxey	S/Maj.Gen.	March 30, 1825
1846	George McClellan	N/Maj.Gen.	December 3, 1826
1846	Innis Newton Palmer	N/Brig.Gen.	March 30, 1824
1846	George Edward Pickett	S/Maj.Gen.	January 28, 1825
1846	Jesse Lee Reno	N/Maj.Gen.	June 20, 1823
1846	Truman Seymour	N/Brig.Gen.	September 24, 1824
1846	William Duncan Smith	S/Brig.Gen.	July 28, 1825
1846	George Stoneman	N/Maj.Gen.	August 22, 1822
1846	Samuel Davis Sturgis	N/Brig.Gen.	June 11, 1822
1846	Cadmus Wilcox	S/Maj.Gen.	May 29, 1824
1847	Romeyn Beck Ayres	N/Brig.Gen.	December 20, 1825
1847	William Wallace Burns	N/Brig.Gen.	September 3, 1825
1847	Ambrose Burnside	N/Maj.Gen.	May 23, 1824
1847	James Barnet Fry	N/Brig.Gen.	February 22, 1827
1847	John Gibbon	N/Maj.Gen.	April 20, 1827
1847	Charles Griffin	N/Maj.Gen.	December 18, 1825
1847	Henry Heth	S/Maj.Gen.	December 16, 1825
1847	Ambrose Powell Hill	S/Lt.Gen.	November 9, 1825
1847	Lewis Cass Hunt	N/Brig.Gen.	February 23, 1824
1847	John Sanford Mason	N/Brig.Gen.	August 21, 1824
1847	Thomas Hewson Neill	N/Brig.Gen.	April 9, 1826
1847	Egbert Ludovicus Viele	N/Brig.Gen.	June 17, 1825
1847	Orlando Willcox	N/Brig.Gen.	April 16, 1823
1848	William Nelson Beall	S/Brig.Gen.	March 20, 1825
1848	John Buford	N/Brig.Gen.	March 4, 1826
1848	Nathan George Evans	S/Brig.Gen.	February 3, 1824
1848	William Edmonson Jones	S/Brig.Gen.	May 9, 1824
1848	George Hume Steuart	S/Brig.Gen.	August 24, 1828
1848	Walter Husted Stevens	S/Brig.Gen.	August 24, 1827
1849	Absalom Baird	N/Brig.Gen.	August 20, 1824
1849	Seth Maxwell Barton	S/Brig.Gen.	September 8, 1829
1849	Alfred Cumming	S/Brig.Gen.	January 30, 1829
1849	Johnson Kelly Duncan	S/Brig.Gen.	March 19, 1827
1849	Charles William Field	S/Maj.Gen.	April 6, 1828
1849	John Wesley Frazer	S/Brig.Gen.	January 6, 1827
1849	Quincy Adams Gillmore	N/Maj.Gen.	February 28, 1825
1849	Richard W. Johnson	N/Brig.Gen.	February 27, 1827
1849	James McQueen McIntosh	S/Brig.Gen.	1828
1849	John Creed Moore	S/Brig.Gen.	February 28, 1824

1849	John Grubb Parke	N/Maj.Gen.	September 22, 1827
1849	Beverly Robertson	S/Brig.Gen.	June 5, 1827
1849	Rufus Saxton	N/Brig.Gen.	October 19, 1824
1850	Richard Arnold	N/Brig.Gen.	April 12, 1828
1850	William Lewis Cabell	S/Brig.Gen.	January 1, 1827
1850	William Carlin	N/Brig.Gen.	November 24, 1829
1850	Eugene Asa Carr	N/Brig.Gen.	March 20, 1830
1850	Cuvier Grover	N/Brig.Gen.	July 29, 1828
1850	Armistead Lindsay Long	S/Brig.Gen.	September 3, 1825
1850	Jean Jacques Mouton	S/Brig.Gen.	February 18, 1829
1850	Robert Ransom,Jr.	S/Maj.Gen.	February 12, 1828
1850	Adam Jacoby Slemmer	N/Brig.Gen.	January 24, 1829
1850	Lucius Marshall Walker	S/Brig.Gen.	October 18, 1829
1850	Gouverneur Warren	N/Maj.Gen.	January 8, 1830
1850	Charles Sidney Winder	S/Brig.Gen.	October 18, 1829
1851	George Leonard Andrews	N/Brig.Gen.	August 31, 1828
1851	Laurence Simmons Baker	S/Brig.Gen.	May 15, 1830
1851	Junius Daniel	S/Brig.Gen.	June 27, 1828
1851	Kenner Garrard	N/Brig.Gen.	September 30, 1827
1851	Alvan Cullem Gillem	N/Brig.Gen.	July 29, 1830
1851	Benjamin Hardin Helm	S/Brig.Gen.	June 2, 1831
1851	William Morris	N/Brig.Gen.	April 22, 1827
1851	James St.Clair Morton	N/Brig.Gen.	September 24, 1829
1851	William Whipple	N/Brig.Gen.	August 2, 1826
1852	George Anderson	S/Brig.Gen.	April 12, 1831
1852	George Blake Cosby	S/Brig.Gen.	January 19, 1830
1852	George Crook	N/Maj.Gen.	September 8, 1828
1852	John Horace Forney	S/Maj.Gen.	August 12, 1829
1852	George Lucas Hartsuff	N/Maj.Gen.	May 28, 1830
1852	Milo Smith Hascall	N/Brig.Gen.	August 5, 1829
1852	John Parker Hawkins	N/Brig.Gen.	September 29, 1830
1852	August Kautz	N/Brig.Gen.	January 5, 1828
1852	Alexander McCook	N/Maj.Gen.	April 22, 1831
1852	Henry Warner Slocum	N/Maj.Gen.	September 24, 1827
1852	David Sloane Stanley	N/Maj.Gen.	June 1, 1828
1852	Charles Robert Woods	N/Brig.Gen.	February 19, 1827
1853	William Boggs	S/Brig.Gen.	March 18, 1829
1853	John Stevens Bowen	S/Maj.Gen.	October 30, 1830
1853	Alexander Chambers	N/Brig.Gen.	August 23, 1832
1853	John Chambliss,Jr.	S/Brig.Gen.	January 23, 1833
1853	Henry Brevard Davidson	S/Brig.Gen.	January 28, 1831
1853	John Bell Hood	S/General	June 1, 1831
1853	James McPherson	N/Maj.Gen.	November 14, 1828
1853	John Schofield	N/Maj.Gen.	September 29, 1831
1853	Philip Henry Sheridan	N/Maj.Gen.	March 6, 1831
1853	Joshua Woodrow Sill	N/Brig.Gen.	December 6, 1831
1853	James Argyle Smith	S/Brig.Gen.	July 1, 1831
1853	William Sooy Smith	N/Brig.Gen.	July 22, 1830
1853	William Rufus Terrill	N/Brig.Gen.	April 21, 1834
1853	Robert Ogden Tyler	N/Brig.Gen.	December 22, 1831
1853	Henry Harrison Walker	S/Brig.Gen.	October 15, 1832
1854	James Deshler	S/Brig.Gen.	February 18, 1833
1854	Archibald Gracie,Jr.	S/Brig.Gen.	December 1, 1832
1854	Oliver Otis Howard	N/Maj.Gen.	November 8, 1830
1854	George Washington Lee	S/Maj.Gen.	September 16, 1832
1854	Stephen Dill Lee	S/Lt.Gen.	September 22, 1833

1854	John Pegram	S/Brig.Gen.	January 24, 1832
1854	William Dorsey Pender	S/Maj.Gen.	February 6, 1834
1854	Thomas Howard Ruger	N/Brig.Gen.	April 2, 1833
1854	James Ewell Stuart	S/Maj.Gen.	February 6, 1833
1854	John Villepigue	S/Brig.Gen.	July 2, 1830
1854	Stephen Weed	N/Brig.Gen.	November 17, 1831
1855	William Woods Averell	N/Brig.Gen.	November 5, 1832
1855	David McMurtrie Gregg	N/Brig.Gen.	April 10, 1833
1855	William Babcock Hazen	N/Maj.Gen.	September 27, 1830
1855	Francis Nicholls	S/Brig.Gen.	August 20, 1834
1855	Francis Asbury Shoup	S/Brig.Gen.	March 22, 1834
1855	Alfred Torbert	N/Brig.Gen.	July 1, 1833
1855	John Wesley Turner	N/Brig.Gen.	July 19, 1833
1855	Alexander Webb	N/Brig.Gen.	February 15, 1835
1855	Godfrey Weitzel	N/Maj.Gen.	November 1, 1835
1856	George Bayard	N/Brig.Gen.	December 18, 1835
1856	Samuel Sprigg Carroll	N/Brig.Gen.	September 21, 1832
1856	William Hicks Jackson	S/Brig.Gen.	October 1, 1835
1856	Fitzhugh Lee	S/Maj.Gen.	November 19, 1835
1856	Lunsford Lomax	S/Maj.Gen.	November 4, 1835
1856	Hylan Benton Lyon	S/Brig.Gen.	February 22, 1836
1856	James Patrick Major	S/Brig.Gen.	May 14, 1836
1856	Orlando Metcalfe Poe	N/Brig.Gen.	March 7, 1832
1856	William Sanders	N/Brig.Gen.	August 12, 1833
1856	Francis Vinton	N/Brig.Gen.	June 1, 1835
1857	Edward Alexander	S/Brig.Gen.	May 26, 1835
1857	Robert Anderson	S/Brig.Gen.	October 1, 1835
1857	Samuel Wragg Ferguson	S/Brig.Gen.	November 3, 1834
1857	John Marmaduke	S/Maj.Gen.	March 14, 1833
1857	George Strong	N/Brig.Gen.	October 16, 1832
1858	Charles Harker	N/Brig.Gen.	December 2, 1835
1858	Bryan Morel Thomas	S/Brig.Gen.	May 8, 1836
1859	Martin Davis Hardin	N/Brig.Gen.	June 26, 1837
1859	Edwin Henry Stoughton	N/Brig.Gen.	June 23, 1838
1859	Joseph Wheeler	S/Maj.Gen.	September 10, 1836
1860	Wesley Merritt	N/Maj.Gen.	June 16, 1834
1860	Stephen Ramseur	S/Maj.Gen.	May 31, 1837
1860	James Wilson	N/Brig.Gen.	September 2, 1837
1861	Adelbert Ames	N/Brig.Gen.	October 31, 1835
1861	George A. Custer	N/Brig.Gen.	December 5, 1839
1861	Hugh Kilpatrick	N/Brig.Gen.	January 14, 1836
1861	Emory Upton	N/Brig.Gen.	August 27, 1839
1862	Ranald Mackenzie	N/Brig.Gen.	July 27, 1840

NOTE: George Baird Hodge, Brigadier General for the Confederacy, was the only Civil War general to graduate from Annapolis (class of 1845).

9

Civil War Generals
by Work Before the War

The professions and work the generals engaged in prior to the
Civil War are listed here alphabetically. The generals are
further listed alphabetically in each category of work. In
some cases it is not known what work if any was engaged in.
What formation that was available is listed. Many of the generals were admitted to the bar, but did not practice law as
their major livelihood. In these cases their other profession
is listed, followed by "/L" to indicate they were also lawyers.
In the column of work after the war, those listed as "Killed"
or "Died" are only those generals dying during wartime.

GENERAL	SIDE/RANK	WORK BEFORE	WORK AFTER
Samuel Allen Rice	N/B	Atty Gen-Iowa	Died-operation
John Stevens Bowen	S/M	Architect	Died-Dysentery
Charles Miller Shelley	S/B	Architect	Congress/Sheriff
Francis Jay Herron	N/M	Bank clerk	U.S.Marshal/L
John Beatty	N/B	Banker	Congress/Banker
Hiram Gregory Berry	N/M	Banker/politics	Killed
Napoleon Buford	N/B	Banker	Civil Service
Montgomery Dent Corse	S/B	Banker	Banker
Napoleon Jackson Dana	N/M	Banker/Soldier	R.R. Business
Hugh Weedon Mercer	S/B	Banker	Merchant
Henry Morris Naglee	N/B	Banker	Banker
John James Peck	N/M	Banker	Insurance
Paul Jones Semmes	S/B	Banker/farmer	Killed
William Henry Seward	N/B	Banker	Banker
Clement Hoffman Stevens	S/B	Banker	Killed
Charles Mynn Thruston	N/B	Banker	Farmer
Edward Henry Hobson	N/B	Bank President	Politics
William Edwin Baldwin	S/B	Book & Stationary	Died-horse fall
George Lafayette Beal	N/B	Bookbinder	St.Treas.-Maine
Luther Bradley	N/B	Bookkeeper	Soldier
Simon Bolivar Buckner	S/L	Business	Gov-Kentucky
Daniel Butterfield	N/M	Business/L	Business
George Cadwalader	N/M	Business	Business
Augustus Louis Chetlain	N/B	Business	Banker
George Pierce Doles	S/B	Business	Killed
Jacob Gartner Lauman	N/B	Business	Unknown

John Baillie McIntosh	N/B Business	Soldier
James Winning McMillan	N/B Business	US Pension Off.
Sullivan Amory Meredith	N/B Business	Drug Merchant
Gershom Mott	N/B Business	R.R. Paymaster
John Wilson Sprague	N/B Business	R.R. Manager
David Addison Weisiger	S/B Business	Banker
Thomas Algeo Rowley	N/B Cabinetmaker	U.S.Marshal/L
Gustavus Adolphus Smith	N/B Carriage Manuf.	I.R. Collector
Thomas Alfred Smyth	N/B Coachmaker	Killed
John Brown Gordon	S/M Coal mine devel.	Governor-Georgia
Jacob Ammen	N/B College Prof.	Engineer
Joshua Chamberlain	N/B College Prof.	Governor-Maine
Raleigh Edward Colston	S/B College Prof.	Soldier
Henry Lawrence Eustis	N/B College Prof.	College Prof.
Daniel Harvey Hill	S/L College Prof.	College President
Thomas Jackson	S/L College Prof.	Killed
James Henry Lane	S/B College Prof.	College Prof.
Henry Hayes Lockwood	N/B College Prof.	College Prof.
John McCausland	S/B College Prof.	Farmer
Ormsby Mitchel	N/M College Prof./L	Died-yellow fever
John Creed Moore	S/B College Prof.	Teacher/writer
Issac Ferdinand Quinby	N/B College Prof.	U.S.Marshal
Joseph Jones Reynolds	N/M College Prof.	Soldier
Claudius Wistar Sears	S/B College Prof.	College Prof.
Alexander Stewart	S/L College Prof.	College Prof.
Arthur Manigault	S/B Commis.business	Farmer/politics
William Barksdale	S/B Congress	Killed
Richard Lee T. Beale	S/B Congress/L	Congress/L
Francis Preston Blair	N/M Congress/L	Senator
Milledge Luke Bonham	S/B Congress/L	R.R.Commissioner
Lawrence Branch	S/B Congress/L	Killed
John Cochrane	N/B Congress/L	Politics
Alfred Holt Colquitt	S/B Congress/L	Governor-Georgia
James Cooper	N/B Congress/L	Died
John Farnsworth	N/B Congress/L	Congress/L
Winfield Featherston	S/B Congress/L	Judge
Lucius Gartrell	S/B Congress/L	Politics
Robert Hopkins Hatton	S/B Congress/L	Killed
James Streshly Jackson	N/B Congress/L	Killed
Albert Jenkins	S/B Congress/L	Killed
William High Keim	N/B Congress	Died-Camp Fever
John Alexander Logan	N/M Congress	Congress
Humphrey Marshall	S/B Congress/L	Lawyer
Gilman Marston	N/B Congress/L	Congress
John McClernand	N/M Congress/L	Politics
John Smith Phelps	N/B Congress/L	Gov-Missouri
William Preston	S/B Congress/L	Politics
Roger Atkinson Pryor	S/B Congress/L	Judge/L
Albert Rust	S/B Congress/L	Farmer
Alfred Moore Scales	S/B Congress/L	Gov-N.Carolina
Robert Cumming Schenck	N/M Congress	Lawyer
Daniel Edgar Sickles	N/M Congress	Congress
David Stuart	N/B Congress	Lawyer
William Vandever	N/B Congress/L	Congress
William Thomas Ward	N/B Congress	Lawyer
Cadwallader Washburn	N/M Congress/L	Gov-Wisconsin

John Wilkins Whitfield	S/B Congress	Politics
Darius Nash Couch	N/M Copper Manuf.	Civil Service
Zachariah Cantey Deas	S/B Cotton Broker	Stock Broker
James Monroe Goggin	S/B Cotton Broker	Unknown
William Edwin Starke	S/B Cotton Broker	Killed
Birkett Davenport Fry	S/B Cotton Manuf.	Cotton Manuf.
John Hunt Morgan	S/B Cotton Manuf.	Killed
Lucius Fairchild	N/B Court Clerk	Gov-Wisconsin
Marcus Joseph Wright	S/B Court Clerk/L	Writer/L
Edward Ferrero	N/B Dance Instructor	Ballroom Manager
Byron Root Pierce	N/B Dentist	Hotel Operator
James Patton Anderson	S/M Dr./US Marshal	Editor
James Blunt	N/M Doctor	Doctor
John Bratton	S/B Doctor	Congress
Samuel Wylie Crawford	N/B Doctor	Soldier
Richard Montgomery Gano	S/B Doctor	Min-Christian Ch.
Thomas Maley Harris	N/B Doctor	Doctor/Politics
James Lawlor Kiernan	N/B Doctor	Doctor
Nathan Kimball	N/B Doctor	St.Treas.-Indiana
Lucius Northrop	S/B Doctor	Farmer
Jerome Robertson	S/B Doctor	Railroad Builder
Edward Augustus Wild	N/B Doctor	Miner
Patrick Cleburne	S/M Druggist/L	Killed
Mahlon Dickerson Manson	N/B Druggist	Congress
William Birney	N/B Editor	Lawyer
William Montague Browne	S/B Editor	College Prof.
Robert Cameron	N/B Editor/Doctor	Warden
George Henry Chapman	N/B Editor/L	Judge
Joseph Roswell Hawley	N/B Editor/L	Gov-Connecticut
Rufus King	N/B Editor	Min-Rome
Stephen Miller	N/B Editor	Gov-Minnesota
James Sidney Robinson	N/B Editor	Congress
Isaac Shepard	N/B Editor	Editor
August Willich	N/B Editor	County Auditor
Micah Jenkins	S/B Educator	Killed
William Flank Perry	S/B Educator	College Prof.
George Leonard Andrews	N/B Engineer	U.S.Marshal
Alexander Asboth	N/B Engineer	Minister-Uruguay
James Barnes	N/B Engineer	R.R.Commissioner
Powell Clayton	N/B Engineer	Gov-Arkansas
Samuel Ryan Curtis	N/M Engineer	Died
Grenville Mellen Dodge	N/M Engineer	Railroad Builder
Alfred Washington Ellet	N/B Engineer	Banker/Railroad
Charles Kinnaird Graham	N/B Engineer/L	Engineer
George Sears Greene	N/B Engineer	Engineer
John Hartranft	N/B Engineer/L	Gov-Pennsylvania
Herman Haupt	N/B Engineer	Engineer
Joseph Hayes	N/B Engineer	Mining
Alexander Hays	N/B Engineer	Killed
Louis Hebert	S/B Engineer	Newspaper Editor
Wladimir Krzyzanowski	N/B Engineer	Civil Service
Frederick West Lander	N/B Engineer	Died
James Hewett Ledlie	N/B Engineer	Engineer
William MacRae	S/B Engineer	R.R.Supt.
William Mahone	S/M Engineer	Senator
Thomas Jefferson McKean	N/B Engineer	Farmer

Jean Jacques Mouton	S/B Engineer	Killed
Thomas Edward G. Ransom	N/B Engineer	Died
Robert Emmett Rodes	S/M Engineer	Killed
Alexander Schimmelfennig	N/B Engineer	Died-TB
William Sooy Smith	N/B Engineer	Engineer
Isaac Munroe St.John	S/B Engineer	Engineer
Lloyd Tilghman	S/B Engineer	Killed
Isaac Ridgeway Trimble	S/M Engineer	Unknown
John Basil Turchin	N/B Engineer	Patent Solicitor
Horatio Van Cleve	N/B Engineer	Postmaster
Alfred Vaughan,Jr	S/B Engineer	Farmer
Egbert Ludovicus Viele	N/B Engineer	Engineer
Francis Laurens Vinton	N/B Engineer	College Prof.
Joseph Dana Webster	N/B Engineer	I.R. Collector
Gabriel Colvin Wharton	S/B Engineer	Politics
David Henry Williams	N/B Engineer	Engineer
William Wirt Adams	S/B Farmer/Banker	Postmaster
William Wirt Allen	S/B Farmer	Farmer/US Marshal
Turner Ashby	S/B Farmer	Killed
Tyree Harris Bell	S/B Farmer	Farmer
Louis Ludwig Blenker	N/B Farmer	Died
William Lindsay Brandon	S/B Farmer	Retired
Goode Bryan	S/B Farmer	Retired
Abraham Buford	S/B Farmer	Farmer
John Chambliss,Jr.	S/B Farmer	Killed
Benjamin Cheatham	S/M Farmer	Postmaster
Philip St.George Cocke	S/B Farmer	Suicide
Joseph Alexander Cooper	N/B Farmer	Farmer
George Deitzler	N/B Farmer	Railroad
Thomas Pleasant Dockery	S/B Farmer	Engineer
Daniel Smith Donelson	S/M Farmer	Died
Thomas Fenwick Drayton	S/B Farmer	Insurance Agent
Stephen Elliott,Jr.	S/B Farmer	Politics
Joseph Finegan	S/B Farmer	Cotton Broker
Nathan Bedford Forrest	S/L Farmer	R.R.President
James Byron Gordon	S/B Farmer	Killed
Daniel Chevilette Govan	S/B Farmer	Indian Agent
Elkanah Brackin Greer	S/B Farmer/Merchant	Unknown
Bryan Grimes	S/M Farmer	Farmer
Charles Smith Hamilton	N/M Farmer	U.S.Marshal
Michael Kelly Lawler	N/B Farmer	Farmer
William Henry F. Lee	S/M Farmer	Congress
St.John Liddell	S/B Farmer	Farmer
James Scott Negley	N/M Farmer	Congress
Marsena Rudolph Patrick	N/B Farmer	Soldier
William Raine Peck	S/B Farmer	Farmer
Abram Sanders Piatt	N/B Farmer	Farmer
Lucius Eugene Polk	S/B Farmer	Farmer
Carnot Posey	S/B Farmer/L	Killed
Edward Elmer Potter	N/B Farmer	Unknown
Thomas Moore Scott	S/B Farmer	Farmer
Marcellus Stovall	S/B Farmer	Cotton Broker
Thomas Hart Taylor	S/B Farmer	Police Chief
Allen Thomas	S/B Farmer/L	Politics/Farmer
Edward Lloyd Thomas	S/B Farmer	Farmer
James Heyward Trapier	S/B Farmer/Soldier	Died

Adolph von Steinwehr	N/B Farmer	College Prof.
Reuben Lindsay Walker	S/B Farmer	Engineer/Farmer
William Henry Wallace	S/B Farmer/L	Judge
Stand Watie	S/B Farmer	Farmer
Thomas Neville Waul	S/B Farmer/L	Lawyer
Elon John Farnsworth	N/B Foragemaster	Killed
George Stannard	N/B Foundry Owner	Customs Collector
Erastus Barnard Tyler	N/B Fur Business	Postmaster
George Hector Tyndale	N/B Glass Importer	Glass Business
John Selden Roane	S/B Gov-Arkansas	Retired
James William Denver	N/B Gov-Colorado	Lawyer
Howell Cobb	S/M Gov-Georgia/L	Business
John White Geary	N/B Gov-Kansas/L	Gov-Pennsylvania
Paul Octave Hebert	S/B Gov-Louisiana	Politics
Nathaniel Prentiss Banks	N/M Gov-Massachusetts	Politics/L
Willis Arnold Gorman	N/B Gov-Minnesota/L	Lawyer
Henry Hastings Sibley	N/B Gov-Minnesota	Banker
Sterling Price	S/M Gov-Missouri	Retired
Edwin Denison Morgan	N/M Gov-New York	Senate
William Bowen Campbell	N/B Gov-Tennessee/L	Politics
Andrew Johnson	N/B Gov-Tennessee	U.S.President
John Buchanan Floyd	S/B Gov-Virginia/L	Died
William Smith	S/M Gov-Virginia/L	Farmer
Henry Alexander Wise	S/B Gov-Virginia/L	Lawyer
Isaac Ingalls Stevens	N/B Gov-Washington	Killed
Jasper Adalmorn Maltby	N/B Gunsmith	Merchant
George Francis McGinnis	N/B Hatter	Postmaster
Max Weber	N/B Hotel operator	I.R.Collector
Giles Alexander Smith	N/B Hotel Owner	A/Postmaster Gen.
Thomas Casimer Devin	N/B House painter	Soldier
Abram Duryee	N/B Importer	Police Chief-NYC
Clinton Bowen Fisk	N/B Insurance	Banker
John McNeil	N/B Insurance	Sheriff
George William Taylor	N/B Iron Manufact.	Killed
William Henry Powell	N/B Iron Works Mgr.	Nail Co.Mgr.
Catharinus Buckingham	N/B Iron Works Owner	Steelworks Pres.
John McArthur	N/B Iron Works Owner	Postmaster
Joseph Reid Anderson	S/B Iron Works Supt.	Iron Works Supt.
John Eugene Smith	N/B Jeweler	Soldier
Julius Stahel	N/M Journalist	Insurance
Henry Lewis Benning	S/B Judge/L	Lawyer
William Plummer Benton	N/B Judge/L	Lawyer
Joseph Tarr Copeland	N/B Judge/L	Retired
Edmund Jackson Davis	N/B Judge/L	Governor-Texas
Thomas Ewing,Jr.	N/B Judge/L	Congress
Samuel Jameson Gholson	S/B Judge/L	Politics
John Gregg	S/B Judge/L	Killed
William Grose	N/B Judge/L	Tax Collector
Pleasant Adam Hackleman	N/B Judge/L	Killed
Isham Nicholas Haynie	N/B Judge/L	Lawyer
Alvin Peterson Hovey	N/B Judge/L	Gov-Indiana
Edmund Winston Pettus	S/B Judge/L	Senator
William Andrew Quarles	S/B Judge/L	Politics
James Camp Tappan	S/B Judge/L	Politics
William Feimster Tucker	S/B Judge/L	Politics/L
Thomas William Sweeny	N/B Laborer	Unknown

Daniel Weisiger Adams	S/B Lawyer	Lawyer
Christopher Andrews	N/B Lawyer	Politics
Alpheus Baker	S/B Lawyer	Lawyer
Francis Channing Barlow	N/B Lawyer	Politics
Rufus Barringer	S/B Lawyer	Politics
Joseph Jackson Bartlett	N/B Lawyer	Minister-Sweden
Cullen Andrews Battle	S/B Lawyer	Newspaper Editor
William Worth Belknap	N/B Lawyer	US Secty/War
David Bell Birney	N/M Lawyer	Died-malaria
Jerimiah Tilford Boyle	N/B Lawyer	R.R.Business
Edward Stuyvesant Bragg	N/B Lawyer	Politics
William Felix Brantley	S/B Lawyer	Lawyer
Mason Brayman	N/B Lawyer	Gov-Idaho Terr
Henry Shaw Briggs	N/B Lawyer	Judge
John Calvin Brown	S/M Lawyer	Gov-Tennessee
Ralph Pomeroy Buckland	N/B Lawyer	Congress
Stephen Gano Burbridge	N/B Lawyer	Unknown
Richard Busteed	N/B Lawyer	Judge
Benjamin Franklin Butler	N/M Lawyer	Gov-Massachusetts
Matthew Calbraith Butler	S/M Lawyer	Senator
Alexander Campbell	S/B Lawyer	Lawyer
Henry Beebee Carrington	N/B Lawyer	Soldier
John Carpenter Carter	S/B Lawyer	Killed
James Ronald Chalmers	S/B Lawyer	Congress
Stephen Gardner Champlin	N/B Lawyer	Killed
James Holt Clanton	S/B Lawyer	Lawyer
John Bullock Clark,Jr.	S/B Lawyer	Congress
Thomas Reade Rootes Cobb	S/B Lawyer	Killed
Francis Marion Cockrell	S/B Lawyer	Senator
Philip Cook	S/B Lawyer	Congress
John Murray Corse	N/B Lawyer	Postmaster
William Ruffin Cox	S/B Lawyer	Congress
Thomas Crittenden	N/M Lawyer	Soldier
Thomas Turpin Crittenden	N/B Lawyer	Lawyer
Marcellus Monroe Crocker	N/B Lawyer	Died-TB
John Thomas Croxton	N/B Lawyer	Min-Bolivia
Henry Eugene Davies	N/B Lawyer	Lawyer
Joseph Robert Davis	S/B Lawyer	Lawyer
William George M. Davis	S/B Lawyer	Lawyer
Philippe deTrobriand	N/B Lawyer	Soldier
Dudley McIver DuBose	S/B Lawyer	Congress
Basil Wilson Duke	S/B Lawyer	Lawyer
Jubal Anderson Early	S/L Lawyer	Lawyer
John Echols	S/B Lawyer	Business
Matthew Duncan Ector	S/B Lawyer	Judge
Hugh Boyle Ewing	N/B Lawyer	Min-Holland
Francis Fessenden	N/B Lawyer	Lawyer
James Deering Fessenden	N/B Lawyer	Lawyer
Manning Ferguson Force	N/B Lawyer	Judge
William Henry Forney	S/B Lawyer	Congress
Speed Smith Fry	N/B Lawyer	Civil Service
Samuel Garland,Jr.	S/B Lawyer	Killed
Randall Lee Gibson	S/B Lawyer	Senator
States Rights Gist	S/B Lawyer	Killed
Henry Gray	S/B Lawyer	Politics
Thomas Green	S/B Lawyer	Killed

Maxcy Gregg	S/B Lawyer	Killed
Walter Quintin Gresham	N/B Lawyer	US Secy/State
Simon Goodell Griffin	N/B Lawyer	Politics
Johnson Hagood	S/B Lawyer	Gov-S.Carolina
Cyrus Hamlin	N/B Lawyer	Lawyer
Edward Harland	N/B Lawyer	Politics/L
Nathaniel Harris	S/B Lawyer	Lawyer
William Harrow	N/B Lawyer	Politics/L
Milo Smith Hascall	N/B Lawyer	Banker
Alexander Hawthorne	S/B Lawyer	Min-Baptist
Rutherford Hayes	N/B Lawyer	U.S.President
James Thadeus Holtzclaw	S/B Lawyer	Politics/L
William Young Humes	S/B Lawyer	Lawyer
Eppa Hunton	S/B Lawyer	Politics
Henry Rootes Jackson	S/B Lawyer	Min-Mexico
John King Jackson	S/B Lawyer	Lawyer
Robert Daniel Johnston	S/B Lawyer	Banker/L
Thomas Leiper Kane	N/B Lawyer	Business
John Reese Kenly	N/B Lawyer	Lawyer
John Doby Kennedy	S/B Lawyer	Politics
Edward Needles Kirk	N/B Lawyer	Killed
Edwin Gray Lee	S/B Lawyer	Unknown
Mortimer Dormer Leggett	N/B Lawyer	Lawyer
Robert Lowry	S/B Lawyer	Gov-Mississippi
William Haines Lytle	N/B Lawyer	Killed
George Ear Maney	S/B Lawyer	Politics
William Thompson Martin	S/M Lawyer	Politics
John Henry Martindale	N/B Lawyer	Atty Gen-New York
Samuel Bell Maxey	S/M Lawyer	Senator/L
Edward Moody McCook	N/B Lawyer	Gov-Colorado
Robert Latimer McCook	N/B Lawyer	Killed
Nathaniel McLean	N/B Lawyer	Farmer
Dandridge McRae	S/B Lawyer	Politics/L
John Franklin Miller	N/B Lawyer	Senator
Robert Huston Milroy	N/M Lawyer	Indian Agent
Robert Mitchell	N/B Lawyer	Gov-New Mexico
George Webb Morell	N/M Lawyer	Farmer
George Morgan	N/B Lawyer	Congress
John Tyler Morgan	S/B Lawyer	Senator/L
Francis Redding Nicholls	S/B Lawyer	Gov-Louisiana
William Ward Orme	N/B Lawyer	U.S.Treasury
Charles Jackson Paine	N/B Lawyer	R.R.Director
Halbert Eleazer Paine	N/B Lawyer	Congress
Elisha Franklin Paxton	S/B Lawyer	Killed
William Henry F. Payne	S/B Lawyer	Politics/L
Abner Monroe Perrin	S/B Lawyer	Killed
Edward Aylesworth Perry	S/B Lawyer	Gov-Florida
Albert Pike	S/B Lawyer	Legal writer
Gideon Johnson Pillow	S/B Lawyer	Lawyer
Robert Brown Potter	N/B Lawyer	R.R.Receiver
Benjamin Franklin Potts	N/B Lawyer	Gov-Montana
Calvin Edward Pratt	N/B Lawyer	Judge
Benjamin Prentiss	N/M Lawyer	Postmaster
James Edwards Rains	S/B Lawyer	Killed
George Wythe Randolph	S/B Lawyer	Died-TB
Green Berry Raum	N/B Lawyer	Congress

John Aaron Rawlins	N/B Lawyer	U.S.Sec'y War
Hugh Thompson Reid	N/B Lawyer	R.R.President
James William Reilly	N/B Lawyer	Bank President
Daniel Harris Reynolds	S/B Lawyer	Politics/L
Elliott Warren Rice	N/B Lawyer	Lawyer
James Clay Rice	N/B Lawyer	Killed
Robert Richardson	S/B Lawyer	R.R.Builder
Leonard Fulton Ross	N/B Lawyer	Farmer
Thomas Howard Ruger	N/B Lawyer	Soldier
John Benjamin Sanborn	N/B Lawyer	Politics
James Shackelford	N/B Lawyer	Judge
Jacob Hunter Sharp	S/B Lawyer	Politics/L
William Sherman	N/M Lawyer	Soldier
James Phillip Simms	S/B Lawyer	Lawyer
William Yarnel Slack	S/B Lawyer	Killed
Henry Warner Slocum	N/M Lawyer	Congress
Green Clay Smith	N/B Lawyer	Min-Baptist
Preston Smith	S/B Lawyer	Killed
Thomas Church H. Smith	N/B Lawyer	Soldier
James Gallant Spears	N/B Lawyer	Lawyer
John Starkweather	N/B Lawyer	Lawyer
Otho French Strahl	S/B Lawyer	Killed
Frederick Stumbaugh	N/B Lawyer	Lawyer
Wager Swayne	N/B Lawyer	Lawyer
Alfred Howe Terry	N/M Lawyer	Soldier
Henry Dwight Terry	N/B Lawyer	Lawyer
William Terry	S/B Lawyer	Congress/L
John Milton Thayer	N/B Lawyer	Gov-Nebraska
Henry Goddard Thomas	N/B Lawyer	Soldier
Edward Dorr Tracy	S/B Lawyer	Killed
Daniel Ullmann	N/B Lawyer	Retired
Adin Ballou Underwood	N/B Lawyer	Surveyor
James Clifford Veatch	N/B Lawyer	I.R.Collector
James Alexander Walker	S/B Lawyer	Congress/L
William Harvey Wallace	N/B Lawyer	Killed
Edward Cary Walthall	S/M Lawyer	Senator/L
John Austin Wharton	S/M Lawyer	Died
Walter Chiles Whitaker	N/B Lawyer	Lawyer
James Williamson	N/B Lawyer	R.R.President
Isaac Jones Wistar	N/B Lawyer	Lawyer
Sterling Alexander Wood	S/B Lawyer	Lawyer
Ambrose Ransom Wright	S/M Lawyer	Politics/L
Zebulon York	S/B Lawyer	Hotel Operator
Neal Dow	N/B Leather Tanner	Politics
Henry Bohlen	N/B Liquor Business	Killed
Charles Leopold Matthies	N/B Liquor Business	Politics
Joseph Bailey	N/B Lumber Business	Sheriff
Hiram Burnham	N/B Lumber Business	Killed
Robert Cowdin	N/B Lumber Business	Unknown
James Isham Gilbert	N/B Lumber Business	Lumber business
Edward Hatch	N/B Lumber Business	Soldier
Charles Davis Jameson	N/B Lumber Business	Died-Camp Fever
William Miller	S/B Lumber Business	Politics
Nathaniel James Jackson	N/B Machinist	Unknown
William Dwight	N/B Manufacturer	R.R.Management
Daniel Marsh Frost	S/B Manufacturer	Farmer

William McComb	S/B Manufacturer	Farmer
Henry Warner Birge	N/B Merchant	Lumber
Thomas Alfred Davies	N/B Merchant	Writer
George Gibbs Dibrell	S/B Merchant/farmer	Congress
Charles Camp Doolittle	N/B Merchant	Banker
Isaac Hardin Duval	N/B Merchant	Congress
Archibald Gracie,Jr.	S/B Merchant	Killed
Benjamin Henry Grierson	N/B Merchant	Soldier
Alfred Eugene Jackson	S/B Merchant	Farmer
Evander McNair	S/B Merchant	Unknown
Patrick Theodore Moore	S/B Merchant	Insurance
James Dada Morgan	N/B Merchant	Banker
Isaac Peace Rodman	N/B Merchant	Killed
William Kerley Strong	N/B Merchant	Retired
William Richard Terry	S/B Merchant	Politics
Robert Brank Vance	S/B Merchant	Congress
John Crawford Vaughn	S/B Merchant	Politics
Melancthon Smith Wade	N/B Merchant	Retired
Lucius Marshall Walker	S/B Merchant	Died-duel
Richard Waterhouse	S/B Merchant	Land Speculator
Thomas Welsh	N/B Merchant	Died-malaria
Henry Baxter	N/B Miller	Min-Honduras
Mark Perrin Lowrey	S/B Min-Baptist	Coll.President
William Nelson Pendleton	S/B Min-Episcopal	Min-Episcopal
Leonidas Polk	S/L Min-Episcopal	Killed
William Anderson Pile	N/B Min-Methodist	Gov-New Mexico
Archibald Godwin	S/B Miner/rancher	Killed
Patrick Edward Connor	N/B Mining	Editor
Walter Paye Lane	S/B Mining	Merchant
William Brimage Bate	S/M Newsp.Editor/L	Gov-Tennessee
Joseph Rodman West	N/B Newspaper Oper.	U.S.Marshal
William Paul Roberts	S/B None	Politics
Alexander Shaler	N/B None/Wealthy	Politics
James Henry Van Alen	N/B None/Wealthy	None/Wealthy
James Nagle	N/B Painter	Unknown
John Morrison Oliver	N/B Pharmacist	Lawyer
Daniel Davidson Bidwell	N/B Police Justice	Killed
Edward Dickinson Baker	N/M Politics-L	Killed
Hamilton Prioleau Bee	S/B Politics	Unknown
Theodore Brevard	S/B Politics/L	Lawyer
Cyrus Bussey	N/B Politics	Merchant/L
Charles Thomas Campbell	N/B Politics	Hotel operator
James Cantey	S/B Politics/L	Farmer
Cassius Marcellus Clay	N/M Politics	Unknown
Henry DeLamar Clayton	S/M Politics/L	Farmer/L
Jacob Dolson Cox	N/M Politics/L	Governor-Ohio
James Craig	N/B Politics/L	R.R.President
John Adams Dix	N/M Politics/L	Gov-New York
Ebenezer Dumont	N/B Politics/L	Congress
John Edwards	N/B Politics/L	Congress
Clement Anselm Evans	S/B Politics/L	Min-Episcopal
James Fleming Fagan	S/M Politics	U.S.Marshal
Orris Sanford Ferry	N/B Politics/L	Politics
Jesse Johnson Finley	S/B Politics/L	Congress
Theophilus Garrard	N/B Politics	Farmer
Martin Witherspoon Gary	S/B Politics/L	Politics

Hiram Bronson Granbury	S/B Politics/L	Killed
Andrew Jackson Hamilton	N/B Politics/L	Judge
Wade Hampton	S/L Politics	Gov-S.Carolina
Roger Weightman Hanson	S/B Politics/L	Killed
Abner Clark Harding	N/B Politics/L	Congress
James Edward Harrison	S/B Politics	Politics
Thomas Harrison	S/B Politics/L	Judge
Harry Thompson Hays	S/M Politics/L	Sheriff
Benjamin Hardin Helm	S/B Politics/L	Killed
Benjamin Jefferson Hill	S/B Politics	Merchant
Edward Winslow Hincks	N/B Politics	Soldier
Thomas Hindman	S/M Politics/L	Lawyer
George Baird Hodge	S/B Politics/L	Politics/L
Joseph Lewis Hogg	S/B Politics/L	Died-dysentery
Joseph Holt	N/B Politics/L	Soldier
Benjamin Grubb Humphreys	S/B Politics/farmer	Gov-Mississippi
Stephen Augustus Hurlbut	N/M Politics/L	Congress
John Daniel Imboden	S/B Politics/L	Lawyer
William Lowther Jackson	S/B Politics/L	Judge
Bradley Tyler Johnson	S/B Politics/L	Politics
George Doherty Johnston	S/B Politics/L	Politics
James Lawson Kemper	S/M Politics/L	Gov-Virginia
Joseph Brevard Kershaw	S/M Politics/L	Judge/politics
Alexander Robert Lawton	S/B Politics/L	Min-Austria
Joseph Horace Lewis	S/B Politics/L	Judge/Congress
Samuel McGowan	S/B Politics/L	Judge/politics
Thomas Francis Meagher	N/B Politics	Secy St-Montana
Allison Nelson	S/B Politics/L	Died-fever
Richard James Oglesby	N/M Politics/L	Gov-Illinois
John McCauley Palmer	N/M Politics/L	Gov-Illinois
Joseph Benjamin Palmer	S/B Politics/L	Lawyer
Mosby Monroe Parsons	S/M Politics/L	Soldier-China
James Johnston Pettigrew	S/B Politics/L	Killed
John Smith Preston	S/B Politics/L	Unknown
Matt Whitaker Ransom	S/B Politics/L	Senator
Lovell Harrison Rousseau	N/M Politics/L	Soldier
Carl Schurz	N/M Politics	Senator
James Shields	N/B Politics/L	Senator
James Richard Slack	N/B Politics/L	Judge
John Potts Slough	N/B Politics	Chief Justice-NM
Francis Spinola	N/B Politics/L	Congress
John Dunlap Stevenson	N/B Politics	Lawyer
William Taliaferro	S/M Politics/L	Judge
Richard Taylor	S/L Politics/farmer	Unknown
Davis Tillson	N/B Politics	Business
Robert Augustus Toombs	S/B Politics/L	Politics
James Samuel Wadsworth	N/M Politics/L	Killed
George Day Wagner	N/B Politics	Lawyer
Leroy Pope Walker	S/B Politics/L	Politics/L
Lewis Wallace	N/M Politics/L	Gov-New Mexico
Fitz-Henry Warren	N/B Politics	Min-Guatemala
Julius White	N/B Politics	Unknown
Williams Carter Wickham	S/B Politics/L	RR President
John Stuart Williams	S/B Politics/L	Politics/Farmer
Jones Mitchell Withers	S/M Politics/L	Cotton Broker
William Tatum Wofford	S/B Politics/L	Politics

Felix Kirk Zollicoffer	S/B Politics	Killed
Michael Corcoran	N/B Postal clerk	Died-accident
Samuel Read Anderson	S/B Postmaster	Merchant
William Henry Carroll	S/B Postmaster	Unknown
Thomas James Churchill	S/M Postmaster	Gov-Mississippi
Adley Hogan Gladden	S/B Postmaster	Killed
Alpheus Williams	N/B Postmaster/L	Congress
James Blair Steedman	N/M Printer	Police Chief
John Wallace Fuller	N/B Publisher	Boot/Shoe Bus.
Egbert Benson Brown	N/B RR Business	Farmer
Joseph Farmer Knipe	N/B RR Business	Postmaster
Thomas Benton Smith	S/B RR Business	RR Business
Gilbert Moxley Sorrel	S/B RR Business	Merchant
Charles Adam Heckman	N/B RR Conductor	Train Dispatcher
Benjamin Franklin Kelley	N/B RR Freight Agt.	Civil Service
James Bowen	N/B RR President	Retired
Charles Cruft	N/B RR President/L	Lawyer
Daniel Tyler	N/B RR President	RR President
Conrad Feger Jackson	N/B RR Worker	Killed
Joseph Orville Shelby	S/B Rope Manufact.	U.S.Marshal
Adelbert Ames	N/B Sailor	Gov-Mississippi
Robert Doak Lilley	S/B Salesman	Financial Agent
Martin Edwin Green	S/B Sawmill Oper.	Killed
Henry Watkins Allen	S/B School Teacher/L	Newspaper Editor
Albert Blanchard	S/B School Teacher	Surveyor
Robert Bullock	S/B School Teacher	Congress/L
Ellison Capers	S/B School Teacher	Min-Episcopal
Charles Clark	S/B School Teacher	Gov-Mississippi/L
Newton Martin Curtis	N/B School Teacher	Politic
George Armstrong Custer	N/B School Teacher	Soldier
Lysander Cutler	N/B School Teacher	Died
James Abram Garfield	N/M School Teacher	U.S.President
Lewis Addison Grant	N/B School Teacher/L	U.S.Secy of War
Richard Griffith	S/B School Teacher	Killed
Bushrod Rust Johnson	S/M School Teacher	Educator
Evander McIvor Law	S/B School Teacher	Educator
William Gaston Lewis	S/B School Teacher	Engineer
Young Marshall Moody	S/B School Teacher	Business
Joshua Thomas Owen	N/B School Teacher	Lawyer
Franz Sigel	N/M School Teacher	U.S.Pension Agt.
Morgan Lewis Smith	N/B School Teacher	Business
John Curtis Caldwell	N/B School Principal	Politics/L
Charles Edward Hovey	N/B School Principal	Lobbyist
John Robert Jones	S/B School Principal	Merchant
James Chesnut, Jr.	S/B Senator/L	Politics
Thomas Lanier Clingman	S/B Senator/L	Lawyer
Peter Burwell Starke	S/B Senator	Sheriff
Louis Trezevant Wigfall	S/B Senator/L	Unknown
Samuel Beatty	N/B Sheriff	Farmer
John Cook	N/B Sheriff	Politics
Philip Dale Roddey	S/B Sheriff	Business
Leroy Augustus Stafford	S/B Sheriff/farmer	Killed
Nelson Taylor	N/B Sheriff/L	Congress
James Madison Tuttle	N/B Sheriff	Mining
Ferdinand Van Derveer	N/B Sheriff/L	Judge
John Joseph Abercrombie	N/B Soldier	Soldier

John Adams	S/B Soldier	Killed
Edward Porter Alexander	S/B Soldier	College Prof.
Robert Allen	N/B Soldier	Soldier
Benjamin Alvord	N/B Soldier	Soldier
George Burgwyn Anderson	S/B Soldier	Killed
George Thomas Anderson	S/B Soldier	Police Chief
Richard Heron Anderson	S/L Soldier	St.Phosphate Agt
Robert Anderson	N/B Soldier	Retired
Robert Anderson	S/B Soldier	Police Chief
James Jay Archer	S/B Soldier/L	Died
Lewis Addison Armistead	S/B Soldier	Killed
Frank Armstrong	S/B Soldier	US Indian Insp.
Lewis Golding Arnold	N/B Soldier	Retired
Richard Arnold	N/B Soldier	Soldier
Christopher Augur	N/M Soldier	Soldier
William Woods Averell	N/B Soldier	Inventor
Romeyn Beck Ayres	N/B Soldier	Soldier
Absalom Baird	N/B Soldier	Soldier
Laurence Simmons Baker	S/B Soldier	R.R.Station Agt.
John Gross Barnard	N/B Soldier	Soldier
Joseph K. Barnes	N/B Soldier/Doctor	Soldier/Doctor
William Farquhar Barry	N/B Soldier	Soldier
Seth Maxwell Barton	S/B Soldier	Unknown
George Dashiell Bayard	N/B Soldier	Killed
William Nelson R. Beall	S/B Soldier	Merchant
Pierre Beauregard	S/G Soldier	R.R.President
Barnard Elliott Bee	S/B Soldier	Killed
Henry Washington Benham	N/B Soldier	Soldier
William Robertson Boggs	S/B Soldier	Engineer
Braxton Bragg	S/G Soldier/Planter	Engineer
John Milton Brannan	N/B Soldier	Soldier
William Thomas Brooks	N/M Soldier	Farmer
Robert Buchanan	N/B Soldier	Soldier
Don Carlos Buell	N/M Soldier	Ironworks Oper.
John Buford	N/B Soldier	Died-typhoid
William Wallace Burns	N/B Soldier	Soldier
Ambrose Burnside	N/M Soldier	Gov-Rhode Island
William Lewis Cabell	S/B Soldier	Lawyer/US Marshal
Edward Richard Canby	N/M Soldier	Soldier
James Henry Carleton	N/B Soldier	Soldier
William Passmore Carlin	N/B Soldier	Soldier
Eugene Asa Carr	N/B Soldier	Soldier
Samuel Sprigg Carroll	N/B Soldier	Soldier
Silas Casey	N/M Soldier	Soldier
Alexander Chambers	N/B Soldier	Soldier
Robert Hall Chilton	S/B Soldier	Pres.Manuf.Co.
Gustave Paul Cluseret	N/B Soldier	Politics(foreign)
John Rogers Cooke	S/B Soldier	Merchant
Philip St.George Cooke	N/B Soldier	Soldier
Samuel Cooper	S/G Soldier	Retired
George Blake Cosby	S/B Soldier	Farmer
George Bibb Crittenden	S/M Soldier	St.Librarian-KY
George Crook	N/M Soldier	Soldier
George Cullum	N/B Soldier	Soldier
Alfred Cumming	S/B Soldier	Farmer
Junius Daniel	S/B Soldier	Killed

Henry Brevard Davidson	S/B Soldier	Engineer
John Wynn Davidson	N/B Soldier	Soldier
Jefferson Davis	N/B Soldier	Soldier
James Dearing	S/B Soldier	Killed
Richard Delafield	N/B Soldier	Retired
Julius Adolph deLagnel	S/B Soldier	Steamship service
Gustavus DeRussy	N/B Soldier	Soldier
James Deshler	S/B Soldier	Killed
Abner Doubleday	N/B Soldier	Soldier
Alfred Napoleon Duffie	N/B Soldier	U.S.Consul-Spain
Johnson Kelly Duncan	S/B Soldier	Died-fever
John Dunovant	S/B Soldier	Killed
Alexander Brydie Dyer	N/B Soldier	Soldier
Amos Beebe Eaton	N/B Soldier	Soldier
Washington Elliott	N/B Soldier	Soldier
Arnold Elzey	S/M Soldier	Farmer
William Hemsley Emory	N/B Soldier	Soldier
Nathan George Evans	S/B Soldier	School Principal
Richard Stoddert Ewell	S/L Soldier	Farmer
Samuel Wragg Ferguson	S/B Soldier	Lawyer
Charles William Field	S/M Soldier	Engineer
John Horace Forney	S/M Soldier	Farmer/Engineer
John Gray Foster	N/M Soldier	Soldier
William Buel Franklin	N/B Soldier	Colt Guns Mgr.
John Wesley Frazer	S/B Soldier	Business
John Charles Fremont	N/M Soldier/politics	Gov-Arizona
Samuel Gibbs French	S/M Soldier/farmer	Farmer
William Henry French	N/M Soldier	Soldier
James Barnet Fry	N/B Soldier	Soldier/writer
Franklin Gardner	S/M Soldier	Farmer
William Gardner	S/B Soldier	Unknown
Richard Brooke Garnett	S/B Soldier	Killed
Robert Selden Garnett	S/B Soldier	Killed
Kenner Garrard	N/B Soldier	Politics
Richard Caswell Gatlin	S/B Soldier	Farmer
George Washington Getty	N/B Soldier	Soldier
John Gibbon	N/M Soldier	Soldier
Alfred Gibbs	N/B Soldier	Soldier
Charles Champion Gilbert	N/B Soldier	Soldier
Alvan Cullem Gillem	N/B Soldier	Soldier
Quincy Adams Gillmore	N/M Soldier	Soldier
Jeremy Francis Gilmer	S/M Soldier	Pres.Gas Co.
George Henry Gordon	N/B Soldier/L	Lawyer
Josiah Gorgas	S/B Soldier	Univ.President
Lawrence Pike Graham	N/B Soldier	Soldier
Gordon Granger	N/M Soldier	Soldier
Robert Seaman Granger	N/B Soldier	Soldier
Ulysses Simpson Grant	N/L Soldier	U.S.President
John Grayson	S/B Soldier	Died
David McMurtrie Gregg	N/B Soldier	Farmer
Charles Griffin	N/M Soldier	Soldier
Cuvier Grover	N/B Soldier	Soldier
Henry Wager Halleck	N/M Soldier/L	Soldier
Schuyler Hamilton	N/M Soldier	Unknown
William Hammond	N/B Soldier/Doctor	Doctor
Winfield Scott Hancock	N/M Soldier	Soldier

William Joseph Hardee	S/L Soldier	Farmer
William Polk Hardeman	S/B Soldier	Farmer
James Allen Hardie	N/B Soldier	Soldier
Martin Davis Hardin	N/B Soldier	Soldier/L
Charles Garrison Harker	N/B Soldier	Killed
William Selby Harney	N/B Soldier	Retired
George Lucas Hartsuff	N/M Soldier	Soldier
Joseph Abel Haskin	N/B Soldier	Soldier
John Porter Hatch	N/B Soldier	Soldier
James Morrison Hawes	S/B Soldier	Merchant
John Parker Hawkins	N/B Soldier	Soldier
William Hays	N/B Soldier	Soldier
William Babcock Hazen	N/M Soldier	Soldier
Samuel Heintzelman	N/M Soldier	Soldier
Henry Heth	S/M Soldier	Insurance
Ambrose Powell Hill	S/L Soldier	Killed
Ethan Allen Hitchcock	N/M Soldier	Retired
Theophilus Holmes	S/L Soldier	Farmer
John Bell Hood	S/G Soldier	Unknown
Joseph Hooker	N/M Soldier	Soldier
Oliver Otis Howard	N/M Soldier	Soldier
Albion Parris Howe	N/B Soldier	Soldier
Benjamin Huger	S/M Soldier	Farmer
Andrew Humphreys	N/M Soldier	Soldier
Henry Jackson Hunt	N/B Soldier	Soldier
Lewis Cass Hunt	N/B Soldier	Soldier
David Hunter	N/M Soldier	Retired
Rufus Ingalls	N/B Soldier	Soldier
Alfred Iverson,Jr.	S/B Soldier	Orange Grower
William Hicks Jackson	S/B Soldier	Farmer
Edward Johnson	S/M Soldier	Farmer
Richard W. Johnson	N/B Soldier	Coll.Professor
Albert Sidney Johnston	S/G Soldier	Killed
Joseph Johnston	S/G Soldier	Politics
David Rumph Jones	S/M Soldier	Died-heart
John Marshall Jones	S/B Soldier	Killed
Samuel Jones	S/M Soldier	Farmer
William Edmonson Jones	S/B Soldier	Killed
Thomas Jordan	S/B Soldier	Editor
Henry Moses Judah	N/B Soldier	Soldier
August Valentine Kautz	N/B Soldier	Soldier
Philip Kearny	N/M Soldier	Killed
William Scott Ketchum	N/B Soldier	Soldier
Erasmus Darwin Keyes	N/M Soldier	Banker/Mining
John Haskell King	N/B Soldier	Soldier
William Whedbee Kirkland	S/B Soldier	Business
Danville Leadbetter	S/B Soldier	Unknown
Fitzhugh Lee	S/M Soldier	Gov-Virginia
George Washington Lee	S/M Soldier	Coll.President
Robert Edward Lee	S/G Soldier	Coll.President
Stephen Dill Lee	S/L Soldier	Farmer/Politics
Collett Leventhorpe	S/B Soldier	Unknown
Joseph Andrew Lightburn	N/B Soldier	Min-Baptist
Lewis Henry Little	S/B Soldier	Killed
Lunsford Lindsay Lomax	S/M Soldier	Coll.President
Armistead Lindsay Long	S/B Soldier	Engineer/Writer

Eli Long	N/B Soldier	Lawyer
James Longstreet	S/L Soldier	Min-Turkey
William Wing Loring	S/M Soldier/L	Soldier
Mansfield Lovell	S/M Soldier	Engineer
Hylan Benton Lyon	S/B Soldier	Farmer
Nathaniel Lyon	N/B Soldier	Killed
William Whann Mackall	S/B Soldier	Farmer
John Bankhead Magruder	S/M Soldier	Soldier(Mexico)
James Patrick Major	S/B Soldier	Farmer
Joseph King Mansfield	N/B Soldier	Killed
Randolph Barnes Marcy	N/B Soldier	Soldier
John Marmaduke	S/M Soldier	Gov-Missouri
James Green Martin	S/B Soldier	Lawyer
John Sanford Mason	N/B Soldier	Soldier
Dabney Herndon Maury	S/M Soldier	Min-Colombia
George Archibald McCall	N/B Soldier	Retired
George Brinton McClellan	N/M Soldier	Gov-New Jersey
Alexander McCook	N/M Soldier	Soldier
John Porter McCown	S/M Soldier	Teacher/Farmer
Irvin McDowell	N/M Soldier	Soldier
James McQueen McIntosh	S/B Soldier	Killed
Justus McKinstry	N/B Soldier	Stockbroker
Lafayette McLaws	S/M Soldier	Insurance
James Birdseye McPherson	N/M Soldier	Killed
George Gordon Meade	N/M Soldier	Soldier
Montgomery Meigs	N/B Soldier	Soldier
Wesley Merritt	N/M Soldier	Soldier
William Montgomery	N/B Soldier	Business
William Hopkins Morris	N/B Soldier	Farmer
James St.Clair Morton	N/B Soldier	Killed
Joseph Anthony Mower	N/M Soldier	Soldier
Thomas Hewson Neill	N/B Soldier	Soldier
John Newton	N/M Soldier	Soldier
Edward Otho C. Ord	N/M Soldier	Soldier
Innis Newton Palmer	N/B Soldier	Soldier
John Grubb Parke	N/M Soldier	Soldier
Francis Engle Patterson	N/B Soldier	Accidently shot
Gabriel Rene Paul	N/B Soldier	Retired
John Pegram	S/B Soldier	Killed
John Clifford Pemberton	S/L Soldier	Farmer
William Dorsey Pender	S/M Soldier	Killed
John Wolcott Phelps	N/B Soldier	Writer
George Edward Pickett	S/M Soldier	Insurance
Thomas Gamble Pitcher	N/B Soldier	Soldier
Alfred Pleasonton	N/M Soldier	Soldier
Joseph Bennett Plummer	N/B Soldier	Died
Orlando Metcalfe Poe	N/B Soldier	Soldier
Camille A.J.M.Polignac	S/M Soldier	Mathematics
John Pope	N/M Soldier	Soldier
Andrew Porter	N/B Soldier	Retired
Fitz John Porter	N/M Soldier	Unknown
Henry Prince	N/B Soldier	Soldier
Gabriel James Rains	S/B Soldier	Govt Clerk
George Douglas Ramsay	N/B Soldier	Soldier
Stephen Dodson Ramseur	S/M Soldier	Killed
Robert Ransom,Jr.	S/M Soldier	Engineer

Jesse Lee Reno	N/M Soldier	Killed
Alexander Reynolds	S/B Soldier	Soldier-Egypt
John Fulton Reynolds	N/M Soldier	Killed
Israel Bush Richardson	N/M Soldier	Killed
James Brewerton Ricketts	N/B Soldier	Soldier
James Wolfe Ripley	N/B Soldier	Retired
Roswell Sabine Ripley	S/B Soldier/business	Manufacturer
Benjamin Stone Roberts	N/B Soldier/L	Soldier
Beverly Robertson	S/B Soldier	Insurance
John Cleveland Robinson	N/B Soldier	Lt.Gov-NY
William Rosecrans	N/M Soldier	Congress
Lawrence Sullivan Ross	S/B Soldier	Gov-Texas
Daniel Henry Rucker	N/B Soldier	Soldier
Daniel Ruggles	S/B Soldier	Unknown
David Allen Russell	N/B Soldier	Killed
William Price Sanders	N/B Soldier	Killed
Rufus Saxton	N/B Soldier	Soldier
Eliakim Parker Scammon	N/B Soldier	Coll.Professor
John Schofield	N/M Soldier	Soldier
Winfield Scott	N/M Soldier	Retired
William Read Scurry	S/B Soldier	Killed
John Sedgwick	N/M Soldier	Killed
Truman Seymour	N/B Soldier	Soldier
Philip Henry Sheridan	N/M Soldier	Soldier
Thomas West Sherman	N/B Soldier	Soldier
Francis Asbury Shoup	S/B Soldier/L	Coll.Professor
Henry Hopkins Sibley	S/B Soldier	Soldier/Egypt
Joshua Woodrow Sill	N/B Soldier	Killed
James Edwin Slaughter	S/B Soldier	Engineer
Adam Jacoby Slemmer	N/B Soldier	Soldier
Andrew Jackson Smith	N/M Soldier	Postmaster
Charles Ferguson Smith	N/M Soldier	Died-infection
Edmund Kirby Smith	S/G Soldier	Coll.Professor
Gustavus Woodson Smith	S/M Soldier/Engineer	Iron Works Supt.
James Argyle Smith	S/B Soldier	Farmer
Martin Luther Smith	S/M Soldier	Unknown
William Duncan Smith	S/B Soldier	Died-yellow fever
William Farrar Smith	N/M Soldier	Engineer
David Sloane Stanley	N/M Soldier	Soldier
Frederick Steele	N/M Soldier	Soldier
William Steele	S/B Soldier	Merchant
George Hume Steuart	S/B Soldier	Farmer
Walter Husted Stevens	S/B Soldier	Engineer
Carter Stevenson	S/M Soldier	Engineer
Charles John Stolbrand	N/B Soldier	Politics
Charles Pomeroy Stone	N/B Soldier	Soldier-Egypt
George Stoneman	N/M Soldier	Gov-California
Edwin Henry Stoughton	N/B Soldier	Lawyer
George Crockett Strong	N/B Soldier	Killed
James Ewell Stuart	S/M Soldier	Killed
Samuel Davis Sturgis	N/B Soldier	Soldier
Alfred Sully	N/B Soldier	Soldier
Edwin Vose Sumner	N/M Soldier	Died
George Sykes	N/M Soldier	Soldier
Joseph Pannell Taylor	N/B Soldier	Died
William Rufus Terrill	N/B Soldier	Killed

Bryan Morel Thomas	S/B Soldier	U.S. Marshal
George Henry Thomas	N/M Soldier	Soldier
Lorenzo Thomas	N/B Soldier	Soldier
John Blair Smith Todd	N/B Soldier/L	Politics
Alfred Thomas A. Torbert	N/B Soldier	Civil Service
Joseph Gilbert Totten	N/B Soldier	Died-pneumonia
Zealous Bates Tower	N/B Soldier	Soldier
John Wesley Turner	N/B Soldier	Soldier
David Emanuel Twiggs	S/M Soldier	Died
Robert Charles Tyler	S/B Soldier	Killed
Robert Ogden Tyler	N/B Soldier	Soldier
Earl Van Dorn	S/M Soldier	Murdered
Stewart Van Vliet	N/B Soldier	Soldier
John Villepigue	S/B Soldier	Died-fever
Israel Vogdes	N/B Soldier	Soldier
Henry Harrison Walker	S/B Soldier	Investment Broker
John George Walker	S/M Soldier	Politics
William Henry T. Walker	S/M Soldier	Killed
William Stephen Walker	S/B Soldier	Unknown
John Henry Hobart Ward	N/B Soldier	Court Clerk
Gouverneur Kemble Warren	N/M Soldier	Soldier
Henry Constantine Wayne	S/B Soldier	Lumber Business
Alexander Stewart Webb	N/B Soldier	Coll.President
Stephen Hinsdale Weed	N/B Soldier	Killed
Godfrey Weitzel	N/M Soldier	Soldier
Henry Walton Wessells	N/B Soldier	Soldier
Frank Wheaton	N/B Soldier	Soldier
Joseph Wheeler	S/M Soldier	Congress
Amiel Weeks Whipple	N/B Soldier	Killed
William Denison Whipple	N/B Soldier	Soldier
William Henry Whiting	S/M Soldier	Killed
Cadmus Marcellus Wilcox	S/M Soldier	Government
Orlando Bolivar Willcox	N/B Soldier/L	Soldier
Seth Williams	N/B Soldier	Soldier
Thomas Williams	N/B Soldier	Killed
James Harrison Wilson	N/B Soldier	Engineer
Charles Sidney Winder	S/B Soldier	Killed
John Henry Winder	S/B Soldier	Died
Thomas John Wood	N/M Soldier	Soldier
Daniel Phineas Woodbury	N/B Soldier	Died-yellow fever
Charles Robert Woods	N/B Soldier	Soldier
John Ellis Wool	N/M Soldier	Retired
George Wright	N/B Soldier	Soldier
Horatio Wright	N/M Soldier	Soldier
Nelson Appleton Miles	N/B Store Clerk	Soldier
Peter Joseph Osterhaus	N/M Store Clerk	Hardware Business
John Decatur Barry	S/B Student	Newspaper Editor
William Francis Bartlett	N/B Student	Business
Selden Connor	N/B Student	Governor-Maine
Robert Frederick Hoke	S/M Student	Unknown
John Herbert Kelly	S/B Student	Killed
Thomas Muldrup Logan	S/B Student	RR Management/L
Ranald Slidell Mackenzie	N/B Student	Soldier
John Grant Mitchell	N/B Student	Lawyer
John Caldwell C. Sanders	S/B Student	Killed
Thomas Fentress Toon	S/B Student	Educator

Emory Upton	N/B Student	Soldier
William Hugh Young	S/B Student	Real Estate/L
Albert Lindley Lee	N/B Supreme Ct.Just.	Business/L
George Washington Gordon	S/B Surveyor	Congress/L
Adam Rankin Johnson	S/B Surveyor	Unknown
Friedrich Salomon	N/B Surveyor	U.S.Survey.Gen.
Charles Carroll Walcutt	N/B Surveyor	Prison Warden
Samuel Kosciuszko Zook	N/B Telegrapher	Killed
Robert Sanford Foster	N/B Tinner	U.S.Marshal
Joseph Bradford Carr	N/B Tobacconist	Secy State-NY
John Rutter Brooke	N/B Unknown	Soldier
Charles Cleveland Dodge	N/B Unknown	Business
Thomas Wilberforce Egan	N/B Unknown	Customs Collector
Victor Jean B. Girardey	S/B Unknown	Killed
Franklin Nickerson	N/B U.S.Customs	Lawyer
James Conner	S/B U.S.Dist.Atty/L	Atty Gen.-S.C.
George Foster Shepley	N/B U.S.Dist.Atty/L	Judge
Douglas Hancock Cooper	S/B U.S.Indian Agent	Indian Rep.
Elias Smith Dennis	N/B U.S.Marshal	Sheriff
Charles Devens,Jr.	N/B U.S.Marshal/L	US Attorney Gen.
Ben McCulloch	S/B U.S.Marshal	Killed
Henry Eustace McCulloch	S/B U.S.Marshal	Farmer
Solomon Meredith	N/B U.S.Marshal	Farmer
Eleazer Arthur Paine	N/B U.S.Marshal	Lawyer
Thomas Kilby Smith	N/B U.S.Marshal	Consul-Panama
Samuel Powhatan Carter	N/B U.S.Navy	U.S.Navy
Edward Higgins	S/B U.S.Navy	Insurance
William Nelson	N/M U.S.Navy	Murdered
Richard Lucian Page	S/B U.S.Navy	School Supt.
Joseph Warren Revere	N/B U.S.Navy	Retired
Jeremiah Cutler Sullivan	N/B U.S.Navy	Clerk
Albin Francisco Schoepf	N/B U.S.Patent Clerk	U.S.Patent Exam.
John Cabell Breckinridge	S/M U.S.Vice Pres.	Lawyer
Thomas Greely Stevenson	N/B Unknown	Killed
Thomas John Lucas	N/B Watchmaker	Postmaster
Hugh Judson Kilpatrick	N/B West Point	Min-Chili
Felix Huston Robertson	S/B West Point	Lawyer
Thomas Lafayette Rosser	S/M West Point	Engineer
Pierce Manning B. Young	S/M West Point	Politics

10

Civil War Generals
by Work After the War

The generals are listed here alphabetically by the work they engaged in following the Civil War, then alphabetically by name
within each profession. In many cases the generals engaged in
several fields of endeavor. Only the most prominent positions
are listed below. A "/L" is included after the professions of
those generals who were also lawyers. Those listed as "died"
are the generals who died during wartime. If it is known what
they died from,this information is included briefly. The "died"
category includes disease, accidents and natural causes. Those
generals listed as "killed" are only those dying from wounds received in actual battles.

GENERAL	SIDE/RANK	BEFORE THE WAR	AFTER THE WAR
Giles Alexander Smith	N/B	Hotel Owner	Asst Postmaster
John Henry Martindale	N/B	Lawyer	Atty Gen.-N.Y.
James Conner	S/B	US Dist.Atty/L	Atty Gen.-S.C.
Edward Ferrero	N/B	Dance Instr.	Ballroom Manager
Augustus Chetlain	N/B	Business	Banker
Montgomery Dent Corse	S/B	Banker	Banker
Charles Camp Doolittle	N/B	Merchant	Banker
Alfred Ellet	N/B	Engineer	Banker
Clinton Bowen Fisk	N/B	Insurance	Banker
Milo Smith Hascall	N/B	Lawyer	Banker
Robert Daniel Johnston	S/B	Lawyer	Banker
Erasmus Darwin Keyes	N/M	Soldier	Banker/Mining
James Dada Morgan	N/B	Merchant	Banker
Henry Morris Naglee	N/B	Banker	Banker
William Henry Seward	N/B	Banker	Banker
Henry Hastings Sibley	N/B	Gov-Minnesota	Banker
James William Reilly	N/B	Lawyer	Banker
David Addison Weisiger	S/B	Business	Banker
John Wallace Fuller	N/B	Publisher	Boot/Shoe Bus.
William Bartlett	N/B	Student	Business
Daniel Butterfield	N/M	Business/L	Business
George Cadwalader	N/M	Business	Business
Howell Cobb	S/M	Gov-Georgia/L	Business
Charles Dodge	N/B	Unknown	Business
John Echols	S/B	Lawyer	Business

John Wesley Frazer	S/B	Soldier	Business
Thomas Leiper Kane	N/B	Lawyer	Business
William Kirkland	S/B	Soldier	Business
Albert Lindley Lee	N/B	Supreme Court	Business/L
William Montgomery	N/B	Soldier	Business
Young Marshall Moody	S/B	Teacher/Merchant	Business
Philip Dale Roddey	S/B	Sheriff	Business
Morgan Lewis Smith	N/B	Teacher	Business
Davis Tillson	N/B	Politics	Business
John Potts Slough	N/B	Politics	Chief Justice-NM
Napoleon Buford	N/B	Banker	Civil Service
Darius Nash Couch	N/M	Copper Manuf.	Civil Service
Speed Smith Fry	N/B	Lawyer	Civil Service
Benjamin Kelley	N/B	RR Freight Agt.	Civil Service
Wladimir Krzyzanowski	N/B	Engineer	Civil Service
Alfred Thomas Torbert	N/B	Soldier	Civil Service
Jeremiah Sullivan	N/B	U.S.Navy	Clerk
Josiah Gorgas	S/B	Soldier	College Pres.
Daniel Harvey Hill	S/L	College Prof.	College Pres.
George Washington Lee	S/M	Soldier	College Pres.
Robert Edward Lee	S/G	Soldier	College Pres.
Lunsford Lindsay Lomax	S/M	Soldier	College Pres.
Mark Perrin Lowrey	S/B	Min-Baptist	College Pres.
Alexander Stewart Webb	N/B	Soldier	College Pres.
Edward Alexander	S/B	Soldier	College Prof.
William Browne	S/B	Editor	College Prof.
Henry Lawrence Eustis	N/B	College Prof.	College Prof.
Richard W. Johnson	N/B	Soldier	College Prof.
James Henry Lane	S/B	College Prof.	College Prof.
Henry Hayes Lockwood	N/B	College Prof.	College Prof.
William Flank Perry	S/B	Educator	College Prof.
Eliakim Parker Scammon	N/B	Soldier	College Prof.
Claudius Wistar Sears	S/B	College Prof.	College Prof.
Francis Asbury Shoup	S/B	Soldier/L	College Prof.
Edmund Kirby Smith	S/G	Soldier	College Prof.
Alexander Stewart	S/L	College Prof.	College Prof.
Francis Laurens Vinton	N/B	Engineer	College Prof.
Adolph vonSteinwehr	N/B	Farmer	College Prof.
William Buel Franklin	N/B	Soldier	Colt Guns Mgr.
Richard Lee T. Beale	S/B	Congress/L.	Congress
John Beatty	N/B	Banker	Congress/Banker
John Bratton	S/B	Doctor	Congress
Ralph Pomeroy Buckland	N/B	Lawyer	Congress
Robert Bullock	S/B	School Teacher	Congress/L
James Ronald Chalmers	S/B	Lawyer	Congress
John Bullock Clark,Jr.	S/B	Lawyer	Congress
Philip Cook	S/B	Lawyer	Congress
William Ruffin Cox	S/B	Lawyer	Congress
George Gibbs Dibrell	S/B	Merchant/farmer	Congress
Dudley McIver DuBose	S/B	Lawyer	Congress
Ebenezer Dumont	N/B	Politics/L	Congress
Isaac Hardin Duval	N/B	Merchant	Congress
John Edwards	N/B	Politics/L	Congress
Thomas Ewing,Jr.	N/B	Judge/L	Congress
John Farnsworth	N/B	Congress/L	Congress
Jesse Johnson Finley	S/B	Politics/L	Congress

William Henry Forney	S/B	Lawyer	Congress
George Gordon	S/B	Surveyor	Congress/L
Abner Clark Harding	N/B	Politics/L	Congress
Stephen Hurlbut	N/M	Politics/L	Congress
William Henry F. Lee	S/M	Farming	Congress
John Alexander Logan	N/M	Congress	Congress
Mahlon Manson	N/B	Druggist	Congress
Gilman Marston	N/B	Congress/L	Congress
George Morgan	N/B	Lawyer	Congress
James Scott Negley	N/M	Farmer	Congress
Halbert Eleazer Paine	N/B	Lawyer	Congress
Green Berry Raum	N/B	Lawyer	Congress
James Sidney Robinson	N/B	Editor	Congress
William Rosecrans	N/M	Soldier	Congress
Charles Miller Shelley	S/B	Architect	Congress/Sheriff
Daniel Edgar Sickles	N/M	Congress	Congress
Henry Warner Slocum	N/M	Lawyer	Congress
Francis Spinola	N/B	Politics/L	Congress
Nelson Taylor	N/B	Sheriff/L	Congress
William Terry	S/B	Lawyer	Congress
Robert Brank Vance	S/B	Merchant	Congress
William Vandever	N/B	Congress/L	Congress
James Alexander Walker	S/B	Lawyer	Congress
Joseph Wheeler	S/M	Soldier	Congress
Alpheus Williams	N/B	Postmaster/L	Congress
Thomas Kilby Smith	N/B	U.S.Marshal	Consul-Panama
Joseph Finegan	S/B	Farmer	Cotton Broker
Marcellus Stovall	S/B	Farmer	Cotton Broker
Jones Mitchell Withers	S/M	Politics/L	Cotton Broker
Birkett Davenport Fry	S/B	Cotton Manuf.	Cotton Manuf.
August Willich	N/B	Editor	County Auditor
John Henry Hobart Ward	N/B	Soldier	Court Clerk
Thomas Egan	N/B	Unknown	Customs Collect.
George Stannard	N/B	Foundry Owner	Customs Collect.
James Jay Archer	S/B	Soldier/L	Died-illness
William Edwin Baldwin	S/B	Book/Stationary	Died-horse fall
David Bell Birney	N/M	Lawyer	Died-malaria
Louis Ludwig Blenker	N/B	Farmer	Died
John Stevens Bowen	S/M	Architect	Died-dysentery
John Buford	N/B	Soldier	Died-typhoid
James Cooper	N/B	Congress/L	Died
Michael Corcoran	N/B	Postal Clerk	Died-accident
Marcellus Crocker	N/B	Lawyer	Died-TB
Samuel Ryan Curtis	N/M	Engineer	Died
Lysander Cutler	N/B	Teacher/business	Died
Daniel Smith Donelson	S/M	Farmer	Died
Johnson Kelly Duncan	S/B	Soldier	Died-fever
John Buchanan Floyd	S/B	Gov-Virginia/L	Died
John Grayson	S/B	Soldier	Died
Joseph Lewis Hogg	S/B	Politics/L	Died-dysentery
Charles Davis Jameson	N/B	Lumber Business	Died-camp fever
David Rumph Jones	S/M	Soldier	Died-heart
William High Keim	N/B	Congress	Died-camp fever
Frederick West Lander	N/B	Engineer	Died
Ormsby Mitchel	N/M	College Prof./L	Died
Allison Nelson	S/B	Politics/L	Died-fever

Name	Code	Occupation	Outcome
Francis Patterson	N/B	Soldier	Died
Joseph Plummer	N/B	Soldier	Died
George Wythe Randolph	S/B	Lawyer	Died-TB
Thomas Edward Ransom	N/B	Engineer	Died
Samuel Allen Rice	N/B	Atty Gen-Iowa	Died-operation
Alexander Schimmelfennig	N/B	Engineer	Died-TB
Charles Ferguson Smith	N/M	Soldier	Died-infection
William Duncan Smith	S/B	Soldier	Died
Edwin Vose Sumner	N/M	Soldier	Died
Joseph Pannell Taylor	N/B	Soldier	Died
Joseph Gilbert Totten	N/B	Soldier	Died-pneumonia
James Heyward Trapier	S/B	Farmer/Soldier	Died
David Emanuel Twiggs	S/M	Soldier	Died
John Villepigue	S/B	Soldier	Died-fever
Lucius Marshall Walker	S/B	Merchant	Died-duel
Thomas Welsh	N/B	Merchant	Died-malaria
John Austin Wharton	S/M	Lawyer	Died
John Henry Winder	S/B	Soldier	Died
Daniel Phineas Woodbury	N/B	Soldier	Died
James Gillpatrick Blunt	N/M	Doctor	Doctor
William Hammond	N/B	Soldier/Doctor	Doctor
Thomas Maley Harris	N/B	Doctor	Doctor/Politics
James Lawlor Kiernan	N/B	Doctor	Doctor
Sullivan Amory Meredith	N/B	Business	Drug Merchant
James Patton Anderson	S/M	Doctor/US Marshal	Editor
Patrick Edward Connor	N/B	Miner	Editor
Thomas Jordan	S/B	Soldier	Editor
Isaac Fitzgerald Shepard	N/B	Editor	Editor
Bushrod Rust Johnson	S/M	Teacher	Educator
Evander McIvor Law	S/B	Teacher	Educator
Thomas Fentress Toon	S/B	Student	Educator
Jacob Ammen	N/B	College Prof.	Engineer
William Robertson Boggs	S/B	Soldier	Engineer
Braxton Bragg	S/G	Soldier/Planter	Engineer
Henry Brevard Davidson	S/B	Soldier	Engineer
Thomas Pleasant Dockery	S/B	Farmer	Engineer
Charles William Field	S/M	Soldier	Engineer
Charles Kinnaird Graham	N/B	Engineer/L	Engineer
George Sears Greene	N/B	Engineer	Engineer
Herman Haupt	N/B	Engineer	Engineer
James Hewett Ledlie	N/B	Engineer	Engineer
William Gaston Lewis	S/B	Teacher/Surveyor	Engineer
Armistead Lindsay Long	S/B	Soldier	Engineer/writer
Mansfield Lovell	S/M	Soldier	Engineer
Robert Ransom,Jr.	S/M	Soldier	Engineer
Thomas Lafayette Rosser	S/M	West Point	Engineer
James Edwin Slaughter	S/B	Soldier	Engineer
William Farrar Smith	N/M	Soldier	Engineer
William Sooy Smith	N/B	Engineer	Engineer
Isaac Munroe St.John	S/B	Engineer	Engineer
Walter Husted Stevens	S/B	Soldier	Engineer
Carter Stevenson	S/M	Soldier	Engineer
Egbert Ludovicus Viele	N/B	Engineer	Engineer
Reuben Lindsay Walker	S/B	Farmer	Engineer/farmer
David Henry Williams	N/B	Engineer	Engineer
James Harrison Wilson	N/B	Soldier	Engineer

Samuel Beatty	N/B	Sheriff	Farmer
Tyree Harris Bell	S/B	Farmer	Farmer
William Thomas Brooks	N/M	Soldier	Farmer
Egbert Benson Brown	N/B	R.R.Business	Farmer
Abraham Buford	S/B	Farmer	Farmer
James Cantey	S/B	Politics/L	Farmer
Henry DeLamar Clayton	S/M	Politics/L	Farmer
Joseph Alexander Cooper	N/B	Farmer	Farmer
George Blake Cosby	S/B	Soldier	Farmer
Alfred Cumming	S/B	Soldier	Farmer
Arnold Elzey	S/M	Soldier	Farmer
Richard Stoddert Ewell	S/L	Soldier	Farmer
John Horace Forney	S/M	Soldier	Farmer/Engineer
Samuel Gibbs French	S/M	Soldier/farmer	Farmer
Daniel Marsh Frost	S/B	Manufacturer	Farmer
Franklin Gardner	S/M	Soldier	Farmer
Theophilus Garrard	N/B	Politics	Farmer
Richard Caswell Gatlin	S/B	Soldier	Farmer
David McMurtrie Gregg	N/B	Soldier	Farmer
Bryan Grimes	S/M	Farmer	Farmer
William Joseph Hardee	S/L	Soldier	Farmer
William Polk Hardeman	S/B	Soldier	Farmer
Theophilus Hunter Holmes	S/L	Soldier	Farmer
Benjamin Huger	S/M	Soldier	Farmer
Alfred Eugene Jackson	S/B	Merchant	Farmer
William Hicks Jackson	S/B	Soldier	Farmer
Edward Johnson	S/M	Soldier	Farmer
Samuel Jones	S/M	Soldier	Farmer
Michael Kelly Lawler	N/B	Farmer	Farmer
Stephen Dill Lee	S/L	Soldier	Farmer/politics
St.John Liddell	S/B	Farmer	Farmer
Hylan Benton Lyon	S/B	Soldier	Farmer
William Whann Mackall	S/B	Soldier	Farmer
James Patrick Major	S/B	Soldier	Farmer
Arthur Manigault	S/B	Commission Bus.	Farmer/politics
John McCausland	S/B	Coll. Professor	Farmer
William McComb	S/B	Manufacturer	Farmer
Henry Eustace McCulloch	S/B	US Marshal	Farmer
Thomas Jefferson McKean	N/B	Engineer	Farmer
Nathaniel McLean	N/B	Lawyer	Farmer
Solomon Meredith	N/B	U.S.Marshal	Farmer
George Webb Morell	N/M	Lawyer	Farmer
William Hopkins Morris	N/B	Soldier	Farmer
Lucius Northrop	S/B	Doctor	Farmer
William Raine Peck	S/B	Farmer	Farmer
John Clifford Pemberton	S/L	Soldier	Farmer
Abram Sanders Piatt	N/B	Farmer	Farmer
Lucius Eugene Polk	S/B	Farmer	Farmer
Leonard Fulton Ross	N/B	Lawyer	Farmer
Albert Rust	S/B	Congress/L	Farmer
Thomas Moore Scott	S/B	Farmer	Farmer
James Argyle Smith	S/B	Soldier	Farmer
William Smith	S/M	Gov-Virginia/L	Farmer
George Hume Steuart	S/B	Soldier	Farmer
Edward Lloyd Thomas	S/B	Farmer	Farmer
Charles Mynn Thruston	N/B	Banker	Farmer

Alfred Vaughan, Jr.	S/B	Engineer	Farmer
Stand Watie	S/B	Farmer	Farmer
Robert Doak Lilley	S/B	Salesman	Financial Agent
George Hector Tyndale	N/B	Glass Importer	Glass Business
John Charles Fremont	N/M	Soldier/politics	Gov-Arizona
Powell Clayton	N/B	Engineer	Gov-Arkansas
George Stoneman	N/M	Soldier	Gov-Calif.
Edward Moody McCook	N/B	Lawyer	Gov-Colorado
Joseph Roswell Hawley	N/B	Editor/L	Gov-Connecticut
Edward Aylesworth Perry	S/B	Lawyer	Gov-Florida
Alfred Holt Colquitt	S/B	Congress/L	Gov-Georgia
John Brown Gordon	S/M	Coal Mine Bus.	Gov-Georgia
Mason Brayman	N/B	Lawyer	Gov-Idaho
Alvin Peterson Hovey	N/B	Judge/L	Gov-Indiana
Richard James Oglesby	N/M	Politics/L	Gov-Illinois
John McCauley Palmer	N/M	Politics/L	Gov-Illinois
Simon Bolivar Buckner	S/L	Business	Gov-Kentucky
Francis Nicholls	S/B	Lawyer	Gov-Louisiana
Joshua Chamberlain	N/B	Coll.Professor	Gov-Maine
Selden Connor	N/B	Student	Gov-Maine
Benjamin Butler	N/M	Lawyer	Gov-Mass.
Stephen Miller	N/B	Editor	Gov-Minnesota
Adelbert Ames	N/B	Sailor	Gov-Mississippi
Thomas James Churchill	S/M	Postmaster	Gov-Mississippi
Charles Clark	S/B	School Teacher	Gov-Mississippi
Benjamin Grubb Humphreys	S/B	Politics/farmer	Gov-Mississippi
Robert Lowry	S/B	Lawyer	Gov-Mississippi
John Marmaduke	S/M	Soldier	Gov-Missouri
John Smith Phelps	N/B	Congress/L	Gov-Missouri
Benjamin Franklin Potts	N/B	Lawyer	Gov-Montana
John Milton Thayer	N/B	Lawyer	Gov-Nebraska
George Brinton McClellan	N/M	Soldier	Gov-New Jersey
Robert Byington Mitchell	N/B	Lawyer	Gov-New Mexico
William Anderson Pile	N/B	Min-Methodist	Gov-New Mexico
Lewis Wallace	N/M	Politics/L	Gov-New Mexico
John Adams Dix	N/M	Politics/L	Gov-New York
Alfred Moore Scales	S/B	Congress/L	Gov-N.Carolina
Jacob Dolson Cox	N/M	Politics/L	Gov-Ohio
John White Geary	N/B	Gov-Kansas/L	Gov-Penna.
John Frederick Hartranft	N/B	Engineer/L	Gov-Penna.
Ambrose Everett Burnside	N/M	Soldier	Gov-Rhode Island
Johnson Hagood	S/B	Lawyer	Gov-S.Carolina
Wade Hampton	S/L	Politics	Gov-S.Carolina
William Brimage Bate	S/M	NewspaperEditor/L	Gov-Tennessee
John Calvin Brown	S/M	Lawyer	Gov-Tennessee
Edmund Jackson Davis	N/B	Judge/L	Gov-Texas
Lawrence Sullivan Ross	S/B	Soldier	Gov-Texas/Sher.
James Lawson Kemper	S/M	Politics/L	Gov-Virginia
Fitzhugh Lee	S/M	Soldier	Gov-Virginia
Lucius Fairchild	N/B	Court Clerk	Gov-Wisconsin
Cadwallader Washburn	N/M	Congress/L	Gov-Wisconsin
Cadmus Marcellus Wilcox	S/M	Soldier	Government
Gabriel James Rains	S/B	Soldier	Govt. Clerk
Peter Joseph Osterhaus	N/M	Store Clerk	Hardware
Charles Thomas Campbell	N/B	Politics	Hotel Operator
Byron Root Pierce	N/B	Dentist	Hotel Operator

Zebulon York	S/B	Lawyer	Hotel Operator
Daniel Chevilette Govan	S/B	Farmer	Indian Agent
Robert Huston Milroy	N/M	Lawyer	Indian Agent
Douglas Hancock Cooper	S/B	U.S.Indian Agt.	Indian Represent.
Thomas Fenwick Drayton	S/B	Farmer	Insurance
Henry Heth	S/M	Soldier	Insurance
Edward Higgins	S/B	US Navy	Insurance
Lafayette McLaws	S/M	Soldier	Insurance
Patrick Theodore Moore	S/B	Merchant	Insurance
John James Peck	N/M	Banker	Insurance
George Edward Pickett	S/M	Soldier	Insurance
Beverly Robertson	S/B	Soldier	Insurance
Julius Stahel	N/M	Journalist	Insurance
Gustavus Adolphus Smith	N/B	Carriage Manuf.	I.R.Collector
James Clifford Veatch	N/B	Lawyer	I.R.Collector
Max Weber	N/B	Hotel operator	I.R.Collector
Joseph Dana Webster	N/B	Engineer	I.R.Collector
William Woods Averell	N/B	Soldier	Inventor
Henry Harrison Walker	S/B	Soldier	Invest.Broker
Don Carlos Buell	N/M	Soldier	Iron Works Oper.
Joseph Reid Anderson	S/B	Iron Works Supt.	Iron Works Supt.
Gustavus Woodson Smith	S/M	Soldier/Engineer	Iron Works Supt.
Henry Shaw Briggs	N/B	Lawyer	Judge
Richard Busteed	N/B	Lawyer	Judge
George Henry Chapman	N/B	Editor/L	Judge
Matthew Duncan Ector	S/B	Lawyer	Judge
Winfield Featherston	S/B	Congress/L	Judge
Manning Ferguson Force	N/B	Lawyer	Judge
Andrew Jackson Hamilton	N/B	Politics/L	Judge
Thomas Harrison	S/B	Politics/L	Judge
William Lowther Jackson	S/B	Politics/L	Judge
Joseph Brevard Kershaw	S/M	Politics/L	Judge/politics
Joseph Horace Lewis	S/B	Politics/L	Judge/Congress
Samuel McGowan	S/B	Politics/L	Judge/politics
Calvin Edward Pratt	N/B	Lawyer	Judge
Roger Atkinson Pryor	S/B	Congress/L	Judge
James Shackelford	N/B	Lawyer	Judge
George Foster Shepley	N/B	U.S.Dist.Atty/L	Judge
James Richard Slack	N/B	Politics/L	Judge
William Taliaferro	S/M	Politics/L	Judge
Ferdinand Van Derveer	N/B	Sheriff/L	Judge
William Henry Wallace	S/B	Farmer/L	Judge
John Adams	S/B	Soldier	Killed
George Burgwyn Anderson	S/B	Soldier	Killed
Lewis Addison Armistead	S/B	Soldier	Killed
Turner Ashby	S/B	Farmer	Killed
Edward Dickinson Baker	N/M	Politics/L	Killed
William Barksdale	S/B	Congress	Killed
George Dashiell Bayard	N/B	Soldier	Killed
Barnard Elliott Bee	S/B	Soldier	Killed
Hiram Gregory Berry	N/M	Banker/politics	Killed
Daniel Davidson Bidwell	N/B	Police Justice	Killed
Henry Bohlen	N/B	Liquor dealer	Killed
Lawrence O'Bryan Branch	S/B	Congress/L	Killed
Hiram Burnham	N/B	Lumberman	Killed
John Carpenter Carter	S/B	Lawyer	Killed

John Chambliss, Jr.	S/B	Farmer	Killed
Stephen Champlin	N/B	Lawyer	Killed
Patrick Cleburne	S/M	Druggist/L	Killed
Thomas Reade Cobb	S/B	Lawyer	Killed
Junius Daniel	S/B	Soldier	Killed
James Dearing	S/B	Soldier	Killed
James Deshler	S/B	Soldier	Killed
George Pierce Doles	S/B	Business	Killed
John Dunovant	S/B	Soldier	Killed
Elon John Farnsworth	N/B	Foragemaster	Killed
Samuel Garland,Jr.	S/B	Lawyer	Killed
Richard Brooke Garnett	S/B	Soldier	Killed
Robert Selden Garnett	S/B	Soldier	Killed
Victor Jean B. Girardey	S/B	Unknown	Killed
States Rights Gist	S/B	Lawyer	Killed
Adley Hogan Gladden	S/B	Postmaster	Killed
Archibald Godwin	S/B	Miner/rancher	Killed
James Byron Gordon	S/B	Farmer/politics	Killed
Archibald Gracie,Jr.	S/B	Merchant	Killed
Hiram Bronson Granbury	S/B	Politics/L	Killed
Martin Edwin Green	S/B	Sawmill Oper.	Killed
Thomas Green	S/B	Lawyer	Killed
John Gregg	S/B	Judge/L	Killed
Maxcy Gregg	S/B	Lawyer	Killed
Richard Griffith	S/B	Teacher	Killed
Pleasant Adam Hackleman	N/B	Judge/L	Killed
Charles Garrison Harker	N/B	Soldier	Killed
Roger Weightman Hanson	S/B	Politics/L	Killed
Robert Hopkins Hatton	S/B	Congress/L	Killed
Alexander Hays	N/B	Engineer	Killed
Benjamin Hardin Helm	S/B	Politics/L	Killed
Ambrose Powell Hill	S/L	Soldier	Killed
Conrad Feger Jackson	N/B	Railroad worker	Killed
James Streshly Jackson	N/B	Congress/L	Killed
Thomas Jonathon Jackson	S/L	College Prof.	Killed
Albert Gallatin Jenkins	S/B	Congress/L	Killed
Micah Jenkins	S/B	Educator	Killed
Albert Sidney Johnston	S/G	Soldier	Killed
John Marshall Jones	S/B	Soldier	Killed
William Edmonson Jones	S/B	Soldier	Killed
Philip Kearny	N/M	Soldier	Killed
John Herbert Kelly	S/B	Student	Killed
Edward Needles Kirk	N/B	Lawyer	Killed
Lewis Henry Little	S/B	Soldier	Killed
Nathaniel Lyon	N/B	Soldier	Killed
William Haines Lytle	N/B	Lawyer	Killed
Joseph King Mansfield	N/B	Soldier	Killed
Robert Latimer McCook	N/B	Lawyer	Killed
Ben McCulloch	S/B	U.S.Marshal	Killed
James McQueen McIntosh	S/B	Soldier	Killed
James Birdseye McPherson	N/M	Soldier	Killed
John Hunt Morgan	S/B	Cotton Manuf.	Killed
James St.Clair Morton	N/B	Soldier	Killed
Jean Jacques Mouton	S/B	Engineer	Killed
Elisha Franklin Paxton	S/B	Lawyer	Killed
John Pegram	S/B	Soldier	Killed

William Dorsey Pender	S/M	Soldier	Killed
Abner Monroe Perrin	S/B	Lawyer	Killed
James Pettigrew	S/B	Politics/L	Killed
Leonidas Polk	S/L	Min-Episcopal	Killed
Carnot Posey	S/B	Farmer/L	Killed
James Edwards Rains	S/B	Lawyer	Killed
Stephen Dodson Ramseur	S/M	Soldier	Killed
Jesse Lee Reno	N/M	Soldier	Killed
John Fulton Reynolds	N/M	Soldier	Killed
James Clay Rice	N/B	Lawyer	Killed
Israel Bush Richardson	N/M	Soldier	Killed
Robert Emmett Rodes	S/M	Engineer	Killed
Isaac Peace Rodman	N/B	Merchant	Killed
David Allen Russell	N/B	Soldier	Killed
John Caldwell Sanders	S/B	Student	Killed
William Price Sanders	N/B	Soldier	Killed
William Read Scurry	S/B	Soldier	Killed
John Sedgwick	N/M	Soldier	Killed
Paul Jones Semmes	S/B	Banker/farmer	Killed
Joshua Woodrow Sill	N/B	Soldier	Killed
William Yarnel Slack	S/B	Lawyer	Killed
Preston Smith	S/B	Lawyer	Killed
Thomas Alfred Smyth	N/B	Coachmaker	Killed
Leroy Augustus Stafford	S/B	Sheriff/farmer	Killed
William Edwin Starke	S/B	Cotton Broker	Killed
Clement Hoffman Stevens	S/B	Banker	Killed
Isaac Ingalls Stevens	N/B	Gov-Washington	Killed
Thomas Greely Stevenson	N/B	Unknown	Killed
Otho French Strahl	S/B	Lawyer	Killed
George Crockett Strong	N/B	Soldier	Killed
James Ewell Stuart	S/M	Soldier	Killed
George William Taylor	N/B	Iron Manuf.	Killed
William Rufus Terrill	N/B	Soldier	Killed
Lloyd Tilghman	S/B	Engineer	Killed
Edward Dorr Tracy	S/B	Lawyer	Killed
Robert Charles Tyler	S/B	Soldier	Killed
James Samuel Wadsworth	N/B	Politics/L	Killed
William Henry T. Walker	S/M	Soldier	Killed
William Harvey Wallace	N/B	Lawyer	Killed
Stephen Hinsdale Weed	N/B	Soldier	Killed
Amiel Weeks Whipple	N/B	Soldier	Killed
Thomas Williams	N/B	Soldier	Killed
William Henry Whiting	S/M	Soldier	Killed
Charles Sidney Winder	S/B	Soldier	Killed
Felix Kirk Zollicoffer	S/B	Politics	Killed
Samuel Kosciuszko Zook	N/B	Telegrapher	Killed
Richard Waterhouse	S/B	Merchant	Land Speculator
Daniel Weisiger Adams	S/B	Lawyer	Lawyer
Alpheus Baker	S/B	Lawyer	Lawyer
Henry Lewis Benning	S/B	Judge/L	Lawyer
William Plummer Benton	N/B	Judge/L	Lawyer
William Birney	N/B	Editor/L	Lawyer
William Felix Brantley	S/B	Lawyer	Lawyer
John Breckinridge	S/M	US Vice Pres.	Lawyer
Theodore Brevard	S/B	Politics/L	Lawyer
William Lewis Cabell	S/B	Soldier	Lawyer

Alexander Campbell	S/B	Lawyer	Lawyer
James Holt Clanton	S/B	Lawyer	Lawyer
Thomas Lanier Clingman	S/B	Senator/L	Lawyer
Thomas Crittenden	N/B	Lawyer	Lawyer
Charles Cruft	N/B	RR Pres./L	Lawyer
Henry Eugene Davies	N/B	Lawyer	Lawyer
Joseph Robert Davis	S/B	Lawyer	Lawyer
William George M. Davis	S/B	Lawyer	Lawyer
James William Denver	N/B	Gov-Colorado	Lawyer
Basil Wilson Duke	S/B	Lawyer	Lawyer
Jubal Anderson Early	S/L	Lawyer	Lawyer
Samuel Wragg Ferguson	S/B	Soldier	Lawyer
Francis Fessenden	N/B	Lawyer	Lawyer
James Deering Fessenden	N/B	Lawyer	Lawyer
George Henry Gordon	N/B	Soldier/L	Lawyer
Willis Arnold Gorman	N/B	Gov-Minnesota	Lawyer
Cyrus Hamlin	N/B	Lawyer	Lawyer
Nathaniel Harris	S/B	Lawyer	Lawyer
Isham Nicholas Haynie	N/B	Judge	Lawyer
Thomas Hindman	S/M	Politics/L	Lawyer
William Young Humes	S/B	Lawyer	Lawyer
John Daniel Imboden	S/B	Politics/L	Lawyer
John King Jackson	S/B	Lawyer	Lawyer
John Reese Kenly	N/B	Lawyer	Lawyer
Mortimer Dormer Leggett	N/B	Lawyer	Lawyer
Eli Long	N/B	Soldier	Lawyer
Humphrey Marshall	S/B	Congress/L	Lawyer
James Green Martin	S/B	Soldier	Lawyer
John Grant Mitchell	N/B	Student	Lawyer
Franklin Nickerson	N/B	U.S.Customs	Lawyer
John Morrison Oliver	N/B	Pharmacist	Lawyer
Joshua Thomas Owen	N/B	Teacher	Lawyer
Eleazer Arthur Paine	N/B	U.S.Marshal	Lawyer
Joseph Benjamin Palmer	S/B	Politics	Lawyer
Gideon Johnson Pillow	S/B	Lawyer	Lawyer
Elliott Warren Rice	N/B	Lawyer	Lawyer
Felix Huston Robertson	S/B	West Point	Lawyer
Robert Cumming Schenck	N/M	Congress	Lawyer
James Phillip Simms	S/B	Lawyer	Lawyer
James Gallant Spears	N/B	Lawyer	Lawyer
John Starkweather	N/B	Lawyer	Lawyer
John Dunlap Stevenson	N/B	Politics	Lawyer
Edwin Henry Stoughton	N/B	Soldier	Lawyer
David Stuart	N/B	Congress	Lawyer
Frederick Stumbaugh	N/B	Lawyer	Lawyer
Wager Swayne	N/B	Lawyer	Lawyer
Henry Dwight Terry	N/B	Lawyer	Lawyer
George Day Wagner	N/B	Politics	Lawyer
William Thomas Ward	N/B	Congress	Lawyer
Thomas Neville Waul	S/B	Farmer	Lawyer
Walter Chiles Whitaker	N/B	Lawyer	Lawyer
Henry Alexander Wise	S/B	Gov-Virginia	Lawyer
Isaac Jones Wistar	N/B	Lawyer	Lawyer
Sterling Alexander Wood	S/B	Lawyer	Lawyer
Albert Pike	S/B	Lawyer	Legal writer
John Cleveland Robinson	N/B	Soldier	Lt.Gov-New York

Charles Edward Hovey	N/B	Principal	Lobbyist
Henry Warner Birge	N/B	Merchant	Lumber business
James Isham Gilbert	N/B	Lumber business	Lumber business
Henry Constantine Wayne	S/B	Soldier	Lumber business
Roswell Sabine Ripley	S/B	Soldier/business	Manufacturer
Camille A.J.M. Polignac	S/M	Soldier	Mathematics
Samuel Read Anderson	S/B	Postmaster	Merchant
William Nelson R. Beall	S/B	Soldier	Merchant
Cyrus Bussey	N/B	Politics	Merchant/L
John Rogers Cooke	S/B	Soldier	Merchant
James Morrison Hawes	S/B	Soldier	Merchant
Benjamin Jefferson Hill	S/B	Politics	Merchant
John Robert Jones	S/B	School Principal	Merchant
Walter Paye Lane	S/B	Mining	Merchant
Jasper Adalmorn Maltby	N/B	Gunsmith	Merchant
Hugh Weedon Mercer	S/B	Banker	Merchant
Gilbert Moxley Sorrel	S/B	Railroad	Merchant
William Steele	S/B	Soldier	Merchant
Alexander Robert Lawton	S/B	Politics/L	Min—Austria
John Thomas Croxton	N/B	Lawyer	Min—Bolivia
Hugh Judson Kilpatrick	N/B	USMA	Min—Chili
Dabney Herndon Maury	S/M	Soldier	Min—Colombia
Fitz-Henry Warren	N/B	Politics	Min—Guatemala
Hugh Boyle Ewing	N/B	Lawyer	Min—Holland
Henry Baxter	N/B	Miller	Min—Honduras
Henry Rootes Jackson	S/B	Lawyer	Min—Mexico
Rufus King	N/B	Editor	Min—Rome
Joseph Jackson Bartlett	N/B	Lawyer	Min—Sweden
James Longstreet	S/L	Soldier	Min—Turkey
Alexander Sandor Asboth	N/B	Engineer	Min—Uruguay
Alexander Hawthorne	S/B	Lawyer	Min—Baptist
Joseph Andrew Lightburn	N/B	Soldier	Min—Baptist
Green Clay Smith	N/B	Lawyer	Min—Baptist
Richard Montgomery Gano	S/B	Doctor	Min—Christ.Church
Ellison Capers	S/B	School Teacher	Min—Episcopal
Clement Anselm Evans	S/B	Politics/L	Min—Episcopal
William Nelson Pendleton	S/B	Min—Episcopal	Min—Episcopal
Joseph Hayes	N/B	Engineer	Mining
James Madison Tuttle	N/B	Sheriff	Mining
Edward Augustus Wild	N/B	Doctor	Mining
William Nelson	N/M	U.S.Navy	Murdered
Earl Van Dorn	S/M	Soldier	Murdered
William Henry Powell	N/B	Iron Works Mgr.	Nail Co.Manager
Henry Watkins Allen	S/B	School Teacher/L	Newspaper Editor
John Decatur Barry	S/B	Student	Newspaper Editor
Cullen Andrews Battle	S/B	Lawyer	Newspaper Editor
Louis Hebert	S/B	Engineer	Newspaper Editor
Alfred Iverson,Jr.	S/B	Soldier	Orange grower
John Basil Turchin	N/B	Engineer	Patent Solicitor
George Thomas Anderson	S/B	Soldier	Police Chief
Robert Anderson	S/B	Soldier	Police Chief
Abram Duryee	N/B	Importer	Police Chief
James Blair Steedman	N/M	Printer	Police Chief
Thomas Hart Taylor	S/B	Farmer	Police Chief
Christopher Andrews	N/B	Lawyer	Politics
Nathaniel Banks	N/M	Gov-Massachusetts	Politics/L

Francis Channing Barlow	N/B	Lawyer	Politics
Rufus Barringer	S/B	Lawyer	Politics
Edward Stuyvesant Bragg	N/B	Lawyer	Politics
John Curtis Caldwell	N/B	Principal	Politics/L
William Bowen Campbell	N/B	Gov-Tennessee/L	Politics
James Chesnut, Jr.	S/B	Senator/L	Politics
Gustave Paul Cluseret	N/B	Soldier	Politics
John Cochrane	N/B	Congress/L	Politics
John Cook	N/B	Sheriff	Politics
Newton Martin Curtis	N/B	Teacher	Politics
Neal Dow	N/B	Leather Tanner	Politics
Stephen Elliott,Jr.	S/B	Farmer	Politics
Orris Sanford Ferry	N/B	Politics/L	Politics
Kenner Garrard	N/B	Soldier	Politics
Lucius Gartrell	S/B	Congress/L	Politics
Martin Witherspoon Gary	S/B	Politics/L	Politics
Samuel Jameson Gholson	S/B	Judge/L	Politics
Henry Gray	S/B	Lawyer	Politics
Simon Goodell Griffin	N/B	Lawyer	Politics
Edward Harland	N/B	Lawyer	Politics
James Edward Harrison	S/B	Politics	Politics
William Harrow	N/B	Lawyer	Politics
Paul Octave Hebert	S/B	Gov-Louisiana	Politics
Edward Henry Hobson	N/B	Bank President	Politics
George Baird Hodge	S/B	Politics/L	Politics
James Thadeus Holtzclaw	S/B	Lawyer	Politics
Eppa Hunton	S/B	Lawyer	Politics
Bradley Tyler Johnson	S/B	Politics/L	Politics
George Doherty Johnston	S/B	Politics/L	Politics
Joseph Johnston	S/G	Soldier	Politics
John Doby Kennedy	S/B	Lawyer	Politics
George Ear Maney	S/B	Lawyer	Politics
William Thompson Martin	S/M	Lawyer	Politics
Charles Matthies	N/B	Liquor Business	Politics
John McClernand	N/M	Congress/L	Politics
Dandridge McRae	S/B	Lawyer	Politics
William Miller	S/B	Lumber business	Politics
William Henry F. Payne	S/B	Lawyer	Politics
William Preston	S/B	Congress/L	Politics
William Andrew Quarles	S/B	Judge/L	Politics
Daniel Harris Reynolds	S/B	Lawyer	Politics
William Paul Roberts	S/B	None	Politics
John Benjamin Sanborn	N/B	Lawyer	Politics
Alexander Shaler	N/B	None/wealthy	Politics
Jacob Hunter Sharp	S/B	Lawyer	Politics
Charles John Stolbrand	N/B	Soldier	Politics
James Camp Tappan	S/B	Judge/L	Politics
William Richard Terry	S/B	Merchant	Politics
Allen Thomas	S/B	Farmer/L	Politics/Farmer
John Blair Smith Todd	N/B	Soldier/L	Politics
Robert Augustus Toombs	S/B	Politics/L	Politics
William Feimster Tucker	S/B	Judge/L	Politics
John Crawford Vaughn	S/B	Merchant	Politics
John George Walker	S/M	Soldier	Politics
Leroy Pope Walker	S/B	Politics/L	Politics
Gabriel Colvin Wharton	S/B	Engineer	Politics

John Wilkins Whitfield	S/B	Congress	Politics
John Stuart Williams	S/B	Politics/L	Politics/Farmer
William Tatum Wofford	S/B	Politics/L	Politics
Ambrose Ransom Wright	S/M	Lawyer	Politics
Pierce Manning Young	S/M	West Point	Politics
William Wirt Adams	S/B	Farmer/Banker	Postmaster
Benjamin Cheatham	S/M	Farmer	Postmaster
John Murray Corse	N/B	Lawyer	Postmaster
Joseph Farmer Knipe	N/B	Railroad	Postmaster
Thomas John Lucas	N/B	Watchmaker	Postmaster
John McArthur	N/B	Iron Works Owner	Postmaster
George Francis McGinnis	N/B	Hatter	Postmaster
Benjamin Prentiss	N/M	Lawyer	Postmaster
Andrew Jackson Smith	N/M	Soldier	Postmaster
Erastus Barnard Tyler	N/B	Fur business	Postmaster
Horatio Van Cleve	N/B	Engineer	Postmaster
Jeremy Francis Gilmer	S/M	Soldier	Pres.Gas Co.
Robert Hall Chilton	S/B	Soldier	Pres.Manuf.Co.
Nathan George Evans	S/B	Soldier	Principal
Charles Carroll Walcutt	N/B	Surveyor	Prison Warden
George Deitzler	N/B	Farmer/Realtor	Railroad
Thomas Benton Smith	S/B	Railroad	Railroad
Grenville Mellen Dodge	N/M	Engineer	R.R. Builder
Robert Richardson	S/B	Lawyer	R.R. Builder
Jerome Robertson	S/B	Doctor	R.R. Builder
Jerimiah Tilford Boyle	N/B	Lawyer	R.R. Business
Napoleon Jackson Dana	N/M	Banker/Soldier	R.R. Business
James Barnes	N/B	Engineer	R.R.Commissioner
Milledge Luke Bonham	S/B	Congress/L	R.R.Commissioner
Charles Jackson Paine	N/B	Lawyer	R.R.Director
William Dwight	N/B	Manufacturer	R.R.Management
Thomas Muldrup Logan	S/B	Student	R.R.Management/L
John Wilson Sprague	N/B	Business	R.R.Management
Gershom Mott	N/B	Business	R.R.Paymaster
Pierre Beauregard	S/G	Soldier	R.R.President
James Craig	N/B	Politics/L	R.R.President
Nathan Bedford Forrest	S/L	Farmer/slave dlr	R.R.President
Hugh Thompson Reid	N/B	Lawyer	R.R.President
Daniel Tyler	N/B	RR President	R.R.President
Williams Carter Wickham	S/B	Politics/L	R.R.President
James Williamson	N/B	Lawyer	R.R.President
Robert Brown Potter	N/B	Lawyer	R.R.Receiver
Laurence Simmons Baker	S/B	Soldier	R.R.Station Agt.
William MacRae	S/B	Engineer	R.R.Supt.
William Hugh Young	S/B	Student	Real Estate/L
Robert Anderson	N/B	Soldier	Retired
Lewis Golding Arnold	N/B	Soldier	Retired
James Bowen	N/B	RR President	Retired
William Lindsay Brandon	S/B	Farmer	Retired
Goode Bryan	S/B	Farmer	Retired
Samuel Cooper	S/G	Soldier	Retired
Joseph Tarr Copeland	N/B	Judge/L	Retired
Richard Delafield	N/B	Soldier	Retired
William Selby Harney	N/B	Soldier	Retired
Ethan Allen Hitchcock	N/M	Soldier	Retired
David Hunter	N/M	Soldier	Retired

George Archibald McCall	N/B	Soldier	Retired
Gabriel Rene Paul	N/B	Soldier	Retired
Andrew Porter	N/B	Soldier	Retired
Sterling Price	S/M	Gov-Missouri	Retired
Joseph Warren Revere	N/B	U.S.Navy	Retired
James Wolfe Ripley	N/B	Soldier	Retired
John Selden Roane	S/B	Gov-Arkansas	Retired
Winfield Scott	N/M	Soldier	Retired
William Kerley Strong	N/B	Merchant	Retired
Daniel Ullmann	N/B	Lawyer	Retired
Melancthon Smith Wade	N/B	Merchant	Retired
John Ellis Wool	N/M	Soldier	Retired
Richard Lucian Page	S/B	U.S. Navy	School Supt.
Thomas Francis Meagher	N/B	Politics	Secy St.-Montana
Joseph Bradford Carr	N/B	Tobacconist	Secy State-N.Y.
Francis Preston Blair	N/M	Congress/L	Senator
Matthew Calbraith Butler	S/M	Lawyer	Senator
Francis Marion Cockrell	S/B	Lawyer	Senator
Randall Lee Gibson	S/B	Lawyer	Senator
William Mahone	S/M	Engineer	Senator
Samuel Bell Maxey	S/M	Lawyer	Senator
Edwin Denison Morgan	N/M	Gov-New York	Senator
John Tyler Morgan	S/B	Lawyer	Senator
John Franklin Miller	N/B	Lawyer	Senator
Edmund Winston Pettus	S/B	Judge/L	Senator
Matt Whitaker Ransom	S/B	Politics/L	Senator
Carl Schurz	N/M	Politics	Senator
James Shields	N/B	Politics/L	Senator
Edward Cary Walthall	S/M	Lawyer	Senator
Joseph Bailey	N/B	Lumberman	Sheriff
Elias Smith Dennis	N/B	U.S.Marshal	Sheriff
Harry Thompson Hays	S/M	Politics/L	Sheriff
John McNeil	N/B	Insurance	Sheriff
Peter Burwell Starke	S/B	Senator	Sheriff
John Joseph Abercrombie	N/B	Soldier	Soldier
Robert Allen	N/B	Soldier	Soldier
Benjamin Alvord	N/B	Soldier	Soldier
Richard Arnold	N/B	Soldier	Soldier
Christopher Augur	N/M	Soldier	Soldier
Romeyn Beck Ayres	N/B	Soldier	Soldier
Absalom Baird	N/B	Soldier	Soldier
John Gross Barnard	N/B	Soldier	Soldier
Joseph K. Barnes	N/B	Soldier/Doctor	Soldier/Doctor
William Farquhar Barry	N/B	Soldier	Soldier
Henry Washington Benham	N/B	Soldier	Soldier
Luther Prentice Bradley	N/B	Bookkeeper	Soldier
John Milton Brannan	N/B	Soldier	Soldier
John Rutter Brooke	N/B	Unknown	Soldier
Robert Christie Buchanan	N/B	Soldier	Soldier
William Wallace Burns	N/B	Soldier	Soldier
Edward Richard S. Canby	N/M	Soldier	Soldier
James Henry Carleton	N/B	Soldier	Soldier
William Passmore Carlin	N/B	Soldier	Soldier
Eugene Asa Carr	N/B	Soldier	Soldier
Henry Beebee Carrington	N/B	Lawyer	Soldier
Samuel Sprigg Carroll	N/B	Soldier	Soldier

Silas Casey	N/M	Soldier	Soldier
Alexander Chambers	N/B	Soldier	Soldier
Raleigh Edward Colston	S/B	College Prof.	Soldier
Philip St.George Cooke	N/B	Soldier	Soldier
Samuel Wylie Crawford	N/B	Doctor	Soldier
Thomas Crittenden	N/M	Lawyer	Soldier
George Crook	N/M	Soldier	Soldier
George Washington Cullum	N/B	Soldier	Soldier
George Armstrong Custer	N/B	Teacher	Soldier
John Wynn Davidson	N/B	Soldier	Soldier
Jefferson Columbus Davis	N/B	Soldier	Soldier
Gustavus DeRussy	N/B	Soldier	Soldier
Philippe deTrobriand	N/B	Lawyer	Soldier
Thomas Casimer Devin	N/B	House painter	Soldier
Abner Doubleday	N/B	Soldier	Soldier
Alexander Brydie Dyer	N/B	Soldier	Soldier
Amos Beebe Eaton	N/B	Soldier	Soldier
Washington Elliott	N/B	Soldier	Soldier
William Hemsley Emory	N/B	Soldier	Soldier
John Gray Foster	N/M	Soldier	Soldier
William Henry French	N/M	Soldier	Soldier
James Barnet Fry	N/B	Soldier	Soldier/writer
George Washington Getty	N/B	Soldier	Soldier
John Gibbon	N/M	Soldier	Soldier
Alfred Gibbs	N/B	Soldier	Soldier
Charles Champion Gilbert	N/B	Soldier	Soldier
Alvan Cullem Gillem	N/B	Soldier	Soldier
Quincy Adams Gillmore	N/M	Soldier	Soldier
Lawrence Pike Graham	N/B	Soldier	Soldier
Gordon Granger	N/M	Soldier	Soldier
Robert Seaman Granger	N/B	Soldier	Soldier
Benjamin Henry Grierson	N/B	Merchant	Soldier
Charles Griffin	N/M	Soldier	Soldier
Cuvier Grover	N/B	Soldier	Soldier
Henry Wager Halleck	N/M	Soldier/L	Soldier
Winfield Scott Hancock	N/M	Soldier	Soldier
James Allen Hardie	N/B	Soldier	Soldier
Martin Davis Hardin	N/B	Soldier	Soldier/L
George Lucas Hartsuff	N/M	Soldier	Soldier
Joseph Abel Haskin	N/B	Soldier	Soldier
Edward Hatch	N/B	Lumber bus.	Soldier
John Porter Hatch	N/B	Soldier	Soldier
John Parker Hawkins	N/B	Soldier	Soldier
William Hays	N/B	Soldier	Soldier
William Babcock Hazen	N/M	Soldier	Soldier
Samuel Heintzelman	N/M	Soldier	Soldier
Edward Winslow Hincks	N/B	Politics	Soldier
Joseph Holt	N/B	Politics/L	Soldier
Joseph Hooker	N/M	Soldier	Soldier
Oliver Otis Howard	N/M	Soldier	Soldier
Albion Parris Howe	N/B	Soldier	Soldier
Andrew Humphreys	N/M	Soldier	Soldier
Henry Jackson Hunt	N/B	Soldier	Soldier
Lewis Cass Hunt	N/B	Soldier	Soldier
Rufus Ingalls	N/B	Soldier	Soldier
Henry Moses Judah	N/B	Soldier	Soldier

August Valentine Kautz	N/B	Soldier	Soldier
William Scott Ketchum	N/B	Soldier	Soldier
John Haskell King	N/B	Soldier	Soldier
William Wing Loring	S/M	Soldier/L	Soldier
Ranald Mackenzie	N/B	Student	Soldier
John Bankhead Magruder	S/M	Soldier	Soldier-Mexico
Randolph Barnes Marcy	N/B	Soldier	Soldier
John Sanford Mason	N/B	Soldier	Soldier
Alexander McCook	N/M	Soldier	Soldier
Irvin McDowell	N/M	Soldier	Soldier
John Baillie McIntosh	N/B	Business	Soldier
George Gordon Meade	N/M	Soldier	Soldier
Montgomery Meigs	N/B	Soldier	Soldier
Wesley Merritt	N/M	Soldier	Soldier
Nelson Appleton Miles	N/B	Store Clerk	Soldier
Joseph Anthony Mower	N/M	Soldier	Soldier
Thomas Hewson Neill	N/B	Soldier	Soldier
John Newton	N/M	Soldier	Soldier
Edward Otho C. Ord	N/M	Soldier	Soldier
Innis Newton Palmer	N/B	Soldier	Soldier
John Grubb Parke	N/M	Soldier	Soldier
Mosby Monroe Parsons	S/M	Politics/L	Soldier-China
Marsena Rudolph Patrick	N/B	Farmer	Soldier
Thomas Gamble Pitcher	N/B	Soldier	Soldier
Alfred Pleasonton	N/M	Soldier	Soldier
Orlando Metcalfe Poe	N/B	Soldier	Soldier
John Pope	N/M	Soldier	Soldier
Henry Prince	N/B	Soldier	Soldier
George Douglas Ramsay	N/B	Soldier	Soldier
Alexander Reynolds	S/B	Soldier	Soldier-Egypt
Joseph Jones Reynolds	N/M	College Prof.	Soldier
James Brewerton Ricketts	N/B	Soldier	Soldier
Benjamin Stone Roberts	N/B	Soldier/L	Soldier
Lovell Harrison Rousseau	N/M	Politics/L	Soldier
Daniel Henry Rucker	N/B	Soldier	Soldier
Thomas Howard Ruger	N/B	Lawyer	Soldier
Rufus Saxton	N/B	Soldier	Soldier
John Schofield	N/M	Soldier	Soldier
Truman Seymour	N/B	Soldier	Soldier
Philip Henry Sheridan	N/M	Soldier	Soldier
Thomas West Sherman	N/B	Soldier	Soldier
William Sherman	N/M	Lawyer	Soldier
Henry Hopkins Sibley	S/B	Soldier	Soldier-Egypt
Adam Jacoby Slemmer	N/B	Soldier	Soldier
John Eugene Smith	N/B	Jeweler	Soldier
Thomas Church H. Smith	N/B	Lawyer	Soldier
David Sloane Stanley	N/M	Soldier	Soldier
Frederick Steele	N/M	Soldier	Soldier
Charles Pomeroy Stone	N/B	Soldier	Soldier-Egypt
Samuel Davis Sturgis	N/B	Soldier	Soldier
Alfred Sully	N/B	Soldier	Soldier
George Sykes	N/M	Soldier	Soldier
Alfred Howe Terry	N/M	Lawyer	Soldier
George Henry Thomas	N/M	Soldier	Soldier
Henry Goddard Thomas	N/B	Lawyer	Soldier
Lorenzo Thomas	N/B	Soldier	Soldier

Zealous Bates Tower	N/B	Soldier	Soldier
John Wesley Turner	N/B	Soldier	Soldier
Robert Ogden Tyler	N/B	Soldier	Soldier
Emory Upton	N/B	Student	Soldier
Stewart Van Vliet	N/B	Soldier	Soldier
Israel Vogdes	N/B	Soldier	Soldier
Gouverneur Warren	N/M	Soldier	Soldier
Godfrey Weitzel	N/M	Soldier	Soldier
Henry Walton Wessells	N/B	Soldier	Soldier
Frank Wheaton	N/B	Soldier	Soldier
William Denison Whipple	N/B	Soldier	Soldier
Orlando Bolivar Willcox	N/B	Soldier/L	Soldier
Seth Williams	N/B	Soldier	Soldier
Thomas John Wood	N/M	Soldier	Soldier
Charles Robert Woods	N/B	Soldier	Soldier
George Wright	N/B	Soldier	Soldier
Horatio Wright	N/M	Soldier	Soldier
George Bibb Crittenden	S/M	Soldier	St.Librarian-KY
Richard Heron Anderson	S/L	Soldier	St.Phosphate Agt
Nathan Kimball	N/B	Doctor	St.Treas.-IN
George Lafayette Beal	N/B	Bookbinder	St.Treas.-Maine
Julius Adolph deLagnel	S/B	Soldier	Steamship serv.
Catharinus Buckingham	N/B	Ironworks Owner	Steelworks Pres.
Zachariah Cantey Deas	S/B	Cotton Broker	Stockbroker
Justus McKinstry	N/B	Soldier	Stockbroker
Philip St.George Cocke	S/B	Farmer	Suicide
Albert Blanchard	S/B	Teacher/merchant	Surveyor
Adin Ballou Underwood	N/B	Lawyer	Surveyor
William Grose	N/B	Judge/L	Tax Collector
John Porter McCown	S/M	Soldier	Teacher/Farmer
John Creed Moore	S/B	Coll.Professor	Teacher/writer
Charles Adam Heckman	N/B	RR Conductor	Train dispatcher
Seth Maxwell Barton	S/B	Soldier	Unknown
Hamilton Prioleau Bee	S/B	Texas legisl.	Unknown
Stephen Gano Burbridge	N/B	Lawyer	Unknown
William Henry Carroll	S/B	Postmaster	Unknown
Cassius Marcellus Clay	N/M	Politics	Unknown
Robert Cowdin	N/B	Lumber business	Unknown
William Gardner	S/B	Soldier	Unknown
James Monroe Goggin	S/B	Cotton Broker	Unknown
Elkanah Brackin Greer	S/B	Farmer/Merchant	Unknown
Schuyler Hamilton	N/M	Soldier	Unknown
Robert Frederick Hoke	S/M	Student	Unknown
John Bell Hood	S/G	Soldier	Unknown
Nathaniel James Jackson	N/B	Machinist	Unknown
Adam Rankin Johnson	S/B	Surveyor	Unknown
Jacob Gartner Lauman	N/B	Business	Unknown
Danville Leadbetter	S/B	Soldier	Unknown
Edwin Gray Lee	S/B	Lawyer	Unknown
Collett Leventhorpe	S/B	Soldier	Unknown
Evander McNair	S/B	Merchant	Unknown
James Nagle	N/B	Painter	Unknown
Fitz John Porter	N/M	Soldier	Unknown
Edward Elmer Potter	N/B	Farmer	Unknown
John Smith Preston	S/B	Politics/L	Unknown
Daniel Ruggles	S/B	Soldier	Unknown

Martin Luther Smith	S/M	Soldier	Unknown
Thomas William Sweeny	N/B	Laborer	Unknown
Richard Taylor	S/L	Politics/farmer	Unknown
Isaac Ridgeway Trimble	S/M	Engineer	Unknown
William Stephen Walker	S/B	Soldier	Unknown
Julius White	N/B	Politics	Unknown
Louis Trezevant Wigfall	S/B	Senator/L	Unknown
Charles Devens,Jr.	N/B	U.S.Marshal/L	U.S.Attny.Gen.
Alfred Napoleon Duffie	N/B	Soldier	U.S.Consul-Spain
Frank Armstrong	S/B	Soldier	U.S.Indian Insp.
William Wirt Allen	S/B	Farmer	U.S.Marshal
George Leonard Andrews	N/B	Engineer	U.S.Marshal
William Lewis Cabell	S/B	Soldier	U.S.Marshal/L
James Fleming Fagan	S/M	Politics	U.S.Marshal
Robert Sanford Foster	N/B	Tinner	U.S.Marshal
Charles Smith Hamilton	N/M	Farmer	U.S.Marshal
Francis Jay Herron	N/M	Bank clerk	U.S.Marshal/L
Issac Ferdinand Quinby	N/B	Coll.Professor	U.S.Marshal
Thomas Algeo Rowley	N/B	Cabinetmaker	U.S.Marshal/L
Joseph Orville Shelby	S/B	Rope Manuf.	U.S.Marshal
Bryan Morel Thomas	S/B	Soldier	U.S.Marshal
Joseph Rodman West	N/B	Newspaper oper.	U.S.Marshal
Samuel Powhatan Carter	N/B	U.S.Navy	U.S.Navy
Albin Francisco Schoepf	N/B	U.S.Patent Clerk	U.S.Patent Exam.
James Winning McMillan	N/B	Business	U.S.Pension Agt.
Franz Sigel	N/M	School Teacher	U.S.Pension Agt.
James Abram Garfield	N/M	School Teacher	U.S.President
Ulysses Simpson Grant	N/L	Soldier	U.S.President
Rutherford Hayes	N/B	Lawyer	U.S.President
Andrew Johnson	N/B	Gov-Tennessee	U.S.President
Walter Quintin Gresham	N/B	Lawyer	U.S.Secy State
William Worth Belknap	N/B	Lawyer	U.S.Secy War
Lewis Addison Grant	N/B	Teacher/L	U.S.Secy War
John Aaron Rawlins	N/B	Lawyer	U.S.Secy War
Friedrich Salomon	N/B	Surveyor	U.S.Survey.Gen.
William Ward Orme	N/B	Lawyer	U.S.Treasury
Robert Cameron	N/B	Editor/Doctor	Warden
James Henry Van Alen	N/B	Wealthy	Wealthy
Thomas Alfred Davies	N/B	Merchant	Writer
John Wolcott Phelps	N/B	Soldier	Writer
Marcus Joseph Wright	S/B	Court Clerk/L	Writer/L

11

Civil War Generals
by Place of Death

The generals are listed here according to their location or residence at the time of their death. They are listed first alphabetically according to the state or country, then by city within that state.

LOCATION OF DEATH	GENERAL	SIDE/RANK
Alabama,Anniston	George Thomas Anderson	S/B
Alabama,Auburn	James Henry Lane	S/B
Alabama,Birmingham	Charles Miller Shelley	S/B
Alabama,Dog River Factory	William Edwin Baldwin	S/B
Alabama,Fort Mitchell	James Cantey	S/B
Alabama,Huntsville	William Thomas Brooks	N/M
Alabama,Huntsville	William Young Humes	S/B
Alabama,Huntsville	Leroy Pope Walker	S/B
Alabama,Jacksonville	John Horace Forney	S/M
Alabama,Jacksonville	William Henry Forney	S/B
Alabama,Midway	Nathan George Evans	S/B
Alabama,Mobile	Jones Mitchell Withers	S/M
Alabama,Montgomery	James Thadeus Holtzclaw	S/B
Alabama,Sheffield	William Wirt Allen	S/B
Alabama,Tuscaloosa	George Doherty Johnston	S/B
Alabama,Tuscaloosa	Henry DeLamar Clayton	S/M
Alabama,Tuscaloosa	Josiah Gorgas	S/B
Arizona,Casa Grande	James Madison Tuttle	N/B
Arizona,Tucson	George Deitzler	N/B
Arkansas,Austin	Allison Nelson	S/B
Arkansas,DeVall's Bluff	Elkanah Brackin Greer	S/B
Arkansas,Eureka Springs	Samuel Bell Maxey	S/M
Arkansas,Eureka Springs	Cadwallader Washburn	N/M
Arkansas,Helena	Thomas Carmichael Hindman	S/M
Arkansas,Helena	Gideon Johnson Pillow	S/B
Arkansas,Helena	James Camp Tappan	S/B
Arkansas,Hot Springs	Randall Lee Gibson	S/B
Arkansas,Lake Village	Daniel Harris Reynolds	S/B
Arkansas,Little Rock	Thomas James Churchill	S/M
Arkansas,Little Rock	James Fleming Fagan	S/M
Arkansas,Little Rock	John Porter McCown	S/M
Arkansas,Little Rock	Albert Rust	S/B

Arkansas,Little Rock	Lucius Marshall Walker	S/B
Arkansas,Mt.Nebo	Richard Caswell Gerios	S/B
Arkansas,Pine Bluff	John Selden Roane	S/B
Arkansas,Searcy	Dandridge McRae	S/B
At sea	James Henry Van Alen	N/B
At sea	George Wright	N/B
Battle/Atlanta	James Birdseye McPherson	N/M
Battle/Atlanta	William Henry T. Walker	S/M
Battle/6vuuSn 6ufdd	Edward Dickinson Baker	N/M
Battle/Baton Rouge	Thomas Williams	N/B
Battle/Bethesda Church	George Pierce Doles	S/B
Battle/Blair's Landing	Thomas Green	S/B
Battle/Bristoe Station	Carnot Posey	S/B
Battle/Bull Run	George William Taylor	N/B
Battle/Cedar Creek	Daniel Davidson Bidwell	N/B
Battle/Cedar Creek	Stephen Dodson Ramseur	S/M
Battle/Cedar Mountain	Charles Sidney Winder	S/B
Battle/Champion's Hill	Lloyd Tilghman	S/B
Battle/Chancellorsville	Hiram Gregory Berry	N/M
Battle/Chancellorsville	Thomas Jonathon Jackson	S/L
Battle/Chancellorsville	Elisha Franklin Paxton	S/B
Battle/Chancellorsville	Amiel Weeks Whipple	N/B
Battle/Chantilly	Philip Kearny	N/M
Battle/Chantilly	Isaac Ingalls Stevens	N/B
Battle/Charles City Road	John Randolph Chambliss	S/B
Battle/Chickamauga	James Deshler	S/B
Battle/Chickamauga	Benjamin Hardin Helm	S/B
Battle/Chickamauga	William Haines Lytle	N/B
Battle/Chickamauga	Preston Smith	S/B
Battle/Cloyd's Mountain	Albert Gallatin Jenkins	S/B
Battle/Corinth	Adley Hogan Gladden	S/B
Battle/Corinth	Pleasant Adam Hackleman	N/B
Battle/Corrick's Ford	Robert Selden Garnett	S/B
Battle/Elkhorn	James McQueen McIntosh	S/B
Battle/Elkhorn	William Yarnel Slack	S/B
Battle/Elkhorn Tavern	Ben McCulloch	S/B
Battle/Falling Waters	James Johnston Pettigrew	S/B
Battle/Farmville	Thomas Alfred Smyth	N/B
Battle/Fort Fisher	William Henry C. Whiting	S/M
Battle/Fort Harrison	Hiram Burnham	N/B
Battle/Fort Harrison	John Dunovant	S/B
Battle/Fort Tyler	Robert Charles Tyler	S/B
Battle/Fort Wagner	George Crockett Strong	N/B
Battle/Franklin	John Adams	S/B
Battle/Franklin	John Carpenter Carter	S/B
Battle/Franklin	Patrick Ronayne Cleburne	S/M
Battle/Franklin	States Rights Gist	S/B
Battle/Franklin	Hiram Bronson Granbury	S/B
Battle/Franklin	John Herbert Kelly	S/B
Battle/Franklin	Otho French Strahl	S/B
Battle/Fredericksburg	George Dashiell Bayard	N/B
Battle/Fredericksburg	Thomas Reade Rootes Cobb	S/B
Battle/Fredericksburg	Maxcy Gregg	S/B
Battle/Fredericksburg	Conrad Feger Jackson	N/B
Battle/Fredericksburg	Abner Monroe Perrin	S/B
Battle/Freeman's Ford	Henry Bohlen	N/B

Battle/Fussell's Mill	Victor Jean B. Girardey	S/B
Battle/Gettysburg	Lewis Addison Armistead	S/B
Battle/Gettysburg	William Barksdale	S/B
Battle/Gettysburg	Elon John Farnsworth	N/B
Battle/Gettysburg	Richard Brooke Garnett	S/B
Battle/Gettysburg	William Dorsey Pender	S/M
Battle/Gettysburg	John Fulton Reynolds	N/M
Battle/Gettysburg	Paul Jones Semmes	S/B
Battle/Gettysburg	Stephen Hinsdale Weed	N/B
Battle/Gettysburg	Samuel Kosciuszko Zook	N/B
Battle/Greenville	John Hunt Morgan	S/B
Battle/Harrisonburg	Turner Ashby	S/B
Battle/Hatcher's Run	John Pegram	S/B
Battle/High Bridge	James Dearing	S/B
Battle/Iuka	Lewis Henry Little	S/B
Battle/Jenkin's Ferry	William Read Scurry	S/B
Battle/Kennesaw Mountain	Charles Garrison Harker	N/B
Battle/Knoxville	William Price Sanders	N/B
Battle/Manassas Junction	Barnard Elliott Bee	S/B
Battle/Mansfield	Jean Jacques A.A. Mouton	S/B
Battle/Meadow Bridge	James Byron Gordon	S/B
Battle/Mill Springs	Felix Kirk Zollicoffer	S/B
Battle/Murfreesboro	Roger Weightman Hanson	S/B
Battle/Murfreesboro	Edward Needles Kirk	N/B
Battle/Murfreesboro	James Edwards Rains	S/B
Battle/Murfreesboro	Joshua Woodrow Sill	N/B
Battle/Peach Tree Creek	Clement Hoffman Stevens	S/B
Battle/Perryville	James Streshly Jackson	N/B
Battle/Perryville	William Rufus Terrill	N/B
Battle/Petersburg	Archibald Gracie,Jr.	S/B
Battle/Petersburg	Ambrose Powell Hill	S/L
Battle/Petersburg	James St.Clair Morton	N/B
Battle/Piedmont	William Edmonson Jones	S/B
Battle/Pine Mountain	Leonidas Polk	S/L
Battle/Port Gibson	Edward Dorr Tracy	S/B
Battle/Richmond	John Gregg	S/B
Battle/Richmond	Thomas Greely Stevenson	N/B
Battle/Savage Station	Richard Griffith	S/B
Battle/Seven Pines	Stephen Gardner Champlin	N/B
Battle/Seven Pines	Robert Hopkins Hatton	S/B
Battle/Sharpsburg	George Burgwyn Anderson	S/B
Battle/Sharpsburg	Lawrence O'Bryan Branch	S/B
Battle/Sharpsburg	Joseph King F. Mansfield	N/B
Battle/Sharpsburg	Israel Bush Richardson	N/M
Battle/Sharpsburg	Isaac Peace Rodman	N/B
Battle/Sharpsburg	William Edwin Starke	S/B
Battle/Shiloh	Albert Sidney Johnston	S/G
Battle/Shiloh	William Harvey Wallace	N/B
Battle/South Mountain	Samuel Garland,Jr.	S/B
Battle/South Mountain	Jesse Lee Reno	N/M
Battle/Spotsylvania	James Clay Rice	N/B
Battle/Spotsylvania	John Sedgwick	N/M
Battle/Spotsylvania Courthse.	Junius Daniel	S/B
Battle/Vicksburg	Martin Edwin Green	S/B
Battle/Weldon Railroad	John Caldwell Sanders	S/B
Battle/Wilderness	Alexander Hays	N/B

Battle/Wilderness	Micah Jenkins	S/B
Battle/Wilderness	John Marshall Jones	S/B
Battle/Wilderness	Leroy Augustus Stafford	S/B
Battle/Wilderness	James Samuel Wadsworth	N/B
Battle/Wilson's Creek	Nathaniel Lyon	N/B
Battle/Winchester	Archibald Campbell Godwin	S/B
Battle/Winchester	Robert Latimer McCook	N/B
Battle/Winchester	Robert Emmett Rodes	S/M
Battle/Winchester	David Allen Russell	N/B
Battle/Yellow Tavern	James Ewell Brown Stuart	S/M
Bolivia	John Thomas Croxton	N/B
Brazil,Buenos Aires	Alexander Sandor Asboth	N/B
California,Livermore	Henry Brevard Davidson	S/B
California,Monrovia	William Anderson Pile	N/B
California,Oakland	George Blake Cosby	S/B
California,Oakland	Jeremiah Cutler Sullivan	N/B
California,Ojai	Thomas Church H. Smith	N/B
California,Redondo Beach	William Starke Rosecrans	N/M
California,San Francisco	Washington Elliott	N/B
California,San Francisco	Edward Higgins	S/B
California,San Francisco	Irvin McDowell	N/M
California,San Francisco	John Franklin Miller	N/B
California,San Francisco	Henry Morris Naglee	N/B
California,San Francisco	George Henry Thomas	N/M
California,San Francisco	Emory Upton	N/B
California,San Mateo	Frederick Steele	N/M
California,Siskiyou County	Edward Richard S. Canby	N/M
California,Ventura	William Vandever	N/B
Canada,Clifton	Danville Leadbetter	S/B
Canada,Coburg	Orlando Bolivar Willcox	N/B
Canada,Montreal	William Henry Carroll	S/B
Chili,Santiago	Hugh Judson Kilpatrick	N/B
China,Nueva Leon	Mosby Monroe Parsons	S/M
Colombia,Medellin	Edward Augustus Wild	N/B
Colorado,Canon City	Robert Alexander Cameron	N/B
Colorado,Leadville	Francis Laurens Vinton	N/B
Connecticut,Hartford	William Buel Franklin	N/B
Connecticut,Hartford	James Wolfe Ripley	N/B
Connecticut,New Haven	Amos Beebe Eaton	N/B
Connecticut,New Haven	Alfred Howe Terry	N/M
Connecticut,Norwalk	Darius Nash Couch	N/M
Connecticut,Norwalk	Orris Sanford Ferry	N/B
Connecticut,Norwich	Edward Harland	N/B
Connecticut,South Norwalk	Nelson Taylor	N/B
Connecticut,Stamford	Thomas Howard Ruger	N/B
Cuba,Havana	Edward Otho C. Ord	N/M
D.C.,Georgetown	Christopher Augur	N/M
D.C.,Georgetown	Henry Hayes Lockwood	N/B
Delaware,Claymont	Isaac Jones Wistar	N/B
Delaware,Dover	Henry Walton Wessells	N/B
Egypt,Alexandria	Alexander Welch Reynolds	S/B
England,London	Henry Prince	N/B
England,London	Philip Dale Roddey	S/B
England,Malvern	Nathaniel Harris	S/B
Florida,Bartow	Evander McIvor Law	S/B
Florida,Cape Canaveral	Alfred Thomas Torbert	N/B

Florida,Key West	Daniel Phineas Woodbury	N/B
Florida,Florala	Samuel Gibbs French	S/M
Florida,Lake City	Jesse Johnson Finley	S/B
Florida,Longwood	George Baird Hodge	S/B
Florida,Miami	John Brown Gordon	S/M
Florida,Ocala	Robert Bullock	S/B
Florida,Orange Park	Joseph Tarr Copeland	N/B
Florida,Orlando	William Selby Harney	N/B
Florida,Ormond	Adelbert Ames	N/B
Florida,Point Washington	William Miller	S/B
Florida,Rutledge	Joseph Finegan	S/B
Florida,St.Augustine	Martin Davis Hardin	N/B
Florida,St.Augustine	John Schofield	N/M
Florida,Tallahassee	Theodore Brevard	S/B
Florida,Tallahassee	John Breckinridge Grayson	S/B
France,Hyeres	Gustave Paul Cluseret	N/B
France,Nice	Robert Anderson	N/B
France,Nice	Erasmus Darwin Keyes	N/M
France,Nice	John Henry Martindale	N/B
France,Paris	Camille A.J.M. Polignac	S/M
France,Paris	Andrew Porter	N/B
Georgia,Athens	William Montague Browne	S/B
Georgia,Atlanta	Philip Cook	S/B
Georgia,Atlanta	Clement Anselm Evans	S/B
Georgia,Atlanta	Lucius Jeremiah Gartrell	S/B
Georgia,Atlanta	Alfred Iverson,Jr.	S/B
Georgia,Atlanta	William Stephen Walker	S/B
Georgia,Augusta	Goode Bryan	S/B
Georgia,Augusta	William MacRae	S/B
Georgia,Augusta	Marcellus Stovall	S/B
Georgia,Augusta	David Emanuel Twiggs	S/M
Georgia,Augusta	Ambrose Ransom Wright	S/M
Georgia,Cass Station	William Tatum Wofford	S/B
Georgia,Columbus	Henry Lewis Benning	S/B
Georgia,Columbus	Robert Hall Chilton	S/B
Georgia,Covington	James Phillip Simms	S/B
Georgia,Dalton	Bryan Morel Thomas	S/B
Georgia,Gainesville	James Longstreet	S/L
Georgia,Milledgeville	John King Jackson	S/B
Georgia,Rome	Alfred Cumming	S/B
Georgia,Rome	Thomas Edward G. Ransom	N/B
Georgia,Savannah	Edward Porter Alexander	S/B
Georgia,Savannah	Robert Houstoun Anderson	S/B
Georgia,Savannah	Jeremy Francis Gilmer	S/M
Georgia,Savannah	Henry Rootes Jackson	S/B
Georgia,Savannah	Lafayette McLaws	S/M
Georgia,Savannah	Martin Luther Smith	S/M
Georgia,Savannah	Henry Constantine Wayne	S/B
Georgia,Sparta	Ethan Allen Hitchcock	N/M
Georgia,Thomasville	John Crawford Vaughn	S/B
Georgia,Washington	Dudley McIver DuBose	S/B
Georgia,Washington	Robert Augustus Toombs	S/B
Germany,Baden-Baden	Hugh Weedon Mercer	S/B
Germany,Duisburg	Peter Joseph Osterhaus	N/M
Illinois,Anna	John Basil Turchin	N/B
Illinois,Belleville	William Henry Powell	N/B

Illinois,Bloomington	William Ward Orme	N/B
Illinois,Bloomington	Giles Alexander Smith	N/B
Illinois,Brighton	Bushrod Rust Johnson	S/M
Illinois,Carlyle	Elias Smith Dennis	N/B
Illinois,Chicago	Catharinus Buckingham	N/B
Illinois,Chicago	Napoleon Bonaparte Buford	N/B
Illinois,Chicago	Augustus Louis Chetlain	N/B
Illinois,Chicago	George Crook	N/M
Illinois,Chicago	Jefferson Columbus Davis	N/B
Illinois,Chicago	John McArthur	N/B
Illinois,Chicago	Edward Moody McCook	N/B
Illinois,Chicago	Green Berry Raum	N/B
Illinois,Chicago	James Richard Slack	N/B
Illinois,Chicago	John Eugene Smith	N/B
Illinois,Chicago	Joseph Dana Webster	N/B
Illinois,Elkhart	Richard James Oglesby	N/M
Illinois,Equality	Michael Kelly Lawler	N/B
Illinois,Evanston	Julius White	N/B
Illinois,Lewistown	Leonard Fulton Ross	N/B
Illinois,Monmouth	Abner Clark Harding	N/B
Illinois,Oak Park	Milo Smith Hascall	N/B
Illinois,Peoria	Dabney Herndon Maury	S/M
Illinois,Quincy	James Dada Morgan	N/B
Illinois,Springfield	Isham Nicholas Haynie	N/B
Illinois,Springfield	John Alexander McClernand	N/M
Illinois,Springfield	John McCauley Palmer	N/M
Illinois,Wilmington	James Harrison Wilson	N/B
Indiana,Cambridge City	Solomon Meredith	N/B
Indiana,Crawfordsville	Mahlon Dickerson Manson	N/B
Indiana,Crawfordsville	Lewis Wallace	N/M
Indiana,Danville	Abraham Buford	S/B
Indiana,Indianapolis	George Henry Chapman	N/B
Indiana,Indianapolis	Ebenezer Dumont	N/B
Indiana,Indianapolis	Robert Sanford Foster	N/B
Indiana,Indianapolis	John Parker Hawkins	N/B
Indiana,Indianapolis	Alvin Peterson Hovey	N/B
Indiana,Indianapolis	George Francis McGinnis	N/B
Indiana,Indianapolis	Alfred Jefferson Vaughan	S/B
Indiana,Indianapolis	George Day Wagner	N/B
Indiana,Lawrenceburg	Thomas John Lucas	N/B
Indiana,New Albany	William Harrow	N/B
Indiana,Rockport	James Clifford Veatch	N/B
Indiana,Terre Haute	Charles Cruft	N/B
Iowa,Burlington	Jacob Gartner Lauman	N/B
Iowa,Burlington	Charles Leopold Matthies	N/B
Iowa,Council Bluffs	Samuel Ryan Curtis	N/M
Iowa,Council Bluffs	Grenville Mellen Dodge	N/M
Iowa,Des Moines	Hugh Thompson Reid	N/B
Iowa,Marion	Thomas Jefferson McKean	N/B
Iowa,Oskaloosa	Samuel Allen Rice	N/B
Iowa,Ottumwa	James Shields	N/B
Iowa,Sioux City	Elliott Warren Rice	N/B
Iowa,Topeka	Frederick Stumbaugh	N/B
Italy,Florence	Truman Seymour	N/B
Kansas,El Dorado	Alfred Washington Ellet	N/B
Kansas,Fort Leavenworth	Alfred Gibbs	N/B

Kansas,Stafford	Joseph Alexander Cooper	N/B
Kansas,Topeka	James Isham Gilbert	N/B
Kentucky,Bowling Green	William Flank Perry	S/B
Kentucky,Covington	James Morrison Hawes	S/B
Kentucky,Danville	George Bibb Crittenden	S/M
Kentucky,Eddyville	Hylan Benton Lyon	S/B
Kentucky,Lexington	John Cabell Breckinridge	S/M
Kentucky,Lexington	William Preston	S/B
Kentucky,Logan County	William Andrew Quarles	S/B
Kentucky,Louisville	Alpheus Baker	S/B
Kentucky,Louisville	Jerimiah Tilford Boyle	N/B
Kentucky,Louisville	Speed Smith Fry	N/B
Kentucky,Louisville	Henry Wager Halleck	N/M
Kentucky,Louisville	William Lowther Jackson	S/B
Kentucky,Louisville	Humphrey Marshall	S/B
Kentucky,Louisville	William Nelson	N/M
Kentucky,Louisville	Thomas Hart Taylor	S/B
Kentucky,Louisville	William Thomas Ward	N/B
Kentucky,Lyndon	Walter Chiles Whitaker	N/B
Kentucky,Madison County	Cassius Marcellus Clay	N/M
Kentucky,Manchester	Theophilus Garrard	N/B
Kentucky,Mt.Sterling	John Stuart Williams	S/B
Kentucky,Munfordville	Simon Bolivar Buckner	S/L
Kentucky,Paradise	Don Carlos Buell	N/M
Kentucky,Scott County	Joseph Horace Lewis	S/B
Louisiana,Catahoula Parish	St.John Liddell	S/B
Louisiana,Coushatta	Henry Gray	S/B
Louisiana,Madison Parish	William Raine Peck	S/B
Louisiana,New Orleans	Daniel Weisiger Adams	S/B
Louisiana,New Orleans	Pierre Beauregard	S/G
Louisiana,New Orleans	Tyree Harris Bell	S/B
Louisiana,New Orleans	William Plummer Benton	N/B
Louisiana,New Orleans	Albert Gallatin Blanchard	S/B
Louisiana,New Orleans	Cyrus Hamlin	N/B
Louisiana,New Orleans	Harry Thompson Hays	S/M
Louisiana,New Orleans	Paul Octave Hebert	S/B
Louisiana,New Orleans	John Bell Hood	S/G
Louisiana,New Orleans	Young Marshall Moody	S/B
Louisiana,New Orleans	Joseph Anthony Mower	N/M
Louisiana,New Orleans	Lovell Harrison Rousseau	N/M
Louisiana,New Orleans	Thomas Moore Scott	S/B
Louisiana,Port Hudson	John Bordenave Villepigue	S/B
Louisiana,St.Martin	Louis Hebert	S/B
Louisiana,Thibodeaux	Francis Redding Nicholls	S/B
Louisiana,Vermillionville	Franklin Gardner	S/M
Maine,Augusta	Selden Connor	N/B
Maine,Bangor	Charles Davis Jameson	N/B
Maine,Bar Harbor	Frank Crawford Armstrong	S/B
Maine,Calais	John Curtis Caldwell	N/B
Maine,Norway	George Lafayette Beal	N/B
Maine,Portland	Joshua Chamberlain	N/B
Maine,Portland	Neal Dow	N/B
Maine,Portland	Francis Fessenden	N/B
Maine,Portland	James Deering Fessenden	N/B
Maine,Portland	George Foster Shepley	N/B
Maine,Rockland	Davis Tillson	N/B

Maryland,Baltimore	William Farquhar Barry	N/B
Maryland,Baltimore	Joseph Jackson Bartlett	N/B
Maryland,Baltimore	Arnold Elzey	S/M
Maryland,Baltimore	John Gibbon	N/M
Maryland,Baltimore	Charles Champion Gilbert	N/B
Maryland,Baltimore	John Reese Kenly	N/B
Maryland,Baltimore	William Scott Ketchum	N/B
Maryland,Baltimore	Isaac Ridgeway Trimble	S/M
Maryland,Baltimore	Erastus Barnard Tyler	N/B
Maryland,Chevy Chase	Innis Newton Palmer	N/B
Maryland,Cumberland	Charles Mynn Thruston	N/B
Maryland,Forest Glen	William Birney	N/B
Maryland,Forest Glen	George Washington Getty	N/B
Maryland,Hyattsville	Albin Francisco Schoepf	N/B
Maryland,Montgomery County	Samuel Sprigg Carroll	N/B
Maryland,Oakland	Benjamin Franklin Kelley	N/B
Maryland,Pikesville	Lucius Bellinger Northrop	S/B
Maryland,Relay	Absalom Baird	N/B
Maryland,South River	George Hume Steuart	S/B
Massachusetts,Bellingham	Isaac Fitzgerald Shepard	N/B
Massachusetts,Boston	Lewis Golding Arnold	N/B
Massachusetts,Boston	Henry Beebee Carrington	N/B
Massachusetts,Boston	Robert Cowdin	N/B
Massachusetts,Boston	Charles Devens,Jr.	N/B
Massachusetts,Boston	William Dwight	N/B
Massachusetts,Boston	William Hays	N/B
Massachusetts,Boston	Franklin Nickerson	N/B
Massachusetts,Boston	Robert Ogden Tyler	N/B
Massachusetts,Boston	Adin Ballou Underwood	N/B
Massachusetts,Boston	Seth Williams	N/B
Massachusetts,Brimfield	Fitz-Henry Warren	N/B
Massachusetts,Brookline	George Leonard Andrews	N/B
Massachusetts,Cambridge	Henry Lawrence Eustis	N/B
Massachusetts,Cambridge	Edward Winslow Hincks	N/B
Massachusetts,Cambridge	Albion Parris Howe	N/B
Massachusetts,Cohasset	Zealous Bates Tower	N/B
Massachusetts,Framingham	George Henry Gordon	N/B
Massachusetts,Gloucester	Jacob Dolson Cox	N/M
Massachusetts,Gloucester	Thomas Turpin Crittenden	N/B
Massachusetts,Middleboro	Henry Eugene Davies	N/B
Massachusetts,Nonquitt	Philip Henry Sheridan	N/M
Massachusetts,Pittsfield	William Francis Bartlett	N/B
Massachusetts,Pittsfield	Henry Shaw Briggs	N/B
Massachusetts,Rochester	Calvin Edward Pratt	N/B
Massachusetts,Springfield	James Barnes	N/B
Massachusetts,Waltham	Nathaniel Prentiss Banks	N/M
Massachusetts,Weston	Charles Jackson Paine	N/B
Massachusetts,Winchester	John Murray Corse	N/B
Mexico,Mexico City	Henry Watkins Allen	S/B
Mexico,Mexico City	James Edwin Slaughter	S/B
Mexico,Vera Cruz	Walter Husted Stevens	S/B
Michigan,Detroit	John Gross Barnard	N/B
Michigan,Detroit	Philip St.George Cooke	N/B
Michigan,Detroit	Gustavus Adolphus DeRussy	N/B
Michigan,Detroit	David Stuart	N/B
Michigan,Grand Rapids	Byron Root Pierce	N/B

Michigan,Jonesville	Henry Baxter	N/B
Michigan,Omena	Benjamin Henry Grierson	N/B
Michigan,Port Huron	James Murrell Shackelford	N/B
Michigan,Ransom	John Cook	N/B
Michigan,Soo	Orlando Metcalfe Poe	N/B
Minnesota,Minneapolis	Lewis Addison Grant	N/B
Minnesota,Minneapolis	Horatio Van Cleve	N/B
Minnesota,St.Paul	Christopher Andrews	N/B
Minnesota,St.Paul	John Wynn Davidson	N/B
Minnesota,St.Paul	Willis Arnold Gorman	N/B
Minnesota,St.Paul	Richard W. Johnson	N/B
Minnesota,St.Paul	John Benjamin Sanborn	N/B
Minnesota,St.Paul	Henry Hastings Sibley	N/B
Minnesota,St.Paul	Samuel Davis Sturgis	N/B
Minnesota,Worthington	Stephen Miller	N/B
Mississippi,Aberdeen	Samuel Jameson Gholson	S/B
Mississippi,Biloxi	Joseph Robert Davis	S/B
Mississippi,Biloxi	Alexander Peter Stewart	S/L
Mississippi,Bolivar County	Charles Clark	S/B
Mississippi,Columbus	Jacob Hunter Sharp	S/B
Mississippi,Corinth	Joseph Lewis Hogg	S/B
Mississippi,Corinth	Joseph Bennett Plummer	N/B
Mississippi,Hattiesburg	Evander McNair	S/B
Mississippi,Holly Springs	Winfield Featherston	S/B
Mississippi,Jackson	William Wirt Adams	S/B
Mississippi,Jackson	Samuel Wragg Ferguson	S/B
Mississippi,Jackson	Robert Lowry	S/B
Mississippi,Jackson	James Argyle Smith	S/B
Mississippi,Leflore County	Benjamin Grubb Humphreys	S/B
Mississippi,Natchez	William Thompson Martin	S/M
Mississippi,Natchez	Zebulon York	S/B
Mississippi,Okolona	William Feimster Tucker	S/B
Mississippi,Oxford	Claudius Wistar Sears	S/B
Mississippi,Raymond	John Stevens Bowen	S/M
Mississippi,Tuscaloosa	Sterling Alexander Wood	S/B
Mississippi,Vicksburg	Stephen Dill Lee	S/L
Mississippi,Vicksburg	Jasper Adalmorn Maltby	N/B
Mississippi,Waveland	Allen Thomas	S/B
Mississippi,Wilkinson County	William Lindsay Brandon	S/B
Mississippi,Winona	William Felix Brantley	S/B
Missouri,Adrian	Joseph Orville Shelby	S/B
Missouri,Bethany	Benjamin Mayberry Prentiss	N/M
Missouri,Clarkton	Robert Vinkler Richardson	S/B
Missouri,Jefferson City	John Sappington Marmaduke	S/M
Missouri,Kansas City	Mason Brayman	N/B
Missouri,Nevada	Joseph Bailey	N/B
Missouri,St.Joseph	James Craig	N/B
Missouri,St.Louis	Francis Preston Blair,Jr.	N/M
Missouri,St.Louis	Justus McKinstry	N/B
Missouri,St.Louis	John McNeil	N/B
Missouri,St.Louis	John Smith Phelps	N/B
Missouri,St.Louis	Sterling Price	S/M
Missouri,St.Louis	Andrew Jackson Smith	N/M
Missouri,St.Louis	John Dunlap Stevenson	N/B
Missouri,St.Louis	John Wesley Turner	N/B
Missouri,St.Louis County	Daniel Marsh Frost	S/B

Missouri,West Plains	Egbert Benson Brown	N/B
Montana,Fort Benton	Thomas Francis Meagher	N/B
Montana,Helena	Benjamin Franklin Potts	N/B
Montana,Little Big Horn	George Armstrong Custer	N/B
Montana,Whitehall	William Passmore Carlin	N/B
Nebraska,Fort Robinson	Edward Hatch	N/B
Nebraska,Lincoln	John Milton Thayer	N/B
Nebraska,Omaha	Charles Carroll Walcutt	N/B
New Hampshire,Exeter	Gilman Marston	N/B
New Hampshire,Isles of Shoals	Joseph Reid Anderson	S/B
New Hampshire,Keene	Simon Goodell Griffin	N/B
New Hampshire,Portsmouth	Napoleon Jackson Dana	N/M
New Jersey,Atlantic City	Cuvier Grover	N/B
New Jersey,Elberon	James Abram Garfield	N/M
New Jersey,Hoboken	Joseph Warren Revere	N/B
New Jersey,Jersey City	Herman Haupt	N/B
New Jersey,Jersey City	Eleazer Arthur Paine	N/B
New Jersey,Jersey City	Morgan Lewis Smith	N/B
New Jersey,Lakewood	Charles Kinnaird Graham	N/B
New Jersey,Long Branch	William Hopkins Morris	N/B
New Jersey,Mendham	Abner Doubleday	N/B
New Jersey,Morristown	George Sears Greene	N/B
New Jersey,Morristown	Fitz John Porter	N/M
New Jersey,Morristown	Henry Harrison Walker	S/B
New Jersey,New Brunswick	John Baillie McIntosh	N/B
New Jersey,Orange	George Brinton McClellan	N/M
New Jersey,Plainfield	James Scott Negley	N/M
New Jersey,West Orange	Randolph Barnes Marcy	N/B
New Mexico,Fort Bayard	Thomas Gamble Pitcher	N/B
New Mexico,Fort Union	Lewis Cass Hunt	N/B
New Mexico,Santa Fe	Gordon Granger	N/M
New Mexico,Santa Fe	John Potts Slough	N/B
New Mexico,Santa Fe	Gustavus Adolphus Smith	N/B
New York,Annandale	Thomas Crittenden	N/M
New York,Astoria	Thomas William Sweeny	N/B
New York,Auburn	William Henry Seward	N/B
New York,Bath	William Woods Averell	N/B
New York,Bayport	Philippe deTrobriand	N/B
New York,Bellport	Nathaniel Collins McLean	N/B
New York,Binghamton	John Cleveland Robinson	N/B
New York,Brooklyn	Stephen Gano Burbridge	N/B
New York,Brooklyn	Silas Casey	N/M
New York,Brooklyn	Quincy Adams Gillmore	N/M
New York,Brooklyn	Henry Warner Slocum	N/M
New York,Brooklyn	Max Weber	N/B
New York,Brooklyn	Joseph Wheeler	S/M
New York,Buffalo	Sullivan Amory Meredith	N/B
New York,Buffalo	George Stoneman	N/M
New York,Buffalo	Adolph von Steinwehr	N/B
New York,Clifton Springs	Alexander Robert Lawton	S/B
New York,Cold Spring	Daniel Butterfield	N/M
New York,Dobbs Ferry	James Bowen	N/B
New York,Fort Hamilton	Romeyn Beck Ayres	N/B
New York,Garden City	Joseph Hooker	N/M
New York,Governors Island	Richard Arnold	N/B
New York,Governors Island	Winfield Scott Hancock	N/M

New York,Jamestown	Nathaniel James Jackson	N/B
New York,Monroe	John Henry Hobart Ward	N/B
New York,Mt.McGregor	Ulysses Simpson Grant	N/L
New York,Nashua	John Gray Foster	N/M
New York,New York City	Francis Channing Barlow	N/B
New York,New York City	Henry Washington Benham	N/B
New York,New York City	Henry Warner Birge	N/B
New York,New York City	John Milton Brannan	N/B
New York,New York City	Richard Busteed	N/B
New York,New York City	Howell Cobb	S/M
New York,New York City	John Cochrane	N/B
New York,New York City	George Washington Cullum	N/B
New York,New York City	Newton Martin Curtis	N/B
New York,New York City	Zachariah Cantey Deas	S/B
New York,New York City	Thomas Casimer Devin	N/B
New York,New York City	John Adams Dix	N/M
New York,New York City	Thomas Pleasant Dockery	S/B
New York,New York City	Charles Cleveland Dodge	N/B
New York,New York City	Basil Wilson Duke	S/B
New York,New York City	Abram Duryee	N/B
New York,New York City	Thomas Wilberforce Egan	N/B
New York,New York City	Thomas Ewing,Jr.	N/B
New York,New York City	Edward Ferrero	N/B
New York,New York City	Clinton Bowen Fisk	N/B
New York,New York City	John Wesley Frazer	S/B
New York,New York City	John Charles Fremont	N/M
New York,New York City	Schuyler Hamilton	N/M
New York,New York City	George Lucas Hartsuff	N/M
New York,New York City	John Porter Hatch	N/B
New York,New York City	Joseph Hayes	N/B
New York,New York City	Francis Jay Herron	N/M
New York,New York City	Rufus Ingalls	N/B
New York,New York City	Thomas Jordan	S/B
New York,New York City	James Lawlor Kiernan	N/B
New York,New York City	Rufus King	N/B
New York,New York City	Wladimir Krzyzanowski	N/B
New York,New York City	Albert Lindley Lee	N/B
New York,New York City	Thomas Muldrup Logan	S/B
New York,New York City	Eli Long	N/B
New York,New York City	William Wing Loring	S/M
New York,New York City	Mansfield Lovell	S/M
New York,New York City	Edwin Denison Morgan	N/M
New York,New York City	Gershom Mott	N/B
New York,New York City	John Newton	N/M
New York,New York City	Edward Elmer Potter	N/B
New York,New York City	Roger Atkinson Pryor	S/B
New York,New York City	Roswell Sabine Ripley	S/B
New York,New York City	Eliakim Parker Scammon	N/B
New York,New York City	Carl Schurz	N/M
New York,New York City	Alexander Shaler	N/B
New York,New York City	William Tecumseh Sherman	N/M
New York,New York City	Daniel Edgar Sickles	N/M
New York,New York City	Franz Sigel	N/M
New York,New York City	Gustavus Woodson Smith	S/M
New York,New York City	Thomas Kilby Smith	N/B
New York,New York City	Julius Stahel	N/M

New York,New York City	Charles Pomeroy Stone	N/B
New York,New York City	Edwin Henry Stoughton	N/B
New York,New York City	William Kerley Strong	N/B
New York,New York City	Wager Swayne	N/B
New York,New York City	Richard Taylor	S/P
New York,New York City	Daniel Tyler	N/B
New York,New York City	Egbert Ludovicus Viele	N/B
New York,New York City	Israel Vogdes	N/B
New York,New York City	William Denison Whipple	N/B
New York,New York City	Pierce Manning Young	S/M
New York,Nyack	Daniel Ullmann	N/B
New York,Ogdensburg	Thomas Alfred Davies	N/B
New York,Oswego	Joseph Abel Haskin	N/B
New York,Plattsburg	Henry Moses Judah	N/B
New York,Riverdale	Alexander Stewart Webb	N/B
New York,Rochester	Issac Ferdinand Quinby	N/B
New York,Rockland County	Louis Ludwig Blenker	N/B
New York,Roslyn	John Joseph Abercrombie	N/B
New York,Scarborough	George Webb Morell	N/M
New York,Staten Island	James Hewett Ledlie	N/B
New York,Staten Island	Ranald Slidell Mackenzie	N/B
New York,Syracuse	John James Peck	N/M
New York,Syracuse	Edwin Vose Sumner	N/M
New York,Troy	Joseph Bradford Carr	N/B
New York,Troy	John Ellis Wool	N/M
New York,West Point	Winfield Scott	N/M
North Carolina,Asheville	James Green Martin	S/B
North Carolina,Asheville	Robert Brank Vance	S/B
North Carolina,Charlotte	Rufus Barringer	S/B
North Carolina,Charlotte	Daniel Harvey Hill	S/L
North Carolina,Fayetteville	Theophilus Hunter Holmes	S/L
North Carolina,Garysburg	Matt Whitaker Ransom	S/B
North Carolina,Goldsboro	William Gaston Lewis	S/B
North Carolina,Greensboro	Cullen Andrews Battle	S/B
North Carolina,Greensboro	Alfred Moore Scales	S/B
North Carolina,Hot Springs	Edmund Winston Pettus	S/B
North Carolina,Morgantown	Thomas Lanier Clingman	S/B
North Carolina,New Bern	Robert Ransom,Jr.	S/M
North Carolina,Pitt County	Bryan Grimes	S/M
North Carolina,Raleigh	Robert Frederick Hoke	S/M
North Carolina,Raleigh	Thomas Fentress Toon	S/B
N.C.,White Sulphur Springs	Milledge Luke Bonham	S/B
North Carolina,Wilkes County	Collett Leventhorpe	S/B
North Carolina,Wilmington	John Decatur Barry	S/B
North Carolina,Winston-Salem	William Robertson Boggs	S/B
Ohio,Cincinnati	Kenner Garrard	N/B
Ohio,Cincinnati	Melancthon Smith Wade	N/B
Ohio,Cincinnati	Thomas Welsh	N/B
Ohio,Cleveland	Edward Henry Hobson	N/B
Ohio,Cleveland	Mortimer Dormer Leggett	N/B
Ohio,Columbus	John Beatty	N/B
Ohio,Columbus	James Cooper	N/B
Ohio,Columbus	John Grant Mitchell	N/B
Ohio,Dayton	Alexander McDowell McCook	N/M
Ohio,Dayton	Marsena Rudolph Patrick	N/B
Ohio,Dayton	Thomas John Wood	N/M

Ohio,Fremont	Ralph Pomeroy Buckland	N/B
Ohio,Hamilton	Ferdinand Van Derveer	N/B
Ohio,Kenton	James Sidney Robinson	N/B
Ohio,Lancaster	Hugh Boyle Ewing	N/B
Ohio,Lockland	Jacob Ammen	N/B
Ohio,Logan County	Abram Sanders Piatt	N/B
Ohio,Massillon	Samuel Beatty	N/B
Ohio,Newark	Charles Robert Woods	N/B
Ohio,New Castle	William Grose	N/B
Ohio,Sandusky	Manning Ferguson Force	N/B
Ohio,Sandusky	John Pope	N/M
Ohio,Spiegel Grove	Rutherford Birchard Hayes	N/B
Ohio,St.Mary's	August Willich	N/B
Ohio,Toledo	Charles Camp Doolittle	N/B
Ohio,Toledo	John Wallace Fuller	N/B
Ohio,Toledo	James Blair Steedman	N/M
Ohio,Wellsville	James William Reilly	N/B
Oklahoma,Bryan County	Douglas Hancock Cooper	S/B
Oklahoma,Delaware County	Stand Watie	S/B
Oklahoma,Oklahoma City	Henry Goddard Thomas	N/B
Oklahoma,South McAlester	Edward Lloyd Thomas	S/B
Oregon,Medford	William Sooy Smith	N/B
Pennsylvania,Belair	George Archibald McCall	N/B
Pennsylvania,BlueRidge Summit	Richard Lucian Page	S/B
Pennsylvania,Bristol	William Reading Montgomery	N/B
Pennsylvania,Broad Run	Joseph Andrew Lightburn	N/B
Pennsylvania,Germantown	Charles Adam Heckman	N/B
Pennsylvania,Harrisburg	John White Geary	N/B
Pennsylvania,Harrisburg	William High Keim	N/B
Pennsylvania,Harrisburg	Joseph Farmer Knipe	N/B
Pennsylvania,Norristown	John Frederick Hartranft	N/B
Pennsylvania,Penllyn	John Clifford Pemberton	S/L
Pennsylvania,Philadelphia	David Bell Birney	N/M
Pennsylvania,Philadelphia	John Rutter Brooke	N/B
Pennsylvania,Philadelphia	George Cadwalader	N/M
Pennsylvania,Philadelphia	Samuel Wylie Crawford	N/B
Pennsylvania,Philadelphia	Thomas Leiper Kane	N/B
Pennsylvania,Philadelphia	George Gordon Meade	N/M
Pennsylvania,Philadelphia	Thomas Hewson Neill	N/B
Pennsylvania,Philadelphia	Joshua Thomas Owen	N/B
Pennsylvania,Philadelphia	William Farrar Smith	N/M
Pennsylvania,Philadelphia	George Hector Tyndale	N/B
Pennsylvania,Philadelphia	Godfrey Weitzel	N/M
Pennsylvania,Pittsburgh	Thomas Algeo Rowley	N/B
Pennsylvania,Pittsburgh	David Henry Williams	N/B
Pennsylvania,Pottsville	James Nagle	N/B
Pennsylvania,Reading	David McMurtrie Gregg	N/B
Pennsylvania,Wernersville	Alexander Schimmelfennig	N/B
Peru,Lima	Stephen Augustus Hurlbut	N/M
Rhode Island,Bristol	Ambrose Everett Burnside	N/M
Rhode Island,Jamestown	James Williamson	N/B
Rhode Island,Newport	James Barnet Fry	N/B
Rhode Island,Newport	Robert Brown Potter	N/B
Rhode Island,Newport	Thomas West Sherman	N/B
Rhode Island,Newport	Gouverneur Kemble Warren	N/M
South Carolina,Abbeville	Samuel McGowan	S/B

South Carolina,Aiken	Stephen Elliott,Jr.	S/B
South Carolina,Aiken	Gabriel James Rains	S/B
South Carolina,Barnwell	Johnson Hagood	S/B
South Carolina,Beaufort	Richard Heron Anderson	S/L
South Carolina,Beaufort	William Wallace Burns	N/B
South Carolina,Camden	James Chesnut, Jr.	S/B
South Carolina,Camden	John Doby Kennedy	S/B
South Carolina,Camden	Joseph Brevard Kershaw	S/M
South Carolina,Charleston	Benjamin Huger	S/M
South Carolina,Charleston	William Duncan Smith	S/B
South Carolina,Charleston	Charles John Stolbrand	N/B
South Carolina,Columbia	Ellison Capers	S/B
South Carolina,Columbia	Wade Hampton	S/L
South Carolina,Columbia	John Smith Preston	S/B
South Carolina,Edgefield Cty.	Martin Witherspoon Gary	S/B
South Carolina,Florence	Thomas Fenwick Drayton	S/B
South Carolina,Florence	John Henry Winder	S/B
South Carolina,Georgetown	James Heyward Trapier	S/B
South Carolina,Georgetown Cty.	Arthur Middleton Manigault	S/B
South Carolina,Hilton Head	Ormsby MacKnight Mitchel	N/M
South Carolina,Union	William Henry Wallace	S/B
South Carolina,Winnsboro	John Bratton	S/B
South Dakota,Scotland	Charles Thomas Campbell	N/B
South Dakota,Yankton County	John Blair Smith Todd	N/B
Spain,Cadiz	Alfred Napoleon A. Duffie	N/B
Switzerland,Geneva	Robert Allen	N/B
Tennessee,Braden's Knob	James Gallant Spears	N/B
Tennessee,Columbia	Lucius Eugene Polk	S/B
Tennessee,Columbia	Francis Asbury Shoup	S/B
Tennessee,Elizabethton	Andrew Johnson	N/B
Tennessee,Jackson	Alexander William Campbell	S/B
Tennessee,Jonesboro	Alfred Eugene Jackson	S/B
Tennessee,Knoxville	James Holt Clanton	S/B
Tennessee,Knoxville	Johnson Kelly Duncan	S/B
Tennessee,Lebanon	William Bowen Campbell	N/B
Tennessee,McMinnville	William Nelson R. Beall	S/B
Tennessee,McMinnville	Benjamin Jefferson Hill	S/B
Tennessee,Memphis	James Patton Anderson	S/M
Tennessee,Memphis	James Ronald Chalmers	S/B
Tennessee,Memphis	Nathan Bedford Forrest	S/L
Tennessee,Memphis	William Montgomery Gardner	S/B
Tennessee,Memphis	George Washington Gordon	S/B
Tennessee,Memphis	Daniel Chevilette Govan	S/B
Tennessee,Middleton	Mark Perrin Lowrey	S/B
Tennessee,Montvale Springs	Daniel Smith Donelson	S/M
Tennessee,Murfreesboro	Joseph Benjamin Palmer	S/B
Tennessee,Nashville	Samuel Read Anderson	S/B
Tennessee,Nashville	Benjamin Franklin Cheatham	S/M
Tennessee,Nashville	Alvan Cullem Gillem	N/B
Tennessee,Nashville	William Hicks Jackson	S/B
Tennessee,Nashville	Thomas Benton Smith	S/B
Tennessee,Red Boiling Springs	John Calvin Brown	S/M
Tennessee,Savannah	Charles Ferguson Smith	N/M
Tennessee,Sparta	George Gibbs Dibrell	S/B
Tennessee,Spring Hill	Richard Stoddert Ewell	S/L
Tennessee,Spring Hill	Earl Van Dorn	S/M

Tennessee,Sewanee	Edmund Kirby Smith	S/G
Texas,Austin	Edmund Jackson Davis	N/B
Texas,Austin	James Monroe Goggin	S/B
Texas,Austin	Andrew Jackson Hamilton	N/B
Texas,Austin	William Polk Hardeman	S/B
Texas,Austin	James Patrick Major	S/B
Texas,Brownsville	George Sykes	N/M
Texas,Burnet	Adam Rankin Johnson	S/B
Texas,College Station	Lawrence Sullivan Ross	S/B
Texas,Dallas	William Lewis Cabell	S/B
Texas,Dallas	Richard Montgomery Gano	S/B
Texas,Dallas	Alexander Hawthorne	S/B
Texas,Galveston	Braxton Bragg	S/G
Texas,Galveston	Charles Griffin	N/M
Texas,Galveston	Louis Trezevant Wigfall	S/B
Texas,Hallettsville	John Wilkins Whitfield	S/B
Texas,Houston	John Bankhead Magruder	S/M
Texas,Houston	John Austin Wharton	S/M
Texas,Hunt County	Thomas Neville Waul	S/B
Texas,Kerrville	Edward Aylesworth Perry	S/B
Texas,Marshall	Walter Paye Lane	S/B
Texas,Osage	John Creed Moore	S/B
Texas,Rockport	Henry Eustace McCulloch	S/B
Texas,San Antonio	Hamilton Prioleau Bee	S/B
Texas,San Antonio	James Henry Carleton	N/B
Texas,San Antonio	Alexander Chambers	N/B
Texas,San Antonio	William Steele	S/B
Texas,San Antonio	William Hugh Young	S/B
Texas,Tyler	Matthew Duncan Ector	S/B
Texas,Waco	James Edward Harrison	S/B
Texas,Waco	Thomas Harrison	S/B
Texas,Waco	Felix Huston Robertson	S/B
Texas,Waco	Jerome Bonaparte Robertson	S/B
Texas,Waco	Richard Waterhouse	S/B
Utah,Ogden	Nathan Kimball	N/B
Utah,Salt Lake City	Patrick Edward Connor	N/B
Utah,Salt Lake City	Friedrich Salomon	N/B
Vermont,Burlington	Oliver Otis Howard	N/M
Vermont,Guilford	John Wolcott Phelps	N/B
Virginia,Abingdon	John Buchanan Floyd	S/B
Virginia,Alexandria	Samuel Cooper	S/G
Virginia,Alexandria	Montgomery Dent Corse	S/B
Virginia,Alexandria	William George M. Davis	S/B
Virginia,Alexandria	George Washington Lee	S/M
Virginia,Alexandria	William Henry F. Lee	S/M
Virginia,Amelia	Bradley Tyler Johnson	S/B
Virginia,Bedford Springs	Samuel Jones	S/M
Virginia,Caroline County	Carter Stevenson	S/M
Virginia,Charlottesville	Armistead Lindsay Long	S/B
Virginia,Charlottesville	George Wythe Randolph	S/B
Virginia,Charlottesville	Thomas Lafayette Rosser	S/M
Virginia,Chesterfield Crt.Hse.	William Richard Terry	S/B
Virginia,Damascus	John Daniel Imboden	S/B
Virginia,Fairfax County	William Whann Mackall	S/B
Virginia,Fairfax Court House	Michael Corcoran	N/B
Virginia,Fluvanna County	Reuben Lindsay Walker	S/B

Virginia,Fort Monroe	George Washington Morgan	N/B
Virginia,Fredericksburg	Daniel Ruggles	S/B
Virginia,Fredericksburg	Henry Hopkins Sibley	S/B
Virginia,Gloucester County	William Booth Taliaferro	S/M
Virginia,Gordonsville	William McComb	S/B
Virginia,Hague	Richard Lee T. Beale	S/B
Virginia,Harrisonburg	John Robert Jones	S/B
Virginia,Harrisville	Thomas Maley Harris	N/B
Virginia,Lawrenceville	Peter Burwell Starke	S/B
Virginia,Lexington	Robert Edward Lee	S/G
Virginia,Lexington	William Nelson Pendleton	S/B
Virginia,Lynchburg	Jubal Anderson Early	S/L
Virginia,Natural Bridge	Wesley Merritt	N/M
Virginia,Norfolk	George Edward Pickett	S/M
Virginia,Norfolk	William Paul Roberts	S/B
Virginia,Occoquan	Francis Engle Patterson	N/B
Virginia,Orange County	James Lawson Kemper	S/M
Virginia,Paw Paw	Frederick West Lander	N/B
Virginia,Powhatan County	Philip St.George Cocke	S/B
Virginia,Radford	Gabriel Colvin Wharton	S/B
Virginia,Richmond	James Jay Archer	S/B
Virginia,Richmond	Raleigh Edward Colston	S/B
Virginia,Richmond	James Conner	S/B
Virginia,Richmond	John Rogers Cooke	S/B
Virginia,Richmond	William Ruffin Cox	S/B
Virginia,Richmond	Birkett Davenport Fry	S/B
Virginia,Richmond	Eppa Hunton	S/B
Virginia,Richmond	Edward Johnson	S/M
Virginia,Richmond	David Rumph Jones	S/M
Virginia,Richmond	Robert Doak Lilley	S/B
Virginia,Richmond	Patrick Theodore Moore	S/B
Virginia,Richmond	David Addison Weisiger	S/B
Virginia,Richmond	Williams Carter Wickham	S/B
Virginia,Richmond	Henry Alexander Wise	S/B
Virginia,Roanoke	Gilbert Moxley Sorrel	S/B
Virginia,Staunton	John Echols	S/B
Virginia,Suffolk	Laurence Simmons Baker	S/B
Virginia,Warrenton	William Smith	S/M
Virginia,Wht.Sulphur Springs	Isaac Munroe St.John	S/B
Virginia,Winchester	Robert Daniel Johnston	S/B
Virginia,Wytheville	William Joseph Hardee	S/L
Virginia,Wytheville	William Terry	S/B
Virginia,Wytheville	James Alexander Walker	S/B
Virginia,Yell.Sulphur Springs	Edwin Gray Lee	S/B
Washington,Fort Vancouver	Alfred Sully	N/B
Washington,Olympia	Robert Huston Milroy	N/M
Washington,Seattle	August Valentine Kautz	N/B
Washington,Tacoma	Luther Prentice Bradley	N/B
Washington,Tacoma	John Wilson Sprague	N/B
West Virginia,Mason County	John McCausland	S/B
West Virginia,Wellsburg	Isaac Hardin Duval	N/B
Washington,D.C.	Benjamin Alvord	N/B
Washington,D.C.	Joseph K. Barnes	N/B
Washington,D.C.	Seth Maxwell Barton	S/B
Washington,D.C.	William Brimage Bate	S/M
Washington,D.C.	William Worth Belknap	N/B

Washington,D.C.	James Gillpatrick Blunt	N/M
Washington,D.C.	Robert Christie Buchanan	N/B
Washington,D.C.	John Buford	N/B
Washington,D.C.	Cyrus Bussey	N/B
Washington,D.C.	Benjamin Franklin Butler	N/M
Washington,D.C.	Matthew Calbraith Butler	S/M
Washington,D.C.	Eugene Asa Carr	N/B
Washington,D.C.	Samuel Powhatan Carter	N/B
Washington,D.C.	John Bullock Clark	S/B
Washington,D.C.	Powell Clayton	N/B
Washington,D.C.	Francis Marion Cockrell	S/B
Washington,D.C.	Alfred Holt Colquitt	S/B
Washington,D.C.	Marcellus Monroe Crocker	N/B
Washington,D.C.	Richard Delafield	N/B
Washington,D.C.	Julius Adolph deLagnel	S/B
Washington,D.C.	James William Denver	N/B
Washington,D.C.	Alexander Brydie Dyer	N/B
Washington,D.C.	John Edwards	N/B
Washington,D.C.	William Hemsley Emory	N/B
Washington,D.C.	John Franklin Farnsworth	N/B
Washington,D.C.	Charles William Field	S/M
Washington,D.C.	William Henry French	N/M
Washington,D.C.	Lawrence Pike Graham	N/B
Washington,D.C.	Robert Seaman Granger	N/B
Washington,D.C.	Walter Quintin Gresham	N/B
Washington,D.C.	William Alexander Hammond	N/B
Washington,D.C.	James Allen Hardie	N/B
Washington,D.C.	Joseph Roswell Hawley	N/B
Washington,D.C.	William Babcock Hazen	N/M
Washington,D.C.	Samuel Peter Heintzelman	N/M
Washington,D.C.	Henry Heth	S/M
Washington,D.C.	Joseph Holt	N/B
Washington,D.C.	Charles Edward Hovey	N/B
Washington,D.C.	Andrew Atkinson Humphreys	N/M
Washington,D.C.	Henry Jackson Hunt	N/B
Washington,D.C.	David Hunter	N/M
Washington,D.C.	Joseph Eggleston Johnston	S/G
Washington,D.C.	John Haskell King	N/B
Washington,D.C.	William Whedbee Kirkland	S/B
Washington,D.C.	Fitzhugh Lee	S/M
Washington,D.C.	John Alexander Logan	N/M
Washington,D.C.	Lunsford Lindsay Lomax	S/M
Washington,D.C.	William Mahone	S/M
Washington,D.C.	George Ear Maney	S/B
Washington,D.C.	John Sanford Mason	N/B
Washington,D.C.	James Winning McMillan	N/B
Washington,D.C.	Montgomery Meigs	N/B
Washington,D.C.	Nelson Appleton Miles	N/B
Washington,D.C.	Robert Byington Mitchell	N/B
Washington,D.C.	John Tyler Morgan	S/B
Washington,D.C.	John Morrison Oliver	N/B
Washington,D.C.	Halbert Eleazer Paine	N/B
Washington,D.C.	John Grubb Parke	N/M
Washington,D.C.	Gabriel Rene Paul	N/B
Washington,D.C.	William Henry Payne	S/B
Washington,D.C.	Albert Pike	S/B

Washington,D.C.	Alfred Pleasonton	N/M
Washington,D.C.	George Douglas Ramsay	N/B
Washington,D.C.	John Aaron Rawlins	N/B
Washington,D.C.	Joseph Jones Reynolds	N/M
Washington,D.C.	James Brewerton Ricketts	N/B
Washington,D.C.	Benjamin Stone Roberts	N/B
Washington,D.C.	Beverly Robertson	S/B
Washington,D.C.	Daniel Henry Rucker	N/B
Washington,D.C.	Rufus Saxton	N/B
Washington,D.C.	Robert Cumming Schenck	N/M
Washington,D.C.	Green Clay Smith	N/B
Washington,D.C.	Francis Barretto Spinola	N/B
Washington,D.C.	David Sloane Stanley	N/M
Washington,D.C.	George Jerrison Stannard	N/B
Washington,D.C.	John Converse Starkweather	N/B
Washington,D.C.	Joseph Pannell Taylor	N/B
Washington,D.C.	Henry Dwight Terry	N/B
Washington,D.C.	Lorenzo Thomas	N/B
Washington,D.C.	Joseph Gilbert Totten	N/B
Washington,D.C.	Stewart Van Vliet	N/B
Washington,D.C.	John George Walker	S/M
Washington,D.C.	Edward Cary Walthall	S/M
Washington,D.C.	Joseph Rodman West	N/B
Washington,D.C.	Frank Wheaton	N/B
Washington,D.C.	Cadmus Marcellus Wilcox	S/M
Washington,D.C.	Alpheus Starkey Williams	N/B
Washington,D.C.	Horatio Gouverneur Wright	N/M
Washington,D.C.	Marcus Joseph Wright	S/B
Wisconsin,Fond du Lac	Edward Stuyvesant Bragg	N/B
Wisconsin,Madison	Lucius Fairchild	N/B
Wisconsin,Milwaukee	Lysander Cutler	N/B
Wisconsin,Milwaukee	Charles Smith Hamilton	N/M
Wyoming,Ft.Laramie	Adam Jacoby Slemmer	N/B

12

Civil War Generals
by Date of Death

This chapter lists all the generals according to the dates
they died.

DATE OF DEATH	GENERAL	SIDE/RANK
July 3, 1861	Robert Selden Garnett	S/Brig.Gen.
July 22, 1861	Barnard Elliott Bee	S/Brig.Gen.
August 10, 1861	Nathaniel Lyon	N/Brig.Gen.
October 21, 1861	Edward Dickinson Baker	N/Maj.Gen.
October 21, 1861	John Breckinridge Grayson	S/Brig.Gen.
December 26, 1861	Philip St.George Cocke	S/Brig.Gen.
January 19, 1862	Felix Kirk Zollicoffer	S/Brig.Gen.
March 2, 1862	Frederick West Lander	N/Brig.Gen.
March 7, 1862	Ben McCulloch	S/Brig.Gen.
March 7, 1862	James McQueen McIntosh	S/Brig.Gen.
March 21, 1862	William Yarnel Slack	S/Brig.Gen.
April 6, 1862	Albert Sidney Johnston	S/General
April 10, 1862	William Harvey L. Wallace	N/Brig.Gen.
April 12, 1862	Adley Hogan Gladden	S/Brig.Gen.
April 25, 1862	Charles Ferguson Smith	N/Maj.Gen.
May 16, 1862	Joseph Lewis Hogg	S/Brig.Gen.
May 18, 1862	William High Keim	N/Brig.Gen.
May 31, 1862	Robert Hopkins Hatton	S/Brig.Gen.
June 6, 1862	Turner Ashby	S/Brig.Gen.
June 29, 1862	Richard Griffith	S/Brig.Gen.
July 15, 1862	David Emanuel Twiggs	S/Maj.Gen.
August 5, 1862	Thomas Williams	N/Brig.Gen.
August 6, 1862	Robert Latimer McCook	N/Brig.Gen.
August 9, 1862	Joseph Bennett Plummer	N/Brig.Gen.
August 9, 1862	Charles Sidney Winder	S/Brig.Gen.
August 22, 1862	Henry Bohlen	N/Brig.Gen.
September 1, 1862	Philip Kearny	N/Maj.Gen.
September 1, 1862	Isaac Ingalls Stevens	N/Brig.Gen.
September 1, 1862	George William Taylor	N/Brig.Gen.
September 14, 1862	Samuel Garland,Jr.	S/Brig.Gen.
September 14, 1862	Jesse Lee Reno	N/Maj.Gen.
September 16, 1862	William Edwin Starke	S/Brig.Gen.
September 17, 1862	Lawrence O'Bryan Branch	S/Brig.Gen.
September 18, 1862	Joseph King F. Mansfield	N/Brig.Gen.

September 19, 1862	Lewis Henry Little	S/Brig.Gen.
September 29, 1862	William Nelson	N/Maj.Gen.
September 30, 1862	Isaac Peace Rodman	N/Brig.Gen.
October 3, 1862	Pleasant Adam Hackleman	N/Brig.Gen.
October 4, 1862	William Duncan Smith	S/Brig.Gen.
October 7, 1862	Allison Nelson	S/Brig.Gen.
October 8, 1862	James Streshly Jackson	N/Brig.Gen.
October 8, 1862	William Rufus Terrill	N/Brig.Gen.
October 16, 1862	George Burgwyn Anderson	S/Brig.Gen.
October 30, 1862	Ormsby MacKnight Mitchel	N/Maj.Gen.
November 3, 1862	Israel Bush Richardson	N/Maj.Gen.
November 6, 1862	Charles Davis Jameson	N/Brig.Gen.
November 9, 1862	John Bordenave Villepigue	S/Brig.Gen.
November 22, 1862	Francis Engle Patterson	N/Brig.Gen.
December 13, 1862	Thomas Reade Rootes Cobb	S/Brig.Gen.
December 13, 1862	Conrad Feger Jackson	N/Brig.Gen.
December 14, 1862	George Dashiell Bayard	N/Brig.Gen.
December 15, 1862	Maxcy Gregg	S/Brig.Gen.
December 18, 1862	Johnson Kelly Duncan	S/Brig.Gen.
December 31, 1862	James Edwards Rains	S/Brig.Gen.
December 31, 1862	Joshua Woodrow Sill	N/Brig.Gen.
January 4, 1863	Roger Weightman Hanson	S/Brig.Gen.
January 15, 1863	David Rumph Jones	S/Maj.Gen.
March 21, 1863	Edwin Vose Sumner	N/Maj.Gen.
March 28, 1863	James Cooper	N/Brig.Gen.
April 17, 1863	Daniel Smith Donelson	S/Maj.Gen.
May 1, 1863	Edward Dorr Tracy	S/Brig.Gen.
May 3, 1863	Hiram Gregory Berry	N/Maj.Gen.
May 3, 1863	Elisha Franklin Paxton	S/Brig.Gen.
May 7, 1863	Earl Van Dorn	S/Maj.Gen.
May 7, 1863	Amiel Weeks Whipple	N/Brig.Gen.
May 10, 1863	Thomas Jonathon Jackson	S/Lt.Gen.
May 16, 1863	Lloyd Tilghman	S/Brig.Gen.
June 25, 1863	Martin Edwin Green	S/Brig.Gen.
July 1, 1863	John Fulton Reynolds	N/Maj.Gen.
July 2, 1863	Stephen Hinsdale Weed	N/Brig.Gen.
July 3, 1863	William Barksdale	S/Brig.Gen.
July 3, 1863	Elon John Farnsworth	N/Brig.Gen.
July 3, 1863	Richard Brooke Garnett	S/Brig.Gen.
July 3, 1863	Samuel Kosciuszko Zook	N/Brig.Gen.
July 5, 1863	Lewis Addison Armistead	S/Brig.Gen.
July 10, 1863	Paul Jones Semmes	S/Brig.Gen.
July 13, 1863	John Stevens Bowen	S/Maj.Gen.
July 17, 1863	James Johnston Pettigrew	S/Brig.Gen.
July 18, 1863	William Dorsey Pender	S/Maj.Gen.
July 21, 1863	Edward Needles Kirk	N/Brig.Gen.
July 30, 1863	George Crockett Strong	N/Brig.Gen.
August 14, 1863	Thomas Welsh	N/Brig.Gen.
August 26, 1863	John Buchanan Floyd	S/Brig.Gen.
September 7, 1863	Lucius Marshall Walker	S/Brig.Gen.
September 19, 1863	Preston Smith	S/Brig.Gen.
September 20, 1863	James Deshler	S/Brig.Gen.
September 20, 1863	Benjamin Hardin Helm	S/Brig.Gen.
September 20, 1863	William Haines Lytle	N/Brig.Gen.
October 31, 1863	Louis Ludwig Blenker	N/Brig.Gen.
November 13, 1863	Carnot Posey	S/Brig.Gen.

November 19, 1863	William Price Sanders	N/Brig.Gen.
December 16, 1863	John Buford	N/Brig.Gen.
December 22, 1863	Michael Corcoran	N/Brig.Gen.
January 24, 1864	Stephen Gardner Champlin	N/Brig.Gen.
February 19, 1864	William Edwin Baldwin	S/Brig.Gen.
April 8, 1864	Jean Jacques A.A. Mouton	S/Brig.Gen.
April 12, 1864	Thomas Green	S/Brig.Gen.
April 22, 1864	Joseph Gilbert Totten	N/Brig.Gen.
April 30, 1864	William Read Scurry	S/Brig.Gen.
May 5, 1864	Alexander Hays	N/Brig.Gen.
May 5, 1864	John Marshall Jones	S/Brig.Gen.
May 6, 1864	Micah Jenkins	S/Brig.Gen.
May 8, 1864	Leroy Augustus Stafford	S/Brig.Gen.
May 8, 1864	James Samuel Wadsworth	N/Brig.Gen.
May 9, 1864	John Sedgwick	N/Maj.Gen.
May 10, 1864	James Clay Rice	N/Brig.Gen.
May 10, 1864	Thomas Greely Stevenson	N/Brig.Gen.
May 12, 1864	Abner Monroe Perrin	S/Brig.Gen.
May 12, 1864	James Ewell Brown Stuart	S/Maj.Gen.
May 13, 1864	Junius Daniel	S/Brig.Gen.
May 18, 1864	James Byron Gordon	S/Brig.Gen.
May 21, 1864	Albert Gallatin Jenkins	S/Brig.Gen.
June 2, 1864	George Pierce Doles	S/Brig.Gen.
June 5, 1864	William Edmonson Jones	S/Brig.Gen.
June 14, 1864	Leonidas Polk	S/Lt.Gen.
June 17, 1864	James St.Clair Morton	N/Brig.Gen.
June 26, 1864	Charles Garrison Harker	N/Brig.Gen.
June 29, 1864	Joseph Pannell Taylor	N/Brig.Gen.
July 6, 1864	Samuel Allen Rice	N/Brig.Gen.
July 22, 1864	James Birdseye McPherson	N/Maj.Gen.
July 22, 1864	William Henry T. Walker	S/Maj.Gen.
July 25, 1864	Clement Hoffman Stevens	S/Brig.Gen.
August 15, 1864	Daniel Phineas Woodbury	N/Brig.Gen.
August 16, 1864	John Randolph Chambliss	S/Brig.Gen.
August 16, 1864	Victor Jean B. Girardey	S/Brig.Gen.
August 21, 1864	John Caldwell C. Sanders	S/Brig.Gen.
September 4, 1864	John Herbert Kelly	S/Brig.Gen.
September 4, 1864	John Hunt Morgan	S/Brig.Gen.
September 19, 1864	Archibald Campbell Godwin	S/Brig.Gen.
September 19, 1864	Robert Emmett Rodes	S/Maj.Gen.
September 19, 1864	David Allen Russell	N/Brig.Gen.
September 29, 1864	Hiram Burnham	N/Brig.Gen.
October 1, 1864	John Dunovant	S/Brig.Gen.
October 7, 1864	John Gregg	S/Brig.Gen.
October 18, 1864	David Bell Birney	N/Maj.Gen.
October 19, 1864	Daniel Davidson Bidwell	N/Brig.Gen.
October 20, 1864	Stephen Dodson Ramseur	S/Maj.Gen.
October 24, 1864	James Jay Archer	S/Brig.Gen.
October 29, 1864	Thomas Edward G. Ransom	N/Brig.Gen.
November 30, 1864	John Adams	S/Brig.Gen.
November 30, 1864	John Carpenter Carter	S/Brig.Gen.
November 30, 1864	Patrick Ronayne Cleburne	S/Maj.Gen.
November 30, 1864	States Rights Gist	S/Brig.Gen.
November 30, 1864	Hiram Bronson Granbury	S/Brig.Gen.
November 30, 1864	Otho French Strahl	S/Brig.Gen.
December 2, 1864	Archibald Gracie,Jr.	S/Brig.Gen.

February 6, 1865	John Pegram	S/Brig.Gen.
February 7, 1865	John Henry Winder	S/Brig.Gen.
March 10, 1865	William Henry C. Whiting	S/Maj.Gen.
April 2, 1865	Ambrose Powell Hill	S/Lt.Gen.
April 6, 1865	John Austin Wharton	S/Maj.Gen.
April 7, 1865	Thomas Alfred Smyth	N/Brig.Gen.
April 16, 1865	Robert Charles Tyler	S/Brig.Gen.
April 23, 1865	James Dearing	S/Brig.Gen.
July 30, 1865	George Wright	N/Brig.Gen.
August 15, 1865	Mosby Monroe Parsons	S/Maj.Gen.
August 26, 1865	Marcellus Monroe Crocker	N/Brig.Gen.
September 5, 1865	Alexander Schimmelfennig	N/Brig.Gen.
December 21, 1865	James Heyward Trapier	S/Brig.Gen.
January 14, 1866	Henry Moses Judah	N/Brig.Gen.
February 21, 1866	Stephen Elliott,Jr.	S/Brig.Gen.
February 27, 1866	John King Jackson	S/Brig.Gen.
March 23, 1866	Seth Williams	N/Brig.Gen.
April 22, 1866	Henry Watkins Allen	S/Brig.Gen.
May 29, 1866	Winfield Scott	N/Maj.Gen.
July 29, 1866	Martin Luther Smith	S/Maj.Gen.
July 30, 1866	Lysander Cutler	N/Brig.Gen.
August 22, 1866	James Nagle	N/Brig.Gen.
September 13, 1866	William Ward Orme	N/Brig.Gen.
September 18, 1866	Young Marshall Moody	S/Brig.Gen.
September 26, 1866	Danville Leadbetter	S/Brig.Gen.
December 26, 1866	Samuel Ryan Curtis	N/Maj.Gen.
February 9, 1867	Jacob Gartner Lauman	N/Brig.Gen.
March 14, 1867	William Plummer Benton	N/Brig.Gen.
March 16, 1867	William Kerley Strong	N/Brig.Gen.
March 21, 1867	Joseph Bailey	N/Brig.Gen.
March 24, 1867	John Decatur Barry	S/Brig.Gen.
April 3, 1867	George Wythe Randolph	S/Brig.Gen.
April 8, 1867	John Selden Roane	S/Brig.Gen.
July 1, 1867	Thomas Francis Meagher	N/Brig.Gen.
August 19, 1867	William Bowen Campbell	N/Brig.Gen.
August 28, 1867	Cyrus Hamlin	N/Brig.Gen.
September 15, 1867	Charles Griffin	N/Maj.Gen.
September 29, 1867	Sterling Price	S/Maj.Gen.
November 12, 1867	Walter Husted Stevens	S/Brig.Gen.
December 12, 1867	Jasper Adalmorn Maltby	N/Brig.Gen.
December 17, 1867	John Potts Slough	N/Brig.Gen.
January 12, 1868	Frederick Steele	N/Maj.Gen.
January 21, 1868	Alexander Sandor Asboth	N/Brig.Gen.
February 26, 1868	George Archibald McCall	N/Brig.Gen.
May 3, 1868	William Henry Carroll	S/Brig.Gen.
May 22, 1868	Isham Nicholas Haynie	N/Brig.Gen.
August 11, 1868	Melancthon Smith Wade	N/Brig.Gen.
September 11, 1868	David Stuart	N/Brig.Gen.
September 28, 1868	Thomas Carmichael Hindman	S/Maj.Gen.
October 7, 1868	Adam Jacoby Slemmer	N/Brig.Gen.
October 9, 1868	Howell Cobb	S/Maj.Gen.
October 16, 1868	Charles Leopold Matthies	N/Brig.Gen.
November 23, 1868	Nathan George Evans	S/Brig.Gen.
December 25, 1868	Edwin Henry Stoughton	N/Brig.Gen.
December 26, 1868	Alfred Gibbs	N#Brig.Gen.
January 7, 1869	Lovell Harrison Rousseau	N/Maj.Gen.

February 12, 1869	James Barnes	N/Brig.Gen.
February 13, 1869	George Day Wagner	N/Brig.Gen.
June 22, 1869	Henry Dwight Terry	N/Brig.Gen.
July 22, 1869	James Gallant Spears	N/Brig.Gen.
September 6, 1869	John Aaron Rawlins	N/Brig.Gen.
November 10, 1869	John Ellis Wool	N/Maj.Gen.
November 29, 1869	James Lawlor Kiernan	N/Brig.Gen.
January 5, 1870	Robert Vinkler Richardson	S/Brig.Gen.
January 6, 1870	Joseph Anthony Mower	N/Maj.Gen.
February 14, 1870	St.John Richardson Liddell	S/Brig.Gen.
March 15, 1870	James Wolfe Ripley	N/Brig.Gen.
March 28, 1870	George Henry Thomas	N/Maj.Gen.
April 4, 1870	Albert Rust	S/Brig.Gen.
April 19, 1870	Thomas Jefferson McKean	N/Brig.Gen.
July 19, 1870	William Thomas H. Brooks	N/Maj.Gen.
August 5, 1870	Ethan Allen Hitchcock	N/Maj.Gen.
August 24, 1870	Edwin Gray Lee	S/Brig.Gen.
October 12, 1870	Robert Edward Lee	S/General
November 2, 1870	William Felix Brantley	S/Brig.Gen.
January 22, 1871	William Raine Peck	S/Brig.Gen.
February 18, 1871	John Bankhead Magruder	S/Maj.Gen.
February 21, 1871	Arnold Elzey	S/Maj.Gen.
April 16, 1871	Ebenezer Dumont	N/Brig.Gen.
June 1, 1871	William Reading Montgomery	N/Brig.Gen.
June 28, 1871	William Scott Ketchum	N/Brig.Gen.
July 28, 1871	Jerimiah Tilford Boyle	N/Brig.Gen.
September 9, 1871	Stand Watie	S/Brig.Gen.
September 22, 1871	Lewis Golding Arnold	N/Brig.Gen.
September 27, 1871	James Holt Clanton	S/Brig.Gen.
October 26, 1871	Robert Anderson	N/Brig.Gen.
January 3, 1872	Andrew Porter	N/Brig.Gen.
January 5, 1872	John Blair Smith Todd	N/Brig.Gen.
January 9, 1872	Henry Wager Halleck	N/Maj.Gen.
January 25, 1872	Richard Stoddert Ewell	S/Lt.Gen.
March 28, 1872	Humphrey Marshall	S/Brig.Gen.
March 30, 1872	John Morrison Oliver	N/Brig.Gen.
June 13, 1872	Daniel Weisiger Adams	S/Brig.Gen.
September 20, 1872	James Patton Anderson	S/Maj.Gen.
September 27, 1872	William Harrow	N/Brig.Gen.
November 6, 1872	George Gordon Meade	N/Maj.Gen.
December 21, 1872	Ambrose Ransom Wright	S/Maj.Gen.
January 7, 1873	James Henry Carleton	N/Brig.Gen.
January 18, 1873	John White Geary	N/Brig.Gen.
February 18, 1873	Charles Mynn Thruston	N/Brig.Gen.
March 2, 1873	Edward Johnson	S/Maj.Gen.
April 11, 1873	Edward Richard S. Canby	N/Maj.Gen.
April 29, 1873	Franklin Gardner	S/Maj.Gen.
November 5, 1873	Richard Delafield	N/Brig.Gen.
November 6, 1873	William Joseph Hardee	S/Lt.Gen.
December 30, 1873	Henry Baxter	N/Brig.Gen.
February 18, 1874	Louis Trezevant Wigfall	S/Brig.Gen.
April 16, 1874	John Thomas Croxton	N/Brig.Gen.
May 20, 1874	Alexander Brydie Dyer	N/Brig.Gen.
June 30, 1874	James Cantey	S/Brig.Gen.
July 9, 1874	Robert Cowdin	N/Brig.Gen.
July 19, 1874	Abner Clark Harding	N/Brig.Gen.

August 3, 1874	Joseph Abel Haskin	N/Brig.Gen.
August 21, 1874	Hugh Thompson Reid	N/Brig.Gen.
September 2, 1874	John Gray Foster	N/Maj.Gen.
December 1, 1874	Robert Ogden Tyler	N/Brig.Gen.
December 26, 1874	Sullivan Amory Meredith	N/Brig.Gen.
December 28, 1874	Morgan Lewis Smith	N/Brig.Gen.
January 29, 1875	Benjamin Stone Roberts	N/Brig.Gen.
January 31, 1875	Edward Higgins	S/Brig.Gen.
February 7, 1875	William Hays	N/Brig.Gen.
February 23, 1875	James Edward Harrison	S/Brig.Gen.
March 2, 1875	Lorenzo Thomas	N/Brig.Gen.
April 11, 1875	Andrew Jackson Hamilton	N/Brig.Gen.
May 17, 1875	John Cabell Breckinridge	S/Maj.Gen.
July 8, 1875	Francis Preston Blair,Jr.	N/Maj.Gen.
July 10, 1875	Henry Lewis Benning	S/Brig.Gen.
July 30, 1875	George Edward Pickett	S/Maj.Gen.
July 31, 1875	Andrew Johnson	N/Brig.Gen.
September 10, 1875	John Crawford Vaughn	S/Brig.Gen.
October 2, 1875	Solomon Meredith	N/Brig.Gen.
November 21, 1875	Orris Sanford Ferry	N/Brig.Gen.
December 2, 1875	Alvan Cullem Gillem	N/Brig.Gen.
January 10, 1876	Gordon Granger	N/Maj.Gen.
March 12, 1876	Joseph Dana Webster	N/Brig.Gen.
March 20, 1876	Richard Waterhouse	S/Brig.Gen.
April 21, 1876	Thomas Moore Scott	S/Brig.Gen.
May 20, 1876	Willis Arnold Gorman	N/Brig.Gen.
May 26, 1876	Alexander Welch Reynolds	S/Brig.Gen.
June 25, 1876	George Armstrong Custer	N/Brig.Gen.
August 21, 1876	Harry Thompson Hays	S/Maj.Gen.
September 12, 1876	Henry Alexander Wise	S/Brig.Gen.
September 27, 1876	Braxton Bragg	S/General
October 13, 1876	Rufus King	N/Brig.Gen.
November 5, 1876	Giles Alexander Smith	N/Brig.Gen.
December 3, 1876	Samuel Cooper	S/General
December 14, 1876	James Allen Hardie	N/Brig.Gen.
December 17, 1876	William Francis Bartlett	N/Brig.Gen.
January 3, 1877	John Joseph Abercrombie	N/Brig.Gen.
February 21, 1877	Amos Beebe Eaton	N/Brig.Gen.
February 25, 1877	Adolph von Steinwehr	N/Brig.Gen.
March 25, 1877	Elkanah Brackin Greer	S/Brig.Gen.
May 7, 1877	James Patrick Major	S/Brig.Gen.
June 9, 1877	Hugh Weedon Mercer	S/Brig.Gen.
October 29, 1877	Nathan Bedford Forrest	S/Lt.Gen.
December 7, 1877	Benjamin Huger	S/Maj.Gen.
December 18, 1877	Charles Clark	S/Brig.Gen.
January 22, 1878	August Willich	N/Brig.Gen.
April 4, 1878	Thomas Casimer Devin	N/Brig.Gen.
April 21, 1878	John James Peck	N/Maj.Gen.
June 21, 1878	Fitz-Henry Warren	N/Brig.Gen.
July 20, 1878	George Foster Shepley	N/Brig.Gen.
October 4, 1878	James Green Martin	S/Brig.Gen.
October 8, 1878	Gideon Johnson Pillow	S/Brig.Gen.
October 12, 1878	William Thomas Ward	N/Brig.Gen.
November 29, 1878	Robert Christie Buchanan	N/Brig.Gen.
December 21, 1878	Alpheus Starkey Williams	N/Brig.Gen.
January 22, 1879	John Porter McCown	S/Maj.Gen.

February 3, 1879	George Cadwalader	N/Maj.Gen.
February 18, 1879	Robert Hall Chilton	S/Brig.Gen.
March 16, 1879	Thomas West Sherman	N/Brig.Gen.
April 12, 1879	Richard Taylor	S/Lt.Gen.
April 21, 1879	John Adams Dix	N/Maj.Gen.
April 27, 1879	Alfred Sully	N/Brig.Gen.
April 29, 1879	Douglas Hancock Cooper	S/Brig.Gen.
May 15, 1879	Kenner Garrard	N/Brig.Gen.
June 1, 1879	James Shields	N/Brig.Gen.
June 26, 1879	Richard Heron Anderson	S/Lt.Gen.
July 18, 1879	William Farquhar Barry	N/Brig.Gen.
August 30, 1879	John Bell Hood	S/General
October 6, 1879	Francis Laurens Vinton	N/Brig.Gen.
October 27, 1879	John Wilkins Whitfield	S/Brig.Gen.
October 29, 1879	Matthew Duncan Ector	S/Brig.Gen.
October 31, 1879	Joseph Hooker	N/Maj.Gen.
November 30, 1879	Jefferson Columbus Davis	N/Brig.Gen.
January 5, 1880	Benjamin Jefferson Hill	S/Brig.Gen.
February 8, 1880	George Sykes	N/Maj.Gen.
March 19, 1880	George Hector Tyndale	N/Brig.Gen.
April 7, 1880	Isaac Munroe St.John	S/Brig.Gen.
April 20, 1880	Joseph Warren Revere	N/Brig.Gen.
May 1, 1880	Samuel Peter Heintzelman	N/Maj.Gen.
June 21, 1880	Theophilus Hunter Holmes	S/Lt.Gen.
August 14, 1880	Bryan Grimes	S/Maj.Gen.
August 29, 1880	Paul Octave Hebert	S/Brig.Gen.
August 29, 1880	Alfred Thomas A. Torbert	N/Brig.Gen.
September 12, 1880	Bushrod Rust Johnson	S/Maj.Gen.
November 8, 1880	Alfred Napoleon A. Duffie	N/Brig.Gen.
November 27, 1880	George Bibb Crittenden	S/Maj.Gen.
March 15, 1881	Emory Upton	N/Brig.Gen.
April 9, 1881	Martin Witherspoon Gary	S/Brig.Gen.
May 1, 1881	John Smith Preston	S/Brig.Gen.
May 20, 1881	William Henry French	N/Maj.Gen.
June 26, 1881	John Wynn Davidson	N/Brig.Gen.
July 13, 1881	John Clifford Pemberton	S/Lt.Gen.
July 27, 1881	James Gillpatrick Blunt	N/Maj.Gen.
July 28, 1881	James Richard Slack	N/Brig.Gen.
August 6, 1881	Gabriel James Rains	S/Brig.Gen.
August 18, 1881	Stephen Miller	N/Brig.Gen.
September 13, 1881	Ambrose Everett Burnside	N/Maj.Gen.
September 14, 1881	William Feimster Tucker	S/Brig.Gen.
September 19, 1881	James Abram Garfield	N/Maj.Gen.
December 4, 1881	Hugh Judson Kilpatrick	N/Brig.Gen.
December 13, 1881	John Henry Martindale	N/Brig.Gen.
January 22, 1882	Silas Casey	N/Maj.Gen.
January 26, 1882	Robert Byington Mitchell	N/Brig.Gen.
February 11, 1882	William MacRae	S/Brig.Gen.
March 6, 1882	Zachariah Cantey Deas	S/Brig.Gen.
March 27, 1882	StephenAugustus Hurlbut	N/Maj.Gen.
May 14, 1882	John Gross Barnard	N/Brig.Gen.
May 14, 1882	Cadwallader Colden Washburn	N/Maj.Gen.
May 23, 1882	George Douglas Ramsay	N/Brig.Gen.
June 16, 1882	George Henry Chapman	N/Brig.Gen.
June 20, 1882	Theodore Washington Brevard	S/Brig.Gen.
June 30, 1882	Joseph K. Barnes	N/Brig.Gen.

July 26, 1882	Michael Kelly Lawler	N/Brig.Gen.
August 8, 1882	Gouverneur Kemble Warren	N/Maj.Gen.
August 15, 1882	James Hewett Ledlie	N/Brig.Gen.
September 11, 1882	William Young Conn Humes	S/Brig.Gen.
November 8, 1882	Richard Arnold	N/Brig.Gen.
November 18, 1882	James Deering Fessenden	N/Brig.Gen.
November 30, 1882	Daniel Tyler	N/Brig.Gen.
December 16, 1882	Eleazer Arthur Paine	N/Brig.Gen.
December 20, 1882	Benjamin Grubb Humphreys	S/Brig.Gen.
January 2, 1883	Samuel Read Anderson	S/Brig.Gen.
January 15, 1883	William Nelson Pendleton	S/Brig.Gen.
February 7, 1883	Edmund Jackson Davis	N/Brig.Gen.
February 11, 1883	George Webb Morell	N/Maj.Gen.
February 14, 1883	Edwin Denison Morgan	N/Maj.Gen.
February 19, 1883	Patrick Theodore Moore	S/Brig.Gen.
March 2, 1883	Dudley McIver DuBose	S/Brig.Gen.
March 15, 1883	Henry Constantine Wayne	S/Brig.Gen.
March 23, 1883	Charles Cruft	N/Brig.Gen.
March 28, 1883	Napoleon Bonaparte Buford	N/Brig.Gen.
April 28, 1883	William Montague Browne	S/Brig.Gen.
May 15, 1883	Josiah Gorgas	S/Brig.Gen.
June 26, 1883	James Conner	S/Brig.Gen.
July 22, 1883	Edward Otho C. Ord	N/Maj.Gen.
July 25, 1883	William Nelson R. Beall	S/Brig.Gen.
October 16, 1883	Samuel Jameson Gholson	S/Brig.Gen.
October 18, 1883	James Blair Steedman	N/Maj.Gen.
December 1, 1883	Jeremy Francis Gilmer	S/Maj.Gen.
December 26, 1883	Thomas Leiper Kane	N/Brig.Gen.
December 27, 1883	Andrew Atkinson Humphreys	N/Maj.Gen.
February 9, 1884	James Isham Gilbert	N/Brig.Gen.
March 19, 1884	Godfrey Weitzel	N/Maj.Gen.
April 11, 1884	George Washington Deitzler	N/Brig.Gen.
May 22, 1884	William Tatum Wofford	S/Brig.Gen.
June 1, 1884	Henry Washington Benham	N/Brig.Gen.
June 1, 1884	Mansfield Lovell	S/Maj.Gen.
June 9, 1884	Abraham Buford	S/Brig.Gen.
August 22, 1884	Leroy Pope Walker	S/Brig.Gen.
October 16, 1884	Benjamin Alvord	N/Brig.Gen.
November 29, 1884	Gershom Mott	N/Brig.Gen.
January 11, 1885	Henry Lawrence Eustis	N/Brig.Gen.
January 12, 1885	William Steele	S/Brig.Gen.
February 1, 1885	James Chesnut, Jr.	S/Brig.Gen.
February 2, 1885	John Wolcott Phelps	N/Brig.Gen.
February 26, 1885	Charles Robert Woods	N/Brig.Gen.
February 27, 1885	Mark Perrin Lowrey	S/Brig.Gen.
March 12, 1885	Thomas Hewson Neill	N/Brig.Gen.
May 4, 1885	Irvin McDowell	N/Maj.Gen.
May 26, 1885	Samuel Beatty	N/Brig.Gen.
June 6, 1885	Cuvier Grover	N/Brig.Gen.
July 23, 1885	Ulysses Simpson Grant	N/Lt.Gen.
August 16, 1885	Goode Bryan	S/Brig.Gen.
October 29, 1885	Joseph Finegan	S/Brig.Gen.
October 29, 1885	George Brinton McClellan	N/Maj.Gen.
December 11, 1885	Gustavus Adolphus Smith	N/Brig.Gen.
December 15, 1885	Robert Augustus Toombs	S/Brig.Gen.
February 2, 1886	David Hunter	N/Maj.Gen.

February 9, 1886	Winfield Scott Hancock	N/Maj.Gen.
March 5, 1886	Henry Morris Naglee	N/Brig.Gen.
March 8, 1886	John Franklin Miller	N/Brig.Gen.
May 5, 1886	Gabriel Rene Paul	N/Brig.Gen.
May 10, 1886	Albin Francisco Schoepf	N/Brig.Gen.
June 1, 1886	George Jerrison Stannard	N/Brig.Gen.
July 22, 1886	James Henry Van Alen	N/Brig.Gen.
August 5, 1886	Robert Allen	N/Brig.Gen.
August 17, 1886	Arthur Middleton Manigault	S/Brig.Gen.
August 23, 1886	Henry Hopkins Sibley	S/Brig.Gen.
August 30, 1886	George Henry Gordon	N/Brig.Gen.
September 4, 1886	Benjamin Franklin Cheatham	S/Maj.Gen.
September 6, 1886	Lewis Cass Hunt	N/Brig.Gen.
September 29, 1886	James Bowen	N/Brig.Gen.
November 12, 1886	Robert Doak Lilley	S/Brig.Gen.
November 20, 1886	John Smith Phelps	N/Brig.Gen.
December 26, 1886	John Alexander Logan	N/Maj.Gen.
December 30, 1886	William Wing Loring	S/Maj.Gen.
January 16, 1887	William Babcock Hazen	N/Maj.Gen.
January 24, 1887	Charles Pomeroy Stone	N/Brig.Gen.
January 31, 1887	Wladimir Krzyzanowski	N/Brig.Gen.
February 19, 1887	Robert Brown Potter	N/Brig.Gen.
February 24, 1887	Thomas Wilberforce Egan	N/Brig.Gen.
March 29, 1887	Roswell Sabine Ripley	S/Brig.Gen.
May 18, 1887	William Smith	S/Maj.Gen.
May 30, 1887	James Phillip Simms	S/Brig.Gen.
June 17, 1887	Benjamin Franklin Potts	N/Brig.Gen.
June 22, 1887	Elliott Warren Rice	N/Brig.Gen.
July 9, 1887	Walter Chiles Whitaker	N/Brig.Gen.
July 31, 1887	Samuel Jones	S/Maj.Gen.
September 21, 1887	William Preston	S/Brig.Gen.
September 22, 1887	James Brewerton Ricketts	N/Brig.Gen.
September 23, 1887	Henry Shaw Briggs	N/Brig.Gen.
November 2, 1887	Randolph Barnes Marcy	N/Brig.Gen.
November 7, 1887	Joshua Thomas Owen	N/Brig.Gen.
December 1, 1887	William Hemsley Emory	N/Brig.Gen.
December 14, 1887	Thomas Kilby Smith	N/Brig.Gen.
December 28, 1887	John Sappington Marmaduke	S/Maj.Gen.
January 2, 1888	Alexander Chambers	N/Brig.Gen.
January 2, 1888	Isaac Ridgeway Trimble	S/Maj.Gen.
January 24, 1888	Adin Ballou Underwood	N/Brig.Gen.
February 8, 1888	Robert Houstoun Anderson	S/Brig.Gen.
April 7, 1888	Quincy Adams Gillmore	N/Maj.Gen.
April 7, 1888	John Haskell King	N/Brig.Gen.
April 21, 1888	William Dwight	N/Brig.Gen.
May 1, 1888	William Wirt Adams	S/Brig.Gen.
May 9, 1888	George Gibbs Dibrell	S/Brig.Gen.
June 1, 1888	Henry Warner Birge	N/Brig.Gen.
June 29, 1888	Washington Elliott	N/Brig.Gen.
June 29, 1888	John Baillie McIntosh	N/Brig.Gen.
July 13, 1888	Peter Burwell Starke	S/Brig.Gen.
July 23, 1888	Williams Carter Wickham	S/Brig.Gen.
July 27, 1888	Marsena Rudolph Patrick	N/Brig.Gen.
August 5, 1888	Philip Henry Sheridan	N/Maj.Gen.
August 15, 1888	Carter Stevenson	S/Maj.Gen.
August 30, 1888	Catharinus Buckingham	N/Brig.Gen.

September 5, 1888	William Terry	S/Brig.Gen.
October 21, 1888	James Craig	N/Brig.Gen.
December 4, 1888	Romeyn Beck Ayres	N/Brig.Gen.
January 12, 1889	Henry Walton Wessells	N/Brig.Gen.
January 19, 1889	Ranald Slidell Mackenzie	N/Brig.Gen.
February 11, 1889	Henry Jackson Hunt	N/Brig.Gen.
April 11, 1889	Edward Hatch	N/Brig.Gen.
April 15, 1889	Charles Kinnaird Graham	N/Brig.Gen.
May 9, 1889	William Selby Harney	N/Brig.Gen.
June 1, 1889	Edward Elmer Potter	N/Brig.Gen.
July 7, 1889	William Anderson Pile	N/Brig.Gen.
August 17, 1889	John Calvin Brown	S/Maj.Gen.
August 25, 1889	Isaac Fitzgerald Shepard	N/Brig.Gen.
September 24, 1889	Daniel Harvey Hill	S/Lt.Gen.
September 28, 1889	Samuel Davis Sturgis	N/Brig.Gen.
October 10, 1889	James Monroe Goggin	S/Brig.Gen.
October 13, 1889	Henry DeLamar Clayton	S/Maj.Gen.
October 15, 1889	Edward Aylesworth Perry	S/Brig.Gen.
October 17, 1889	John Frederick Hartranft	N/Brig.Gen.
October 30, 1889	Alfred Eugene Jackson	S/Brig.Gen.
November 22, 1889	James Morrison Hawes	S/Brig.Gen.
December 1, 1889	Collett Leventhorpe	S/Brig.Gen.
December 7, 1889	Israel Vogdes	N/Brig.Gen.
March 13, 1890	Jones Mitchell Withers	S/Maj.Gen.
March 21, 1890	George Crook	N/Maj.Gen.
March 23, 1890	Robert Cumming Schenck	N/Maj.Gen.
March 24, 1890	William Lowther Jackson	S/Brig.Gen.
March 29, 1890	Robert Huston Milroy	N/Maj.Gen.
May 12, 1890	Julius White	N/Brig.Gen.
June 7, 1890	Reuben Lindsay Walker	S/Brig.Gen.
July 3, 1890	Gilman Marston	N/Brig.Gen.
July 9, 1890	Clinton Bowen Fisk	N/Brig.Gen.
July 13, 1890	John Charles Fremont	N/Maj.Gen.
August 27, 1890	Milledge Luke Bonham	S/Brig.Gen.
September 20, 1890	John Alexander McClernand	N/Maj.Gen.
September 27, 1890	Abram Duryee	N/Brig.Gen.
October 8, 1890	William Lindsay Brandon	S/Brig.Gen.
October 13, 1890	William Worth Belknap	N/Brig.Gen.
October 21, 1890	Jeremiah Cutler Sullivan	N/Brig.Gen.
November 4, 1890	Joseph Benjamin Palmer	S/Brig.Gen.
November 14, 1890	John Converse Starkweather	N/Brig.Gen.
December 2, 1890	Cadmus Marcellus Wilcox	S/Maj.Gen.
December 16, 1890	Alfred Howe Terry	N/Maj.Gen.
January 7, 1891	Charles Devens,Jr.	N/Brig.Gen.
January 7, 1891	Jerome Bonaparte Robertson	S/Brig.Gen.
January 9, 1891	Erastus Barnard Tyler	N/Brig.Gen.
January 21, 1891	Birkett Davenport Fry	S/Brig.Gen.
January 26, 1891	Sterling Alexander Wood	S/Brig.Gen.
February 14, 1891	William Tecumseh Sherman	N/Maj.Gen.
February 15, 1891	Claudius Wistar Sears	S/Brig.Gen.
February 18, 1891	Thomas Fenwick Drayton	S/Brig.Gen.
February 18, 1891	Henry Hastings Sibley	N/Brig.Gen.
March 12, 1891	John Wallace Fuller	N/Brig.Gen.
March 21, 1891	Joseph Johnston	S/General
April 2, 1891	Albert Pike	S/Brig.Gen.
April 7, 1891	Lucius Jeremiah Gartrell	S/Brig.Gen.

April 10, 1891	John Rogers Cooke	S/Brig.Gen.
April 17, 1891	Charles Smith Hamilton	N/Maj.Gen.
April 24, 1891	Horatio Van Cleve	N/Brig.Gen.
April 29, 1891	Armistead Lindsay Long	S/Brig.Gen.
May 26, 1891	Samuel Powhatan Carter	N/Brig.Gen.
May 28, 1891	Winfield Featherston	S/Brig.Gen.
May 29, 1891	Gustavus Adolphus DeRussy	N/Brig.Gen.
June 1, 189`	David Henry Williams	N/Brig.Gen.
June 8, 1891	John McNeil	N/Brig.Gen.
June 21, 1891	Albert Gallatin Blanchard	S/Brig.Gen.
July 14, 1891	Thomas Harrison	S/Brig.Gen.
July 16, 1891	Benjamin Franklin Kelley	N/Brig.Gen.
August 12, 1891	William Whann Mackall	S/Brig.Gen.
August 28, 1891	Edward Augustus Wild	N/Brig.Gen.
September 18, 1891	Issac Ferdinand Quinby	N/Brig.Gen.
October 2, 1891	Alpheus Baker	S/Brig.Gen.
October 15, 1891	William Henry F. Lee	S/Maj.Gen.
October 30, 1891	Truman Seymour	N/Brig.Gen.
November 23, 1891	Alvin Peterson Hovey	N/Brig.Gen.
December 17, 1891	Patrick Edward Connor	N/Brig.Gen.
December 20, 1891	John Reese Kenly	N/Brig.Gen.
January 2, 1892	Montgomery Meigs	N/Brig.Gen.
January 14, 1892	Robert Ransom,Jr.	S/Maj.Gen.
January 14, 1892	James Sidney Robinson	N/Brig.Gen.
January 28, 1892	Walter Paye Lane	S/Brig.Gen.
February 8, 1892	Alfred Moore Scales	S/Brig.Gen.
February 29, 1892	George Washington Cullum	N/Brig.Gen.
April 9, 1892	Charles William Field	S/Maj.Gen.
April 10, 1892	Thomas William Sweeny	N/Brig.Gen.
April 19, 1892	William Wallace Burns	N/Brig.Gen.
April 21, 1892	Nathaniel James Jackson	N/Brig.Gen.
May 14, 1892	Thomas Algeo Rowley	N/Brig.Gen.
May 27, 1892	Ralph Pomeroy Buckland	N/Brig.Gen.
August 1, 1892	Speed Smith Fry	N/Brig.Gen.
August 1, 1892	George Baird Hodge	S/Brig.Gen.
August 9, 1892	James William Denver	N/Brig.Gen.
August 19, 1892	Henry Prince	N/Brig.Gen.
September 7, 1892	Joseph Reid Anderson	S/Brig.Gen.
September 20, 1892	Daniel Ullmann	N/Brig.Gen.
September 23, 1892	John Pope	N/Maj.Gen.
October 24, 1892	James Madison Tuttle	N/Brig.Gen.
November 3, 1892	Samuel Wylie Crawford	N/Brig.Gen.
November 5, 1892	Ferdinand Van Derveer	N/Brig.Gen.
December 1, 1892	Lucius Eugene Polk	S/Brig.Gen.
December 11, 1892	Henry Gray	S/Brig.Gen.
December 15, 1892	Randall Lee Gibson	S/Brig.Gen.
December 16, 1892	John Milton Brannan	N/Brig.Gen.
January 11, 1893	Benjamin Franklin Butler	N/Maj.Gen.
January 13, 1893	Rutherford Birchard Hayes	N/Brig.Gen.
January 14, 1893	Joseph Jackson Bartlett	N/Brig.Gen.
January 15, 1893	Rufus Ingalls	N/Brig.Gen.
January 26, 1893	Abner Doubleday	N/Brig.Gen.
January 28, 1893	Samuel Sprigg Carroll	N/Brig.Gen.
February 20, 1893	Pierre Gustave Beauregard	S/General
March 28, 1893	Edmund Kirby Smith	S/General
April 21, 1893	Richard Lee T. Beale	S/Brig.Gen.

April 27, 1893	John Murray Corse	N/Brig.Gen.
May 6, 1893	Joseph Tarr Copeland	N/Brig.Gen.
June 13, 1893	Alexander Campbell	S/Brig.Gen.
July 19, 1893	James Thadeus Holtzclaw	S/Brig.Gen.
July 20, 1893	John George Walker	S/Maj.Gen.
July 23, 1893	William Vandever	N/Brig.Gen.
July 26, 1893	George Washington Morgan	N/Brig.Gen.
September 1, 1893	James Fleming Fagan	S/Maj.Gen.
October 23, 1893	Thomas Crittenden	N/Maj.Gen.
December 24, 1893	John Wilson Sprague	N/Brig.Gen.
December 28, 1893	William Andrew Quarles	S/Brig.Gen.
January 16, 1894	William Henry Forney	S/Brig.Gen.
January 16, 1894	Nelson Taylor	N/Brig.Gen.
February 3, 1894	Charles John Stolbrand	N/Brig.Gen.
February 6, 1894	Jacob Ammen	N/Brig.Gen.
February 9, 1894	Lucius Bellinger Northrop	S/Brig.Gen.
February 14, 1894	Edward Winslow Hincks	N/Brig.Gen.
March 2, 1894	Jubal Anderson Early	S/Lt.Gen.
March 15, 1894	Robert Alexander Cameron	N/Brig.Gen.
March 26, 1894	Alfred Holt Colquitt	S/Brig.Gen.
April 8, 1894	John Edwards	N/Brig.Gen.
April 13, 1894	Joseph Brevard Kershaw	S/Maj.Gen.
April 14, 1894	Henry Warner Slocum	N/Maj.Gen.
April 25, 1894	Robert Seaman Granger	N/Brig.Gen.
May 21, 1894	Philip Cook	S/Brig.Gen.
July 11, 1894	James Barnet Fry	N/Brig.Gen.
August 1, 1894	Joseph Holt	N/Brig.Gen.
September 1, 1894	Nathaniel Prentiss Banks	N/Maj.Gen.
September 5, 1894	George Stoneman	N/Maj.Gen.
September 7, 1894	Henry Eugene Davies	N/Brig.Gen.
November 7, 1894	John Grant Mitchell	N/Brig.Gen.
November 24, 1894	William Wirt Allen	S/Brig.Gen.
December 2, 1894	Stephen Gano Burbridge	N/Brig.Gen.
December 7, 1894	Eliakim Parker Scammon	N/Brig.Gen.
December 17, 1894	Elias Smith Dennis	N/Brig.Gen.
January 9, 1895	Alfred Washington Ellet	N/Brig.Gen.
February 3, 1895	Rufus Barringer	S/Brig.Gen.
February 4, 1895	Mahlon Dickerson Manson	N/Brig.Gen.
February 11, 1895	Montgomery Dent Corse	S/Brig.Gen.
February 24, 1895	Joseph Bradford Carr	N/Brig.Gen.
February 27, 1895	Mason Brayman	N/Brig.Gen.
March 12, 1895	Henry Eustace McCulloch	S/Brig.Gen.
March 20, 1895	Philip St.George Cooke	N/Brig.Gen.
April 7, 1895	James Lawson Kemper	S/Maj.Gen.
April 15, 1895	Charles Thomas Campbell	N/Brig.Gen.
April 30, 1895	Davis Tillson	N/Brig.Gen.
May 1, 1895	John Newton	N/Maj.Gen.
May 28, 1895	Walter Quintin Gresham	N/Brig.Gen.
June 29, 1895	Green Clay Smith	N/Brig.Gen.
August 4, 1895	Marcellus Augustus Stovall	S/Brig.Gen.
August 15, 1895	John Daniel Imboden	S/Brig.Gen.
August 16, 1895	Samuel Bell Maxey	S/Maj.Gen.
September 4, 1895	August Valentine Kautz	N/Brig.Gen.
October 2, 1895	Orlando Metcalfe Poe	N/Brig.Gen.
October 8, 1895	William Mahone	S/Maj.Gen.
October 14, 1895	Erasmus Darwin Keyes	N/Maj.Gen.

October 21, 1895	Thomas Gamble Pitcher	N/Brig.Gen.
November 27, 1895	Thomas Jordan	S/Brig.Gen.
December 22, 1895	James Clifford Veatch	N/Brig.Gen.
January 6, 1896	Mortimer Dormer Leggett	N/Brig.Gen.
January 11, 1896	Francis Channing Barlow	N/Brig.Gen.
January 14, 1896	Charles Adam Heckman	N/Brig.Gen.
January 21, 1896	Thomas Ewing,Jr.	N/Brig.Gen.
February 6, 1896	John Gibbon	N/Maj.Gen.
April 14, 1896	John Doby Kennedy	S/Brig.Gen.
May 23, 1896	Lucius Fairchild	N/Brig.Gen.
May 24, 1896	John Echols	S/Brig.Gen.
June 24, 1896	Gustavus Woodson Smith	S/Maj.Gen.
July 2, 1896	Alexander Robert Lawton	S/Brig.Gen.
July 6, 1896	Pierce Manning B. Young	S/Maj.Gen.
July 29, 1896	Raleigh Edward Colston	S/Brig.Gen.
August 3, 1896	Calvin Edward Pratt	N/Brig.Gen.
September 4, 1896	Francis Asbury Shoup	S/Brig.Gen.
September 8, 1896	Richard Caswell Gatlin	S/Brig.Gen.
September 12, 1896	James Dada Morgan	N/Brig.Gen.
September 15, 1896	Joseph Robert Davis	S/Brig.Gen.
December 11, 1896	George Lafayette Beal	N/Brig.Gen.
January 22, 1897	John Dunlap Stevenson	N/Brig.Gen.
January 23, 1897	Henry Goddard Thomas	N/Brig.Gen.
January 25, 1897	Albion Parris Howe	N/Brig.Gen.
January 29, 1897	John Eugene Smith	N/Brig.Gen.
January 30, 1897	Andrew Jackson Smith	N/Maj.Gen.
February 12, 1897	Darius Nash Couch	N/Maj.Gen.
February 13, 1897	Joseph Orville Shelby	S/Brig.Gen.
February 17, 1897	Alfred Pleasonton	N/Maj.Gen.
February 18, 1897	John Cleveland Robinson	N/Brig.Gen.
February 25, 1897	Frederick Stumbaugh	N/Brig.Gen.
March 8, 1897	Friedrich Salomon	N/Brig.Gen.
March 28, 1897	William Richard Terry	S/Brig.Gen.
April 8, 1897	Thomas Church H. Smith	N/Brig.Gen.
April 21, 1897	Richard W. Johnson	N/Brig.Gen.
June 1, 1897	Daniel Ruggles	S/Brig.Gen.
July 14, 1897	John Franklin Farnsworth	N/Brig.Gen.
July 15, 1897	Philippe Regis deTrobriand	N/Brig.Gen.
July 20, 1897	Philip Dale Roddey	S/Brig.Gen.
July 24, 1897	Lafayette McLaws	S/Maj.Gen.
August 9, 1897	Samuel McGowan	S/Brig.Gen.
October 2, 1897	Neal Dow	N/Brig.Gen.
October 3, 1897	Hamilton Prioleau Bee	S/Brig.Gen.
November 3, 1897	Thomas Lanier Clingman	S/Brig.Gen.
November 17, 1897	Charles Edward Hovey	N/Brig.Gen.
November 29, 1897	John Sanford Mason	N/Brig.Gen.
December 3, 1897	Allen Thomas	S/Brig.Gen.
December 11, 1897	Justus McKinstry	N/Brig.Gen.
January 3, 1898	Lawrence Sullivan Ross	S/Brig.Gen.
January 4, 1898	Johnson Hagood	S/Brig.Gen.
January 12, 1898	John Bratton	S/Brig.Gen.
January 16, 1898	Christopher Columbus Augur	N/Maj.Gen.
January 21, 1898	Nathan Kimball	N/Brig.Gen.
February 7, 1898	John Cochrane	N/Brig.Gen.
February 27, 1898	Thomas Pleasant Dockery	S/Brig.Gen.
March 8, 1898	Edward Lloyd Thomas	S/Brig.Gen.

March 11, 1898	William George M. Davis	S/Brig.Gen.
March 11, 1898	William Starke Rosecrans	N/Maj.Gen.
April 8, 1898	William Polk Hardeman	S/Brig.Gen.
April 9, 1898	James Ronald Chalmers	S/Brig.Gen.
April 21, 1898	Edward Cary Walthall	S/Maj.Gen.
May 2, 1898	Charles Carroll Walcutt	N/Brig.Gen.
May 23, 1898	Henry Rootes Jackson	S/Brig.Gen.
July 17, 1898	John Stuart Williams	S/Brig.Gen.
September 14, 1898	Richard Busteed	N/Brig.Gen.
November 19, 1898	Don Carlos Buell	N/Maj.Gen.
December 27, 1898	William Booth Taliaferro	S/Maj.Gen.
January 28, 1899	George Sears Greene	N/Brig.Gen.
February 23, 1899	David Addison Weisiger	S/Brig.Gen.
February 25, 1899	Joseph Jones Reynolds	N/Maj.Gen.
March 4, 1899	Henry Brevard Davidson	S/Brig.Gen.
April 4, 1899	George Leonard Andrews	N/Brig.Gen.
April 8, 1899	John Wesley Turner	N/Brig.Gen.
April 23, 1899	Dandridge McRae	S/Brig.Gen.
April 24, 1899	Richard James Oglesby	N/Maj.Gen.
May 8, 1899	Manning Ferguson Force	N/Brig.Gen.
May 31, 1899	Alexander Hawthorne	S/Brig.Gen.
June 7, 1899	William Stephen Walker	S/Brig.Gen.
July 2, 1899	Horatio Gouverneur Wright	N/Maj.Gen.
August 19, 1899	Thomas Alfred Davies	N/Brig.Gen.
September 27, 1899	Henry Heth	S/Maj.Gen.
October 1, 1899	Alfred Jefferson Vaughan	S/Brig.Gen.
November 28, 1899	Robert Brank Vance	S/Brig.Gen.
December 7, 1899	Henry Hayes Lockwood	N/Brig.Gen.
December 11, 1899	Edward Ferrero	N/Brig.Gen.
January 5, 1900	William Alexander Hammond	N/Brig.Gen.
January 11, 1900	Dabney Herndon Maury	S/Maj.Gen.
February 3, 1900	William Woods Averell	N/Brig.Gen.
March 20, 1900	Zealous Bates Tower	N/Brig.Gen.
April 11, 1900	Seth Maxwell Barton	S/Brig.Gen.
July 30, 1900	William Grose	N/Brig.Gen.
August 4, 1900	Jacob Dolson Cox	N/Maj.Gen.
August 5, 1900	Zebulon York	S/Brig.Gen.
August 22, 1900	Gustave Paul Cluseret	N/Brig.Gen.
August 23, 1900	Nathaniel Harrison Harris	S/Brig.Gen.
August 26, 1900	William Hopkins Morris	N/Brig.Gen.
September 9, 1900	Innis Newton Palmer	N/Brig.Gen.
September 25, 1900	John McCauley Palmer	N/Maj.Gen.
October 29, 1900	Daniel Marsh Frost	S/Brig.Gen.
December 16, 1900	John Grubb Parke	N/Maj.Gen.
January 1, 1901	James Edwin Slaughter	S/Brig.Gen.
January 7, 1901	Louis Hebert	S/Brig.Gen.
January 7, 1901	William Gaston Lewis	S/Brig.Gen.
January 17, 1901	Leonard Fulton Ross	N/Brig.Gen.
February 8, 1901	Benjamin Mayberry Prentiss	N/Maj.Gen.
February 9, 1901	George Ear Maney	S/Brig.Gen.
March 21, 1901	William Henry Wallace	S/Brig.Gen.
March 28, 1901	Stewart Van Vliet	N/Brig.Gen.
April 1, 1901	John Robert Jones	S/Brig.Gen.
April 4, 1901	George Thomas Anderson	S/Brig.Gen.
April 12, 1901	John Porter Hatch	N/Brig.Gen.
April 12, 1901	Thomas Hart Taylor	S/Brig.Gen.

May 17, 1901	Joseph Andrew Lightburn	N/Brig.Gen.
May 21, 1901	Fitz John Porter	N/Maj.Gen.
June 15, 1901	Max Weber	N/Brig.Gen.
June 16, 1901	William Montgomery Gardner	S/Brig.Gen.
June 19, 1901	John Basil Turchin	N/Brig.Gen.
July 17, 1901	Daniel Butterfield	N/Maj.Gen.
August 7, 1901	James Scott Negley	N/Maj.Gen.
August 9, 1901	Richard Lucian Page	S/Brig.Gen.
August 10, 1901	Gilbert Moxley Sorrel	S/Brig.Gen.
August 18, 1901	Joseph Farmer Knipe	N/Brig.Gen.
September 14, 1901	Edward Henry Hobson	N/Brig.Gen.
October 1, 1901	George Washington Getty	N/Brig.Gen.
October 20, 1901	James Alexander Walker	S/Brig.Gen.
November 28, 1901	William Hugh Young	S/Brig.Gen.
December 6, 1901	James Argyle Smith	S/Brig.Gen.
December 18, 1901	William Flank Perry	S/Brig.Gen.
January 8, 1902	Francis Jay Herron	N/Maj.Gen.
January 14, 1902	Simon Goodell Griffin	N/Brig.Gen.
February 11, 1902	Egbert Benson Brown	N/Brig.Gen.
February 19, 1902	Thomas Fentress Toon	S/Brig.Gen.
March 13, 1902	David Sloane Stanley	N/Maj.Gen.
March 14, 1902	Daniel Harris Reynolds	S/Brig.Gen.
March 15, 1902	Theophilus Toulmin Garrard	N/Brig.Gen.
April 1, 1902	William Denison Whipple	N/Brig.Gen.
April 11, 1902	Wade Hampton	S/Lt.Gen.
April 22, 1902	Egbert Ludovicus Viele	N/Brig.Gen.
July 10, 1902	Isaac Hardin Duval	N/Brig.Gen.
August 21, 1902	Franz Sigel	N/Maj.Gen.
September 1, 1902	Tyree Harris Bell	S/Brig.Gen.
September 7, 1902	James Alexander Williamson	N/Brig.Gen.
September 13, 1902	John Horace Forney	S/Maj.Gen.
November 13, 1902	Evander McNair	S/Brig.Gen.
December 18, 1902	Wager Swayne	N/Brig.Gen.
January 5, 1903	Eli Long	N/Brig.Gen.
January 17, 1903	Charles Champion Gilbert	N/Brig.Gen.
February 20, 1903	Charles Camp Doolittle	N/Brig.Gen.
February 28, 1903	William Farrar Smith	N/Maj.Gen.
March 3, 1903	Robert Sanford Foster	N/Brig.Gen.
March 8, 1903	William Buel Franklin	N/Brig.Gen.
March 8, 1903	Schuyler Hamilton	N/Maj.Gen.
March 9, 1903	James Winning McMillan	N/Brig.Gen.
March 30, 1903	William Hicks Jackson	S/Brig.Gen.
June 12, 1903	Alexander McDowell McCook	N/Maj.Gen.
June 18, 1903	Frank Wheaton	N/Brig.Gen.
July 22, 1903	Cassius Marcellus Clay	N/Maj.Gen.
July 24, 1903	John Henry Hobart Ward	N/Brig.Gen.
July 28, 1903	Thomas Neville Waul	S/Brig.Gen.
September 7, 1903	John Bullock Clark,Jr.	S/Brig.Gen.
October 4, 1903	William Passmore Carlin	N/Brig.Gen.
October 5, 1903	Bradley Tyler Johnson	S/Brig.Gen.
November 22, 1903	George Hume Steuart	S/Brig.Gen.
January 2, 1904	James Longstreet	S/Lt.Gen.
January 9, 1904	John Brown Gordon	S/Maj.Gen.
March 29, 1904	William Henry F. Payne	S/Brig.Gen.
May 16, 1904	John Benjamin Sanborn	N/Brig.Gen.
July 6, 1904	Joseph Horace Lewis	S/Brig.Gen.

August 30, 1904	Milo Smith Hascall	N/Brig.Gen.
October 8, 1904	Matt Whitaker Ransom	S/Brig.Gen.
November 6, 1904	Jesse Johnson Finley	S/Brig.Gen.
December 26, 1904	William Henry Powell	N/Brig.Gen.
January 4, 1905	Nathaniel Collins McLean	N/Brig.Gen.
February 15, 1905	Lewis Wallace	N/Maj.Gen.
March 9, 1905	William Brimage Bate	S/Maj.Gen.
March 18, 1905	Joseph Roswell Hawley	N/Brig.Gen.
April 8, 1905	Cullen Andrews Battle	S/Brig.Gen.
April 14, 1905	Halbert Eleazer Paine	N/Brig.Gen.
April 28, 1905	Fitzhugh Lee	S/Maj.Gen.
May 14, 1905	Thomas James Churchill	S/Maj.Gen.
June 14, 1905	Absalom Baird	N/Brig.Gen.
June 30, 1905	Hugh Boyle Ewing	N/Brig.Gen.
July 15, 1905	Napoleon Jackson Dana	N/Maj.Gen.
July 16, 1905	Bryan Morel Thomas	S/Brig.Gen.
July 27, 1905	Robert Bullock	S/Brig.Gen.
September 5, 1905	Thomas Turpin Crittenden	N/Brig.Gen.
September 12, 1905	Lawrence Pike Graham	N/Brig.Gen.
September 18, 1905	Isaac Jones Wistar	N/Brig.Gen.
November 6, 1905	James William Reilly	N/Brig.Gen.
December 14, 1905	Herman Haupt	N/Brig.Gen.
January 2, 1906	Francis Fessenden	N/Brig.Gen.
January 25, 1906	Joseph Wheeler	S/Maj.Gen.
February 25, 1906	Thomas John Wood	N/Maj.Gen.
March 4, 1906	John McAllister Schofield	N/Maj.Gen.
March 19, 1906	James Camp Tappan	S/Brig.Gen.
March 19, 1906	John Milton Thayer	N/Brig.Gen.
March 31, 1906	John Wesley Frazer	S/Brig.Gen.
May 12, 1906	Gabriel Colvin Wharton	S/Brig.Gen.
May 14, 1906	Carl Schurz	N/Maj.Gen.
May 15, 1906	John McArthur	N/Brig.Gen.
September 30, 1906	Thomas Maley Harris	N/Brig.Gen.
January 20, 1907	Charles Miller Shelley	S/Brig.Gen.
April 10, 1907	Laurence Simmons Baker	S/Brig.Gen.
April 25, 1907	Hylan Benton Lyon	S/Brig.Gen.
May 10, 1907	Orlando Bolivar Willcox	N/Brig.Gen.
June 3, 1907	Thomas Howard Ruger	N/Brig.Gen.
June 11, 1907	John Tyler Morgan	S/Brig.Gen.
July 27, 1907	Edmund Winston Pettus	S/Brig.Gen.
August 14, 1907	William Birney	N/Brig.Gen.
September 15, 1907	Jacob Hunter Sharp	S/Brig.Gen.
September 21, 1907	James Henry Lane	S/Brig.Gen.
December 31, 1907	Albert Lindley Lee	N/Brig.Gen.
February 23, 1908	Rufus Saxton	N/Brig.Gen.
March 16, 1908	Abram Sanders Piatt	N/Brig.Gen.
April 22, 1908	Ellison Capers	S/Brig.Gen.
May 28, 1908	Stephen Dill Lee	S/Lt.Gen.
August 30, 1908	Alexander Peter Stewart	S/Lt.Gen.
October 11, 1908	Eppa Hunton	S/Brig.Gen.
November 16, 1908	Thomas John Lucas	N/Brig.Gen.
April 14, 1909	Matthew Calbraith Butler	S/Maj.Gen.
June 29, 1909	George Blake Cosby	S/Brig.Gen.
August 8, 1909	William Miller	S/Brig.Gen.
September 7, 1909	James Murrell Shackelford	N/Brig.Gen.
September 8, 1909	Frank Crawford Armstrong	S/Brig.Gen.

September 9, 1909	Edward Moody McCook	N/Brig.Gen.
October 26, 1909	Oliver Otis Howard	N/Maj.Gen.
December 18, 1909	Green Berry Raum	N/Brig.Gen.
January 6, 1910	Daniel Henry Rucker	N/Brig.Gen.
January 8, 1910	Newton Martin Curtis	N/Brig.Gen.
January 19, 1910	Robert Lowry	S/Brig.Gen.
March 13, 1910	Luther Prentice Bradley	N/Brig.Gen.
March 16, 1910	William Thompson Martin	S/Maj.Gen.
March 28, 1910	William Paul Roberts	S/Brig.Gen.
March 29, 1910	Thomas Lafayette Rosser	S/Maj.Gen.
April 20, 1910	Samuel Gibbs French	S/Maj.Gen.
April 28, 1910	Edward Porter Alexander	S/Brig.Gen.
May 20, 1910	Joseph Alexander Cooper	N/Brig.Gen.
May 29, 1910	George Francis McGinnis	N/Brig.Gen.
October 13, 1910	John Cook	N/Brig.Gen.
November 4, 1910	Charles Cleveland Dodge	N/Brig.Gen.
November 12, 1910	Beverly Holcombe Robertson	S/Brig.Gen.
December 2, 1910	Eugene Asa Carr	N/Brig.Gen.
December 3, 1910	Wesley Merritt	N/Maj.Gen.
December 5, 1910	Alfred Cumming	S/Brig.Gen.
December 8, 1910	George Doherty Johnston	S/Brig.Gen.
December 31, 1910	John Creed Moore	S/Brig.Gen.
February 12, 1911	Alexander Stewart Webb	N/Brig.Gen.
February 22, 1911	William Lewis Cabell	S/Brig.Gen.
March 12, 1911	Daniel Chevilette Govan	S/Brig.Gen.
March 31, 1911	Alfred Iverson,Jr.	S/Brig.Gen.
July 2, 1911	Clement Anselm Evans	S/Brig.Gen.
August 9, 1911	George Washington Gordon	S/Brig.Gen.
September 1, 1911	Benjamin Henry Grierson	N/Brig.Gen.
September 11, 1911	William Robertson Boggs	S/Brig.Gen.
December 28, 1911	Alexander Shaler	N/Brig.Gen.
January 4, 1912	Francis Redding Nicholls	S/Brig.Gen.
March 22, 1912	Henry Harrison Walker	S/Brig.Gen.
June 3, 1912	Julius Adolph deLagnel	S/Brig.Gen.
June 20, 1912	Edward Stuyvesant Bragg	N/Brig.Gen.
July 3, 1912	Robert Frederick Hoke	S/Maj.Gen.
August 19, 1912	Joseph Hayes	N/Brig.Gen.
August 31, 1912	John Curtis Caldwell	N/Brig.Gen.
October 26, 1912	Henry Beebee Carrington	N/Brig.Gen.
December 4, 1912	Julius Stahel	N/Maj.Gen.
February 18, 1913	George Washington C. Lee	S/Maj.Gen.
March 27, 1913	Richard Montgomery Gano	S/Brig.Gen.
May 28, 1913	Lunsford Lindsay Lomax	S/Maj.Gen.
November 15, 1913	Camille A.J.M.P. Polignac	S/Maj.Gen.
January 8, 1914	Simon Bolivar Buckner	S/Lt.Gen.
February 7, 1914	John Parker Hawkins	N/Brig.Gen.
February 24, 1914	Joshua Chamberlain	N/Brig.Gen.
March 15, 1914	Augustus Louis Chetlain	N/Brig.Gen.
May 3, 1914	Daniel Edgar Sickles	N/Maj.Gen.
August 11, 1914	Thomas Muldrup Logan	S/Brig.Gen.
August 25, 1914	Powell Clayton	N/Brig.Gen.
December 21, 1914	John Beatty	N/Brig.Gen.
March 2, 1915	Cyrus Bussey	N/Brig.Gen.
March 9, 1915	Edward Harland	N/Brig.Gen.
May 12, 1915	William Whedbee Kirkland	S/Brig.Gen.
December 13, 1915	Francis Marion Cockrell	S/Brig.Gen.

January 3, 1916	Grenville Mellen Dodge	N/Maj.Gen.
March 4, 1916	William Sooy Smith	N/Brig.Gen.
August 7, 1916	David McMurtrie Gregg	N/Brig.Gen.
August 12, 1916	Charles Jackson Paine	N/Brig.Gen.
September 16, 1916	Basil Wilson Duke	S/Brig.Gen.
January 2, 1917	Peter Joseph Osterhaus	N/Maj.Gen.
January 23, 1917	Franklin Nickerson	N/Brig.Gen.
February 3, 1917	Samuel Wragg Ferguson	S/Brig.Gen.
July 9, 1917	Selden Connor	N/Brig.Gen.
March 20, 1918	Lewis Addison Grant	N/Brig.Gen.
July 21, 1918	William McComb	S/Brig.Gen.
February 1, 1919	Robert Daniel Johnston	S/Brig.Gen.
March 14, 1919	Roger Atkinson Pryor	S/Brig.Gen.
December 26, 1919	William Ruffin Cox	S/Brig.Gen.
April 26, 1920	William Henry Seward,Jr.	N/Brig.Gen.
October 31, 1920	Evander McIvor Law	S/Brig.Gen.
September 21, 1922	Christopher Andrews	N/Brig.Gen.
October 20, 1922	Adam Rankin Johnson	S/Brig.Gen.
December 27, 1922	Marcus Joseph Wright	S/Brig.Gen.
May 21, 1923	Thomas Benton Smith	S/Brig.Gen.
December 12, 1923	Martin Davis Hardin	N/Brig.Gen.
July 10, 1924	Byron Root Pierce	N/Brig.Gen.
February 23, 1925	James Harrison Wilson	N/Brig.Gen.
May 15, 1925	Nelson Appleton Miles	N/Brig.Gen.
September 5, 1926	John Rutter Brooke	N/Brig.Gen.
January 22, 1927	John McCausland	S/Brig.Gen.
April 20, 1928	Felix Huston Robertson	S/Brig.Gen.
April 13, 1933	Adelbert Ames	N/Brig.Gen.

Civil War Generals
by Month of Death

In this chapter all the generals are listed by the month when they died.

DATE OF DEATH	GENERAL	SIDE/RANK
January 1, 1901	James Edwin Slaughter	S/Brig.Gen.
January 2, 1883	Samuel Read Anderson	S/Brig.Gen.
January 2, 1888	Alexander Chambers	N/Brig.Gen.
January 2, 1888	Isaac Ridgeway Trimble	S/Maj.Gen.
January 2, 1892	Montgomery Cunningham Meigs	N/Brig.Gen.
January 2, 1904	James Longstreet	S/Lt.Gen.
January 2, 1906	Francis Fessenden	N/Brig.Gen.
January 2, 1917	Peter Joseph Osterhaus	N/Maj.Gen.
January 3, 1872	Andrew Porter	N/Brig.Gen.
January 3, 1877	John Joseph Abercrombie	N/Brig.Gen.
January 3, 1898	Lawrence Sullivan Ross	S/Brig.Gen.
January 3, 1916	Grenville Mellen Dodge	N/Maj.Gen.
January 4, 1905	Nathaniel Collins McLean	N/Brig.Gen.
January 4, 1912	Francis Redding T. Nicholls	S/Brig.Gen.
January 4, 1863	Roger Weightman Hanson	S/Brig.Gen.
January 4, 1898	Johnson Hagood	S/Brig.Gen.
January 5, 1870	Robert Vinkler Richardson	S/Brig.Gen.
January 5, 1872	John Blair Smith Todd	N/Brig.Gen.
January 5, 1880	Benjamin Jefferson Hill	S/Brig.Gen.
January 5, 1900	William Alexander Hammond	N/Brig.Gen.
January 5, 1903	Eli Long	N/Brig.Gen.
January 6, 1870	Joseph Anthony Mower	N/Maj.Gen.
January 6, 1896	Mortimer Dormer Leggett	N/Brig.Gen.
January 6, 1910	Daniel Henry Rucker	N/Brig.Gen.
January 7, 1869	Lovell Harrison Rousseau	N/Maj.Gen.
January 7, 1873	James Henry Carleton	N/Brig.Gen.
January 7, 1891	Charles Devens,Jr.	N/Brig.Gen.
January 7, 1891	Jerome Bonaparte Robertson	S/Brig.Gen.
January 7, 1901	Louis Hebert	S/Brig.Gen.
January 7, 1901	William Gaston Lewis	S/Brig.Gen.
January 8, 1902	Francis Jay Herron	N/Maj.Gen.
January 8, 1910	Newton Martin Curtis	N/Brig.Gen.
January 8, 1914	Simon Bolivar Buckner	S/Lt.Gen.
January 9, 1872	Henry Wager Halleck	N/Maj.Gen.

January 9, 1895	Alfred Washington Ellet	N/Brig.Gen.
January 9, 1904	John Brown Gordon	S/Maj.Gen.
January 10, 1876	Gordon Granger	N/Maj.Gen.
January 11, 1885	Henry Lawrence Eustis	N/Brig.Gen.
January 11, 1893	Benjamin Franklin Butler	N/Maj.Gen.
January 11, 1896	Francis Channing Barlow	N/Brig.Gen.
January 11, 1900	Dabney Herndon Maury	S/Maj.Gen.
January 12, 1868	Frederick Steele	N/Maj.Gen.
January 12, 1885	William Steele	S/Brig.Gen.
January 12, 1889	Henry Walton Wessells	N/Brig.Gen.
January 12, 1898	John Bratton	S/Brig.Gen.
January 13, 1893	Rutherford Birchard Hayes	N/Brig.Gen.
January 14, 1866	Henry Moses Judah	N/Brig.Gen.
January 14, 1892	Robert Ransom,Jr.	S/Maj.Gen.
January 14, 1892	James Sidney Robinson	N/Brig.Gen.
January 14, 1893	Joseph Jackson Bartlett	N/Brig.Gen.
January 14, 1896	Charles Adam Heckman	N/Brig.Gen.
January 14, 1902	Simon Goodell Griffin	N/Brig.Gen.
January 15, 1863	David Rumph Jones	S/Maj.Gen.
January 15, 1883	William Nelson Pendleton	S/Brig.Gen.
January 15, 1893	Rufus Ingalls	N/Brig.Gen.
January 16, 1887	William Babcock Hazen	N/Maj.Gen.
January 16, 1894	William Henry Forney	S/Brig.Gen.
January 16, 1894	Nelson Taylor	N/Brig.Gen.
January 16, 1898	Christopher Columbus Augur	N/Maj.Gen.
January 17, 1901	Leonard Fulton Ross	N/Brig.Gen.
January 17, 1903	Charles Champion Gilbert	N/Brig.Gen.
January 18, 1873	John White Geary	N/Brig.Gen.
January 19, 1862	Felix Kirk Zollicoffer	S/Brig.Gen.
January 19, 1889	Ranald Slidell Mackenzie	N/Brig.Gen.
January 19, 1910	Robert Lowry	S/Brig.Gen.
January 20, 1907	Charles Miller Shelley	S/Brig.Gen.
January 21, 1868	Alexander Sandor Asboth	N/Brig.Gen.
January 21, 1891	Birkett Davenport Fry	S/Brig.Gen.
January 21, 1896	Thomas Ewing,Jr.	N/Brig.Gen.
January 21, 1898	Nathan Kimball	N/Brig.Gen.
January 22, 1871	William Raine Peck	S/Brig.Gen.
January 22, 1878	August Willich	N/Brig.Gen.
January 22, 1879	John Porter McCown	S/Maj.Gen.
January 22, 1882	Silas Casey	N/Maj.Gen.
January 22, 1897	John Dunlap Stevenson	N/Brig.Gen.
January 22, 1927	John McCausland	S/Brig.Gen.
January 23, 1897	Henry Goddard Thomas	N/Brig.Gen.
January 23, 1917	Franklin Stillman Nickerson	N/Brig.Gen.
January 24, 1864	Stephen Gardner Champlin	N/Brig.Gen.
January 24, 1887	Charles Pomeroy Stone	N/Brig.Gen.
January 24, 1888	Adin Ballou Underwood	N/Brig.Gen.
January 25, 1872	Richard Stoddert Ewell	S/Lt.Gen.
January 25, 1897	Albion Parris Howe	N/Brig.Gen.
January 25, 1906	Joseph Wheeler	S/Maj.Gen.
January 26, 1882	Robert Byington Mitchell	N/Brig.Gen.
January 26, 1891	Sterling Alexander M. Wood	S/Brig.Gen.
January 26, 1893	Abner Doubleday	N/Brig.Gen.
January 28, 1892	Walter Paye Lane	S/Brig.Gen.
January 28, 1893	Samuel Sprigg Carroll	N/Brig.Gen.
January 28, 1899	George Sears Greene	N/Brig.Gen.

January 29, 1875	Benjamin Stone Roberts	N/Brig.Gen.
January 29, 1897	John Eugene Smith	N/Brig.Gen.
January 30, 1897	Andrew Jackson Smith	N/Maj.Gen.
January 31, 1875	Edward Higgins	S/Brig.Gen.
January 31, 1887	Wladimir Krzyzanowski	N/Brig.Gen.
February 1, 1919	Robert Daniel Johnston	S/Brig.Gen.
February 1, 1885	James Chesnut, Jr.	S/Brig.Gen.
February 2, 1885	John Wolcott Phelps	N/Brig.Gen.
February 2, 1886	David Hunter	N/Maj.Gen.
February 3, 1879	George Cadwalader	N/Maj.Gen.
February 3, 1894	Charles John Stolbrand	N/Brig.Gen.
February 3, 1895	Rufus Barringer	S/Brig.Gen.
February 3, 1900	William Woods Averell	N/Brig.Gen.
February 3, 1917	Samuel Wragg Ferguson	S/Brig.Gen.
February 4, 1895	Mahlon Dickerson Manson	N/Brig.Gen.
February 6, 1865	John Pegram	S/Brig.Gen.
February 6, 1894	Jacob Ammen	N/Brig.Gen.
February 6, 1896	John Gibbon	N/Maj.Gen.
February 7, 1865	John Henry Winder	S/Brig.Gen.
February 7, 1875	William Hays	N/Brig.Gen.
February 7, 1883	Edmund Jackson Davis	N/Brig.Gen.
February 7, 1898	John Cochrane	N/Brig.Gen.
February 7, 1914	John Parker Hawkins	N/Brig.Gen.
February 8, 1880	George Sykes	N/Maj.Gen.
February 8, 1888	Robert Houstoun Anderson	S/Brig.Gen.
February 8, 1892	Alfred Moore Scales	S/Brig.Gen.
February 8, 1901	Benjamin Mayberry Prentiss	N/Maj.Gen.
February 9, 1867	Jacob Gartner Lauman	N/Brig.Gen.
February 9, 1884	James Isham Gilbert	N/Brig.Gen.
February 9, 1886	Winfield Scott Hancock	N/Maj.Gen.
February 9, 1894	Lucius Bellinger Northrop	S/Brig.Gen.
February 9, 1901	George Earl Maney	S/Brig.Gen.
February 11, 1882	William MacRae	S/Brig.Gen.
February 11, 1883	George Webb Morell	N/Maj.Gen.
February 11, 1889	Henry Jackson Hunt	N/Brig.Gen.
February 11, 1895	Montgomery Dent Corse	S/Brig.Gen.
February 11, 1902	Egbert Benson Brown	N/Brig.Gen.
February 12, 1869	James Barnes	N/Brig.Gen.
February 12, 1897	Darius Nash Couch	N/Maj.Gen.
February 12, 1911	Alexander Stewart Webb	N/Brig.Gen.
February 13, 1869	George Day Wagner	N/Brig.Gen.
February 13, 1897	Joseph Orville Shelby	S/Brig.Gen.
February 14, 1870	St.John Richardson Liddell	S/Brig.Gen.
February 14, 1883	Edwin Denison Morgan	N/Maj.Gen.
February 14, 1891	William Tecumseh Sherman	N/Maj.Gen.
February 14, 1894	Edward Winslow Hincks	N/Brig.Gen.
February 15, 1891	Claudius Wistar Sears	S/Brig.Gen.
February 15, 1905	Lewis Wallace	N/Maj.Gen.
February 17, 1897	Alfred Pleasonton	N/Maj.Gen.
February 18, 1871	John Bankhead Magruder	S/Maj.Gen.
February 18, 1873	Charles Mynn Thruston	N/Brig.Gen.
February 18, 1874	Louis Trezevant Wigfall	S/Brig.Gen.
February 18, 1879	Robert Hall Chilton	S/Brig.Gen.
February 18, 1891	Thomas Fenwick Drayton	S/Brig.Gen.
February 18, 1891	Henry Hastings Sibley	N/Brig.Gen.
February 18, 1897	John Cleveland Robinson	N/Brig.Gen.

February 18, 1913	George Washington C. Lee	S/Maj.Gen.
February 19, 1864	William Edwin Baldwin	S/Brig.Gen.
February 19, 1883	Patrick Theodore Moore	S/Brig.Gen.
February 19, 1887	Robert Brown Potter	N/Brig.Gen.
February 19, 1902	Thomas Fentress Toon	S/Brig.Gen.
February 20, 1893	Pierre Gustave T. Beauregard	S/General
February 20, 1903	Charles Camp Doolittle	N/Brig.Gen.
February 21, 1866	Stephen Elliott,Jr.	S/Brig.Gen.
February 21, 1871	Arnold Elzey	S/Maj.Gen.
February 21, 1877	Amos Beebe Eaton	N/Brig.Gen.
February 22, 1911	William Lewis Cabell	S/Brig.Gen.
February 23, 1875	James Edward Harrison	S/Brig.Gen.
February 23, 1899	David Addison Weisiger	S/Brig.Gen.
February 23, 1908	Rufus Saxton	N/Brig.Gen.
February 23, 1925	James Harrison Wilson	N/Brig.Gen.
February 24, 1887	Thomas Wilberforce Egan	N/Brig.Gen.
February 24, 1895	Joseph Bradford Carr	N/Brig.Gen.
February 24, 1914	Joshua Lawrence Chamberlain	N/Brig.Gen.
February 25, 1877	Adolph Wilhelm von Steinwehr	N/Brig.Gen.
February 25, 1897	Frederick Shearer Stumbaugh	N/Brig.Gen.
February 25, 1899	Joseph Jones Reynolds	N/Maj.Gen.
February 25, 1906	Thomas John Wood	N/Maj.Gen.
February 26, 1868	George Archibald McCall	N/Brig.Gen.
February 26, 1885	Charles Robert Woods	N/Brig.Gen.
February 27, 1866	John King Jackson	S/Brig.Gen.
February 27, 1885	Mark Perrin Lowrey	S/Brig.Gen.
February 27, 1895	Mason Brayman	N/Brig.Gen.
February 27, 1898	Thomas Pleasant Dockery	S/Brig.Gen.
February 28, 1903	William Farrar Smith	N/Maj.Gen.
February 29, 1892	George Washington Cullum	N/Brig.Gen.
March 2, 1862	Frederick West Lander	N/Brig.Gen.
March 2, 1873	Edward Johnson	S/Maj.Gen.
March 2, 1875	Lorenzo Thomas	N/Brig.Gen.
March 2, 1883	Dudley McIver DuBose	S/Brig.Gen.
March 2, 1894	Jubal Anderson Early	S/Lt.Gen.
March 2, 1915	Cyrus Bussey	N/Brig.Gen.
March 3, 1903	Robert Sanford Foster	N/Brig.Gen.
March 4, 1899	Henry Brevard Davidson	S/Brig.Gen.
March 4, 1906	John McAllister Schofield	N/Maj.Gen.
March 4, 1916	William Sooy Smith	N/Brig.Gen.
March 5, 1886	Henry Morris Naglee	N/Brig.Gen.
March 6, 1882	Zachariah Cantey Deas	S/Brig.Gen.
March 7, 1862	Ben McCulloch	S/Brig.Gen.
March 7, 1862	James McQueen McIntosh	S/Brig.Gen.
March 8, 1886	John Franklin Miller	N/Brig.Gen.
March 8, 1897	Friedrich Salomon	N/Brig.Gen.
March 8, 1898	Edward Lloyd Thomas	S/Brig.Gen.
March 8, 1903	William Buel Franklin	N/Brig.Gen.
March 8, 1903	Schuyler Hamilton	N/Maj.Gen.
March 9, 1903	James Winning McMillan	N/Brig.Gen.
March 9, 1905	William Brimage Bate	S/Maj.Gen.
March 9, 1915	Edward Harland	N/Brig.Gen.
March 10, 1865	William Henry C. Whiting	S/Maj.Gen.
March 11, 1898	William George M. Davis	S/Brig.Gen.
March 11, 1898	William Starke Rosecrans	N/Maj.Gen.
March 12, 1876	Joseph Dana Webster	N/Brig.Gen.

March 12, 1885	Thomas Hewson Neill	N/Brig.Gen.
March 12, 1891	John Wallace Fuller	N/Brig.Gen.
March 12, 1895	Henry Eustace McCulloch	S/Brig.Gen.
March 12, 1911	Daniel Chevilette Govan	S/Brig.Gen.
March 13, 1890	Jones Mitchell Withers	S/Maj.Gen.
March 13, 1902	David Sloane Stanley	N/Maj.Gen.
March 13, 1910	Luther Prentice Bradley	N/Brig.Gen.
March 14, 1867	William Plummer Benton	N/Brig.Gen.
March 14, 1902	Daniel Harris Reynolds	S/Brig.Gen.
March 14, 1919	Roger Atkinson Pryor	S/Brig.Gen.
March 15, 1870	James Wolfe Ripley	N/Brig.Gen.
March 15, 1881	Emory Upton	N/Brig.Gen.
March 15, 1883	Henry Constantine Wayne	S/Brig.Gen.
March 15, 1894	Robert Alexander Cameron	N/Brig.Gen.
March 15, 1902	Theophilus Toulmin Garrard	N/Brig.Gen.
March 15, 1914	Augustus Louis Chetlain	N/Brig.Gen.
March 16, 1867	William Kerley Strong	N/Brig.Gen.
March 16, 1879	Thomas West Sherman	N/Brig.Gen.
March 16, 1910	William Thompson Martin	S/Maj.Gen.
March 16, 1908	Abram Sanders Piatt	N/Brig.Gen.
March 18, 1905	Joseph Roswell Hawley	N/Brig.Gen.
March 19, 1880	George Hector Tyndale	N/Brig.Gen.
March 19, 1884	Godfrey Weitzel	N/Maj.Gen.
March 19, 1906	James Camp Tappan	S/Brig.Gen.
March 19, 1906	John Milton Thayer	N/Brig.Gen.
March 20, 1876	Richard Waterhouse	S/Brig.Gen.
March 20, 1895	Philip St.George Cooke	N/Brig.Gen.
March 20, 1900	Zealous Bates Tower	N/Brig.Gen.
March 20, 1918	Lewis Addison Grant	N/Brig.Gen.
March 21, 1862	William Yarnel Slack	S/Brig.Gen.
March 21, 1863	Edwin Vose Sumner	N/Maj.Gen.
March 21, 1867	Joseph Bailey	N/Brig.Gen.
March 21, 1890	George Crook	N/Maj.Gen.
March 21, 1891	Joseph Eggleston Johnston	S/General
March 21, 1901	William Henry Wallace	S/Brig.Gen.
March 22, 1912	Henry Harrison Walker	S/Brig.Gen.
March 23, 1866	Seth Williams	N/Brig.Gen.
March 23, 1883	Charles Cruft	N/Brig.Gen.
March 23, 1890	Robert Cumming Schenck	N/Maj.Gen.
March 24, 1867	John Decatur Barry	S/Brig.Gen.
March 24, 1890	William Lowther Jackson	S/Brig.Gen.
March 25, 1877	Elkanah Brackin Greer	S/Brig.Gen.
March 26, 1894	Alfred Holt Colquitt	S/Brig.Gen.
March 27, 1882	Stephen Augustus Hurlbut	N/Maj.Gen.
March 27, 1913	Richard Montgomery Gano	S/Brig.Gen.
March 28, 1863	James Cooper	N/Brig.Gen.
March 28, 1870	George Henry Thomas	N/Maj.Gen.
March 28, 1872	Humphrey Marshall	S/Brig.Gen.
March 28, 1883	Napoleon Bonaparte Buford	N/Brig.Gen.
March 28, 1893	Edmund Kirby Smith	S/General
March 28, 1897	William Richard Terry	S/Brig.Gen.
March 28, 1901	Stewart Van Vliet	N/Brig.Gen.
March 28, 1910	William Paul Roberts	S/Brig.Gen.
March 29, 1887	Roswell Sabine Ripley	S/Brig.Gen.
March 29, 1890	Robert Huston Milroy	N/Maj.Gen.
March 29, 1904	William Henry F. Payne	S/Brig.Gen.

March 29, 1910	Thomas Lafayette Rosser	S/Maj.Gen.
March 30, 1872	John Morrison Oliver	N/Brig.Gen.
March 30, 1903	William Hicks Jackson	S/Brig.Gen.
March 31, 1906	John Wesley Frazer	S/Brig.Gen.
March 31, 1911	Alfred Iverson,Jr.	S/Brig.Gen.
April 1, 1901	John Robert Jones	S/Brig.Gen.
April 1, 1902	William Denison Whipple	N/Brig.Gen.
April 2, 1865	Ambrose Powell Hill	S/Lt.Gen.
April 2, 1891	Albert Pike	S/Brig.Gen.
April 3, 1867	George Wythe Randolph	S/Brig.Gen.
April 4, 1870	Albert Rust	S/Brig.Gen.
April 4, 1878	Thomas Casimer Devin	N/Brig.Gen.
April 4, 1899	George Leonard Andrews	N/Brig.Gen.
April 4, 1901	George Thomas Anderson	S/Brig.Gen.
April 6, 1862	Albert Sidney Johnston	S/General
April 6, 1865	John Austin Wharton	S/Maj.Gen.
April 7, 1865	Thomas Alfred Smyth	N/Brig.Gen.
April 7, 1880	Isaac Munroe St.John	S/Brig.Gen.
April 7, 1888	Quincy Adams Gillmore	N/Maj.Gen.
April 7, 1888	John Haskell King	N/Brig.Gen.
April 7, 1891	Lucius Jeremiah Gartrell	S/Brig.Gen.
April 7, 1895	James Lawson Kemper	S/Maj.Gen.
April 8, 1864	Jean Jacques A.A. Mouton	S/Brig.Gen.
April 8, 1867	John Selden Roane	S/Brig.Gen.
April 8, 1894	John Edwards	N/Brig.Gen.
April 8, 1897	Thomas Church H. Smith	N/Brig.Gen.
April 8, 1898	William Polk Hardeman	S/Brig.Gen.
April 8, 1899	John Wesley Turner	N/Brig.Gen.
April 8, 1905	Cullen Andrews Battle	S/Brig.Gen.
April 9, 1881	Martin Witherspoon Gary	S/Brig.Gen.
April 9, 1892	Charles William Field	S/Maj.Gen.
April 9, 1898	James Ronald Chalmers	S/Brig.Gen.
April 10, 1862	William Harvey L. Wallace	N/Brig.Gen.
April 10, 1891	John Rogers Cooke	S/Brig.Gen.
April 10, 1892	Thomas William Sweeny	N/Brig.Gen.
April 10, 1907	Laurence Simmons Baker	S/Brig.Gen.
April 11, 1873	Edward Richard S. Canby	N/Maj.Gen.
April 11, 1875	Andrew Jackson Hamilton	N/Brig.Gen.
April 11, 1884	George Washington Deitzler	N/Brig.Gen.
April 11, 1889	Edward Hatch	N/Brig.Gen.
April 11, 1900	Seth Maxwell Barton	S/Brig.Gen.
April 11, 1902	Wade Hampton	S/Lt.Gen.
April 12, 1862	Adley Hogan Gladden	S/Brig.Gen.
April 12, 1864	Thomas Green	S/Brig.Gen.
April 12, 1879	Richard Taylor	S/Lt.Gen.
April 12, 1901	John Porter Hatch	N/Brig.Gen.
April 12, 1901	Thomas Hart Taylor	S/Brig.Gen.
April 13, 1894	Joseph Brevard Kershaw	S/Maj.Gen.
April 13, 1933	Adelbert Ames	N/Brig.Gen.
April 14, 1894	Henry Warner Slocum	N/Maj.Gen.
April 14, 1896	John Doby Kennedy	S/Brig.Gen.
April 14, 1905	Halbert Eleazer Paine	N/Brig.Gen.
April 14, 1909	Matthew Calbraith Butler	S/Maj.Gen.
April 15, 1889	Charles Kinnaird Graham	N/Brig.Gen.
April 15, 1895	Charles Thomas Campbell	N/Brig.Gen.
April 16, 1865	Robert Charles Tyler	S/Brig.Gen.

April 16, 1871	Ebenezer Dumont	N/Brig.Gen.
April 16, 1874	John Thomas Croxton	N/Brig.Gen.
April 17, 1863	Daniel Smith Donelson	S/Maj.Gen.
April 17, 1891	Charles Smith Hamilton	N/Maj.Gen.
April 19, 1870	Thomas Jefferson McKean	N/Brig.Gen.
April 19, 1892	William Wallace Burns	N/Brig.Gen.
April 20, 1880	Joseph Warren Revere	N/Brig.Gen.
April 20, 1910	Samuel Gibbs French	S/Maj.Gen.
April 20, 1928	Felix Huston Robertson	S/Brig.Gen.
April 21, 1876	Thomas Moore Scott	S/Brig.Gen.
April 21, 1878	John James Peck	N/Maj.Gen.
April 21, 1879	John Adams Dix	N/Maj.Gen.
April 21, 1888	William Dwight	N/Brig.Gen.
April 21, 1892	Nathaniel James Jackson	N/Brig.Gen.
April 21, 1893	Richard Lee T. Beale	S/Brig.Gen.
April 21, 1897	Richard W. Johnson	N/Brig.Gen.
April 21, 1898	Edward Cary Walthall	S/Maj.Gen.
April 22, 1864	Joseph Gilbert Totten	N/Brig.Gen.
April 22, 1866	Henry Watkins Allen	S/Brig.Gen.
April 22, 1902	Egbert Ludovicus Viele	N/Brig.Gen.
April 22, 1908	Ellison Capers	S/Brig.Gen.
April 23, 1865	James Dearing	S/Brig.Gen.
April 23, 1899	Dandridge McRae	S/Brig.Gen.
April 24, 1891	Horatio Phillips Van Cleve	N/Brig.Gen.
April 24, 1899	Richard James Oglesby	N/Maj.Gen.
April 25, 1862	Charles Ferguson Smith	N/Maj.Gen.
April 25, 1894	Robert Seaman Granger	N/Brig.Gen.
April 25, 1907	Hylan Benton Lyon	S/Brig.Gen.
April 26, 1920	William Henry Seward,Jr.	N/Brig.Gen.
April 27, 1879	Alfred Sully	N/Brig.Gen.
April 27, 1893	John Murray Corse	N/Brig.Gen.
April 28, 1883	William Montague Browne	S/Brig.Gen.
April 28, 1905	Fitzhugh Lee	S/Maj.Gen.
April 28, 1910	Edward Porter Alexander	S/Brig.Gen.
April 29, 1873	Franklin Gardner	S/Maj.Gen.
April 29, 1879	Douglas Hancock Cooper	S/Brig.Gen.
April 29, 1891	Armistead Lindsay Long	S/Brig.Gen.
April 30, 1864	William Read Scurry	S/Brig.Gen.
April 30, 1895	Davis Tillson	N/Brig.Gen.
May 1, 1863	Edward Dorr Tracy	S/Brig.Gen.
May 1, 1880	Samuel Peter Heintzelman	N/Maj.Gen.
May 1, 1881	John Smith Preston	S/Brig.Gen.
May 1, 1888	William Wirt Adams	S/Brig.Gen.
May 1, 1895	John Newton	N/Maj.Gen.
May 2, 1898	Charles Carroll Walcutt	N/Brig.Gen.
May 3, 1863	Hiram Gregory Berry	N/Maj.Gen.
May 3, 1863	Elisha Franklin Paxton	S/Brig.Gen.
May 3, 1868	William Henry Carroll	S/Brig.Gen.
May 3, 1914	Daniel Edgar Sickles	N/Maj.Gen.
May 4, 1885	Irvin McDowell	N/Maj.Gen.
May 5, 1864	Alexander Hays	N/Brig.Gen.
May 5, 1864	John Marshall Jones	S/Brig.Gen.
May 5, 1886	Gabriel Rene Paul	N/Brig.Gen.
May 6, 1864	Micah Jenkins	S/Brig.Gen.
May 6, 1893	Joseph Tarr Copeland	N/Brig.Gen.
May 7, 1863	Amiel Weeks Whipple	N/Brig.Gen.

May 7, 1863	Earl Van Dorn	S/Maj.Gen.
May 7, 1877	James Patrick Major	S/Brig.Gen.
May 8, 1864	Leroy Augustus Stafford	S/Brig.Gen.
May 8, 1864	James Samuel Wadsworth	N/Brig.Gen.
May 8, 1899	Manning Ferguson Force	N/Brig.Gen.
May 9, 1864	John Sedgwick	N/Maj.Gen.
May 9, 1888	George Gibbs Dibrell	S/Brig.Gen.
May 9, 1889	William Selby Harney	N/Brig.Gen.
May 10, 1863	Thomas Jonathon Jackson	S/Lt.Gen.
May 10, 1864	James Clay Rice	N/Brig.Gen.
May 10, 1864	Thomas Greely Stevenson	N/Brig.Gen.
May 10, 1886	Albin Francisco Schoepf	N/Brig.Gen.
May 10, 1907	Orlando Bolivar Willcox	N/Brig.Gen.
May 12, 1864	Abner Monroe Perrin	S/Brig.Gen.
May 12, 1864	James Ewell Brown Stuart	S/Maj.Gen.
May 12, 1890	Julius White	N/Brig.Gen.
May 12, 1906	Gabriel Colvin Wharton	S/Brig.Gen.
May 12, 1915	William Whedbee Kirkland	S/Brig.Gen.
May 13, 1864	Junius Daniel	S/Brig.Gen.
May 14, 1882	John Gross Barnard	N/Brig.Gen.
May 14, 1882	Cadwallader Colden Washburn	N/Maj.Gen.
May 14, 1892	Thomas Algeo Rowley	N/Brig.Gen.
May 14, 1905	Thomas James Churchill	S/Maj.Gen.
May 15, 1879	Kenner Garrard	N/Brig.Gen.
May 15, 1883	Josiah Gorgas	S/Brig.Gen.
May 15, 1906	John McArthur	N/Brig.Gen.
May 15, 1925	Nelson Appleton Miles	N/Brig.Gen.
May 16, 1862	Joseph Lewis Hogg	S/Brig.Gen.
May 16, 1863	Lloyd Tilghman	S/Brig.Gen.
May 16, 1904	John Benjamin Sanborn	N/Brig.Gen.
May 17, 1875	John Cabell Breckinridge	S/Maj.Gen.
May 17, 1901	Joseph Andrew J. Lightburn	N/Brig.Gen.
May 18, 1862	William High Keim	N/Brig.Gen.
May 18, 1864	James Byron Gordon	S/Brig.Gen.
May 18, 1887	William Smith	S/Maj.Gen.
May 20, 1874	Alexander Brydie Dyer	N/Brig.Gen.
May 20, 1876	Willis Arnold Gorman	N/Brig.Gen.
May 20, 1881	William Henry French	N/Maj.Gen.
May 20, 1910	Joseph Alexander Cooper	N/Brig.Gen.
May 21, 1864	Albert Gallatin Jenkins	S/Brig.Gen.
May 21, 1894	Philip Cook	S/Brig.Gen.
May 21, 1901	Fitz John Porter	N/Maj.Gen.
May 21, 1923	Thomas Benton Smith	S/Brig.Gen.
May 22, 1868	Isham Nicholas Haynie	N/Brig.Gen.
May 22, 1884	William Tatum Wofford	S/Brig.Gen.
May 23, 1882	George Douglas Ramsay	N/Brig.Gen.
May 23, 1896	Lucius Fairchild	N/Brig.Gen.
May 23, 1898	Henry Rootes Jackson	S/Brig.Gen.
May 24, 1896	John Echols	S/Brig.Gen.
May 26, 1876	Alexander Welch Reynolds	S/Brig.Gen.
May 26, 1885	Samuel Beatty	N/Brig.Gen.
May 26, 1891	Samuel Powhatan Carter	N/Brig.Gen.
May 27, 1892	Ralph Pomeroy Buckland	N/Brig.Gen.
May 28, 1891	Winfield Scott Featherston	S/Brig.Gen.
May 28, 1895	Walter Quintin Gresham	N/Brig.Gen.
May 28, 1908	Stephen Dill Lee	S/Lt.Gen.

May 28, 1913	Lunsford Lindsay Lomax	S/Maj.Gen.
May 29, 1866	Winfield Scott	N/Maj.Gen.
May 29, 1891	Gustavus Adolphus DeRussy	N/Brig.Gen.
May 29, 1910	George Francis McGinnis	N/Brig.Gen.
May 30, 1887	James Phillip Simms	S/Brig.Gen.
May 31, 1862	Robert Hopkins Hatton	S/Brig.Gen.
May 31, 1899	Alexander Travis Hawthorne	S/Brig.Gen.
June 1, 1871	William Reading Montgomery	N/Brig.Gen.
June 1, 1879	James Shields	N/Brig.Gen.
June 1, 1884	Henry Washington Benham	N/Brig.Gen.
June 1, 1884	Mansfield Lovell	S/Maj.Gen.
June 1, 1886	George Jerrison Stannard	N/Brig.Gen.
June 1, 1888	Henry Warner Birge	N/Brig.Gen.
June 1, 1889	Edward Elmer Potter	N/Brig.Gen.
June 1, 1891	David Henry Williams	N/Brig.Gen.
June 1, 1897	Daniel Ruggles	S/Brig.Gen.
June 2, 1864	George Pierce Doles	S/Brig.Gen.
June 3, 1907	Thomas Howard Ruger	N/Brig.Gen.
June 3, 1912	Julius Adolph deLagnel	S/Brig.Gen.
June 5, 1864	William Edmonson Jones	S/Brig.Gen.
June 6, 1862	Turner Ashby	S/Brig.Gen.
June 6, 1885	Cuvier Grover	N/Brig.Gen.
June 7, 1890	Reuben Lindsay Walker	S/Brig.Gen.
June 7, 1899	William Stephen Walker	S/Brig.Gen.
June 8, 1891	John McNeil	N/Brig.Gen.
June 9, 1877	Hugh Weedon Mercer	S/Brig.Gen.
June 9, 1884	Abraham Buford	S/Brig.Gen.
June 11, 1907	John Tyler Morgan	S/Brig.Gen.
June 12, 1903	Alexander McDowell McCook	N/Maj.Gen.
June 13, 1872	Daniel Weisiger Adams	S/Brig.Gen.
June 13, 1893	Alexander William Campbell	S/Brig.Gen.
June 14, 1864	Leonidas Polk	S/Lt.Gen.
June 14, 1905	Absalom Baird	N/Brig.Gen.
June 15, 1901	Max Weber	N/Brig.Gen.
June 16, 1882	George Henry Chapman	N/Brig.Gen.
June 16, 1901	William Montgomery Gardner	S/Brig.Gen.
June 17, 1864	James St.Clair Morton	N/Brig.Gen.
June 17, 1887	Benjamin Franklin Potts	N/Brig.Gen.
June 18, 1903	Frank Wheaton	N/Brig.Gen.
June 19, 1901	John Basil Turchin	N/Brig.Gen.
June 20, 1882	Theodore Washington Brevard	S/Brig.Gen.
June 20, 1912	Edward Stuyvesant Bragg	N/Brig.Gen.
June 21, 1878	Fitz-Henry Warren	N/Brig.Gen.
June 21, 1880	Theophilus Hunter Holmes	S/Lt.Gen.
June 21, 1891	Albert Gallatin Blanchard	S/Brig.Gen.
June 22, 1869	Henry Dwight Terry	N/Brig.Gen.
June 22, 1887	Elliott Warren Rice	N/Brig.Gen.
June 24, 1896	Gustavus Woodson Smith	S/Maj.Gen.
June 25, 1863	Martin Edwin Green	S/Brig.Gen.
June 25, 1876	George Armstrong Custer	N/Brig.Gen.
June 26, 1864	Charles Garrison Harker	N/Brig.Gen.
June 26, 1879	Richard Heron Anderson	S/Lt.Gen.
June 26, 1881	John Wynn Davidson	N/Brig.Gen.
June 26, 1883	James Conner	S/Brig.Gen.
June 28, 1871	William Scott Ketchum	N/Brig.Gen.
June 29, 1862	Richard Griffith	S/Brig.Gen.

June 29, 1864	Joseph Pannell Taylor	N/Brig.Gen.
June 29, 1888	Washington Lafayette Elliott	N/Brig.Gen.
June 29, 1888	John Baillie McIntosh	N/Brig.Gen.
June 29, 1895	Green Clay Smith	N/Brig.Gen.
June 29, 1909	George Blake Cosby	S/Brig.Gen.
June 30, 1874	James Cantey	S/Brig.Gen.
June 30, 1882	Joseph K. Barnes	N/Brig.Gen.
June 30, 1905	Hugh Boyle Ewing	N/Brig.Gen.
July 1, 1863	John Fulton Reynolds	N/Maj.Gen.
July 1, 1867	Thomas Francis Meagher	N/Brig.Gen.
July 2, 1863	Stephen Hinsdale Weed	N/Brig.Gen.
July 2, 1896	Alexander Robert Lawton	S/Brig.Gen.
July 2, 1899	Horatio Gouverneur Wright	N/Maj.Gen.
July 2, 1911	Clement Anselm Evans	S/Brig.Gen.
July 3, 1861	Robert Selden Garnett	S/Brig.Gen.
July 3, 1863	William Barksdale	S/Brig.Gen.
July 3, 1863	Elon John Farnsworth	N/Brig.Gen.
July 3, 1863	Richard Brooke Garnett	S/Brig.Gen.
July 3, 1863	Samuel Kosciuszko Zook	N/Brig.Gen.
July 3, 1890	Gilman Marston	N/Brig.Gen.
July 3, 1912	Robert Frederick Hoke	S/Maj.Gen.
July 5, 1863	Lewis Addison Armistead	S/Brig.Gen.
July 6, 1864	Samuel Allen Rice	N/Brig.Gen.
July 6, 1896	Pierce Manning B. Young	S/Maj.Gen.
July 6, 1904	Joseph Horace Lewis	S/Brig.Gen.
July 7, 1889	William Anderson Pile	N/Brig.Gen.
July 8, 1875	Francis Preston Blair,Jr.	N/Maj.Gen.
July 9, 1874	Robert Cowdin	N/Brig.Gen.
July 9, 1887	Walter Chiles Whitaker	N/Brig.Gen.
July 9, 1890	Clinton Bowen Fisk	N/Brig.Gen.
July 9, 1917	Selden Connor	N/Brig.Gen.
July 10, 1863	Paul Jones Semmes	S/Brig.Gen.
July 10, 1875	Henry Lewis Benning	S/Brig.Gen.
July 10, 1902	Isaac Hardin Duval	N/Brig.Gen.
July 10, 1924	Byron Root Pierce	N/Brig.Gen.
July 11, 1894	James Barnet Fry	N/Brig.Gen.
July 13, 1863	John Stevens Bowen	S/Maj.Gen.
July 13, 1881	John Clifford Pemberton	S/Lt.Gen.
July 13, 1888	Peter Burwell Starke	S/Brig.Gen.
July 13, 1890	John Charles Fremont	N/Maj.Gen.
July 14, 1891	Thomas Harrison	S/Brig.Gen.
July 14, 1897	John Franklin Farnsworth	N/Brig.Gen.
July 15, 1862	David Emanuel Twiggs	S/Maj.Gen.
July 15, 1897	Philippe Regis deTrobriand	N/Brig.Gen.
July 15, 1905	Napoleon Jackson T. Dana	N/Maj.Gen.
July 16, 1891	Benjamin Franklin Kelley	N/Brig.Gen.
July 16, 1905	Bryan Morel Thomas	S/Brig.Gen.
July 17, 1863	James Johnston Pettigrew	S/Brig.Gen.
July 17, 1898	John Stuart Williams	S/Brig.Gen.
July 17, 1901	Daniel Butterfield	N/Maj.Gen.
July 18, 1863	William Dorsey Pender	S/Maj.Gen.
July 18, 1879	William Farquhar Barry	N/Brig.Gen.
July 19, 1870	William Thomas H. Brooks	N/Maj.Gen.
July 19, 1874	Abner Clark Harding	N/Brig.Gen.
July 19, 1893	James Thadeus Holtzclaw	S/Brig.Gen.
July 20, 1878	George Foster Shepley	N/Brig.Gen.

July 20, 1893	John George Walker	S/Maj.Gen.
July 20, 1897	Philip Dale Roddey	S/Brig.Gen.
July 21, 1863	Edward Needles Kirk	N/Brig.Gen.
July 21, 1918	William McComb	S/Brig.Gen.
July 22, 1861	Barnard Elliott Bee	S/Brig.Gen.
July 22, 1864	James Birdseye McPherson	N/Maj.Gen.
July 22, 1864	William Henry T. Walker	S/Maj.Gen.
July 22, 1869	James Gallant Spears	N/Brig.Gen.
July 22, 1883	Edward Otho C. Ord	N/Maj.Gen.
July 22, 1886	James Henry Van Alen	N/Brig.Gen.
July 22, 1903	Cassius Marcellus Clay	N/Maj.Gen.
July 23, 1885	Ulysses Simpson Grant	N/Lt.Gen.
July 23, 1888	Williams Carter Wickham	S/Brig.Gen.
July 23, 1893	William Vandever	N/Brig.Gen.
July 24, 1897	Lafayette McLaws	S/Maj.Gen.
July 24, 1903	John Henry Hobart Ward	N/Brig.Gen.
July 25, 1864	Clement Hoffman Stevens	S/Brig.Gen.
July 25, 1883	William Nelson R. Beall	S/Brig.Gen.
July 26, 1882	Michael Kelly Lawler	N/Brig.Gen.
July 26, 1893	George Washington Morgan	N/Brig.Gen.
July 27, 1881	James Gillpatrick Blunt	N/Maj.Gen.
July 27, 1888	Marsena Rudolph Patrick	N/Brig.Gen.
July 27, 1905	Robert Bullock	S/Brig.Gen.
July 27, 1907	Edmund Winston Pettus	S/Brig.Gen.
July 28, 1871	Jerimiah Tilford Boyle	N/Brig.Gen.
July 28, 1881	James Richard Slack	N/Brig.Gen.
July 28, 1903	Thomas Neville Waul	S/Brig.Gen.
July 29, 1866	Martin Luther Smith	S/Maj.Gen.
July 29, 1896	Raleigh Edward Colston	S/Brig.Gen.
July 30, 1863	George Crockett Strong	N/Brig.Gen.
July 30, 1865	George Wright	N/Brig.Gen.
July 30, 1866	Lysander Cutler	N/Brig.Gen.
July 30, 1875	George Edward Pickett	S/Maj.Gen.
July 30, 1900	William Grose	N/Brig.Gen.
July 31, 1875	Andrew Johnson	N/Brig.Gen.
July 31, 1887	Samuel Jones	S/Maj.Gen.
August 1, 1892	Speed Smith Fry	N/Brig.Gen.
August 1, 1892	George Baird Hodge	S/Brig.Gen.
August 1, 1894	Joseph Holt	N/Brig.Gen.
August 3, 1874	Joseph Abel Haskin	N/Brig.Gen.
August 3, 1896	Calvin Edward Pratt	N/Brig.Gen.
August 4, 1895	Marcellus Augustus Stovall	S/Brig.Gen.
August 4, 1900	Jacob Dolson Cox	N/Maj.Gen.
August 5, 1862	Thomas Williams	N/Brig.Gen.
August 5, 1870	Ethan Allen Hitchcock	N/Maj.Gen.
August 5, 1886	Robert Allen	N/Brig.Gen.
August 5, 1888	Philip Henry Sheridan	N/Maj.Gen.
August 5, 1900	Zebulon York	S/Brig.Gen.
August 6, 1862	Robert Latimer McCook	N/Brig.Gen.
August 6, 1881	Gabriel James Rains	S/Brig.Gen.
August 7, 1901	James Scott Negley	N/Maj.Gen.
August 7, 1916	David McMurtrie Gregg	N/Brig.Gen.
August 8, 1882	Gouverneur Kemble Warren	N/Maj.Gen.
August 8, 1909	William Miller	S/Brig.Gen.
August 9, 1862	Joseph Bennett Plummer	N/Brig.Gen.
August 9, 1862	Charles Sidney Winder	S/Brig.Gen.

August 9, 1892	James William Denver	N/Brig.Gen.
August 9, 1897	Samuel McGowan	S/Brig.Gen.
August 9, 1901	Richard Lucian Page	S/Brig.Gen.
August 9, 1911	George Washington Gordon	S/Brig.Gen.
August 10, 1861	Nathaniel Lyon	N/Brig.Gen.
August 10, 1901	Gilbert Moxley Sorrel	S/Brig.Gen.
August 11, 1868	Melancthon Smith Wade	N/Brig.Gen.
August 11, 1914	Thomas Muldrup Logan	S/Brig.Gen.
August 12, 1891	William Whann Mackall	S/Brig.Gen.
August 12, 1916	Charles Jackson Paine	N/Brig.Gen.
August 14, 1863	Thomas Welsh	N/Brig.Gen.
August 14, 1880	Bryan Grimes	S/Maj.Gen.
August 14, 1907	William Birney	N/Brig.Gen.
August 15, 1864	Daniel Phineas Woodbury	N/Brig.Gen.
August 15, 1865	Mosby Monroe Parsons	S/Maj.Gen.
August 15, 1882	James Hewett Ledlie	N/Brig.Gen.
August 15, 1888	Carter Littlepage Stevenson	S/Maj.Gen.
August 15, 1895	John Daniel Imboden	S/Brig.Gen.
August 16, 1864	John Randolph Chambliss,Jr.	S/Brig.Gen.
August 16, 1864	Victor Jean B. Girardey	S/Brig.Gen.
August 16, 1885	Goode Bryan	S/Brig.Gen.
August 16, 1895	Samuel Bell Maxey	S/Maj.Gen.
August 17, 1886	Arthur Middleton Manigault	S/Brig.Gen.
August 17, 1889	John Calvin Brown	S/Maj.Gen.
August 18, 1881	Stephen Miller	N/Brig.Gen.
August 18, 1901	Joseph Farmer Knipe	N/Brig.Gen.
August 19, 1867	William Bowen Campbell	N/Brig.Gen.
August 19, 1892	Henry Prince	N/Brig.Gen.
August 19, 1899	Thomas Alfred Davies	N/Brig.Gen.
August 19, 1912	Joseph Hayes	N/Brig.Gen.
August 21, 1864	John Caldwell C. Sanders	S/Brig.Gen.
August 21, 1874	Hugh Thompson Reid	N/Brig.Gen.
August 21, 1876	Harry Thompson Hays	S/Maj.Gen.
August 21, 1902	Franz Sigel	N/Maj.Gen.
August 22, 1862	Henry Bohlen	N/Brig.Gen.
August 22, 1866	James Nagle	N/Brig.Gen.
August 22, 1884	Leroy Pope Walker	S/Brig.Gen.
August 22, 1900	Gustave Paul Cluseret	N/Brig.Gen.
August 23, 1886	Henry Hopkins Sibley	S/Brig.Gen.
August 23, 1900	Nathaniel Harrison Harris	S/Brig.Gen.
August 24, 1870	Edwin Gray Lee	S/Brig.Gen.
August 25, 1889	Isaac Fitzgerald Shepard	N/Brig.Gen.
August 25, 1914	Powell Clayton	N/Brig.Gen.
August 26, 1863	John Buchanan Floyd	S/Brig.Gen.
August 26, 1865	Marcellus Monroe Crocker	N/Brig.Gen.
August 26, 1900	William Hopkins Morris	N/Brig.Gen.
August 27, 1890	Milledge Luke Bonham	S/Brig.Gen.
August 28, 1867	Cyrus Hamlin	N/Brig.Gen.
August 28, 1891	Edward Augustus Wild	N/Brig.Gen.
August 29, 1880	Paul Octave Hebert	S/Brig.Gen.
August 29, 1880	Alfred Thomas A. Torbert	N/Brig.Gen.
August 30, 1879	John Bell Hood	S/General
August 30, 1886	George Henry Gordon	N/Brig.Gen.
August 30, 1888	Catharinus Putnam Buckingham	N/Brig.Gen.
August 30, 1904	Milo Smith Hascall	N/Brig.Gen.
August 30, 1908	Alexander Peter Stewart	S/Lt.Gen.

August 31, 1912	John Curtis Caldwell	N/Brig.Gen.
September 1, 1862	Philip Kearny	N/Maj.Gen.
September 1, 1862	Isaac Ingalls Stevens	N/Brig.Gen.
September 1, 1862	George William Taylor	N/Brig.Gen.
September 1, 1893	James Fleming Fagan	S/Maj.Gen.
September 1, 1894	Nathaniel Prentiss Banks	N/Maj.Gen.
September 1, 1902	Tyree Harris Bell	S/Brig.Gen.
September 1, 1911	Benjamin Henry Grierson	N/Brig.Gen.
September 2, 1874	John Gray Foster	N/Maj.Gen.
September 4, 1864	John Herbert Kelly	S/Brig.Gen.
September 4, 1864	John Hunt Morgan	S/Brig.Gen.
September 4, 1886	Benjamin Franklin Cheatham	S/Maj.Gen.
September 4, 1895	August Valentine Kautz	N/Brig.Gen.
September 4, 1896	Francis Asbury Shoup	S/Brig.Gen.
September 5, 1865	Alexander Schimmelfennig	N/Brig.Gen.
September 5, 1888	William Terry	S/BrigGen.
September 5, 1894	George Stoneman	N/Maj.Gen.
September 5, 1905	Thomas Turpin Crittenden	N/Brig.Gen.
September 5, 1926	John Rutter Brooke	N/Brig.Gen.
September 6, 1869	John Aaron Rawlins	N/Brig.Gen.
September 6, 1886	Lewis Cass Hunt	N/Brig.Gen.
September 7, 1863	Lucius Marshall Walker	S/Brig.Gen.
September 7, 1892	Joseph Reid Anderson	S/Brig.Gen.
September 7, 1894	Henry Eugene Davies	N/Brig.Gen.
September 7, 1902	James Alexander Williamson	N/Brig.Gen.
September 7, 1903	John Bullock Clark,Jr.	S/Brig.Gen.
September 7, 1909	James Murrell Shackelford	N/Brig.Gen.
September 8, 1896	Richard Caswell Gatlin	S/Brig.Gen.
September 8, 1909	Frank Crawford Armstrong	S/Brig.Gen.
September 9, 1871	Stand Watie	S/Brig.Gen.
September 9, 1900	Innis Newton Palmer	N/Brig.Gen.
September 9, 1909	Edward Moody McCook	N/Brig.Gen.
September 10, 1875	John Crawford Vaughn	S/Brig.Gen.
September 11, 1868	David Stuart	N/Brig.Gen.
September 11, 1882	William Young Conn Humes	S/Brig.Gen.
September 11, 1911	William Robertson Boggs	S/Brig.Gen.
September 12, 1876	Henry Alexander Wise	S/Brig.Gen.
September 12, 1880	Bushrod Rust Johnson	S/Maj.Gen.
September 12, 1896	James Dada Morgan	N/Brig.Gen.
September 12, 1905	Lawrence Pike Graham	N/Brig.Gen.
September 13, 1866	William Ward Orme	N/Brig.Gen.
September 13, 1881	Ambrose Everett Burnside	N/Maj.Gen.
September 13, 1902	John Horace Forney	S/Maj.Gen.
September 14, 1862	Samuel Garland,Jr.	S/Brig.Gen.
September 14, 1862	Jesse Lee Reno	N/Maj.Gen.
September 14, 1881	William Feimster Tucker	S/Brig.Gen.
September 14, 1898	Richard Busteed	N/Brig.Gen.
September 14, 1901	Edward Henry Hobson	N/Brig.Gen.
September 15, 1867	Charles Griffin	N/Maj.Gen.
September 15, 1896	Joseph Robert Davis	S/Brig.Gen.
September 15, 1907	Jacob Hunter Sharp	S/Brig.Gen.
September 16, 1862	William Edwin Starke	S/Brig.Gen.
September 16, 1916	Basil Wilson Duke	S/Brig.Gen.
September 17, 1862	Lawrence O'Bryan Branch	S/Brig.Gen.
September 18, 1862	Joseph King F. Mansfield	N/Brig.Gen.
September 18, 1866	Young Marshall Moody	S/Brig.Gen.

September 18, 1891	Issac Ferdinand Quinby	N/Brig.Gen.
September 18, 1905	Isaac Jones Wistar	N/Brig.Gen.
September 19, 1862	Lewis Henry Little	S/Brig.Gen.
September 19, 1863	Preston Smith	S/Brig.Gen.
September 19, 1864	Archibald Campbell Godwin	S/Brig.Gen.
September 19, 1864	Robert Emmett Rodes	S/Maj.Gen.
September 19, 1864	David Allen Russell	N/Brig.Gen.
September 19, 1881	James Abram Garfield	N/Maj.Gen.
September 20, 1863	James Deshler	S/Brig.Gen.
September 20, 1863	Benjamin Hardin Helm	S/Brig.Gen.
September 20, 1863	William Haines Lytle	N/Brig.Gen.
September 20, 1872	James Patton Anderson	S/Maj.Gen.
September 20, 1890	John Alexander McClernand	N/Maj.Gen.
September 20, 1892	Daniel Ullmann	N/Brig.Gen.
September 21, 1887	William Preston	S/Brig.Gen.
September 21, 1907	James Henry Lane	S/Brig.Gen.
September 21, 1922	Christopher Columbus Andrews	N/Brig.Gen.
September 22, 1871	Lewis Golding Arnold	N/Brig.Gen.
September 22, 1887	James Brewerton Ricketts	N/Brig.Gen.
September 23, 1887	Henry Shaw Briggs	N/Brig.Gen.
September 23, 1892	John Pope	N/Maj.Gen.
September 24, 1889	Daniel Harvey Hill	S/Lt.Gen.
September 25, 1900	John McCauley Palmer	N/Maj.Gen.
September 26, 1866	Danville Leadbetter	S/Brig.Gen.
September 27, 1871	James Holt Clanton	S/Brig.Gen.
September 27, 1872	William Harrow	N/Brig.Gen.
September 27, 1876	Braxton Bragg	S/General
September 27, 1890	Abram Duryee	N/Brig.Gen.
September 27, 1899	Henry Heth	S/Maj.Gen.
September 28, 1868	Thomas Carmichael Hindman	S/Maj.Gen.
September 28, 1889	Samuel Davis Sturgis	N/Brig.Gen.
September 29, 1862	William Nelson	N/Maj.Gen.
September 29, 1864	Hiram Burnham	N/Brig.Gen.
September 29, 1867	Sterling Price	S/Maj.Gen.
September 29, 1886	James Bowen	N/Brig.Gen.
September 30, 1862	Isaac Peace Rodman	N/Brig.Gen.
September 30, 1906	Thomas Maley Harris	N/Brig.Gen.
October 1, 1864	John Dunovant	S/Brig.Gen.
October 1, 1899	Alfred Jefferson Vaughan,Jr	S/Brig.Gen.
October 1, 1901	George Washington Getty	N/Brig.Gen.
October 2, 1875	Solomon Meredith	N/Brig.Gen.
October 2, 1891	Alpheus Baker	S/Brig.Gen.
October 2, 1895	Orlando Metcalfe Poe	N/Brig.Gen.
October 2, 1897	Neal Dow	N/Brig.Gen.
October 3, 1862	Pleasant Adam Hackleman	N/Brig.Gen.
October 3, 1897	Hamilton Prioleau Bee	S/Brig.Gen.
October 4, 1862	William Duncan Smith	S/Brig.Gen.
October 4, 1878	James Green Martin	S/Brig.Gen.
October 4, 1903	William Passmore Carlin	N/Brig.Gen.
October 5, 1903	Bradley Tyler Johnson	S/Brig.Gen.
October 6, 1879	Francis Laurens Vinton	N/Brig.Gen.
October 7, 1862	Allison Nelson	S/Brig.Gen.
October 7, 1864	John Gregg	S/Brig.Gen.
October 7, 1868	Adam Jacoby Slemmer	N/Brig.Gen.
October 8, 1862	James Streshly Jackson	N/Brig.Gen.
October 8, 1862	William Rufus Terrill	N/Brig.Gen.

October 8, 1878	Gideon Johnson Pillow	S/Brig.Gen.
October 8, 1890	William Lindsay Brandon	S/Brig.Gen.
October 8, 1895	William Mahone	S/Maj.Gen.
October 8, 1904	Matt Whitaker Ransom	S/Brig.Gen.
October 9, 1868	Howell Cobb	S/Maj.Gen.
October 10, 1889	James Monroe Goggin	S/Brig.Gen.
October 11, 1908	Eppa Hunton	S/Brig.Gen.
October 12, 1870	Robert Edward Lee	S/General
October 12, 1878	William Thomas Ward	N/Brig.Gen.
October 13, 1876	Rufus King	N/Brig.Gen.
October 13, 1889	Henry DeLamar Clayton	S/Maj.Gen.
October 13, 1890	William Worth Belknap	N/Brig.Gen.
October 13, 1910	John Cook	N/Brig.Gen.
October 14, 1895	Erasmus Darwin Keyes	N/Maj.Gen.
October 15, 1889	Edward Aylesworth Perry	S/Brig.Gen.
October 15, 1891	William Henry F. Lee	S/Maj.Gen.
October 16, 1862	George Burgwyn Anderson	S/Brig.Gen.
October 16, 1868	Charles Leopold Matthies	N/Brig.Gen.
October 16, 1883	Samuel Jameson Gholson	S/Brig.Gen.
October 16, 1884	Benjamin Alvord	N/Brig.Gen.
October 17, 1889	John Frederick Hartranft	N/Brig.Gen.
October 18, 1864	David Bell Birney	N/Maj.Gen.
October 18, 1883	James Blair Steedman	N/Maj.Gen.
October 19, 1864	Daniel Davidson Bidwell	N/Brig.Gen.
October 20, 1864	Stephen Dodson Ramseur	S/Maj.Gen.
October 20, 1901	James Alexander Walker	S/Brig.Gen.
October 20, 1922	Adam Rankin Johnson	S/Brig.Gen.
October 21, 1861	Edward Dickinson Baker	N/Maj.Gen.
October 21, 1861	John Breckinridge Grayson	S/Brig.Gen.
October 21, 1888	James Craig	N/Brig.Gen.
October 21, 1890	Jeremiah Cutler Sullivan	N/Brig.Gen.
October 21, 1895	Thomas Gamble Pitcher	N/Brig.Gen.
October 23, 1893	Thomas Leonidas Crittenden	N/Maj.Gen.
October 24, 1864	James Jay Archer	S/Brig.Gen.
October 24, 1892	James Madison Tuttle	N/Brig.Gen.
October 26, 1871	Robert Anderson	N/Brig.Gen.
October 26, 1909	Oliver Otis Howard	N/Maj.Gen.
October 26, 1912	Henry Beebee Carrington	N/Brig.Gen.
October 27, 1879	John Wilkins Whitfield	S/Brig.Gen.
October 29, 1864	Thomas Edward G. Ransom	N/Brig.Gen.
October 29, 1877	Nathan Bedford Forrest	S/Lt.Gen.
October 29, 1879	Matthew Duncan Ector	S/Brig.Gen.
October 29, 1885	Joseph Finegan	S/Brig.Gen.
October 29, 1885	George Brinton McClellan	N/Maj.Gen.
October 29, 1900	Daniel Marsh Frost	S/Brig.Gen.
October 30, 1862	Ormsby MacKnight Mitchel	N/Maj.Gen.
October 30, 1889	Alfred Eugene Jackson	S/Brig.Gen.
October 30, 1891	Truman Seymour	N/Brig.Gen.
October 31, 1863	Louis Ludwig Blenker	N/Brig.Gen.
October 31, 1879	Joseph Hooker	N/Maj.Gen.
October 31, 1898	Joseph Rodman West	N/Brig.Gen.
October 31, 1920	Evander McIvor Law	S/Brig.Gen.
November 2, 1870	William Felix Brantley	S/Brig.Gen.
November 2, 1887	Randolph Barnes Marcy	N/Brig.Gen.
November 3, 1862	Israel Bush Richardson	N/Maj.Gen.
November 3, 1892	Samuel Wylie Crawford	N/Brig.Gen.

November 3, 1897	Thomas Lanier Clingman	S/Brig.Gen.
November 4, 1890	Joseph Benjamin Palmer	S/Brig.Gen.
November 4, 1910	Charles Cleveland Dodge	N/Brig.Gen.
November 5, 1873	Richard Delafield	N/Brig.Gen.
November 5, 1876	Giles Alexander Smith	N/Brig.Gen.
November 5, 1892	Ferdinand Van Derveer	N/Brig.Gen.
November 6, 1862	Charles Davis Jameson	N/Brig.Gen.
November 6, 1872	George Gordon Meade	N/Maj.Gen.
November 6, 1873	William Joseph Hardee	S/Lt.Gen.
November 6, 1904	Jesse Johnson Finley	S/Brig.Gen.
November 6, 1905	James William Reilly	N/Brig.Gen.
November 7, 1887	Joshua Thomas Owen	N/Brig.Gen.
November 7, 1894	John Grant Mitchell	N/Brig.Gen.
November 8, 1880	Alfred Napoleon A. Duffie	N/Brig.Gen.
November 8, 1882	Richard Arnold	N/Brig.Gen.
November 9, 1862	John Bordenave Villepigue	S/Brig.Gen.
November 10, 1869	John Ellis Wool	N/Maj.Gen.
November 12, 1867	Walter Husted Stevens	S/Brig.Gen.
November 12, 1886	Robert Doak Lilley	S/Brig.Gen.
November 12, 1910	Beverly Holcombe Robertson	S/Brig.Gen.
November 13, 1863	Carnot Posey	S/Brig.Gen.
November 13, 1902	Evander McNair	S/Brig.Gen.
November 14, 1890	John Converse Starkweather	N/Brig.Gen.
November 15, 1913	Camille A.J.M.P. Polignac	S/Maj.Gen.
November 16, 1908	Thomas John Lucas	N/Brig.Gen.
November 17, 1897	Charles Edward Hovey	N/Brig.Gen.
November 18, 1882	James Deering Fessenden	N/Brig.Gen.
November 19, 1863	William Price Sanders	N/Brig.Gen.
November 19, 1898	Don Carlos Buell	N/Maj.Gen.
November 20, 1886	John Smith Phelps	N/Brig.Gen.
November 21, 1875	Orris Sanford Ferry	N/Brig.Gen.
November 22, 1862	Francis Engle Patterson	N/Brig.Gen.
November 22, 1889	James Morrison Hawes	S/Brig.Gen.
November 22, 1903	George Hume Steuart	S/Brig.Gen.
November 23, 1868	Nathan George Evans	S/Brig.Gen.
November 23, 1891	Alvin Peterson Hovey	N/Brig.Gen.
November 24, 1894	William Wirt Allen	S/Brig.Gen.
November 27, 1880	George Bibb Crittenden	S/Maj.Gen.
November 27, 1895	Thomas Jordan	S/Brig.Gen.
November 28, 1899	Robert Brank Vance	S/Brig.Gen.
November 28, 1901	William Hugh Young	S/Brig.Gen.
November 29, 1869	James Lawlor Kiernan	N/Brig.Gen.
November 29, 1878	Robert Christie Buchanan	N/Brig.Gen.
November 29, 1884	Gershom Mott	N/Brig.Gen.
November 29, 1897	John Sanford Mason	N/Brig.Gen.
November 30, 1864	John Adams	S/Brig.Gen.
November 30, 1864	John Carpenter Carter	S/Brig.Gen.
November 30, 1864	Patrick Ronayne Cleburne	S/Maj.Gen.
November 30, 1864	States Rights Gist	S/Brig.Gen.
November 30, 1864	Hiram Bronson Granbury	S/Brig.Gen.
November 30, 1864	Otho French Strahl	S/Brig.Gen.
November 30, 1879	Jefferson Columbus Davis	N/Brig.Gen.
November 30, 1882	Daniel Tyler	N/Brig.Gen.
December 1, 1874	Robert Ogden Tyler	N/Brig.Gen.
December 1, 1883	Jeremy Francis Gilmer	S/Maj.Gen.
December 1, 1887	William Hemsley Emory	N/Brig.Gen.

December 1, 1889	Collett Leventhorpe	S/Brig.Gen.
December 1, 1892	Lucius Eugene Polk	S/Brig.Gen.
December 2, 1864	Archibald Gracie,Jr.	S/Brig.Gen.
December 2, 1875	Alvan Cullem Gillem	N/Brig.Gen.
December 2, 1890	Cadmus Marcellus Wilcox	S/Maj.Gen.
December 2, 1894	Stephen Gano Burbridge	N/Brig.Gen.
December 2, 1910	Eugene Asa Carr	N/Brig.Gen.
December 3, 1876	Samuel Cooper	S/General
December 3, 1897	Allen Thomas	S/Brig.Gen.
December 3, 1910	Wesley Merritt	N/Maj.Gen.
December 4, 1881	Hugh Judson Kilpatrick	N/Brig.Gen.
December 4, 1888	Romeyn Beck Ayres	N/Brig.Gen.
December 4, 1912	Julius Stahel	N/Maj.Gen.
December 5, 1910	Alfred Cumming	S/Brig.Gen.
December 6, 1901	James Argyle Smith	S/Brig.Gen.
December 7, 1877	Benjamin Huger	S/Maj.Gen.
December 7, 1889	Israel Vogdes	N/Brig.Gen.
December 7, 1894	Eliakim Parker Scammon	N/Brig.Gen.
December 7, 1899	Henry Hayes Lockwood	N/Brig.Gen.
December 8, 1910	George Doherty Johnston	S/Brig.Gen.
December 11, 1885	Gustavus Adolphus Smith	N/Brig.Gen.
December 11, 1892	Henry Gray	S/Brig.Gen.
December 11, 1896	George Lafayette Beal	N/Brig.Gen.
December 11, 1897	Justus McKinstry	N/Brig.Gen.
December 11, 1899	Edward Ferrero	N/Brig.Gen.
December 12, 1867	Jasper Adalmorn Maltby	N/Brig.Gen.
December 12, 1923	Martin Davis Hardin	N/Brig.Gen.
December 13, 1862	Thomas Reade Rootes Cobb	S/Brig.Gen.
December 13, 1862	Conrad Feger Jackson	N/Brig.Gen.
December 13, 1881	John Henry Martindale	N/Brig.Gen.
December 13, 1915	Francis Marion Cockrell	S/Brig.Gen.
December 14, 1862	George Dashiell Bayard	N/Brig.Gen.
December 14, 1876	James Allen Hardie	N/Brig.Gen.
December 14, 1887	Thomas Kilby Smith	N/Brig.Gen.
December 14, 1905	Herman Haupt	N/Brig.Gen.
December 15, 1862	Maxcy Gregg	S/Brig.Gen.
December 15, 1885	Robert Augustus Toombs	S/Brig.Gen.
December 15, 1892	Randall Lee Gibson	S/Brig.Gen.
December 16, 1863	John Buford	N/Brig.Gen.
December 16, 1882	Eleazer Arthur Paine	N/Brig.Gen.
December 16, 1890	Alfred Howe Terry	N/Maj.Gen.
December 16, 1892	John Milton Brannan	N/Brig.Gen.
December 16, 1900	John Grubb Parke	N/Maj.Gen.
December 17, 1867	John Potts Slough	N/Brig.Gen.
December 17, 1876	William Francis Bartlett	N/Brig.Gen.
December 17, 1891	Patrick Edward Connor	N/Brig.Gen.
December 17, 1894	Elias Smith Dennis	N/Brig.Gen.
December 18, 1862	Johnson Kelly Duncan	S/Brig.Gen.
December 18, 1877	Charles Clark	S/Brig.Gen.
December 18, 1901	William Flank Perry	S/Brig.Gen.
December 18, 1902	Wager Swayne	N/Brig.Gen.
December 18, 1909	Green Berry Raum	N/Brig.Gen.
December 20, 1882	Benjamin Grubb Humphreys	S/Brig.Gen.
December 20, 1891	John Reese Kenly	N/Brig.Gen.
December 21, 1865	James Heyward Trapier	S/Brig.Gen.
December 21, 1872	Ambrose Ransom Wright	S/Maj.Gen.

December 21, 1878	Alpheus Starkey Williams	N/Brig.Gen.
December 21, 1914	John Beatty	N/Brig.Gen.
December 22, 1863	Michael Corcoran	N/Brig.Gen.
December 22, 1895	James Clifford Veatch	N/Brig.Gen.
December 24, 1893	John Wilson Sprague	N/Brig.Gen.
December 25, 1868	Edwin Henry Stoughton	N/Brig.Gen.
December 26, 1861	Philip St.George Cocke	S/Brig.Gen.
December 26, 1866	Samuel Ryan Curtis	N/Maj.Gen.
December 26, 1868	Alfred Gibbs	N/Brig.Gen.
December 26, 1874	Sullivan Amory Meredith	N/Brig.Gen.
December 26, 1883	Thomas Leiper Kane	N/Brig.Gen.
December 26, 1886	John Alexander Logan	N/Maj.Gen.
December 26, 1904	William Henry Powell	N/Brig.Gen.
December 26, 1919	William Ruffin Cox	S/Brig.Gen.
December 27, 1883	Andrew Atkinson Humphreys	N/Maj.Gen.
December 27, 1898	William Booth Taliaferro	S/Maj.Gen.
December 27, 1922	Marcus Joseph Wright	S/Brig.Gen.
December 28, 1874	Morgan Lewis Smith	N/Brig.Gen.
December 28, 1887	John Sappington Marmaduke	S/Maj.Gen.
December 28, 1893	William Andrew Quarles	S/Brig.Gen.
December 28, 1911	Alexander Shaler	N/Brig.Gen.
December 30, 1873	Henry Baxter	N/Brig.Gen.
December 30, 1886	William Wing Loring	S/Maj.Gen.
December 31, 1862	James Edwards Rains	S/Brig.Gen.
December 31, 1862	Joshua Woodrow Sill	N/Brig.Gen.
December 31, 1907	Albert Lindley Lee	N/Brig.Gen.
December 31, 1910	John Creed Moore	S/Brig.Gen.

_____14_____

Civil War Generals
Killed in Battle, by Battle

This chapter arranges the generals killed during the war by the
battles where they met their death. In some cases there was
more than one action at a battle location, therefore generals
killed at a battle location were not necessarily all killed in
the same month or year.

GENERAL	SIDE/RANK	KILLED IN BATTLE AT:
James Birdseye McPherson	N/M	Atlanta,Georgia
William Henry T. Walker	S/M	Atlanta,Georgia
Edward Dickinson Baker	N/M	Ball's Bluff,Virginia
Thomas Williams	N/B	Baton Rouge,Louisiana
George Pierce Doles	S/B	Bethesda Church,Virginia
Thomas Green	S/B	Blair's Landing,Louisiana
Carnot Posey	S/B	Bristoe Station,Virginia
George William Taylor	N/B	Bull Run,Virginia
Daniel Davidson Bidwell	N/B	Cedar Creek,Virginia
Stephen Dodson Ramseur	S/M	Cedar Creek,Virginia
Charles Sidney Winder	S/B	Cedar Mountain,Virginia
Lloyd Tilghman	S/B	Champion's Hills,Miss.
Hiram Gregory Berry	N/M	Chancellorsville,Virginia
Thomas Jonathon Jackson	S/L	Chancellorsville,Virginia
Elisha Franklin Paxton	S/B	Chancellorsville,Virginia
Amiel Weeks Whipple	N/B	Chancellorsville,Virginia
Philip Kearny	N/M	Chantilly,Virginia
Isaac Ingalls Stevens	N/B	Chantilly,Virginia
John Randolph Chambliss	S/B	Charles City Road,Virginia
James Deshler	S/B	Chickamauga,Georgia
Benjamin Hardin Helm	S/B	Chickamauga,Georgia
William Haines Lytle	N/B	Chickamauga,Georgia
Preston Smith	S/B	Chickamauga,Georgia
Albert Gallatin Jenkins	S/B	Cloyd's Mountain,Virginia
Adley Hogan Gladden	S/B	Corinth,Mississippi
Pleasant Adam Hackleman	N/B	Corinth,Mississippi
Robert Selden Garnett	S/B	Carrick's Ford,Virginia
James McQueen McIntosh	S/B	Elkhorn Tavern,Arkansas
William Yarnel Slack	S/B	Elkhorn Tavern,Arkansas
Ben McCulloch	S/B	Elkhorn Tavern,Arkansas
James Johnston Pettigrew	S/B	Falling Waters,Maryland

Thomas Alfred Smyth	N/B	Farmville,Virginia
William Henry C. Whiting	S/M	Fort Fisher,North Carolina
Hiram Burnham	N/B	Fort Harrison,Virginia
John Dunovant	S/B	Fort Harrison,Virginia
Robert Charles Tyler	S/B	Fort Tyler,Virginia
George Crockett Strong	N/B	Fort Wagner,South Carolina
John Adams	S/B	Franklin,Tennessee
John Carpenter Carter	S/B	Franklin,Tennessee
Patrick Ronayne Cleburne	S/M	Franklin,Tennessee
States Rights Gist	S/B	Franklin,Tennessee
Hiram Bronson Granbury	S/B	Franklin,Tennessee
John Herbert Kelly	S/B	Franklin,Tennessee
Otho French Strahl	S/B	Franklin,Tennessee
George Dashiell Bayard	N/B	Fredericksburg,Virginia
Thomas Reade Rootes Cobb	S/B	Fredericksburg,Virginia
Maxcy Gregg	S/B	Fredericksburg,Virginia
Conrad Feger Jackson	N/B	Fredericksburg,Virginia
Abner Monroe Perrin	S/B	Fredericksburg,Virginia
Henry Bohlen	N/B	Freeman's Ford,Virginia
Victor Jean B. Girardey	S/B	Fussell's Mill,Virginia
Lewis Addison Armistead	S/B	Gettysburg,Pennsylvania
William Barksdale	S/B	Gettysburg,Pennsylvania
Elon John Farnsworth	N/B	Gettysburg,Pennsylvania
Richard Brooke Garnett	S/B	Gettysburg,Pennsylvania
William Dorsey Pender	S/M	Gettysburg,Pennsylvania
John Fulton Reynolds	N/M	Gettysburg,Pennsylvania
Paul Jones Semmes	S/B	Gettysburg,Pennsylvania
Stephen Hinsdale Weed	N/B	Gettysbueg,Pennsylvania
Samuel Kosciuszko Zook	N/B	Gettysburg,Pennsylvania
John Hunt Morgan	S/B	Greenville,Tennessee
Turner Ashby	S/B	Harrisonburg,Virginia
John Pegram	S/B	Hatcher's Run,Virginia
Lewis Henry Little	S/B	Iuka,Mississippi
Samuel Allen Rice	N/B	Jenkin's Ferry,Arkansas
William Read Scurry	S/B	Jenkin's Ferry,Arkansas
Charles Garrison Harker	N/B	Kennesaw Mountain,Georgia
William Price Sanders	N/B	Knoxville,Tennessee
Barnard Elliott Bee	S/B	Manassas,Virginia
Jean Jacques A.A. Mouton	S/B	Mansfield,Louisiana
James Byron Gordon	S/B	Meadow Bridge,Virginia
Felix Kirk Zollicoffer	S/B	Mill Springs,Kentucky
Roger Weightman Hanson	S/B	Murfreesboro,Tennessee
Edward Needles Kirk	N/B	Murfreesboro,Tennessee
James Edwards Rains	S/B	Murfreesboro,Tennessee
Joshua Woodrow Sill	N/B	Murfreesboro,Tennessee
Clement Hoffman Stevens	S/B	Peach Tree Creek,Georgia
James Streshly Jackson	N/B	Perryville,Kentucky
William Rufus Terrill	N/B	Perryville,Kentucky
Archibald Gracie,Jr.	S/B	Petersburg,Virginia
Ambrose Powell Hill	S/L	Petersburg,Virginia
James St.Clair Morton	N/B	Petersburg,Virginia
William Edmonson Jones	S/B	Piedmont,West Virginia
Leonidas Polk	S/L	Pine Mountain,Georgia
Edward Dorr Tracy	S/B	Port Gibson,Mississippi
John Gregg	S/B	Richmond,Virginia
Thomas Greely Stevenson	N/B	Richmond,Virginia

Thomas Edward G. Ransom	N/B	Sabine Crossroads, La.
Richard Griffith	S/B	Savage Station, Virginia
Robert Hopkins Hatton	S/B	Seven Pines, Virginia
George Burgwyn Anderson	S/B	Sharpsburg, Maryland
Lawrence O'Bryan Branch	S/B	Sharpsburg, Maryland
Joseph King F. Mansfield	N/B	Sharpsburg, Maryland
Israel Bush Richardson	N/M	Sharpsburg, Maryland
Isaac Peace Rodman	N/B	Sharpsburg, Maryland
William Edwin Starke	S/B	Sharpsburg, Maryland
Albert Sidney Johnston	S/G	Shiloh, Tennessee
William Harvey Wallace	N/B	Shiloh, Tennessee
Samuel Garland, Jr.	S/B	South Mountain, Maryland
Jesse Lee Reno	N/M	South Mountain, Maryland
James Clay Rice	N/B	Spotsylvania, Virginia
John Sedgwick	N/M	Spotsylvania, Virginia
Junius Daniel	S/B	Spotsylvania, Virginia
Martin Edwin Green	S/B	Vicksburg, Mississippi
John Caldwell Sanders	S/B	Weldon Railroad, Virginia
Alexander Hays	N/B	Wilderness, Virginia
Micah Jenkins	S/B	Wilderness, Virginia
John Marshall Jones	S/B	Wilderness, Virginia
Leroy Augustus Stafford	S/B	Wilderness, Virginia
James Samuel Wadsworth	N/B	Wilderness, Virginia
Nathaniel Lyon	N/B	Wilson's Creek, Missouri
Archibald Campbell Godwin	S/B	Winchester, Virginia
Robert Latimer McCook	N/B	Winchester, Virginia
Robert Emmett Rodes	S/M	Winchester, Virginia
David Allen Russell	N/B	Winchester, Virginia
James Ewell Brown Stuart	S/M	Yellow Tavern, Virginia

15

Civil War Generals
Killed in Battle, Alphabetically

All generals killed in battle during the civil war from both
sides are listed here in alphabetical order.

GENERAL	SIDE/RANK	DATE WOUNDED	DATE OF DEATH
John Adams	S/B	November 30,1864	November 30,1864
George B. Anderson	S/B	September 17,1862	October 16,1862
Lewis Armistead	S/B	July 3,1863	July 5,1863
Turner Ashby	S/B	June 6,1862	June 6,1862
Edward D. Baker	N/M	October 21,1861	October 21,1861
William Barksdale	S/B	July 2,1863	July 3,1863
George D. Bayard	N/B	December 13,1862	December 14,1862
Barnard Elliott Bee	S/B	July 21,1861	July 22,1861
Hiram Gregory Berry	N/M	May 3,1863	May 3,1863
Daniel D. Bidwell	N/B	October 19,1864	October 19,1864
Henry Bohlen	N/B	August 22,1862	August 22,1862
Lawrence Branch	S/B	September 17,1862	September 17,1862
Hiram Burnham	N/B	September 29,1864	September 29,1864
John C. Carter	S/B	November 30,1864	December 10,1864
John Chambliss	S/B	August 16,1864	August 16,1864
Patrick Cleburne	S/M	November 30,1864	November 30,1864
Thomas R.R. Cobb	S/B	December 13,1862	December 13,1862
Junius Daniel	S/B	May 12,1864	May 13,1864
James Deshler	S/B	September 20,1863	September 20,1864
George Pierce Doles	S/B	June 2,1864	June 2,1864
John Dunovant	S/B	October 1,1864	October 1,1864
Elon Farnsworth	N/B	July 3,1863	July 3,1863
Samuel Garland,Jr.	S/B	September 14,1862	September 14,1862
Richard B. Garnett	S/B	July 3,1863	July 3,1863
Robert S. Garnett	S/B	July 13,1861	July 13,1861
Victor Girardey	S/B	August 16,1864	August 16,1864
States Rights Gist	S/B	November 30,1864	November 30,1864
Adley Hogan Gladden	S/B	April 6,1862	April 12,1862
Archibald Godwin	S/B	September 19,1864	September 19,1864
James Byron Gordon	S/B	May 13,1864	May 18,1864
Archibald Gracie	S/B	December 2,1864	December 2,1864
Hiram Granbury	S/B	November 30,1864	November 30,1864
Martin Edwin Green	S/B	June 25,1863	June 25,1863
Thomas Green	S/B	April 12,1864	April 12,1864

John Gregg	S/B	October 7,1864	October 7,1864
Maxcy Gregg	S/B	December 13,1862	December 15,1862
Richard Griffith	S/B	June 29,1862	June 29,1862
Pleasant Hackleman	N/B	October 3,1862	October 3,1862
Roger W. Hanson	S/B	January 2,1863	January 4,1863
Charles G. Harker	N/B	June 26,1864	June 26,1864
Robert Hatton	S/B	May 31,1862	May 31,1862
Alexander Hays	N/B	May 5,1864	May 5,1864
Benjamin Helm	S/B	September 20,1863	September 21,1863
Ambrose P. Hill	S/L	April 2,1865	April 2,1865
Conrad Feger Jackson	N/B	December 13,1862	December 13,1862
James S. Jackson	N/B	October 8,1862	October 8,1862
Thomas J. Jackson	S/L	May 2,1863	May 10,1863
Albert Jenkins	S/B	May 9,1864	May 21,1864
Micah Jenkins	S/B	May 6,1864	May 6,1864
Albert Johnston	S/G	April 6,1862	April 6,1862
John Marshall Jones	S/B	May 5,1864	May 5,1864
William E. Jones	S/B	June 5,1864	June 5,1864
Philip Kearny	N/M	September 1,1862	September 1,1862
John Herbert Kelly	S/B	September 2,1864	September 4,1864
Edward Needles Kirk	N/B	December 31,1862	July 21,1863
Lewis Henry Little	S/B	September 19,1862	September 19,1864
Nathaniel Lyon	N/B	August 10,1861	August 10,1861
William Lytle	N/B	September 20,1863	September 20,1863
Joseph Mansfield	N/B	September 17,1862	September 18,1862
Robert L. McCook	N/B	August 5,1862	August 6,1862
Ben McCulloch	S/B	March 7,1862	March 7,1862
James McIntosh	S/B	March 7,1862	March 7,1862
James McPherson	N/M	July 22,1864	July 22,1864
John Hunt Morgan	S/B	September 4,1864	September 4,1864
James Morton	N/B	June 17,1864	June 17,1864
Jean Jacques Mouton	S/B	April 8,1864	April 8,1864
Elisha Paxton	S/B	May 3,1863	May 3,1863
John Pegram	S/B	February 6,1865	February 6,1865
William Pender	S/M	July 2,1863	July 18,1863
Abner Monroe Perrin	S/B	May 12,1864	May 12,1864
James Pettigrew	S/B	July 14,1863	July 17,1863
Leonidas Polk	S/L	June 14,1864	June 14,1864
Carnot Posey	S/B	October 14,1863	November 13,1863
James Edwards Rains	S/B	December 31,1862	December 31,1862
Stephen Ramseur	S/M	October 19,1864	October 20,1864
Thomas Edward Ransom	S/B	April 8,1864	October 29,1864
Jesse Lee Reno	N/M	September 14,1862	September 14,1862
John Fulton Reynolds	N/M	July 1,1863	July 1,1863
James Clay Rice	N/B	May 10,1864	May 10,1864
Samuel Allen Rice	N/B	April 30,1864	July 6,1864
Israel Richardson	N/M	September 17,1862	November 3,1862
Robert Emmett Rodes	S/M	September 19,1864	September 19,1864
Isaac Peace Rodman	N/B	September 17,1862	September 30,1862
David Allen Russell	N/B	September 19,1864	September 19,1864
John C. Sanders	S/B	August 21,1864	August 21,1864
William Sanders	N/B	November 18,1863	November 19,1863
William Read Scurry	S/B	April 30,1864	April 30,1864
John Sedgwick	N/M	May 9,1864	May 9,1864
Paul Jones Semmes	S/B	July 2,1863	July 10,1863
Joshua Woodrow Sill	N/B	December 31,1862	December 31,1862

William Yarnel Slack	S/B	March 7,1862	March 21,1862
Preston Smith	S/B	September 19,1863	September 19,1863
Thomas Alfred Smyth	N/B	April 7,1865	April 9,1865
Leroy Stafford	S/B	May 5,1864	May 8,1864
William Edwin Starke	S/B	September 17,1862	September 17,1862
Clement Stevens	S/B	July 20,1864	July 25,1864
Isaac Ingalls Stevens	N/B	September 1,1862	September 1,1862
Thomas Stevenson	N/B	May 10,1864	May 10,1864
Otho French Strahl	S/B	November 30,1864	November 30,1864
George Strong	N/B	July 18,1863	July 30,1863
James E.B. Stuart	S/M	May 11,1864	May 12,1864
George Taylor	N/B	August 30,1862	September 1,1862
William Terrill	N/B	October 8,1862	October 8,1862
Lloyd Tilghman	S/B	May 16,1863	May 16,1863
Edward Dorr Tracy	S/B	May 1,1863	May 1,1863
Robert Charles Tyler	S/B	April 16,1865	April 16,1865
James Wadsworth	N/B	May 6,1864	May 8,1864
William Henry Walker	S/M	July 22,1864	July 22,1864
William Wallace	N/B	April 7,1862	April 10,1862
Stephen Weed	N/B	July 2,1863	July 2,1863
Amiel Weeks Whipple	N/B	May 4,1863	May 7,1863
William Whiting	S/M	January 15,1865	March 10,1865
Thomas Williams	N/B	August 5,1862	August 5,1862
Charles Winder	S/B	August 9,1862	August 9,1862
Felix Zollicoffer	S/B	January 19,1862	January 19,1862
Samuel Zook	N/B	July 2,1863	July 3,1863

16

Civil War Generals
Killed in Battle, by Date

This chapter arranges the generals killed in battle by the date of their death.

DIED	GENERAL	SIDE/RANK	BATTLE
1-8-6-1			
July 3	Robert Selden Garnett	S/B	Carrick's Ford,VA
July 22	Barnard Elliott Bee	S/B	Manassas,VA
August 10	Nathaniel Lyon	N/B	Wilson's Creek,MO
October 21	Edward Dickinson Baker	N/M	Ball's Bluff,VA
1-8-6-2			
January 19	Felix Kirk Zollicoffer	S/B	Mill Springs,KY
March 7	Ben McCulloch	S/B	Elkhorn Tavern,AR
March 7	James McQueen McIntosh	S/B	Elkhorn Tavern,AR
March 21	William Yarnel Slack	S/B	Elkhorn Tavern,AR
April 6	Albert Sidney Johnston	S/G	Shiloh,TN
April 10	William Harvey Wallace	N/B	Shiloh,TN
April 12	Adley Hogan Gladden	S/B	Corinth,MS
May 31	Robert Hopkins Hatton	S/B	Seven Pines,VA
June 6	Turner Ashby	S/B	Harrisonburg,VA
June 29	Richard Griffith	S/B	Savage Station,VA
August 5	Thomas Williams	N/B	Baton Rouge,LA
August 6	Robert Latimer McCook	N/B	Winchester,VA
August 9	Charles Sidney Winder	S/B	Cedar Mountain,VA
August 22	Henry Bohlen	N/B	Freeman's Ford,VA
September 1	Philip Kearny	N/M	Chantilly,VA
September 1	Isaac Ingalls Stevens	N/B	Chantilly,VA
September 1	George William Taylor	N/B	Bull Run,VA
September 14	Samuel Garland,Jr.	S/B	South Mountain,MD
September 14	Jesse Lee Reno	N/M	South Mountain,MD
September 16	William Edwin Starke	S/B	Sharpsburg,MD
September 17	Lawrence O'Bryan Branch	S/B	Sharpsburg,MD
September 18	Joseph King Mansfield	N/B	Sharpsburg,MD
September 19	Lewis Henry Little	S/B	Iuka,MS
September 30	Isaac Peace Rodman	N/B	Sharpsburg,MD
October 3	Pleasant Hackleman	N/B	Corinth,MS
October 8	James Streshly Jackson	N/B	Perryville,KY

October 8	William Rufus Terrill	N/B	Perryville,KY
October 16	George Burgwyn Anderson	S/B	Sharpsburg,MD
November 3	Israel Bush Richardson	N/M	Sharpsburg,MD
December 13	Thomas Reade Cobb	S/B	Fredericksburg,VA
December 13	Conrad Feger Jackson	N/B	Fredericksburg,VA
December 14	George Dashiell Bayard	N/B	Fredericksburg,VA
December 15	Maxcy Gregg	S/B	Fredericksburg,VA
December 31	James Edwards Rains	S/B	Murfreesboro,TN
December 31	Joshua Woodrow Sill	N/B	Murfreesboro,TN

1-8-6-3

January 4	Roger Weightman Hanson	S/B	Murfreesboro,TN
May 1	Edward Dorr Tracy	S/B	Port Gibson,MS
May 3	Hiram Gregory Berry	N/M	Chancellorsville,VA
May 3	Elisha Franklin Paxton	S/B	Chancellorsville,VA
May 7	Amiel Weeks Whipple	N/B	Chancellorsville,VA
May 10	Thomas Jonathon Jackson	S/L	Chancellorsville,VA
May 16	Lloyd Tilghman	S/B	Champion's Hills,MS
June 25	Martin Edwin Green	S/B	Vicksburg,MS
July 1	John Fulton Reynolds	N/M	Gettysburg,PA
July 2	Stephen Hinsdale Weed	N/B	Gettysburg,PA
July 3	William Barksdale	S/B	Gettysburg,PA
July 3	Elon John Farnsworth	N/B	Gettysburg,PA
July 3	Richard Brooke Garnett	S/B	Gettysburg,PA
July 3	Samuel Kosciuszko Zook	N/B	Gettysburg,PA
July 5	Lewis Armistead	S/B	Gettysburg,PA
July 10	Paul Jones Semmes	S/B	Gettysburg,PA
July 17	James Pettigrew	S/B	Falling Waters,MD
July 18	William Dorsey Pender	S/M	Gettysburg,PA
July 21	Edward Needles Kirk	N/B	Murfreesboro,TN
July 30	George Crockett Strong	N/B	Fort Wagner,SC
September 19	Preston Smith	S/B	Chickamauga,GA
September 20	James Deshler	S/B	Chickamauga,GA
September 20	Benjamin Hardin Helm	S/B	Chickamauga,GA
September 20	William Haines Lytle	N/B	Chickamauga,GA
November 13	Carnot Posey	S/B	Bristoe Station,VA
November 19	William Price Sanders	N/B	Knoxville,TN

1-8-6-4

April 8	Jean Jacques Mouton	S/B	Mansfield,LA
April 12	Thomas Green	S/B	Blair's Landing,LA
April 30	William Read Scurry	S/B	Jenkin's Ferry,AR
May 5	Alexander Hays	N/B	Wilderness,VA
May 5	John Marshall Jones	S/B	Wilderness,VA
May 6	Micah Jenkins	S/B	Wilderness,VA
May 8	Leroy Augustus Stafford	S/B	Wilderness,VA
May 8	James Samuel Wadsworth	N/B	Wilderness,VA
May 9	John Sedgwick	N/M	Spotsylvania,VA
May 10	James Clay Rice	N/B	Spotsylvania,VA
May 10	Thomas Greely Stevenson	N/B	Richmond,VA
May 12	Abner Monroe Perrin	S/B	Fredericksburg,VA
May 12	James Ewell Stuart	S/M	Yellow Tavern,VA
May 13	Junius Daniel	S/B	Spotsylvania,VA
May 18	James Byron Gordon	S/B	Meadow Bridge,VA
May 21	Albert Gallatin Jenkins	S/B	Cloyd's Mountain,VA

June 2	George Pierce Doles	S/B	Bethesda Church,VA
June 5	William Edmonson Jones	S/B	Piedmont,West VA
June 14	Leonidas Polk	S/L	Pine Mountain,GA
June 17	James St.Clair Morton	N/B	Petersburg,VA
June 26	Charles Garrison Harker	N/B	Kennesaw Mountain,GA
July 6	Samuel Allen Rice	N/B	Jenkin's Ferry,AR
July 22	James McPherson	N/M	Atlanta,GA
July 22	William Henry T. Walker	S/M	Atlanta,GA
July 25	Clement Hoffman Stevens	S/B	Peach Tree Creek,GA
August 16	John Randolph Chambliss	S/B	Charles City Rd.,VA
August 16	Victor Jean B. Girardey	S/B	Fussell's Mill,VA
August 21	John Caldwell Sanders	S/B	Weldon Railroad,VA
September 4	John Herbert Kelly	S/B	Franklin,TN
September 4	John Hunt Morgan	S/B	Greenville,TN
September 19	Archibald Godwin	S/B	Winchester,VA
September 19	Robert Emmett Rodes	S/M	Winchester,VA
September 19	David Allen Russell	N/B	Winchester,VA
September 29	Hiram Burnham	N/B	Fort Harrison,VA
October 1	John Dunovant	S/B	Fort Harrison,VA
October 7	John Gregg	S/B	Richmond,VA
October 19	Daniel Davidson Bidwell	N/B	Cedar Creek,VA
October 20	Stephen Dodson Ramseur	S/M	Cedar Creek,VA
October 29	Thomas Edward G. Ransom	N/B	Sabine Cross Rd.,LA
November 30	John Adams	S/B	Franklin,TN
November 30	John Carpenter Carter	S/B	Franklin,TN
November 30	Patrick Cleburne	S/M	Franklin,TN
November 30	States Rights Gist	S/B	Franklin,TN
November 30	Hiram Bronson Granbury	S/B	Franklin,TN
November 30	Otho French Strahl	S/B	Franklin,TN
December 2	Archibald Gracie,Jr.	S/B	Petersburg,VA

1-8-6-5

February 6	John Pegram	S/B	Hatcher's Run,VA
March 10	William Henry Whiting	S/M	Fort Fisher,NC
April 2	Ambrose Powell Hill	S/L	Petersburg,VA
April 7	Thomas Alfred Smyth	N/B	Farmville,VA
April 16	Robert Charles Tyler	S/B	Fort Tyler,VA

17

Biographies

This chapter lists a concise biography of each of the Civil War generals from both sides in alphabetical order.

ABERCROMBIE, JOHN JOSEPH. Union Brigadier General, born March 4, 1798 in Baltimore, Maryland. Graduated from West Point 1822 and served in the army before and after the war. Died January 3, 1877 at Roslyn, New York.

ADAMS, DANIEL WEISIGER. Confederate Brigadier General, born in June 1821 at Frankfort, Kentucky. Brother of William Adams. Lawyer before and after the war. Died June 13, 1872 in New Orleans, Louisiana.

ADAMS, JOHN. Confederate Brigadier General, born July 1, 1825 at Nashville, Tennessee. Graduated from West Point 1846 and served in the army before the war. Killed November 30, 1864 at the battle of Franklin, Tennessee.

ADAMS, WILLIAM WIRT. Confederate Brigadier General, born March 22, 1819 at Frankfort, Kentucky. Brother of Daniel Adams. Farmer and banker before the war and Postmaster after. Killed in street argument with a newspaper editor May 1, 1888 at Jackson, Mississippi.

ALEXANDER, EDWARD PORTER. Confederate Brigadier General, born May 26, 1835 at Washington, Georgia. Graduated from West Point 1857 and served in the army before the war. College professor of engineering after the war. Died April 28, 1910 at Savannah, Georgia.

ALLEN, HENRY WATKINS. Confederate Brigadier General, born April 29, 1820 in Prince Edward County, Virginia. Attended Marion College, and was a school teacher and lawyer before the war; following the war a newspaper editor. Died April 22, 1866 in Mexico City, Mexico.

ALLEN, ROBERT. Union Brigadier General, born March 15, 1811 in West Point, Ohio. Graduated from West Point 1836 and served in the army before and after the war. Died August 5, 1886 at Geneva, Switzerland.

ALLEN, WILLIAM WIRT.   Confederate Brigadier General,born September 11,1835 in New York City, New York.   Attended Princeton University, a farmer before and after the war, also a U.S. Marshal. Died November 24,1894 at Sheffield, Alabama.

ALVORD, BENJAMIN.   Union Brigadier General, born August 18, 1813 in Rutland,Vermont.   Graduated West Point 1833 and served in the army before and after the war.   Died October 16,1884 at Washington, D.C.

AMES, ADELBERT.   Union Brigadier General, born October 31, 1835 in Rockland,Maine.   Graduated from West Point 1861.   Governor of Mississippi following the war.   Died April 13, 1933 at Ormond, Florida.

AMMEN, JACOB.   Union Brigadier General, born January 7, 1806 in Botetourt County,Virginia.   Graduated from West Point 1831, college professor before the war, an engineer after.   Died February 6,1894 in Lockland, Ohio.

ANDERSON, GEORGE BURGWYN.   Confederate Brigadier General, born April 12,1831 in Hillsboro, North Carolina.   Attended University of North Carolina,then graduated from West Point 1852 and served in the army before the war.   Wounded September 17,1862 in battle at Sharpsburg, Maryland and died October 16,1862.

ANDERSON, GEORGE THOMAS. Confederate Brigadier General,born February 3, 1824 at Covington, Georgia.   Attended Emory College and served in the army before the war.   Police Chief of Atlanta following the war. Died April 4,1901 at Anniston, Alabama.

ANDERSON, JAMES PATTON.   Confederate Major General, born February 16,1822 in Franklin County,Tennessee.   A doctor and U.S.Marshal before the war, editor after.   Died September 20, 1872 in Memphis, Tennessee.

ANDERSON, JOSEPH REID.   Confederate Brigadier General, born February 16,1813 in Botetourt County,Virginia.   Graduated from West Point 1836.   Iron works Superintendent before and after the war. Died September 7,1892 at Isles of Shoals, New Hampshire.

ANDERSON, RICHARD HERON.   Confederate Lieutenant General, born October 7,1821 in Sumter County, South Carolina.   Graduated from West Point 1842 and served in the army before the war.   State Phosphate agent following the war.   Died June 26, 1879 in Beaufort, South Carolina.

ANDERSON, ROBERT. Union Brigadier General, born June 14,1805 at Louisville, Kentucky.   Graduated from West Point 1825, served in the army before the war, retired after.   Died October 26,1871 in Nice, France.

ANDERSON, ROBERT HOUSTOWN.   Confederate Brigadier General, born October 1, 1835 at Savannah, Georgia.   Graduated from West Point 1857 and served in the army until the war.   Police Chief after the war. Died February 8,1888 in Savannah, Georgia.

ANDERSON, SAMUEL READ. Confederate Brigadier General, born February 17,1804 in Bedford County,Virginia. Postmaster before the war and merchant after. Died January 2,1893 in Nashville, Tennessee.

ANDREWS, CHRISTOPHER COLUMBUS. Union Brigadier General,born October 27,1829 at Hillsboro, New Hampshire. Attended Harvard Law School,lawyer before the war and in politics after. Died September 21,1922 at St. Paul, Minnesota.

ANDREWS, GEORGE LEONARD. Union Brigadier General,born August 31, 1828 in Bridgewater, Massachusetts.   Graduated from West Point 1851. An engineer before the war and U.S. Marshal after.   Died April 4,1899 at Brookline, Massachusetts.

ARCHER, JAMES JAY.   Confederate Brigadier General, born December 19,1817 at Bel Air,Maryland. Attenoed Princeton University, was a lawyer and served in the army before the war. Died of illness during the war at Richmond, Virginia October 24,1864.

ARMISTEAD, LEWIS ADDISON.   Confederate Brigadier General, born October 18,1817 at New Bern, North Carolina. Served in the army before the war.   Wounded in battle July 3, 1863 at Gettysburg, Pennsylvania, died on July 5,1863.

ARMSTRONG, FRANK CRAWFORD.   Confederate Brigadier General, born November 22, 1835 at Scullyville, Oklahoma. Attended Holy Cross Academy, then served in the army until the war. U.S. Indian Inspector after the war.   Died September 8, 1909 at Bar Harbor, Maine.

ARNOLD, LEWIS GOLDING. Union Brigadier General,born January 15, 1817 in Perth Amboy,New Jersey. Graduated from West Point 1837, served in the army before the war, retired after.   Died September 22,1871 in Boston, Massachusetts.

ARNOLD, RICHARD.   Union Brigadier General, born April 12, 1828 in Providence, Rhode Island. Graduated from West Point 1850 and served in the army before and after the war.   Died November 8, 1882 at Governor's Island, New York.

ASBOTH, ALEXANDER SANDOR.   Union Brigadier General, born December 18,1811 at Keszthely,Hungary. Engineer before the war, U.S. Minister to Uruguay after. Died January 21,1868 at Buenos Aires, Brazil.

ASHBY, TURNER.   Confederate Brigadier General, born October 23, 1828 in Fauquier County,Virginia. Farmer before the war. Killed in battle June 6, 1862 at Harrisonburg, Virginia.

AUGUR, CHRISTOPHER COLUMBUS. Union Major General, born July 10, 1821 in Kendall, New York. Graduated from West Point 1843 and served in the army before and after the war.   Died January 16, 1898 at Georgetown, D.C.

AVERELL, WILLIAM WOODS.   Union Brigadier General, born November 5,1832 at Cameron,New York. Graduated from West Point 1855, served in the army before the war.   Worked as inventor after. Died February 3,1900 at Bath, New York.

AYRES, ROMEYN BECK.   Union Brigadier General, born December 20, 1825 at East Creek,New York. Graduated from West Point 1847 and served in the army before and after the war.   Died December 4, 1888 at Fort Hamilton, New York.

BAILEY, JOSEPH.   Union Brigadier General, born May 6, 1825 in Pennsville,Ohio. Lumberman before the war, sheriff after. Died March 21,1867 at Nevada,Missouri after being shot by two prisoners he had arrested.

BAIRD, ABSALOM. Union Brigadier General, born August 20,1824 at Washington,Pennsylvania. Attended Washington College, graduated from West Point 1849.   Served in the army both before and after the war. Died June 14,1905 at Relay, Maryland.

BAKER, ALPHEUS. Confederate Brigadier General, born May 28,1828 in Abbeville District, South Carolina.   Lawyer before and after the war. Died October 2,1891 at Louisville, Kentucky.

BAKER, EDWARD DICKINSON. Union Major General, born February 24, 1811 in London,England. A lawyer and in politics before the war. Killed in battle October 21,1861 at Ball's Bluff, Virginia.

BAKER, LAURENCE SIMMONS.   Confederate Brigadier General, born May 15,1830 in Gates County,North Carolina. Graduated from West Point 1851,then served in the army until the war. Railroad station agent following the war.   Died April 10, 1907 at Suffolk, Virginia.

BALDWIN, WILLIAM EDWIN.   Confederate Brigadier General, born July 28,1827 at Statesburg, South Carolina. Book ana stationery business before the war.   Died February 19, 1864 near Dog River Factory, Alabama after falling from his horse.

BANKS, NATHANIEL PRENTISS. Union Major General,born January 30, 1816 in Waltham,Massachusetts. Governor of Massachusetts before the war, lawyer, politics and U.S. Marshal after.   Died September 1,1894 at Waltham, Massachusetts.

BARKSDALE,WILLIAM. Confederate Brigadier General,born August 21, 1821 at Smyrna, Tennessee. Attended University of Nashville and served in Congress before the war. Wounded in battle July 2,1863 at Gettysburg, Pennsylvania and died the following day.

BARLOW, FRANCIS CHANNING.   Union Brigadier General, born October 19,1834 in Brooklyn, New York. Attended Harvard University. Lawyer before the war,politics and U.S. Marshal after. Died January 11,1896 at New York City, New York.

BARNARD, JOHN GROSS. Union Brigadier General, born May 19, 1815 in Sheffield, Massachusetts. Graduated from West Point 1833 and served in the army before and after the war. Died May 14,1882 in

Detroit, Michigan.

BARNES, JAMES.   Union Brigadier General, born December 28, 1801 in Boston,Massachusetts. Graduated from West Point 1829. Engineer before the war,on railroad commission after. Died February 12,1869 in Springfield, Massachusetts.

BARNES, JOSEPH K.(initial only)   Union Brigadier General, born July 21,1817 in Philadelphia, Pennsylvania. Attended University of Pennsylvania.   Doctor in the army before and after the war. Died June 30,1882 at Washington, D.C.

BARRINGER, RUFUS. Confederate Brigadier General,born December 2, 1821 in Cabarrus County, North Carolina. Attended University of North Carolina. Lawyer before the war, in politics after. Died February 3,1895 at Charlotte, North Carolina.

BARRY, JOHN DECATUR. Confederate Brigadier General,born June 21, 1839 in Wilmington,North Carolina. Attended University of North Carolina until the war, newspaper editor after.   Died March 24, 1867 in Wilmington,North Carolina.

BARRY, WILLIAM FARQUHAR. Union Brigadier General,born August 18, 1818 in New York City,New York. Graduated from West Point 1838, then served in the army before and after the war. Died July 18, 1879 in Baltimore, Maryland.

BARTLETT, JOSEPH JACKSON.   Union Brigadier General, born November 21,1834 in Binghamton,New York. Lawyer before the war, U.S. Minister to Sweden after.   Died January 14, 1893 at Baltimore, Maryland.

BARTLETT, WILLIAM FRANCIS. Union Brigadier General,born June 6, 1840 in Haverhill, Massachusetts. Attended Harvard University until the war, business after. Died December 17, 1876 at Pittsford, Massachusetts.

BARTON, SETH MAXWELL.   Confederate Brigadier General, born September 8, 1829 in Fredericksburg, Virginia. Graduated from West Point 1849 and served in the army before the war. Died April 11, 1900 at Washington, D.C.

BATE, WILLIAM BRIMAGE. Confederate Major General,born October 7, 1826 at Bledsoe's Lick, Tennessee.   Newspaper editor before the war, Governor of Tennessee after. Died March 9,1905 at Washington, D.C.

BATTLE, CULLEN ANDREWS.   Confederate Brigadier General, born June 1, 1829 in Powelton, Georgia. Lawyer before the war, newspaper editor after. Died April 8,1905 at Greensboro,North Carolina.

BAXTER, HENRY.   Union Brigadier General, born September 8, 1821 at Sidney Plains, New York. Miller before the war, U.S.Minister to Honduras after. Died December 30,1873 at Jonesville,Michigan.

BAYARD, GEORGE DASHIELL.   Union Brigadier General, born December 18,1835 at Seneca Falls,New York.   Graduated from West Point 1856 and served in the army before the war.   Wounded in battle December 13, 1862 at Fredericksburg, Virginia, and died the next day.

BEAL, GEORGE LAFAYETTE. Union Brigadier General,born May 21,1825 at Norway,Maine. Attended Westbrook Seminary. Bookbinder before the war, State Treasurer of Maine after. Died December 11, 1896 at Norway, Maine.

BEALE, RICHARD LEE TURBERVILLE.   Confederate Brigadier General, born May 22,1819 at Hickory Hill, Virginia.   Attended University of Virginia. Lawyer and served in Congress before and after the war. Died April 21,1893 at Hague, Virginia.

BEALL, WILLIAM NELSON RECTOR.   Confederate Brigadier General, born March 20, 1825 at Bardstown, Kentucky. Graduated from West Point 1848,then served in the army until the war. Worked as merchant following the war. Died July 25,1883 in McMinnville, Tennessee.

BEATTY, JOHN. Union Brigadier General, born December 16,1828 at Sandusky,Ohio.   Banker before the war, banker and served in Congress after. Died December 21,1914 at Columbus, Ohio.

BEATTY, SAMUEL. Union Brigadier General, born December 16, 1820 in Mifflin County,Pennsylvania. Sheriff before the war and farmer after. Died May 26,1885 at Massillon, Ohio.

BEAUREGARD, PIERRE GUSTAVE TOUTANT.   Confederate General, born May 28,1818 in St. Bernard Parish,Louisiana. Graduated from West Point 1838 and served in the army before the war, railroad president after.   Died February 20, 1918 at New Orleans, Louisiana.

BEE, BARNARD ELLIOTT.   Confederate Brigadier General, born February 8,1824 in Charleston, South Carolina.   Brother of Hamilton Bee.   Graduated from West Point 1845, then served in the army until the war. Wounded in battle July 21,1861 at Manassas Junction, Virginia, and died the next day.

BEE, HAMILTON PRIOLEAU.   Confederate Brigadier General, born July 22, 1822 in Charleston, South Carolina.   Brother of Barnard Bee. In politics before the war.   Died October 3, 1897 in San Antonio, Texas.

BELKNAP, WILLIAM WORTH.   Union Brigadier General, born September 22,1829 at Newburgh,New York. Attended Princeton University. Lawyer before the war, U.S. Secretary of War after. Died October 13,1890 in Washington, D.C.

BELL, TYREE HARRIS. Confederate Brigadier General, born September 5,1815 in Covington, Tennessee. Farmer before and after the war.   Died September 1, 1902 at New Orleans, Louisiana.

BENHAM, HENRY WASHINGTON. Union Brigadier General,born April 17,

1813 in Meriden,Connecticut. Attended Yale University,then graduated from West Point 1837.   Soldier before and after the war.
Died June 1,1894 in New York City, New York.

BENNING,HENRY LEWIS. Confederate Brigadier General,born April 2,
1814 in Columbia County,Georgia. Attended University of Georgia.
Judge before the war, lawyer after.   Died July 10,1875 at Columbus, Georgia.

BENTON, WILLIAM PLUMMER.   Union Brigadier General, born December 25,1828 at New Market,Maryland.   Judge before the war,lawyer
after.   Died of yellow fever March 14,1867 in New Orleans, Louisiana.

BERRY, HIRAM GREGORY.   Union Major General, born August 27,1824
in Rockland,Maine.   Banker and in politics before the war. Killed in battle May 3, 1863 at Chancellorsville, Virginia.

BIDWELL,DANIEL DAVIDSON. Union Brigadier General,born August 12,
1819 in Black Rock, New York.   Police Justice before the war.
Killed in battle October 19, 1864 at Cedar Creek, Virginia.

BIRGE, HENRY WARNER.   Union Brigadier General, born August 25,
1825 at Hartford,Connecticut. Merchant before the war and in the
lumber business after.   Died June 1, 1888 in New York City, New
York.

BIRNEY, DAVID BELL.   Union Major General, born May 29, 1825 in
Huntsville, Alabama.   Brother of William Birney.   Lawyer before
the war.   Died of malaria October 18,1864 at Philadelphia, Pennsylvania.

BIRNEY, WILLIAM.   Union Brigadier General, born May 28, 1819 in
Madison County, Alabama.   Brother of David Birney.   Editor and
lawyer before the war,lawyer after.   Died August 14,1907 at Forest Glen, Maryland.

BLAIR, JR., FRANCIS PRESTON.   Union Major General, born Februar-
y 19,1821 in Lexington,Kentucky.   Attended Princeton University.
Lawyer and served in Congress before the war, U.S.Senator after.
Died July 8, 1875 at St.Louis, Missouri.

BLANCHARD, ALBERT GALLATIN.   Confederate Brigadier General, born
September 10,1810 at Charlestown, Massachusetts.   Graduated from
West Point 1829.   Teacher and merchant before the war, surveyor
after.   Died June 21,1891 in New Orleans, Louisiana.

BLENKER, LOUIS LUDWIG. Union Brigadier General,born May 12,1812
at Worms, Germany.   Farmer before the war.   Died October 31,1863
in Rockland County, New York.

BLUNT, JAMES GILLPATRICK.   Union Major General,born July 21,1826
in Trenton,Maine. Doctor before and after the war. Died July 27,
1881 at Washington, D.C.

BOGGS, WILLIAM ROBERTSON.   Confederate Brigadier General, born

March 18, 1829 in Augusta, Georgia.   Graduated from West Point
1853, then soldier   until the war.   Engineer following the war.
Died September 11, 1911 at Winston-Salem, North Carolina.

BOHLEN, HENRY.   Union Brigadier General, born October 22,1810 at
Bremen,Germany.   Liquor dealer before the war.   Killed in battle
August 22, 1862 at Freeman's Ford, Virginia.

BONHAM, MILLEDGE LUKE.   Confederate Brigadier General, born December 25, 1813 in Edgefield District, South Carolina.   Attended
University of South Carolina.   Lawyer and served in Congress before the war, railroad commissioner after.   Died August 27, 1890
at White Sulphur Springs, North Carolina.

BOWEN, JAMES.   Union Brigadier General, born February 25, 1808
in New York City, New York.   Railroad president before the war,
retired after.   Died September 29,1886 at Dobbs Ferry, New York.

BOWEN, JOHN STEVENS.   Confederate Major General,born October 30,
1830 in Savannah,Georgia. Graduated from West Point 1853.   Worked as architect until the war. Died of dysentery July 13,1863 at
Raymond, Mississippi.

BOYLE, JERIMIAH TILFORD.   Union Brigadier General, born May 22,
1818 in Mercer County, Kentucky.   Attended Princeton University.
Lawyer before the war,in railroad business after.   Died July 28,
1871 at Louisville, Kentucky.

BRADLEY, LUTHER PRENTICE.   Union Brigadier General, born December 8,1822 in New Haven,Connecticut.   Bookkeeper before the war,
served in the army after.   Died March 13,1910 at Tacoma,Washing-
ton.

BRAGG, BRAXTON.   Confederate General, born March 22,1817 in Warrenton, North Carolina.   Graduated from West Point 1837.   Served
in the army until the war, farmer and engineer after.   Died September 27, 1876 at Galveston, Texas.

BRAGG, EDWARD STUYVESANT.   Union Brigadier General, born February 20,1827 in Unadilla,New York.   Attended Hobart College. Lawyer before the war,in politics after.   Died June 20,1912 at Fond
du Lac, Wisconsin.

BRANCH, LAWRENCE O'BRYAN.   Confederate Brigadier General, born
November 28,1820 in Enfield, North Carolina.   Attended Princeton
University, then a lawyer and served in Congress before the war.
Killed in battle September 17, 1862 at Sharpsburg, Maryland.

BRANDON, WILLIAM LINDSAY. Confederate Brigadier General,born in
1802 in Washington, Mississippi.   Attended Princeton University.
A farmer before the war, retired after.   Died October 8, 1890 in
Wilkinson County, Mississippi.

BRANNAN, JOHN MILTON.   Union Brigadier General, born July 1,1819
in Washington,D.C.   Graduated from West Point 1841 and served in
the army before and after the war.   Died December 16,1892 in New

York City, New York.

BRANTLEY, WILLIAM FELIX.   Confederate Brigadier General, born
March 12,1830 in Greene County,Alabama. Lawyer before and after
the war. Murdered by unknown killer November 2,1870 while riding
in a buggy near Winona, Mississippi.

BRATTON, JOHN. Confederate Brigadier General, born March 7,1831
at Winnsboro,South Carolina. Attended University of South Carolina.   Practiced medicine before the war, served in Congress
after. Died January 12, 1898 in Winnsboro, South Carolina.

BRAYMAN, MASON.   Union Brigadier General, born May 23, 1813 in
Buffalo,New York. Lawyer before the war, Governor of Idaho Territory after.   Died February 27, 1895 at Kansas City, Missouri.

BRECKINRIDGE, JOHN CABELL. Confederate Major General, born January 15, 1821 at Lexington, Kentucky.   Attended Centre College.
U.S. Vice President before the war, lawyer after.   Died May 17,
1875 in Lexington, Kentucky.

BREVARD, THEODORE WASHINGTON.   Confederate Brigadier General,
born August 26, 1835 in Tuskegee, Alabama.   Attended University
of Virginia.   In politics before the war, practiced law after.
Died June 20,1882 at Tallahassee, Florida.

BRIGGS, HENRY SHAW. Union Brigadier General, born August 1,1824
in Lanesboro,Massachusetts. Attended Williams College,then lawyer before the war. Judge following the war. Died September 23,
1887 at Pittsfield, Massachusetts.

BROOKE, JOHN RUTTER. Union Brigadier General, born July 21,1838
in Montgomery County,Pennsylvania. Served in the army following
the war. Died September 5, 1926 in Philadelphia, Pennsylvania.

BROOKS, WILLIAM THOMAS HARBAUGH. Union Major General, born January 28, 1821 in Lisbon, Ohio.   Graduated from West Point 1841.
Served in the army before the war, farmer after. Died July 19,
1870 at Huntsville, Alabama.

BROWN, EGBERT BENSON.   Union Brigadier General, born October 4,
1816 in Brownsville, New York.   In railroad business before the
war,farmer after. Died February 11,1902 at West Plains,Missouri.

BROWN, JOHN CALVIN.   Confederate Major General, born January 6,
1827 in Giles County,Tennessee. Attended Jackson College. Lawyer before the war,Governor of Tennessee after.   Died August 17,
1889 at Red Boiling Springs, Tennessee.

BROWNE, WILLIAM MONTAGUE. Confederate Brigadier General,born in
1823 in Dublin, Ireland. Attended National University.   Editor
before the war, college professor after. Died April 28, 1883 at
Athens, Georgia.

BRYAN, GOODE. Confederate Brigadier General,born August 31,1811
in Hancock County,Georgia. Graduated from West Point 1834. Farm-

er before the war,retired after. Died August 16,1885 in Augusta, Georgia.

BUCHANAN, ROBERT CHRISTIE. Union Brigadier General,born March 1, 1811 in Baltimore, Maryland. Graduated from West Point 1830 and served in the army before and after the war.   Died November 29, 1878 at Washington, D.C.

BUCKINGHAM, CATHARINUS PUTNAM.   Union Brigadier General, born March 14, 1808 in Zanesville, Ohio.   Graduated from West Point 1829. Ironworks owner before the war,steelworks president after. Died August 30, 1888 at Chicago, Illinois.

BUCKLAND, RALPH POMEROY.   Union Brigadier General, born January-y 20,1812 at Leyden,Massachusetts.   Lawyer before the war,served in Congress after.   Died May 27,1892 in Fremont, Ohio.

BUCKNER, SIMON BOLIVAR.   Confederate Lieutenant General,   born April 1,1823 in Hart County,Kentucky. Graduated from West Point 1844. In business until the war,Governor of Kentucky after. Died January 8, 1914 at Munfordville, Kentucky.

BUELL, DON CARLOS.   Union Major General, born March 23, 1818 at Lowell, Ohio. Graduated from West Point 1841, and served in the army before the war.   Ironworks operator after the war. Died November 19, 1898 in Paradise, Kentucky.

BUFORD, ABRAHAM. Confederate Brigadier General,born January 18, 1820 at Woodford,Kentucky. Attended Centre College and graduated from West Point 1841. Farmer before and after the war. Two cousins were Federal generals. Committed suicide June 9,1884 at Danville, Indiana.

BUFORD, JOHN. Union Brigadier General,born March 4,1826 in Woodford County,Kentucky. Graduated from West Point 1848 and served in the army before the war. Brother of Napoleon Buford. Died of typhoid fever December 16, 1863 at Washington, D.C.

BUFORD, NAPOLEON BONAPARTE. Union Brigadier General, born January 13,1807 in Woodford County,Kentucky. Brother of John Buford. Graduated from West Point 1827. Banker before the war and worked in civil service after.   Died March 28,1883 in Chicago,Illinois.

BULLOCK, ROBERT. Confederate Brigadier General,born December 8, 1828 at Greenville, North Carolina.   School teacher before the war, lawyer and served in Congress after.   Died July 27, 1905 in Ocala, Florida.

BURBRIDGE, STEPHEN GANO. Union Brigadier General,born August 19, 1831 in Scott County, Kentucky. Attended Georgetown College and practiced law before the war. Died December 2,1894 in Brooklyn, New York.

BURNHAM, HIRAM. Union Brigadier General,about 1814 in Narraguagus, Maine and worked as a lumberman before the war.   Killed in battle September 29, 1864 at Fort Harrison, Virginia.

BURNS, WILLIAM WALLACE.   Union Brigadier General, born September 3,1825 in Coshocton,Ohio. Graduated from West Point 1847 and served in the army before and after the war.   Died April 19,1892 at Beaufort, South Carolina.

BURNSIDE, AMBROSE EVERETT.   Union Major General,born May 23,1824 at Liberty,Indiana.   Graduated from West Point 1847.   In business and served in Congress before the war,   Governor of Rhode Island after.   Died September 13, 1881 at Bristol, Rhode Island.

BUSSEY, CYRUS.   Union Brigadier General, born October 5, 1833 at Hubbard, Ohio.   In politics before the war, lawyer and merchant after.   Died March 2, 1915 in Washington, D.C.

BUSTEED, RICHARD.   Union Brigadier General,born February 16,1822 at Cavan,Ireland.   Lawyer before the war,judge after.   Died September 14, 1922 in New York City, New York.

BUTLER, BENJAMIN FRANKLIN.   Union Major General,born November 5, 1818 at Deerfield,   New Hampshire.   Attended Colby College and practiced law before the war.   Governor of Massachusetts after the war.   Died January 11, 1893 at Washington,D.C.

BUTLER, MATTHEW CALBRAITH.   Confederate Major General,   born March 8, 1836 at Greenville, South Carolina.   Lawyer before the war, U.S. Senator after.   Died April 14, 1909 at Washington,D.C.

BUTTERFIELD, DANIEL.   Union Major General, born October 31,1831 in Utica,New York.   Attended Union College.   Lawyer and in business before and after the war. Died July 17,1901 at Cold Spring, New York.

CABELL, WILLIAM LEWIS.   Confederate Brigadier General, born January 1,1827 at Danville,Virginia. Graduated from West Point 1850 and served in the army before the war.   Following the war worked as lawyer and U.S. Marshal.   Died   February 22, 1911 in Dallas, Texas.

CADWALADER, GEORGE.   Union Major General, born May 16, 1806 in Philadelphia,Pennsylvania. In business before and after the war. Died February 3, 1879 at Philadelphia, Pennsylvania.

CALDWELL, JOHN CURTIS.   Union Brigadier General, born April 17, 1833 at Lowell, Vermont.   Attended Amherst College.   School principal before the war,lawyer and in politics after.   Died August 31,1912 in Calais, Maine.

CAMERON, ROBERT ALEXANDER. Union Brigadier General,born February 22, 1828 in Brooklyn,New York.   Attended Indiana Medical College.   Editor before the war, prison warden after.   Apparently never practiced medicine.   Died March 15, 1894 at Canon City, Colorado.

CAMPBELL, ALEXANDER WILLIAM.   Confederate Brigadier General, born June 4,1828 at Nashville, Tennessee. Attended West Tennessee College, then   practiced law before and after the war.   Died

June 13, 1893 in Jackson, Tennessee.

CAMPBELL, CHARLES THOMAS.   Union Brigadier General, born August 10, 1823 in Franklin County, Pennsylvania. In politics before the war,hotel operator after. Died April 15, 1895 in Scotland, South Dakota after falling on the steps at his hotel.

CAMPBELL, WILLIAM BOWEN.   Union Brigadier General, born February 1,1807 in Sumner County, Tennessee.   Lawyer and Governor of Tennessee before the war, in politics after.   Died August 19, 1867 at Lebanon, Tennessee.

CANBY, EDWARD RICHARD SPRIGG.   Union Major General, born November 9, 1817 at Piatt's Landing, Kentucky.   Attended Wabash College and graduated from West Point 1839. Served in the army before and after the war.   Killed by Indians while negotiating a treaty in Siskiyou County, California on April 11, 1873.

CANTEY, JAMES. Confederate Brigadier General, born December 30, 1818 at Camden,South Carolina. Attended South Carolina College, lawyer and in politics before the war. Farmer following the war. Died June 30, 1874 at Fort Mitchell, Alabama.

CAPERS, ELLISON. Confederate Brigadier General,born October 14, 1837 in Charleston,South Carolina. Attended South Carolina Military Academy. Teacher before the war,Episcopal minister after. Died April 22, 1908 at Columbia, South Carolina.

CARLETON, JAMES HENRY. Union Brigadier General,born December 27, 1814 at Lubec, Maine.   Served in the army before and after the war.   Died of pneumonia January 7, 1873 at San Antonio, Texas.

CARLIN, WILLIAM PASSMORE.   Union Brigadier General, born November 24, 1829 at Carrollton, Illinois. Graduated from West Point 1850 and served in the army before and after the war.   Died October 4, 1903 at Whitehall, Montana.

CARR, EUGENE ASA.   Union Brigadier General, born March 20, 1830 in Erie County, New York.   Graduated from West Point 1850 and served in the army before and after the war.   Died December 2, 1910 in Washington, D.C.

CARR, JOSEPH BRADFORD. Union Brigadier General, born August 16, 1828 in Albany, New York. Tobacconist before the war, Secretary of State for New York after. Died February 24,1895 at Troy, New York.

CARRINGTON, HENRY BEEBEE. Union Brigadier General,born March 2, 1824 at Wallingford,Connecticut. Attended Yale University,practiced law before the war and served in the army after. Died October 26, 1912 in Boston, Massachusetts.

CARROLL, SAMUEL SPRIGG.   Union Brigadier General, born September 21, 1832 in Washington, D.C. Graduated from West Point 1856 and served in the army before and after the war.   Died January 28, 1893 in Montgomery County, Maryland.

CARROLL, WILLIAM HENRY. Confederate Brigadier General,born about 1810 in Nashville, Tennessee. Postmaster before the war.   Died May 3, 1868 at Montreal, Canada.

CARTER, JOHN CARPENTER. Confederate Brigadier General, born December 19, 1837 at Waynesboro, Georgia.   Attended University of Virginia and practiced law before the war. Killed in battle November 30, 1864 at Franklin, Tennessee.

CARTER, SAMUEL POWHATAN. Union Brigadier General,born August 6, 1819 in Elizabethton, Tennessee.   Attended Princeton University and graduated from Annapolis in 1846. Served in the U.S.Navy before and after the war.   Possibly the only officer in U.S. history to achieve the ranks of Brigadier General in the army and Commodore in the navy.   Died May 26, 1891 in Washington, D.C.

CASEY, SILAS.   Union Major General, born July 12, 1807 in East Greenwich,Rhode Island. Graduated from West Point 1826 and served in the army before and after the war.   Died January 22, 1882 at Brooklyn, New York

CHALMERS, JAMES RONALD. Confederate Brigadier General,born January 11, 1831 in Halifax County, Virginia. Attended South Carolina College.   Lawyer before the war, served in Congress after. Died April 9, 1898 at Memphis, Tennessee.

CHAMBERLAIN, JOSHUA LAWRENCE. Union Brigadier General,born September 8, 1828 in Brewer, Maine. Attended Bowdoin College, college professor before the war,Governor of Maine after. Died February 24, 1914 at Portland, Maine.

CHAMBERS, ALEXANDER.   Union Brigadier General, born August 23, 1832 at Great Valley, New York.   Graduated from West Point 1853 and served in the army before and after the war. Died January 2, 1888 in San Antonio, Texas.

CHAMBLISS JR., JOHN RANDOLPH.   Confederate Brigadier General, born January 23, 1833 at Hicksford, Virginia. Farmer before the war.   Killed in battle August 16, 1864 on Charles City Road, Virginia.

CHAMPLIN, STEPHEN GARDNER.   Union Brigadier General,born July 1, 1827 in Kingston,New York. Attended Rhinebeck Academy and practiced law before the war. Wounded in spring of 1862 in battle of Seven Pines, Virginia.   Died of these wounds January 24, 1864.

CHAPMAN, GEORGE HENRY. Union Brigadier General,born November 22, 1832 at Holland,Massachusetts. Attended Marion County Seminary. Lawyer and editor before the war,Judge after.   Died June 16,1882 in Indianapolis, Indiana.

CHEATHAM, BENJAMIN FRANKLIN. Confederate Major General,born October 20, 1820 at Nashville, Tennessee.   Farmer before the war, postmaster after. Died September 4,1886 in Nashville,Tennessee.

CHESNUT JR., JAMES. Confederate Brigadier General, born January 18,1815 in Camden, South Carolina. Attended Princeton University. A lawyer and U.S. Senator before the war, in politics after. Died February 1, 1885 at Camden, South Carolina.

CHETLAIN, AUGUSTUS LOUIS.   Union Brigadier General, born December 26,1824 in St. Louis, Missouri. In business before the war, banker after.   Died March 15, 1914 at Chicago, Illinois.

CHILTON, ROBERT HALL.   Confederate Brigadier General, born February 25, 1815 in Loudoun County, Virginia. Graduated from West Point 1837 and served in the army before the war.   President of manufacturing company after the war.   Died February 18, 1879 in Columbus, Georgia.

CHURCHILL,THOMAS JAMES. Confederate Major General,born March 10, 1824 in Jefferson County, Kentucky. Attended St. Mary's College. Postmaster before the war, Governor of Mississippi after.   Died May 14, 1905 in Little Rock, Arkansas.

CLANTON, JAMES HOLT.   Confederate Brigadier General, born January 8,1827 in Columbia County, Georgia. Lawyer before and after the war. Murdered on September 27, 1871 by a drunken ex-federal officer in Knoxville, Tennessee.

CLARK, CHARLES. Confederate Brigadier General, born May 24,1811 in Lebanon,Kentucky. School teacher before the war, Governor of Mississippi after. Died December 18,1877 in Bolivar County,Mississippi.

CLARK JR., JOHN BULLOCK.   Confederate Brigadier General, born January 14,1831 at Fayette, Missouri. Attended Missouri University, practiced law before the war and served in Congress after. Died September 7, 1903 in Washington, D.C.

CLAY, CASSIUS MARCELLUS.   Union Major General, born October 19, 1810 in Madison County, Kentucky. Attended Yale University. In politics before the war.   Died July 22, 1903 in Madison County, Kentucky.

CLAYTON, HENRY DELAMAR. Confederate Major General,born March 7, 1827 in Pulaski County, Georgia.   Attended Emory and Henry College. Lawyer and in politics before the war,farmer after.   Died October 13, 1889 at Tuskaloosa, Alabama.

CLAYTON, POWELL.   Union Brigadier General, born August 7, 1833 in Delaware County,Pennsylvania.   Engineer before the war, Governor of Arkansas after. Died August 25,1914 in Washington,D.C.

CLEBURNE, PATRICK RONAYNE.   Confederate Major General, born March 17,1828 at Bridgepark Cottage,Ireland. Lawyer and druggist before the war.   Killed in battle on November 30,1864 at Franklin, Tennessee.

CLINGMAN, THOMAS LANIER.   Confederate Brigadier General, born July 27,1812 at Huntsville, North Carolina. Attended University of North Carolina. U.S.Senator and practiced law before and after the war. Died November 3,1897 in Morgantown,North Carolina.

CLUSERET, GUSTAVE PAUL.   Union Brigadier General, born June 13, 1823 at Suresnes,France.   Soldier before the war,in foreign politics after. Died August 22, 1900 at Hyeres, France.

COBB, HOWELL.   Confederate Major General, born September 7, 1815 in Jefferson County, Georgia. Brother of Thomas Cobb. Attended University of Georgia. Lawyer and Governor of Georgia before the war, in business after.   Died October 9, 1915 in New York City, New York.

COBB, THOMAS READE ROOTES.   Confederate Brigadier General, born April 10, 1823 in Jefferson County, Georgia.   Brother of Howell Cobb. Attended University of Georgia and practiced law before the war. Killed in battle on December 13,1862 at Fredericksburg, Virginia.

COCKRANE, JOHN.   Union Brigadier General, born August 27, 1813 in Palatine,New York. Attended Hamilton College. Practiced law and served in Congress before the war, in politics after.   Died February 7, 1898 in New York City, New York

COCKE, PHILIP ST. GEORGE.   Confederate Brigadier General, born April 17,1809 in Fluvanna County, Virginia. Graduated from West Point 1832.   Farmer before the war.   Committed suicide December 26, 1861 in Powhatan County, Virginia.

COCKRELL, FRANCIS MARION.   Confederate Brigadier General, born October 1, 1834 at Warrensburg, Missouri.   Attended Chapel Hill College. Lawyer before the war, U.S.Senator after. Died December 13, 1915 in Washington, D.C.

COLQUITT, ALFRED HOLT.   Confederate Brigadier General, born April 20,1824 at Monroe,Georgia.   Attended Princeton University. Lawyer and served in Congress before the war,Governor of Georgia after. Died March 26, 1894 in Washington, D.C.

COLSTON, RALEIGH EDWARD.   Confederate Brigadier General, born October 31,1825 in Paris,France. Attended Virginia Military Institute.   Professor of French before the war,served in the Egyptian army after. Died July 29, 1896 at Richmond, Virginia.

CONNER, JAMES. Confederate Brigadier General, born September 1, 1829 at Charleston,South Carolina. Attended South Carolina College. Lawyer and U.S.District Attorney before the war, Attorney General of South Carolina after. Died June 26,1883 at Richmond, Virginia.

CONNOR, PATRICK EDWARD. Union Brigadier General, born March 17, 1820 in County Kerry, Ireland.   Miner before the war, newspaper editor after.   Died December 17, 1891 at Salt Lake City, Utah.

CONNOR, SELDEN.   Union Brigadier General, born January 25, 1839 at Fairfield,Maine. Attended Tufts College before the war, Governor of Maine after.   Died July 9, 1917 in Augusta, Maine.

COOK, JOHN. Union Brigadier General,born June 12,1825 at Belle-ville,Illinois. Sheriff before the war,in politics after. Died October 13, 1910 in Ransom, Michigan.

COOK, PHILIP. Confederate Brigadier General, born July 31, 1817 in Twiggs County,Georgia. Attended Oglethorpe University. Prac-ticed law before the war,served in Congress after. Died May 21, 1894 at Atlanta, Georgia.

COOKE, JOHN ROGERS. Confederate Brigadier General, born June 9, 1833 at Jefferson Barracks,Missouri. Attended Harvard Universi-ty. Served in the army before the war, merchant after. Son of Philip St.George Cooke. Died April 10,1891 in Richmond,Virginia.

COOKE, PHILIP ST. GEORGE. Union Brigadier General,born June 13, 1809 in Leesburg,Virginia. Father of John Cooke. Graduated from West Point 1827, then served in the army before and after the war. Died March 20, 1895 at Detroit, Michigan.

COOPER, DOUGLAS HANCOCK. Confederate Brigadier General,born No-vember 1, 1815 in Amite County, Mississippi. Attended Virginia University. U.S. Indian Agent before the war, Indian Represent-ative after. Died April 29, 1879 in Bryan County, Oklahoma.

COOPER, JAMES. Union Brigadier General,born May 8,1810 in Fred-erick County,Maryland. Attended Washington College. Lawyer and served in Congress before the war. Died March 28,1863 at Colum-bus, Ohio.

COOPER, JOSEPH ALEXANDER. Union Brigadier General, born Novem-ber 25,1823 at Cumberland Falls,Kentucky. Farmer before and af-ter the war. Died May 20, 1910 in Stafford, Kansas.

COOPER, SAMUEL. Confederate General, born June 12,1798 in Hack-ensack,New Jersey. Graduated from West Point 1815 and served in the army before the war.   Died December 3, 1876 at Alexandria, Virginia.

COPELAND, JOSEPH TARR. Union Brigadier General, born May 6,1813 in Newcastle,Maine. Attended Harvard University, then practiced law and was Judge before the war.   Died May 6, 1893 at Orange Park, Florida.

CORCORAN, MICHAEL. Union Brigadier General, born September 21, 1827 at Carrowkeel, Ireland. Postal clerk before the war. Died December 22, 1863 at Fairfax Courthouse, Virginia when his horse fell on him.

CORSE, JOHN MURRAY. Union Brigadier General, born April 27,1835 at Pittsburg,Pennsylvania. Lawyer before the war,postmaster af-ter.   Died April 27, 1893 in Winchester, Massachusetts.

CORSE, MONTGOMERY DENT. Confederate Brigadier General, born March 14, 1816 at Alexandria, Virginia. Banker before and after the war. Died February 11, 1895 in Alexandria, Virginia.

COSBY, GEORGE BLAKE.   Confederate Brigadier General, born January 19, 1830 in Louisville, Kentucky. Graduated from West Point 1852, served in the army before the war and farmer after.   Died June 29, 1909 at Oakland, California.

COUCH, DARIUS NASH.   Union Major General, born July 23, 1822 in Putnam County,New York. Graduated from West Point 1846. Copper manufacturer before the war, in civil service after.   Died February 12, 1897 at Norwalk, Connecticut.

COWDIN, ROBERT. Union Brigadier General, born September 18,1805 at Jamaica,Vermont. In the lumber business before the war. Died July 9, 1874 in Boston, Massachusetts.

COX, JACOB DOLSON. Union Major General, born October 27,1828 in Montreal, Canada. Attended Oberlin College.   Lawyer before the war, Governor of Ohio after. Died August 4, 1900 at Gloucester, Massachusetts.

COX,WILLIAM RUFFIN. Confederate Brigadier General,born March 11, 1832 at Scotland Neck,North Carolina. Lawyer before the war and in Congress after.   Died December 26,1919 in Richmond,Virginia.

CRAIG, JAMES.   Union Brigadier General, born February 28, 1817 in Washington County,Pennsylvania. Lawyer and in politics before the war, railroad president after. Died October 21, 1888 at St. Joseph, Missouri.

CRAWFORD, SAMUEL WYLIE.   Union Brigadier General, born November 8,1829 in Franklin County, Pennsylania. Attended University of Pennsylvania,then practiced medicine before the war.   Continued serving in the army following the war. Died November 3,1892 in Philadelphia, Pennsylvania.

CRITTENDEN,GEORGE BIBB. Confederate Major General,born March 20, 1812 at Russellville,Kentucky. Brother of Thomas Leonidas Crittenden.   Graduated from West Point 1832 and served in the army before the war.   State Librarian of Kentucky following the war. Died November 27, 1880 in Danville, Kentucky.

CRITTENDEN, THOMAS LEONIDAS.   Union Major General, born May 15, 1819 in Russellville, Kentucky.   Lawyer before the war, served in the army after. Brother of George Crittenden and first cousin of Thomas T. Crittenden.   Died October 23,1893 at Annandale,New York.

CRITTENDEN, THOMAS TURPIN.   Union Brigadier General, born October 16, 1825 in Huntsville, Alabama. Attended Transylvania College, practiced law before and after the war. Died September 8, 1905 at Gloucester, Massachusetts.

CROCKER, MARCELLUS MONROE. Union Brigadier General, born February 6, 1830 at Franklin, Indiana. Attended West Point for two years, then practiced law before the war.   Died of tuberculosis August 26, 1865 in Washington, D.C.

CROOK, GEORGE.   Union Major General, born September 8, 1828 at Dayton, Ohio. Graduated from West Point 1852 and served in the army before and after the war.   Died March 21, 1890 in Chicago, Illinois.

CROXTON, JOHN THOMAS.   Union Brigadier General,born November 20, 1836 in Bourbon County, Kentucky.   Attended Yale University and practiced law before the war,U.S.Minister to Bolivia after. Died April 16, 1874 in Bolivia.

CRUFT, CHARLES.   Union Brigadier General, born January 12, 1826 at Terre Haute, Indiana.   Attended Wabash College.   Lawyer and railroad president before the war,lawyer after.   Died March 23, 1883 in Terre Haute, Indiana.

CULLUM, GEORGE WASHINGTON.   Union Brigadier General, born February 25,1809 in New York City,New York. Graduated from West Point 1833 and served in the army before and after the war.   Died February 29, 1892 at New York City, New York.

CUMMING, ALFRED.   Confederate Brigadier General,born January 30, 1829 in Augusta,Georgia. Graduated from West Point 1849, served in the army before the war, farmer after.   Died December 5,1910 at Rome, Georgia.

CURTIS, NEWTON MARTIN.   Union Brigadier General,born May 21,1835 at DePeyster, New York.   School Teacher before the war, in politics after.   Died January 8, 1910 in New York City, New York.

CURTIS, SAMUEL RYAN.   Union Major General, born February 3, 1805 in Clinton County,New York. Graduated from West Point 1831,then worked as engineer before the war.   Died December 26, 1866 at Council Bluffs, Iowa.

CUSTER, GEORGE ARMSTRONG.   Union Brigadier General, born December 5, 1839 in New Rumley, Ohio. Graduated from West Point 1861 and served in the army before and after the war.   Killed by Indians on June 25, 1876 at Little Big Horn, Montana.

CUTLER, LYSANDER.   Union Brigadier General,born February 16,1807 in Worcester County, Massachusetts.   School teacher before the war. Died July 30, 1866 at Milwaukee, Wisconsin.

DANA, NAPOLEON JACKSON TECUMSEH.   Union Major General, born April 15,1822 in Eastport,Maine. Graduated from West Point 1842. Served in the army and banker before the war, in railroad business after.   Died July 15, 1905 at Portsmouth, New Hampshire.

DANIEL, JUNIUS. Confederate Brigadier General,born June 27,1828 at Halifax, North Carolina.   Graduated from West Point 1852 and served in the army before the war. Wounded in battle May 12,1864 at Spotsylvania Courthouse,Virginia, and died the following day.

DAVIDSON, JOHN WYNN Union Brigadier General,born August 18,1824 in Fairfax County, Virginia. Graduated from West Point 1845 and served in the army before and after the war. Died June 26, 1881 at St. Paul, Minnesota.

DAVIDSON, HENRY BREVARD. Confederate Brigadier General, born on January 28, 1831 in Shelbyville, Tennessee. Graduated from West Point 1853, served in the army before the war. Worked as an engineer after the war. Died March 4,1899 at Livermore,California.

DAVIES, HENRY EUGENE. Union Brigadier General, born July 2,1836 in New York City,New York. Attended Columbia College, then lawyer before and after the war. Nephew of Thomas Davies. Died on September 7, 1894 at Middleboro, Massachusetts.

DAVIES, THOMAS ALFRED. Union Brigadier General,born December 3, 1809 in St. Lawrence County,New York. Graduated from West Point 1829. Merchant before the war, writer after. Died August 19,1899 at Ogdensburg, New York.

DAVIS, EDMUND JACKSON. Union Brigadier General, born October 2, 1827 at St. Augustine,Florida. Lawyer and judge before the war, Governor of Texas after. Died February 7,1883 at Austin,Texas.

DAVIS, JEFFERSON COLUMBUS. Union Brigadier General,born March 2, 1828 in Clark County,Indiana. Served in the army before and after the war. Shot down Federal Major General William Nelson in cold blood during a personal feud. Died on November 30,1879 at Chicago, Illinois.

DAVIS, JOSEPH ROBERT. Confederate Brigadier General, born January 12,1825 at Woodville, Mississippi. Attended Miami University, Oxford, Ohio, then a lawyer before and after the war. Died September 15, 1896 in Biloxi, Mississippi.

DAVIS, WILLIAM GEORGE MACKEY. Confederate Brigadier General,born May 9, 1812 at Portsmouth,Virginia. Lawyer before and after the war. Died March 11, 1898 in Alexandria, Virginia.

DEARING, JAMES. Confederate Brigadier General,born on April 25, 1840 in Campbell County,Virginia. Served in the army before the war. Killed in battle April 23, 1865 at High Bridge, Virginia.

DEAS, ZACHARIAH CANTEY. Confederate Brigadier General, born October 25, 1819 in Camden, South Carolina. Cotton broker before the war, stock broker after. Cousin of James Chestnut. Died on March 6, 1882 at New York City, New York.

DEITZLER, GEORGE WASHINGTON. Union Brigadier General, born November 30,1826 at Pine Grove,Pennsylvania. Farmer until the war, worked real estate after. Died April 11,1884 in Tucson,Arizona.

DELAFIELD, RICHARD. Union Brigadier General, born September 1, 1798 in New York City,New York. Graduated from West Point 1818, soldier before the war. Died November 5,1873 at Washington,D.C.

DE LAGNEL, JULIUS ADOLPH. Confederate Brigadier General,born on July 24, 1827 at Newark, New Jersey. Soldier before the war, in steamship business after. Died June 3, 1912 in Washington, D.C.

DE TROBRIAND, PHILIPPE REGIS DENIS DE KEREDERN. Union Brigadier General, born June 4, 1816 at Tours, France. Lawyer before the war, soldier after. Died July 15, 1897 in Bayport, New York.

DENNIS, ELIAS SMITH. Union Brigadier General, born December 4, 1812 in Newburgh, New York. U.S. Marshal before the war, sheriff after. Died December 17, 1894 at Carlyle, Illinois.

DENVER, JAMES WILLIAM. Union Brigadier General, born October 23, 1817 at Winchester, Virginia. Governor of Colorado before the war, practiced law after. Died August 9,1892 in Washington,D.C.

DERUSSY, GUSTAVUS ADOLPHUS. Union Brigadier General, born November 3,1818 in Brooklyn, New York. Attended West Point for three years without graduating. Served in the army before and after the war. Died May 29, 1891 at Detroit, Michigan.

DESHLER, JAMES. Confederate Brigadier General, born February 18, 1833 at Tuscumbia, Alabama. Graduated from West Point 1854 and served in the army before the war. Killed in battle on September 20, 1863 at Chickamauga, Georgia.

DEVENS JR., CHARLES. Union Brigadier General, born April 4,1820 at Charlestown,Massachusetts. Attended Harvard University,practiced law, and was U.S.Marshal before the war, U.S.Attorney General after the war. Died January 7,1891 in Boston,Massachusetts.

DEVIN, THOMAS CASIMER. Union Brigadier General,born December 10, 1822 in New York City, New York. House painter before the war, soldier after. Died April 4, 1878 at New York City, New York.

DIBRELL, GEORGE GIBBS. Confederate Brigadier General, born on April 12,1822 at Sparta, Tennessee. Merchant before the war and served in Congress after. Died May 9,1888 in Sparta, Tennessee.

DIX, JOHN ADAMS. Union Major General, born on July 24, 1798 at Boscawen, New Hampshire. Lawyer before the war, Governor of New York after. Died April 21, 1879 in New York City, New York.

DOCKERY, THOMAS PLEASANT. Confederate Brigadier General, born December 18, 1833 in Montgomery County, North Carolina. Farmer before the war,engineer after. Died February 27,1898 in New York City, New York.

DODGE, CHARLES CLEVELAND. Union Brigadier General, born on September 16, 1841 in Plainfield, New Jersey. In business following the war. Died November 4, 1910 at New York City, New York.

DODGE, GRENVILLE MELLEN. Union Major General, born on April 12, 1831 in Danvers, Massachusetts. Engineer before the war, railroad builder after. Died January 3,1916 at Council Bluffs, Iowa.

DOLES, GEORGE PIERCE. Confederate Brigadier General, born on May 14, 1830 in Milledgeville, Georgia. In business before the war. Killed in battle June 2,1864 at Bethesda Church, Virginia.

DONELSON, DANIEL SMITH. Confederate Major General,born June 23, 1801 in Sumner County,Tennessee. Graduated from West Point 1825. Nephew of President Andrew Jackson. Farmer before the war. Died April 17, 1863 at Montvale Springs, Tennessee.

DOOLITTLE, CHARLES CAMP. Union Brigadier General,born March 16, 1832 in Burlington,Vermont. Merchant before the war, banker after. Died February 20, 1903 at Toledo, Ohio.

DOUBLEDAY, ABNER. Union Brigadier General, born June 26,1819 at Ballston Spa, New York. Graduated from West Point 1842, served in the army before and after the war. Died January 26, 1893 in Mendham,New Jersey

DOW, NEAL. Union Brigadier General, born March 20,1804 at Portland, Maine. Leather tanner before the war, in politics after. Died October 2, 1897 in Portland, Maine.

DRAYTON, THOMAS FENWICK. Confederate Brigadier General,born August 24,1808 in Charleston, South Carolina. Graduated from West Point 1828. Farmer before the war, insurance agent after. Died February 18, 1891 at Florence, South Carolina.

DUBOSE, DUDLEY MCIVER. Confederate Brigadier General, born October 28,1834 in Shelby County, Tennessee. Attended Mississippi University,practiced law before the war,in Congress after. Died March 2, 1883 at Washington, Georgia.

DUFFIE, ALFRED NAPOLEON ALEXANDER. Union Brigadier General,born May 1,1835 in Paris, France. Attended St. Cyr Military College. Soldier before the war, U.S. Consul to Spain after. Died November 8, 1880 at Cadiz, Spain.

DUKE, BASIL WILSON. Confederate Brigadier General, born May 28, 1838 in Scott County,Kentucky. Attended Centre College. Lawyer before and after the war. Died on September 16,1916 at New York City, New York.

DUMONT, EBENEZER. Union Brigadier General,born November 23,1814 at Vevay, Indiana. Attended Indiana University. Lawyer and in politics before the war,served in Congress after. Died April 16, 1871 in Indianapolis, Indiana.

DUNCAN, JOHNSON KELLY. Confederate Brigadier General, born on March 19, 1827 in York, Pennsylvania. Graduated from West Point 1849 and served in the army before the war. Died of fever December 18, 1862 at Knoxville, Tennessee.

DUNOVANT, JOHN. Confederate Brigadier General,born March 5,1825 at Chester, South Carolina. Served in the army before the war. Killed in battle October 1, 1864 at Fort Harrison, Virginia.

DURYEE, ABRAM. Union Brigadier General, born April 29, 1815 in New York City,New York. Importer before the war,Chief of Police after. Died September 27, 1890 at New York City, New York.

DUVAL, ISAAC HARDIN. Union Brigadier General, born September 1, 1824 at Wellsburg, West Virginia.   Merchant before the war, in Congress after. Died July 10, 1902 in Wellsburg, West Virginia.

DWIGHT, WILLIAM. Union Brigadier General, born July 14, 1831 at Springfield, Massachusetts. Manufacturer before the war, worked in railroad management after. Died on April 21, 1888 in Boston, Massachusetts.

DYER, ALEXANDER BRYDIE. Union Brigadier General,born January 10, 1815 at Richmond, Virginia.   Graduated from West Point 1837 and served in the army before and after the war. Died at Washington, D.C. on May 20, 1874.

EARLY, JUBAL ANDERSON. Confederate Lieutenant General, born November 3,1816 in Franklin County, Virginia. Graduated from West Point 1837,then practiced law before and after the war. Died on March 2, 1894 at Lynchburg, Virginia.

EATON, AMOS BEEBE. Union Brigadier General, born May 12,1806 at Catskill, New York. Graduated from West Point 1826, then served in the army before and after the war. Died February 21, 1877 in New Haven, Connecticut.

ECHOLS, JOHN. Confederate Brigadier General, born March 20,1823 in Lynchburg,Virginia. Attended Washington College. Lawyer before the war, in business after. Died May 24, 1896 at Staunton, Virginia.

ECTOR, MATTHEW DUNCAN. Confederate Brigadier General, born February 28,1822 in Putnam County,Georgia. Attended Centre College. Lawyer before the war, Judge after. Died on October 29, 1879 at Tyler, Texas.

EDWARDS, JOHN. Union Brigadier General, born on October 24,1815 at Louisville, Kentucky. Lawyer and in politics before the war, served in Congress after. Died April 8,1894 in Washington, D.C.

EGAN, THOMAS WILBERFORCE. Union Brigadier General,born June 14, 1834 at Watervliet, New York.   Customs collector following the war.   Died February 24, 1887 in New York City, New York.

ELLET, ALFRED WASHINGTON.   Union Brigadier General, born November 11, 1820 at Penn's Manor, Pennsylvania. Attended Bristol Academy. Engineer before the war,banker and in railroad business after. Died January 9, 1895 in El Dorado, Kansas.

ELLIOTT JR., STEPHEN. Confederate Brigadier General, born October 26,1830 in Beaufort,South Carolina. Attended South Carolina College. Farmer before the war, in politics after. Died February 21, 1866 at Aiken, South Carolina.

ELLIOTT, WASHINGTON LAFAYETTE. Union Brigadier General, on born March 31,1825 in Carlisle,Pennsylvania. Attended Dickinson College. Also went to West Point 1841-44,without graduating. Served in the army before and after the war.   Died June 29,1888 at San

Francisco, California.

ELZEY, ARNOLD. Confederate Major General, born December 18,1816 in Somerset County,Maryland. Graduated from West Point 1837 and served in the army before the war,a farmer after. Died February 21,1871 at Baltimore, Maryland.

EMORY,WILLIAM HEMSLEY. Union Brigadier General,born September 7, 1811 in Queen Anne's County,Maryland. Graduated from West Point 1831 and served in the army before and after the war. Died December 1,1887 at Washington, D.C.

EUSTIS, HENRY LAWRENCE. Union Brigadier General,born February 1, 1819 at Boston,Massachusetts. Attended Harvard University, then graduated from West Point 1842. College professor before and after the war. Died January 11,1885 in Cambridge, Massachusetts.

EVANS, CLEMENT ANSELM. Confederate Brigadier General, born February 25,1833 in Stewart County,Georgia. Lawyer and in politics before the war, Episcopal minister after.   Died July 2, 1911 at Atlanta, Georgia.

EVANS, NATHAN GEORGE.   Confederate Brigadier General, born February 3,1824 at Marion, South Carolina. Attended Randolph-Macon College,then graduated from West Point 1848. Served in the army before the war, high school principal after.   Died November 23, 1868 in Midway, Alabama.

EWELL, RICHARD STODDERT.   Confederate Lieutenant General, born February 8, 1817 at Georgetown, D.C.   Graduated from West Point 1840, then served in the army before the war.   Farmer following the war. Died January 25,1872 at Spring Hill, Tennessee.

EWING, HUGH BOYLE. Union Brigadier General,born October 31,1826 at Lancaster, Ohio. Brother of Thomas Ewing, Jr. Attended West Point 1844-48, but did not graduate because of bad grades. Lawyer before the war,U.S.Minister to Holland after. Died June 30, 1905 in Lancaster, Ohio.

EWING JR., THOMAS. Union Brigadier General, born August 7, 1829 in Lancaster,Ohio. Brother of Hugh Ewing. Lawyer and judge before the war,served in Congress after.   Died January 21,1896 at New York City, New York.

FAGAN, JAMES FLEMING.   Confederate Major General, born March 1, 1828 in Clark County,Kentucky. In politics before the war, U.S. Marshal after. Died September 1,1893 at Little Rock, Arkansas.

FAIRCHILD, LUCIUS.   Union Brigadier General, born December 27, 1831 in Portage County, Ohio.   Attended Carroll College. Court clerk before the war, Governor of Wisconsin after. Died May 23, 1896 at Madison, Wisconsin.

FARNSWORTH, ELON JOHN.   Union Brigadier General, born July 30, 1837 at Green Oak,Michigan. Attended Michigan University. Foragemaster before the war. Killed July 3, 1863 in battle at Gettysburg, Pennsylvania.

FARNSWORTH,JOHN FRANKLIN. Union Brigadier General,born March 27, 1820 at Eaton,Quebec, Canada. Uncle of Elon Farnsworth. Lawyer and served in Congress before and after the war. Died July 14, 1897 in Washington, D.C.

FEATHERSTON, WINFIELD SCOTT. Confederate Brigadier General,born August 8,1820 in Murfreesboro,Tennessee. Lawyer and in Congress before the war, Judge after. Died May 28,1891 at Holly Springs, Mississippi.

FERGUSON, SAMUEL WRAGG. Confederate Brigadier General, born November 3,1834 in Charleston,South Carolina. Graduated from West Point 1857,served in the army before the war,lawyer after. Died February 3,1917 at Jackson, Mississippi.

FERRERO, EDWARD. Union Brigadier General, born January 18, 1831 at Granada, Spain. Dance instructor before the war, a ballroom manager after. Died December 11,1899 in New York City,New York.

FERRY, ORRIS SANFORD. Union Brigadier General, born August 15, 1823 at Bethel,Connecticut. Attended Yale University,lawyer and in politics before and after the war. Died November 21, 1875 in Norwalk, Connecticut.

FESSENDEN, FRANCIS. Union Brigadier General, born March 18,1839 in Portland,Maine. Brother of James Fessenden. Attended Bowdoin College, then practiced law before and after the war. Died January 2,1906 at Portland, Maine.

FESSENDEN, JAMES DEERING. Union Brigadier General, born September 28, 1833 at Westbrook, Maine. Brother of Francis Fessenden. Attended Bowdoin College,then practiced law before and after the war. Died November 18, 1882 in Portland, Maine.

FIELD, CHARLES WILLIAM. Confederate Major General,born April 6, 1828 in Woodford County, Kentucky. Graduated from West Point 1849. Served in the army before the war, engineer after. Died April 9,1892 at Washington, D.C.

FINEGAN, JOSEPH. Confederate Brigadier General,born November 17, 1814 in Clones, Ireland. Farmer before the war, cotton broker after. Died October 29,1885 at Rutledge, Florida.

FINLEY, JESSE JOHNSON. Confederate Brigadier General, born November 18, 1812 in Wilson County, Tennessee. Lawyer before the war,served in Congress after. Died November 6,1904 at Lake City, Florida.

FISK, CLINTON BOWEN. Union Brigadier General, born December 8, 1828 in York,New York. In insurance before the war,banker after. Died July 9, 1890 at New York City, New York.

FLOYD, JOHN BUCHANAN. Confederate Brigadier General,born June 1, 1806 in Montgomery County,Virginia. Attended South Carolina Col-

lege. Lawyer and Governor of Virginia before the war.   Died of
illness August 26, 1863 at Abingdon, Virginia.

FORCE, MANNING FERGUSON.   Union Brigadier General, born December 17,1824 in Washington,D.C. Attended Harvard University. Lawyer before the war, judge after.   Died May 8, 1899 at Sandusky,
Ohio.

FORNEY, JOHN HORACE. Confederate Major General, born August 12,
1829 at Lincolnton, North Carolina.   Brother of William Forney.
Graduated from West Point 1852.   Served in the army before the
war,farmer and engineer after.   Died September 13,1902 in Jacksonville,Alabama.

FORNEY, WILLIAM HENRY.   Confederate Brigadier General, born November 9, 1823 at Lincolnton, North Carolina.   Brother of John
Forney. Attended University of Alabama,then practiced law until
the war,in Congress after. Died January 16,1894 in Jacksonville,
Alabama.

FORREST, NATHAN BEDFORD.   Confederate Lieutenant General, born
July 13,1821 in Bedford County,Tennessee. Farmer and slave dealer before the war, railroad president after.   Died October 29,
1877 at Memphis, Tennessee.

FOSTER, JOHN GRAY.   Union Major General, born May 27, 1823 at
Whitefield, New Hampshire.   Graduated from West Point 1846 and
served in the army before and after the war.   Died September 2,
1874 in Nashua, New York

FOSTER, ROBERT SANFORD. Union Brigadier General,born January 27,
1834 in Vernon, Indiana. Tinner before the war, U.S.Marshal after. Died March 3,1903 at Indianapolis, Indiana.

FRANKLIN, WILLIAM BUEL.   Union Brigadier General, born Februar-
y 27,1823 at York, Pennsylvania. Graduated from West Point 1843
and served in the army before the war. Manager of Colt Guns following the war. Died March 8,1903 in Hartford, Connecticut.

FRAZER, JOHN WESLEY.   Confederate Brigadier General, born January 6,1827 in Hardin County,Tennessee. Graduated from West Point
1849. Served in the army before the war, in business after. Died
March 31, 1906 at New York City, New York.

FREMONT, JOHN CHARLES. Union Major General,born January 21,1813
in Savannah,Georgia. Attended Charleston College. Served in the
army before the war, Governor of Arizona after.   Died July 13,
1890 at New York City, New York.

FRENCH, SAMUEL GIBBS.   Confederate Major General, born November 22, 1818 in Gloucester County, New Jersey.   Graduated from
West Point 1843. Served in the army before the war,then a farmer
after. Died April 20, 1910 at Florala, Florida.

FRENCH, WILLIAM HENRY. Union Major General,born January 13,1815
in Baltimore,Maryland. Graduated from West Point 1837,then serv-

ed in the army before and after the war.   Died May 20, 1881 at Washington, D.C.

FROST, DANIEL MARSH.   Confederate Brigadier General, born August 9,1823 in Schenectady County,New York. Graduated from West Point 1844. Manufacturer before the war,farmer after. Died October 29, 1900 at St. Louis County, Missouri.

FRY, BIRKETT DAVENPORT.   Confederate Brigadier General, born June 24,1822 in Kanasha County,West Virginia. Attended Virginia Military Institute.   Cotton manufacturer before and after the war. Died January 21, 1891 at Richmond, Virginia.

FRY, JAMES BARNET. Union Brigadier General,born February 22,1827 at Carrollton,Illinois. Graduated from West Point 1847 and served in the army before and after the war.   Died July 11, 1894 in Newport, Rhode Island.

FRY, SPEED SMITH. Union Brigadier General,born September 9,1817 in Boyle County, Kentucky. Attended Wabash College. Lawyer before the war, in civil service after.   Died August 1, 1892 at Louisville, Kentucky.

FULLER, JOHN WALLACE.   Union Brigadier General,born July 28,1827 in Harston, England.   Publisher before the war, in the boot and shoe business after. Died March 12, 1891 at Toledo, Ohio.

GANO, RICHARD MONTGOMERY.   Confederate Brigadier General, born June 17,1830 in Bourbon County,Kentucky. Attended Bacon College. Practiced medicine before the war, Christian Church minister after. Died March 27, 1913 at Dallas, Texas.

GARDNER, FRANKLIN.   Confederate Major General, born January 29, 1823 in New York City, New York. Graduated from West Point 1843 and served in the army before the war, farmer after.   Died April 29, 1873 at Vermillionville, Louisiana.

GARDNER, WILLIAM MONTGOMERY. Confederate Brigadier General,born June 8,1824 in Augusta, Georgia. Graduated from West Point 1846 and served in the army before the war.   Died June 16, 1901 at Memphis, Tennessee.

GARFIELD, JAMES ABRAM. Union Major General,born November 19,1831 in Cuyahoga County, Ohio.   Attended Williams College.   School teacher before the war, U.S.President after. Died September 19, 1881 at Elberon, New Jersey.

GARLAND JR., SAMUEL. Confederate Brigadier General, born December 16,1830 in Lynchburg, Virginia. Attended University of Virginia and practiced law before the war. Killed in battle September 14, 1862 at South Mountain, Maryland.

GARNETT, RICHARD BROOKE.   Confederate Brigadier General, born November 21, 1817 in Essex County, Virginia.   Cousin of Robert Garnett.   Graduated from West Point 1841 and served in the army before the war. Killed in battle July 3,1863 at Gettysburg,Pennsylvania.

GARNETT, ROBERT SELDEN. Confederate Brigadier General, born December 16,1819 in Essex County,Virginia. Cousin of Richard Garnett. Graduated from West Point 1841 and served in the army before the war. Killed in battle July 3, 1861 at Carrick's Ford, Virginia.

GARRARD, KENNER. Union Brigadier General,born September 30,1827 at Fairfield, Kentucky. Attended Harvard University, then graduated from West Point 1851 and served in the army until the war. In politics following the war. Died May 15, 1879 in Cincinnati, Ohio.

GARRARD, THEOPHILUS TOULMIN. Union Brigadier General, born June 7,1812 in Manchester,Kentucky. In politics before the war, farmer after. Died March 15, 1902 at Manchester, Kentucky.

GARTRELL, LUCIUS JEREMIAH. Confederate Brigadier General, born January 7,1821 in Wilkes County,Georgia. Attended Franklin College. Lawyer and in Congress before the war, in politics after. Died April 7, 1891 at Atlanta, Georgia.

GARY, MARTIN WITHERSPOON. Confederate Brigadier General, born March 25,1831 at Cokesbury, South Carolina. Attended Harvard University. Lawyer and in politics before and after the war. Died April 9, 1881 in Edgefield County, South Carolina.

GATLIN, RICHARD CASWELL. Confederate Brigadier General,born January 18, 1819 born in Lenoir County, North Carolina. Attended University of North Carolina and graduated from West Point 1832. Served in the army before the war, farmer after. Died September 8, 1896 at Mt. Nebo, Arkansas.

GEARY, JOHN WHITE. Union Brigadier General, born December 30, 1819 in Mt. Pleasant, Pennsylvania. Attended Jefferson College. Governor of Kansas before the war, Governor of Pennsylvania after. Died January 18, 1873 at Harrisburg, Pennsylvania.

GETTY, GEORGE WASHINGTON. Union Brigadier General, born October 2, 1819 at Georgetown, D.C. Graduated from West Point 1840 and served in the army before and after the war. Died October 1, 1901 in Forest Glen, Maryland.

GHOLSON, SAMUEL JAMESON. Confederate Brigadier General, born May 19,1808 in Madison County,Kentucky. Lawyer and judge before the war, in politics after. Died October 16, 1893 at Aberdeen, Mississippi.

GIBBON, JOHN. Union Major General, born April 20,1827 in Philadelphia,Pennsylvania. Graduated from West Point 1847 and served in the army before and after the war. Died February 6, 1896 at Baltimore, Maryland.

GIBBS, ALFRED. Union Brigadier General, born April 22, 1823 at Astoria, New York. Attended Dartmouth College, then graduated from West Point 1846 and served in the army before and after the war. Died December 26, 1868 in Fort Leavenworth, Kansas.

GIBSON, RANDALL LEE. Confederate Brigadier General,born September 10, 1832 at Versailles, Kentucky. Attended Yale University. Lawyer before the war, U.S.Senator after. Died December 15,1892 in Hot Springs, Arkansas.

GILBERT, CHARLES CHAMPION. Union Brigadier General,born March 1, 1822 in Zanesville, Ohio. Graduated from West Point 1846 and served in the army before and after the war. Died January 17, 1903 at Baltimore, Maryland.

GILBERT, JAMES ISHAM. Union Brigadier General,born July 16,1823 at Louisville,Kentucky. In the lumber business before and after the war. Died February 9, 1884 in Topeka, Kansas.

GILLEM, ALVAN CULLEM. Union Brigadier General,born July 29,1830 in Gainesboro, Tennessee. Graduated from West Point 1851 and served in the army before and after the war. Died December 2, 1875 at Nashville, Tennessee.

GILLMORE, QUINCY ADAMS. Union Major General, born February 28, 1825 at Lorain, Ohio. Graduated from West Point 1849 and served in the army before and after the war. Died April 7, 1888 in Brooklyn, New York.

GILMER, JEREMY FRANCIS. Confederate Major General, born February 23, 1818 in Guilford County, North Carolina. Graduated from West Point 1839. Served in the army before the war, president of gas company after. Died December 1,1883 at Savannah, Georgia.

GIRARDEY, VICTOR JEAN BAPTISTE. Confederate Brigadier General, born June 26, 1837 at Lauw, France. Killed in battle August 16, 1864 at Fussell's Mill, Virginia.

GIST, STATES RIGHTS. Confederate Brigadier General, born September 3,1831 in Union District, South Carolina. Attended South Carolina College and practiced law before the war. Killed in battle November 30, 1864 at Franklin, Tennessee.

GLADDEN, ADLEY HOGAN. Confederate Brigadier General, born October 28, 1810 in Fairfield District, South Carolina. Postmaster before the war. Wounded in battle April 6,1862 at Corinth,Mississippi, and died April 12, 1862.

GODWIN, ARCHIBALD CAMPBELL. Confederate Brigadier General, born in 1831 in Nansemond County, Virginia. Miner and rancher before the war. Killed in battle September 19,1864 at Winchester,Virginia.

GOGGIN, JAMES MONROE. Confederate Brigadier General, born October 23, 1820 in Bedford County, Virginia. Cotton broker before the war. Died October 10, 1889 at Austin, Texas.

GORDON, GEORGE HENRY. Union Brigadier General,born July 19,1823

at Charlestown, Massachusetts.   Graduated from West Point 1846.
Served in the army before the war,lawyer after.   Died August 30,
1886 at Framingham, Massachusetts.

GORDON, GEORGE WASHINGTON.   Confederate Brigadier General, born
October 5,1836 in Giles County,Tennessee.   Attended Western Military Institute.   Surveyor before the war,lawyer and in Congress
after.   Died August 9, 1911 at Memphis, Tennessee.

GORDON, JAMES BYRON.   Confederate Brigadier General, born November 2, 1822 in Wilkesboro, North Carolina.   Attended Emory and
Henry College.   Farmer and in politics before the war.   Wounded
in battle May 13,1864 at Meadow Bridge,Virginia,and died May 18,
1864.

GORDON, JOHN BROWN.   Confederate Major General, born February 6,
1832 in Upson County,Georgia.   Attended Georgia University. Coal
mine developer before the war, Governor of Georgia after.   Died
January 9, 1904 at Miami, Florida.

GORGAS, JOSIAH.   Confederate Brigadier General, born July 1,1818
in Running Pumps, Pennsylvania.   Graduated from West Point 1841.
Served in the army before the war, university president after.
Died May 15, 1883 at Tuskaloosa, Alabama.

GORMAN, WILLIS ARNOLD.   Union Brigadier General,born January 12,
1816 in Flemingsburg,Kentucky.   Governor of Minnesota before the
war,practiced law after.   Died May 20,1876 at St.Paul,Minnesota.

GOVAN, DANIEL CHEVILETTE.   Confederate Brigadier General, born
July 4,1829 in Northampton County,North Carolina.   Attended University of South Carolina.   Farmer before the war, Indian agent
after.   Died March 12, 1911 at Memphis, Tennessee.

GRACIE JR., ARCHIBALD.   Confederate Brigadier General, born December 1, 1832 in New York City, New York.   Graduated from West
Point 1854.   Worked as a merchant before the war. Killed in battle December 2, 1864 at Petersburg, Virginia.

GRAHAM, CHARLES KINNAIRD.   Union Brigadier General,born June 3,
1824 in New York City, New York.   Lawyer and engineer before and
after the war.   Died April 15, 1889 at Lakewood, New Jersey.

GRAHAM, LAWRENCE PIKE.   Union Brigadier General, born January 8,
1815 in Amelia County, Virginia.   Served in the army before and
after the war.   Died September 12, 1905 at Washington, D.C.

GRANBURY, HIRAM BRONSON.   Confederate Brigadier General, born
March 1,1831 in Copiah County,Mississippi. Attended Oakland Col-
lege.   Lawyer and in politics before the war.   Killed in battle
November 30, 1864 at Franklin, Tennessee.

GRANGER, GORDON.   Union Major General, born November 6,1822 at
Joy, New York. Graduated from West Point 1845 and served in the
army before and after the war. Died January 10,1876 in Santa Fe,
New Mexico.

GRANGER, ROBERT SEAMAN.   Union Brigadier General, born May 24, 1816 at Zanesville, Ohio. Graduated from West Point 1838 and served in the army before and after the war. Died April 25,1894 in Washington, D.C.

GRANT, LEWIS ADDISON. Union Brigadier General, born January 17, 1828 in Winhall, Vermont.   Teacher and lawyer before the war, U.S. Secretary of War after. Died March 20,1918 at Minneapolis, Minnesota.

GRANT, ULYSSES SIMPSON. Union Lieutenant General,born April 27, 1822 at Point Pleasant, Ohio.   Graduated from West Point 1843 and served in the army before the war. U.S. President following the war. Died July 23, 1885 in Mt.McGregor, New York.

GRAY, HENRY. Confederate Brigadier General,born January 19,1816 in Laurens District,South Carolina. Attended University of South Carolina. Lawyer before the war and in politics after.   Died December 11, 1892 at Coushatta, Louisiana.

GRAYSON, JOHN BRECKINRIDGE. Confederate Brigadier General, born October 18,1806 in Fayette County,Kentucky. Graduated from West Point 1826 and served in the army before the war.   Died October 21, 1861 of lung disease at Tallahassee, Florida.

GREEN, GEORGE SEARS.   Union Brigadier General, born May 6, 1801 at Apponaug,Rhode Island. Graduated from West Point 1823. Worked as an engineer before and after the war. Died January 28,1899 in Morristown, New Jersey.

GREEN, MARTIN EDWIN. Confederate Brigadier General,born June 3, 1815 in Fauquier County, Virginia.   Sawmill operator before the war. Killed in battle June 25, 1863 at Vicksburg, Mississippi.

GREEN, THOMAS. Confederate Brigadier General, born January 8, 1814 in Amelia County, Virginia.   Attended University of Nashville, then practiced law before the war.   Killed in battle April 12, 1864 at Blair's Landing, Louisiana.

GREER, ELKANAH BRACKIN. Confederate Brigadier General, born October 11,1825 in Paris,Tennessee. Farmer and merchant before the war. Died March 25, 1877 at DeVall's Bluff, Arkansas.

GREGG, DAVID MCMURTRIE. Union Brigadier General, born April 10, 1833 in Huntingdon,Pennslyvania. Graduated from West Point 1855. Served in the army before the war, farmer after. Died August 7, 1916 at Reading, Pennsylvania.

GREGG, JOHN. Confederate Brigadier General, born September 28, 1828 in Lawrence County, Alabama.   Attended LaGrange College, a lawyer and judge before the war. Killed in battle October 7,1864 at Richmond, Virginia.

GREGG, MAXCY. Confederate Brigadier General, born August 1,1814 in Charleston, South Carolina.   Attended South Carolina College and practiced law before the war. Wounded in battle December 13,

1862 at Fredericksburg, Virginia, died two days later.

GRESHAM, WALTER QUINTIN. Union Brigadier General,born March 17, 1832 in Lanesville, Indiana. Lawyer before the war, U.S. Secretary of State after. Died May 28, 1895 at Washington, D.C.

GRIERSON, BENJAMIN HENRY. Union Brigadier General, born July 8, 1826 at Pittsburgh, Pennsylvania. Merchant before the war,served in the army after. Died September 1,1911 in Omena, Michigan.

GRIFFIN, CHARLES. Union Major General, born December 18,1825 at Granville,Ohio. Graduated from West Point 1847 and served in the army before and after the war. Died September 15,1867 in Galveston, Texas.

GRIFFIN, SIMON GOODELL. Union Brigadier General, born August 9, 1824 at Nelson, New Hampshire. Lawyer before the war, politics after. Died January 14, 1902 in Keene, New Hampshire.

GRIFFITH, RICHARD. Confederate Brigadier General, born January 11,1814 in Philadelphia, Pennsylvania. Attended University of Ohio. Teacher and U.S.Marshal before the war. Killed in battle June 29, 1862 at Savage Station, Virginia.

GRIMES, BRYAN. Confederate Major General, born November 2, 1828 in Pitt County,North Carolina. Attended University of North Carolina. Farmer before and after the war. Assasinated from ambush August 14, 1880 in Pitt County, North Carolina.

GROSE, WILLIAM. Union Brigadier General, born December 16, 1812 at Dayton, Ohio. Lawyer and Judge before the war, tax collector after. Died July 30, 1900 in New Castle, Ohio.

GROVER, CUVIER.   Union Brigadier General, born July 29, 1828 in Bethel, Maine.   Graduated from West Point 1850 and served in the army before and after the war. Died June 6,1885 at Atlantic City, New Jersey.

HACKLEMAN, PLEASANT ADAM.   Union Brigadier General, born November 15,1814 in Franklin County,Indiana. Lawyer and judge before the war. Killed in battle at Corinth,Mississippi October 3,1862.

HAGOOD, JOHNSON. Confederate Brigadier General,born February 21, 1829 at Barnwell, South Carolina. Attended South Carolina Military Academy. Lawyer before the war, Governor of South Carolina after. Died January 4, 1898 in Barnwell, South Carolina.

HALLECK, HENRY WAGER. Union Major General, born January 16,1815 in Westernville,New York. Attended Union College,then graduated from West Point 1839. Lawyer and soldier before and after the war. Died January 9, 1872 at Louisville, Kentucky.

HAMILTON, ANDREW JACKSON.   Union Brigadier General, born January 28, 1815 in Huntsville, Alabama. Lawyer and in politics before the war, judge after. Died April 11,1875 at Austin, Texas.

HAMILTON, CHARLES SMITH.   Union Major General, born November 16, 1822 in Westernville, New York. Graduated from West Point 1843. Farmer before the war, U.S.Marshal after. Died April 17,1891 at Milwaukee, Wisconsin.

HAMILTON, SCHUYLER.   Union Major General, born July 25, 1822 at New York City,New York. Graduated from West Point 1841 and served in the army before the war.   Died March 8, 1903 in New York City, New York.

HAMLIN, CYRUS.   Union Brigadier General, born April 26, 1839 at Hampden, Maine.   Attended Colby College and practiced law before and after the war. Died August 28,1867 in New Orleans,Louisiana.

HAMMOND, WILLIAM ALEXANDER.   Union Brigadier General, born August 28,1828 at Annapolis, Maryland.   Attended New York Medical College,soldier and practiced medicine before and after the war. Died January 5, 1900 in Washington, D.C.

HAMPTON, WADE.   Confederate Lieutenant General, born March 28, 1818 at Charleston,South Carolina.   Attended South Carolina College.   In politics before the war,Governor of South Carolina after.   Died April 11, 1902 in Columbia, South Carolina.

HANCOCK, WINFIELD SCOTT.   Union Major General, born February 14, 1824 at Montgomery Square, Pennsylvania.   Graduated from West Point 1844 and served in the army before and after the war. Died February 9, 1886 on Governors Island, New York.

HANSON, ROGER WEIGHTMAN.   Confederate Brigadier General,born August 27, 1827 in Clark County, Kentucky.   Lawyer and in politics before the war.   Wounded in battle January 2, 1863 at Murfreesboro, Tennessee, died January 4, 1863.

HARDEE, WILLIAM JOSEPH.   Confederate Lieutenant General,born October 12, 1815 in Camden County, Georgia.   Graduated from West Point 1838 and served in the army before the war, farmer after. Died November 6, 1873 at Wytheville, Virginia.

HARDEMAN, WILLIAM POLK.   Confederate Brigadier General, born November 4,1816 in Williamson County,Tennessee. Served in the army before the war,farmer after.   Died April 8,1898 at Austin,Texas.

HARDIE, JAMES ALLEN.   Union Brigadier General, born May 5, 1823 at New York City, New York.   Graduated from West Point 1843 and served in the army before and after the war.   Died December 14, 1876 in Washington, D.C.

HARDIN, MARTIN DAVIS.   Union Brigadier General,born June 26,1837 at Jacksonville, Illinois.   Graduated from West Point 1859 and served in the army before and after the war.   Died December 12, 1923 in St.Augustine, Florida.

HARDING, ABNER CLARK.   Union Brigadier General,born February 10, 1807 at East Hampton,Connecticut. Lawyer and in politics before the war,served in Congress after. Died July 19,1874 in Monmouth,

Illinois.

HARKER, CHARLES GARRISON.   Union Brigadier General, born December 2,1835 in Swedesboro, New Jersey.   Graduated from West Point 1858 and served in the army before the war.   Killed in battle June 26, 1864 at Kennesaw Mountain, Georgia.

HARLAND, EDWARD.   Union Brigadier General, born June 24, 1832 in Norwich, Connecticut. Attended Yale University and practiced law before and after the war. Died March 9,1915 at Norwich,Connecticut.

HARNEY, WILLIAM SELBY.   Union Brigadier General, born August 27, 1800 in Haysboro, Tennessee.   Served in the army before the war, retired after.   Died May 9, 1889 at Orlando, Florida

HARRIS, NATHANIEL HARRISON.   Confederate Brigadier General, born August 22, 1834 at Natchez, Mississippi.   Attended University of Louisiana,then practiced law before and after the war.   Died August 23, 1900 in Malvern, England.

HARRIS, THOMAS MALEY.   Union Brigadier General,born June 17,1817 in Wood County, West Virginia.   Doctor before and after the war. Died September 30, 1906 at Harrisville, Virginia.

HARRISON, JAMES EDWARD.   Confederate Brigadier General, born April 24, 1815 in Greenville District, South Carolina.   Brother of Thomas Harrison.   In politics before and after the war.   Died February 23, 1875 at Waco, Texas.

HARRISON, THOMAS.   Confederate Brigadier General,born May 1,1823 in Jefferson County,Alabama.   Brother of James Harrison.   Lawyer and judge before and after the war.   Died July 14, 1891 at Waco, Texas.

HARROW, WILLIAM.   Union Brigadier General, born November 14,1822 at Winchester, Kentucky.   Lawyer before and after the war.   Died September 27, 1872 in New Albany, Indiana.

HARTRANFT, JOHN FREDERICK.   Union Brigadier General, born December 16,1830 in Pottstown, Pennsylvania.   Attended Union College. Lawyer and engineer before the war, Governor of Pennsylvania after.   Died October 17, 1889 at Norristown, Pennsylvania.

HARTSUFF, GEORGE LUCAS.   Union Major General, born May 28, 1830 at Tyre, New York.   Graduated from West Point 1852 and served in the army before and after the war.   Died in New York City, New York, date unknown.

HASCALL, MILO SMITH.   Union Brigadier General,born August 5,1829 in LeRoy, New York.   Graduated from West Point 1852.   Lawyer before the war, banker after.   Died August 30, 1904 at Oak Park, Illinois.

HASKIN, JOSEPH ABEL.   Union Brigadier General, born June 21,1818 at Troy, New York.   Graduated from West Point 1839 and served in the army before and after the war. Died August 3,1874 in Oswego, New York.

HATCH, EDWARD. Union Brigadier General,born December 22,1832 in Bangor,Maine. Attended Norwich University. In the lumber business before the war, served in the army after. Died April 11, 1889 at Fort Robinson, Nebraska.

HATCH, JOHN PORTER. Union Brigadier General,born January 9,1822 at Oswego, New York. Graduated from West Point 1845 and served in the army before and after the war. Died April 12,1901 in New York City, New York.

HATTON, ROBERT HOPKINS. Confederate Brigadier General, born November 2, 1826 at Youngstown, Ohio. Attended Cumberland University, lawyer and served in Congress before the war. Killed in battle May 31, 1862 at Seven Pines, Virginia.

HAUPT, HERMAN. Union Brigadier General, born March 26, 1817 in Philadelphia,Pennsylvania. Graduated from West Point 1835, then worked as engineer before and after the war. Died December 14, 1905 at Jersey City, New Jersey.

HAWES, JAMES MORRISON. Confederate Brigadier General, born January 7, 1824 at Lexington, Kentucky. Graduated from West Point 1845. Served in the army before the war, merchant after. Died November 22, 1889 in Covington, Kentucky.

HAWKINS, JOHN PARKER. Union Brigadier General,born September 29, 1830 in Indianapolis, Indiana. Graduated from West Point 1852 and served in the army before and after the war. Died February 7, 1914 at Indianapolis, Indiana.

HAWLEY, JOSEPH ROSWELL. Union Brigadier General,born October 31, 1826 in Stewartsville,North Carolina. Attended Hamilton College. Lawyer and editor before the war, Governor of Connecticut after. Died March 18, 1905 at Washington, D.C.

HAWTHORNE, ALEXANDER TRAVIS. Confederate Brigadier General,born January 10,1825 in Evergreen,Alabama. Attended Yale University. Lawyer before the war, Baptist minister after. Died May 31,1899 at Dallas, Texas.

HAYES, JOSEPH. Union Brigadier General, born September 14,1835 in South Berwick, Maine. Attended Harvard University. An engineer before the war,in mining after. Died August 19,1912 at New York City, New York.

HAYES, RUTHERFORD BIRCHARD. Union Brigadier General, born October 4,1822 at Delaware, Ohio. Attended Harvard Law School, then practiced law before the war. Governor of Ohio and U.S.President following the war. Died January 13,1893 in Spiegel Grove, Ohio.

HAYNIE, ISHAM NICHOLAS. Union Brigadier General, born November 18, 1824 at Dover, Tennessee. Attended Kentucky Law School and practiced law before and after the war. Died May 22,1868 in

Springfield, Illinois.

HAYS, ALEXANDER.   Union Brigadier General, born July 8,1819 in Franklin, Pennsylvania.   Attended Allegheny College, then graduated from West Point 1844.   Engineer before the war.   Killed in battle May 5, 1864 at the Wilderness, Virginia.

HAYS, HARRY THOMPSON.   Confederate Major General, born April 14, 1820 in Wilson County, Tennessee.   Attended St. Mary's College. Lawyer and in politics before the war, sheriff after.   Died August 21, 1876 at New Orleans, Louisiana.

HAYS, WILLIAM.   Union Brigadier General,born May 9,1819 in Richmond,Virginia.   Graduated from West Point 1840 and served in the army before and after the war.   Died February 7, 1875 at Boston Harbor, Massachusetts.

HAZEN, WILLIAM BABCOCK.   Union Major General, born September 27, 1830 at West Hartford, Vermont.   Graduated from West Point 1855 and served in the army before and after the war.   Died January 16, 1887 in Washington, D.C.

HEBERT, LOUIS.   Confederate Brigadier General,born March 13,1820 in Iberville Parish,Louisiana.   First cousin of Paul Hebert. Attended Jefferson College, then graduated from West Point 1845. Engineer before the war, newspaper editor after. Died January 7, 1901 at St. Martin, Louisiana.

HEBERT, PAUL OCTAVE.   Confederate Brigadier General, born December 12,1818 in Iberville Parish,Louisiana. First cousin of Louis Hebert.   Attended Jefferson College, then graduated from West Point 1840.   Governor of Louisiana before the war, in politics after.   Died August 29, 1880 at New Orleans, Louisiana.

HECKMAN, CHARLES ADAM.   Union Brigadier General,born December 3, 1822 in Easton,Pennsylvania.   Railroad conductor before the war, train dispatcher after. Died January 14,1896 at Germantown,Pennsylvania.

HEINTZELMAN, SAMUEL PETER.   Union Major General, born September 30,1805 at Manheim, Pennsylvania.   Graduated from West Point 1826 and served in the army before and after the war.   Died on May 1, 1880 in Washington, D.C.

HELM, BENJAMIN HARDIN.   Confederate Brigadier General, born June 2, 1831 in Bardstown, Kentucky.   Graduated from West Point 1851.   Lawyer and in politics before the war.   Wounded in battle September 20,1863 at Chickamauga,Georgia,died the following day.

HERRON, FRANCIS JAY.   Union Major General, born February 17,1837 in Pittsburgh,Pennsylvania. Attended Pitt University. Bank clerk before the war, lawyer and U.S. Marshal after.   Died January 8, 1902 at New York City, New York.

HETH, HENRY.   Confederate Major General, born December 16, 1825 in Chesterfield County,Virginia. Graduated from West Point 1847.

Served in the army before the war,insurance business after. Died September 27, 1899 at Washington, D.C.

HIGGINS, EDWARD. Confederate Brigadier General, born in 1821 in Norfolk, Virginia. Served in the U.S.Navy before the war,in insurance after. Died January 31,1875 at San Francisco,California.

HILL, AMBROSE POWELL. Confederate Lieutenant General, born November 9,1825 in Culpeper, Virginia. Graduated from West Point 1847 and served in the army before the war. Killed in battle April 2, 1865 at Petersburg, Virginia.

HILL, BENJAMIN JEFFERSON. Confederate Brigadier General, born June 13, 1825 in McMinnville, Tennessee. In politics before the war, merchant after. Died January 5,1880 at McMinnville,Tennessee.

HILL,DANIEL HARVEY. Confederate Lieutenant General,born July 12, 1821 in York District,South Carolina. Graduated from West Point 1842. College professor before the war,college president after. Died September 24, 1889 at Charlotte, North Carolina.

HINCKS, EDWARD WINSLOW. Union Brigadier General,born May 30,1830 at Bucksport, Maine. In politics before the war, served in the army after. Died February 14,1894 in Cambridge, Massachusetts.

HINDMAN, THOMAS CARMICHAEL. Confederate Major General,born January 28, 1828 in Knoxville, Tennessee. Lawyer before and after the war. Murdered in his home September 28,1868 at Helena, Arkansas by an unknown assailant.

HITCHCOCK, ETHAN ALLEN. Union Major General,born May 18,1798 at Vergennes,Vermont. Graduated from West Point 1817 and served in the army before the war. Died August 5, 1870 in Sparta,Georgia.

HOBSON, EDWARD HENRY. Union Brigadier General,born July 11,1825 at Greensburg, Kentucky. Bank president before the war, in politics after. Died September 14, 1901 in Cleveland, Ohio.

HODGE, GEORGE BAIRD. Confederate Brigadier General,born April 8, 1828 in Fleming County,Kentucky. Graduated from Annapolis 1845. Lawyer and in politics before and after the war. Died August 1, 1892 at Longwood, Florida.

HOGG, JOSEPH LEWIS. Confederate Brigadier General, born September 13, 1806 in Morgan County, Georgia. Lawyer and in politics before the war. Died of dysentery May 16, 1862 at Corinth, Mississippi.

HOKE, ROBERT FREDERICK. Confederate Major General, born May 27, 1837 in Lincolnton, North Carolina. Attended Kentucky Military Institute until the war. Died July 3,1912 at Raleigh,North Carolina.

HOLMES, THEOPHILUS HUNTER. Confederate Lieutenant General, born November 13, 1804 in Sampson County, North Carolina. Graduated

from West Point 1829. Served in the army before the war, farmer
after. Died June 21, 1880 at Fayetteville, North Carolina.

HOLT, JOSEPH.   Union Brigadier General, born January 6, 1807 in
Breckinridge County, Kentucky. Attended Centre College. Lawyer
and in politics before the war, served in the army after.   Died
August 1, 1894 at Washington, D.C.

HOLTZCLAW, JAMES THADEUS. Confederate Brigadier General,born December 17, 1833 at McDonough, Georgia.   Lawyer before the war,
politics after.   Died July 19, 1893 in Montgomery, Alabama.

HOOD, JOHN BELL. Confederate General,born June 1,1831 in Owings-
ville,Kentucky. Graduated from West Point 1853 and served in the
army before the war. Died August 30, 1879 at New Orleans, Louisiana.

HOOKER, JOSEPH.   Union Major General, born November 13, 1814 at
Hadley,Massachusetts. Graduated from West Point 1837 and served
in the army before and after the war.   Died October 31, 1879 in
Garden City, New York.

HOVEY, ALVIN PETERSON.   Union Brigadier General, born Septem-
ber 26, 1821 at Mt. Vernon, Indiana.   Cousin of Charles Hovey.
Lawyer and judge before the war,Governor of Indiana after. Died
November 23, 1891 in Indianapolis, Indiana.

HOVEY, CHARLES EDWARD.   Union Brigadier General, born April 26,
1827 at Thetford, Vermont.   Attended Dartmouth College. School
principal before the war, lobbyist after. Died November 17,1897
in Washington, D.C.

HOWARD, OLIVER OTIS.   Union Major General, born November 8,1830
in Leeds, Maine.   Attended Bowdoin College, then graduated from
West Point 1854.   Served in the army before and after the war.
Died October 26, 1909 at Burlington, Vermont.

HOWE, ALBION PARRIS. Union Brigadier General,born March 13,1818
at Standish, Maine. Graduated from West Point 1841 and served in
the army before and after the war. Died January 25,1897 in Cambridge, Massachusetts.

HUGER, BENJAMIN.   Confederate Major General, born November 22,
1805 in Charleston, South Carolina.   Graduated from West Point
1825.   Served in the army before the war,farmer after. Died December 7, 1877 at Charleston, South Carolina.

HUMES, WILLIAM YOUNG CONN.   Confederate Brigadier General, born
May 1, 1830 at Abingdon, Virginia.   Attended Virginia Military
Institute, then worked as lawyer before and after the war. Died
September 11, 1882 in Huntsville, Alabama.

HUMPHREYS, ANDREW ATKINSON. Union Major General,born November 2,
1810 in Philadelphia, Pennsylvania.   Graduated from West Point
1831 then served in the army before and after the war. Died December 27, 1883 at Washington, D.C.

HUMPHREYS, BENJAMIN GRUBB.   Confederate Brigadier General, born
August 24, 1808 in Claiborne County, Mississippi.   Farmer and in
politics before the war,Governor of Mississippi after.   Died December 20, 1882 in Leflore County, Mississippi.

HUNT, HENRY JACKSON.   Union Brigadier General,born September 14,
1819 at Detroit, Michigan.   Brother of Lewis Hunt.   Graduated
from West Point 1839 and served in the army before and after the
war.   Died February 11, 1889 in Washington, D.C.

HUNT, LEWIS CASS.   Union Brigadier General,born February 23,1824
at Green Bay, Wisconsin.   Brother of Henry Hunt.   Graduated from
West Point 1847, then a soldier before and after the war.   Died
September 6, 1886 in Fort Union, New Mexico.

HUNTER, DAVID.   Union Major General, born July 21,1802 in Washington, D.C.   Graduated from West Point 1822 and served in the
army before the war.   Died February 2, 1886 at Washington, D.C.

HUNTON, EPPA.   Confederate Brigadier General, born September 22,
1822 in Fauquier County, Virginia.   Attended New Baltimore Academy.   Practiced law before the war, in politics after.   Died October 11, 1908 at Richmond, Virginia.

HURLBUT, STEPHEN AUGUSTUS. Union Major General,born November 29,
1815 in Charleston, South Carolina.   Lawyer before the war, in
U.S. Congress after.   Died March 27, 1882 at Lima, Peru.

IMBODEN, JOHN DANIEL.   Confederate Brigadier General, born February 16,1823 at Staunton,Virginia. Attended Washington College,
then practiced law before and after the war. Died August 15,1895
in Damascus, Virginia.

INGALLS, RUFUS.   Union Brigadier General,born August 23,1818 at
Denmark,Maine.   Graduated from West Point 1843 and served in the
army before and after the war.   Died January 15,1893 in New York
City, New York.

IVERSON JR., ALFRED.   Confederate Brigadier General, born February 14, 1829 in Clinton, Georgia.   Served in the army before the
war,orange grower after.   Died March 31,1911 at Atlanta,Georgia.

JACKSON, ALFRED EUGENE.   Confederate Brigadier General,born January 11,1807 in Davidson County, Tennessee.   Attended Washington
and Greeneville College.   Merchant before the war, farmer after.
Died October 30, 1889 at Jonesboro, Tennessee.

JACKSON, CONRAD FEGER.   Union Brigadier General, born September 11,1813 in Alsace, Pennsylvania.   Railroad worker before the
war.   Killed in battle December 13, 1862 at Fredericksburg, Virginia.

JACKSON, HENRY ROOTES.   Confederate Brigadier General, born on
June 24,1820 at Athens,Georgia.   Attended Yale University.   Lawyer before the war, U.S. Minister to Mexico after.   Died May 23,
1898 in Savannah, Georgia.

JACKSON, JAMES STRESHLY.   Union Brigadier General, born September 27,1823 in Fayette County,Kentucky. Attended Centre College. Lawyer and in U.S.Congress before the war.   Killed in battle October 8, 1862 at Perryville, Kentucky.

JACKSON, JOHN KING.   Confederate Brigadier General, born February 8,1828 in Augusta,Georgia. Attended University of South Carolina, then practiced law before and after the war. Died February 27, 1866 at Milledgeville, Georgia.

JACKSON, NATHANIEL JAMES.   Union Brigadier General,born July 28, 1818 in Newburyport, Massachusetts.   Machinist before the war. Died April 21, 1892 at Jamestown, New York.

JACKSON, THOMAS JONATHON.   Confederate Lieutenant General, born January 21,1824 in Clarksburg,West Virginia. Graduated from West Point 1846. College professor before the war.   Accidently shot by his own men May 5, 1863 (died 5/10/63) at Chancellorsville, Virginia.

JACKSON, WILLIAM HICKS. Confederate Brigadier General, born October 1,1835 in Paris, Tennessee.   Attended West Tennessee College, then graduated from West Point 1856.   Served in the army before the war, farmer after. Died March 30, 1903 at Nashville, Tennessee.

JACKSON, WILLIAM LOWTHER.   Confederate Brigadier General,born on February 3,1825 in Clarksburg, West Virginia.   Second cousin of Thomas Jackson.   Lawyer before the war, judge after.   Died on March 24, 1890 at Louisville, Kentucky.

JAMESON, CHARLES DAVIS.   Union Brigadier General, born February 24,1827 in Orono,Maine. In the lumber business before the war. Died of camp fever November 6, 1862 at Bangor, Maine.

JENKINS, ALBERT GALLATIN. Confederate Brigadier General,born November 10,1830 in Cabell County,West Virginia.   Attended Jefferson College,then practiced law and served in Congress before the war.   Wounded in battle May 9,1864 at Cloyd's Mountain,Virginia, died May 21,1864.

JENKINS, MICAH. Confederate Brigadier General, born December 1, 1835 on Edisto Island, South Carolina.   Attended South Carolina Military Academy and was an educator before the war.   Killed by his own men May 6, 1864 near where Stonewall Jackson was shot in the Wilderness, Virginia.

JOHNSON, ADAM RANKIN.   Confederate Brigadier General,born February 8,1834 in Henderson,Kentucky. Surveyor before the war. Died October 20, 1922 at Burnet,Texas.

JOHNSON, ANDREW. Union Brigadier General, born December 29,1808 at Raleigh,North Carolina. Governor of Tennessee before the war, U.S. President after.   Died July 31, 1875 in Elizabethton, Tennessee.

JOHNSON, BRADLEY TYLER. Confederate Brigadier General,born September 29, 1829 in Frederick, Maryland. Attended Princeton University. Lawyer and in politics before and after the war. Died October 5, 1903 at Amelia, Virginia.

JOHNSON, BUSHROD RUST. Confederate Major General,born October 7, 1817, in Belmont County, Ohio.   Graduated from West Point 1840. School teacher before the war,educator after. Died September 12, 1880 at Brighton, Illinois.

JOHNSON, EDWARD. Confederate Major General, born April 16, 1816 at Salisbury, Virginia. Graduated from West Point 1838. Served in the army before the war, farmer after. Died March 2, 1873 in Richmond, Virginia.

JOHNSON, RICHARD W.   Union Brigadier General, born February 27, 1827 in Smithland, Kentucky.   Graduated from West Point 1849. Served in the army before the war,college professor after. Died April 21, 1897 at St.Paul, Minnesota.

JOHNSTON, ALBERT SIDNEY. Confederate General, born February 2, 1803 in Washington, Kentucky. Attended Transylvania University. Graduated from West Point 1826 and served in the army before the war. Killed in battle April 6, 1862 at Shiloh, Tennessee.

JOHNSTON, GEORGE DOHERTY.   Confederate Brigadier General, born May 30, 1832 in Hillsboro, North Carolina.   Attended Cumberland University.   Lawyer and in politics before and after the war. Died December 8, 1910 at Tuscaloosa, Alabama.

JOHNSTON, JOSEPH EGGLESTON.   Confederate General, born February 3,1807 in Farmville,Virginia. Graduated from West Point 1829. Served in the army before the war, in politics after.   Died on March 21, 1891 at Washington, D.C.

JOHNSTON, ROBERT DANIEL.   Confederate Brigadier General, born March 19, 1837 in Lincoln County, North Carolina. Attended University of North Carolina. Lawyer before the war, banker after. Died February 1, 1919 at Winchester, Virginia.

JONES, DAVID RUMPH. Confederate Major General,born April 5,1825 in Orangeburg District,South Carolina. Graduated from West Point 1846 and served in the army before the war. Died of heart trouble January 15, 1863 at Richmond, Virginia.

JONES, JOHN MARSHALL.   Confederate Brigadier General, born on July 26,1820 in Charlottesville, Virginia.   Graduated from West Point 1841 and served in the army before the war. Killed in battle May 5, 1864 at the Wilderness, Virginia.

JONES, JOHN ROBERT.   Confederate Brigadier General, born on March 12,1827 in Harrisonburg, Virginia. Attended Virginia Military Institute. School principal before the war,merchant after. Died April 1, 1901 at Harrisonburg, Virginia.

JONES, SAMUEL. Confederate Major General, born December 17,1819

in Powhatan County, Virginia.   Graduated from West Point 1841.
Served in the army before the war, farmer after.   Died July 31,
1887 at Bedford Springs, Virginia.

JONES, WILLIAM EDMONSON.   Confederate Brigadier General, born on
May 9, 1824 in Washington County, Virginia.   Attended Emory and
Henry College, then graduated from West Point 1848 and served in
the army before the war.   Killed in battle June 5, 1864 at Pied-
mont, West Virginia.

JORDAN, THOMAS. Confederate Brigadier General,born September 30,
1819 in Luray, Virginia. Graduated from West Point 1840.   Served
in the army before the war, editor after.   Died November 27,1895
at New York City, New York.

JUDAH, HENRY MOSES.   Union Brigadier General, born June 12,1821
in Snow Hill,Maryland. Graduated from West Point 1843 and served
in the army before and after the war.   Died January 14, 1866 at
Plattsburg, New York.

KANE, THOMAS LEIPER.   Union Brigadier General, born January 27,
1822 in Philadelphia, Pennsylvania.   Lawyer before the war, in
business after.   Died December 26,1883 in Philadelphia, Pennsylvania.

KAUTZ, AUGUST VALENTINE. Union Brigadier General,born January 5,
1828 in Baden,Germany.   Graduated from West Point 1852 and served in the army before and after the war.   Died September 4, 1895
at Seattle, Washington.

KEARNY, PHILIP.   Union Major General, born June 2, 1815 in New
York City,New York.   Attended Columbia University,then served in
the army before the war.   Killed in battle September 1, 1862 at
Chantilly, Virginia.

KEIM, WILLIAM HIGH.   Union Brigadier General, born June 25,1813
in Reading,Pennsylvania. Served in Congress before the war. Died
of camp fever May 18, 1862 at Harrisburg, Pennsylvania.

KELLEY, BENJAMIN FRANKLIN.   Union Brigadier General, born on
April 10, 1807 in New Hampton, New Hampshire.   Railroad freight
agent before the war, in civil service after.   Died July 16,1891
at Oakland, Maryland.

KELLY, JOHN HERBERT.   Confederate Brigadier General, born on
March 31,1840 in Carrollton,Alabama.   College student before the
war.   Wounded in battle September 2, 1864 at Franklin,Tennessee,
died two days later.

KEMPER, JAMES LAWSON.   Confederate Major General, born June 11,
1823 in Madison County, Virginia.   Attended Washington College.
Lawyer before the war,Governor of Virginia after.   Died April 7,
1895 in Orange County, Virginia.

KENLY, JOHN REESE. Union Brigadier General,born January 11,1818
in Baltimore, Maryland. Lawyer before and after the war.   Died

December 20, 1891 at Baltimore, Maryland.

KENNEDY, JOHN DOBY. Confederate Brigadier General, born January 5,1840 in Camden,South Carolina. Attended University of South Carolina. Lawyer before the war, in politics after. Died on April 14, 1896 at Camden, South Carolina.

KERSHAW, JOSEPH BREVARD. Confederate Major General,born on January 5, 1822 in Camden, South Carolina. Lawyer before the war, judge after. Died April 13, 1894 at Camden, South Carolina.

KETCHUM, WILLIAM SCOTT. Union Brigadier General,born July 7,1813 in Norwalk,Connecticut. Graduated from West Point 1834 and served in the army before and after the war. Murdered by poison on June 28, 1871 at Baltimore, Maryland.

KEYES, ERASMUS DARWIN. Union Major General, born May 29, 1810 in Brimfield, Massachusetts. Graduated from West Point 1832. before the war,banker and in mining after. Died October 14,1895 at Nice, France.

KIERNAN, JAMES LAWLOR. Union Brigadier General,born October 26, 1837 in Galway, Ireland. Attended New York University of Medicine, then practiced medicine before and after the war. Died on November 29, 1869 in New York City, New York.

KILPATRICK, HUGH JUDSON. Union Brigadier General, born on January 14,1836 in Deckertown,New Jersey. Graduated from West Point 1861. U.S.Minister to Chile after the war. Died December 4,1881 at Santiago, Chili.

KIMBALL, NATHAN. Union Brigadier General, born November 22,1822 in Fredericksburg, Indiana. Attended DePauw University. Doctor before the war, State Treasurer of Indiana after. Died on January 21, 1898 at Ogden, Utah.

KING, JOHN HASKELL. Union Brigadier General,born on February 19, 1820 in Sackets Harbor, New York. Served in the army before and after the war. Died April 7, 1888 at Washington, D.C.

KING, RUFUS. Union Brigadier General, born January 26, 1814 in New York City, New York. Graduated from West Point 1833. Editor before the war,U.S.Minister to Rome after. Died October 13,1876 in New York City, New York.

KIRK, EDWARD NEEDLES. Union Brigadier General,born February 29, 1828 in Jefferson County, Ohio. Lawyer before the war. Wounded in battle December 31, 1862 at Murfreesboro, Tennessee, died on July 21, 1863.

KIRKLAND, WILLIAM WHEDBEE. Confederate Brigadier General, born February 13,1833 at Hillsboro,North Carolina. Served in the army before the war, in business after. Died May 12,1915 in Washington, D.C.

KNIPE, JOSEPH FARMER. Union Brigadier General, born March 30,

1823 at Mount Joy, Pennsylvania.   Worked on the railroad before the war, postmaster after.   Died August 18, 1901 in Harrisburg, Pennsylvania.

KRZYZANOWSKI, WLADIMIR.   Union Brigadier General, born July 8, 1824 at Raznova,Germany.   Engineer before the war, in civil service after.   Died January 31, 1887 in New York City, New York.

LANDER, FREDERICK WEST.   Union Brigadier General, born on December 17, 1821 at Salem, Massachusetts.   Engineer before the war. Died March 2, 1862 at Paw Paw, Virginia.

LANE, JAMES HENRY.   Confederate Brigadier General,born July 28, 1833 at Mathews Court House, Virginia.   Attended University of Virginia, then college professor before and after the war.   Died September 21, 1907 in Auburn, Alabama.

LANE, WALTER PAYE.   Confederate Brigadier General, born February 18,1817 in County Cork,Ireland.   Miner before the war,merchant after.   Died January 28, 1892 at Marshall, Texas.

LAUMAN, JACOB GARTNER.   Union Brigadier General,born January 20, 1813 at Taneytown, Maryland.   In business before the war.   Died February 9, 1867 in Burlington, Iowa.

LAW, EVANDER McIVOR.   Confederate Brigadier General, born on August 7,1836 in Darlington, South Carolina.   Attended South Carolina Military Academy,then a teacher before the war and educator after.   Died October 31, 1920 at Bartow, Florida.

LAWLER, MICHAEL KELLY. Union Brigadier General,born November 16, 1814 in County Kildare,Ireland. Farmer before and after the war. Died July 26, 1882 at Equality, Illinois.

LAWTON, ALEXANDER ROBERT.   Confederate Brigadier General, born November 4, 1818 in Beaufort District, South Carolina.   Attended Harvard Law School,practiced law and in politics before the war, U.S. Minister to Austria after.   Died on July 2, 1896 at Clifton Springs, New York.

LEADBETTER, DANVILLE.   Confederate Brigadier General, born August 26,1811 in Leeds,Maine.   Graduated from West Point 1836 and served in the army before the war.   Died on September 26,1866 at Clifton, Canada.

LEDLIE, JAMES HEWETT.   Union Brigadier General, born April 14, 1832 in Utica,New York.   Attended Union College, engineer before and after the war.   Died August 15, 1882 at Staten Island, New York.

LEE, ALBERT LINDLEY.   Union Brigadier General, born January 16, 1834 at Fulton, New York.   Attended Union College, lawyer and a Supreme Court Justice before the war.   In business after.   Died December 31, 1907 in New York City, New York.

LEE, EDWIN GRAY. Confederate Brigadier General,born May 27,1836

at Leeland,Virginia. Attended William and Mary College and practiced law before the war.   Died August 24,1870 in Yellow Sulphur
Springs, Virginia.

LEE, FITZHUGH.   Confederate Major General, born November 19,1835
in Fairfax County, Virginia.   Nephew of General Robert E. Lee.
Graduated from West Point 1856,and served in the army before the
war.   Governor of Virginia after.   Died April 28,1905 at Washington, D.C.

LEE, GEORGE WASHINGTON CUSTIS.   Confederate Major General, born
September 16, 1832 at Fortress Monroe, Virginia.   Eldest son of
General Robert E. Lee. Graduated from West Point 1854,served in
the army before the war, college president after.   Died Februar-
y 18, 1913 in Alexandria, Virginia.

LEE, ROBERT EDWARD.   Confederate General, born January 19, 1807
in Westmoreland County,Virginia. Graduated from West Point 1829.
Served in the army before the war,college president after.   Died
October 12, 1870 at Lexington, Virginia.

LEE, STEPHEN DILL.   Confederate Lieutenant General, born September 22, 1833 in Charleston, South Carolina.   Graduated from West
Point 1854. Served in the army before the war,farmer and in politics after.   Died May 28, 1908 at Vicksburg, Mississippi.

LEE, WILLIAM HENRY FITZHUGHS.   Confederate Major General, born
May 31,1837 at Arlington,Virginia.   Second son of General Robert
E.Lee.   Attended Harvard University. Farmer before the war,serv-
ed in U.S. Congress after.   Died October 15,1891 in Alexandria,
Virginia.

LEGGETT, MORTIMER DORMER. Union Brigadier General,born April 19,
1821 in Ithaca,New York.   Lawyer before and after the war.   Died
January 6, 1896 at Cleveland, Ohio.

LEVENTHORPE, COLLETT. Confederate Brigadier General,born May 15,
1815 at Devonshire, England.   Served in the army before the war.
Died December 1, 1889 in Wilkes County, North Carolina.

LEWIS, JOSEPH HORACE.   Confederate Brigadier General,   born on
October 29,1824 at Glasgow, Kentucky.   Attended Centre College.
A lawyer before the war, judge and in U.S.Congress after.   Died
July 6, 1904 in Scott County, Kentucky.

LEWIS, WILLIAM GASTON.   Confederate Brigadier General, born on
September 3, 1835 at Rocky Mount, North Carolina.   Attended the
University of North Carolina. School teacher and surveyor before
the war, engineer after.   Died January 7,1901 in Goldsboro,North
Carolina.

LIDDELL, ST.JOHN RICHARDSON. Confederate Brigadier General,born
September 6, 1815 in Woodville, Mississippi.   Farmer before and
after the war.   Murdered on February 14, 1870 by a neighboring
planter at Catahoula Parish, Louisiana.

LIGHTBURN, JOSEPH ANDREW JACKSON.   Union Brigadier General, born
September 21, 1824 in Webster, Pennsylvania.   Served in the army
before the war, a Baptist minister after.   Died May 17, 1901 at
Broad Run, Pennsylvania.

LILLEY, ROBERT DOAK.   Confederate Brigadier General, born January 28, 1836 in Greenville, Virginia.   Attended Washington College.   Salesman before the war, financial agent after.   Died on
November 12, 1886 at Richmond, Virginia.

LITTLE, LEWIS HENRY.   Confederate Brigadier General, born on
March 19, 1817 in Baltimore,Maryland.   Served in the army before
the war.   Killed in battle on September 19,1862 at Iuka, Mississippi.

LOCKWOOD, HENRY HAYES.   Union Brigadier General, born August 17,
1814 in Kent County, Delaware.   Graduated from West Point 1836.
College professor before and after the war.   Died December 7,
1899 at Georgetown, D.C.

LOGAN, JOHN ALEXANDER.   Union Major General, born on February 9,
1826 in Jackson County, Illinois.   Served in U.S.Congress before
and after the war.   Died December 26, 1886 at Washington, D.C.

LOGAN, THOMAS MULDRUP.   Confederate Brigadier General, born on
November 3,1840 in Charleston, South Carolina.   Attended University of South Carolina until the war, in railroad management after.   Died August 11, 1914 in New York City, New York.

LOMAX, LUNSFORD LINDSAY.   Confederate Major General, born November 4, 1835 in Newport, Rhode Island.   Graduated from West Point
1856.   Served in the army before the war, college president after.   Died May 28, 1913 at Washington, D.C.

LONG, ARMISTEAD LINDSAY.   Confederate Brigadier General, born
September 3, 1825 in Campbell County, Virginia.   Graduated from
West Point 1850.   Served in the army before the war,engineer and
writer after.   Died April 29, 1891 at Charlottesville, Virginia.

LONG, ELI.   Union Brigadier General, born June 16, 1837 in Woodford County,Kentucky.   Attended Frankfort Military Academy, then
served in the army before the war,lawyer after.   Died January 5,
1903 at New York City, New York.

LONGSTREET, JAMES.   Confederate Lieutenant General, born January 8,1821 in Edgefield District,South Carolina.   Graduated from
West Point 1842 and served in the army before the war.   The U.S.
Minister to Turkey after the war. Died January 2,1904 at Gaines-
ville, Georgia.

LORING, WILLIAM WING.   Confederate Major General, born December 4, 1818 at Wilmington, North Carolina.   Lawyer and served in
the army before the war.   Served in Egypian army following the
war.   Died December 30, 1886 in New York City, New York.

LOVELL, MANSFIELD.   Confederate Major General, born October 20, 1822 in Washington, D.C. Graduated from West Point 1842. Served in the army before the war, engineer and Street Commissioner after. Died June 1, 1884 at New York City, New York.

LOWREY, MARK PERRIN. Confederate Brigadier General, born December 30, 1828 in McNairy County, Tennessee. Baptist minister before the war, college president after.   Died February 27, 1885 at Middleton, Tennessee.

LOWRY, ROBERT. Confederate Brigadier General, born March 10,1830 in Chesterfield District, South Carolina. Lawyer before the war, Governor of Mississippi after. Died January 19,1910 at Jackson, Mississippi.

LUCAS, THOMAS JOHN.   Union Brigadier General, born September 9, 1826 in Lawrenceburg, Indiana. Watchmaker before the war, postmaster after.   Died November 16, 1908 at Lawrenceburg, Indiana.

LYON, HYLAN BENTON.   Confederate Brigadier General, born February 22, 1836 in Caldwell County, Kentucky.   Graduated from West Point 1856.   Served in the army before the war, farmer after. Died April 25, 1907 at Eddyville, Kentucky.

LYON, NATHANIEL. Union Brigadier General, born on July 14, 1818 in Ashford, Connecticut.   Graduated from West Point in 1841 and served in the army before the war.   Killed in battle August 10, 1861 at Wilson's Creek, Missouri.

LYTLE, WILLIAM HAINES. Union Brigadier General, born November 2, 1826 in Cincinnati, Ohio. Practiced law before the war. Killed in battle September 20, 1863 at Chickamauga, Georgia.

MACKALL, WILLIAM WHANN.   Confederate Brigadier General, born on January 18, 1817 in Cecil County, Maryland. Graduated from West Point 1837.   Served in the army before the war, a farmer after. Died August 12, 1891 in Fairfax County, Virginia.

MACKENZIE, RANALD SLIDELL. Union Brigadier General, born July 27, 1840 in Westchester County, New York. Attended Williams College, then graduated from West Point 1862, and served in the army following the war. Died January 19,1889 at Staten Island, New York.

MACRAE, WILLIAM. Confederate Brigadier General, born September 9, 1834 in Wilmington, North Carolina. An engineer before the war, railroad superintendent after. Died February 11,1882 at Augusta, Georgia.

MAGRUDER, JOHN BANKHEAD.   Confederate Major General, born May 1, 1807 at Port Royal, Virginia.   Graduated from West Point 1830. Served in the army before the war and with the Mexican army after. Died February 18, 1871 in Houston, Texas.

MAHONE, WILLIAM. Confederate Major General, born December 1,1826 in Southhampton County, Virginia. Attended Virginia Military Institute. Worked as engineer before the war, U.S. Senator after.

Died October 8, 1895 at Washington, D.C.

MAJOR, JAMES PATRICK. Confederate Brigadier General,born May 14, 1836 at Fayette,Missouri. Graduated from West Point 1856. Served in the army before the war,farmer after. Died May 7, 1877 in Austin, Texas.

MALTBY,JASPER ADALMORN. Union Brigadier General,born November 3, 1826 at Kingsville, Ohio. Gunsmith before the war, merchant after. Died December 12, 1867 in Vicksburg, Mississippi.

MANEY, GEORGE EAR. Confederate Brigadier General,born August 24, 1826 at Franklin,Tennessee. Attended Nashville University. Lawyer before the war, in politics after. Died February 9, 1901 in Washington, D.C.

MANIGAULT, ARTHUR MIDDLETON. Confederate Brigadier General,born October 26,1824 at Charleston,South Carolina. In business before the war, farmer and in politics after. Died August 17, 1886 in Georgetown County, South Carolina.

MANSFIELD, JOSEPH KING FENNO. Union Brigadier General, born December 22, 1803 in New Haven, Connecticut. Graduated from West Point 1822 and served in the army before the war. Wounded in battle on September 17,1862 and died the next day at Sharpsburg, Maryland.

MANSON, MAHLON DICKERSON. Union Brigadier General, born February 20,1820 in Piqua, Ohio. Druggist before the war,in U.S.Congress after. Died February 4, 1895 at Crawfordsville, Indiana.

MARCY, RANDOLPH BARNES. Union Brigadier General, born April 9, 1812 at Greenwich,Massachusetts. Graduated from West Point 1832 and served in the army before and after the war. Died on November 2, 1887 in West Orange, New Jersey.

MARMADUKE, JOHN SAPPINGTON. Confederate Major General, born on March 14,1833 at Arrow Rock,Missouri. Graduated from West Point 1857 and served in the army before the war. Governor of Missouri following the war. Died December 28,1887 in Jefferson City, Missouri.

MARSHALL, HUMPHREY. Confederate Brigadier General, born January 13,1812 at Frankfort,Kentucky. Graduated from West Point 1832. Lawyer and served in U.S. Congress before the war, lawyer after. Died March 28, 1872 in Louisville, Kentucky.

MARSTON, GILMAN. Union Brigadier General, born August 20, 1811 at Orford, New Hampshire. Attended Harvard University. Lawyer and served in U.S. Congress before and after the war. Died on July 3, 1890 in Exeter, New Hampshire.

MARTIN, JAMES GREEN. Confederate Brigadier General, born February 14,1819 in Elizabeth County, North Carolina. Graduated from West Point 1840. Served in the army before the war,lawyer after. Died October 4, 1878 at Asheville, North Carolina.

MARTIN, WILLIAM THOMPSON.   Confederate Major General, born on March 25, 1823 in Glasgow, Kentucky.   Attended Centre College. Practiced law before the war,in politics after.   Died March 16, 1910 at Natchez, Mississippi.

MARTINDALE, JOHN HENRY. Union Brigadier General, born March 20, 1815 in Hudson Falls, New York. Graduated from West Point 1835. Lawyer before the war, Attorney General of New York after. Died December 13, 1881 at Nice, France.

MASON, JOHN SANFORD.   Union Brigadier General, born August 21, 1824 at Steubenville, Ohio.   Graduated from West Point 1847 and served in the army before and after the war.   Died November 29, 1897 in Washington, D.C.

MATTHIES, CHARLES LEOPOLD. Union Brigadier General,born May 31, 1824 in Bromberg, Germany. Attended Halle University. In the liquor business before the war,politics after. Died October 16, 1868 at Burlington, Iowa.

MAURY, DABNEY HERNDON.   Confederate Major General, born May 21, 1822 in Fredericksburg,Virginia. Attended the University of Virginia, then graduated from West Point 1846.   Served in the army before the war,U.S.Minister to Colombia after. Died January 11, 1900 at Peoria, Illinois.

MAXEY, SAMUEL BELL.   Confederate Major General, born March 30, 1825 at Tompkinsville,Kentucky. Graduated from West Point 1846. Lawyer before the war, U.S. Senator after. Died August 16, 1895 in Eureka Springs, Arkansas.

MCARTHUR, JOHN.   Union Brigadier General, born November 17,1826 in Erskine,Scotland. Irons works owner before the war,postmaster after. Died May 15, 1906 at Chicago, Illinois.

MCCALL, GEORGE ARCHIBALD. Union Brigadier General,born March 16, 1802 at Philadelphia, Pennsylvania.   Graduated from West Point 1825 and served in the army until the war. Died February 26,1868 in Belair, Pennsylvania.

MCCAUSLAND, JOHN.   Confederate Brigadier General, born September 13, 1836 at St. Louis, Missouri. Attended Virginia Military Institute. College professor before the war,farmer after. Died January 22, 1927 in Mason County, West Virginia.

MCCLELLAN, GEORGE BRINTON. Union Major General,born December 3, 1826 in Philadelphia,Pennsylvania. Attended University of Pennsylvania,then graduated from West Point 1846. Served in the army before the war, Governor of New Jersey after.   Died October 29, 1885 at Orange, New Jersey.

MCCLERNAND, JOHN ALEXANDER.   Union Major General, born May 30, 1812 in Hardinsburg,Kentucky. Lawyer and served in U.S.Congress before the war, in politics after. Died on September 20,1890 at Springfield, Illinois.

MCCOMB, WILLIAM. Confederate Brigadier General,born November 21, 1828 in Mercer County,Pennsylvania. Manufacturer before the war, farmer after.   Died July 21, 1918 at Gordonsville, Virginia.

MCCOOK, ALEXANDER MCDOWELL. Union Major General, born April 22, 1831 in Columbiana County, Ohio.   Graduated from West Point 1852 and served in the army before and after the war.   Brother of Edward McCook, first cousin of Robert McCook. Died June 12,1903 at Dayton, Ohio.

MCCOOK, EDWARD MOODY. Union Brigadier General,born June 15,1833 in Steubenville,Ohio. Lawyer before the war,Governor of Colorado Territory after.   Died September 9, 1909 at Chicago, Illinois.

MCCOOK, ROBERT LATIMER. Union Brigadier General, born on December 28,1827 in New Lisbon, Ohio. Lawyer before the war. Wounded in battle August 5,1862 and died the next day at Winchester,Virginia.

MCCOWN, JOHN PORTER. Confederate Major General, born August 19, 1815 at Sevierville, Tennessee. Graduated from West Point 1840. Served in the army before the war, school teacher and farmer after.   Died January 22, 1879 in Little Rock, Arkansas.

MCCULLOCH, BEN. Confederate Brigadier General,born November 11, 1811 in Rutherford County,Tennessee. Brother of Henry McCulloch. U.S. Marshal before the war.   Killed in battle March 7, 1862 at Elkhorn Tavern, Arkansas.

MCCULLOCH, HENRY EUSTACE.   Confederate Brigadier General, born December 6,1816 in Rutherford County, Tennessee. Brother of Ben McCulloch.   U.S. Marshal before the war, farmer after. Died on March 12, 1895 at Rockport, Texas.

MCDOWELL, IRVIN.   Union Major General, born October 15, 1818 at Columbus, Ohio.   Graduated from West Point 1838, then served in the army before and after the war. Died May 4,1885 in San Francisco, California.

MCGINNIS, GEORGE FRANCIS. Union Brigadier General,born March 19, 1826 at Boston,Massachusetts. Hatter before the war, postmaster after. Died May 29, 1910 in Indianapolis, Indiana.

MCGOWAN, SAMUEL. Confederate Brigadier General, born October 9, 1819 in Laurens District,South Carolina. Attended South Carolina College. Lawyer and in politics before the war,judge and in politics after.   Died August 9, 1897 at Abbeville, South Carolina.

MCINTOSH, JAMES MCQUEEN. Confederate Brigadier General, born in 1828 in Tampa,Florida. Brother of John McIntosh. Graduated from West Point 1849 and served in the army before the war. Killed in battle March 7, 1862 at Elkhorn Tavern, Arkansas.

MCINTOSH, JOHN BAILLIE. Union Brigadier General,born June 6,1829 at Fort Brooke,Florida. Brother of James McIntosh. In business before the war,served in the army after.   Died June 29, 1888 in

New Brunswick, New Jersey.

MCKEAN, THOMAS JEFFERSON.   Union Brigadier General, born on August 21, 1810 in Burlington, Pennsylvania.   Graduated from West Point 1831. Engineer before the war,farmer after. Died April 19, 1870 at Marion, Iowa.

MCKINSTRY, JUSTUS.   Union Brigadier General, born July 6, 1814 in Columbia County, New York.   Graduated from West Point 1838. Served in the army before the war, stockbroker after.   The only general from either side cashiered during the war.   Died December 11, 1897 at St. Louis, Missouri.

MCLAWS, LAFAYETTE.   Confederate Major General, born January 15, 1821 in Augusta,Georgia.   Graduated from West Point 1842. Served in the army before the war,in insurance after. Died July 24,1897 at Savannah, Georgia.

MCLEAN, NATHANIEL COLLINS.   Union Brigadier General, born February 2, 1815 at Ridgeville, Ohio.   Attended Harvard University. Lawyer before the war, farmer after.   Died on January 4, 1905 in Bellport, New York.

MCMILLAN, JAMES WINNING.   Union Brigadier General,born April 28, 1825 in Clark County, Kentucky.   In business before the war,U.S. Pension Officer after.   Died March 9, 1903 at Washington, D.C.

MCNAIR, EVANDER.   Confederate Brigadier General, born April 15, 1820 in Richmond County,North Carolina. Merchant before the war. Died November 13, 1902 at Hattiesburg, Mississippi.

MCNEIL, JOHN. Union Brigadier General, born February 14,1813 at Halifax,Nova Scotia. Worked in insurance before the war,sheriff after. Died June 8, 1891 in St. Louis, Missouri.

MCPHERSON, JAMES BIRDSEYE. Union Major General,born November 14, 1828 in Clyde, Ohio.   Attended Norwalk Academy, then graduated from West Point 1853. Served in the army before the war. Killed in battle July 22, 1864 at Atlanta, Georgia.

MCRAE, DANDRIDGE. Confederate Brigadier General,born October 10, 1829 in Baldwin County, Alabama.   Attended University of South Carolina. Lawyer before the war, in politics after. Died on April 23, 1899 at Searcy, Arkansas.

MEADE, GEORGE GORDON. Union Major General,born December 31,1815 in Cadiz, Spain.   Graduated from West Point 1835 and served in the army before and after the war.   Died on November 6, 1872 at Philadelphia, Pennsylvania.

MEAGHER, THOMAS FRANCIS. Union Brigadier General,born August 3, 1823 in Waterford, Ireland. In politics before the war, Montana Secretary of State after the war.   Died on July 1, 1867 at Fort Benton, Montana.

MEIGS, MONTGOMERY CUNNINGHAM.   Union Brigadier General, born on May 3,1816 at Augusta, Georgia.   Attended University of Pennsylvania.   Graduated from West Point 1836, then served in the army before and after the war.   Died on January 2,1892 in Washington, D.C.

MERCER, HUGH WEEDON.   Confederate Brigadier General, born November 27, 1808 in Fredericksburg, Virginia.   Graduated from West Point 1828.   Banker before the war,merchant after.   Died June 9, 1877 at Baden-Baden, Germany.

MEREDITH, SOLOMON.   Union Brigadier General, born May 29, 1810 in Guilford County, North Carolina.   U.S.Marshal before the war, farmer after.   Died October 2, 1875 at Cambridge City, Indiana.

MEREDITH, SULLIVAN AMORY.   Union Brigadier General, born July 4, 1816 at Philadelphia, Pennsylvania.   In business before the war, drug merchant after.   Died December 26,1874 in Buffalo, New York.

MERRITT, WESLEY.   Union Major General, born June 16, 1834 in New York City, New York.   Graduated from West Point 1860 and served in the army before and after the war.   Died December 3, 1910 at Natural Bridge, Virginia.

MILES, NELSON APPLETON.   Union Brigadier General, born August 8, 1839 in Westminster,Massachusetts.   Store clerk before the war, served in the army after.   Died May 15, 1925 at Washington, D.C.

MILLER, JOHN FRANKLIN.   Union Brigadier General, born on November 21,1831 at South Bend, Indiana.   Lawyer before the war, U.S. Senator after.   Died March 8, 1886 in San Francisco, California.

MILLER, STEPHEN.   Union Brigadier General, born January 7, 1816 at Carroll, Pennsylvania.   An editor before the war, Governor of Minnesota after.   Died August 18, 1881 in Worthington, Minnesota.

MILLER, WILLIAM.   Confederate Brigadier General, born August 3, 1820 in Ithaca, New York.   Attended Louisiana College.   In the lumber business before the war, politics after.   Died August 8, 1909 at Point Washington, Florida.

MILROY, ROBERT HUSTON.   Union Major General, born June 11, 1816 in Salem,Indiana. Attended Captain Partridge's Military Academy. Lawyer before the war, Indian Agent after.   Died March 29, 1890 at Olympia, Washington.

MITCHEL, ORMSBY MACKNIGHT.   Union Major General, born July 28, 1809 at Morganfield, Kentucky.   Graduated from West Point 1829. Lawyer and college professor before the war.   Died from Yellow Fever October 30, 1862 at Hilton Head, South Carolina.

MITCHELL, JOHN GRANT.   Union Brigadier General, born November 6, 1838 in Piqua,Ohio.   Attended Kenyon College before the war,lawyer after.   Died November 7, 1894 at Columbus, Ohio.

MITCHELL, ROBERT BYINGTON. Union Brigadier General,born April 4,

1823 in Mansfield,Ohio. Attended Kenyon College. Lawyer before
the war, Governor of New Mexico after. Died January 26, 1882 at
Washington, D.C.

MONTGOMERY, WILLIAM READING.   Union Brigadier General, born on
July 10,1801 in Monmouth County,New Jersey. Graduated from West
Point 1825. Served in the army before the war,in business after.
Died June 1, 1871 at Bristol, Pennsylvania.

MOODY, YOUNG MARSHALL.   Confederate Brigadier General, born on
June 23, 1822 in Chesterfield County, Virginia.   School teacher
before the war, merchant after.   Died September 18, 1866 at New
Orleans, Louisiana.

MOORE, JOHN CREED.   Confederate Brigadier General, born Februar-
y 28,1824 in Hawkins County,Tennessee. Attended Emory and Henry
College, then graduated from West Point 1849.   College professor
before the war, school teacher and writer after.   Died on December 31, 1910 at Osage, Texas.

MOORE, PATRICK THEODORE.   Confederate Brigadier General, born on
September 22, 1821 at Galway, Ireland.   Merchant before the war,
in insurance after.   Died February 19,1883 in Richmond,Virginia.

MORELL, GEORGE WEBB.   Union Major General, born January 8, 1815
in Cooperstown,New York. Graduated from West Point 1835. Lawyer
before the war, farmer after. Died on February 11,1883 at Scar-
borough, New York.

MORGAN, EDWIN DENISON. Union Major General,born February 8,1811
at Washington, Massachusetts.   Governor of New York before the
war, U.S.Senator after.   Died February 14,1883 in New York City,
New York.

MORGAN, GEORGE WASHINGTON. Union Brigadier General,born September 20, 1820 in Washington County, Pennsylvania.   Lawyer before
the war, in U.S. Congress after.   Died on July 26, 1893 at Fort
Monroe, Virginia.

MORGAN, JAMES DADA. Union Brigadier General, born August 1,1810
in Boston,Massachusetts. Merchant before the war, banker after.
Died September 12, 1896 at Quincy, Illinois.

MORGAN, JOHN HUNT.   Confederate Brigadier General, born June 1,
1825 in Huntsville, Alabama.   Attended Transylvania College. A
cotton manufacturer before the war. Killed in battle on September 4, 1864 at Greenville, Tennessee.

MORGAN, JOHN TYLER. Confederate Brigadier General,born June 20,
1824 at Athens, Tennessee.   Lawyer before the war, U.S. Senator
after. Died June 11, 1907 in Washington, D.C.

MORRIS, WILLIAM HOPKINS. Union Brigadier General,born April 22,
1827 in New York City,New York. Graduated from West Point 1851.
Served in the army before the war,farmer after. Died August 26,
1900 at Long Branch, New Jersey.

MORTON, JAMES ST. CLAIR.   Union Brigadier General, born September 24, 1829 in Philadelphia, Pennsylvania.   Attended University of Pennsylvania.   Graduated from West Point 1851 and served in the army before the war.   Killed in battle on June 17, 1864 at Petersburg, Virginia.

MOTT, GERSHOM.   Union Brigadier General, born on April 7,1822 at Lamberton,New Jersey.   In business before the war, railroad paymaster after.   Died November 29,1884 in New York City, New York.

MOUTON,JEAN JACQUES ALFRED ALEXANDER. Confederate Brigadier General, born February 18, 1829 in Opelousas, Louisiana.   Graduated from West Point 1850.   Engineer before the war. Killed in battle April 8, 1864 at Mansfield, Louisiana.

MOWER, JOSEPH ANTHONY.   Union Major General, born August 22,1827 in Woodstock, Vermont.   Attended Norwich Academy.   Served in the army before and after the war. Died on January 6,1870 at New Orleans, Louisiana.

NAGLE, JAMES.   Union Brigadier General, born April 5, 1822 in Reading, Pennsylvania.   Painter before the war.   Died August 22, 1866 at Pottsville, Pennsylvania.

NAGLEE, HENRY MORRIS.   Union Brigadier General, born January 15, 1815 in Philadelphia,Pennsylvania.   Graduated from West Point in 1835. Banker before and after the war.   Died March 5,1886 at San Francisco, California.

NEGLEY, JAMES SCOTT.   Union Major General, born December 22,1826 in Pittsburgh, Pennsylvania.   Attended Pitt University.   Farmer before the war,in Congresss after.   Died August 7,1901 at Plainfield, New Jersey.

NEILL, THOMAS HEWSON.   Union Brigadier General,born April 9,1826 in Philadelphia, Pennsylvania.   Attended University of Pennsylvania, then graduated from West Point 1847.   Served in the army before and after the war.   Died March 12, 1885 at Philadelphia, Pennsylvania.

NELSON, ALLISON.   Confederate Brigadier General, born March 11, 1822 in Fulton County, Georgia.   Lawyer and in politics before the war.   Died of fever October 7, 1862 at Austin, Arkansas.

NELSON, WILLIAM.   Union Major General, born September 27,1824 at Maysville,Kentucky.   Attended Norwich University, then served in the U.S. Navy before the war.   Following an argument, shot down September 29, 1862 by Union Brigadier General Jefferson Davis in Louisville, Kentucky.

NEWTON, JOHN.   Union Major General, born August 25, 1822 in Norfolk,Virginia.   Graduated from West Point 1842 and served in the army before and after the war. Died May 1,1895 at New York City, New York.

NICHOLLS, FRANCIS REDDING TILLOU. Confederate Brigadier General, born August 20,1834 in Donaldsonville,Louisiana.   Attended University of Louisiana, then graduated from West Point 1855. Lawyer before the war,Governor of Louisiana after. Died January 4, 1912 at Thibodeaux, Louisiana.

NICKERSON, FRANKLIN STILLMAN. Union Brigadier General, born August 27,1826 in Swanville,Maine. U.S.Customs officer before the war,lawyer after. Died January 23,1917 at Boston,Massachusetts.

NORTHROP, LUCIUS BELLINGER. Confederate Brigadier General, born September 8, 1811 at Charleston, South Carolina. Graduated from West Point 1831. Doctor before the war,farmer after. Died February 9, 1894 in Pikesville, Maryland.

OGLESBY, RICHARD JAMES. Union Major General, born July 25, 1824 in Oldham County, Kentucky. Lawyer before the war, Governor of Illinois after. Died April 24, 1899 at Elkhart, Illinois.

OLIVER, JOHN MORRISON. Union Brigadier General,born September 6, 1828 in Penn Yan, New York. Attended St.John's College. Pharmacist before the war, lawyer after. Died on March 30, 1872 at Washington, D.C.

ORD, EDWARD OTHO CRESAP. Union Major General, born October 18, 1818 at Cumberland,Maryland. Graduated from West Point 1839 and served in the army before and after the war. Died July 22, 1883 in Havana, Cuba.

ORME, WILLIAM WARD. Union Brigadier General, born February 17, 1832 in Washington, D.C. Attended Mt.St.Mary's College. Lawyer before the war, in the U.S. Treasury Department after. Died on September 13, 1866 at Bloomington, Illinois.

OSTERHAUS, PETER JOSEPH. Union Major General, born January 4, 1823 at Coblenz, Germany. Store clerk before the war, in hardware business after. Died January 2, 1917 in Duisburg, Germany.

OWEN, JOSHUA THOMAS. Union Brigadier General,born March 29,1821 at Caermarthen,Wales. Attended Jefferson College. School teacher before the war, lawyer after. Died November 7,1887 in Philadelphia, Pennsylvania.

PAGE, RICHARD LUCIAN. Confederate Brigadier General,born December 20,1807 in Clarke County, Virginia. Served in the U.S. Navy before the war,school superintendent after. Died August 9, 1901 at Blue Ridge Summit, Pennsylvania.

PAINE, CHARLES JACKSON. Union Brigadier General,born August 26, 1833 at Boston,Massachusetts. Attended Harvard University. Lawyer before the war,railroad director after. Died August 12,1916 in Weston, Massachusetts.

PAINE, ELEAZER ARTHUR. Union Brigadier General, born on September 10,1815 in Parkman,Ohio. Cousin of Halbert Paine. Graduated from West Point 1839. U.S.Marshal before the war, lawyer after. Died December 16, 1882 at Jersey City, New Jersey.

PAINE, HALBERT ELEAZER. Union Brigadier General,born February 4, 1826 at Chardon,Ohio. Cousin of Eleazer Paine. Attended Western Reserve University. Lawyer before the war, served in Congress after. Died April 14, 1905 in Washington, D.C.

PALMER, JOSEPH BENJAMIN. Confederate Brigadier General,born November 1, 1825 in Rutherford County, Tennessee. Attended Union University, then a lawyer before and after the war. Died November 4, 1890 at Murfreesboro, Tennessee.

PALMER, INNIS NEWTON. Union Brigadier General,born on March 30, 1824 at Buffalo, New York.   Graduated from West Point 1846 and served in the army before and after the war.   Died September 9, 1900 in Chevy Chase, Maryland.

PALMER, JOHN MCCAULEY.   Union Major General, born September 13, 1817 in Scott County,Kentucky. Attended Shurtleff College. Lawyer before the war, Governor of Illinois after. Died on September 25, 1900 at Springfield, Illinois.

PARKE, JOHN GRUBB. Union Major General, born September 22, 1827 at Coatesville, Pennsylvania. Attended University of Pennsylvania, then graduated from West Point 1849 and served in the army before and after the war.   Died December 16,1900 in Washington, D.C.

PARSONS, MOSBY MONROE.   Confederate Major General, born May 21, 1822 in Charlottesville,Virginia.   Lawyer before the war,served in the Chinese army after.   Died August 15, 1865 at Nueva Leon, China.

PATRICK, MARSENA RUDOLPH. Union Brigadier General,born March 11, 1811 in Watertown, New York. Graduated from West Point in 1835. Farmer before the war, served in the army after.   Died July 27, 1888 at Dayton, Ohio.

PATTERSON, FRANCIS ENGLE.   Union Brigadier General, born May 7, 1821 in Philadelphia, Pennsylvania.   Served in the army before the war.   Died November 22, 1862 after being accidently shot at Occoquan, Virginia.

PAUL, GABRIEL RENE. Union Brigader General, born March 22, 1813 in St.Louis,Missouri. Graduated from West Point 1834 and served in the army before the war. Died May 5, 1886 at Washington,D.C.

PAXTON, ELISHA FRANKLIN. Confederate Brigadier General, born on March 4,1828 in Rockbridge County, Virginia. Attended Yale University. Lawyer before the war. Killed in battle May 3,1863 at Chancellorsville, Virginia.

PAYNE, WILLIAM HENRY FITZHUGH.   Confederate Brigadier General, born January 27,1830 in Fauquier County,Virginia. Attended University of Virginia. Lawyer before and after the war. Died on March 29, 1904 at Washington, D.C.

PECK, JOHN JAMES.   Union Major General, born January 4, 1821 in

Manlius,New York. Banker before the war,in the insurance after.
Died April 21, 1921 at Syracuse, New York.

PECK, WILLIAM RAINE.   Confederate Brigadier General, born January 31, 1818 in Jefferson County, Tennessee.   Farmer before and
after the war. Died January 22,1871 in Madison Parish,Louisiana.

PEGRAM, JOHN. Confederate Brigadier General,born January 24,1832
in Petersburg,Virginia. Graduated from West Point 1854 and served in the army before the war. Killed in battle February 6,1865
at Hatcher's Run, Virginia.

PEMBERTON, JOHN CLIFFORD.   Confederate Lieutenant General, born
August 10,1814 in Philadelphia,Pennsylvania. Graduated from West
Point 1837. Served in the army before the war,farmer after. Died
July 13, 1881 at Penllyn, Pennsylvania.

PENDER, WILLIAM DORSEY. Confederate Major General,born Februar-
y 6,1834 in Edgecomb County,North Carolina. Graduated from West
Point 1854, and served in the army before the war.   Wounded in
battle July 2,1863 at Gettysburg, Pennsylvania, died on July 18,
1863.

PENDLETON, WILLIAM NELSON.   Confederate Brigadier General, born
December 26,1809 at Richmond,Virginia. Graduated from West Point
1830. Episcopal minister before and after the war.   Died Januar-
y 15, 1883 in Lexington, Virginia.

PERRIN, ABNER MONROE. Confederate Brigadier General,born February 2,1827 in Edgefield District, South Carolina. Lawyer before
the war. Killed in battle on May 12,1864 at Fredericksburg,Vir-
ginia.

PERRY, EDWARD AYLESWORTH. Confederate Brigadier General,born on
March 15,1831 in Richmond,Massachusetts. Lawyer before the war,
Governor of Florida after.   Died October 15, 1889 at Kerrville,
Texas.

PERRY, WILLIAM FLANK.   Confederate Brigadier General, was born
March 12, 1823 in Jackson County, Georgia.   Although he had no
formal education,lawyer and educator before the war, and college
professor after.   Died December 18, 1901 at Bowling Green, Kentucky.

PETTIGREW, JAMES JOHNSTON.   Confederate Brigadier General, born
July 4,1828 in Tyrrell County,North Carolina. Lawyer before the
war. Wounded in battle July 14,1863 at Falling Waters,Maryland,
died July 17, 1863.

PETTUS, EDMUND WINSTON.   Confederate Brigadier General, born on
July 6,1821 in Limestone County, Alabama. Attended Clinton Col-
lege. Lawyer and judge before the war, U.S.Senator after.   Died
July 27, 1907 at Hot Springs, North Carolina.

PHELPS, JOHN SMITH.   Union Brigadier General, born December 22,
1814 in Simsbury,Connecticut. Attended Trinity College. Lawyer

and in U.S. Congress before the war, Governor of Missouri after. Died on November 20, 1886 at St. Louis, Missouri.

PHELPS, JOHN WOLCOTT. Union Brigadier General,born November 13, 1813 in Guilford,Vermont. Graduated from West Point 1836. Served in the army before the war, writer after.   Died February 2,1885 at Guilford, Vermont.

PIATT, ABRAM SANDERS. Union Brigadier General, born May 2, 1821 at Cincinnati, Ohio. Farmer before and after the war.   Died on March 16, 1908 in Logan County, Ohio.

PIERCE, BYRON ROOT. Union Brigadier General, born September 20, 1829 at East Bloomfield,New York. Dentist before the war, hotel operator after.   Died July 10, 1924 in Grand Rapids, Michigan.

PICKETT, GEORGE EDWARD. Confederate Major General, born on January 28, 1825 at Richmond, Virginia.   Graduated from West Point 1846. Served in the army before the war,in insurance after. Died July 30, 1875 in Norfolk, Virginia.

PIKE, ALBERT.   Confederate Brigadier General, born December 29, 1809 in Boston,Massachusetts. Lawyer before the war,legal writer after. Died April 2, 1891 at Washington, D.C.

PILE, WILLIAM ANDERSON. Union Brigadier General, born on February 11,1829 in Indianapolis, Indiana. Methodist minister before the war, Governor of New Mexico after.   Died on July 7, 1889 at Monrovia, California.

PILLOW, GIDEON JOHNSON.   Confederate Brigadier General, born on June 8,1806 in Williamson County, Tennessee. Attended University of Nashville, then a lawyer before and after the war.   Died October 8, 1878 at Helena, Arkansas.

PITCHER, THOMAS GAMBLE. Union Brigadier General,born October 23, 1824 in Rockport,Indiana. Graduated from West Point in 1845 and served in the army before and after the war. Died on October 21, 1895 at Fort Bayard, New Mexico.

PLEASONTON, ALFRED. Union Major General, born on July 7,1824 in Washington,D.C. Graduated from West Point 1844 and served in the army before and after the war. Died on February 17,1897 at Washington, D.C.

PLUMMER, JOSEPH BENNETT. Union Brigadier General,born on November 15, 1816 in Barre, Massachusetts. Graduated from West Point 1841,then served in the army before the war. Died August 9,1862 at Corinth, Mississippi.

POE, ORLANDO METCALFE. Union Brigadier General,born March 7,1832 in Navarre, Ohio. Graduated from West Point 1856,then served in the army before and after the war. Died October 2, 1895 at Soo, Michigan.

POLIGNAC, CAMILLE ARMAND JULES MARIE PRINCE DE.Confederate Major

General, born February 16, 1832 in Millemont, France. Served in the French army before the war, engaged in study of mathematics after. Died November 15, 1913 at Paris, France.

POLK, LEONIDAS.   Confederate Lieutenant General, born April 10, 1806 in Raleigh,North Carolina. Uncle of Lucius Polk.   Graduated from West Point 1827.   Episcopal Bishop before the war.   Killed in battle June 14, 1864 at Pine Mountain, Georgia.

POLK, LUCIUS EUGENE. Confederate Brigadier General,born July 10, 1833 in Salisbury,North Carolina.   Nephew of Leonidas Polk. Attended University of Virginia. Farmer before and after the war. Died December 1, 1892 at Columbia, Tennessee.

POPE, JOHN. Union Major General,born on March 16,1822 in Louisville, Kentucky. Graduated from West Point 1842, then served in the army before and after the war. Died on September 23,1892 at Sandusky, Ohio.

PORTER, ANDREW.   Union Brigadier General, born July 10, 1820 in Lancaster, Pennsylvania. Served in the army before the war, retired after. Died January 3, 1872 at Paris, France.

PORTER, FITZ JOHN. Union Major General, born August 31, 1822 at Portsmouth, New Hampshire. Graduated from West Point 1845, then served in the army before the war. Died May 21, 1901 in Morristown, New Jersey.

POSEY, CARNOT. Confederate Brigadier General,born August 5,1818 in Wilkinson County,Mississippi. Attended University of Virginia. Lawyer and farmer before the war.   Wounded in battle October 14,1863 at Bristoe Station, Virginia, died November 13,1863.

POTTER, EDWARD ELMER. Union Brigadier General,born June 21,1823 in New York City,New York. Attended Columbia University. Farmer before the war. Died June 1, 1889 at New York City, New York.

POTTER, ROBERT BROWN. Union Brigadier General,born July 16,1829 in Schenectady,New York. Attended Union College. Lawyer before the war, railroad receiver after. Died February 19,1887 at Newport, Rhode Island.

POTTS, BENJAMIN FRANKLIN. Union Brigadier General, born on January 29,1836 in Carroll County,Ohio. Lawyer before the war,Governor of Montana Territory after. Died June 17, 1887 at Helena, Montana.

POWELL, WILLIAM HENRY. Union Brigadier General,born May 10,1825 at Pontypool,South Wales. Iron works manager before the war,nail company manager after. Died on December 26, 1904 in Belleville, Illinois.

PRATT, CALVIN EDWARD. Union Brigadier General, born January 23, 1828 at Shrewsbury, Massachusetts. Lawyer before the war, judge after. Died August 3, 1896 in Rochester, Massachusetts.

PRENTISS, BENJAMIN MAYBERRY. Union Major General,born on November 23,1819 in Belleville,West Virginia. Lawyer before the war, postmaster after.   Died February 8, 1901 at Bethany, Missouri.

PRESTON, JOHN SMITH.   Confederate Brigadier General, born on April 20,1809 in Abingdon,Virginia. Attended Harvard University. Lawyer and in politics before the war.   Died on May 1, 1881 at Columbia, South Carolina.

PRESTON, WILLIAM. Confederate Brigadier General,born October 16, 1816 in Louisville,Kentucky. Attended Harvard University. Lawyer and served in U.S. Congress before the war, politics after. Died September 21, 1887 at Lexington, Kentucky.

PRICE, STERLING.   Confederate Major General, born September 20, 1809 in Prince Edward County, Virginia. Attended Hampden-Sydney College. Governor of Missouri before the war,retired after. Died September 29, 1867 at St. Louis, Missouri.

PRINCE, HENRY. Union Brigadier General, born on June 19,1811 at Eastport, Maine.   Graduated from West Point 1835 then served in the army before and after the war. Committed suicide August 19, 1892 in London, England.

PRYON, ROGER ATKINSON.   Confederate Brigadier General, born on July 19, 1828 in Petersburg, Virginia.   Attended Hampden-Sydney College. Lawyer and served in Congress before the war,Judge after. Died March 14, 1919 at New York City, New York.

QUARLES, WILLIAM ANDREW. Confederate Brigadier General, born on July 4,1825 at Jamestown, Virginia. Attended University of Virginia. Lawyer and judge before the war,politics after. Died on December 28, 1893 in Logan County, Kentucky.

QUINBY, ISSAC FERDINAND. Union Brigadier General, born on January 29,1821 in Morristown,New Jersey. Graduated from West Point 1843. College professor before the war,U.S.Marshall after. Died September 18, 1891 at Rochester, New York.

RAINS, GABRIEL JAMES. Confederate Brigadier General,born June 4, 1803 in Craven County,North Carolina. Graduated from West Point 1827. Served in the army before the war,government clerk after. Died August 6, 1881 at Aiken, South Carolina.

RAINS, JAMES EDWARDS. Confederate Brigadier General, born on April 10,1833 in Nashville, Tennessee. Attended Yale University. Lawyer before the war. Killed in battle on December 31, 1862 at Murfreesboro, Tennessee.

RAMSAY, GEORGE DOUGLAS. Union Brigadier General, born on February 21,1802 at Dumfries, Virginia. Graduated from West Point in 1820, then served in the army before and after the war. Died on May 23, 1882 in Washington, D.C.

RAMSEUR, STEPHEN DODSON. Confederate Major General,born May 31, 1837 in Lincolnton,North Carolina. Graduated from West Point in

1860 and served in the army before the war. Wounded in battle on October 19,1864 at Cedar Creek, Virginia. Died October 20,1864.

RANDOLPH, GEORGE WYTHE. Confederate Brigadier General, born on March 10,1818 at Charlottesville, Virginia. Attended University of Virginia. Lawyer before the war. Died of tuberculosus on A-pril 3, 1867 in Charlottesville, Virginia.

RANSOM, MATT WHITAKER. Confederate Brigadier General,born October 8,1826 in Warren County,North Carolina. Attended University of North Carolina. Brother of Robert Ransom. Lawyer before the war, U.S.Senator after. Died October 8,1904 at Garysburg, North Carolina.

RANSOM JR., ROBERT. Confederate Major General,born February 12, 1828 in Warren County, North Carolina. Brother of Matt Ransom. Graduated from West Point 1850. Served in the army before the war, an engineer after. Died January 14,1892 at New Bern, North Carolina.

RANSOM, THOMAS EDWARD GREENFIELD. Union Brigadier General, born November 29,1834 in Norwich,Vermont. Attended Norwich Universi-ty. Engineer before the war. Died October 29,1864 at Rome,Geor-gia after being wounded in battle at Sabine Crossroads,Louisiana on April 8, 1864.

RAUM, GREEN BERRY. Union Brigadier General,born December 3,1829 at Golconda,Illinois. Lawyer before the war, served in Congress after. Died December 18, 1909 in Chicago, Illinois.

RAWLINS, JOHN AARON. Union Brigadier General, born February 13, 1831 at Galena, Illinois. Lawyer before the war, U.S. Secretary of War after. Died September 6, 1869 in Washington, D.C.

REID, HUGH THOMPSON. Union Brigadier General, born October 18, 1811 in Union County,Indiana. Attended Bloomington College. Law-yer before the war,railroad president after. Died August 21,1874 at Des Moines, Iowa.

REILLY, JAMES WILLIAM. Union Brigadier General,born May 20,1828 in Akron, Ohio. Attended Mt. St. Mary's College. Lawyer before the war, bank president after. Died November 6, 1905 at Wells-ville, Ohio.

RENO, JESSE LEE. Union Major General, born on June 20, 1823 in Wheeling,West Virginia. Graduated from West Point 1846 and serv-ed in the army before the war. Killed in battle September 14, 1862 at South Mountain, Maryland.

REVERE, JOSEPH WARREN. Union Brigadier General,born May 17,1812 in Boston,Massachusetts. Served in the U.S.Navy before the war, retired after. Died April 20, 1880 at Hoboken, New Jersey.

REYNOLDS, ALEXANDER WELCH. Confederate Brigadier General, born in April of 1816 in Clarke County,Virginia. Graduated from West Point 1838. Served in the army before the war and the Egyptian army after. Died May 26, 1876 at Alexandria, Egypt.

REYNOLDS, DANIEL HARRIS. Confederate Brigadier General, born on December 14,1832 in Centerburg,Ohio. Attended Ohio Wesleyan University. Lawyer before the war,in politics after. Died March 14, 1902 at Lake Village, Arkansas.

REYNOLDS, JOHN FULTON.   Union Major General, born September 20, 1820 in Lancaster,Pennsylvania. Graduated from West Point 1841, then served in the army before the war. Killed in battle July 1, 1863 at Gettysburg, Pennsylvania.

REYNOLDS, JOSEPH JONES. Union Major General,born January 4,1822 in Flemingsburg,Kentucky. Attended Wabash College. College professor before the war, served in the army after. Died on February 25, 1899 at Washington, D.C.

RICE, ELLIOTT WARREN. Union Brigadier General,born November 16, 1835 in Pittsburg, Pennsylvania.   Brother of Samuel Rice.   Attended Franklin College. Lawyer before and after the war. Died June 22, 1887 at Sioux City, Iowa.

RICE, JAMES CLAY. Union Brigadier General,born December 27,1829 in Worthington,Massachusetts. Attended Yale University. Lawyer before the war.   Killed in battle May 10, 1864 at Spotsylvania, Virginia.

RICE, SAMUEL ALLEN. Union Brigadier General,born on January 27, 1828 in Cattaraugus County,New York. Attended Union College. Attorney General of Iowa before the war.   Died on July 6, 1864 at Oskaloose,Iowa from wounds received in battle at Jenkin's Ferry, Arkansas on April 30, 1864.

RICHARDSON, ISRAEL BUSH. Union Major General, born December 26, 1815 in Fairfax, Vermont. Graduated from West Point in 1841 and served in the army before the war. Wounded in battle on September 17, 1862 at Sharpsburg, Maryland.   Died November 3, 1862.

RICHARDSON, ROBERT VINKLER. Confederate Brigadier General, born November 4,1820 in Granville County, North Carolina. Lawyer before the war, railroad builder after. Died on January 5,1870 at Clarkton, Missouri.

RICKETTS, JAMES BREWERTON. Union Brigadier General,born June 21, 1817 in New York City,New York. Graduated from West Point 1839, then served in the army before and after the war.   Died September 22, 1887 at Washington, D.C.

RIPLEY, JAMES WOLFE. Union Brigadier General, born December 10, 1794 in Windham County, Connecticut.   Graduated from West Point 1814. Uncle of Roswell Ripley. Served in the army until the war, retired after.   Died March 15, 1870 at Hartford, Connecticut.

RIPLEY, ROSWELL SABINE.   Confederate Brigadier General, born on March 14, 1823 at Worthington, Ohio.   Graduated from West Point 1843. Served in the army before the war,manufacturer after. Died

March 29, 1887 in New York City, New York.

ROANE, JOHN SELDEN. Confederate Brigadier General, born on January 8,1817 in Wilson County,Tennessee. Attended Cumberland College. Governor of Arkansas before the war, retired after. Died April 8, 1867 at Pine Bluff, Arkansas.

ROBERTS, BENJAMIN STONE. Union Brigadier General,born on November 18,1810 at Manchester,Vermont. Graduated from West Point in 1835. Lawyer and soldier before and after the war. Died January 29, 1875 in Washington, D.C.

ROBERTS, WILLIAM PAUL.   Confederate Brigadier General, born on July 11, 1841 in Gates County, North Carolina. In politics following the war.   Youngest Confederate Brigadier General.   Died March 28, 1910 at Norfolk, Virginia.

ROBERTSON, BEVERLY HOLCOMBE. Confederate Brigadier General,born June 5,1827 in Amelia County,Virginia. Graduated from West Point 1849. Served in the army before the war,in insurance after. Died at Washington, D.C. on November 12, 1910.

ROBERTSON, FELIX HUSTON. Confederate Brigadier General, born on March 9,1839 in Washington,Texas. Attended Baylor University and was at West Point when war broke out. Lawyer after the war. Son of Jerome Robertson. Died April 20, 1928 at Waco, Texas.

ROBERTSON, JEROME BONAPARTE. Confederate Brigadier General,born March 14, 1815 in Woodford County, Kentucky.   Father of Felix Robertson. Attended Transylvania University. Doctor before the war, railroad builder after. Died January 7,1891 at Waco,Texas.

ROBINSON, JAMES SIDNEY. Union Brigadier General,born October 14, 1827 in Mansfield, Ohio. Editor before the war, in U.S.Congress after. Died January 14, 1927 at Kenton, Ohio.

ROBINSON, JOHN CLEVELAND. Union Brigadier General,born April 10, 1817 in Binghamton,New York. Served in the army before the war, Lieutenant Governor of New York after. Died February 18,1897 at Binghamton, New York.

RODDEY, PHILIP DALE. Confederate Brigadier General,born April 2, 1826 in Moulton, Alabama.   Sheriff before the war, in business after. Died July 20, 1897 at London, England.

RODES, ROBERT EMMETT. Confederate Major General, born March 29, 1829 in Lynchburg, Virginia.   Attended Virginia Military Institute. Engineer before the war.   Killed in battle September 19, 1864 at Winchester, Virginia.

RODMAN, ISSAC PEACE. Union Brigadier General,born August 18,1822 in South Kingstown,Rhode Island. Merchant before the war. Wounded in battle September 17,1862 at Sharpsburg, Maryland. Died on September 30, 1862.

ROSECRANS, WILLIAM STARKE. Union Major General, born on September 6, 1819 in Delaware County, Ohio. Graduated from West Point 1842. Served in the army before the war and U.S.Congress after. Died March 11, 1898 at Redondo Beach, California.

ROSS, LAWRENCE SULLIVAN. Confederate Brigadier General, born on September 27,1838 in Bentonsport,Iowa. Attended Wesleyan University. Served in the army before the war,sheriff and Governor of Texas after. Died January 3, 1898 at College Station, Texas.

ROSS, LEONARD FULTON. Union Brigadier General, born on July 18, 1823 in Lewistown,Illinois. Attended Jacksonville College. Lawyer before the war,farmer after. Died January 17,1901 at Lewistown, Illinois.

ROSSER, THOMAS LAFAYETTE. Confederate Major General, born October 15,1836 in Campbell County,Virginia. In West Point when the war started, engineer following the war. Died March 29, 1910 at Charlottesville, Virginia.

ROUSSEAU, LOVELL HARRISON.   Union Major General, born August 4, 1818 at Stanford, Kentucky. Lawyer before the war, served in the army after. Died January 7, 1869 at New Orleans, Louisiana.

ROWLEY, THOMAS ALGEO.   Union Brigadier General, born October 5, 1808 in Pittsburgh, Pennsylvania.   Cabinetmaker before the war, lawyer and U.S.Marshal after.   Died May 14, 1892 at Pittsburgh, Pennsylvania.

RUCKER, DANIEL HENRY. Union Brigadier General,born April 28,1812 in Belleville, New Jersey.   Served in the army before and after the war. Died January 6, 1910.

RUGER, THOMAS HOWARD. Union Brigadier General,born April 2,1833 in Lima,New York. Graduated from West Point 1854. Lawyer before the war,served in the army after. Died June 3,1907 at Stamford, Connecticut.

RUGGLES, DANIEL. Confederate Brigadier General,born January 31, 1810 in Barre,Massachusetts. Graduated from West Point 1833 and served in the army before the war. Died on June 1,1897 at Fredericksburg, Virginia.

RUSSELL, DAVID ALLEN. Union Brigadier General,born December 10, 1820 in Salem,New York. Graduated from West Point 1845 and served in the army before the war.   Killed in battle September 19, 1864 at Winchester, Virginia.

RUST, ALBERT. Confederate Brigadier General, born about 1818 in Fauquier County,Virginia. Lawyer and in U.S.Congress before the war, farmer after. Died April 4, 1870 at Little Rock, Arkansas.

SALOMON, FRIEDRICH.   Union Brigadier General, born April 7,1826 in Strobeck,Germany. Surveyor before the war, U.S.Surveyor General after.   Died March 8, 1897 at Salt Lake City, Utah.

SANBORN, JOHN BENJAMIN. Union Brigadier General,born December 5,

1826 in Epsom, New Hampshire. Attended Dartmouth College. Lawyer before the war, in politics after.   Died on May 16, 1904 at St.Paul, Minnesota.

SANDERS, JOHN CALDWELL CALHOUN.   Confederate Brigadier General, born April 4,1840 in Tuscaloosa,Alabama. Attended University of Alabama before the war.   Killed in battle on August 21, 1864 at Weldon Railroad, Virginia.

SANDERS, WILLIAM PRICE. Union Brigadier General,born August 12, 1833 in Frankfort, Kentucky. Graduated from West Point 1856 and served in the army before the war.   Wounded in battle on November 18, 1863 at Knoxville, Tennessee, died the next day.

SAXTON, RUFUS. Union Brigadier General, born October 19,1824 in Greenfield,Massachusetts. Graduated from West Point in 1849 and served in the army before and after the war.   Died February 23, 1908 at Washington, D.C.

SCALES, ALFRED MOORE. Confederate Brigadier General,born November 26, 1827 in Reidsville, North Carolina. Attended University of North Carolina. Lawyer and in Congress before the war, Governor of North Carolina after. Died February 8,1892 at Greensboro, North Carolina.

SCAMMON, ELIAKIM PARKER. Union Brigadier General,born on December 27,1816 in Whitefield,Maine. Graduated from West Point 1837. Served in the army before the war,college professor after. Died December 7, 1894 at New York City, New York.

SCHENCK, ROBERT CUMMING. Union Major General,born October 4,1809 in Franklin,Ohio. Attended Miami University. Served in Congress before the war, lawyer after. Died March 23,1890 at Washington, D.C.

SCHIMMELFENNIG, ALEXANDER. Union Brigadier General,born July 20, 1824 in Lithauen, Germany. Engineer before the war. Died of TB September 5, 1865 at Wernersville, Pennsylvania.

SCHOEPF, ALBIN FRANCISCO. Union Brigadier General,born March 1, 1822 in Podgorz, Poland. U.S. Patent clerk before the war, U.S. Patent Examiner after. Died May 10, 1886 Hyattsville, Maryland.

SCHOFIELD, JOHN MCALLISTER. Union Major General,born on September 29, 1831 in Gerry, New York. Graduated from West Point 1853 and served in the army before and after the war.   Died March 4, 1906 at St.Augustine, Florida.

SCHURZ, CARL. Union Major General, born March 2,1829 in Liblar, Germany. Attended Bonn University. Politics before the war,U.S. Senator after.   Died May 14, 1906 at New York City, New York.

SCOTT, THOMAS MOORE.   Confederate Brigadier General, born about 1829 in Athens, Georgia. Farmer before and after the war. Died April 21, 1876 at New Orleans, Louisiana.

SCOTT, WINFIELD. Union Major General,born June 13,1786 in Petersburg,Virginia. Attended William and Mary College,then served in the army before the war.   Died May 29, 1866 at West Point, New York.

SCURRY, WILLIAM READ. Confederate Brigadier General,born February 10,1821 in Gallatin,Tennessee. Served in the army before the war. Killed in battle April 30,1864 at Jenkin's Ferry,Arkansas.

SEARS, CLAUDIUS WISTAR. Confederate Brigadier General, born November 8,1817 in Peru, Massachusetts. Graduated from West Point 1841.   College professor before and after the war. Died February 15, 1891 at Oxford, Mississippi.

SEDGWICK, JOHN. Union Major General, born September 13, 1813 in Cornwall Hollow,Connecticut. Attended Sharon Academy,then graduated from West Point 1837.   Served in the army before the war. Killed in battle May 9, 1864 at Spotsylvania, Virginia.

SEMMES, PAUL JONES. Confederate Brigadier General, born June 4, 1815 in Wilkes County,Georgia. Attended University of Virginia. Farmer and banker before the war. Wounded July 2,1863 at battle of Gettysburg, Pennsylvania and died July 10, 1863.

SEWARD JR., WILLIAM HENRY. Union Brigadier General,born June 18, 1839 in Auburn, New York. Banker before and after the war. Died April 26, 1920 at Auburn, New York.

SEYMOUR, TRUMAN. Union Brigadier General,born September 24,1824 in Burlington, Vermont. Attended Norwich Universtiy, then graduated from West Point 1846. Served in the army before and after the war. Died October 30, 1891 at Florence, Italy.

SHACKELFORD, JAMES MURRELL. Union Brigadier General,born July 7, 1827 in Lincoln County, Kentucky.   Lawyer before the war, judge after. Died September 7, 1909 at Port Huron, Michigan.

SHALER, ALEXANDER. Union Brigadier General, born March 19, 1827 in Haddam, Connecticut. Independently wealthy before the war, in politics after. Died December 28,1911 at New York City,New York.

SHARP, JACOB HUNTER. Confederate Brigadier General, born February 6,1833 in Pickensville,Alabama. Attended University of Alabama. Lawyer before the war,in politics after. Died on September 15, 1907 at Columbus, Mississippi.

SHELBY, JOSEPH ORVILLE. Confederate Brigadier General, born December 12,1830 in Lexington,Kentucky. Attended Transylvania University.   Rope manufacturer before the war, U.S. Marshal after. Died February 13, 1897 at Adrian, Missouri.

SHELLEY, CHARLES MILLER.   Confederate Brigadier General, born December 28, 1833 in Sullivan County, Tennessee.   Architect before the war, Sheriff and served in U.S. Congress after.   Died January 20, 1907 at Birmingham, Alabama.

SHEPARD, ISAAC FITZGERALD. Union Brigadier General,born July 7, 1816 in Natick,Massachusetts. Attended Harvard University. Editor before and after the war. Died August 25, 1889 at Bellingham, Massachusetts.

SHEPLEY, GEORGE FOSTER. Union Brigadier General, born January 1, 1819 in Saco,Maine. Attended Dartmouth College. Lawyer and U.S. District Attorney before the war, judge after.   Died July 20, 1878 at Portland, Maine.

SHERIDAN, PHILIP HENRY. Union Major General, born March 6, 1831 in Albany, New York. Graduated from West Point 1853 and served in the army before and after the war. Died on August 5, 1888 at Nonquitt, Massachusetts.

SHERMAN, THOMAS WEST.   Union Brigadier General, born March 26, 1813 in Newport, Rhode Island.   Graduated from West Point 1836 and served in the army before and after the war. Died March 16, 1879 at Newport, Rhode Island.

SHERMAN, WILLIAM TECUMSEH. Union Major General, born February 8, 1820 in Lancaster, Ohio.   Graduated from West Point 1840.   Lawyer before the war, served in the army after. Died February 14, 1891 at New York City, New York.

SHIELDS, JAMES.   Union Brigadier General, born May 10, 1810 in County Tyrone, Ireland.   Lawyer and in politics before the war, U.S. Senator after. Died June 1, 1879 at Ottumwa, Iowa.

SHOUP, FRANCIS ASBURY.   Confederate Brigadier General, born on March 22,1834 in Laurel, Indiana. Attended Asbury College, then graduated from West Point 1855.   Lawyer and served in the army before the war, college professor after. Died September 4, 1896 at Columbia, Tennessee.

SIBLEY, HENRY HASTINGS. Union Brigadier General, born on February 29, 1811 in Detroit, Michigan. Governor of Minnesota before the war, banker after. Cousin of Henry Sibley.   Died on February 18, 1891 at St. Paul, Minnesota.

SIBLEY, HENRY HOPKINS.   Confederate Brigadier General, born on May 25, 1816 at Natchitoches, Louisiana.   Graduated from West Point 1838.   Served in the army before the war and in the Egyptian army after. Died on August 23, 1886 in Fredericksburg,Virginia.

SICKLES, DANIEL EDGAR.   Union Major General, born October 20, 1819 in New York City, New York.   Attended New York University. Served in Congress before and after the war. Died May 3,1914 at New York City, New York.

SIGEL, FRANZ. Union Major General, born on November 18, 1824 at Sinsheim, Germany. School teacher before the war, U.S. Pension Agent after.   Died August 21, 1902 in New York City, New York.

SILL, JOSHUA WOODROW. Union Brigadier General, born December 6,

1831 in Chillicothe, Ohio.   Graduated from West Point 1853 and
served in the army before the war.   Killed in battle on December 31, 1862 at Murfreesboro, Tennessee.

SIMMS, JAMES PHILLIP.   Confederate Brigadier General, born January 16,1837 in Covington, Georgia. Lawyer before and after the
war. Died May 30, 1887 at Covington, Georgia.

SLACK, JAMES RICHARD.   Union Brigadier General, born on September 28, 1818 in Bucks County, Pennsylvania.   Lawyer before the
war, judge after. Died July 28, 1881 at Chicago, Illinois.

SLACK, WILLIAM YARNEL.   Confederate Brigadier General, born Au-
gust 1, 1816 in Mason County, Kentucky.   Lawyer before the war.
Wounded in battle March 7,1862 at Elkhorn Tavern, Arkansas. Died
March 21, 1862.

SLAUGHTER, JAMES EDWIN.   Confederate Brigadier General, born in
June 1827 at Cedar Mountain, Virginia.   Attended Virginia Military Institute.   Served in the army before the war, an engineer
after. Died January 1, 1901 in Mexico City, Mexico.

SLEMMER, ADAM JACOBY.   Union Brigadier General,born January 24,
1829 in Montgomery County, Pennsylvania.   Graduated from West
Point 1850, then served in the army before and after the war.
Died October 7, 1868 at Fort Laramie, Wyoming.

SLOCUM, HENRY WARNER.   Union Major General, born September 24,
1827 in Delphi,New York. Attended Cazenovia Seminary,then graduated from West Point 1852. Lawyer before the war, served in U.
S. Congress after. Died April 14, 1894 at Brooklyn, New York.

SLOUGH, JOHN POTTS.   Union Brigadier General, born February 1,
1829 in Cincinnati,Ohio. In politics before the war, then Chief
Justice of New Mexico after. Died December 17,1867 at Santa Fe,
New Mexico.

SMITH, ANDREW JACKSON. Union Major General, born April 28, 1815
in Bucks County, Pennsylvania.   Graduated from West Point 1838
and served in the army before the war. Postmaster after the war.
Died January 30, 1897 at St. Louis, Missouri.

SMITH, CHARLES FERGUSON. Union Major General,born April 24,1807
at Philadelphia, Pennsylvania.   Graduated from West Point 1825
and served in the army before the war.   Died of infection on A-
pril 25, 1862 in Savannah, Tennessee.

SMITH, EDMUND KIRBY. Confederate General,born on May 16,1824 at
St. Augustine,Florida. Graduated from West Point 1845 and serv-
ed in the army before the war, college professor after. Died on
March 28, 1893 in Sewanee, Tennessee.

SMITH, GILES ALEXANDER. Union Brigadier General,born on Septem-
ber 29, 1829 in Jefferson County, New York.   Brother of Morgan
Smith.   Hotel owner before the war, Assistant Postmaster after.
Died November 5, 1876 at Bloomington, Illinois.

SMITH, GREEN CLAY. Union Brigadier General, born July 4,1826 in Richmond,Kentucky. Attended Transylvania College. Lawyer before the war,Baptist minister after. Died June 29,1895 at Washington, D.C.

SMITH, GUSTAVUS ADOLPHUS.   Union Brigadier General, born December 26,1820 in Philadelphia,Pennsylvania. Carriage manufacturer before the war,Internal Revenue Collector after. Died on December 11, 1885 at Santa Fe, New Mexico.

SMITH, GUSTAVUS WOODSON. Confederate Major General, born November 30, 1821 in Georgetown, Kentucky. Graduated from West Point 1842. Engineer and served in the army before the war,iron works superintendent after. Died June 24, 1896 at New York City, New York.

SMITH, JAMES ARGYLE. Confederate Brigadier General,born July 1, 1831 in Maury County,Tennessee. Graduated from West Point 1853. Served in the army before the war, farmer after. Died on December 6, 1901 at Jackson, Mississippi.

SMITH, JOHN EUGENE. Union Brigadier General, born August 3,1816 in Berne,Switzerland. Jeweler before the war, served in the army after. Died January 29, 1897 at Chicago, Illinois.

SMITH, MARTIN LUTHER. Confederate Major General,born on September 9, 1819 in Danby, New York. Graduated from West Point 1842 and served in the army before the war. Died on July 29, 1866 at Savannah, Georgia.

SMITH, MORGAN LEWIS. Union Brigadier General, born March 8,1821 in Mexico,New York. Brother of Giles Smith. School teacher before the war,in business after. Died December 28,1874 at Jersey City, New Jersey.

SMITH, PRESTON. Confederate Brigadier General,born December 25, 1823 in Giles County, Tennessee. Attended Jackson College, then practiced law before the war. Killed in battle September 19,1863 at Chickamauga, Georgia.

SMITH, THOMAS BENTON. Confederate Brigadier General,born February 24,1838 in Mechanicsville,Tennessee. Attended Nashville Military Academy. Worked on the railroad before and after the war. Died May 21, 1923 at Nashville, Tennessee.

SMITH, THOMAS CHURCH HASKELL.   Union Brigadier General, born on March 24,1819 in Acushnet, Massachusetts. Attended Harvard University. Lawyer before the war, served in the army after. Died April 8,1897 at Ojai, California.

SMITH, THOMAS KILBY. Union Brigadier General,born September 23, 1820 in Dorchester, Massachusetts. Attended Cincinnati College. U.S. Marshal before the war, U.S. Consul to Panama after. Died December 14, 1887 at New York City, New York.

SMITH, WILLIAM. Confederate Major General,born September 6,1797 in King George County,Virginia. Lawyer and Governor of Virginia before the war, farmer after. Died on May 18,1887 at Warrenton, Virginia.

SMITH, WILLIAM DUNCAN.   Confederate Brigadier General, born on July 28,1825 in Augusta,Georgia. Graduated from West Point 1846 and served in the army before the war. Died of yellow fever October 4, 1862 at Charleston, South Carolina.

SMITH, WILLIAM FARRAR. Union Major General,born February 17,1824 at St. Albans, Vermont. Graduated from West Point 1845. Served in the army before the war,an engineer after. Died February 28, 1903 in Philadelphia, Pennsylvania.

SMITH, WILLIAM SOOY. Union Brigadier General, born July 22,1830 in Tarlton, Ohio. Attended Ohio University, then graduated from West Point in 1853. Engineer before and after the war. Died on March 4, 1916 at Medford, Oregon.

SMYTH, THOMAS ALFRED. Union Brigadier General,born December 25, 1832 in County Cork,Ireland. Coachmaker before the war. Wounded in battle April 7, 1865 at Farmville,Virginia. Died on April 9, 1865.

SORREL, GILBERT MOXLEY. Confederate Brigadier General,born February 23,1838 in Savannah, Georgia. In railroad work before the war, merchant after. Died August 10, 1901 at Roanoke, Virginia.

SPEARS, JAMES GALLANT.   Union Brigadier General, born March 29, 1816 in Bledsoe County, Tennessee.   Lawyer before and after the war. Died July 22, 1869 at Braden's Knob, Tennessee.

SPINOLA,FRANCIS BARRETTO. Union Brigadier General,born March 19, 1821 at Stony Brook,New York. Lawyer before the war,in U.S.Congress after. Died at Washington, D.C., date unknown.

SPRAGUE, JOHN WILSON. Union Brigadier General,born April 4,1817 at White Creek, New York.   In business before the war, railroad mananger after. Died December 24, 1893 in Tacoma, Washington.

STAFFORD, LEROY AUGUSTUS. Confederate Brigadier General,born on April 13,1822 in Cheneyville, Louisiana. Farmer and sheriff before the war.   Wounded in battle May 5, 1864 at the Wilderness, Virginia, died May 8, 1864.

STAHEL, JULIUS. Union Major General, born on November 5,1825 in Szeged, Hungary. Journalist before the war, in insurance after. Died December 4, 1912 at New York City, New York.

STANLEY, DAVID SLOANE. Union Major General, born June 1,1828 in Cedar Valley,Ohio. Graduated from West Point 1852 and served in the army before and after the war. Died March 13, 1902 at Washington, D.C.

STANNARD, GEORGE JERRISON. Union Brigadier General, born on October 20,1820 in Georgia,Vermont. Foundry owner before the war,

U.S.Customs Collector after. Died June 1,1886 at Washington,D.C.

STARKE, PETER BURWELL. Confederate Brigadier General,born about 1815 in Brunswick County, Virginia.   Brother of William Starke. U.S. Senator before the war, sheriff after.   Died July 13, 1888 at Lawrenceville, Virginia.

STARKE, WILLIAM EDWIN. Confederate Brigadier General,born about 1814 in Brunswick County,Virginia. Brother of Peter Starke. Cotton broker before the war. Killed in battle September 16,1862 at Sharpsburg, Maryland.

STARKWEATHER, JOHN CONVERSE.   Union Brigadier General, born on May 11,1830 at Cooperstown,New York. Attended Union College,then a lawyer before and after the war. Died on November 14, 1890 in Washington, D.C.

STEEDMAN, JAMES BLAIR.   Union Major General,born July 29,1817 in Northumberland,Pennsylvania. Printer before the war,Police Chief after.   Died October 18, 1883 at Toledo, Ohio.

STEELE, FREDERICK. Union Major General, born January 14,1819 in Delhi,New York. Graduated from West Point 1843 and served in the army before and after the war.   Died on January 12, 1868 at San Mateo, California.

STEELE, WILLIAM. Confederate Brigadier General, born May 1,1819 in Albany, New York. Graduated from West Point 1840.   Served in the army before the war,merchant after. Died January 12,1885 at San Antonio, Texas.

STEUART, GEORGE HUME. Confederate Brigadier General,born on August 24, 1828 in Baltimore, Maryland.   Graduated from West Point 1848.   Served in the army before the war, farmer after.   Died on November 22, 1903 at South River, Maryland.

STEVENS, CLEMENT HOFFMAN. Confederate Brigadier General,born on August 14, 1821 in Norwich, Connecticut.   Banker before the war. Wounded in battle July 20,1864 at Peach Tree Creek,Georgia. Died July 25, 1864.

STEVENS, ISAAC INGALLS. Union Brigadier General, born March 25, 1818 in Andover,Massachusetts. Attended Philips-Andover College, then graduated from West Point 1839.   Governor of Washington before the war.   Killed in battle September 1, 1862 at Chantilly, Virginia.

STEVENS, WALTER HUSTED.   Confederate Brigadier General, born on August 24,1827 in Penn Yan, New York.   Graduated from West Point 1848.   Served in the army before the war, engineer after.   Died November 12, 1867 at Vera Cruz, Mexico.

STEVENSON, CARTER LITTLEPAGE.   Confederate Major General, born September 21, 1817 at Fredericksburg, Virginia.   Graduated from West Point 1838.   Served in the army before the war,an engineer after. Died August 15, 1888 in Caroline County, Virginia.

STEVENSON, JOHN DUNLAP. Union Brigadier General,born June 8,1821 in Staunton, Virginia. Attended South Carolina College. In politics before the war, a lawyer after. Died January 22, 1897 at St. Louis, Missouri.

STEVENSON, THOMAS GREELY. Union Brigadier General, born on February 3,1836 in Boston, Massachusetts. Killed in battle May 10, 1864 at Richmond, Virginia.

STEWART, ALEXANDER PETER.   Confederate Lieutenant General, born October 2, 1821 in Rogersville, Tennessee.   Graduated from West Point 1842, then a college professor before and after the war. Died August 30, 1908 at Biloxi, Mississippi.

ST.JOHN, ISAAC MUNROE.   Confederate Brigadier General, born November 19,1827 in Augusta,Georgia. Attended Yale University,then an engineer before and after the war. Died April 7,1880 at White Sulphur Springs, Virginia.

STOLBRAND, CHARLES JOHN.   Union Brigadier General, born May 11, 1821 at Kristianstad,Sweden. Served in the army before the war, in politics after.   Died February 3, 1894 in Charleston, South Carolina.

STONE, CHARLES POMEROY. Union Brigadier General,born on September 30, 1824 at Greenfield, Massachusetts.   Graduated from West Point 1845. Served in the army until the war, the Egyptian army after. Died January 24, 1887 in New York City, New York.

STONEMAN, GEORGE.   Union Major General, born August 22, 1822 in Busti, New York. Graduated from West Point 1846. Served in the army before the war, Governor of California after. Died September 5, 1894 at Buffalo, New York.

STOUGHTON, EDWIN HENRY.   Union Brigadier General, born June 23, 1838 in Chester,Vermont. Graduated from West Point 1859. Served in the army before the war, lawyer after.   Died December 25, 1868 at New York City, New York.

STOVALL, MARCELLUS AUGUSTUS. Confederate Brigadier General, born September 18, 1818 in Sparta, Georgia. Farmer before the war, a cotton broker after.   Died August 4, 1895 at Augusta, Georgia.

STRAHL, OTHO FRENCH. Confederate Brigadier General,born June 3, 1831 in McConnelsville,Ohio. Attended Ohio Wesleyan University, then a lawyer before the war. Killed in battle November 30,1864 at Franklin, Tennessee.

STRONG, GEORGE CROCKETT. Union Brigadier General, born on October 16, 1832 in Stockbridge, Vermont. Graduated from West Point 1857 and served in the army before the war.   Wounded in battle July 18, 1863 at Fort Wagner, South Carolina, died July 30, 1863 at New York City, New York.

STRONG, WILLIAM KERLEY. Union Brigadier General, born April 30, 1805 in Duanesburg, New York.   Merchant before the war, retired after. Died March 16, 1867 at New York City, New York.

STUART, DAVID.   Union Brigadier General, born March 12, 1816 in Brooklyn, New York. Served in U.S.Congress before the war, lawyer after. Died September 11, 1868 at Detroit, Michigan.

STUART, JAMES EWELL BROWN. Confederate Major General, born February 6, 1833 in Patrick County, Virginia.   Graduated from West Point in 1854 and served in the army before the war. Wounded in battle May 11,1864 at Yellow Tavern,Virginia, died the next day.

STUMBAUGH, FREDERICK SHEARER.   Union Brigadier General, born on April 14, 1817 in Shippensburg, Pennsylvania. Lawyer before and after the war. Died February 25, 1897 at Topeka, Iowa.

STURGIS, SAMUEL DAVIS. Union Brigadier General,born June 11,1822 in Shippensburg,Pennsylvania. Graduated from West Point 1846 and served in the army before and after the war. Died September 28, 1889 at St.Paul, Minnesota.

SULLIVAN, JEREMIAH CUTLER. Union Brigadier General, born on October 1,1830 in Madison,Indiana.   Served in the U.S. navy before the war,clerk after. Died October 21,1890 at Oakland,California.

SULLY, ALFRED. Union Brigadier General, born on May 22, 1820 in Philadelphia, Pennsylvania.   Graduated from West Point 1841 and served in the army before and after the war. Died April 27,1879 at Fort Vancouver, Washington.

SUMNER, EDWIN VOSE. Union Major General,born January 30,1797 in Boston, Massachusetts. Served in the army before the war. Died March 21, 1863 at Syracuse, New York.

SWAYNE, WAGER.   Union Brigadier General, born November 10, 1834 in Columbus, Ohio. Attended Yale University, then practiced law before and after the war. Died on December 18, 1902 at New York City, New York.

SWEENY, THOMAS WILLIAM. Union Brigadier General, born on December 25, 1820 in County Cork, Ireland.   Laborer before the war. Died April 10, 1892 at Astoria, New York.

SYKES, GEORGE. Union Major General,born October 9,1822 in Dover, Delaware. Graduated from West Point 1842 and served in the army before and after the war. Died February 8, 1880 at Brownsville, Texas.

TALIAFERRO, WILLIAM BOOTH. Confederate Major General,born December 28,1822 in Gloucester County,Virginia. Attended William and Mary College. Lawyer before the war, judge after. Died on December 27, 1898 in Gloucester County, Virginia.

TAPPAN, JAMES CAMP. Confederate Brigadier General, born September 9,1825 in Newburyport, Massachusetts. Attended Yale University. Lawyer and judge before the war, in politics after. Died March 19, 1906 at Helena, Arkansas.

TAYLOR, GEORGE WILLIAM. Union Brigadier General, born cn November 22, 1808 in Hunterdon County, New Jersey. Attended Captain Partridge's Military College. Iron manufacturer before the war. Wounded in battle August 30,1862 at Bull Run, Virginia. Died on September 1, 1862.

TAYLOR, JOSEPH PANNELL. Union Brigadier General,born May 4,1796 in Louisville, Kentucky. Brother of President Zachary Taylor. Served in the army before the war. Died on June 29,1864 at Washington, D.C.

TAYLOR, NELSON. Union Brigadier General, born on June 8,1821 in Norwalk, Connecticut. Attended Harvard Law School. Sheriff and lawyer before the war, in Congress after. Died January 16, 1894 at South Norwalk, Connecticut.

TAYLOR, RICHARD. Confederate Lieutenant General,born January 27, 1826 in Louisville, Kentucky. Son of President Zachary Taylor. Attended Yale University. Farmer and in politics before the war. Died April 12, 1879 at New York City, New York.

TAYLOR, THOMAS HART. Confederate Brigadier General,born July 31, 1825 in Frankfort,Kentucky. Attended Centre College. Farmer before the war, police chief and Deputy U.S. Marshal after.   Died April 12, 1901 at Louisville, Kentucky.

TERRILL, WILLIAM RUFUS. Union Brigadier General, born April 21, 1834 in Covington, Virginia. Graduated from West Point 1853 and served in the army before the war.   Killed in battle October 8, 1862 at Perryville, Kentucky.

TERRY, ALFRED HOWE. Union Major General, born November 10, 1827 in Hartford, Connecticut. Attended Yale Law School. Lawyer before the war,served in the army after. Died December 16,1890 at New Haven, Connecticut.

TERRY, HENRY DWIGHT. Union Brigadier General,born March 16,1812 in Hartford, Connecticut. Lawyer before and after the war. Died June 22, 1869 at Washington, D.C.

TERRY, WILLIAM.   Confederate Brigadier General, born August 14, 1824 in Amherst County,Virginia. Attended the University of Virginia.   Lawyer before the war, in Congress after. Died on September 5, 1888 at Wytheville, Virginia.

TERRY, WILLIAM RICHARD.   Confederate Brigadier General, born on March 12,1827 at Liberty, Virginia. Attended University of Virginia. Merchant before the war,in politics after. Died March 28, 1897 in Chesterfield Court House, Virginia.

THAYER, JOHN MILTON.   Union Brigadier General, born January 24, 1820 in Bellingham, Massachusetts.   Attended Brown University. Lawyer before the war,Governor of Nebraska and Wyoming Territory after. Died March 19, 1906 at Lincoln, Nebraska.

THOMAS, ALLEN.   Confederate Brigadier General, born December 4,

1830 in Howard County, Maryland. Attended Princeton University. Lawyer and farmer before and after the war. Died on December 3, 1897 at Waveland, Mississippi.

THOMAS, BRYAN MOREL. Confederate Brigadier General, born May 8, 1836 in Milledgeville, Georgia. Graduated from West Point 1858. Served in the army before the war, U.S. Marshal after.   Died on July 16, 1905 at Dalton, Georgia.

THOMAS, EDWARD LLOYD.   Confederate Brigadier General, born on March 23,1825 in Clarke County,Georgia. Attended Emory College. Farmer before and after the war. Died on March 8, 1898 at South McAlester, Oklahoma.

THOMAS, GEORGE HENRY. Union Major General, born July 31,1816 in Southampton County,Virginia. Graduated from West Point 1840 and served in the army before and after the war. Died March 28,1870 at San Francisco, California.

THOMAS, HENRY GODDARD. Union Brigadier General,born April 4,1837 in Portland, Maine. Attended Amherst College. Lawyer before the war, served in the army after. Died January 23,1897 at Oklahoma City, Oklahoma.

THOMAS, LORENZO.   Union Brigadier General, born October 26,1804 in New Castle,Delaware. Graduated from West Point 1823 and served in the army before and after the war. Died March 2, 1875 at Washington, D.C.

THRUSTON, CHARLES MYNN. Union Brigadier General, born on February 22,1798 in Lexington,Kentucky. Graduated from West Point in 1814. Banker before the war,farmer after. Died February 18,1873 at Cumberland, Maryland.

TILGHMAN, LLOYD. Confederate Brigadier General,born January 26, 1816 in Baltimore,Maryland. Graduated from West Point 1836,then worked as an engineer before the war.   Killed in battle May 16, 1863 at Champion's Hills, Mississippi.

TILLSON, DAVIS. Union Brigadier General, born April 14, 1830 in Rockland,Maine. In politics before the war,business after.   Died April 30, 1895 at Rockland, Maine.

TODD, JOHN BLAIR SMITH.   Union Brigadier General, born April 4, 1814 in Lexington, Kentucky. Graduated from West Point in 1837. Lawyer and served in the army before the war, in politics after. Died January 5, 1872 in Yankton County, South Dakota.

TOOMBS, ROBERT AUGUSTUS. Confederate Brigadier General, born on July 2, 1810 in Wilkes County, Georgia. Attended Union College. Lawyer and in politics before and after the war. Died on December 15, 1885 at Washington, Georgia.

TOON, THOMAS FENTRESS.   Confederate Brigadier General, born on June 10, 1840 in Columbus County, North Carolina. Attended Wake Forrest College until the war,an educator after. Died on February 19, 1902 at Raleigh, North Carolina.

TORBERT, ALFRED THOMAS ARCHIMEDES. Union Brigadier General,born
July 1, 1833 in Georgetown, Delaware. Graduated from West Point
1855. Served in the army before the war,in civil service after.
Died August 29, 1880 at Cape Canaveral, Florida.

TOTTEN, JOSEPH GILBERT. Union Brigadier General, born April 17,
1788 in New Haven, Connecticut. Graduated from West Point 1805
and served in the army before the war. Died of pneumonia on A-
pril 22, 1864 at Washington, D.C.

TOWER, ZEALOUS BATES. Union Brigadier General, born January 12,
1819 in Cohasset,Massachusetts. Graduated from West Point 1841,
and served in the army before and after the war. Died March 20,
1900 at Cohasset, Massachusetts.

TRACY, EDWARD DORR. Confederate Brigadier General, born on November 5,1833 in Macon, Georgia. Lawyer before the war. Killed
in battle May 1, 1863 at Port Gibson, Mississippi.

TRAPIER, JAMES HEYWARD. Confederate Brigadier General, born No-
vember 24,1815 in Georgetown,South Carolina. Graduated from West
Point 1838. Farmer and served in the army before the war. Died
December 21, 1865 at Georgetown, South Carolina.

TRIMBLE, ISAAC RIDGEWAY. Confederate Major General,born May 15,
1802 in Culpeper County, Virginia. Graduated from West Point in
1822. Engineer before the war. Died January 2,1888 at Baltimore,
Maryland.

TUCKER, WILLIAM FEIMSTER. Confederate Brigadier General,born on
May 9,1827 in Iredell County,North Carolina. Attended Emory and
Henry College. Lawyer and judge before the war, in politics af-
ter. Died September 14, 1881 at Okolona, Mississippi.

TURCHIN, JOHN BASIL. Union Brigadier General, born January 30,
1822 in Don,Russia. Attended Imperial Military School. Engineer
before the war, patent solicitor after. Died on June 19,1901 at
Anna, Illinois.

TURNER, JOHN WESLEY. Union Brigadier General, born July 19,1833
in Saratoga,New York. Graduated from West Point 1855 and served
in the army before and after the war. Died on April 8, 1899 at
St.Louis, Missouri.

TUTTLE, JAMES MADISON. Union Brigadier General, born on September 24, 1823 in Summerfield, Ohio. Sheriff before the war, then
in mining after. Died October 24, 1892 at Casa Grande, Arizona.

TWIGGS, DAVID EMANUEL. Confederate Major General,born about 1790
in Richmond County, Georgia. Served in the army before the war.
Died July 15, 1862 at Augusta, Georgia.

TYLER, DANIEL. Union Brigadier General, born January 7, 1799 in
Brooklyn,Connecticut. Graduated from West Point 1819. Railroad

president before and after the war. Died November 30,1882 in New York City, New York.

TYLER, ERASTUS BARNARD. Union Brigadier General, born April 24, 1822 in West Bloomfield, New York.   Attended Granville College. In the fur business before the war, postmaster after. Died January 9, 1891 at Baltimore, Maryland.

TYLER, ROBERT CHARLES. Confederate Brigadier General,born about 1833 in Baltimore, Maryland. Served in the army before the war. Killed in battle April 16, 1865 at Fort Tyler, Virginia.

TYLER, ROBERT OGDEN. Union Brigadier General, born December 22, 1831 in Hunter, New York.   Graduated from West Point 1853, then served in the army before and after the war.   Died December 1, 1874 at Boston, Massachusetts.

TYNDALE, GEORGE HECTOR. Union Brigadier General, born March 24, 1821 in Philadelphia,Pennsylvania.   A glass importer before the war, in the glass business after. Died March 19, 1880 at Philadelphia, Pennsylvania.

ULLMAN, DANIEL. Union Brigadier General, born April 28, 1810 in Wilmington, Delaware.   Attended Yale University. Lawyer before the war,retired after. Died September 20,1892 at Nyack,New York.

UNDERWOOD, ADIN BALLOU. Union Brigadier General,born May 19,1828 in Milford,Massachusetts. Attended Brown University. Lawyer before the war, surveyor after.   Died January 24, 1888 at Boston, Massachusetts.

UPTON, EMORY.   Union Brigadier General, born August 27, 1839 in Batavia,New York. Attended Oberlin College, then graduated from West Point 1861.   Continued serving in the army following the war. Committed suicide March 15,1881 at his headquarters at San Francisco, California.

VAN ALEN, JAMES HENRY. Union Brigadier General, born August 17, 1819 in Kinderhook,New York. Independently wealthy. Fell overboard at sea on July 22, 1886.

VANCE, ROBERT BRANK.   Confederate Brigadier General, born on April 24,1828 in Buncombe County,North Carolina. Merchant before the war, in U.S. Congress after. Died November 28,1899 at Asheville, North Carolina.

VAN CLEVE, HORATIO PHILLIPS. Union Brigadier General,born on November 23,1809 in Princeton,New Jersey. Attended Princeton University,then graduated from West Point 1831. Engineer before the war, postmaster after.   Died on April 24, 1891 at Minneapolis, Minnesota.

VAN DERVEER, FERDINAND. Union Brigadier General, born on February 27, 1823 in Butler County, Ohio.   Sheriff and lawyer before the war, judge after.   Died November 5, 1892 at Hamilton, Ohio.

VANDEVER, WILLIAM.   Union Brigadier General, born March 31, 1817 in Baltimore,Maryland.   Lawyer and served in Congress before and after the war.   Died July 23, 1893 at Ventura, California.

VAN DORN, EARL.   Confederate Major General, born September 17, 1820 in Port Gibson,Mississippi.   Graduated from West Point 1842 and served in the army before the war.   Murdered May 7, 1863 at his headquarters in Spring Hill, Tennessee.

VAN VLIET, STEWART.   Union Brigadier General, born July 21,1815 in Ferrisburg,Vermont. Graduated from West Point 1840 and served in the army before and after the war.   Died on March 28, 1901 at Washington, D.C.

VAUGHAN JR., ALFRED JEFFERSON.   Confederate Brigadier General, born May 10,1830 in Dinwiddie County,Virginia.   Attended Virginia Military Institute.   An engineer before the war, farmerafter. Died October 1, 1899 at Indianapolis, Indiana.

VAUGHN, JOHN CRAWFORD.   Confederate Brigadier General, born February 24, 1824 in Roane County, Tennessee.   Merchant before the war, in politics after.   Died September 10,1875 at Thomasville, Georgia.

VEATCH, JAMES CLIFFORD.   Union Brigadier General, born on December 19, 1819 in Elizabethtown, Indiana.   Lawyer before the war, Internal Revenue Collector after.   Died on December 22, 1895 at Rockport, Indiana.

VIELE, EGBERT LUDOVICUS.   Union Brigadier General, born June 17, 1825 in Waterford,New York.   Attended Albany Academy, then graduated from West Point 1847.   Engineer before and after the war. Died April 22, 1902 at New York City, New York.

VILLEPIGUE, JOHN BORDENAVE.   Confederate Brigadier General, born July 2,1830 in Camden,South Carolina.   Graduated from West Point 1854 and served in the army before the war. Died of fever on November 9, 1862 at Port Hudson, Louisiana.

VINTON, FRANCIS LAURENS.   Union Brigadier General, born June 1, 1835 in Fort Preble,Maine.   Graduated from West Point 1856.   Engineer before the war, college professor after.   Died October 6, 1879 at Leadville, Colorado.

VOGDES, ISRAEL.   Union Brigadier General, born August 4,1816 in Willistown, Pennsylvania.   Graduated from West Point 1837, then served in the army before and after the war.   Died December 7, 1889 at New York City, New York.

VON STEINWEHR, ADOLPH WILHELM AUGUST FRIEDRICH.   Union Brigadier General,born September 25,1822 at Blankenburg,Germany.   Attended Brunswick Military Academy.   Farmer and soldier before the war, college professor after.   Died February 25, 1877 in Buffalo, New York.

WADE, MELANCTHON SMITH. Union Brigadier General,born December 2,

1802 in Cincinnati,Ohio. Merchant before the war,retired after.
Died August 11, 1868 at Cincinnati, Ohio.

WADSWORTH, JAMES SAMUEL. Union Brigadier General, born on Octo-
ber 30, 1807 in Geneseo, New York. Attended Harvard University.
Lawyer before the war. Wounded in battle on May 6,1864.   Died
May 8, 1864 at the Wilderness, Virginia.

WAGNER, GEORGE DAY. Union Brigadier General, born September 22,
1829 in Ross County,Ohio. Politics before the war,lawyer after.
Died February 13, 1869 at Indianapolis, Indiana.

WALCUTT, CHARLES CARROLL. Union Brigadier General, born on February 12,1838 in Columbus, Ohio. Attended Kentucky Military Institute. Surveyor before the war, prison warden after. Died on
May 2, 1898 at Omaha, Nebraska.

WALKER, HENRY HARRISON. Confederate Brigadier General, born October 15, 1832 in Sussex County, Virginia.   Graduated from West
Point 1853. Served in the army before the war,investment broker
after. Died March 22, 1912 at Morristown, New Jersey.

WALKER, JAMES ALEXANDER. Confederate Brigadier General, born on
August 27,1832 in Mount Sidney,Virginia. Attended University of
Virginia. Lawyer before the war, Congress after. Died on Octo-
ber 20, 1901 at Wytheville, Virginia.

WALKER, JOHN GEORGE. Confederate Major General,born July 22,1822
in Cole County,Missouri. Attended Jesuit College. Served in the
army before the war, in politics after. Died on July 20,1893 at
Washington, D.C.

WALKER, LEROY POPE. Confederate Brigadier General, born on Feb-
ruary 7,1817 in Huntsville, Alabama. Attended the University of
Alabama. Lawyer and in politics before and after the war. Died
August 22, 1884 at Huntsville, Alabama.

WALKER, LUCIUS MARSHALL. Confederate Brigadier General, born on
October 18,1829 in Columbia,Tennessee. Graduated from West Point
1850.   Merchant before the war.   Wounded September 6,1863 in a
duel with Brigadier General John Marmaduke, died the next day at
Little Rock, Arkansas.

WALKER, REUBEN LINDSAY. Confederate Brigadier General, born on
May 29,1827 in Logan,Virginia. Attended Virginia Military Insti-
tute. Farmer before the war, engineer and farmer after.   Died
June 7, 1890 in Fluvanna County, Virginia.

WALKER, WILLIAM HENRY TALBOT. Confederate Major General,born on
November 26,1816 in Augusta, Georgia. Graduated from West Point
1837 and served in the army before the war. Killed in battle on
July 22, 1864 at Atlanta, Georgia.

WALKER, WILLIAM STEPHEN. Confederate Brigadier General, born on
April 13,1822 in Pittsburg,Pennsylvania. Served in the army before the war. Died June 7, 1899 at Atlanta, Georgia.

WALLACE, LEWIS. Union Major General,born April 10,1827 in Brook-
ville, Indiana.   Lawyer before the war, Governor of New Mexico
Territory after.   Died on February 15, 1905 at Crawfordsville,
Indiana.

WALLACE, WILLIAM HARVEY LAMB.   Union Brigadier General, born on
July 8,1821 in Urbana, Ohio. Lawyer before the war. Wounded in
battle April 7, 1862 at Shiloh, Tennessee. Died April 10, 1862.

WALLACE, WILLIAM HENRY.   Confederate Brigadier General, born on
March 24,1827 in Laurens District, South Carolina. Attended the
University of South Carolina. Farmer and lawyer before the war,
judge after.   Died March 21, 1901 in Union, South Carolina.

WALTHALL, EDWARD CARY. Confederate Major General, born April 4,
1831 in Richmond, Virginia. Lawyer before the war, U.S. Senator
after. Died April 21, 1898 at Washington, D.C.

WARD, JOHN HENRY HOBART. Union Brigadier General, born June 17,
1823 in New York City, New York.   Served in the army before the
war, court clerk after. Ran over by a train on July 24, 1903 at
Monroe, New York.

WARD, WILLIAM THOMAS. Union Brigadier General,born on August 9,
1808 in Amelia County,Virginia. Attended St.Mary's College. In
Congress before the war, lawyer after.   Died October 12,1878 at
Louisville, Kentucky.

WARREN, FITZ-HENRY.   Union Brigadier General, born January 11,
1816 in Brimfield,Massachusetts. In politics before the war,U.S.
Minister to Guatemala after.   Died June 21, 1878 at Brimfield,
Massachusetts.

WARREN, GOUVERNEUR KEMBLE. Union Major General, born January 8,
1830 in Cold Spring,New York. Graduated from West Point 1850 and
served in the army before and after the war. Died August 8,1882
at Newport, Rhode Island.

WASHBURN, CADWALLADER COLDEN. Union Major General,born April 22,
1818 in Livermore, Maine. Lawyer and in Congress before the war,
Governor of Wisconsin after. Died May 14,1882 at Eureka Springs,
Arkansas.

WATERHOUSE, RICHARD. Confederate Brigadier General,born on January 12,1832 in Rhea County,Tennessee. Merchant before the war,
land speculator after. Died of pneumonia March 20,1876 at Waco,
Texas.

WATIE, STAND.   Confederate Brigadier General, born December 12,
1806 in Rome,Georgia. A three-fourths blood Cherokee Indian. A
farmer before and after the war. Died September 9,1871 in Delaware County, Oklahoma.

WAUL, THOMAS NEVILLE. Confederate Brigadier General, born January 5,1813 in Sumter District, South Carolina. Attended University of South Carolina. Farmer and lawyer before the war,lawyer

after. Died July 28, 1903 in Hunt County, Texas.

WAYNE, HENRY CONSTANTINE. Confederate Brigadier General,born on September 18,1815 in Savannah,Georgia. Graduated from West Point 1838. Served in the army before the war, in lumber business after. Died March 15, 1883 at Savannah, Georgia.

WEBB, ALEXANDER STEWART. Union Brigadier General,born on February 15,1835 in New York City,New York. Graduated from West Point 1855. Served in the army before the war,college president after. Died February 12, 1911 at Riverdale, New York.

WEBER, MAX. Union Brigadier General, born on August 27,1824 in Achern,Germany. Attended Karlsruhe Military School. Hotel operator before the war, Internal Revenue collector after. Died on June 15, 1901 at Brooklyn, New York.

WEBSTER, JOSEPH DANA. Union Brigadier General, born August 25, 1811 at Hampton,New Hampshire. Attended Dartmouth College. Engineer before the war, Internal Revenue collector after. Died March 12, 1876 at Chicago, Illinois.

WEED, STEPHEN HINSDALE. Union Brigadier General, born on November 17,1831 in Potsdam,New York. Graduated from West Point 1854 and served in the army before the war. Killed in battle July 2, 1863 at Gettysburg, Pennsylvania.

WEISIGER, DAVID ADDISON. Confederate Brigadier General, born on December 23, 1818 in Chesterfield County, Virginia. In business before the war,banker after. Died February 23,1899 at Richmond, Virginia.

WEITZEL, GODFREY. Union Major General, born November 1,1835 in Cincinnati,Ohio. Graduated from West Point in 1855 and served in the army before and after the war. Died March 19,1884 at Philadelphia, Pennsylvania.

WELSH, THOMAS. Union Brigadier General, born on May 5, 1824 in Columbia,Pennsylvania. Merchant before the war. Died of malaria August 14, 1863 at Cincinnati, Ohio.

WESSELLS, HENRY WALTON. Union Brigadier General, born on February 20,1809 in Litchfield,Connecticut. Graduated from West Point 1833 and served in the army before and after the war. Died January 12, 1889 at Dover, Delaware.

WEST, JOSEPH RODMAN. Union Brigadier General,born September 19, 1822 in New Orleans, Louisiana. Attended University of Pennsylvania. Operated a newspaper before the war, U.S. Marshal after. Died October 31, 1898 at Washington, D.C.

WHARTON, GABRIEL COLVIN. Confederate Brigadier General, born on July 23,1824 in Culpeper County,Virginia. Attended Virginia Military Institute. Engineer before the war,in politics after. Died May 12, 1906 at Radford, Virginia.

WHARTON, JOHN AUSTIN. Confederate Major General,born July 3,1828 in Nashville,Tennessee.   Attended University of South Carolina, then a lawyer before the war.   Shot in an argument with Colonel George Baylor April 6, 1865 at Houston, Texas.   *

WHEATON, FRANK. Union Brigadier General, born on May 8, 1833 in Providence, Rhode Island. Attended Brown University. Served in the army before and after the war. Died July 18,1903 at Washington, D.C.

WHEELER, JOSEPH.   Confederate Major General, born September 10, 1836 in Augusta,Georgia. Graduated from West Point 1859. Served in the army before the war,Congress after. Died January 25,1906 at Brooklyn, New York.

WHIPPLE, AMIEL WEEKS. Union Brigadier General, born October 15, 1816 in Greenwich,Massachusetts. Attended Amherst College, then graduated from West Point in 1841. Served in the army before the war.   Wounded in battle on May 4,1863, died May 7,1863 at Chancellorsville, Virginia.

WHIPPLE, WILLIAM DENISON. Union Brigadier General,born August 2, 1826 in Nelson, New York. Graduated from West Point 1851, then served in the army before and after the war. Died April 1, 1902 at New York City, New York.

WHITAKER, WALTER CHILES. Union Brigadier General,born August 8, 1823 in Shelbyville, Kentucky.   Attended Bethany College, then practiced law before and after the war. Died on July 9, 1887 at Lyndon, Kentucky.

WHITE, JULIUS.   Union Brigadier General, born September 23,1816 in Cazenovia,New York. In politics before the war. Died May 12, 1890 at Evanston, Illinois.

WHITFIELD, JOHN WILKINS. Confederate Brigadier General, born on March 11,1818 in Franklin,Tennessee. In Congress before the war, politics after.   Died October 27, 1879 at Hallettsville, Texas.

WHITING, WILLIAM HENRY CHASE. Confederate Major General,born on March 22,1824 in Biloxi,Mississippi.   Graduated from West Point 1845 and served in the army before the war. Wounded in battle on January 15, 1865.   Died on March 10, 1865 at Fort Fisher, North Carolina.

WICKHAM, WILLIAMS CARTER. Confederate Brigadier General, born on September 21,1820 in Richmond, Virginia. Attended University of Virginia. Lawyer and in politics before the war, railroad president after. Died July 23, 1888 at Richmond, Virginia.

WIGFALL, LOUIS TREZEVANT. Confederate Brigadier General,born on April 21,1816 in Edgefield, South Carolina. Attended University of South Carolina. Lawyer and U.S.Senator before the war. Died February 18, 1874 at Galveston, Texas.

WILCOX, CADMUS MARCELLUS. Confederate Major General,born May 29,

1824 in Wayne County,North Carolina. Attended Nashville University, then graduated from West Point 1846.   Served in the army before the war, in civil service after. Died December 2,1890 at Washington, D.C.

WILD, EDWARD AUGUSTUS. Union Brigadier General,born November 25, 1825 in Brookline, Massachusetts.   Attended Harvard University. Doctor before the war, in mining after. Died August 28, 1891 at Medellin, Colombia.

WILLCOX, ORLANDO BOLIVAR. Union Brigadier General,born April 16, 1823 in Detroit,Michigan. Graduated from West Point 1847. Lawyer and served in the army before and after the war.   Died May 10, 1907 at Coburg, Ontario.

WILLIAMS, ALPHEUS STARKEY. Union Brigadier General,born September 20,1810 in Saybrook, Connecticut. Attended Yale University. Lawyer and postmaster before the war,in Congress after. Died on December 21, 1878 at Washington, D.C.

WILLIAMS, DAVID HENRY.   Union Brigadier General, born March 19, 1819 in Otsego County, New York.   Engineer before and after the war. Died June 1, 1891 at Pittsburgh, Pennsylvania.

WILLIAMS, JOHN STUART.   Confederate Brigadier General, born on July 10,1818 in Mount Sterling,Kentucky. Attended Miami University. Lawyer and in politics before the war,farmer after. Died July 17, 1898 at Mount Sterling, Kentucky.

WILLIAMS, SETH.   Union Brigadier General, born March 22,1822 in Augusta, Maine. Graduated from West Point 1842 and served in the army before and after the war. Died on March 23,1866 at Boston, Massachusetts.

WILLIAMS, THOMAS. Union Brigadier General, born January 10,1815 in Albany, New York.   Graduated from West Point 1837 and served in the army before the war.   Killed in battle August 5, 1862 at Baton Rouge, Louisiana.

WILLIAMSON, JAMES ALEXANDER. Union Brigadier General, born February 8, 1829 in Adair County, Kentucky. Attended Knox College. Lawyer before the war,railroad president after. Died on September 7, 1902 at Jamestown, Rhode Island.

WILLICH, AUGUST. Union Brigadier General, born November 19,1810 in Braunsberg,Germany. Attended Berlin Military Academy. Editor before the war, county auditor after.   Died January 22, 1878 at St.Mary's, Ohio.

WILSON, JAMES HARRISON. Union Brigadier General,born on September 2,1837 in Shawneetown,Illinois. Attended McKendree College, then graduated from West Point 1860.   Served in the army before the war, engineer after.   Died February 23, 1925 at Wilmington, Illinois.

WINDER, CHARLES SIDNEY. Confederate Brigadier General, born Oc-

tober 18, 1829 in Talbot County, Maryland.   Graduated from West
Point 1850 and served in the army before the war. Killed in battle August 9, 1862 at Cedar Mountain, Virginia.

WINDER, JOHN HENRY.   Confederate Brigadier General, born February 21, 1800 in Somerset County, Maryland.   Graduated from West
Point 1820 and served in the army before the war.   Died on February 7, 1865 at Florence, South Carolina.

WISE, HENRY ALEXANDER.   Confederate Brigadier General, born December 3,1806 in Drummondtown,Virginia. Attended Washington College.   Governor of Virginia before the war, lawyer after.   Died
September 12, 1876 at Richmond, Virginia.

WISTAR, ISAAC JONES.   Union Brigadier General, born November 14,
1827 in Philadelphia, Pennsylvania.   Attended Haverford College,
then practices law before and after the war.   Died September 18,
1905 at Claymont, Delaware.

WITHERS, JONES MITCHELL.   Confederate Major General, born January 12,1814 in Madison County,Alabama. Graduated from West Point
1835.   Lawyer before the war,cotton broker after. Died March 13,
1890 at Mobile, Alabama.

WOFFORD, WILLIAM TATUM.   Confederate Brigadier General, born on
June 28,1824 in Habersham County,Georgia. Lawyer and in politics
before and after the war.   Died on May 22,1884 at Cass Station,
Georgia.

WOOD, STERLING ALEXANDER MARTIN.   Confederate Brigadier General,
born March 17,1823 in Florence,Alabama. Attended Jesuit College,
then a lawyer before and after the war.   Died January 26,1891 at
Tuscaloosa, Mississippi.

WOOD, THOMAS JOHN.   Union Major General, born September 25,1823
in Munfordville, Kentucky.   Graduated from West Point 1845 then
served in the army before and after the war.   Died February 25,
1906 at Dayton, Ohio.

WOODBURY, DANIEL PHINEAS.   Union Brigadier General, born December 16,1812 in New London,New Hampshire. Attended Dartmouth College, then graduated from West Point 1836.   Served in the army
before the war.   Died from yellow fever on August 15,1864 at Key
West, Florida.

WOODS, CHARLES ROBERT. Union Brigadier General,born February 19,
1827 in Newark,Ohio.   Graduated from West Point 1852 then served
in the army before and after the war.   Died February 26,1885 at
Newark, Ohio.

WOOL, JOHN ELLIS.   Union Major General, born February 29,1784 in
Newburgh, New York.   Served in the army before the war, retired
after.   Died November 10, 1869 at Troy, New York.

WRIGHT, AMBROSE RANSOM. Confederate Major General,born April 26,
1826 in Louisville, Georgia.   Lawyer before the war, in politics

after. Died December 21, 1872 at Augusta, Georgia.

WRIGHT, GEORGE. Union Brigadier General,born October 21,1801 in Norwich, Vermont. Attended Captain Partridge's Military School, then graduated from West Point 1822.   Served in the army before and after the war.   Died on July 30,1865 in a shipwreck off the California coast.

WRIGHT, HORATIO GOUVERNEUR.   Union Major General, born March 6, 1820 in Clinton, Connecticut. Graduated from West Point in 1841, then served in the army before and after the war.   Died July 2, 1899 at Washington, D.C.

WRIGHT, MARCUS JOSEPH.   Confederate Brigadier General, born on June 5,1831 in Purdy, Tennessee.   Court clerk and lawyer before the war, writer after. Died December 27,1922 at Washington,D.C.

YORK, ZEBULON.   Confederate Brigadier General, born October 10, 1819 in Avon, Maine.   Attended University of Louisiana. Lawyer before the war, hotel operator after.   Died on August 5,1900 at Natchez, Mississippi.

YOUNG, PIERCE MANNING BUTLER.   Confederate Major General, born November 15, 1836 in Spartanburg, South Carolina. Attended West Point until the war, in politics after. Died July 6,1896 at New York City, New York.

YOUNG, WILLIAM HUGH. Confederate Brigadier General,born on January 1,1838 in Booneville, Missouri. Attended the University of Virginia until the war, in real estate and a lawyer after. Died November 28, 1901 at San Antonio, Texas.

ZOLLICOFFER, FELIX KIRK. Confederate Brigadier General, born on May 19, 1812 in Maury County, Tennessee. In politics before the war. Killed in battle January 19,1862 at Mill Springs,Kentucky.

ZOOK, SAMUEL KOSCIUSZKO. Union Brigadier General,born March 27, 1821 in Chester County,Pennsylvania. Telegrapher before the war. Wounded in battle July 2,1863 at Gettysburg,Pennsylvania.   Died the next day.

Index

ARMISTEAD, LEWIS ADDISON, 7,
32, 39, 63, 76, 102, 132,
145, 159, 176, 202, 212,
214, 218, 222
ARMSTRONG, FRANK CRAWFORD, 7,
25, 42, 64, 87, 104, 109,
132, 156, 163, 190, 205,
222
ARNOLD, LEWIS GOLDING, 13,
32, 44, 60, 75, 90, 115,
132, 151, 164, 179, 206,
222
ARNOLD, RICHARD, 13, 33, 66,
83, 94, 119, 132, 152, 166,
182, 208, 222
ASBOTH, ALEXANDER SANDOR, 13,
21, 50, 55, 73, 105, 123,
149, 160, 178, 194, 222
ASHBY, TURNER, 7, 36, 69, 83,
103, 124, 145, 159, 175,
201, 212, 214, 217, 222
AUGUR, CHRISTOPHER COLUMBUS,
5, 23, 42, 61, 78, 98, 117,
132, 152, 160, 187, 194,
222
AVERELL, WILLIAM WOODS, 13,
36, 52, 61, 86, 103, 120,
132, 145, 166, 188, 195,
222
AYRES, ROMEYN BECK, 13, 34,
40, 61, 81, 105, 118, 132,
152, 166, 184, 209, 223
BAILEY, JOSEPH, 13, 31, 64,
81, 95, 128, 152, 165, 178,
197, 223

B

BAIRD, ABSALOM, 13, 21, 66,
81, 100, 112, 118, 132,
152, 164, 190, 201, 223
BAKER, ALPHEUS, 7, 22, 66,
83, 96, 126, 147, 163,
185, 206, 223
BAKER, EDWARD DICKINSON, 5,
24, 42, 54, 73, 92, 129,
145, 158, 175, 207, 211,
214, 217, 223
BAKER, LAURENCE SIMMONS, 7,
32, 50, 63, 84, 96, 119,
132, 151, 172, 190, 198,
223
BALDWIN, WILLIAM EDWIN, 7,
37, 43, 67, 83, 99, 121,
141, 157, 177, 196, 223
BANKS, NATHANIEL PRENTISS, 5,

33, 49, 60, 75, 91, 125,
149, 164, 186, 205, 223
BARKSDALE, WILLIAM, 7, 36, 68,
78, 100, 110, 122, 145, 159,
176, 202, 212, 214, 218, 223
BARLOW, FRANCIS CHANNING, 13,
25, 41, 60, 87, 102, 109,
126, 150, 167, 186, 194, 223
BARNARD, JOHN GROSS, 13, 29,
44, 60, 74, 96, 115, 132,
152, 164, 181, 200, 223
BARNES, JAMES, 13, 28, 59, 71,
106, 115, 123, 151, 164,
178, 195, 224
BARNES, JOSEPH K., 13, 31, 65,
76, 98, 110, 132, 152, 172,
181, 202, 224
BARRINGER, RUFUS, 7, 34, 63,
78, 105, 110, 126, 150, 168,
186, 195, 224
BARRY, JOHN DECATUR, 7, 29,
42, 63, 88, 97, 110, 137,
149, 168, 178, 197, 224
BARRY, WILLIAM FARQUHAR, 13,
37, 43, 62, 76, 100, 116,
132, 152, 164, 181, 202,
224
BARTLETT, JOSEPH JACKSON, 13,
31, 46, 61, 87, 104, 126,
149, 164, 185, 194, 224
BARTLETT, WILLIAM FRANCIS, 13,
37, 43, 59, 88, 97, 109,
137, 139, 164, 180, 209, 224
BARTON, SETH MAXWELL, 7, 35,
47, 69, 84, 101, 118, 132,
155, 172, 188, 198, 224
BATE, WILLIAM BRIMAGE, 4, 37,
41, 67, 82, 102, 129, 144,
172, 190, 196, 224
BATTLE, CULLEN ANDREWS, 7, 23,
40, 55, 84, 97, 107, 126,
149, 168, 190, 198, 224
BAXTER, HENRY, 13, 26, 62, 78,
101, 129, 149, 165, 179,
210, 224
BAYARD, GEORGE DASHIELL, 13,
25, 42, 62, 87, 105, 120,
132, 145, 158, 176, 209,
212, 214, 218, 225
BEAL, GEORGE LAFAYETTE, 13,
26, 47, 58, 81, 96, 112, 121,
155, 163, 187, 209, 225
BEALE, RICHARD LEE TURBERVILLE,
7, 34, 47, 69, 77, 96, 112,
122, 140, 172, 185, 199, 225
BEALL, WILLIAM NELSON RECTOR,

200, 267
MCCALL, GEORGE ARCHIBALD, 17,
26, 40, 65, 71, 93, 114,
135, 152, 169, 178, 196, 267
MCCAUSLAND, JOHN, 10, 29, 60,
87, 101, 112, 122, 143, 172,
192, 194, 267
MCCLELLAN, GEORGE BRINTON, 6,
26, 41, 65, 82, 105, 110,
118, 135, 144, 166, 182,
207, 267
MCCLERNAND, JOHN ALEXANDER, 6,
30, 39, 57, 73, 96, 122,
150, 162, 184, 206, 267
MCCOMB, WILLIAM, 10, 36, 65,
84, 104, 129, 143, 172, 192,
203, 268
MCCOOK, ALEXANDER MCDOWELL, 6,
21, 47, 64, 85, 95, 119,
135, 154, 168, 189, 201, 268
MCCOOK, EDWARD MOODY, 17, 24,
48, 64, 86, 97, 127, 144,
162, 191, 205, 268
MCCOOK, ROBERT LATIMER, 17,
34, 47, 64, 83, 106, 127,
146, 160, 175, 203, 213,
215, 217, 268
MCCOWN, JOHN PORTER, 4, 30,
49, 68, 74, 100, 116, 135,
155, 157, 180, 194, 268
MCCULLOCH, BEN, 10, 22, 68,
73, 104, 138, 146, 158,
175, 196, 211, 215, 217, 268
MCCULLOCH, HENRY EUSTACE, 10,
27, 43, 68, 75, 105, 138,
143, 171, 186, 197, 268
MCDOWELL, IRVIN, 6, 27, 64,
76, 102, 116, 135, 154,
160, 182, 199, 268
MCGINNIS, GEORGE FRANCIS, 17,
26, 43, 59, 82, 93, 125,
151, 162, 191, 201, 268
MCGOWAN, SAMUEL, 10, 34, 67,
77, 102, 111, 130, 145,
169, 187, 204, 268
MCINTOSH, JAMES MCQUEEN, 11,
28, 48, 54, 83, 118, 135,
146, 158, 175, 196, 211,
215, 217, 268
MCINTOSH, JOHN BAILLIE, 17,
30, 40, 54, 84, 97, 122,
154, 166, 183, 202, 268
MCKEAN, THOMAS JEFFERSON,
17, 36, 46, 65, 73, 100,
115, 123, 143, 162, 179,
199, 269

MCKINSTRY, JUSTUS, 17, 32,
61, 74, 98, 116, 135,
155, 165, 187, 209, 269
MCLAWS, LAFAYETTE, 4, 32,
54, 78, 90, 117, 135,
145, 161, 187, 203, 269
MCLEAN, NATHANIEL COLLINS,
17, 33, 42, 64, 74, 91,
109, 127, 143, 166, 190,
193, 269
MCMILLAN, JAMES WINNING, 17,
28, 52, 56, 81, 95, 122,
156, 173, 189, 196, 269
MCNAIR, EVANDER, 11, 25, 63,
77, 94, 129, 155, 165,
189, 208, 269
MCNEIL, JOHN, 17, 29, 62,
73, 91, 125, 152, 165,
185, 201, 269
MCPHERSON, JAMES BIRDSEYE,
6, 28, 40, 64, 84, 104,
110, 119, 135, 146, 158,
177, 203, 211, 215, 219, 269
MCRAE, DANDRIDGE, 11, 23, 53,
84, 102, 111, 127, 150, 158,
188, 199, 269
MEADE, GEORGE GORDON, 6, 26,
44, 67, 75, 106, 115, 135,
154, 169, 179, 208, 269
MEAGHER, THOMAS FRANCIS, 17,
36, 43, 56, 80, 99, 130,
152, 166, 178, 202, 269
MEIGS, MONTGOMERY CUNNINGHAM,
17, 33, 42, 54, 75, 95,
110, 115, 135, 154, 173,
185, 193, 270
MERCER, HUGH WEEDON, 11, 27,
51, 69, 72, 104, 114, 121,
149, 161, 180, 201, 270
MEREDITH, SOLOMON, 17, 35,
39, 63, 73, 96, 138, 143,
162, 180, 206, 270
MEREDITH, SULLIVAN AMORY, 17,
35, 65, 75, 98, 122, 142,
166, 180, 210, 270
MERRITT, WESLEY, 6, 36, 62,
86, 97, 120, 135, 154, 172,
191, 209, 270
MILES, NELSON APPLETON, 17,
33, 40, 60, 88, 99, 137,
154, 173, 192, 200, 270
MILLER, JOHN FRANKLIN, 17,
30, 44, 56, 85, 104, 127,
152, 160, 183, 196, 270
MILLER, STEPHEN, 17, 35, 65,
75, 89, 123, 144, 165,

140, 166, 180, 196, 296

W

WADE, MELANCTHON SMITH, 20, 32, 50, 64, 71, 105, 129, 152, 168, 178, 204, 296

WADSWORTH, JAMES SAMUEL, 20, 29, 50, 61, 72, 103, 109, 130, 147, 160, 177, 200, 213, 216, 218, 297

WAGNER, GEORGE DAY, 20, 26, 42, 64, 84, 101, 130, 148, 162, 179, 195, 297

WALCUTT, CHARLES CARROLL, 20, 23, 41, 64, 88, 91, 109, 138, 151, 166, 188, 199, 297

WALKER, HENRY HARRISON, 12, 27, 44, 70, 86, 102, 119, 137, 145, 166, 191, 197, 297

WALKER, JAMES ALEXANDER, 12, 29, 39, 69, 86, 100, 112, 128, 141, 172, 189, 207, 297

WALKER, JOHN GEORGE, 5, 31, 44, 60, 79, 99, 109, 137, 150, 174, 186, 203, 297

WALKER, LEROY POPE, 12, 32, 49, 53, 75, 91, 107, 130, 150, 157, 182, 204, 297

WALKER, LUCIUS MARSHALL, 12, 32, 47, 67, 84, 102, 119, 129, 142, 158, 176, 205, 297

WALKER, REUBEN LINDSAY, 12, 33, 47, 69, 82, 96, 112, 125, 142, 171, 184, 201, 297

WALKER, WILLIAM HENRY TALBOT, 5, 38, 45, 55, 75, 104, 116, 137, 147, 158, 177, 203, 211, 216, 219, 297

WALKER, WILLIAM STEPHEN, 12, 38, 50, 65, 79, 94, 137, 156, 161, 188, 201, 297

WALLACE, LEWIS, 7, 32, 56, 82, 94, 130, 144, 162, 190, 195, 297

WALLACE, WILLIAM HARVEY LAMB, 12, 38, 44, 64, 78, 98, 128, 147, 159, 175, 198, 213, 216, 217, 298

WALLACE, WILLIAM HENRY, 20, 38, 45, 67, 82, 93, 111,

125, 145, 170, 188, 197, 298

WALTHALL, EDWARD CARY, 5, 24, 41, 70, 85, 94, 128, 152, 174, 188, 199, 298

WARD, JOHN HENRY HOBART, 20, 31, 45, 62, 80, 97, 137, 141, 167, 189, 203, 298

WARD, WILLIAM THOMAS, 20, 38, 51, 68, 72, 99, 111, 122, 148, 163, 180, 207, 298

WARREN, FITZ-HENRY, 20, 25, 59, 75, 90, 130, 149, 164, 180, 201, 298

WARREN, GOUVERNEUR KEMBLE, 7, 26, 46, 61, 84, 89, 119, 137, 155, 169, 182, 203, 298

WASHBURN, CADWALLADER COLDEN, 7, 23, 42, 58, 76, 95, 122, 144, 157, 181, 200, 298

WATERHOUSE, RICHARD, 12, 34, 67, 85, 90, 129, 147, 171, 180, 197, 298

WATIE, STAND, 12, 35, 55, 72, 105, 125, 144, 169, 179, 205, 298

WAUL, THOMAS NEVILLE, 12, 36, 48, 67, 73, 89, 111, 125, 148, 171, 189, 203, 298

WAYNE, HENRY CONSTANTINE, 12, 27, 42, 55, 75, 101, 116, 137, 149, 161, 182, 197, 299

WEBB, ALEXANDER STEWART, 20, 22, 50, 62, 87, 91, 120, 137, 140, 168, 191, 195, 299

WEBER, MAX, 20, 32, 55, 81, 100, 109, 125, 145, 166, 189, 201, 299

WEBSTER, JOSEPH DANA, 20, 31, 42, 60, 73, 100, 108, 124, 145, 162, 180, 196, 299

WEED, STEPHEN HINSDALE, 20, 35, 45, 62, 85, 104, 120, 137, 147, 159, 176, 202, 212, 216, 218, 299

WEISIGER, DAVID ADDISON, 12, 24, 39, 69, 76, 105, 122, 139, 172, 188, 196, 299

WEITZEL, GODFREY, 7, 26, 64, 87, 103, 120, 137, 155, 169, 182, 197, 299

WELSH, THOMAS, 20, 35, 65, 80, 95, 129, 142, 168, 176, 204, 299

WESSELLS, HENRY WALTON, 20,

ABOUT THE COMPILER

JAMES SPENCER recently retired from a career in law enforcement.